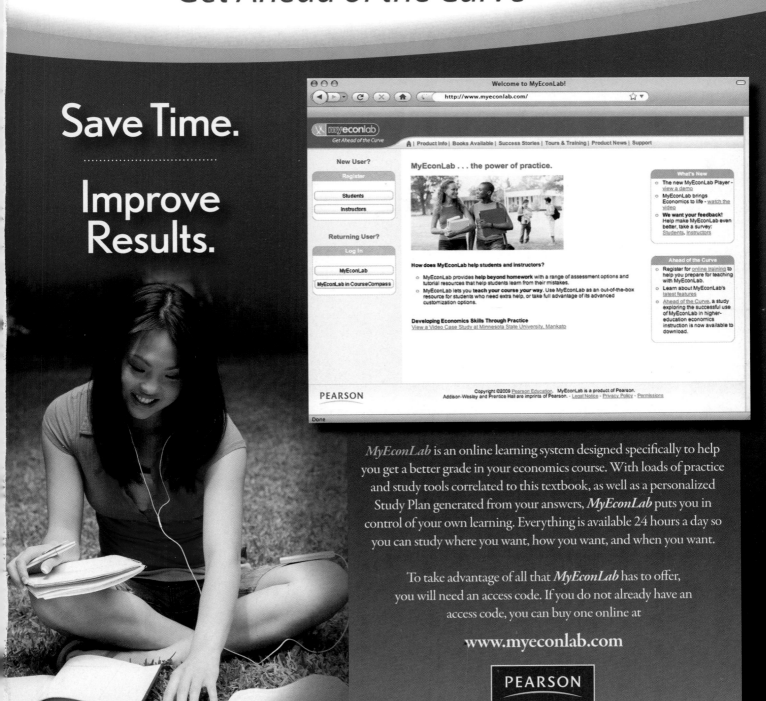

Get Ahead of the Curve

Personalized Learning!

The *MyEconLab* Study Plan is based on your specific learning needs.

Auto-Graded Tests and Assignments

MyEconLab comes with two pre-loaded Sample Tests for each chapter so you can self-assess your understanding of the material.

Personalized Study Plan

A Study Plan is generated based on your results on Sample Tests and instructor assignments. You can clearly see which topics you have mastered and, more importantly, which topics you need to work on!

"I just wanted to let you know how helpful the Study Plan in MyEconLab is. Everything's clicking... so two thumbs up!"
—Student, Ryerson University

Practice Problems

Use the Study Plan exercises to get practice where you need it. To check how you're doing, click Results to get an overview of all your scores.

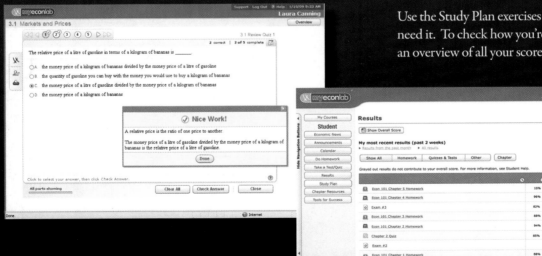

Save Time. Improve Results. www.myeconlab.com

Unlimited Practice!

MyEconLab offers a wide variety of problems that let you practise the theories and models being learned.

Graphing Tools and Questions

MyEconLab offers questions that allow you to draw graphs and plot data, as well as manipulate interactive model-based graphs.

Practice Problems

Many Study Plan and instructor-assigned problems contain algorithmically generated values, ensuring you get as much practice as you need.

Learning Resources

Each problem links to the eText page discussing the very concept being applied. You also have access to guided solutions and a suite of other practice tools.

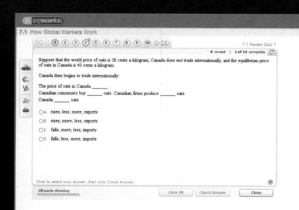

MACROECONOMICS

CANADA IN THE GLOBAL ENVIRONMENT

SEVENTH EDITION

SEE THE ECONOMICS BEHIND REAL ISSUES

From the global food shortage to the global financial climate, economic issues permeate your everyday life. By applying economic theory to today's events, news, and research, Parkin and Bade train you to think the way economists do. You learn to see the economic forces that shape our world, so you can make more informed decisions in your own life.

Chapter Openers
Each chapter begins with a current issue that demonstrates the real-world application of theoretical concepts.

2 The Economic Problem

After studying this chapter, you will be able to

- Define the production possibilities frontier and calculate opportunity cost
- Distinguish between production possibilities and preferences and describe an efficient allocation of resources
- Explain how current production choices expand future production possibilities
- Explain how specialization and trade expand our production possibilities
- Describe the economic institutions that coordinate decisions

Why does food cost much more today

than it did a few years ago? One reason is that many countries now use part of their corn crops to produce ethanol, a clean biofuel substitute for gasoline. Another reason is that drought in some parts of the world has decreased global [...] an economic [...] and you will [...] ave increased [...] how to assess

whether it is a good idea to increase corn production to produce fuel; how we can expand our production possibilities; how we gain by trading with others; and why the social institutions of firms, markets, property rights, and money that make trade possible have evolved. At the end of the chapter, in *Reading Between the Lines*, we'll apply what you've learned to understanding why ethanol production is raising the cost of food.

Economic Growth

Hong Kong Overtakes Canada

In 1968, the production possibilities per person in Canada were much larger than those in Hong Kong (see the figure). Canada devotes one-fifth of its resources to accumulating capital and in 1968 was at point *A* on its *PPF*. Hong Kong devotes one-third of its resources to accumulating capital and in 1968, Hong Kong was at point *A* on its *PPF*.

Since 1968, both countries have experienced economic growth, but because Hong Kong devotes a bigger fraction of its resources to accumulating capital, its production possibilities have expanded more quickly.

By 2008, production possibilities per person in Hong Kong had exceeded those in Canada. If Hong Kong continues to devote more resources to accumulating capital than Canada does (at point *B* on its 2008 *PPF*), Hong Kong will continue to grow more rapidly. But if Hong Kong decreases capital accumulation (moving to point *D* on its 2008 *PPF*), then its rate of economic growth will slow.

Hong Kong is typical of the fast-growing Asian economies, which include Taiwan, Thailand, South Korea, and China. Production possibilities expand in these countries by between 5 and 10 percent a year. If such high economic growth rates are maintained, these other Asian countries will continue to close the gap between themselves and Canada.

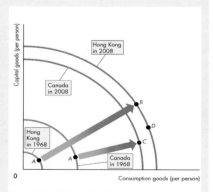

Economic Growth in Canada and Hong Kong

To catch up with Hong Kong, Canada must devote more than one-third of its resources to accumulating capital.

Issues of Our Global Economy
Economic issues that confront today's world are integrated into applications, end-of-chapter news analysis problems, and MyEconLab.

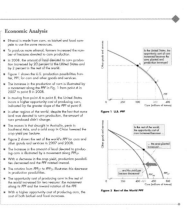

Reading Between the Lines

At the end of each chapter, *Reading Between the Lines* uses economic tools to critically evaluate a news article about the chapter-opening issue.

News-based End-of-Chapter Problems

New end-of-chapter problems based on current news stories are also available for practice in MyEconLab.

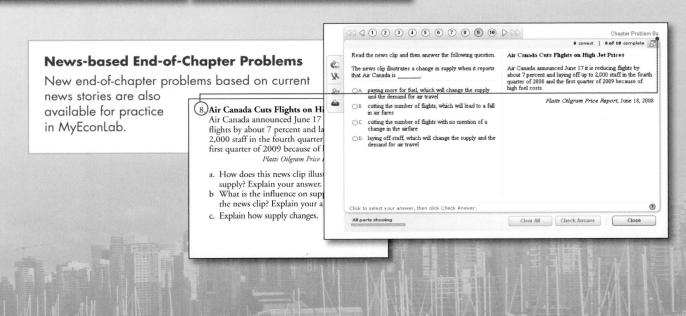

8. **Air Canada Cuts Flights on Hi**
Air Canada announced June 17 flights by about 7 percent and la 2,000 staff in the fourth quarter first quarter of 2009 because of

Platts Oilgram Price

a. How does this news clip illus supply? Explain your answer.

b What is the influence on supp the news clip? Explain your a

c. Explain how supply changes.

Air Canada Cuts Flights on High Jet Prices

Air Canada announced June 17 it is reducing flights by about 7 percent and laying off up to 2,000 staff in the fourth quarter of 2008 and the first quarter of 2009 because of high fuel costs.

Platts Oilgram Price Report, June 18, 2008

Read the news clip and then answer the following question.

The news clip illustrates a change in supply when it reports that Air Canada is _____.

- A. paying more for fuel, which will change the supply and the demand for air travel
- B. cutting the number of flights, which will lead to a fall in air fares
- C. cutting the number of flights with no mention of a change in the airfare
- D. laying off staff, which will change the supply and the demand for air travel

Economics in the News *myeconlab*

To keep you informed about the latest economic news, Parkin and Bade upload two relevant articles daily, one each covering microeconomic and macroeconomic topics. They also include discussion questions, links to additional online resources, and references to related textbook chapters.

MICHAEL PARKIN ◆ ROBIN BADE
University of Western Ontario

MACROECONOMICS

CANADA IN THE GLOBAL ENVIRONMENT

SEVENTH EDITION

Pearson Canada
Toronto

Library and Archives Canada Cataloguing in Publication

Parkin, Michael, 1939-
     Macroeconomics : Canada in the global environment / Michael
Parkin, Robin Bade. -- 7th ed.
Includes index.
ISBN 978-0-321-56390-3
     1. Macroeconomics--Textbooks. 2. Canada--Economic
conditions--1991- --Textbooks. I. Bade, Robin II. Title.
HB172.5.P363 2010   339   C2009-900493-3

ISBN-13: 978-0-321-56390-3

ISBN-10: 0-321-56390-5

Vice President, Editorial Director: Gary Bennett
Acquisitions Editor: Gary Bennett
Marketing Manager: Leigh-Ann Graham
Associate Editor: Catherine Belshaw
Production Editor: Leanne Rancourt/Cheryl Jackson
Copy Editor: Sally Glover
Proofreader: Lu Cormier
Production Coordinator: Deborah Starks
Compositor: Christine Velakis
Photo/Permissions Researcher: Lisa Brant
Art Director: Julia Hall
Technical Illustrator: Richard Parkin
Cover and Interior Designer: Anthony Leung
Cover Image: Getty Images

1 2 3 4 5   13 12 11 10 09

Printed and bound in the United States.

TO

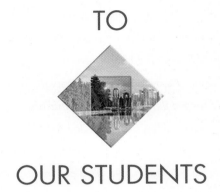

OUR STUDENTS

Michael Parkin received his training as an economist at the Universities of Leicester and Essex in England. Currently in the Department of Economics at the University of Western Ontario, Canada, Professor Parkin has held faculty appointments at Brown University, the University of Manchester, the University of Essex, and Bond University. He is a past president of the Canadian Economics Association and has served on the editorial boards of the *American Economic Review* and the *Journal of Monetary Economics* and as managing editor of the *Canadian Journal of Economics*. Professor Parkin's research on macroeconomics, monetary economics, and international economics has resulted in over 160 publications in journals and edited volumes, including the *American Economic Review*, the *Journal of Political Economy*, the *Review of Economic Studies*, the *Journal of Monetary Economics*, and the *Journal of Money, Credit and Banking*. He became most visible to the public with his work on inflation that discredited the use of wage and price controls. Michael Parkin also spearheaded the movement towards European monetary union.

Robin Bade earned degrees in mathematics and economics at the University of Queensland and her Ph.D. at the Australian National University. She has held faculty appointments at the University of Edinburgh in Scotland, at Bond University in Australia, and at the Universities of Manitoba, Toronto, and Western Ontario in Canada. Her research on international capital flows appears in the *International Economic Review* and the *Economic Record*.

Professor Parkin and Dr. Bade are the joint authors of *Foundations of Economics* (Addison Wesley), *Modern Macroeconomics* (Pearson Education Canada), an intermediate text, and have collabrated on many research and textbook writing projects. They are both experienced and dedicated teachers of introductory economics.

BRIEF CONTENTS

PREFACE

Historic is a big word. Yet it accurately describes the economic events and policy responses that followed the subprime mortgage crisis of August 2007. Economics moved from the business pages to the front page as fear gripped producers, consumers, financial institutions, and governments. The unimaginable repeat of a Great Depression gradually became imaginable as U.S. house prices plunged, credit markets froze, financial institutions failed, governments in Canada, the United States, and around the world mounted massive bailouts and rescues, central banks made loans and bought debts of a quality that they don't normally touch, and the prices of items from gasoline and food to stocks and currencies fluctuated wildly.

Even the *idea* that the market is an efficient mechanism for allocating scarce resources came into question as some political leaders trumpeted the end of capitalism and the dawn of a new economic order in which tighter regulation reigned in unfettered greed.

Rarely do teachers of economics have such a rich feast on which to draw. And rarely are the principles of economics more surely needed to provide the solid foundation on which to think about economic events and navigate the turbulence of economic life.

Although thinking like an economist can bring a clearer perspective to and deeper understanding of today's events, students don't find the economic way of thinking easy or natural. *Economics* seeks to put clarity and understanding in the grasp of the student through its careful and vivid exploration of the tension between self-interest and the social interest, the role and power of incentives—of opportunity cost and marginal benefit—and demonstrating the possibility that markets, supplemented by other mechanisms, might allocate resources efficiently.

Parkin and Bade students begin to think about issues the way real economists do and learn how to explore difficult policy problems and make more informed decisions in their own economic lives.

The Seventh Edition Revision

The seventh edition of *Economics* retains all of the improvements achieved in its predecessors: a thorough and detailed presentation of the principles of economics, an emphasis on real-world examples and applications, the development of critical thinking skills, diagrams renowned for pedagogy and precision, and path-breaking technology.

This comprehensive revision also incorporates and responds to the suggestions for improvements made by reviewers and users, in both the broad architecture of the text and chapter-by-chapter.

Current issues organize each chapter. News stories about today's major economic events tie each chapter together, from new chapter-opening vignettes to end-of-chapter problems and online practice. Students learn to use economic tools to analyze their own daily decisions and recent real-world events and issues.

Each chapter includes a discussion of a critical issue of our time to demonstrate how economic theory can be applied to explore a particular debate or question. Issues of central importance include

- Gains and tensions from globalization, the rise of Asia, and the changing structure of the global economy in Chapters 2, 22, and 31
- High and rising cost of food in Chapters 2 and 3
- Fluctuations in gas and oil prices and the effects of high gas prices on auto sales in Chapters 3, 4, and 18
- Bank of Canada and government rescues and bailouts in Chapters 23 and 30
- Financial instability of 2008 in Chapters 23, 26, and 30
- Currency fluctuations in Chapter 25
- Recession of 2008–2009 in Chapters 26, 27, 28, and 29
- Real-world examples and applications appear in the body of each chapter and in the end-of-chapter problems and applications. Each chapter has approximately 10 additional problems tied to current news and events. All of these problems have parallel questions in MyEconLab.
  Questions that appear weekly in *Economics in the News* in MyEconLab are also available for assignment in MyEconLab as homework, quizzes, or tests.

Highlights of the Macro Revision

The thoroughly updated coverage of macroeconomics is now organized in four parts: *monitoring the trends and fluctuations, understanding the trends, understanding the fluctuations,* and *macroeconomic policy.*

The introductory chapter of previous editions is redistributed across the other chapters as needed. Economic growth and the long-term trends in output growth have been brought forward and the content of the previous edition's chapter on the classical model of potential GDP is incorporated into the economic growth chapter.

Following economic growth is a new chapter on financial markets. This chapter enables students to understand the financial crisis of 2007–2008. Then follows two chapters on money and the exchange rate in which the emphasis is on understanding inflation and exchange rate trends.

The aggregate supply–aggregate demand model, the Keynesian model of aggregate expenditure, and the short-run tradeoff between real variables and inflation come next. This group of chapters can be covered right after Chapter 21 if desired.

The treatment of fiscal policy and monetary policy is radically revised to pay attention to the roles of policy in influencing both trends and fluctuations. The chapter in previous editions on fiscal and monetary interaction has been dropped from this edition.

In addition to these organizational changes, the chapters feature the following nine major revisions:

1. ***Measuring GDP and Economic Growth*** (Chapter 20): This chapter now includes a description and discussion of the recent history of real GDP growth and fluctuations found in the previous edition's introductory macro chapter. The explanation of the real GDP calculation has been simplified, and the current chain-dollar method of real GDP calculation is presented in a new Mathematical Note at the end of the chapter.

2. ***Monitoring Jobs and Inflation*** (Chapter 21): This substantially revised chapter has a simplified coverage of the anatomy and types of unemployment, but a more comprehensive explanation of the sources of unemployment. As today's unemployment is compared with that of the Great Depression, the empirical relationship between cyclical unemployment and the output gap is more clearly illustrated. The measurement of the price level and inflation is motivated with a discussion of inflation and why it is a problem. The chapter also includes new material on alternative price indexes, including the personal consumption expenditure deflator as well as the concept of core inflation. The chapter now concludes with a brief section on the general use of real variables in macroeconomics.

3. ***Economic Growth*** (Chapter 22): The process of economic growth now begins with an explanation of what determines potential GDP (adapted from the previous edition's classical model chapter), which is followed by an explanation of what makes potential GDP grow. The sources of labour productivity growth are thoroughly explored.

4. ***Finance, Saving, and Investment*** (Chapter 23): New to the seventh edition, this chapter provides a thorough and extensive explanation of financial markets and institutions and their role in providing the funds for investment, an engine of economic growth. The circular flow model of Chapter 20 is extended to include the flows in the market for loanable funds that finance investment. The chapter explains the role of government in the market for loanable funds and explains crowding out and the role of debt and the government budget deficit. The chapter also includes a discussion of borrowing and lending in the global loanable funds market. The credit crisis of 2008 is a central example used to illustrate the working of this vital macroeconomic market.

5. ***Money, the Price Level, and Inflation*** (Chapter 24): This chapter is heavily revised to simplify the explanation of the money creation process. A Mathematical Note at the end of the chapter provides a more comprehensive analysis of this process. The chapter includes an explanation of the role and functions of the Bank of Canada. It also includes coverage of the U.S. Federal Reserve's role in the 2008 credit crisis.

6. ***The Exchange Rate and the Balance of Payments*** (Chapter 25): This chapter is heavily revised to incorporate an explanation of the

determination of the balance of payments found in the international trade chapter of the previous edition. The chapter also looks at the recent dramatic fluctuations in the Canadian dollar in 2007 and 2008.

7. ***Aggregate Supply and Aggregate Demand*** (Chapter 26): This chapter is a streamlined version of the previous edition's content, but with a new and more detailed explanation and illustration of Canada's business cycle. The added clarity and focus of this chapter reflects the tone and goals of the seventh edition.

8. ***Fiscal Policy*** (Chapter 29) and ***Monetary Policy*** (Chapter 30): These chapters are revised to incorporate the dramatic policy responses to the ongoing slowdown and increasingly likely recession of 2008–2009.

9. ***International Trade Policy*** (Chapter 31): This new chapter explains the sources and effects of international trade, its winners and losers, and the effects of trade protection (tariffs and import quotas) on economic welfare. The chapter applies the tools of demand and supply. Offshore outsourcing and the ongoing failure of the Doha negotiations feature in this chapter.

 ## Features to Enhance Teaching and Learning

Chapter Objectives

Each chapter opens with a list of learning objectives, which enables students to see exactly where the chapter is going and to set their goals before they begin.

Chapter Openers

Each chapter opens with a student-friendly vignette that raises questions to motivate the student and focus the chapter. This chapter-opening story is woven into the main body of the chapter and is explored in the *Reading Between the Lines* feature that ends each chapter.

Key Terms

Highlighted terms simplify the student's task of learning the vocabulary of economics. Each highlighted term appears in an end-of-chapter list with page numbers, in an end-of-book glossary with page numbers, boldfaced in the index, in the Web glossary, and in the Web Flash Cards.

Diagrams that Show the Action

Through the past six editions, this book has set new standards of clarity in its diagrams; the seventh edition continues to uphold this tradition. Our goal has always been to show "where the economic action is." The diagrams in this book continue to generate an enormously positive response, which confirms our view that graphical analysis is the most powerful tool available for teaching and learning economics.

Because many students find graphs hard to work with, we have developed the entire art program with the study and review needs of the student in mind.

The diagrams feature

- Original curves consistently shown in blue
- Shifted curves, equilibrium points, and other important features highlighted in red
- Colour-blended arrows to suggest movement
- Graphs paired with data tables
- Diagrams labelled with boxed notes
- Extended captions that make each diagram and its caption a self-contained object for study and review.

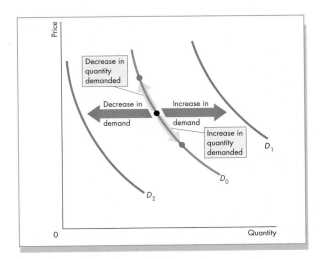

Reading Between the Lines

In *Reading Between the Lines*, which appears at the end of each chapter, students apply the tools they have just learned by analyzing an article from a newspaper or news Web site. Each article sheds additional light on the questions first raised in the Chapter Opener.

Questions about the article also appear with the end-of-chapter problems and applications.

In-Text Review Quizzes

A review quiz at the end of each major section enables students to determine whether a topic needs further study before moving on. This feature includes a reference to the appropriate MyEconLab Study Plan to help students further test their understanding.

End-of-Chapter Study Material

Each chapter closes with a concise summary organized by major topics, lists of key terms, figures and tables (all with page references), and problems and applications. These learning tools provide students with a summary for review and exam preparation.

News-Based End-of-Chapter Problems and Applications

Each chapter's problems and applications section now includes an additional set of news-based real-world problems that are new to the seventh edition. All of the problems and applications are also available for self-assessment or assignment as homework, a quiz, or a test in MyEconLab.

Interviews with Economists

Each major part of the text closes with a summary feature that includes an interview with a leading economist whose research and expertise correlates to what the student has just learned. These interviews explore the background, education, and research these prominent economists have conducted, as well as advice for those who want to continue the study of economics. New interviewees in this seventh edition are Susan Athey of Harvard University, Jadgish Baghwati, Xavier Sala-i-Martin, and Stephanie Schmitt-Grohé of Columbia University, and Ricardo Cabellaro of MIT. The interview with Peter Howitt of Brown University has been updated.

For the Instructor

This book enables you to achieve three objectives in your principles course:

- Focus on the economic way of thinking
- Explain the issues and problems of our time
- Choose your own course structure

Focus on the Economic Way of Thinking

As an instructor, you know how hard it is to encourage a student to think like an economist. But that is your goal. Consistent with this goal, the text focuses on and repeatedly uses the central ideas: choice; tradeoff; opportunity cost; the margin; incentives; the gains from voluntary exchange; the forces of demand, supply, and equilibrium; the pursuit of economic rent; the tension between self-interest and the social interest; and the scope and limitations of government actions.

Explain the Issues of Our Global Economy

Students must *use* the central ideas and tools if they are to begin to *understand* them. There is no better way to motivate students than by using the tools of economics to explain the issues that confront today's world. Issues such as globalization and the emergence of China and India as major economic forces; the credit crisis, the recent bankruptcy, absorption, or government-funded bailout of U.S. banks, stock market fluctuations, the new economy with new near-monopolies such as eBay and Google; the widening income gap between rich and poor; the reallocation of resources towards counterterrorism; disappearing tropical rainforests and the challenge that this tragedy of the commons creates; the challenge of managing the world's water resources; rising international deficits and debt; and the fluctuating value of currencies on the foreign exchange market.

Flexible Structure

You have preferences for how you want to teach your course. We have organized this book to enable you to do so. The flexibility chart and alternative sequences tables that appear on pages xx–xxi demonstrate this book's flexibility. Whether you want to teach a traditional course that blends theory and policy or focuses on current policy issues, *Economics: Canada in the Global Environment* gives you the choice.

Supplemental Resources

Instructor's Manual We have streamlined and reorganized the Instructor's Manual to reflect the focus and intuition of the seventh edition. The Instructor's Manual integrates the teaching and learning package and serves as a guide to all the supplements.

Each chapter contains

- A chapter overview
- A list of what's new in the seventh edition
- *Lecture Notes* Ready-to-use lecture notes from each chapter enable a new user of Parkin and Bade to walk into a classroom ready to deliver a polished lecture. The lecture notes provide an outline of the chapter; concise statements of key material; alternate tables and figures, key terms, definitions, and boxes that highlight key concepts, provide an interesting anecdote, or suggest how to handle a difficult idea; additional discussion questions; and additional problems with solutions. The chapter outline and teaching suggestions sections are keyed to the PowerPoint® lecture notes.

Solutions Manual For ease of use and instructor reference, a comprehensive Solutions Manual provides instructors with solutions to the Review Quizzes and the end-of-chapter problems. The Solutions Manual is available in hard copy and electronically on the Instructor's Resource Centre CD-ROM, and in the instructor's resources section of MyEconLab and on the Instructor's Resource Centre.

Test Bank The seventh edition Test Bank, with more than 3,000 multiple-choice questions, has been prepared by Jeannie Gillmore of the University of Western Ontario. Jeannie has reviewed and edited all questions in the sixth edition Test Bank to ensure their clarity and consistency with the seventh edition and has incorporated new questions. These new questions follow the style and format of the end-of chapter text problems and provide the instructor with a whole new set of testing opportunities and/or homework assignments. Additionally, end-of-part tests contain questions that cover all the chapters in the part and feature integrative questions that span more than one chapter.

Computerized Test Bank in TestGen Pearson TestGen enables instructors to view and edit test bank questions, generate tests, and print tests in a variety of formats. Powerful search and sort functions make it easy to locate questions and arrange them in any order desired. TestGen also enables instructors to administer tests on a local area network, have tests graded electronically, and have the results prepared in electronic or printed reports. Pearson TestGen is compatible with Windows® or Macintosh® systems. This test bank is also available as a Test Item File in Microsoft Word® and Adobe Acrobat® formats

PowerPoint® Resources We have developed a full-colour Microsoft PowerPoint® Lecture Presentation for each chapter that includes all the figures and tables from the text, animated graphs, and speaking notes. The lecture notes in the Instructor's Manual and the slide outlines are correlated, and the speaking notes are based on the Instructor's Manual teaching suggestions.

A separate set of PowerPoint® files containing large-scale versions of all the text's figures (most of them animated) and tables are also available. The presentations can be used electronically in the classroom or can be printed to create hard copy transparency masters. This item is available for Macintosh® and Windows®.

Clicker-Ready PowerPoint ® Resources This edition features the addition of clicker-ready PowerPoint® slides for the Personal Response System you use. Each chapter of the text includes 10 multiple-choice questions that test important concepts. Instructors can assign these as in-class assignments or review quizzes.

Instructor's Resource Centre CD-ROM The Instructor's Resource CD includes all of the instructor supplements for the seventh edition: the Instructor's Manual in Microsoft Word® and Adobe Acrobat® formats, Solutions Manual, Test Bank, PowerPoint® Resources, and Clicker Questions. The Instructor's Resource CD is compatible with both Windows® and Macintosh® systems.

Most of these instructor supplements are also available for download from a password-protected section of Pearson Education Canada's online catalogue (vig. pearsoned.ca). Navigate to this book's catalogue page to view a list of the supplements that are available. See your local sales representative for details and access.

Technology Specialists Pearson's technology specialists work with faculty and campus course designers to ensure that Pearson technology products, assessment tools, and online course materials are tailored to meet your specific needs. This highly qualified team is dedicated to helping schools take full advantage of a wide range of educational resources by assisting in the integration of a variety of instructional materials and media formats. Your local Pearson Education sales representative can provide you with more details on this service program.

Study Guide The seventh edition Study Guide by Harvey King of the University of Regina is carefully coordinated with the text, MyEconLab, and the Test Bank. Each chapter of the Study Guide contains

- Key concepts
- Helpful hints
- True/false/uncertain questions that ask students to explain their answers
- Multiple-choice questions
- Short-answer questions
- Each Part Wrapup allows students to test their cumulative understanding with questions that go across chapters and to work a sample midterm examination.

MyEconLab Pearson Canada's online resource, MyEconLab, offers instructors and students all of their resources in one place, written and designed to accompany this text. MyEconLab creates a perfect pedagogical loop that provides not only text-specific assessment and practice problems, but also tutorial support to make sure students learn from their mistakes.

MyEconLab is available to instructors by going to www.myeconlab.com and following the instructions. Students access MyEconLab with an access code that is available with the purchase of a new text.

At the core of MyEconLab are the following features:

Auto-Graded Tests and Assignments MyEconLab comes with two preloaded Sample Tests for each chapter. Students can use these tests for self-assessment and obtain immediate feedback. Instructors can assign the

Sample Tests or use them along with Test Bank questions or their own exercises to create tests or quizzes.

Study Plan   A Study Plan is generated from each student's results on Sample Tests and instructor assignments. Students can clearly see which topics they have mastered—and, more importantly, which they need to work on. The Study Plan consists of material from the in-text Review Quizzes and end-of-chapter Problems and Applications. The Study Plan links to additional practice problems and tutorial help on those topics.

Unlimited Practice   Many Study Plan and instructor-assigned exercises contain algorithmically generated values to ensure that students get as much practice as they need. Every problem links students to learning resources that further reinforce concepts they need to master.

Learning Resources   Each practice problem contains a link to the eText page that discusses the concept being applied. Students also have access to guided solutions, animated graphs with audio narrative, flashcards, and live tutoring.

Economics in the News   Weekly news updates during the school year are available in MyEconLab. Each week, the authors post links to two news articles from the week's headlines. One links students to a microeconomics article, and the other to a macroeconomics article. Each article is accompanied by additional links, discussion questions, and a reference to relevant textbook chapters. An archive of *Economics in the News* articles and questions is also available.

New to the seventh edition are instructor-assignable *Economics in the News* questions. These news analysis questions are updated routinely to ensure that the latest news and news analysis problems are available for assignment.

Economics Videos and Assignable Questions Featuring ⓐⓑⓒNEWS
Economics videos featuring ABC news enliven your course with short news clips featuring real-world issues. These 10 videos, available in MyEconLab, feature news footage and commentary by economists. Questions and problems for each video clip are available for assignment in MyEconLab.

Pearson Tutoring Services powered by SMARTHINKING
A subscription to MyEconLab includes complimentary access to Pearson Tutor Services, powered by SMARTHINKING Inc. Highly qualified tutors use whiteboard technology and feedback tools to help students understand and master the major concepts of economics. Students can receive real-time, one-on-one instruction, submit questions for a response within 24 hours, and view archives of past sessions.

Access to MyEconLab and the Complete eText
A student access code card for MyEconLab is packaged with every new copy of this book. Students may purchase access to MyEconLab online at www.myeconlab.com or through their campus bookstore.

CourseSmart eTextbook
CourseSmart is a new way for instructors and students to access this textbook online anytime from anywhere. With thousands of titles across hundreds of courses, CourseSmart helps instructors chose the best textbook for their class and give their students a new option for buying the assigned textbook as a lower cost eTextbook. For more information visit www.coursesmart.com.

◆ Acknowledgments

We thank our current and former colleagues and friends at the University of Western Ontario who have taught us so much. They are Jim Davies, Jeremy Greenwood, Ig Horstmann, Peter Howitt, Greg Huffman, David Laidler, Phil Reny, Chris Robinson, John Whalley, and Ron Wonnacott. We also thank Doug McTaggart and Christopher Findlay, co-authors of the Australian edition, and Melanie Powell and Kent Matthews, co-authors of the European edition. Suggestions arising from their adaptations of earlier editions have been helpful to us in preparing this edition.

We thank the several thousand students whom we have been privileged to teach. The instant response that comes from the look of puzzlement or enlightenment has taught us how to teach economics.

It is a special joy to thank the many outstanding editors, media specialists, and others at Pearson Education Canada who contributed to the concerted publishing effort that brought this edition to completion. Allan Reynolds, President and CEO, and Steve O'Hern, President of Higher Education, have once again provided outstanding corporate direction. They have worked hard to build a culture that brings out the best in its editors and authors. Gary Bennett, Vice-President and Editorial Director for Higher Education, played a major role in bringing this new edition to completion. Gary, ably assisted by Catherine Belshaw, found and managed a team of outstanding supplements authors and editorial resources.

Leanne Rancourt brought a fresh eye to the development and production process. Anthony Leung designed the cover and text. Jennifer Parks directed the development and production of MyEconLab and ensured that all our media assets were correctly assembled. Leigh-Anne Graham provided inspired marketing strategy and direction. Sally Glover provided a careful, consistent, and intelligent copy edit, Lu Cormier, our proofreader, caught many slips, and Kit Pasula, our accuracy checker, found some errors of substance, which we are relieved to have had the opportunity to correct. We thank Lisa Brant, our photo researcher and permissions editor, for her thorough work.

We thank Luke Armstrong of Lee College for providing the news-based applications that appear at the end of each chapter. Luke has been using this type of material with his students and has now shared his talent with a wider audience.

We thank our talented seventh edition supplements authors—Avi Cohen and Harvey King wrote the Study Guide, Jeannie Gillmore updated and revised the Test Bank.

We thank the many exceptional reviewers who have shared their insights through the various editions of this book. Their contributions have been invaluable.

We thank the people who work directly with us. Jeannie Gillmore provided outstanding research assistance on many topics, including the *Reading Between the Lines* news articles. Richard Parkin created the electronic art files and offered many ideas that improved the figures in this book. He also created all the animated figures for the ebook and the PowerPoint® slides. And Laurel Davies managed an ever-growing and ever more complex MyEconLab database.

Classroom experience will test the value of this book. We would appreciate hearing from instructors and students about how we can continue to improve it in future editions.

Michael Parkin
Robin Bade
London, Ontario, Canada
michael.parkin@uwo.ca
robin@econ100.com

◆ Reviewers

Syed Ahmed, Red Deer Community College
Ather H. Akbari, Saint Mary's University
Benjamin Amoah, University of Guelph
Terri Anderson, Fanshawe College
Torben Andersen, Red Deer College
Syed Ashan, Concordia University
Fred Aswani, McMaster University
Iris Au, University of Toronto, Scarborough
Keith Baxter, Bishop's University
Andy Baziliauskas, University of Winnipeg
Dick Beason, University of Alberta
Karl Bennett, University of Waterloo
Ronald Bodkin, University of Ottawa
Caroline Boivin, Concordia University
Paul Booth, University of Alberta
John Boyd, University of British Columbia
John Brander, University of New Brunswick
Larry Brown, Selkirk College
Bogdan Buduru, Concordia University
Lutz-Alexander Busch, University of Waterloo
Alan Tak Yan Chan, Atlantic Baptist University
Beverly J. Cameron, University of Manitoba
Norman Cameron, University of Manitoba
Emanuel Carvalho, University of Waterloo
Francois Casas, University of Toronto
Robert Cherneff, University of Victoria
Jason Childs, University of New Brunswick, Saint John
Saud Choudhry, Trent University
Louis Christofides, University of Guelph
Kam Hon Chu, Memorial University of Newfoundland
George Churchman, University of Manitoba
Avi J. Cohen, York University
Marilyn Cottrell, Brock University
Rosilyn Coulson, Douglas College
Brian Coulter, University College of the Fraser Valley
Stanya Cunningham, Concordia Universiry College of Alberta
Douglas Curtis, Trent University
Garth Davies, OIds College
Vaughan Dickson, University of New Brunswick (Fredericton)
Mohammed Dore, Brock University
Torben Drewes, Trent University
Byron Eastman, Laurentian Universty
Fahira Eston, Humber College
Brian Ferguson, University of Guelph
Len Fitzpatrick, Carleton University
Peter Fortura, Algonquin College
Oliver Franke, Athabasca University

Bruno Fullone, George Brown College
Donald Garrie, Georgian College
Philippe Ghayad, Dawson College and Concordia University
David Gray, University of Ottawa
Rod Hill, University of New Brunswick
Eric Kam, Ryerson University
Susan Kamp, University of Alberta
Cevat Burc Kayahan, University of Guelph
Peter Kennedy, Simon Fraser University
Harvey King, University of Regina
Patricia Koss, Concordia University
Robert Kunimoto, Mt. Royal College
David Johnson, Wilfrid Laurier University
Eva Lau, University of Waterloo
Gordon Lee, University of Alberta
Anastasia M. Lintner, University of Guelph
Scott Lynch, Memorial University
Dan MacKay, SIAST
Keith MacKinnon, York University
Mohammad Mahbobi, Thompson Rivers University
S. Manchouri, University of Alberta
Christian Marfels, Dalhousie University
Raimo Martalla, Malaspina University College
Perry Martens, University of Regina
Roberto Martínez-Espíneira, St. Francis Xavier University
Livio Di Matteo, Lakehead University
Dennis McGuire, Okanagan University College
Rob Moir, University of New Brunswick Saint John
Saeed Moshiri, University of Manitoba
Joseph Muldoon, Trent University
David Murrell, University of New Brunswick (Fredericton)
Robin Neill, Carleton University
A. Gyasi Nimarko, Vanier College
Sonia Novkovic, Saint Mary's University
John O'Brien, Concordia University
Arne Paus-Jenssen, University of Saskatchewan
Derek Pyne, Memorial University of Newfoundland.
Stephen Rakoczy, Humber College
Don Reddick, Kwantlen University College
E. Riser, Memorial University
Roberta Robb, Brock University
Nick Rowe, Carleton University
Michael Rushton, University of Regina
Balbir Sahni, Concordia University
Brian Scarfe, University of Regina
Marlyce Searcy, SIAST Palliser
Jim Sentance, University of Prince Edward Island
Lance Shandler, Kwantlen University College
Stan Shedd, University of Calgary

Peter Sinclair, Wilfrid Laurier University

Ian Skaith, Fanshawe College

Judith Skuce, Georgian College

George Slasor, University of Toronto

Norman Smith, Georgian College

Bert Somers, John Abbott College

Lewis Soroka, Brock University

Glen Stirling, University of Western Ontario

Irene Trela, University of Western Ontario

Russell Uhler, University of British Columbia

Jane Waples, Memorial University of Newfoundland

Tony Ward, Brock University

Bruce Wilkinson, University of Alberta

Christopher Willmore, University of Victoria

Arthur Younger, Humber College Institute of Technology and Advanced Learning

Andrew Wong, Grant MacEwan College

Peter Wylie, University of British Colombia, Okanagan

Ayoub Yousefi, University of Western Ontario

Weiqiu Yu, University of New Brunswick (Fredericton)

FLEXIBILITY
BY CHAPTER

THREE ALTERNATIVE
MACRO SEQUENCES

Classical Perspective

1 What Is Economics?

2 The Economic Problem

3 Demand and Supply

20 Measuring GDP and Economic Growth

21 Monitoring Jobs and Inflation

22 Economic Growth

23 Finance, Saving, and Investment

24 Money, the Price Level, and Inflation

25 The Exchange Rate and the Balance of Payments

26 Aggregate Supply and Aggregate Demand

28 Canadian Inflation, Unemployment, and Business Cycle

29 Fiscal Policy

30 Monetary Policy

31 International Trade Policy

Keynesian Perspective

1 What Is Economics?

2 The Economic Problem

3 Demand and Supply

20 Measuring GDP and Economic Growth

21 Monitoring Jobs and Inflation

27 Expenditure Multipliers: The Keynesian Model

26 Aggregate Supply and Aggregate Demand

28 Canadian Inflation, Unemployment, and Business Cycle (omit real business cycles)

29 Fiscal Policy (omit supply-side sections)

24 Money, the Price Level, and Inflation

30 Monetary Policy

22 Economic Growth

23 Finance, Saving, and Investment

25 The Exchange Rate and the Balance of Payments

31 International Trade Policy

Monetarist Perspective

1 What Is Economics?

2 The Economic Problem

3 Demand and Supply

20 Measuring GDP and Economic Growth

21 Monitoring Jobs and Inflation

24 Money, the Price Level, and Inflation

25 The Exchange Rate and the Balance of Payments

26 Aggregate Supply and Aggregate Demand

28 Canadian Inflation, Unemployment, and Business Cycle (omit real business cycles)

30 Monetary Policy

29 Fiscal Policy

22 Economic Growth

23 Finance, Saving, and Investment

31 International Trade Policy

TABLE OF
CONTENTS

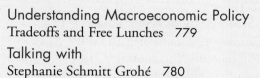

1 What Is Economics?

After studying this chapter, you will be able to

- Define economics and distinguish between microeconomics and macroeconomics
- Explain the two big questions of economics
- Explain the key ideas that define the economic way of thinking
- Explain how economists go about their work as social scientists

You are studying economics at a time of extraordinary change. Canada is one of the world's richest nations, but China, India, Brazil, and Russia, nations with a combined population that dwarfs our own, are emerging to play ever greater roles in an expanding global economy. The technological change that is driving this expansion has brought us the laptops, wireless broadband, iPods, DVDs, cell phones, and video games that have transformed the way Canadians work and play. But this expanding global economy has also brought us sky-rocketing food and fuel prices and is contributing to global warming and climate change.

Your life will be shaped by the challenges you face and the opportunities you create. But to face those challenges and seize the opportunities they present, you must understand the powerful forces at play. The economics that you're about to learn will become your most reliable guide. This chapter gets you started. It describes the questions that economists try to answer and the ways in which they search for the answers.

1

◆ Definition of Economics

All economic questions arise because we want more than we can get. We want a peaceful and secure world. We want clean air, lakes, and rivers. We want long and healthy lives. We want good schools, colleges, and universities. We want spacious and comfortable homes. We want an enormous range of sports and recreational gear, from running shoes to jet skis. We want the time to enjoy sports, games, novels, movies, music, travel, and hanging out with our friends.

What each one of us can get is limited by time, by the incomes we earn, and by the prices we must pay. Everyone ends up with some unsatisfied wants. What we can get as a society is limited by our productive resources. These resources include the gifts of nature, human labour and ingenuity, and tools and equipment that we have produced.

Our inability to satisfy all our wants is called **scarcity**. The poor and the rich alike face scarcity. A child wants a $1.00 can of pop and two 50¢ packs of gum but has only $1.00 in his pocket. He faces scarcity. A millionaire wants to spend the weekend playing golf *and* spend the same weekend attending a business strategy meeting. She faces scarcity. A society wants to provide improved health care, install a computer in every classroom, upgrade the public transit system, clean polluted lakes and rivers, and so on. Society faces scarcity. Even parrots face scarcity!

Faced with scarcity, we must *choose* among the available alternatives. The child must *choose* the pop *or* the gum. The millionaire must *choose* the golf game *or* the meeting. As a society, we must *choose* among health care, national defence, and education.

Not only do I want a cracker—we all want a cracker!

The choices that we make depend on the incentives that we face. An **incentive** is a reward that encourages an action or a penalty that discourages one. If the price of pop falls, the child has an *incentive* to choose more pop. If a profit of $10 million is at stake, the millionaire has an *incentive* to skip the golf game. As computer prices tumble, school boards have an *incentive* to connect more classrooms to the Internet.

Economics is the social science that studies the *choices* that individuals, businesses, governments, and entire societies make as they cope with *scarcity* and the *incentives* that influence and reconcile those choices. The subject divides into two main parts:

- Microeconomics
- Macroeconomics

Microeconomics

Microeconomics is the study of the choices that individuals and businesses make, the way these choices interact in markets, and the influence of governments. Some examples of microeconomic questions are: Why are people buying more DVDs and fewer movie tickets? How would a tax on e-commerce affect eBay?

Macroeconomics

Macroeconomics is the study of the performance of the national economy and the global economy. Some examples of macroeconomic questions are: Why did inflation in Canada start to increase in 2008? Can the Bank of Canada keep our inflation rate under control by raising interest rates?

Review Quiz ◆

1 List some examples of scarcity in Canada today.
2 Use the headlines in today's news to provide some examples of scarcity around the world.
3 Use today's news to illustrate the distinction between microeconomics and macroeconomics.

 Work Study Plan 1.1 and get instant feedback.

Two Big Economic Questions

Two big questions summarize the scope of economics:

- How do choices end up determining *what, how,* and *for whom* goods and services are produced?
- How can choices made in the pursuit of *self-interest* also promote the *social interest*?

What, How, and For Whom?

Goods and services are the objects that people value and produce to satisfy human wants. *Goods* are physical objects, such as cell phones and automobiles. *Services* are tasks performed for people, such as cell phone service and auto-repair service.

What? What we produce changes over time. Sixty-five years ago, almost 20 percent of Canadians worked on farms. That number has shrunk to less than 3 percent today. Over the same period, the number of people who produce goods—in mining, construction, and manufacturing—has shrunk from 60 percent to less than 25 percent. The decrease in farming and manufacturing is reflected in an increase in services. Sixty-five years ago, 20 percent of the population produced services. Today, more than 75 percent of working Canadians have service jobs. Figure 1.1 shows these trends.

What determines these patterns of production? How do choices end up determining the quantities of cell phones, automobiles, cell phone service, auto-repair service, and the millions of other items that are produced in Canada and around the world?

How? Goods and services are produced by using productive resources that economists call **factors of production**. Factors of production are grouped into four categories:

- Land
- Labour
- Capital
- Entrepreneurship

Land The "gifts of nature" that we use to produce goods and services are called **land**. In economics, land is what in everyday language we call *natural resources*. It includes land in the everyday sense together with minerals, oil, gas, coal, water, air, forests, and fish.

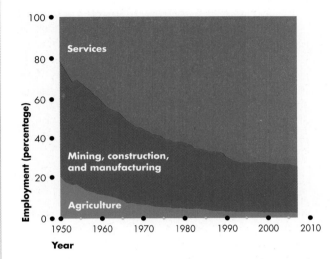

FIGURE 1.1 Trends in What We Produce

Services have expanded and agriculture, mining, construction, and manufacturing have shrunk.

Source of data: Statistics Canada.

Our land surface and water resources are renewable and some of our mineral resources can be recycled. But the resources that we use to create energy are nonrenewable—they can be used only once.

Labour The work time and work effort that people devote to producing goods and services is called **labour**. Labour includes the physical and mental efforts of all the people who work on farms and construction sites and in factories, shops, and offices.

The *quality* of labour depends on **human capital**, which is the knowledge and skill that people obtain from education, on-the-job training, and work experience. You are building your own human capital right now as you work on your economics course, and your human capital will continue to grow as you gain work experience.

Human capital expands over time. Today, 92 percent of the adult population of Canada have completed high school and more than 62 percent have a college or university degree. Figure 1.2 shows these measures of the growth of human capital in Canada over the past few decades.

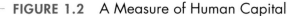

FIGURE 1.2   A Measure of Human Capital

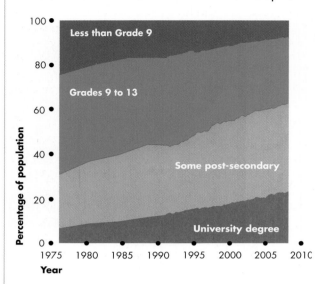

Today, 23 percent of the adult population have university degrees and another 40 percent have post-secondary certificates. A further 30 percent have completed high school.

Source of data: Statistics Canada.

Capital The tools, instruments, machines, buildings, and other constructions that businesses use to produce goods and services are called **capital**.

In everyday language, we talk about money, stocks, and bonds as being "capital." These items are *financial* capital. Financial capital plays an important role in enabling businesses to borrow the funds that they use to buy physical capital. But because financial capital is not used to produce goods and services, it is not a productive resource.

Entrepreneurship The human resource that organizes labour, land, and capital is called **entrepreneurship**. Entrepreneurs come up with new ideas about what and how to produce, make business decisions, and bear the risks that arise from these decisions.

What determines the quantities of factors of production that are used to produce goods and services?

For Whom? Who consumes the goods and services that are produced depends on the incomes that people earn. A large income enables a person to buy large

quantities of goods and services. A small income leaves a person with few options and small quantities of goods and services.

People earn their incomes by selling the services of the factors of production they own:

- Land earns **rent**.
- Labour earns **wages**.
- Capital earns **interest**.
- Entrepreneurship earns **profit**.

Which factor of production earns the most income? The answer is labour. Wages and fringe benefits are around 70 percent of total income. Land, capital, and entrepreneurship share the rest. These percentages have been remarkably constant over time.

Knowing how income is shared among the factors of production doesn't tell us how it is shared among individuals. And the distribution of income among individuals is extremely unequal. You know of some people who earn very large incomes: Mike Lazaridis of Research in Motion earned more than $2.66 billion in 2007 and Frank Stronach, chairman of Canada's largest auto parts company, was paid more than $27 million.

You know of even more people who earn very small incomes. Servers at Tim Hortons average about $8.75 an hour; checkout clerks, cleaners, and textile workers all earn less than $10 an hour.

You probably know about other persistent differences in incomes. Men, on the average, earn more than women; whites earn more than minorities; college graduates earn more than high-school graduates.

We can get a good sense of who consumes the goods and services produced by looking at the percentages of total income earned by different groups of people. The poorest 20 percent of the population earn about 5 percent of total income; the richest 20 percent earn close to 50 percent of total income. So the richest 20 percent, on average, earn more than 10 times what the poorest 20 percent earn.

Why is the distribution of income so unequal? Why do women and minorities earn less than men?

Economics provides some answers to all these questions about what, how, and for whom goods and services are produced and much of the rest of this book will help you to understand those answers.

We're now going to look at the second big question of economics: When does the pursuit of self-interest promote the social interest? This question is a difficult one both to appreciate and to answer.

How Can the Pursuit of Self-Interest Promote the Social Interest?

Every day, you and 32 million other Canadians, along with 6.7 billion people in the rest of the world, make economic choices that result in *what*, *how*, and *for whom* goods and services are produced.

Self-Interest A choice is in your **self-interest** if you think that choice is the best one available for you. You make most of your choices in your self-interest. You use your time and other resources in the ways that make most sense to you, and you don't think too much about how your choices affect other people. You order a home delivery pizza because you're hungry and want to eat. You don't order it thinking that the delivery person needs an income.

When you act on your self-interested economic choices, you come into contact with thousands of other people who produce and deliver the goods and services that you decide to buy or who buy the things that you sell. These people have made their own choices—what to produce and how to produce it, who to hire or whom to work for, and so on—in their self-interest. When the pizza delivery person shows up at your door, he's not doing you a favour. He's earning his income and hoping for a good tip.

Social Interest Self-interested choices promote the **social interest** if they lead to an outcome that is the best for society as a whole—an outcome that uses resources efficiently and distributes goods and services equitably (or fairly) among individuals.

Resources are used efficiently when goods and services are produced

1. At the lowest possible cost, and
2. In the quantities that give the greatest possible benefit.

The Big Question How can we organize our economic lives so that when each one of us makes choices that are in our self-interest, it turns out that these choices also promote the social interest? Does voluntary trading in free markets achieve the social interest? Do we need government action to guide our choices to achieve the social interest? Do we need international cooperation and treaties to achieve the global social interest?

Let's put some flesh on these broad questions with some examples.

Self-Interest and the Social Interest

To get started thinking about the tension between self-interest and the social interest, we'll consider five topics that generate discussion in today's world. Here, we will briefly introduce the topics and identify some of the economic questions that they pose. We'll return to each one of them as you learn more of the economic ideas and tools that can be used to understand these issues. The topics are

- Globalization
- The information-age economy
- Global warming
- Natural resource depletion
- Economic instability

Globalization The term *globalization* means the expansion of international trade, borrowing and lending, and investment.

Whose self-interest does globalization serve? Is it only in the self-interest of the multinational firms that produce in low-cost regions and sell in high-price regions? Is globalization in the interest of consumers who buy lower-cost goods? Is globalization in the interest of the worker in Malaysia who sews your new running shoes? Is globalization in your self-interest and in the social interest? Or should we limit globalization and restrict imports of cheap foreign-produced goods and services?

Globalization Today

Life in a Small and Ever-Shrinking World

Every day, 40,000 people travel by air between North America and Asia and Europe. A phone call or a video conference with people who live 15,000 kilometres away is a common and easily affordable event.

When Roots produces yoga pants, people in Taiwan get work. When Apple designs a new generation iPod, electronics factories in China, Japan, Korea, and Taiwan produce and assemble the parts. When Nintendo creates a new game for the Wii, programmers in India write the code. And when China Airlines buys new regional jets, Canadians who work at Bombardier build them.

While globalization brings expanded production and job opportunities for Asian workers, it destroys many North American jobs. Workers across the manufacturing industries must learn new skills, or take lower-paid service jobs, or retire earlier than planned.

The Information-Age Economy The technological change of the 1990s and 2000s has been called the *Information Revolution.*

During the Information Revolution were scarce resources used in the best possible way? Who benefitted from Bill Gates' decision to quit Harvard and create Microsoft? Did Microsoft produce operating systems for the personal computer that served the social interest? Did it sell its programs for prices that served the social interest? Did Bill Gates have to be paid what has now grown to $55 billion to produce successive generations of Windows, Microsoft Office, and other programs? Did Intel make the right quality of chips and sell them in the right quantities for the right prices? Or was the quality too low and the price too high? Would the social interest have been better served if Microsoft and Intel had faced competition from other firms?

The Source of the Information Age

So Much from One Tiny Chip

The microprocessor or computer chip created the information age. Gordon Moore of Intel predicted in 1965 that the number of transistors that could be placed on one chip would double every 18 months (Moore's law). This prediction turned out to be remarkably accurate. In 1980, an Intel chip had 60,000 transistors. In 2008, Intel's Core 2 Duo processor—that you might be using on your personal computer—has 291 million transistors.

The spinoffs from faster and cheaper computing were widespread. Telecommunications became clearer and faster; music and movie recording became more realistic; routine tasks that previously required human decision and action were automated.

All the new products and processes, and the low-cost computing power that made them possible, were produced by people who made choices in their own self-interest. They did not result from any grand design or government economic plan.

When Gordon Moore set up Intel and started making chips, no one had told him to do so, and he wasn't thinking how much easier it would be for you to turn in your essay on time if you had a faster laptop. When Bill Gates quit Harvard to set up Microsoft, he wasn't thinking about making it easier to use a computer. Moore, Gates, and thousands of other entrepreneurs were in hot pursuit of the big prizes that many of them succeeded in winning.

Global Warming Global warming and its effect on climate change is a huge political issue today. Every serious political leader is acutely aware of the problem and of the popularity of having proposals that might lower carbon emissions.

Every day, when you make self-interested choices to use electricity and gasoline, you contribute to carbon emissions; you leave your carbon footprint. You can lessen your carbon footprint by walking, riding a bike, taking a cold shower, or planting a tree.

But can each one of us be relied upon to make decisions that affect the Earth's carbon-dioxide concentration in the social interest? Must governments change the incentives we face so that our self-interested choices advance the social interest? How can governments change incentives? How can we encourage the use of wind and solar power to replace the burning of fossil fuels that bring climate change?

A Hotter Planet

Melting Ice and the Changing Climate

Retreating polar icecaps are a vivid illustration of a warming planet. Over the past 100 years, Earth's surface air temperature is estimated to have risen by about three-quarters of a degree Celsius. Uncertainty surrounds the causes, likely future amount, and effects of this temperature increase.

The consensus is that the temperature is rising because the amount of carbon dioxide in the Earth's atmosphere is increasing, and that human economic activity is a source of the increased carbon concentration.

Forests convert carbon dioxide to oxygen and so act as carbon sinks, but they are shrinking.

Two-thirds of the world's carbon emissions come from the United States, China, the European Union, Russia, and India. The fastest growing emissions are coming from India and China.

Burning fossil fuels—coal and oil—to generate electricity and to power airplanes, automobiles, and trucks pours a staggering 28 billion tonnes, or 4 tonnes per person, of carbon dioxide into the atmosphere each year.

The amount of future global warming and its effects are uncertain. If the temperature rise continues, the Earth's climate will change, ocean levels will rise, and low-lying coastal areas will need to be protected against the rising tides by expensive barriers.

Natural Resource Depletion Tropical rainforests and ocean fish stocks are disappearing quickly. No one owns these resources and everyone is free to take what they want. When Japanese, Spanish, and Russian trawlers scoop up fish in international waters, no one keeps track of the quantities of fish they catch and no one makes them pay. The fish are free.

Each one of us makes self-interested economic choices to buy products that destroy natural resources and kill wild fish stocks. When you buy soap or shampoo or eat fish and contribute to the depletion of natural resources, are your self-interested choices damaging the social interest? If they are, what can be done to change your choices so that they serve the social interest?

Economic Instability The past 20 years have been ones of remarkable economic stability, so much so that they've been called the *Great Moderation*. Even the economic shockwaves after 9/11 brought only a small dip in the strong pace of Canadian and global economic expansion. But in August 2007, a period of financial stress began.

Running Out of Natural Resources

Disappearing Forests and Fish

Tropical rainforests in South America, Africa, and Asia support the lives of 30 million species of plants, animals, and insects—approaching 50 percent of all the species on the planet. These rainforests provide us with the ingredients for many goods, including soaps, mouthwashes, shampoos, food preservatives, rubber, nuts, and fruits. The Amazon rainforest alone converts about 1 trillion pounds of carbon dioxide into oxygen each year.

Yet tropical rainforests cover less than 2 percent of the earth's surface and are heading for extinction. Logging, cattle ranching, mining, oil extraction, hydroelectric dams, and subsistence farming destroy an area the size of two football fields every second, or an area larger than New York City every day. At the current rate of destruction, almost all the tropical rainforest ecosystems will be gone by 2030.

What is happening to the tropical rainforests is also happening to ocean fish stocks. Overfishing has almost eliminated cod from the Atlantic Ocean and the southern bluefin tuna from the South Pacific Ocean. Many other species of fish are on the edge of extinction in the wild and are now available only from fish farms.

Banks' choices to lend and people's choices to borrow were made in self-interest. But did this lending and borrowing serve the social interest? Did the Federal Reserve's bailout of troubled U.S. banks serve the global social interest? Or might the Federal Reserve's rescue action encourage U.S. banks around the world to repeat their dangerous lending in the future?

The End of the Great Moderation

A Credit Crunch

Flush with funds, and offering record low interest rates, U.S. banks went on a lending spree to home buyers. Rapidly rising U.S. home prices made home owners feel well off and they were happy to borrow and spend. Home loans were bundled into securities that were sold and resold to banks around the world.

In 2006, U.S. interest rates began to rise, the rate of rise in home prices slowed, and borrowers defaulted on their loans. What started as a trickle became a flood. By mid-2007, banks took losses that totalled billions of dollars as more people defaulted.

Global credit markets stopped working, and people began to fear a prolonged slowdown in economic activity. Some even feared the return of the economic trauma of the *Great Depression* of the 1930s. The Federal Reserve, determined to avoid a catastrophe, started lending on a very large scale to the troubled U.S. banks.

Review Quiz

1 Describe the broad facts about *what*, *how*, and *for whom* goods and services are produced.
2 Use headlines from the recent news to illustrate the potential for conflict between self-interest and the social interest.

  Work Study Plan 1.2 and get instant feedback.

We've looked at five topics that illustrate the big question: How can choices made in the pursuit of self-interest also promote the social interest? While working through this book, you will encounter the principles that help economists figure out when the social interest is being served, when it is not, and what might be done when the social interest is not being served.

◆The Economic Way of Thinking

The questions that economics tries to answer tell us about the *scope of economics*. But they don't tell us how economists *think* about these questions and go about seeking answers to them.

You're now going to begin to see how economists approach economic questions. We'll look at the ideas that define the *economic way of thinking*. This way of thinking needs practice, but it is powerful, and as you become more familiar with it, you'll begin to see the world around you with a new and sharper focus.

Choices and Tradeoffs

Because we face scarcity, we must make choices. And when we make a choice, we select from the available alternatives. For example, you can spend Saturday night studying for your next economics test or having fun with your friends, but you can't do both of these activities at the same time. You must choose how much time to devote to each. Whatever choice you make, you could have chosen something else.

You can think about your choice as a tradeoff. A **tradeoff** is an exchange—giving up one thing to get something else. When you choose how to spend your Saturday night, you face a tradeoff between studying and hanging out with your friends.

Guns Versus Butter The classic tradeoff is between guns and butter. "Guns" and "butter" stand for any pair of goods. They might actually be guns and butter. Or they might be broader categories, such as national defence and food. Or they might be any pair of specific goods or services, such as cola and pizza, baseball bats and tennis rackets, colleges and hospitals, realtor services and career counseling.

Regardless of the specific objects that guns and butter represent, the guns-versus-butter tradeoff captures a hard fact of life: If we want more of one thing, we must give up something else to get it: to get more "guns" we must give up some "butter."

The idea of a tradeoff is central to economics. We'll look at some examples, beginning with the big questions: What, How, and For Whom goods and services are produced? We can view each of these questions in terms of tradeoffs.

What, How, and For Whom Tradeoffs

The questions what, how, and for whom goods and services are produced all involve tradeoffs that are similar to that between guns and butter.

What Tradeoffs What goods and services are produced depends on choices made by each one of us, by our government, and by the businesses that produce the things we buy. Each of these choices involves a tradeoff.

Each of us faces a tradeoff when we choose how to spend our income. You go to the movies this week, but you forgo a few cups of coffee to buy the movie ticket. You trade off coffee for a movie.

The federal government faces a tradeoff when it chooses how to spend our tax dollars. It votes for more national defence but cuts back on educational programs. The government trades off education for national defence.

Businesses face a tradeoff when they decide what to produce. Nike hires Tiger Woods and allocates resources to designing and marketing a new golf ball but cuts back on its development of a new running shoe. Nike trades off running shoes for golf balls.

How Tradeoffs How businesses produce the goods and services we buy depends on their choices. These choices involve tradeoffs. For example, when Tim Hortons opens a new store with an automated production line and closes one with a traditional kitchen, it trades off labour for capital. When Air Canada replaces check-in agents with self check-in kiosks, it also trades off labour for capital.

For Whom Tradeoffs For whom goods and services are produced depends on the distribution of buying power. Buying power can be redistributed—transferred from one person to another—in three ways: by voluntary payments, by theft, or through taxes and benefits organized by the government. Redistribution brings tradeoffs.

Each of us faces a tradeoff when we choose how much to contribute to the United Nations' famine relief fund. You donate $50 and cut your spending. You trade off your own spending for a small increase in economic equality. We also face a tradeoff when we vote to increase the resources for catching thieves and enforcing the law. We trade off goods and services for an increase in the security of our property.

We also face a *for whom* tradeoff when we vote for taxes and social programs that redistribute buying power from the rich to the poor. These redistribution programs confront society with what has been called the **big tradeoff**—the tradeoff between equality and efficiency. Taxing the rich and making transfers to the poor brings greater economic equality. But taxing productive activities such as running a business, working hard, and developing a more productive technology discourages these activities. So taxing productive activities means producing less. A more equal distribution means there is less to share.

Think of the problem of how to share a pie that everyone contributes to baking. If each person receives a share of the pie that is proportional to her or his effort, everyone will work hard and the pie will be as large as possible. But if the pie is shared equally, regardless of contribution, some talented bakers will slack off and the pie will shrink. The big tradeoff is one between the size of the pie and how equally it is shared. We trade off some pie for increased equality.

Choices Bring Change

What, how, and for whom goods and services are produced changes over time. The quantity and range of goods and services available today is much greater than it was a generation ago. But the quality of economic life (and its rate of improvement) does not depend purely on nature and on luck. It depends on many of the choices made by each one of us, by governments, and by businesses. These choices also involve tradeoffs.

One choice is how much of our income to consume and how much to save. Our saving can be channelled through the financial system to finance businesses and pay for new capital that increases production. The more we save, the more financial capital is available for businesses to use to buy physcial capital, so the more goods and services we can produce in the future. When you decide to save an extra $1,000 and forgo a vacation, you trade off the vacation for a higher future income. If everyone saves an extra $1,000 and businesses buy more equipment that increases production, future consumption per person rises. As a society, we trade off current consumption for economic growth and higher future consumption.

A second choice is how much effort to devote to education and training. By becoming better educated and more highly skilled, we become more productive

and are able to produce more goods and services. When you decide to remain in school for another two years to complete a professional degree and forgo a huge chunk of leisure time, you trade off leisure today for a higher future income. If everyone becomes better educated, production increases and income per person rises. As a society, we trade off current consumption and leisure time for economic growth and higher future consumption.

A third choice is how much effort to devote to research and the development of new products and production methods. Ford Motor Company can hire people either to design a new robotic assembly line or to operate the existing plant and produce cars. The robotic plant brings greater productivity in the future but means less current production—a tradeoff of current production for greater future production.

Seeing choices as tradeoffs emphasizes the idea that to get something, we must give up something. What we give up is the cost of what we get. Economists call this cost the *opportunity cost*.

Opportunity Cost

"There's no such thing as a free lunch" expresses the central idea of economics: Every choice has a cost. The **opportunity cost** of something is the highest-valued alternative that we must give up to get it.

For example, you face an opportunity cost of being in school. That opportunity cost is the highest-valued alternative that you would do if you were not in school. If you quit school and take a job at Tim Hortons, you will earn enough to go to hockey games and movies and will have lots of free time to spend with your friends. If you remain in school, you can't afford these things. You will be able to buy them when you graduate and get a job, and that is one of the payoffs from being in school. But for now, when you've bought your books, you have nothing left for games and movies. Working on assignments leaves even less time for hanging out with your friends. Giving up hockey games, movies, and free time is part of the opportunity cost of being in school.

All the *what*, *how*, and *for whom* tradeoffs involve opportunity costs. The opportunity cost of a gun is the butter forgone; the opportunity cost of a movie ticket is the number of cups of coffee forgone.

The choices that bring change also involve opportunity costs. The opportunity cost of more goods and services in the future is less consumption today.

Choosing at the Margin

You can allocate the next hour between studying and instant messaging your friends. But the choice is not all or nothing. You must decide how many minutes to allocate to each activity. To make this decision, you compare the benefit of a little bit more study time with its cost—you make your choice at the **margin**.

The benefit that arises from an increase in an activity is called **marginal benefit**. For example, suppose that you're spending four nights a week studying and your grade point average (GPA) is 3.0. You decide that you want a higher GPA, so you study an extra night each week. Your GPA rises to 3.5. The marginal benefit from studying for one extra night a week is the 0.5 increase in your GPA. It is *not* the 3.5. You already have a 3.0 from studying for four nights a week, so we don't count this benefit as resulting from the decision you are now making.

The cost of an increase in an activity is called **marginal cost**. For you, the marginal cost of increasing your study time by one night a week is the cost of the additional night not spent with your friends (if that is your best alternative use of the time). It does not include the cost of the four nights you are already studying.

To make your decision, you compare the marginal benefit from an extra night of studying with its marginal cost. If the marginal benefit exceeds the marginal cost, you study the extra night. If the marginal cost exceeds the marginal benefit, you do not study the extra night.

By evaluating marginal benefits and marginal costs and choosing only those actions that bring greater benefit than cost, we use our scarce resources in the way that makes us as well off as possible.

Responding to Incentives

When we make choices we respond to incentives. A change in marginal cost or a change in marginal benefit changes the incentives that we face and leads us to change our choice.

For example, suppose your economics instructor gives you a set of problems and tells you that all the problems will be on the next test. The marginal benefit from working these problems is large, so you diligently work them all. In contrast, if your math instructor gives you a set of problems and tells you that none of the problems will be on the next test, the marginal benefit from working these problems is lower, so you skip most of them.

The central idea of economics is that we can predict how choices will change by looking at changes in incentives. More of an activity is undertaken when its marginal cost falls or its marginal benefit rises; less of an activity is undertaken when its marginal cost rises or its marginal benefit falls.

Incentives are also the key to reconciling self-interest and social interest. When our choices are *not* in the social interest, it is because of the incentives we face. One of the challenges for economists is to figure out the incentive systems that result in self-interested choices also being in the social interest.

Human Nature, Incentives, and Institutions

Economists take human nature as given and view people as acting in their self-interest. All people—consumers, producers, politicians, and public servants—pursue their self-interest.

Self-interested actions are not necessarily *selfish* actions. You might decide to use your resources in ways that bring pleasure to others as well as to yourself. But a self-interested act gets the most value for *you* based on *your* view about value.

If human nature is given and if people act in their self-interest, how can we take care of the social interest? Economists answer this question by emphasizing the crucial role that institutions play in influencing the incentives that people face as they pursue their self-interest.

A system of laws that protects private property and markets that enable voluntary exchange are the fundamental institutions. You will learn as you progress with your study of economics that where these institutions exist, self-interest can indeed promote the social interest.

Review Quiz

1 Provide three everyday examples of tradeoffs and describe the opportunity cost involved in each.
2 Provide three everyday examples to illustrate what we mean by choosing at the margin.
3 How do economists predict changes in choices?
4 What do economists say about the role of institutions in promoting the social interest?

 Work Study Plan 1.3 and get instant feedback.

◆ Economics as Social Science and Policy Tool

Economics is both a science and a set of tools that can be used to make policy decisions.

Economics as Social Science

As social scientists, economists seek to discover how the economic world works. In pursuit of this goal, like all scientists, they distinguish between two types of statements: positive and normative.

Positive Statements *Positive* statements are about what is. They say what is currently believed about the way the world operates. A positive statement might be right or wrong, but we can test a positive statement by checking it against the facts. "Our planet is warming because of the amount of coal that we're burning" is a positive statement. "A rise in the minimum wage will bring more teenage unemployment" is another positive statement. Each statement might be right or wrong, and it can be tested.

A central task of economists is to test positive statements about how the economic world works and to weed out those that are wrong. Economics first got off the ground in the late 1700s, so economics is a young subject compared with, for example, math and physics, and much remains to be discovered.

Normative Statements *Normative* statements are statements about what ought to be. These statements depend on values and cannot be tested. The statement "We ought to cut back on our use of coal" is a normative statement. "The minimum wage should not be increased" is another normative statement. You may agree or disagree with either of these statements, but you can't test them. They express an opinion, but they don't assert a fact that can be checked. They are not economics.

Unscrambling Cause and Effect Economists are especially interested in positive statements about cause and effect. Are computers getting cheaper because people are buying them in greater quantities? Or are people buying computers in greater quantities because they are getting cheaper? Or is some third factor causing both the price of a computer to fall and the quantity of computers bought to increase?

To answer questions such as these, economists create and test economic models. An **economic model** is a description of some aspect of the economic world that includes only those features that are needed for the purpose at hand. For example, an economic model of a cell phone network might include features such as the prices of calls, the number of users, and the volume of calls. But the model would ignore details such as cell phone colours and ringtones.

A model is tested by comparing its predictions with the facts. But testing an economic model is difficult because we observe the outcomes of the simultaneous operation of many factors. To cope with this problem, economists use natural experiments, statistical investigations, and economic experiments.

Natural Experiment A natural experiment is a situation that arises in the ordinary course of economic life in which the one factor of interest is different and other things are equal (or similar). For example, Canada has higher unemployment benefits than the United States, but the people in the two nations are similar. So to study the effect of unemployment benefits on the unemployment rate, economists might compare Canada with the United States.

Statistical Investigation A statistical investigation looks for correlation—a tendency for the values of two variables to move together (either in the same direction or in opposite directions) in a predictable and related way. For example, cigarette smoking and lung cancer are correlated. Sometimes a correlation shows a causal influence of one variable on the other. For example, smoking causes lung cancer. But sometimes the direction of causation is hard to determine.

Steven Levitt, the author of *Freakonomics* and whom you can meet on pp. 224–226, is a master in the use of a combination of the natural experiment and statistical investigation to unscramble cause and effect. He has used the tools of economics to investigate the effects of good parenting on education (not very strong), to explain why drug dealers live with their mothers (because they don't earn enough to live independently), and (controversially) the effects of abortion law on crime.

Economic Experiment An economic experiment puts people in a decision-making situation and varies the influence of one factor at a time to discover how they respond.

Economics as Policy Tool

Economics is useful. It is a toolkit for making decisions. And you don't need to be a fully fledged economist to think like one and to use the insights of economics as a policy tool.

Economics provides a way of approaching problems in all aspects of our lives. Here, we'll focus on the three broad areas of:

- Personal economic policy
- Business economic policy
- Government economic policy

Personal Economic Policy Should you take out a student loan? Should you get a weekend job? Should you buy a used car or a new one? Should you rent an apartment or take out a loan and buy a condominium? Should you pay off your credit card balance or make just the minimum payment? How should you allocate your time between study, working for a wage, caring for family members, and having fun? How should you allocate your time between studying economics and your other subjects? Should you quit school after getting a bachelor's degree or should you go for a master's or a professional qualification?

All these questions involve a marginal benefit and a marginal cost. And although some of the numbers might be hard to pin down, you will make more solid decisions if you approach these questions with the tools of economics.

Business Economic Policy Should Sony make only flat panel televisions and stop making conventional ones? Should Bell Canada outsource its online customer services to India or run the operation from Quebec? Should Encana explore the Deep Panuke natural gas field off the coast of Nova Scotia or expand its oil sands project in North Alberta? Can Microsoft compete with Google in the search engine business? Can eBay compete with the surge of new Internet auction services? Is Allan Burnett really worth $13,200,000 to the Blue Jays?

Like personal economic questions, these business questions involve the evaluation of a marginal benefit and a marginal cost. Some of the questions require a broader investigation of the interactions of individuals and firms. But again, by approaching these questions with the tools of economics and by hiring economists as advisors, businesses can make better decisions.

Government Economic Policy How can provincial and federal governments balance their budgets? Should the federal governments cut taxes? Should provincial governments raise taxes? How can the Canadian tax system be simplified? Should people be permitted to buy private health insurance just as they already buy private travel insurance? Should there be a special tax to penalize corporations that send jobs overseas? Should cheap foreign imports of furniture and textiles be limited? Should egg, dairy, and milk farmers receive subsidies? Should wheat and barley growers be able to sell their output on the world market and not be restricted to sell to the Canadian Wheat Board?

These government policy questions call for decisions that involve the evaluation of a marginal benefit and a marginal cost and an investigation of the interactions of individuals and businesses. Yet again, by approaching these questions with the tools of economics, governments make better decisions.

Notice that all the policy questions we've just posed involve a blend of the positive and the normative. Economics can't help with the normative part—the objective. But for a given objective, economics provides a method of evaluating alternative solutions. That method is to evaluate the marginal benefits and marginal costs and to find the solution that brings the greatest available gain.

Review Quiz

1 What is the distinction between a positive statement and a normative statement? Provide an example (different from those in the chapter) of each type of statement.

2 What is a model? Can you think of a model that you might use (probably without thinking of it as a model) in your everyday life?

3 What are the three ways in which economists try to disentangle cause and effect?

4 How is economics used as a policy tool?

5 What is the role of marginal benefit and marginal cost in the use of economics as a policy tool?

 Work Study Plan 1.4 and get instant feedback.

SUMMARY ◈

Key Points

Definition of Economics (p. 2)

■ All economic questions arise from scarcity—from the fact that wants exceed the resources available to satisfy them.

■ Economics is the social science that studies the choices that people make as they cope with scarcity.

■ The subject divides into microeconomics and macroeconomics.

Two Big Economic Questions (pp. 3–7)

■ Two big questions summarize the scope of economics:

1. How do choices end up determining *what*, *how*, and *for whom* goods and services are produced?
2. When do choices made in the pursuit of *self-interest* also promote the *social interest*?

The Economic Way of Thinking (pp. 8–10)

■ Every choice is a tradeoff—exchanging more of something for less of something else.

■ The classic guns-versus-butter tradeoff represents all tradeoffs.

■ All economic questions involve tradeoffs.

■ The big social tradeoff is that between equality and efficiency.

■ The highest-valued alternative forgone is the opportunity cost of what is chosen.

■ Choices are made at the margin and respond to incentives.

Economics as Social Science and Policy Tool (pp. 11–12)

■ Economists distinguish between positive statements—what is—and normative statements—what ought to be.

■ To explain the economic world, economists create and test economic models.

■ Economics is used in personal, business, and government economic policy decisions.

■ The main policy tool is the evaluation and comparison of marginal cost and marginal benefit.

Key Terms

Big tradeoff, 9
Capital, 4
Economic model, 11
Economics, 2
Entrepreneurship, 4
Factors of production, 3
Goods and services, 3
Human capital, 3
Incentive, 2

Interest, 4
Labour, 3
Land, 3
Macroeconomics, 2
Margin, 10
Marginal benefit, 10
Marginal cost, 10
Microeconomics, 2
Opportunity cost, 9

Profit, 4
Rent, 4
Scarcity, 2
Self-interest, 5
Social interest, 5
Tradeoff, 8
Wages, 4

PROBLEMS and APPLICATIONS

 Work problems 1–6 in Chapter 1 Study Plan and get instant feedback.
Work problems 7–11 as Homework, a Quiz, or a Test if assigned by your instructor.

1. Apple Computer Inc. decides to make songs freely available in unlimited quantities at the iTunes Store.
   a. How does Apple's decision change the opportunity cost of downloading a song?
   b. Does Apple's decision change the incentives that people face?
   c. Is Apple's decision an example of a microeconomic or a macroeconomic issue?

2. Which of the following pairs does not match?
   a. Labour and wages
   b. Land and rent
   c. Entrepreneurship and profit
   d. Capital and profit

3. Explain how the following news headlines concern self-interest and the social interest:
   a. Roots Expands in China
   b. McDonald's Moves into Salads
   c. Food Must Be Labelled with Nutrition Information

4. The night before a test, you decide to go to the movies instead of working your MyEconLab Study Plan. You get 50 percent on your test, not the 70 percent that you normally score.
   a. Did you face a tradeoff?
   b. What was the opportunity cost of your evening at the movies?

5. Which of the following statements is positive, which is normative, and which can be tested?
   a. The federal government should increase production of biofuels.
   b. China is Canada's largest trading partner.
   c. If the price of antiretroviral drugs increases, HIV/AIDS sufferers will decrease their consumption of the drugs.

6. As London prepares to host the 2012 Olympic Games, concern about the cost of the event is increasing. An example:

   Costs Soar for London Olympics

   The regeneration of East London is set to add extra £1.5 billion to taxpayers' bill.

   The Times, London, July 6, 2006

   Is the cost of regenerating East London an opportunity cost of hosting the 2012 Olympic Games? Explain why or why not.

7. Before starring as Tony Stark in *Iron Man*, Robert Downey Jr. had acted in 45 movies that had average first-weekend box office revenues of a bit less than $5 million. *Iron Man* grossed $102 million on its opening weekend.
   a. How do you expect the success of *Iron Man* to influence the opportunity cost of hiring Robert Downey Jr.?
   b. How have the incentives for a movie producer to hire Robert Downey Jr. changed?

8. How would you classify a movie star as a factor of production?

9. How does the creation of a successful movie influence what, how, and for whom goods and services are produced?

10. How does the creation of a successful movie illustrate self-interested choices that are also in the social interest?

11. Look at today's *National Post*.
    a. What is the top economic news story? With which of the big questions does it deal? (It must deal with at least one of them and might deal with more than one.)
    b. What tradeoffs does the news item discuss or imply?
    c. Write a brief summary of the news item using the economic vocabulary that you have learned in this chapter and as many as possible of the key terms listed on p. 13.

12. Use the link in MyEconLab (Textbook Resources, Chapter 1) to visit *Resources for Economists on the Internet*. This Web site is a good place from which to search for economic information on the Internet. Click on "Blogs, Commentaries, and Podcasts" and then click on the Becker-Posner Blog.
    a. Read the latest blog by these two outstanding economists.
    b. As you read this blog, think about what it is saying about the "what," "how," and "for whom" questions.
    c. As you read the blog, also think about what it is saying about self-interest and the social interest.

APPENDIX

Graphs in Economics

After studying this appendix, you will be able to

- Make and interpret a time-series graph, a cross-section graph, and a scatter diagram
- Distinguish between linear and nonlinear relationships and between relationships that have a maximum and a minimum
- Define and calculate the slope of a line
- Graph relationships among more than two variables

Graphing Data

A graph represents a quantity as a distance on a line. In Fig. A1.1, a distance on the horizontal line represents temperature, measured in degrees Celsius. A movement from left to right shows an increase in temperature. The point 0 represents zero degrees Celsius. To the right of 0, the temperature is positive. To the left of 0 (as indicated by the minus sign), the temperature is negative. A distance on the vertical line represents height, measured in thousands of feet. The point 0 represents sea level. Points above 0 represent feet above sea level. Points below 0 (indicated by a minus sign) represent feet below sea level.

By setting two scales perpendicular to each other, as in Fig. A1.1, we can visualize the relationship between two variables. The scale lines are called *axes*. The vertical line is the *y*-axis, and the horizontal line is the *x*-axis. Each axis has a zero point, which is shared by the two axes and called the *origin*.

We need two bits of information to make a two-variable graph: the value of the *x* variable and the value of the *y* variable. For example, off the coast of British Columbia, the temperature is 10 degrees—the value of *x*. A fishing boat is located at 0 feet above sea level—the value of *y*. These two bits of information appear as point *A* in Fig. A1.1. A climber at the top of Mount McKinley on a cold day is 6,194 metres

FIGURE A1.1 Making a Graph

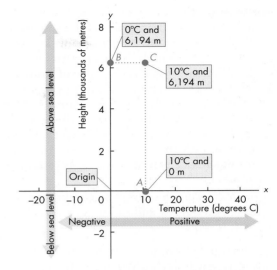

Graphs have axes that measure quantities as distances. Here, the horizontal axis (*x*-axis) measures temperature, and the vertical axis (*y*-axis) measures height. Point *A* represents a fishing boat at sea level (0 on the *y*-axis) on a day when the temperature is 10°C. Point *B* represents a climber at the top of Mt. McKinley, 6,194 metres above sea level in a zero-degree gale. Point *C* represents a climber at the top of Mt. McKinley, 6,194 metres above sea level, at a temperature of 10°C.

myeconlab   animation

above sea level in a zero-degree gale. These two pieces of information appear as point *B*. On a warmer day, a climber might be at the peak of Mt. McKinley when the temperature is 10 degrees, at point *C*.

We can draw two lines, called *coordinates*, from point *C*. One, called the *y*-coordinate, runs from *C* to the horizontal axis. Its length is the same as the value marked off on the *y*-axis. The other, called the *x*-coordinate, runs from *C* to the vertical axis. Its length is the same as the value marked off on the *x*-axis. We describe a point on a graph by the values of its *x*-coordinate and its *y*-coordinate.

Graphs like that in Fig. A1.1 can show any type of quantitative data on two variables. Economists use three types of graphs based on the principles in Fig. A1.1 to reveal and describe the relationships among variables. They are

- Time-series graphs
- Cross-section graphs
- Scatter diagrams

Time-Series Graphs

A **time-series graph** measures time (for example, months or years) on the *x*-axis and the variable or variables in which we are interested on the *y*-axis. Figure A1.2 is an example of a time-series graph. It provides information about the price of gasoline (the variable we're interested in). In this figure, we measure time in months starting in January 2006. We measure the price of gasoline on the *y*-axis.

The point of a time-series graph is to enable us to visualize how a variable has changed over time and how its value in one period relates to its value in another period.

A time-series graph conveys an enormous amount of information quickly and easily, as this example illustrates. It shows

- The *level* of the price of gasoline—when it is *high* and *low*. When the line is a long way from the *x*-axis, the price is high, as it was, for example, in May 2008. When the line is close to the *x*-axis, the price is low, as it was, for example, in October 2006.
- How the price *changes*—whether it *rises* or *falls*. When the line slopes upward, as in January 2008, the price is rising. When the line slopes downward, as in July 2007, the price is falling.
- The *speed* with which the price changes—whether it rises or falls *quickly* or *slowly*. If the line is very steep, then the price rises or falls quickly. If the line is not steep, the price rises or falls slowly. For example, the price rose quickly between March 2008 and May 2008 and slowly between December 2007 and February 2008. The price fell quickly between August 2006 and September 2006 and slowly between July 2007 and August 2007.

A time-series graph also reveals whether there is a **trend**—a general tendency for a variable to move in one direction. A trend might be upward or downward. In Fig. A1.2, the price of gasoline had a general tendency to rise from January 2006 to May 2008. Although the price rose and fell, the general tendency was for it to rise—the price had an upward trend. A time-series graph also helps us to detect fluctuations in a variable around its trend. You can see some peaks and troughs in the price of gasoline in Fig. A1.2.

Finally, a time-series graph also lets us quickly compare the variable in different periods. Figure A1.2 shows that the price of gasoline fluctuated more

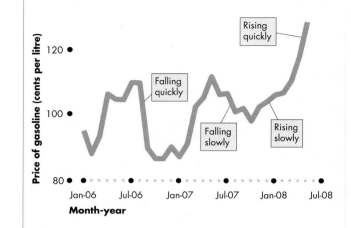

FIGURE A1.2 A Time-Series Graph

Rising quickly

Falling quickly

Falling slowly

Rising slowly

Price of gasoline (cents per litre)

120

100

80

Jan-06   Jul-06   Jan-07   Jul-07   Jan-08   Jul-08

Month-year

A time-series graph plots the level of a variable on the *y*-axis against time (day, week, month, or year) on the *x*-axis. This graph shows the price of gasoline (in 2006 dollars per litre) each month from January 2006 to July 2008. It shows us when the price of gasoline was *high* and when it was *low*, when the price *increased* and when it *decreased*, and when the price changed *quickly* and when it changed *slowly*.

myeconlab animation

during 2006 and 2007 than it did in the first six months of 2008.

You can see that a time-series graph conveys a wealth of information, and it does so in much less space than we have used to describe only some of its features. But you do have to "read" the graph to obtain all this information.

Cross-Section Graphs

A **cross-section graph** shows the values of an economic variable for different groups or categories at a point in time. Figure A1.3, called a *bar chart*, is an example of a cross-section graph.

The bar chart in Fig. A1.3 shows the number of visitors to each province in 2004. The length of each bar indicates the number of visitors. This figure enables you to compare the number of visitors across the provinces. And you can do so much more quickly and clearly than you could by looking at a list of numbers.

FIGURE A1.3   A Cross-Section Graph

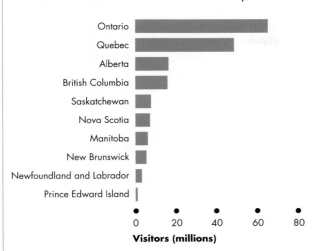

A cross-section graph shows the level of a variable across categories or groups. This bar chart shows the number of visitors to each province in 2004.

Scatter Diagrams

A **scatter diagram** plots the value of one variable against the value of another variable. Such a graph reveals whether a relationship exists between two variables and describes their relationship. Figure A1.4(a) shows the relationship between expenditure and income. Each point shows expenditure per person and income per person in a given year from 1997 to 2007. The points are "scattered" within the graph. The point labelled *A* tells us that in 2000, income per person was $20,840 and expenditure per person was $19,421. The dots in this graph form a pattern, which reveals that as income increases, expenditure increases.

Figure A1.4(b) shows the relationship between the number of computers sold and the price of a computer. This graph shows that as the price of a computer falls, number of computers sold increases.

Figure A1.4(c) shows a scatter diagram of the inflation rate and the unemployment rate in Canada. Here, the dots show no clear relationship between these two variables.

FIGURE A1.4   Scatter Diagrams

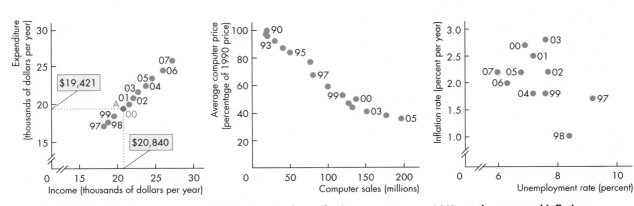

(a) Expenditure and income   **(b) Computer sales and prices**   **(c) Unemployment and inflation**

A scatter diagram reveals the relationship between two variables. Part (a) shows the relationship between expenditure and income. Each point shows the values of the two variables in a specific year. For example, point A shows that in 2000, average income was $20,840 and average expenditure was $19,421. The pattern formed by the points shows that as income increases, expenditure increases.

Part (b) shows the relationship between the price of a computer and the number of computers sold from 1990 to 2006. This graph shows that as the price of a computer falls, the number of computers sold increases.

Part (c) shows a scatter diagram of the inflation rate and the unemployment rate from 1997 to 2007. This graph shows that inflation and unemployment are not closely related.

Breaks in the Axes Two of the graphs you've just looked at, Fig. A1.4(a) and Fig. A1.4(c), have breaks in their axes, as shown by the small gaps. The breaks indicate that there are jumps from the origin, 0, to the first values recorded.

In Fig. A1.4(a), the breaks are used because the lowest value of expenditure exceeds $15,000 and the lowest value of income exceeds $15,000. With no breaks in the axes, there would be a lot of empty space, all the points would be crowded into the top right corner, and we would not be able to see whether a relationship exists between these two variables. By breaking the axes, we are able to bring the relationship into view.

Putting a break in one or both axes is like using a zoom lens to bring the relationship into the centre of the graph and magnify it so that the relationship fills the graph.

Misleading Graphs Breaks can be used to highlight a relationship, but they can also be used to mislead—to make a graph that lies. The most common way of making a graph lie is to use axis breaks and either to stretch or to compress a scale. For example, suppose that in Fig. A1.4(a), the *y*-axis that measures expenditure ran from zero to $30,000 while the *x*-axis was the same as the one shown. The graph would now create the impression that despite a huge increase in income, expenditure had barely changed.

To avoid being misled, it is a good idea to get into the habit of always looking closely at the values and the labels on the axes of a graph before you start to interpret it.

Correlation and Causation A scatter diagram that shows a clear relationship between two variables, such as Fig. A1.4(a) or Fig. A1.4(b), tells us that the two variables have a high correlation. When a high correlation is present, we can predict the value of one variable from the value of the other variable. But correlation does not imply causation.

Sometimes a high correlation is a coincidence, but sometimes it does arise from a causal relationship. It is likely, for example, that rising income causes rising expenditure, in Fig. A1.4(a), and that the falling price of a computer causes more computers to be sold, in Fig. A1.4(b).

You've now seen how we can use graphs in economics to show economic data and to reveal relationships. Next, we'll learn how economists use graphs to construct and display economic models.

◆ Graphs Used in Economic Models

The graphs used in economics are not always designed to show real-world data. Often they are used to show general relationships among the variables in an economic model.

An *economic model* is a stripped-down, simplified description of an economy or of a component of an economy such as a business or a household. It consists of statements about economic behaviour that can be expressed as equations or as curves in a graph. Economists use models to explore the effects of different policies or other influences on the economy in ways that are similar to the use of model airplanes in wind tunnels and models of the climate.

You will encounter many different kinds of graphs in economic models, but there are some repeating patterns. Once you've learned to recognize these patterns, you will instantly understand the meaning of a graph. Here, we'll look at the different types of curves that are used in economic models, and we'll see some everyday examples of each type of curve. The patterns to look for in graphs are the four cases in which

- Variables move in the same direction.
- Variables move in opposite directions.
- Variables have a maximum or a minimum.
- Variables are unrelated.

Let's look at these four cases.

Variables That Move in the Same Direction

Figure A1.5 shows graphs of the relationships between two variables that move up and down together. A relationship between two variables that move in the same direction is called a **positive relationship** or a **direct relationship**. A line that slopes upward shows such a relationship.

Figure A1.5 shows three types of relationships: one that has a straight line and two that have curved lines. But all the lines in these three graphs are called curves. Any line on a graph—no matter whether it is straight or curved—is called a *curve*.

A relationship shown by a straight line is called a linear relationship. Figure A1.5(a) shows a **linear relationship** between the number of kilometres travelled in 5 hours and speed. For example, point *A* shows that we will travel 200 kilometres in 5 hours if our

FIGURE A1.5   Positive (Direct) Relationships

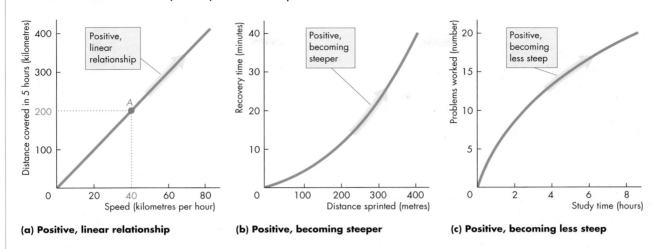

(a) Positive, linear relationship   **(b) Positive, becoming steeper**   **(c) Positive, becoming less steep**

Each part of this figure shows a positive (direct) relationship between two variables. That is, as the value of the variable measured on the *x*-axis increases, so does the value of the variable measured on the *y*-axis. Part (a) shows a linear relationship—as the two variables increase together, we move along a straight line. Part (b) shows a positive relationship such that as the two variables increase together, we move along a curve that becomes steeper. Part (c) shows a positive relationship such that as the two variables increase together, we move along a curve that becomes flatter.

myeconlab animation

speed is 40 kilometres an hour. If we double our speed to 80 kilometres an hour, we will travel 400 kilometres in 5 hours.

Figure A1.5(b) shows the relationship between distance sprinted and recovery time (the time it takes the heart rate to return to its normal resting rate). This relationship is an upward-sloping one that starts out quite flat but then becomes steeper as we move along the curve away from the origin. The reason this curve slopes upward and becomes steeper is because the additional recovery time needed from sprinting an additional 100 metres increases. It takes less than 5 minutes to recover from sprinting 100 metres but more than 10 minutes to recover from sprinting 200 metres.

Figure A1.5(c) shows the relationship between the number of problems worked by a student and the amount of study time. This relationship is an upward-sloping one that starts out quite steep and becomes flatter as we move along the curve away from the origin. Study time becomes less productive as the student spends more hours studying and becomes more tired.

Variables That Move in Opposite Directions

Figure A1.6 shows relationships between things that move in opposite directions. A relationship between variables that move in opposite directions is called a **negative relationship** or an **inverse relationship**.

Figure A1.6(a) shows the relationship between the hours spent playing squash and the hours spent playing tennis when the total number of hours available is 5. One extra hour spent playing tennis means one hour less playing squash and vice versa. This relationship is negative and linear.

Figure A1.6(b) shows the relationship between the cost per kilometre travelled and the length of a journey. The longer the journey, the lower is the cost per kilometre. But as the journey length increases, even though the cost per kilometre decreases, the fall in the cost is smaller. This feature of the relationship is shown by the fact that the curve slopes downward, starting out steep at a short journey length and then becoming flatter as the journey length increases. This relationship arises because some of the costs don't depend on the journey length, such as auto insurance, and these costs are spread over a longer journey.

FIGURE A1.6 Negative (Inverse) Relationships

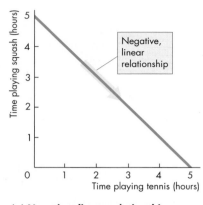

(a) Negative, linear relationship

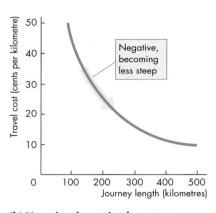

(b) Negative, becoming less steep

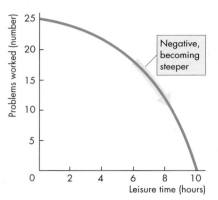

(c) Negative, becoming steeper

Each part of this figure shows a negative (inverse) relationship between two variables. That is, as the value of the variable measured on the x-axis increases, the value of the variable measured on the y-axis decreases. Part (a) shows a linear relationship. The total time spent playing tennis and squash is 5 hours. As the time spent playing tennis increases, the time spent playing squash decreases, and we move along a straight line.

Part (b) shows a negative relationship such that as the journey length increases, the travel cost decreases as we move along a curve that becomes less steep.

Part (c) shows a negative relationship such that as leisure time increases, the number of problems worked decreases as we move along a curve that becomes steeper.

myeconlab animation

Figure A1.6(c) shows the relationship between the amount of leisure time and the number of problems worked by a student. Increasing leisure time produces an increasingly large reduction in the number of problems worked. This relationship is a negative one that starts out with a gentle slope at a small number of leisure hours and becomes steeper as the number of leisure hours increases. This relationship is a different view of the idea shown in Fig. A1.5(c).

Variables That Have a Maximum or a Minimum

Many relationships in economic models have a maximum or a minimum. For example, firms try to make the maximum possible profit and to produce at the lowest possible cost. Figure A1.7 shows relationships that have a maximum or a minimum.

Figure A1.7(a) shows the relationship between rainfall and wheat yield. When there is no rainfall, wheat will not grow, so the yield is zero. As the rainfall increases up to 10 days a month, the wheat yield increases. With 10 rainy days each month, the wheat yield reaches its maximum at 2 tonnes per hectare (point *A*). Rain in excess of 10 days a month starts to lower the yield of wheat. If every day is rainy, the wheat suffers from a lack of sunshine and the yield decreases to zero. This relationship is one that starts out sloping upward, reaches a maximum, and then slopes downward.

Figure A1.7(b) shows the reverse case—a relationship that begins sloping downward, falls to a minimum, and then slopes upward. Most economic costs are like this relationship. An example is the relationship between the cost per kilometre and speed for a car trip. At low speeds, the car is creeping in a traffic jam. The number of kilometres per litre is low, so the cost per kilometre is high. At high speeds, the car is travelling faster than its efficient speed, using a large quantity of gasoline, and again the number of kilometres per litre is low and the cost per kilometre is high. At a speed of 100 kilometres an hour, the cost per kilometre is at its minimum (point *B*). This relationship is one that starts out sloping downward, reaches a minimum, and then slopes upward.

FIGURE A1.7 Maximum and Minimum Points

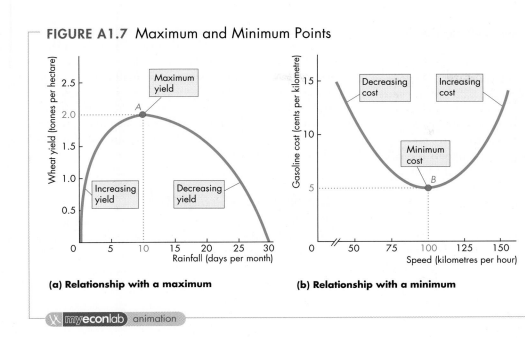

(a) Relationship with a maximum

(b) Relationship with a minimum

Part (a) shows a relationship that has a maximum point, A. The curve slopes upward as it rises to its maximum point, is flat at its maximum, and then slopes downward.

Part (b) shows a relationship with a minimum point, B. The curve slopes downward as it falls to its minimum, is flat at its minimum, and then slopes upward.

Variables That Are Unrelated

There are many situations in which no matter what happens to the value of one variable, the other variable remains constant. Sometimes we want to show the independence between two variables in a graph, and Fig. A1.8 illustrates two ways of achieving this.

In describing the graphs in Fig. A1.5 through A1.7, we have talked about curves that slope upward or slope downward, and curves that become less steep or steeper. Let's spend a little time discussing exactly what we mean by slope and how we measure the slope of a curve.

FIGURE A1.8 Variables That Are Unrelated

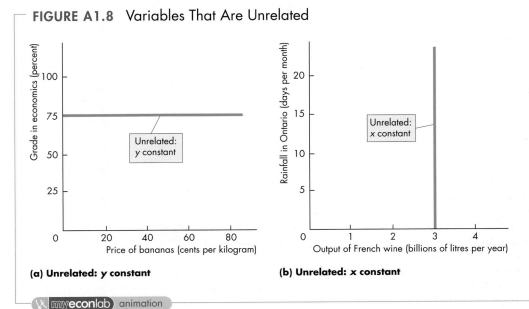

(a) Unrelated: *y* constant

(b) Unrelated: *x* constant

This figure shows how we can graph two variables that are unrelated. In part (a), a student's grade in economics is plotted at 75 percent on the *y*-axis regardless of the price of bananas on the *x*-axis. The curve is horizontal.

In part (b), the output of the vineyards of France on the *x*-axis does not vary with the rainfall in Ontario on the *y*-axis. The curve is vertical.

◆ The Slope of a Relationship

We can measure the influence of one variable on another by the slope of the relationship. The **slope** of a relationship is the change in the value of the variable measured on the *y*-axis divided by the change in the value of the variable measured on the *x*-axis. We use the Greek letter Δ (*delta*) to represent "change in." Thus Δ*y* means the change in the value of the variable measured on the *y*-axis, and Δ*x* means the change in the value of the variable measured on the *x*-axis. Therefore the slope of the relationship is

$$\Delta y\,/\Delta x.$$

If a large change in the variable measured on the *y*-axis (Δ*y*) is associated with a small change in the variable measured on the *x*-axis (Δ*x*), the slope is large and the curve is steep. If a small change in the variable measured on the *y*-axis (Δ*y*) is associated with a large change in the variable measured on the *x*-axis (Δ*x*), the slope is small and the curve is flat.

We can make the idea of slope clearer by doing some calculations.

The Slope of a Straight Line

The slope of a straight line is the same regardless of where on the line you calculate it. The slope of a

FIGURE A1.9 The Slope of a Straight Line

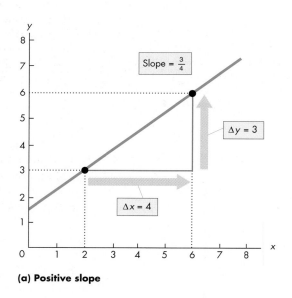

(a) Positive slope

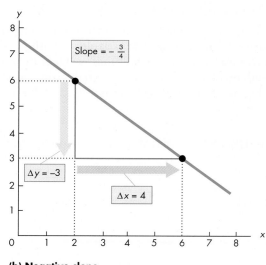

(b) Negative slope

To calculate the slope of a straight line, we divide the change in the value of the variable measured on the *y*-axis (Δ*y*) by the change in the value of the variable measured on the *x*-axis (Δ*x*) as we move along the curve.

Part (a) shows the calculation of a positive slope. When *x* increases from 2 to 6, Δ*x* equals 4. That change in *x* brings about an increase in *y* from 3 to 6, so Δ*y* equals 3. The slope (Δ*y*/Δ*x*) equals 3/4.

Part (b) shows the calculation of a negative slope. When *x* increases from 2 to 6, Δ*x* equals 4. That increase in *x* brings about a decrease in *y* from 6 to 3, so Δ*y* equals –3. The slope (Δ*y*/Δ*x*) equals –3/4.

 myeconlab animation

straight line is constant. Let's calculate the slopes of the lines in Fig. A1.9. In part (a), when x increases from 2 to 6, y increases from 3 to 6. The change in x is +4—that is, Δx is 4. The change in y is +3—that is, Δy is 3. The slope of that line is

$$\frac{\Delta y}{\Delta x} = \frac{3}{4}.$$

In part (b), when x increases from 2 to 6, y decreases from 6 to 3. The change in y is *minus* 3—that is, Δy is –3. The change in x is *plus* 4—that is, Δx is 4. The slope of the curve is

$$\frac{\Delta y}{\Delta x} = \frac{-3}{4}.$$

Notice that the two slopes have the same magnitude (3/4), but the slope of the line in part (a) is positive (+3/+4 = 3/4) while the slope in part (b) is negative (–3/+4 = –3/4). The slope of a positive relationship is positive; the slope of a negative relationship is negative.

The Slope of a Curved Line

The slope of a curved line is trickier. The slope of a curved line is not constant, so the slope depends on where on the curved line we calculate it. There are two ways to calculate the slope of a curved line: You can calculate the slope at a point, or you can calculate the slope across an arc of the curve. Let's look at the two alternatives.

Slope at a Point To calculate the slope at a point on a curve, you need to construct a straight line that has the same slope as the curve at the point in question. Figure A1.10 shows how this is done. Suppose you want to calculate the slope of the curve at point A. Place a ruler on the graph so that it touches point A and no other point on the curve, then draw a straight line along the edge of the ruler. The straight red line is this line, and it is the tangent to the curve at point A. If the ruler touches the curve only at point A, then the slope of the curve at point A must be the same as the slope of the edge of the ruler. If the curve and the ruler do not have the same slope, the line along the edge of the ruler will cut the curve instead of just touching it.

Now that you have found a straight line with the same slope as the curve at point A, you can calculate

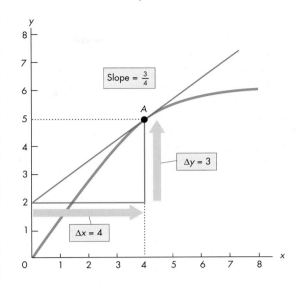

FIGURE A1.10   Slope at a Point

To calculate the slope of the curve at point A, draw the red line that just touches the curve at A—the tangent. The slope of this straight line is calculated by dividing the change in y by the change in x along the line. When x increases from 0 to 4, Δx equals 4. That change in x is associated with an increase in y from 2 to 5, so Δy equals 3. The slope of the red line is 3/4. So the slope of the curve at point A is 3/4.

the slope of the curve at point A by calculating the slope of the straight line. Along the straight line, as x increases from 0 to 4 ($\Delta x = 4$) y increases from 2 to 5 ($\Delta y = 3$). Therefore the slope of the straight line is

$$\frac{\Delta y}{\Delta x} = \frac{3}{4}.$$

So the slope of the curve at point A is 3/4.

Slope Across an Arc An arc of a curve is a piece of a curve. In Fig. A1.11, you are looking at the same curve as in Fig. A1.10. But instead of calculating the slope at point A, we are going to calculate the slope across the arc from B to C. You can see that the slope at B is greater than at C. When we calculate the slope across an arc, we are calculating the average slope between two points. As we move along the arc from B to C, x increases from 3 to 5 and y increases from 4 to

FIGURE A1.11   Slope Across an Arc

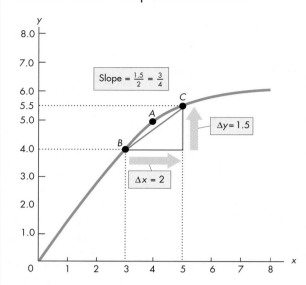

To calculate the average slope of the curve along the arc *BC*, draw a straight line from *B* to *C*. The slope of the line *BC* is calculated by dividing the change in *y* by the change in *x*. In moving from *B* to *C*, Δx equals 2 and Δy equals 1.5. The slope of the line *BC* is 1.5 divided by 2, or 3/4. So the slope of the curve across the arc *BC* is 3/4.

myeconlab animation

5.5. The change in *x* is 2 ($\Delta x = 2$), and the change in *y* is 1.5 ($\Delta y = 1.5$). Therefore the slope is

$$\frac{\Delta y}{\Delta x} = \frac{1.5}{2} = \frac{3}{4}.$$

So the slope of the curve across the arc *BC* is 3/4.

This calculation gives us the slope of the curve between points *B* and *C*. The actual slope calculated is the slope of the straight line from *B* to *C*. This slope approximates the average slope of the curve along the arc *BC*. In this particular example, the slope across the arc *BC* is identical to the slope of the curve at point *A*. But the calculation of the slope of a curve does not always work out so neatly. You might have fun constructing some more examples and a few counterexamples.

You now know how to make and interpret a graph. But so far, we've limited our attention to graphs of two variables. We're now going to learn how to graph more than two variables.

Graphing Relationships Among More Than Two Variables

We have seen that we can graph the relationship between two variables as a point formed by the *x*- and *y*-coordinates in a two-dimensional graph. You might be thinking that although a two-dimensional graph is informative, most of the things in which you are likely to be interested involve relationships among many variables, not just two. For example, the amount of ice cream consumed depends on the price of ice cream and the temperature. If ice cream is expensive and the temperature is low, people eat much less ice cream than when ice cream is inexpensive and the temperature is high. For any given price of ice cream, the quantity consumed varies with the temperature; and for any given temperature, the quantity of ice cream consumed varies with its price.

Figure A1.12 shows a relationship among three variables. The table shows the number of litres of ice cream consumed each day at various temperatures and ice cream prices. How can we graph these numbers?

To graph a relationship that involves more than two variables, we use the *ceteris paribus* assumption.

Ceteris Paribus ***Ceteris paribus*** means "if all other relevant things remain the same." To isolate the relationship of interest in a laboratory experiment, we hold other things constant. We use the same method to graph a relationship with more than two variables.

Figure A1.12(a) shows an example. There, you can see what happens to the quantity of ice cream consumed when the price of ice cream varies when the temperature is held constant. The line labelled 21°C shows the relationship between ice cream consumption and the price of ice cream if the temperature remains at 21°C. The numbers used to plot that line are those in the third column of the table in Fig. A1.12. For example, if the temperature is 21°C, 10 litres are consumed when the price is 60¢ a scoop, and 18 litres are consumed when the price is 30¢ a scoop. The curve labelled 32°C shows consumption as the price varies if the temperature remains at 32°C.

We can also show the relationship between ice cream consumption and temperature when the price of ice cream remains constant, as shown in Fig. A1.12(b). The curve labelled 60¢ shows how the consumption of ice cream varies with the

FIGURE A1.12   Graphing a Relationship Among Three Variables

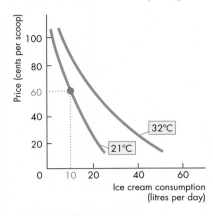

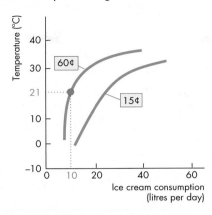

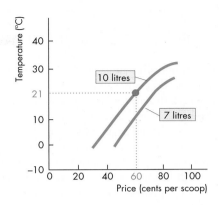

(a) Price and consumption at a given temperature

(b) Temperature and consumption at a given price

(c) Temperature and price at a given consumption

Price (cents per scoop)	Ice cream consumption (litres per day)			
	−10°C	10°C	21°C	32°C
15	12	18	25	50
30	10	12	18	37
45	7	10	13	27
60	5	7	10	20
75	3	5	7	14
90	2	3	5	10
105	1	2	3	6

Ice cream consumption depends on its price and the temperature. The table tells us how many litres of ice cream are consumed each day at different prices and different temperatures. For example, if the price is 60¢ a scoop and the temperature is 21°C, 10 litres of ice cream are consumed. This set of values is highlighted in the table and each part of the figure.

To graph a relationship among three variables, the value of one variable is held constant. Part (a) shows the relationship between price and consumption when temperature is held constant. One curve holds temperature at 32°C and the other holds it at 21°C. Part (b) shows the relationship between temperature and consumption when price is held constant. One curve holds the price at 60¢ a scoop and the other holds it at 15¢ a scoop. Part (c) shows the relationship between temperature and price when consumption is held constant. One curve holds consumption at 10 litres and the other holds it at 7 litres.

temperature when the price of ice cream is 60¢ a scoop, and a second curve shows the relationship when the price is 15¢ a scoop. For example, at 60¢ a scoop, 10 litres are consumed when the temperature is 21°C and 20 litres are consumed when the temperature is 32°C.

Figure A1.12(c) shows the combinations of temperature and price that result in a constant consumption of ice cream. One curve shows the combinations that result in 10 litres a day being consumed, and the other shows the combinations that result in 7 litres a

day being consumed. A high price and a high temperature lead to the same consumption as a lower price and a lower temperature. For example, 10 litres of ice cream are consumed at 21°C and 60¢ a scoop, at 32°C and 90¢ a scoop, and at 10°C and 45¢ a scoop.

With what you have learned about graphs, you can move forward with your study of economics. There are no graphs in this book that are more complicated than those that have been explained in this appendix.

MATHEMATICAL NOTE

Equations of Straight Lines

If a straight line in a graph describes the relationship between two variables, we call it a linear relationship. Figure 1 shows the *linear relationship* between a person's expenditure and income. This person spends $100 a week (by borrowing or spending previous savings) when income is zero. And out of each dollar earned, this person spends 50 cents (and saves 50 cents).

All linear relationships are described by the same general equation. We call the quantity that is measured on the horizontal axis (or *x*-axis) *x*, and we call the quantity that is measured on the vertical axis (or *y*-axis) *y*. In the case of Fig. 1, *x* is income and *y* is expenditure.

A Linear Equation

The equation that describes a straight-line relationship between *x* and *y* is

$$y = a + bx.$$

In this equation, *a* and *b* are fixed numbers and they are called constants. The values of *x* and *y* vary, so these numbers are called variables. Because the equation describes a straight line, the equation is called a *linear equation.*

The equation tells us that when the value of *x* is zero, the value of *y* is *a*. We call the constant *a* the *y*-axis intercept. The reason is that on the graph the straight line hits the *y*-axis at a value equal to *a*. Figure 1 illustrates the *y*-axis intercept.

For positive values of *x*, the value of *y* exceeds *a*. The constant *b* tells us by how much *y* increases above *a* as *x* increases. The constant *b* is the slope of the line.

Slope of Line

As we defined in the chapter, the *slope* of a relationship is the change in the value of *y* divided by the change in the value of *x*. We use the Greek letter Δ (*delta*) to represent "change in." So Δy means the change in the value of the variable measured on the *y*-axis, and Δx means the change in the value of the variable measured on the *x*-axis. Therefore the slope of the relationship is

$$\Delta y/\Delta x.$$

To see why the slope is *b*, suppose that initially the value of *x* is x_1, or $200 in Fig. 2. The corresponding value of *y* is y_1, also $200 in Fig. 2. The equation of the line tells us that

$$y_1 = a + bx_1. \tag{1}$$

Now the value of *x* increases by Δx to $x_1 + \Delta x$ (or $400 in Fig. 2). And the value of *y* increases by Δy to $y_1 + \Delta y$ (or $300 in Fig. 2).

The equation of the line now tells us that

$$y_1 + \Delta y = a + b(x_1 + \Delta x). \tag{2}$$

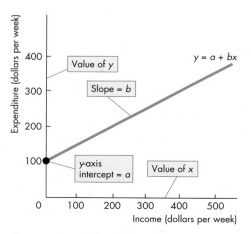

Figure 1 Linear relationship

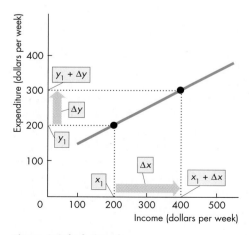

Figure 2 Calculating slope

To calculate the slope of the line, subtract equation (1) from equation (2) to obtain

$$\Delta y = b\Delta x \qquad (3)$$

and now divide equation (3) by Δx to obtain

$$\Delta y/\Delta x = b.$$

So the slope of the line is b.

Position of Line

The y-axis intercept determines the position of the line on the graph. Figure 3 illustrates the relationship between the y-axis intercept and the position of the line. In this graph, the y-axis measures saving and the x-axis measures income.

When the y-axis intercept, a, is positive, the line hits the y-axis at a positive value of y—as the blue line does. Its y-axis intercept is 100. When the y-axis intercept, a, is zero, the line hits the y-axis at the origin—as the purple line does. Its y-axis intercept is 0. When the y-axis intercept, a, is negative, the line hits the y-axis at a negative value of y—as the red line does. Its y-axis intercept is –100.

As the equations of the three lines show, the value of the y-axis intercept does not influence the slope. All three lines have a slope equal to 0.5.

Positive Relationships

Figure 1 shows a positive relationship—the two variables x and y move in the same direction. All positive relationships have a slope that is positive. In the equation of the line, the constant b is positive. In this example, the y-axis intercept, a, is 100. The slope b equals $\Delta y/\Delta x$, which in Fig. 2 is 100/200 or 0.5. The equation of the line is

$$y = 100 + 0.5x.$$

Negative Relationships

Figure 4 shows a negative relationship—the two variables x and y move in the opposite direction. All negative relationships have a slope that is negative. In the equation of the line, the constant b is negative. In the example in Fig. 4, the y-axis intercept, a, is 30. The slope, b, equals $\Delta y/\Delta x$, which is –20/2 or –10. The equation of the line is

$$y = 30 + (-10)x$$

or

$$y = 30 - 10x.$$

Example

A straight line has a y-axis intercept of 50 and a slope of 2. What is the equation of this line? The equation of a straight line is

$$y = a + bx$$

where a is the y-axis intercept and b is the slope. The equation is

$$y = 50 + 2x.$$

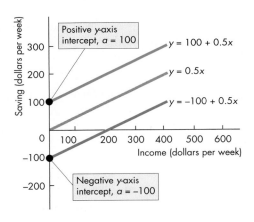

Figure 3 The y-axis intercept

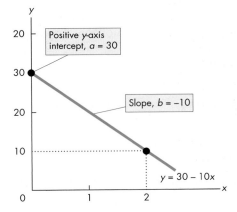

Figure 4 Negative relationship

Review Quiz

1 What are the three types of graphs used to show economic data?
2 Give an example of a time-series graph.
3 List three things that a time-series graph shows quickly and easily.
4 Give three examples, different from those in the chapter, of scatter diagrams that show a positive relationship, a negative relationship, and no relationship.
5 Draw some graphs to show the relationships between two variables that
   a. Move in the same direction.
   b. Move in opposite directions.
   c. Have a maximum and have a minimum.
6 Which of the relationships in question 5 is a positive relationship and which is a negative relationship?
7 What are the two ways of calculating the slope of a curved line?
8 How do we graph a relationship among more than two variables?

 Work Study Plan 1.A and get instant feedback.

SUMMARY

Key Points

Graphing Data (pp. 15–18)

- A time-series graph shows the trend and fluctuations in a variable over time.
- A cross-section graph shows how the value of a variable changes across the members of a population.
- A scatter diagram shows the relationship between two variables. It shows whether two variables are positively related, negatively related, or unrelated.

Graphs Used in Economic Models (pp. 18–21)

- Graphs are used to show relationships among variables in economic models.
- Relationships can be positive (an upward-sloping curve), negative (a downward-sloping curve), positive and then negative (have a maximum point), negative and then positive (have a minimum point), or unrelated (a horizontal or vertical curve).

The Slope of a Relationship (pp. 22–24)

- The slope of a relationship is calculated as the change in the value of the variable measured on the y-axis divided by the change in the value of the variable measured on the x-axis—that is, $\Delta y/\Delta x$.
- A straight line has a constant slope.
- A curved line has a varying slope. To calculate the slope of a curved line, we calculate the slope at a point or across an arc.

Graphing Relationships Among More Than Two Variables (pp. 24–25)

- To graph a relationship among more than two variables, we hold constant the values of all the variables except two.
- We then plot the value of one of the variables against the value of another.

Key Figures

Figure A1.1	Making a Graph, 15	
Figure A1.5	Positive (Direct) Relationships, 19	
Figure A1.6	Negative (Inverse) Relationships, 20	

Figure A1.7	Maximum and Minimum Points, 21	
Figure A1.9	The Slope of a Straight Line, 22	
Figure A1.10	Slope at a Point, 23	
Figure A1.11	Slope Across an Arc, 24	

Key Terms

Ceteris paribus, 24
Cross-section graph, 16
Direct relationship, 18
Inverse relationship, 19

Linear relationship, 18
Negative relationship, 19
Positive relationship, 18
Scatter diagram, 17

Slope, 22
Time-series graph, 16
Trend, 16

PROBLEMS and APPLICATIONS ◆

 Work problems 1–5 in Chapter 1A Study Plan and get instant feedback.
Work problems 6–10 as Homework, a Quiz, or a Test if assigned by your instructor.

1. The spreadsheet provides data on the Canadian economy: Column A is the year, column B is the inflation rate, column C is the interest rate, column D is the growth rate, and column E is the unemployment rate.

	A	B	C	D	E
1	1997	1.6	3.6	4.2	9.2
2	1998	0.9	5.0	4.1	8.4
3	1999	1.7	4.9	5.6	7.6
4	2000	3.1	5.7	5.2	6.8
5	2001	2.1	3.9	1.8	7.2
6	2002	2.2	2.9	2.9	7.7
7	2003	2.8	2.3	1.9	7.6
8	2004	1.8	2.8	3.1	7.2
9	2005	2.2	4.2	2.9	6.8
10	2006	2.0	4.6	3.1	6.3
11	2007	2.2	3.5	2.7	6.0

a. Draw a time-series graph of the inflation rate.
b. In which year(s) (i) was inflation highest, (ii) was inflation lowest, (iii) did it increase, (iv) did it decrease, (v) did it increase most, and (vi) did it decrease most?
c. What was the main trend in inflation?
d. Draw a scatter diagram of the inflation rate and the interest rate. Describe the relationship.
e. Draw a scatter diagram of the growth rate and the unemployment rate. Describe the relationship.

2. **"Hulk" Tops Box Office with Sales of $54.5 Million**

Movie	Theatres (number)	Revenue (dollars per theatre)
Hulk	3,505	15,560
The Happening	2,986	10,214
Zohan	3,462	4,737
Crystal Skull	3,804	3,561

Bloomberg.com, June 15, 2008

a. Draw a graph to show the relationship between the revenue per theatre on the *y*-axis and the number of theatres on the *x*-axis. Describe the relationship.
b. Calculate the slope of the relationship between 3,462 and 3,804 theatres.

3. Calculate the slope of the following relationship.

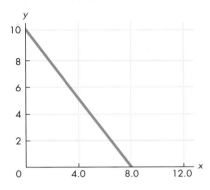

4. Calculate the slope of the following relationship:
   a. At point *A* and at point *B*.
   b. Across the arc *AB*.

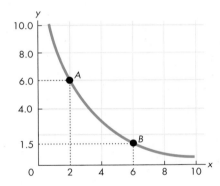

5. The table gives the price of a balloon ride, the temperature, and the number of rides a day.

Price (dollars per ride)	Balloon rides (number per day) 10°C	20°C	30°C
5	32	40	50
10	27	32	40
15	18	27	32

Draw graphs to show the relationship between
a. The price and the number of rides, holding the temperature constant. Describe this relationship.
b. The number of rides and temperature, holding the price constant.

6. The spreadsheet provides data on oil and gasoline: Column A is the year, column B is the price of crude oil (dollars per barrel), column C is the price of motor gasoline (cents per litre), column D is the quantity of crude oil produced, and column E is the quantity of motor gasoline produced (both in millions of cubic metres).

	A	B	C	D	E
1	1997	16	60.6	38.6	112.7
2	1998	9	56.2	38.7	117.1
3	1999	24	58.3	41.0	111.0
4	2000	22	70.9	42.2	116.4
5	2001	18	78.7	43.8	118.2
6	2002	30	72.5	45.9	126.9
7	2003	28	72.2	45.8	134.7
8	2004	36	91.8	44.9	139.3
9	2005	52	92.2	43.9	136.2
10	2006	57	97.0	42.0	143.8
11	2007	90	101.4	43.8	150.3

a. Draw a time-series graph of the quantity of motor gasoline.
b. In which year(s) (i) was the quantity of motor gasoline highest, (ii) was the quantity of motor gasoline lowest, (iii) did it increase, (iv) did it decrease, (v) did it increase most, and (vi) did it decrease most?
c. What was the main trend in this quantity?
d. Draw a scatter diagram of the price of crude oil and the quantity of crude oil. Describe the relationship.
e. Draw a scatter diagram of the price of motor gasoline and the quantity of motor gasoline. Describe the relationship.

7. Draw a graph that shows the relationship between the two variables x and y:

x	0	1	2	3	4	5
y	25	24	22	18	12	0

a. Is the relationship positive or negative?
b. Does the slope of the relationship increase or decrease as the value of x increases?
c. Think of some economic relationships that might be similar to this one.
d. Calculate the slope of the relationship between x and y when x equals 3.
e. Calculate the slope of the relationship across the arc as x increases from 4 to 5.

8. Calculate the slope of the relationship at point A.

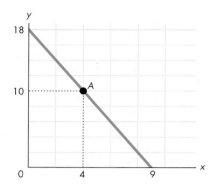

9. Calculate the slope of the relationship:

a. At point A and at point B.
b. Across the arc AB.

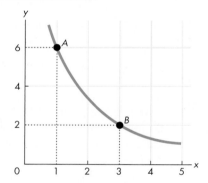

10. The table gives information about umbrellas: price, the number purchased, and rainfall.

Price (dollars per umbrella)	Umbrellas (number per day)		
	0	1	2
	(mms of rainfall)		
20	4	7	8
30	2	4	7
40	1	2	4

Draw graphs to show the relationship between

a. Price and the number of umbrellas purchased, holding the amount of rainfall constant. Describe this relationship.
b. The number of umbrellas purchased and the amount of rainfall, holding the price constant. Describe this relationship.

2  The Economic Problem

After studying this chapter, you will be able to

- Define the production possibilities frontier and calculate opportunity cost

- Distinguish between production possibilities and preferences and describe an efficient allocation of resources

- Explain how current production choices expand future production possibilities

- Explain how specialization and trade expand our production possibilities

- Describe the economic institutions that coordinate decisions

Why does food cost much more today

than it did a few years ago? One reason is that many countries now use part of their corn crops to produce ethanol, a clean biofuel substitute for gasoline. Another reason is that drought in some parts of the world has decreased global grain production. In this chapter, you will study an economic model—the production possibilities frontier—and you will learn why ethanol production and drought have increased the cost of producing food. You will also learn how to assess whether it is a good idea to increase corn production to produce fuel; how we can expand our production possibilities; how we gain by trading with others; and why the social institutions of firms, markets, property rights, and money that make trade possible have evolved. At the end of the chapter, in *Reading Between the Lines*, we'll apply what you've learned to understanding why ethanol production is raising the cost of food.

Production Possibilities and Opportunity Cost

Every working day, in mines, factories, shops, and offices and on farms and construction sites across Canada, 18 million people produce a vast variety of goods and services valued at $5 billion. But the quantities of goods and services that we can produce are limited both by our available resources and by technology. And if we want to increase our production of one good, we must decrease our production of something else—we face a tradeoff. You are going to learn about the production possibilities frontier, which describes the limit to what we can produce and provides a neat way of thinking about and illustrating the idea of a tradeoff.

The **production possibilities frontier** (*PPF*) is the boundary between those combinations of goods and services that can be produced and those that cannot. To illustrate the *PPF*, we focus on two goods at a time and hold the quantities produced of all the other goods and services constant. That is, we look at a *model* economy in which everything remains the same except for the production of the two goods we are considering.

Let's look at the production possibilities frontier for cola and pizza, which stand for *any* pair of goods or services.

Production Possibilities Frontier

The *production possibilities frontier* for cola and pizza shows the limits to the production of these two goods, given the total resources and technology available to produce them. Figure 2.1 shows this production possibilities frontier. The table lists some combinations of the quantities of pizza and cola that can be produced in a month given the resources available. The figure graphs these combinations. The *x*-axis shows the quantity of pizzas produced, and the *y*-axis shows the quantity of cola produced.

The *PPF* illustrates *scarcity* because we cannot attain the points outside the frontier. These points describe wants that can't be satisfied. We can produce at any point *inside* the *PPF* or *on* the *PPF*. These points are attainable. Suppose that in a typical month, we produce 4 million pizzas and 5 million cans of cola. Figure 2.1 shows this combination as point *E* and as possibility *E* in the table. The figure

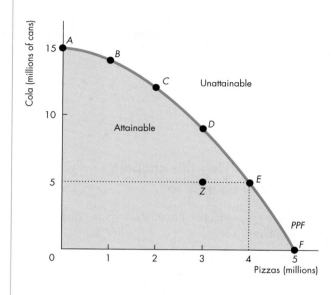

FIGURE 2.1 Production Possibilities Frontier

Possibility	Pizzas (millions)		Cola (millions of cans)
A	0	and	15
B	1	and	14
C	2	and	12
D	3	and	9
E	4	and	5
F	5	and	0

The table lists six production possibilities for cola and pizzas. Row *A* tells us that if we produce no pizza, the maximum quantity of cola we can produce is 15 million cans. Points *A, B, C, D, E,* and *F* in the figure represent the rows of the table. The curve passing through these points is the production possibilities frontier (*PPF*).

The *PPF* separates the attainable from the unattainable. Production is possible at any point *inside* the orange area or *on* the frontier. Points outside the frontier are unattainable. Points inside the frontier, such as point *Z*, are inefficient because resources are wasted or misallocated. At such points, it is possible to use the available resources to produce more of either or both goods.

myeconlab animation

also shows other production possibilities. For example, we might stop producing pizza and move all the people who produce it into producing cola. Point *A* in the figure and possibility *A* in the table show this case. The quantity of cola produced increases to 15 million cans, and pizza production dries up. Alternatively, we might close the cola factories and switch all the resources into producing pizza. In this situation, we produce 5 million pizzas. Point *F* in the figure and possibility *F* in the table show this case.

Production Efficiency

We achieve **production efficiency** if we produce goods and services at the lowest possible cost. This outcome occurs at all the points *on* the *PPF*. At points *inside* the *PPF*, production is inefficient because we are giving up more than necessary of one good to produce a given quantity of the other good.

For example, at point *Z* in Fig. 2.1, we produce 3 million pizzas and 5 million cans of cola. But we could produce 3 million pizzas and 9 million cans of cola. Our pizzas cost more cola than necessary. We can get them for a lower cost. Only when we produce *on* the *PPF* do we incur the lowest possible cost of production.

Production is *inefficient* inside the *PPF* because resources are either *unused* or *misallocated* or both.

Resources are *unused* when they are idle but could be working. For example, we might leave some of the factories idle or some workers unemployed.

Resources are *misallocated* when they are assigned to tasks for which they are not the best match. For example, we might assign skilled pizza chefs to work in a cola factory and skilled cola producers to work in a pizza shop. We could get more pizzas *and* more cola from these same workers if we reassigned them to the tasks that more closely match their skills.

Tradeoff Along the *PPF*

Every choice *along* the *PPF* involves a *tradeoff*. On the *PPF* in Fig. 2.1, we trade off cola for pizzas.

Tradeoffs arise in every imaginable real-world situation, and you reviewed several of them in Chapter 1. At any given point in time, we have a fixed amount of labour, land, capital, and entrepreneurship. By using our available technologies, we can employ these resources to produce goods and services, but we are limited in what we can produce. This limit defines a boundary between what we can attain and what we cannot attain. This boundary is the real world's production possibilities frontier, and it defines the tradeoffs that we must make. On our real-world *PPF*, we can produce more of any one good or service only if we produce less of some other goods or services.

When doctors want to spend more on AIDS and cancer research, they face a tradeoff: more medical research for less of some other things. When the prime minister wants to spend more on education and health care, he faces a tradeoff: more education and health care for less national defence or less private spending (because of higher taxes). When an environmental group argues for less logging, it is suggesting a tradeoff: greater conservation of endangered wildlife for less paper. When you want to study more, you face a tradeoff: more study time for less leisure or sleep.

All tradeoffs involve a cost—an opportunity cost.

Opportunity Cost

The **opportunity cost** of an action is the highest-valued alternative forgone. The *PPF* makes this idea precise and enables us to calculate opportunity cost. Along the *PPF*, there are only two goods, so there is only one alternative forgone: some quantity of the other good. Given our current resources and technology, we can produce more pizzas only if we produce less cola. The opportunity cost of producing an additional pizza is the cola we *must* forgo. Similarly, the opportunity cost of producing an additional can of cola is the quantity of pizza we must forgo.

In Fig. 2.1, if we move from point *C* to point *D*, we get 1 million more pizzas but 3 million fewer cans of cola. The additional 1 million pizzas *cost* 3 million cans of cola. One pizza costs 3 cans of cola.

We can also work out the opportunity cost of moving in the opposite direction. In Fig. 2.1, if we move from point *D* to point *C*, the quantity of cola produced increases by 3 million cans and the quantity of pizzas produced decreases by 1 million. So if we choose point *C* over point *D*, the additional 3 million cans of cola *cost* 1 million pizzas. One can of cola costs 1/3 of a pizza.

Opportunity Cost Is a Ratio Opportunity cost is a ratio. It is the decrease in the quantity produced of one good divided by the increase in the quantity produced of another good as we move along the production possibilities frontier.

Because opportunity cost is a ratio, the opportunity cost of producing an additional can of cola is equal to the *inverse* of the opportunity cost of producing an additional pizza. Check this proposition by returning to the calculations we've just worked through. When we move along the *PPF* from *C* to *D*, the opportunity cost of a pizza is 3 cans of cola. The inverse of 3 is 1/3. If we decrease the production of pizza and increase the production of cola by moving from *D* to *C*, the opportunity cost of a can of cola must be 1/3 of a pizza. That is exactly the number that we calculated for the move from *D* to *C*.

Increasing Opportunity Cost   The opportunity cost of a pizza increases as the quantity of pizzas produced increases. The outward-bowed shape of the *PPF* reflects increasing opportunity cost. When we produce a large quantity of cola and a small quantity of pizzas—between points *A* and *B* in Fig. 2.1—the frontier has a gentle slope. An increase in the quantity of pizzas costs a small decrease in the quantity of cola—the opportunity cost of a pizza is a small quantity of cola.

Increasing Opportunity Cost

Opportunity Cost on the Oil Patch

It costs about $30 a barrel to get crude oil out of the ground and into a tanker or pipeline to deliver it to a refinery. So for every barrel of oil produced, we forgo $30-worth of other goods and services.

Between 2003 and 2006, the price of crude oil on the global oil market doubled; and between 2006 and 2008, it doubled again. With the price of oil at such levels, it becomes worthwhile for owners of oil resources to pump them at a faster rate and to extract from higher-cost sources.

Such changes have taken place on the Alberta and Newfoundland oil patches. The opportunity cost of extracting oil in these regions is probably around $30-worth of other goods and services. But as production increases, the opportunity cost rises.

In Alberta, production increased by 12 percent from 2003 to 2006 and by 3 percent in 2007. The marginal oil in Alberta is in tar sands, and the opportunity cost of extracting this oil is around $50 a barrel.

As Canada produces more crude oil, we slide around our *PPF* and the opportunity cost of producing oil rises.

When we produce a large quantity of pizzas and a small quantity of cola—between points *E* and *F* in Fig. 2.1—the frontier is steep. A given increase in the quantity of pizzas *costs* a large decrease in the quantity of cola, so the opportunity cost of a pizza is a large quantity of cola.

The *PPF* is bowed outward because resources are not all equally productive in all activities. People with many years of experience working for PepsiCo are good at producing cola but not very good at making pizzas. So if we move some of these people from PepsiCo to Domino's, we get a small increase in the quantity of pizzas but a large decrease in the quantity of cola.

Similarly, people who have spent years working at Domino's are good at producing pizzas, but they have no idea how to produce cola. So if we move some of these people from Domino's to PepsiCo, we get a small increase in the quantity of cola but a large decrease in the quantity of pizzas. The more of either good we try to produce, the less productive are the additional resources we use to produce that good and the larger is the opportunity cost of a unit of that good.

Review Quiz

1 How does the production possibilities frontier illustrate scarcity?

2 How does the production possibilities frontier illustrate production efficiency?

3 How does the production possibilities frontier show that every choice involves a tradeoff?

4 How does the production possibilities frontier illustrate opportunity cost?

5 Why is opportunity cost a ratio?

6 Why does the *PPF* for most goods bow outward so that opportunity cost increases as the quantity of the good produced increases?

 Work Study Plan 2.1 and get instant feedback.

We've seen that what we can produce is limited by the production possibilities frontier. We've also seen that production on the *PPF* is efficient. But we can produce many different quantities on the *PPF*. How do we choose among them? How do we know which point on the *PPF* is the best one?

◆ Using Resources Efficiently

We achieve *production efficiency* at every point on the *PPF*. But which point is best? The answer is the point on the *PPF* at which goods and services are produced in the quantities that provide the greatest possible benefit. When goods and services are produced at the lowest possible cost and in the quantities that provide the greatest possible benefit, we have achieved **allocative efficiency**.

The questions that we raised when we reviewed the five big issues in Chapter 1 are questions about allocative efficiency. To answer such questions, we must measure and compare costs and benefits.

The *PPF* and Marginal Cost

The **marginal cost** of a good is the opportunity cost of producing one more unit of it. We calculate marginal cost from the slope of the *PPF*. As the quantity of pizzas produced increases, the *PPF* gets steeper and the marginal cost of a pizza increases. Figure 2.2 illustrates the calculation of the marginal cost of a pizza.

Begin by finding the opportunity cost of pizza in blocks of 1 million pizzas. The cost of the first million pizzas is 1 million cans of cola; the cost of the second million pizzas is 2 million cans of cola; the cost of the third million pizzas is 3 million cans of cola, and so on. The bars in part (a) illustrate these calculations.

The bars in part (b) show the cost of an average pizza in each of the 1 million pizza blocks. Focus on the third million pizzas—the move from *C* to *D* in part (a). Over this range, because 1 million pizzas cost 3 million cans of cola, one of these pizzas, on average, costs 3 cans of cola—the height of the bar in part (b).

Next, find the opportunity cost of each additional pizza—the marginal cost of a pizza. The marginal cost of a pizza increases as the quantity of pizzas produced increases. The marginal cost at point *C* is less than it is at point *D*. On the average over the range from *C* to *D*, the marginal cost of a pizza is 3 cans of cola. But it exactly equals 3 cans of cola only in the middle of the range between *C* and *D*.

The red dot in part (b) indicates that the marginal cost of a pizza is 3 cans of cola when 2.5 million pizzas are produced. Each black dot in part (b) is interpreted in the same way. The red curve that passes through these dots, labelled *MC*, is the marginal cost curve. It shows the marginal cost of a pizza at each quantity of pizzas as we move along the *PPF*.

FIGURE 2.2 The *PPF* and Marginal Cost

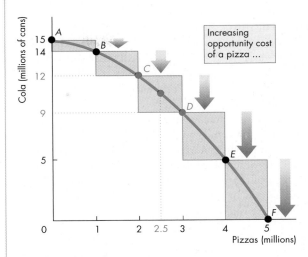

(a) PPF and opportunity cost

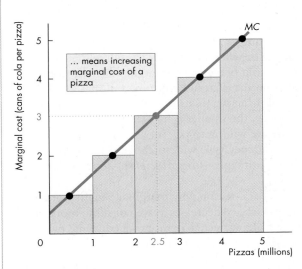

(b) Marginal cost

Marginal cost is calculated from the slope of the *PPF*. As the quantity of pizzas produced increases, the *PPF* gets steeper and the marginal cost of a pizza increases. The bars in part (a) show the opportunity cost of pizza in blocks of 1 million pizzas. The bars in part (b) show the cost of an average pizza in each of these 1 million blocks. The red curve, *MC*, shows the marginal cost of a pizza at each point along the *PPF*. This curve passes through the centre of each of the bars in part (b).

Preferences and Marginal Benefit

Look around your classroom and notice the wide variety of shirts, pants, and shoes that you and your fellow students are wearing today. Why is there such a huge variety? Why don't you all wear the same styles and colours? The answer lies in what economists call preferences. **Preferences** are a description of a person's likes and dislikes.

You've seen that we have a concrete way of describing the limits to production: the *PPF*. We need a similarly concrete way of describing preferences. To describe preferences, economists use the concept of marginal benefit. The **marginal benefit** from a good or service is the benefit received from consuming one more unit of it.

We measure the marginal benefit from a good or service by the most that people are *willing to pay* for an additional unit of it. The idea is that you are willing to pay less for a good than it is worth to you but you are not willing to pay more than it is worth. So the most you are willing to pay for something measures its marginal benefit.

Economists illustrate preferences using the **marginal benefit curve**, which is a curve that shows the relationship between the marginal benefit from a good and the quantity consumed of that good. It is a general principle that the more we have of any good or service, the smaller is its marginal benefit and the less we are willing to pay for an additional unit of it. This tendency is so widespread and strong that we call it a principle—the *principle of decreasing marginal benefit*.

The basic reason why marginal benefit from a good or service decreases as we consume more of it is that we like variety. The more we consume of any one good or service, the more we tire of it and would prefer to switch to something else.

Think about your willingness to pay for a pizza. If pizza is hard to come by and you can buy only a few slices a year, you might be willing to pay a high price to get an additional slice. But if pizza is all you've eaten for the past few days, you are willing to pay almost nothing for another slice.

You've learned to think about cost as opportunity cost, not as a dollar cost. You can think about marginal benefit and willingness to pay in the same way. The marginal benefit, measured by what you are willing to pay for something, is the quantity of other goods and services that you are willing to forgo. Let's continue with the example of cola and pizza and illustrate preferences this way.

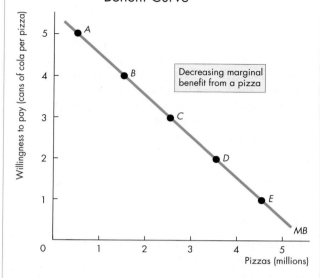

FIGURE 2.3 Preferences and the Marginal Benefit Curve

Possibility	Pizzas (millions)	Willingness to pay (cans of cola per pizza)
A	0.5	5
B	1.5	4
C	2.5	3
D	3.5	2
E	4.5	1

The smaller the quantity of pizzas produced, the more cola people are willing to give up for an additional pizza. If pizza production is 0.5 million, people are willing to pay 5 cans of cola per pizza. But if pizza production is 4.5 million, people are willing to pay only 1 can of cola per pizza. Willingness to pay measures marginal benefit. A universal feature of people's preferences is that marginal benefit decreases.

myeconlab animation

Figure 2.3 illustrates preferences as the willingness to pay for pizza in terms of cola. In row *A*, pizza production is 0.5 million, and at that quantity, people are willing to pay 5 cans of cola per pizza. As the quantity of pizzas produced increases, the amount that people are willing to pay for a pizza falls. When pizza production is 4.5 million, people are willing to pay only 1 can of cola per pizza.

Let's now use the concepts of marginal cost and marginal benefit to describe allocative efficiency.

FIGURE 2.4   Efficient Use of Resources

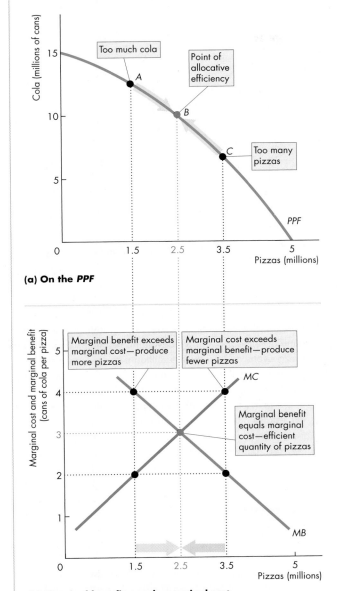

(a) On the PPF

(b) Marginal benefit equals marginal cost

The greater the quantity of pizzas produced, the smaller is the marginal benefit (*MB*) from pizza—the less cola people are willing to give up to get an additional pizza. But the greater the quantity of pizzas produced, the greater is the marginal cost (*MC*) of a pizza—the more cola people must give up to get an additional pizza. When marginal benefit equals marginal cost, resources are being used efficiently.

 animation

Allocative Efficiency

At *any* point on the *PPF*, we cannot produce more of one good without giving up some other good. At the *best* point on the *PPF*, we cannot produce more of one good without giving up some other good that provides greater benefit. We are producing at the point of allocative efficiency—the point on the *PPF* that we prefer above all other points.

Suppose that in Fig. 2.4, we produce 1.5 million pizzas. The marginal cost of a pizza is 2 cans of cola, and the marginal benefit from a pizza is 4 cans of cola. Because someone values an additional pizza more highly than it costs to produce, we can get more value from our resources by moving some of them out of producing cola and into producing pizza.

Now suppose we produce 3.5 million pizzas. The marginal cost of a pizza is now 4 cans of cola, but the marginal benefit from a pizza is only 2 cans of cola. Because the additional pizza costs more to produce than anyone thinks it is worth, we can get more value from our resources by moving some of them away from producing pizza and into producing cola.

Suppose we produce 2.5 million pizzas. Marginal cost and marginal benefit are now equal at 3 cans of cola. This allocation of resources between pizza and cola is efficient. If more pizzas are produced, the forgone cola is worth more than the additional pizzas. If fewer pizzas are produced, the forgone pizzas are worth more than the additional cola.

Review Quiz

1 What is marginal cost? How is it measured?
2 What is marginal benefit? How is it measured?
3 How does the marginal benefit from a good change as the quantity produced of that good increases?
4 What is allocative efficiency and how does it relate to the production possibilities frontier?
5 What conditions must be satisfied if resources are used efficiently?

 Work Study Plan 2.2 and get instant feedback.

You now understand the limits to production and the conditions under which resources are used efficiently. Your next task is to study the expansion of production possibilities.

Economic Growth

During the past 30 years, production per person in Canada has doubled. Such an expansion of production is called **economic growth**. Economic growth increases our *standard of living*, but it doesn't overcome scarcity and avoid opportunity cost. To make our economy grow, we face a tradeoff—the faster we make production grow, the greater is the opportunity cost of economic growth.

The Cost of Economic Growth

Economic growth comes from technological change and capital accumulation. **Technological change** is the development of new goods and of better ways of producing goods and services. **Capital accumulation** is the growth of capital resources, including *human capital*.

Because of technological change and capital accumulation, we have an enormous quantity of cars that provide us with more transportation than was available when we had only horses and carriages; we have satellites that provide global communications on a much larger scale than that available with the earlier cable technology. But if we use our resources to develop new technologies and produce capital, we must decrease our production of consumption goods and services. New technologies and new capital have an opportunity cost. Let's look at this opportunity cost.

Instead of studying the *PPF* of pizza and cola, we'll hold the quantity of cola produced constant and examine the *PPF* for pizzas and pizza ovens. Figure 2.5 shows this *PPF* as the blue curve *ABC*. If we devote no resources to producing pizza ovens, we produce at point *A*. If we produce 3 million pizzas, we can produce 6 pizza ovens at point *B*. If we produce no pizza, we can produce 10 ovens at point *C*.

The amount by which our production possibilities expand depends on the resources we devote to technological change and capital accumulation. If we devote no resources to this activity (point *A*), our *PPF* remains at *ABC*—the blue curve in Fig. 2.5. If we cut the current production of pizza and produce 6 ovens (point *B*), then in the future, we'll have more capital and our *PPF* will rotate outward to the position shown by the red curve. The fewer resources we use for producing pizza and the more resources we use for producing ovens, the greater is the future expansion of our production possibilities.

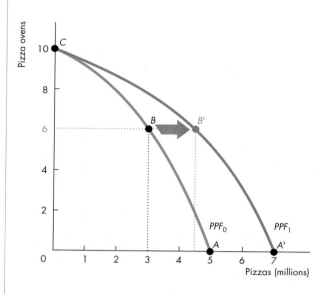

FIGURE 2.5 Economic Growth

PPF_0 shows the limits to the production of pizza and pizza ovens, with the production of all other goods and services remaining the same. If we devote no resources to producing pizza ovens and produce 5 million pizzas, our production possibilities will remain the same PPF_0. But if we decrease pizza production to 3 million and produce 6 ovens, at point *B*, our production possibilities expand. After one period, the *PPF* rotates outward to PPF_1 and we can produce at point *B'*, a point outside the original PPF_0. We can rotate the *PPF* outward, but we cannot avoid opportunity cost. The opportunity cost of producing more pizzas in the future is fewer pizzas today.

myeconlab animation

Economic growth is not free. To make it happen, we use more resources to produce new ovens and fewer resources to produce pizzas. In Fig. 2.5, we move from *A* to *B*. There is no free lunch. The opportunity cost of more pizzas in the future is fewer pizzas today. Also, economic growth is no magic formula for abolishing scarcity. On the new production possibilities frontier, we continue to face a tradeoff and opportunity cost.

The ideas about economic growth that we have explored in the setting of the pizza industry also apply to nations. Hong Kong and Canada provide an interesting case study.

Economic Growth

Hong Kong Overtakes Canada

In 1968, the production possibilities per person in Canada were much larger than those in Hong Kong (see the figure). Canada devotes one-fifth of its resources to accumulating capital and in 1968 was at point *A* on its *PPF*. Hong Kong devotes one-third of its resources to accumulating capital and in 1968, Hong Kong was at point *A* on its *PPF*.

Since 1968, both countries have experienced economic growth, but because Hong Kong devotes a bigger fraction of its resources to accumulating capital, its production possibilities have expanded more quickly.

By 2008, production possibilities per person in Hong Kong had exceeded those in Canada. If Hong Kong continues to devote more resources to accumulating capital than Canada does (at point *B* on its 2008 *PPF*), Hong Kong will continue to grow more rapidly. But if Hong Kong decreases capital accumulation (moving to point *D* on its 2008 *PPF*), then its rate of economic growth will slow.

Hong Kong is typical of the fast-growing Asian economies, which include Taiwan, Thailand, South Korea, and China. Production possibilities expand in these countries by between 5 and 10 percent a year. If such high economic growth rates are maintained, these other Asian countries will continue to close the gap between themselves and Canada.

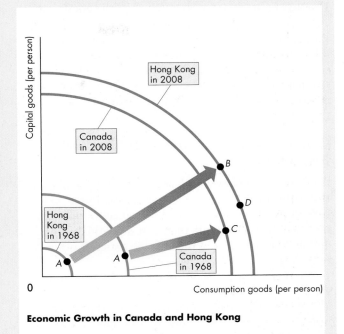

Economic Growth in Canada and Hong Kong

To catch up with Hong Kong, Canada must devote more than one-third of its resources to accumulating capital.

A Nation's Economic Growth

The experiences of Canada and Hong Kong make a striking example of the effects of our choices about what to produce and how to produce it on the rate of economic growth.

If a nation devotes all its factors of production to producing consumption goods and services and none to advancing technology and accumulating capital, its production possibilities in the future will be the same as they are today.

To expand production possibilities in the future, a nation must devote fewer resources to producing consumption goods and services and some resources to accumulating capital and developing new technologies. As production possibilities expand, consumption in the future can increase. The decrease in today's consumption is the opportunity cost of tomorrow's increase in consumption.

Review Quiz

1 What generates economic growth?
2 How does economic growth influence the production possibilities frontier?
3 What is the opportunity cost of economic growth?
4 Why has Hong Kong experienced faster economic growth than Canada?
5 Does economic growth overcome scarcity?

 Work Study Plan 2.3 and get instant feedback.

Next, we're going to study another way in which we expand our production possibilities—the amazing fact that *both* buyers and sellers gain from specialization and trade.

◆ Gains from Trade

People can produce for themselves all the goods and services that they consume, or they can produce one good or a few goods and trade with others. Producing only one good or a few goods is called *specialization*. We are going to learn how people gain by specializing in the production of the good in which they have a *comparative advantage* and trading with others.

Comparative Advantage and Absolute Advantage

A person has a **comparative advantage** in an activity if that person can perform the activity at a lower opportunity cost than anyone else. Differences in opportunity costs arise from differences in individual abilities and from differences in the characteristics of other resources.

No one excels at everything. One person is an outstanding pitcher but a poor catcher; another person is a brilliant lawyer but a poor teacher. In almost all human endeavours, what one person does easily, someone else finds difficult. The same applies to land and capital. One plot of land is fertile but has no mineral deposits; another plot of land has outstanding views but is infertile. One machine has great precision but is difficult to operate; another is fast but often breaks down.

Although no one excels at everything, some people excel and can outperform others in a large number of activities—perhaps even in all activities. A person who is more productive than others has an **absolute advantage**.

Absolute advantage involves comparing productivities—production per hour—whereas comparative advantage involves comparing opportunity costs.

Notice that a person who has an absolute advantage does not have a *comparative* advantage in every activity. Joni Mitchell is a better folk singer and a better painter than most people. She has an absolute advantage in these two activities. But compared to others, she is a better folk singer than a painter, so her *comparative* advantage is in folk singing.

Because ability and resources vary from one person to another, people have different opportunity costs of producing various goods. These differences in opportunity cost are the source of comparative advantage.

Let's explore the idea of comparative advantage by looking at two smoothie bars: one operated by Liz and the other operated by Joe.

Liz's Smoothie Bar Liz produces smoothies and salads. In Liz's high-tech bar, she can turn out either a smoothie or a salad every 2 minutes—see Table 2.1. If Liz spends all her time making smoothies, she can produce 30 an hour. And if she spends all her time making salads, she can also produce 30 an hour. If she splits her time equally between the two, she can produce 15 smoothies and 15 salads an hour. For each additional smoothie Liz produces, she must decrease her production of salads by one, and for each additional salad she produces, she must decrease her production of smoothies by one. So

Liz's opportunity cost of producing 1 smoothie is 1 salad,

and

Liz's opportunity cost of producing 1 salad is 1 smoothie.

Liz's customers buy smoothies and salads in equal quantities, so she splits her time equally between the two items and produces 15 smoothies and 15 salads an hour.

Joe's Smoothie Bar Joe also produces smoothies and salads, but his bar is smaller than Liz's. Also, Joe has only one blender, and it's a slow, old machine. Even if Joe uses all his resources to produce smoothies, he can produce only 6 an hour—see Table 2.2. But Joe is good at making salads, so if he uses all his resources to make salads, he can produce 30 an hour.

Joe's ability to make smoothies and salads is the same regardless of how he splits an hour between the two tasks. He can make a salad in 2 minutes or a smoothie in 10 minutes. For each additional

TABLE 2.1 Liz's Production Possibilities

Item	Minutes to produce 1	Quantity per hour
Smoothies	2	30
Salads	2	30

TABLE 2.2   Joe's Production Possibilities

Item	Minutes to produce 1	Quantity per hour
Smoothies	10	6
Salads	2	30

smoothie Joe produces, he must decrease his production of salads by 5. And for each additional salad he produces, he must decrease his production of smoothies by 1/5 of a smoothie. So

Joe's opportunity cost of producing 1 smoothie is 5 salads,

and

Joe's opportunity cost of producing 1 salad is 1/5 of a smoothie.

Joe's customers, like Liz's, buy smoothies and salads in equal quantities. So Joe spends 50 minutes of each hour making smoothies and 10 minutes of each hour making salads. With this division of his time, Joe produces 5 smoothies and 5 salads an hour.

Liz's Absolute Advantage   Table 2.3(a) summarizes the production of Liz and Joe. You can see that Liz is three times as productive as Joe—her 15 smoothies and salads an hour are three times Joe's 5. Liz has an absolute advantage over Joe in producing both smoothies and salads. But Liz has a comparative advantage in only one of the activities.

Liz's Comparative Advantage   In which of the two activities does Liz have a comparative advantage? Recall that comparative advantage is a situation in which one person's opportunity cost of producing a good is lower than another person's opportunity cost of producing that same good. Liz has a comparative advantage in producing smoothies. Her opportunity cost of a smoothie is 1 salad, whereas Joe's opportunity cost of a smoothie is 5 salads.

Joe's Comparative Advantage   If Liz has a comparative advantage in producing smoothies, Joe must have a comparative advantage in producing salads. Joe's opportunity cost of a salad is 1/5 of a smoothie, whereas Liz's opportunity cost of a salad is 1 smoothie.

Achieving the Gains from Trade

Liz and Joe run into each other one evening in a singles bar. After a few minutes of getting acquainted, Liz tells Joe about her amazing smoothie business. Her only problem, she tells Joe, is that she would like to produce more because potential customers leave when her lines get too long.

Joe isn't sure whether to risk spoiling his chances by telling Liz about his own struggling business. But he takes the risk. When he explains to Liz that he spends 50 minutes of every hour making 5 smoothies and 10 minutes making 5 salads, Liz's eyes pop. "Have I got a deal for you!" she exclaims.

Here's the deal that Liz sketches on a table napkin. Joe stops making smoothies and allocates all his time to producing salads. And Liz stops making salads and allocates all her time to producing smoothies. That is, they both specialize in producing the good in which they have a comparative advantage. Together they produce 30 smoothies and 30 salads—see Table 2.3(b).

TABLE 2.3   Liz and Joe Gain from Trade

(a) Before trade	Liz	Joe
Smoothies	15	5
Salads	15	5
(b) Specialization	**Liz**	**Joe**
Smoothies	30	0
Salads	0	30
(c) Trade	**Liz**	**Joe**
Smoothies	sell 10	buy 10
Salads	buy 20	sell 20
(d) After trade	**Liz**	**Joe**
Smoothies	20	10
Salads	20	10
(e) Gains from trade	**Liz**	**Joe**
Smoothies	+5	+5
Salads	+5	+5

They then trade. Liz sells Joe 10 smoothies and Joe sells Liz 20 salads—the price of a smoothie is 2 salads—see Table 2.3(c).

After the trade, Joe has 10 salads—the 30 he produces minus the 20 he sells to Liz. He also has the 10 smoothies that he buys from Liz. So Joe now has increased the quantities of smoothies and salads that he can sell—see Table 2.3(d).

Liz has 20 smoothies—the 30 she produces minus the 10 she sells to Joe. She also has the 20 salads that she buys from Joe. Liz has increased the quantities of smoothies and salads that she can sell—see Table 2.3(d). Liz and Joe both gain 5 smoothies and 5 salads an hour—see Table 2.3(e).

To illustrate her idea, Liz grabs a fresh napkin and draws the graphs in Fig. 2.6. The blue *PPF* in part (a) shows Joe's production possibilities. Before trade, he is producing 5 smoothies and 5 salads an hour at point *A*.

The blue *PPF* in part (b) shows Liz's production possibilities. Before trade, she is producing 15 smoothies and 15 salads an hour at point *A*.

Liz's proposal is that they each specialize in producing the good in which they have a comparative advantage. Joe produces 30 salads and no smoothies at point *B* on his *PPF*. Liz produces 30 smoothies and no salads at point *B* on her *PPF*.

Liz and Joe then trade smoothies and salads at a price of 2 salads per smoothie or 1/2 a smoothie per salad. Joe gets smoothies from Liz for 2 salads each, which is less than the 5 salads it costs him to produce a smoothie. Liz gets salads from Joe for 1/2 a smoothie each, which is less than the 1 smoothie that it costs her to produce a salad.

With trade, Joe has 10 smoothies and 10 salads at point *C*—a gain of 5 smoothies and 5 salads. Joe moves to a point *outside* his *PPF*.

FIGURE 2.6   The Gains from Trade

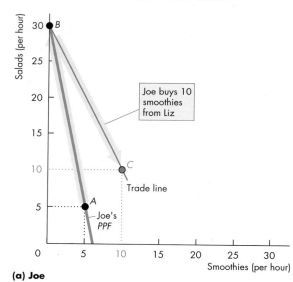

(a) Joe

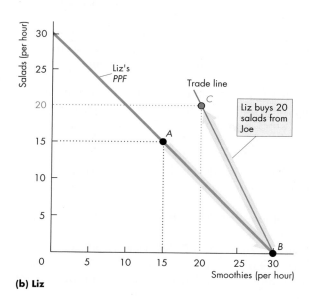

(b) Liz

Joe initially produces at point *A* on his *PPF* in part (a), and Liz initially produces at point *A* on her *PPF* in part (b). Joe's opportunity cost of producing a salad is less than Liz's, so Joe has a comparative advantage in producing salads. Liz's opportunity cost of producing a smoothie is less than Joe's, so Liz has a comparative advantage in producing smoothies. If Joe specializes in making salads, he produces 30 salads and no smoothies at point *B* on his *PPF*. If Liz specializes in

making smoothies, she produces 30 smoothies and no salads at point *B* on her *PPF*. They exchange salads for smoothies along the red "Trade line." Liz buys salads from Joe for less than her opportunity cost of producing them. Joe buys smoothies from Liz for less than his opportunity cost of producing them. Each goes to point *C*—a point outside his or her *PPF*. Both Joe and Liz increase production by 5 smoothies and 5 salads with no change in resources.

With trade, Liz has 20 smoothies and 20 salads at point *C*—a gain of 5 smoothies and 5 salads. Liz moves to a point *outside* her *PPF.*

Despite Liz's absolute advantage in producing smoothies and salads, both Liz and Joe gain from specializing—producing the good in which they have a comparative advantage—and trading.

The gains that we achieve from international trade are similar to those achieved by Joe and Liz in this example. When Canadians buy T-shirts from China and when China buys regional jets from Canada, both countries gain. We get our shirts at a lower cost than that at which we can produce them, and China gets its regional jets at a lower cost than that at which it can produce them.

Dynamic Comparative Advantage

At any given point in time, the resources and technologies available determine the comparative advantages that individuals and nations have. But just by repeatedly producing a particular good or service, people become more productive in that activity, a phenomenon called **learning-by-doing.** Learning-by-doing is the basis of *dynamic* comparative advantage. **Dynamic comparative advantage** is a comparative advantage that a person (or country) has acquired by specializing in an activity and becoming the lowest-cost producer as a result of learning-by-doing.

Singapore, for example, pursued dynamic comparative advantage when it decided to begin a biotechnology industry in which it initially didn't have a comparative advantage.

Review Quiz

1 What gives a person a comparative advantage?
2 Distinguish between comparative advantage and absolute advantage.
3 Why do people specialize and trade?
4 What are the gains from specialization and trade?
5 What is the source of the gains from trade?
6 How does dynamic comparative advantage arise?

 Work Study Plan 2.4 and get instant feedback.

Economic Coordination

People gain by specializing in the production of those goods and services in which they have a comparative advantage and then trading with each other. Liz and Joe, whose production of salads and smoothies we studied earlier in this chapter, can get together and make a deal that enables them to enjoy the gains from specialization and trade. But for billions of individuals to specialize and produce millions of different goods and services, their choices must somehow be coordinated.

Two competing economic coordination systems have been used: central economic planning and decentralized markets.

Central economic planning might appear to be the best system because it can express national priorities. But when this system was tried in Russia for 60 years and in China for 30 years, it was a miserable failure. Today, most previously planned economies are adopting a decentralized market system.

To make decentralized coordination work, four complementary social institutions that have evolved over many centuries are needed. They are

- Firms
- Markets
- Property rights
- Money

Firms

A **firm** is an economic unit that hires factors of production and organizes those factors to produce and sell goods and services. Examples of firms are your local gas station, Canadian Tire, and Roots.

Firms coordinate a huge amount of economic activity. For example, Canadian Tire buys or rents large buildings, equips them with storage shelves and checkout lanes, and hires labour. Canadian Tire directs the labour and decides what goods to buy and sell.

But Canadian Tire doesn't produce the goods that it sells. It could do so. It could own and coordinate the production of all the things that it sells in all its stores. It could also produce all the raw materials that are used to produce the things that it sells. But John W. and Alfred J. Billes would not have created one of Canada's great retailers if they had followed that path.

The reason is that if a firm gets too big, it can't keep track of all the information needed to coordinate its activities. It is more efficient for firms to specialize (just as Liz and Joe did) and trade with each other. This trade between firms takes place in markets.

Markets

In ordinary speech, the word *market* means a place where people buy and sell goods such as fish, meat, fruits, and vegetables. In economics, a *market* has a more general meaning. A **market** is any arrangement that enables buyers and sellers to get information and to do business with each other. An example is the market in which oil is bought and sold—the world oil market. The world oil market is not a place. It is the network of oil producers, oil users, wholesalers, and brokers who buy and sell oil. These decision makers do not meet physically. They make deals by telephone, fax, and direct computer link.

Markets have evolved because they facilitate trade. Without organized markets, we would miss out on a substantial part of the potential gains from trade. Enterprising individuals and firms, each pursuing their own self-interest, have profited from making markets—standing ready to buy or sell the items in which they specialize. But markets can work only when property rights exist.

Property Rights

The social arrangements that govern the ownership, use, and disposal of anything that people value are called **property rights**. *Real property* includes land and buildings—the things we call property in ordinary speech—and durable goods such as plant and equipment. *Financial property* includes stocks and bonds and money in the bank. *Intellectual property* is the intangible product of creative effort. This type of property includes books, music, computer programs, and inventions of all kinds and is protected by copyrights and patents.

Where property rights are enforced, people have the incentive to specialize and produce the goods in which they have a comparative advantage. Where people can steal the production of others, resources are devoted not to production but to protecting possessions. Without property rights, we would still be hunting and gathering as our Stone Age ancestors did.

Money

Money is any commodity or token that is generally acceptable as a means of payment. Liz and Joe didn't use money in the example above. They exchanged salads and smoothies. In principle, trade in markets can exchange any item for any other item. But you can perhaps imagine how complicated life would be if we exchanged goods for other goods. The "invention" of money makes trading in markets much more efficient.

Circular Flows Through Markets

Figure 2.7 shows the flows that result from the choices that households and firms make. Households specialize and choose the quantities of labour, land, capital, and entrepreneurial services to sell or rent to firms. Firms choose the quantities of factors of production to hire. These (red) flows go through the *factor markets*. Households choose the quantities of goods and services to buy, and firms choose the quantities to produce. These (red) flows go through the *goods markets*. Households receive incomes and make expenditures on goods and services (the green flows).

How do markets coordinate all these decisions?

Coordinating Decisions

Markets coordinate decisions through price adjustments. To see how, think about your local market for hamburgers. Suppose that too few hamburgers are available and some people who want to buy hamburgers are not able to do so. To make buying and selling plans the same, either more hamburgers must be offered for sale or buyers must scale down their appetites (or both). A rise in the price of a hamburger produces this outcome. A higher price encourages producers to offer more hamburgers for sale. It also encourages some people to change their lunch plans. Fewer people buy hamburgers, and more buy hot dogs. More hamburgers (and more hot dogs) are offered for sale.

Alternatively, suppose that more hamburgers are available than people want to buy. In this case, to make the choices of buyers and sellers compatible, more hamburgers must be bought or fewer hamburgers must be offered for sale (or both). A fall in the price of a hamburger achieves this outcome. A lower price encourages firms to produce a smaller quantity of hamburgers. It also encourages people to buy more hamburgers.

FIGURE 2.7 Circular Flows in the Market Economy

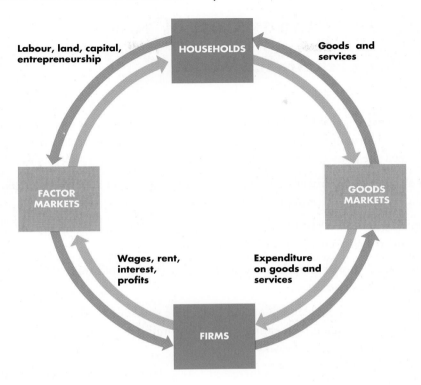

Households and firms make economic choices and markets coordinate these choices.

Households choose the quantities of labour, land, capital, and entrepreneurial services to sell or rent to firms in exchange for wages, rent, interest, and profit. Households also choose how to spend their incomes on the various types of goods and services available.

Firms choose the quantities of factors of production to hire and the quantities of goods and services to produce.

Goods markets and factor markets coordinate these choices of households and firms.

The counterclockwise red flows are real flows—the flow of factors of production from households to firms and the flow of goods and services from firms to households. The clockwise green flows are the payments for the red flows. They are the flow of incomes from firms to households and the flow of expenditure on goods and services from households to firms.

 animation

Review Quiz

1 Why are social institutions such as firms, markets, property rights, and money necessary?
2 What are the main functions of markets?
3 What are the flows in the market economy that go from firms to households and the flows from households to firms?

  Work Study Plan 2.5 and get instant feedback.

You have now begun to see how economists approach economic questions. Scarcity, choice, and divergent opportunity costs explain why we specialize and trade and why firms, markets, property rights, and money have developed. You can see all around you the lessons you've learned in this chapter. *Reading Between the Lines* on pp. 46–47 provides an opportunity to apply the *PPF* model to deepen your understanding of the reasons for the increase in the cost of food associated with the increase in corn production.

The Rising Opportunity Cost of Food

Food Crisis Being Felt Around World

April 1, 2008

Sharply rising prices have triggered food riots in recent weeks in Mexico, Morocco, Senegal, Uzbekistan, Guinea, Mauritania and Yemen, and aid agencies around the world worry they may be unable to feed the poorest of the poor. …

Rising prices for all the world's crucial cereal crops and growing fears of scarcity are careening through international markets, creating turmoil. …

With crude oil soaring above US$100 a barrel, higher fuel prices have driven up the cost of production and increased transportation costs for all foods.

Pests in Southeast Asia, a 10-year drought in Australia, and a 45-day cold snap in China have combined to aggravate the situation.

At the same time, millions of people in China and India have suddenly become relatively wealthy and are changing their eating habits, consuming more meat and chicken, which places a huge demand on cereal stocks.

In China, per-capita meat consumption has increased 150% since the 1980s. But producing more meat requires more feed to raise more animals. …

Also influencing the food crisis is the move in North America and Europe to biofuel in an effort to ease global warming and reduce reliance on imported energy.

A surge in demand for biofuel has resulted in a sharp decline in agricultural land planted for food crops. About 16% of U.S. agricultural land formerly planted with soybeans and wheat is now growing corn for biofuel.

Material reprinted with the express permission of "The National Post Company," a Canwest Partnership.

Essence of the Story

- A swelling global population explains only part of the problem of food shortages.

- The dramatic price rises have been driven by factors such as turning food into fuel, high crude oil prices (which boost trucking costs), and greater consumption of meat products as incomes rise (which raises the demand for animal feedstuffs).

- Pests in Southeast Asia, a long drought in Australia, and a 45-day cold snap in China have limited grain production and also raised the cost of food.

- Driven by fears of global warming, biofuel has become big business, especially in the United States and the European Union.

Economic Analysis

- Ethanol is made from corn, so biofuel and food compete to use the same resources.

- To produce more ethanol, farmers increased the number of hectares devoted to corn production.

- In 2008, the amount of land devoted to corn production increased by 20 percent in the United States and by 2 percent in the rest of the world.

- Figure 1 shows the U.S. production possibilities frontier, PPF, for corn and other goods and services.

- The increase in the production of corn is illustrated by a movement along the PPF in Fig. 1 from point A in 2007 to point B in 2008.

- In moving from point A to point B, the United States incurs a higher opportunity cost of producing corn, indicated by the greater slope of the PPF at point B.

- In other regions of the world, despite the fact that more land was devoted to corn production, the amount of corn produced didn't change.

- The reason is that drought in Australia, pests in Southeast Asia, and a cold snap in China lowered the crop yield per hectare.

- Figure 2 shows the rest of the world's PPF for corn and other goods and services in 2007 and 2008.

- The increase in the amount of land devoted to producing corn is illustrated by a movement along PPF_{07}.

- With a decrease in the crop yield, production possibilities decreased and the PPF rotated inward.

- The rotation from PPF_{07} to PPF_{08} illustrates this decrease in production possibilities.

- The opportunity cost of producing corn in the rest of the world increased for two reasons: the movement along its PPF and the inward rotation of the PPF.

- With a higher opportunity cost of producing corn, the cost of both biofuel and food increases.

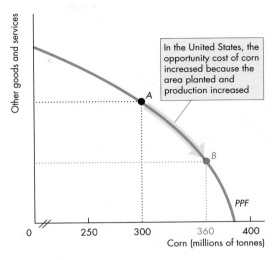

In the United States, the opportunity cost of corn increased because the area planted and production increased

Figure 1 U.S. _PPF_

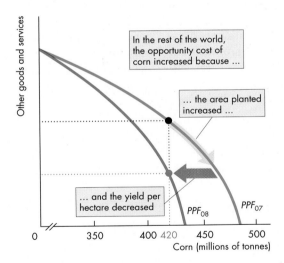

In the rest of the world, the opportunity cost of corn increased because ...

... the area planted increased ...

... and the yield per hectare decreased

Figure 2 Rest of the World _PPF_

SUMMARY ◆

Key Points

Production Possibilities and Opportunity Cost
(pp. 32–34)

- The production possibilities frontier, *PPF*, is the boundary between production levels that are attainable and those that are not attainable when all the available resources are used efficiently.
- Production efficiency occurs at points on the *PPF*.
- Along the *PPF*, the opportunity cost of producing more of one good is the amount of the other good that must be given up.
- The opportunity cost of all goods increases as the production of the good increases.

Using Resources Efficiently (pp. 35–37)

- Allocative efficiency occurs when goods and services are produced at the least possible cost and in the quantities that bring the greatest possible benefit.
- The marginal cost of a good is the opportunity cost of producing one more unit.
- The marginal benefit from a good is the benefit received from consuming one more unit of it, measured by the willingness to pay for it.
- The marginal benefit of a good decreases as the amount of the good available increases.
- Resources are used efficiently when the marginal cost of each good is equal to its marginal benefit.

Economic Growth (pp. 38–39)

- Economic growth, which is the expansion of production possibilities, results from capital accumulation and technological change.
- The opportunity cost of economic growth is forgone current consumption.

Gains from Trade (pp. 40–43)

- A person has a comparative advantage in producing a good if that person can produce the good at a lower opportunity cost than everyone else.
- People gain by specializing in the activity in which they have a comparative advantage and trading with others.
- Dynamic comparative advantage arises from learning-by-doing.

Economic Coordination (pp. 43–45)

- Firms coordinate a large amount of economic activity, but there is a limit to the efficient size of a firm.
- Markets coordinate the economic choices of people and firms.
- Markets can work efficiently only when property rights exist.
- Money makes trading in markets more efficient.

Key Figures

Key Terms

PROBLEMS and APPLICATIONS

 Work problems 1–11 in Chapter 2 Study Plan and get instant feedback.
Work problems 12–21 as Homework, a Quiz, or a Test if assigned by your instructor.

1. Brazil produces ethanol from sugar, and the land used to grow sugar can be used to grow food crops. Suppose that Brazil's production possibilities for ethanol and food crops are as follows:

Ethanol (barrels per day)		Food crops (tonnes per day)
70	and	0
64	and	1
54	and	2
40	and	3
22	and	4
0	and	5

   a. Draw a graph of Brazil's *PPF* and explain how your graph illustrates scarcity.
   b. If Brazil produces 40 barrels of ethanol a day, how much food must it produce if it achieves production efficiency?
   c. Why does Brazil face a tradeoff on its *PPF*?
   d. If Brazil increases its production of ethanol from 40 barrels per day to 54 barrels per day, what is the opportunity cost of the additional ethanol?
   e. If Brazil increases its production of food crops from 2 tonnes per day to 3 tonnes per day, what is the opportunity cost of the additional food?
   f. What is the relationship between your answers to d and e?
   g. Does Brazil face an increasing opportunity cost of ethanol? What feature of the *PPF* that you've drawn illustrates increasing opportunity cost?

2. Define marginal cost and use the information provided in problem 1 to calculate the marginal cost of producing a tonne of food when the quantity produced is 2.5 tonnes per day.

3. Define marginal benefit, explain how it is measured, and explain why the information provided in the table in problem 1 does not enable you to calculate the marginal benefit of food.

4. Distinguish between *production efficiency* and *allocative efficiency*. Explain why many production possibilities achieve production efficiency but only one achieves allocative efficiency.

5. Harry enjoys tennis but wants a high grade in his economics course. The figure shows the limits to what he can achieve: his *PPF*.

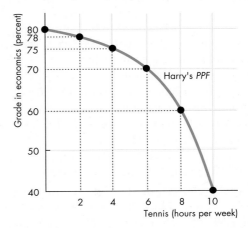

The following figure shows Harry's *MB* curve for tennis.

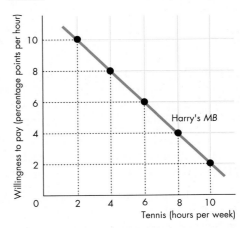

   a. What is Harry's marginal cost of tennis if he plays for (i) 3 hours a week; (ii) 5 hours a week; and (iii) 7 hours a week?
   b. If Harry uses his time to achieve allocative efficiency, what is his economics grade and how many hours of tennis does he play?
   c. Explain why Harry would be worse off getting a grade higher than your answer to b.
   d. If Harry becomes a tennis superstar with big earnings from tennis, what happens to his *PPF*, *MB* curve, and efficient time allocation?

e. If Harry suddenly finds high grades in economics easier to attain, what happens to his *PPF*, *MB* curve, and efficient time allocation?

6. A farm grows wheat and produces pork. The marginal cost of producing each of these products increases as more of it is produced.

   a. Make a graph that illustrates the farm's *PPF*.
   b. The farm adopts a new technology that allows it to use fewer resources to fatten pigs. Use your graph to illustrate the impact of the new technology on the farm's *PPF*.
   c. With the farm using the new technology described in b, has the opportunity cost of producing a tonne of wheat increased, decreased, or remained the same? Explain and illustrate your answer.
   d. Is the farm more efficient with the new technology than it was with the old one? Why?

7. In an hour, Sue can produce 40 caps or 4 jackets and Tessa can produce 80 caps or 4 jackets.

   a. Calculate Sue's opportunity cost of producing a cap.
   b. Calculate Tessa's opportunity cost of producing a cap.
   c. Who has a comparative advantage in producing caps?
   d. If Sue and Tessa specialize in producing the good in which each of them has a comparative advantage, and they trade 1 jacket for 15 caps, who gains from the specialization and trade?

8. Suppose that Tessa buys a new machine for making jackets that enables her to make 20 jackets an hour. (She can still make only 80 caps per hour.)

   a. Who now has a comparative advantage in producing jackets?
   b. Can Sue and Tessa still gain from trade?
   c. Would Sue and Tessa still be willing to trade 1 jacket for 15 caps? Explain your answer.

9. "America's baby-boomers are embracing tea for its health benefits," said the *Economist* (July 8, 2005, p. 65). The article went on to say, "Even though the climate is suitable, tea-growing [in the United States] is simply too costly, since the process is labour-intensive and resists automation."

   Using this information:
   a. Sketch a *PPF* for the production of tea and other goods and services in India.
   b. Sketch a *PPF* for the production of tea and other goods and services in the United States.
   c. Sketch a marginal cost curve for the production of tea in India.
   d. Sketch a marginal cost curve for the production of tea in the United States.
   e. Sketch the marginal benefit curve for tea in the United States before and after the baby-boomers began to appreciate the health benefits of tea.
   f. Explain why the United States does not produce tea and instead imports it from India.
   g. Explain how the quantity of tea that achieves allocative efficiency has changed.
   h. Does the change in preferences towards tea affect the opportunity cost of producing tea?

10. Brazil produces ethanol from sugar at a cost of 22 cents per litre. The United States produces ethanol from corn at a cost of 30 cents per litre. Sugar grown on one hectare of land produces twice the quantity of ethanol as the corn grown on a hectare. The United States imports 5 percent of its ethanol consumption and produces the rest itself. Since 2003, U.S. ethanol production has more than doubled and U.S. corn production has increased by 45 percent.

    a. Does Brazil or the United States have a comparative advantage in producing ethanol?
    b. Do you expect the opportunity cost of producing ethanol in the United States to have increased since 2003? Explain why.
    c. Sketch the *PPF* for ethanol and other goods and services for the United States.
    d. Sketch the *PPF* for ethanol and other goods and services for Brazil.
    e. Sketch a figure similar to Fig. 2.6 on p. 42 to show how both the United States and Brazil can gain from specialization and trade.
    f. Do you think the United States has achieved production efficiency in its manufacture of ethanol? Explain why or why not.
    g. Do you think the United States has achieved allocative efficiency in its manufacture of ethanol? Explain why or why not.

11. For 50 years, Cuba has had a centrally planned economy in which the government decides the allocation of resources. Why would you expect Cuba's production possibilities (per person) to be smaller than those of Canada? What social institutions that help the Canadian economy achieve allocative efficiency are missing in Cuba?

12. Suppose that a country's production possibilities are

Food (kilograms per month)		Sunscreen (litres per month)
300	and	0
200	and	50
100	and	100
0	and	150

  a. Draw a graph of the country's *PPF* and explain how your graph illustrates a tradeoff.
  b. If the country produces 150 kilograms of food per month, how much sunscreen must it produce to achieve production efficiency?
  c. What is the opportunity cost of producing 1 kilogram of food?
  d. What is the opportunity cost of producing 1 litre of sunscreen?
  e. What is the relationship between your answers to c and d?
  f. Does the country face an increasing opportunity cost of food? What feature of a *PPF* illustrates increasing opportunity cost and why does your *PPF* not have this feature?

13. What is the marginal cost of a kilogram of food in the country in problem 12 when the quantity produced is 150 kilograms a month? What is special about the marginal cost of food in this country?

14. The table describes the preferences in the country in problem 12.

Sunscreen (litres per month)	Willingness to pay (kilograms of food per litre)
25	3
75	2
125	1

  a. What is the marginal benefit from sunscreen and how is it measured?
  b. What information provided in the table above and the table in problem 12 do we need to be able to calculate the marginal benefit from sunscreen?
  c. Draw a graph of the marginal benefit from sunscreen.

15. "Dr. Arata Kochi, the World Health Organization malaria chief, ... [says that] eradication is counterproductive. With enough money, he said, current tools like nets, medicines, and DDT could drive down malaria cases 90 percent. 'But eliminating the last 10 percent is a tremen-

dous task and very expensive,' Dr. Kochi said. 'Even places like South Africa should think twice before taking this path.'"

New York Times, March 4, 2008

  a. Is Dr. Kochi talking about *production efficiency* or *allocative efficiency* or both?
  b. Make a graph with the percentage of malaria cases eliminated on the *x*-axis and the marginal cost and marginal benefit of driving down malaria cases on the *y*-axis. On your graph,
   (i) Draw a marginal cost curve that is consistent with Dr. Kochi's opinion reported in the news article.
   (ii) Draw a marginal benefit curve that is consistent with Dr. Kochi's opinion reported in the news article.
   (iii) Identify the quantity of malaria eradicated that achieves allocative efficiency.

16. Capital accumulation and technological change bring economic growth, which means that the *PPF* keeps shifting outward: Production that was unattainable yesterday becomes attainable today; and production that is unattainable today will become attainable tomorrow. Why doesn't this process of economic growth mean that scarcity is being defeated and will one day be gone?

17. "Inexpensive broadband access has done far more for online video than enable the success of services like YouTube and iTunes. By unchaining video watchers from their TV sets, it has opened the floodgates to a generation of TV producers for whom the Internet is their native medium."

New York Times, December 2, 2007

  a. How has inexpensive broadband changed the production possibilities of video entertainment and other goods and services?
  b. Sketch a *PPF* for video entertainment and other goods and services before broadband.
  c. Show how the arrival of inexpensive broadband has changed the *PPF*.
  d. Sketch a marginal benefit curve for video entertainment. Show how opening the "floodgates to a generation of TV producers for whom the Internet is their native medium" might have changed the marginal benefit from video entertainment.
  e. Explain how the quantity of video entertainment that achieves allocative efficiency has changed.

18. Kim can produce 40 pies an hour or 400 cookies an hour. Liam can produce 100 pies an hour or 200 cookies an hour.

    a. Calculate Kim's opportunity cost of producing a pie and Liam's opportunity cost of producing a pie. Who has a comparative advantage in producing pies?
    b. If Kim and Liam spend 30 minutes of each hour producing pies and 30 minutes producing cookies, how many pies and cookies does each of them produce?
    c. Suppose that Kim and Liam increase the time they spend producing the good in which they have a comparative advantage by 15 minutes. What will be the increase in the total number of pies and cookies they produce?
    d. What is the highest price of a pie at which Kim and Liam would agree to trade pies and cookies?
    e. If Kim and Liam specialize and trade, what are the gains from trade?

19. Tony and Patty produce skis and snowboards. The tables show their production possibilities. Each week, Tony produces 5 snowboards and 40 skis and Patty produces 10 snowboards and 5 skis.

Tony's Production Possibilities

Snowboards (per week)		Skis (per week)
25	and	0
20	and	10
15	and	20
10	and	30
5	and	40
0	and	50

Patty's Production Possibilities

Snowboards (per week)		Skis (per week)
20	and	0
10	and	5
0	and	10

    a. Who has a comparative advantage in producing snowboards? And who has a comparative advantage in producing skis?
    b. If Tony and Patty specialize and trade 1 snowboard for 1 ski, what are the gains from trade?

20. "A two-time N.B.A. All-Star, Barron Davis has quietly been moonlighting as a [movie] producer since 2005, when he and a high school buddy, Cash Warren, formed a production company called Verso Entertainment.

    In January, Verso's first feature-length effort, "Made in America," had its premiere to good reviews at Sundance Film Festival and is being courted by distributors."

    New York Times, February 24, 2008

    a. Does Barron Davis have an absolute advantage in basketball and movie directing and is this the reason for his success in both activities?
    b. Does Barron Davis have a comparative advantage in basketball or movie directing or both and is this the reason for his success in both activities?
    c. Sketch a *PPF* between playing basketball and producing other goods and services for Barron Davis and for yourself.
    d. How do you (and people like you) and Barron Davis (and people like him) gain from specialization and trade?

21. After you have studied *Reading Between the Lines* on pp. 46–47, answer the following questions:

    a. Why has corn production in the United States increased?
    b. Why would you expect an increase in the quantity of corn produced to raise the opportunity cost of producing corn?
    c. Why did the cost of producing corn increase in the rest of the world?
    d. Is it possible that the increased quantity of corn produced, despite the higher cost of production, moves the United States closer to allocative efficiency?

22. Use the links on MyEconLab (Textbook Resources, Chapter 2, Weblinks) to obtain data on the tuition and other costs of enrolling in the MBA program at a school that interests you.

    a. Draw a *PPF* that shows the tradeoff that you would face if you decided to enroll in the MBA program.
    b. Do you think your marginal benefit of an MBA exceeds your marginal cost?
    c. Based on your answer to b, do you plan to enroll in an MBA program? Is your answer to this question consistent with using your time to achieve your self-interest?

UNDERSTANDING THE SCOPE OF ECONOMICS

Your Economic Revolution

Three periods in human history stand out as ones of economic revolution. The first, the *Agricultural Revolution*, occurred 10,000 years ago. In what is today Iraq, people learned to domesticate animals and plant crops. People stopped roaming in search of food and settled in villages, towns, and cities, where they specialized in the activities in which they had a comparative advantage and developed markets in which to exchange their products. Wealth increased enormously.

You are studying economics at a time that future historians will call the *Information Revolution*. Over the entire world, people are embracing new information technologies and prospering on an unprecedented scale.

Economics was born during the *Industrial Revolution*, which began in England during the 1760s. For the first time, people began to apply science and create new technologies for the manufacture of textiles and iron, to create steam engines, and to boost the output of farms.

During all three economic revolutions, many have prospered but many have been left behind. It is the range of human progress that poses the greatest question for economics and the one that Adam Smith addressed in the first work of economic science: What causes the differences in wealth among nations?

Many people had written about economics before **Adam Smith**, *but he made economics a science. Born in 1723 in Kirkcaldy, a small fishing town near Edinburgh, Scotland, Smith was the only child of the town's customs officer. Lured from his professorship (he was a full professor at 28) by a wealthy Scottish duke who gave him a pension of £300 a year—ten times the average income at that time—Smith devoted ten years to writing his masterpiece:* An Inquiry into the Nature and Causes of the **Wealth of Nations**, *published in 1776.*

Why, Adam Smith asked, are some nations wealthy while others are poor? He was pondering these questions at the height of the Industrial Revolution, and he answered by emphasizing the role of the division of labour and free markets.

To illustrate his argument, Adam Smith described two pin factories. In the first, one person, using the hand tools available in the 1770s, could make 20 pins a day. In the other, by using those same hand tools but breaking the process into a number of individually small operations in which people specialize—by the division of labour—ten people could make a staggering 48,000 pins a day. One

"It is not from the benevolence of the butcher, the brewer, or the baker that we expect our dinner, but from their regard to their own interest."

ADAM SMITH
The Wealth of Nations

draws out the wire, another straightens it, a third cuts it, a fourth points it, a fifth grinds it. Three specialists make the head, and a fourth attaches it. Finally, the pin is polished and packaged.

But a large market is needed to support the division of labour: One factory employing ten workers would need to sell more than 15 million pins a year to stay in business!

Jagdish Bhagwati

Jagdish Bhagwati is University Professor at Columbia University. Born in India in 1934, he studied at Cambridge University in England, MIT, and Oxford University before returning to India. He returned to teach at MIT in 1968 and moved to Columbia in 1980. A prolific scholar, Professor Bhagwati also writes in leading newspapers and magazines throughout the world. He has been much honoured for both his scientific work and his impact on public policy. His greatest contributions are in international trade but extend also to developmental problems and the study of political economy.

Michael Parkin and Robin Bade talked with Jagdish Bhagwati about his work and the progress that economists have made in understanding the benefits of economic growth and international trade since the pioneering work of Adam Smith.

Professor Bhagwati, what attracted you to economics?

When you come from India, where poverty hits the eye, it is easy to be attracted to economics, which can be used to bring prosperity and create jobs to pull up the poor into gainful employment.

I learned later that there are two broad types of economist: those who treat the subject as an arid mathematical toy and those who see it as a serious social science.

If Cambridge, where I went as an undergraduate, had been interested in esoteric mathematical economics, I would have opted for something else. But the Cambridge economists from whom I learned—many among the greatest figures in the discipline—saw economics as a social science. I therefore saw the power of economics as a tool to address India's poverty and was immediately hooked.

Who had the greatest impact on you at Cambridge?

Most of all, it was Harry Johnson, a young Canadian of immense energy and profound analytical gifts. Quite unlike the shy and reserved British dons, Johnson was friendly, effusive, and supportive of students who flocked around him. He would later move to Chicago, where he became one of the most influential members of the market-oriented Chicago school. Another was Joan Robinson, arguably the world's most impressive female economist.

When I left Cambridge for MIT, going from one Cambridge to the other, I was lucky to transition from one phenomenal set of economists to another. At MIT, I learned much from future Nobel laureates Paul Samuelson and Robert Solow. Both would later become great friends and colleagues when I joined the MIT faculty in 1968.

After Cambridge and MIT, you went to Oxford and then back to India. What did you do in India?

I joined the Planning Commission in New Delhi, where my first big job was to find ways of raising the bottom 30 percent of India's population out of poverty to a "minimum income" level.

And what did you prescribe?

My main prescription was to "grow the pie." My research suggested that the share of the bottom 30 percent of the pie did not seem to vary dramatically with differences in economic and political systems. So growth in the pie seemed to be the principal (but not the only) component of an anti-poverty strategy. To supplement growth's good effects on the poor, the Indian planners were also dedicated to education, health, social reforms, and land reforms. Also, the access of the lowest-income and socially disadvantaged groups to the growth process and its benefits was to be improved in many ways, such as extension of credit without collateral.

Today, this strategy has no rivals. Much empirical work shows that where growth has occurred, poverty has lessened. It is nice to know that one's basic take on an issue of such central importance to humanity's well-being has been borne out by experience!

You left India in 1968 to come to the United States and an academic job at MIT. Why?

While the decision to emigrate often reflects personal factors—and they were present in my case—the offer of a professorship from MIT certainly helped me make up my mind. At the time, it was easily the world's most celebrated department. Serendipitously, the highest-ranked departments at MIT were not in engineering and the sciences but in linguistics (which had Noam Chomsky) and economics (which had Paul Samuelson). Joining the MIT faculty was a dramatic breakthrough: I felt stimulated each year by several fantastic students and by several of the world's most creative economists.

We hear a lot in the popular press about fair trade and level playing fields. What's the distinction between free trade and fair trade? How can the playing field be unlevel?

Free trade simply means allowing no trade barriers such as tariffs, subsidies, and quotas. Trade barriers

> My main prescription was to "grow the pie" ... Today, this strategy has no rivals. Much empirical work shows that where growth has occurred, poverty has lessened.

> Fair trade ... is almost always a sneaky way of objecting to free trade.

make domestic prices different from world prices for traded goods. When this happens, resources are not being used efficiently. Basic economics from the time of Adam Smith tells us why free trade is good for us and why barriers to trade harm us, though our understanding of this doctrine today is far more nuanced and profound than it was at its creation.

Fair trade, on the other hand, is almost always a sneaky way of objecting to free trade. If your rivals are hard to compete with, you are not likely to get protection simply by saying that you cannot hack it. But if you say that your rival is an "unfair" trader, that is an easier sell! As international competition has grown fiercer, cries of "unfair trade" have therefore multiplied. The lesser rogues among the protectionists ask for "free and fair trade," whereas the worst ones ask for "fair, not free, trade."

At the end of World War II, the General Agreement of Tariffs and Trade (GATT) was established and there followed several rounds of multilateral trade negotiations and reductions in barriers to trade. How do you assess the contribution of GATT and its successor, the World Trade Organization (WTO)?

The GATT has made a huge contribution by overseeing massive trade liberalization in industrial goods among the developed countries. GATT rules, which "bind" tariffs to negotiated ceilings, prevent the raising of tariffs and have prevented tariff wars like those of the 1930s in which mutual and retaliatory tariff barriers were raised, to the detriment of everyone.

The GATT was folded into the WTO at the end of the Uruguay Round of trade negotiations, and the WTO is institutionally stronger. For instance, it has a binding dispute settlement mechanism, whereas the GATT had no such teeth. It is also more ambitious in its scope, extending to new areas such as the environment, intellectual property protection, and investment rules.

Running alongside the pursuit of multilateral free trade has been the emergence of bilateral trade agreements such as NAFTA and the European Union (EU). How do you view the bilateral free trade areas in today's world?

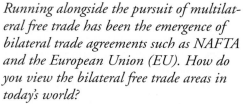

We now have a world of uncoordinated and inefficient trade policies.

Unfortunately, there has been an explosion of bilateral free trade areas today. By some estimates, the ones in place and others being plotted approach 400! Each bilateral agreement gives preferential treatment to its trading partner over others. Because there are now so many bilateral agreements, such as those between the United States and Israel and between the United States and Jordan, the result is a chaotic pattern of different tariffs depending on where a product comes from. Also, "rules of origin" must be agreed upon to determine whether a product is, say, Jordanian or Taiwanese if Jordan qualifies for a preferential tariff but Taiwan does not and Taiwanese inputs enter the Jordanian manufacture of the product.

I have called the resulting crisscrossing of preferences and rules of origin the "spaghetti bowl" problem. The world trading system is choking under these proliferating bilateral deals. Contrast this complexity with the simplicity of a multilateral system with common tariffs for all WTO members.

We now have a world of uncoordinated and inefficient trade policies. The EU makes bilateral free trade agreements with different non-EU countries, so the United States follows with its own bilateral agreements; and with Europe and the United States doing it, the Asian countries, long wedded to multilateralism, have now succumbed to the mania.

Instead, if the United States had provided leadership by rewriting rules to make the signing of such bilateral agreements extremely difficult, this plague on the trading system today might well have been averted.

Despite the benefits that economics points to from multilateral free trade, the main organization that pursues this goal, the WTO, is having a very hard time with the anti-globalization movement. What can we say

about globalization that puts the WTO and its work in proper perspective?

The anti-globalization movement contains a diverse set of activists. Essentially, they all claim to be stakeholders in the globalization phenomenon. But there are those who want to drive a stake through the system, as in Dracula films, and there are those who want to exercise their stake in the system. The former want to be heard; the latter, to be listened to. For a while, the two disparate sets of critics were milling around together, seeking targets of opportunity at international conferences such as WTO's November 2000 meeting in Seattle, where the riots broke out. Now things have settled down, and the groups that want to work systematically and seriously at improving the global economy's functioning are much more in play.

But the WTO is also seen, inaccurately for the most part, as imposing trade sanctions that override concerns such as environmental protection. For example, U.S. legislation bans the importing of shrimp that is harvested without the use of turtle-excluding devices. India and others complained, but the WTO upheld the U.S. legislation. Ignorant of the facts, demonstrators took to the streets dressed as turtles protesting the WTO decision!

What advice do you have for a student who is just starting to study economics? Is economics a good subject in which to major?

I would say: enormously so. In particular, we economists bring three unique insights to good policy making.

First, economists look for second- and subsequent-round effects of actions.

Second, we correctly emphasize that a policy cannot be judged without using a counterfactual. It is a witticism that an economist, when asked how her husband was, said, "compared to what?"

Third, we uniquely and systematically bring the principle of social cost and social benefit to our policy analysis.

3  Demand and Supply

After studying this chapter, you will be able to

- Describe a competitive market and think about price as an opportunity cost
- Explain the influences on demand
- Explain the influences on supply
- Explain how demand and supply determine prices and quantities bought and sold
- Use the demand and supply model to make predictions about changes in prices and quantities

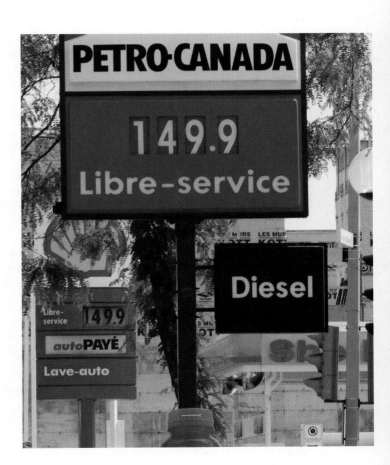

What makes the prices of oil and gasoline double in just one year? Will these prices keep on rising? Are the oil companies taking advantage of people? This chapter enables you to answer these and similar questions about prices—prices that rise, prices that fall, and prices that fluctuate.

You already know that economics is about the choices people make to cope with scarcity and how those choices respond to incentives. Prices act as incentives. You're going to see how people respond to prices and how prices get determined by demand and supply. The demand and supply model that you study in this chapter is the main tool of economics. It helps us to answer the big economic question: What, how,

and for whom are goods and services produced? It also helps us to say more about what it takes for the pursuit of self-interest to promote the social interest.

At the end of the chapter, in *Reading Between the Lines*, we'll apply the model to the market for gasoline and explain why the price is expected to rise again by 2010.

◆ Markets and Prices

When you need a new pair of running shoes, want a bagel and a latte, plan to upgrade your cell phone, or need to fly home for Thanksgiving, you must find a place where people sell those items or offer those services. The place in which you find them is a *market*. You learned in Chapter 2 (p. 44) that a market is any arrangement that enables buyers and sellers to get information and to do business with each other.

A market has two sides: buyers and sellers. There are markets for *goods* such as apples and hiking boots, for *services* such as haircuts and tennis lessons, for *resources* such as computer programmers and earth-movers, and for other manufactured *inputs* such as memory chips and auto parts. There are also markets for money such as Japanese yen and for financial securities such as Yahoo! stock. Only our imagination limits what can be traded in markets.

Some markets are physical places where buyers and sellers meet and where an auctioneer or a broker helps to determine the prices. Examples of this type of market are live car auction markets and wholesale fish, meat, and produce markets.

Some markets are groups of people spread around the world who never meet and know little about each other but are connected through the Internet or by telephone and fax. Examples are the e-commerce markets and the markets for foreign currency.

But most markets are unorganized collections of buyers and sellers. You do most of your trading in this type of market. An example is the market for basketball shoes. The buyers in this $3 billion-a-year market are the 45 million North Americans who play basketball (or who want to make a fashion statement). The sellers are the tens of thousands of retail sports equipment and footwear stores. Each buyer can visit several different stores, and each seller knows that the buyer has a choice of stores.

Markets vary in the intensity of competition that buyers and sellers face. In this chapter, we're going to study a **competitive market**—a market that has many buyers and many sellers, so no single buyer or seller can influence the price.

Producers offer items for sale only if the price is high enough to cover their opportunity cost. And consumers respond to changing opportunity cost by seeking cheaper alternatives to expensive items.

We are going to study how people respond to *prices* and the forces that determine prices. But to pursue these tasks, we need to understand the relationship between a price and an opportunity cost.

In everyday life, the *price* of an object is the number of dollars that must be given up in exchange for it. Economists refer to this price as the **money price**.

The *opportunity cost* of an action is the highest-valued alternative forgone. If, when you buy a cup of coffee, the highest-valued thing you forgo is some gum, then the opportunity cost of the coffee is the *quantity* of gum forgone. We can calculate the quantity of gum forgone from the money prices of the coffee and the gum.

If the money price of coffee is $2 a cup and the money price of gum is $1 a pack, then the opportunity cost of one cup of coffee is two packs of gum. To calculate this opportunity cost, we divide the price of a cup of coffee by the price of a pack of gum and find the *ratio* of one price to the other. The ratio of one price to another is called a **relative price**, and a *relative price is an opportunity cost.*

We can express the relative price of coffee in terms of gum or any other good. The normal way of expressing a relative price is in terms of a "basket" of all goods and services. To calculate this relative price, we divide the money price of a good by the money price of a "basket" of all goods (called a *price index*). The resulting relative price tells us the opportunity cost of the good in terms of how much of the "basket" we must give up to buy it.

The demand and supply model that we are about to study determines *relative prices,* and the word "price" means *relative* price. When we predict that a price will fall, we do not mean that its *money* price will fall—although it might. We mean that its *relative* price will fall. That is, its price will fall *relative* to the average price of other goods and services.

Review Quiz ◆

1 What is the distinction between a money price and a relative price?

2 Explain why a relative price is an opportunity cost.

3 Think of examples of goods whose relative price has risen or fallen by a large amount.

 Work Study Plan 3.1 and get instant feedback.

Let's begin our study of demand and supply, starting with demand.

Demand

If you demand something, then you

1. Want it,
2. Can afford it, and
3. Plan to buy it.

Wants are the unlimited desires or wishes that people have for goods and services. How many times have you thought that you would like something "if only you could afford it" or "if it weren't so expensive"? Scarcity guarantees that many—perhaps most—of our wants will never be satisfied. Demand reflects a decision about which wants to satisfy.

The **quantity demanded** of a good or service is the amount that consumers plan to buy during a given time period at a particular price. The quantity demanded is not necessarily the same as the quantity actually bought. Sometimes the quantity demanded exceeds the amount of goods available, so the quantity bought is less than the quantity demanded.

The quantity demanded is measured as an amount per unit of time. For example, suppose that you buy one cup of coffee a day. The quantity of coffee that you demand can be expressed as 1 cup per day, 7 cups per week, or 365 cups per year.

Many factors influence buying plans, and one of them is the price. We look first at the relationship between the quantity demanded of a good and its price. To study this relationship, we keep all other influences on buying plans the same and we ask: How, other things remaining the same, does the quantity demanded of a good change as its price changes?

The law of demand provides the answer.

The Law of Demand

The **law of demand** states

Other things remaining the same, the higher the price of a good, the smaller is the quantity demanded; and the lower the price of a good, the greater is the quantity demanded.

Why does a higher price reduce the quantity demanded? For two reasons:

■ Substitution effect
■ Income effect

Substitution Effect When the price of a good rises, other things remaining the same, its *relative* price—its opportunity cost—rises. Although each good is unique, it has *substitutes*—other goods that can be used in its place. As the opportunity cost of a good rises, the incentive to economize on its use and switch to a substitute becomes stronger.

Income Effect When a price rises, other things remaining the same, the price rises *relative* to income. Faced with a higher price and an unchanged income, people cannot afford to buy all the things they previously bought. They must decrease the quantities demanded of at least some goods and services. Normally, the good whose price has increased will be one of the goods that people buy less of.

To see the substitution effect and the income effect at work, think about the effects of a change in the price of an energy bar. Several different goods are substitutes for an energy bar. For example, an energy drink could be consumed instead of an energy bar.

Suppose that an energy bar initially sells for $3 and then its price falls to $1.50. People now substitute energy bars for energy drinks—the substitution effect. And with a budget that now has some slack from the lower price of an energy bar, people buy even more energy bars—the income effect. The quantity of energy bars demanded increases for these two reasons.

Now suppose that an energy bar initially sells for $3 and then the price doubles to $6. People now buy fewer energy bars and more energy drinks—the substitution effect. And faced with a tighter budget, people buy even fewer energy bars—the income effect. The quantity of energy bars demanded decreases for these two reasons.

Demand Curve and Demand Schedule

You are now about to study one of the two most used curves in economics: the demand curve. And you are going to encounter one of the most critical distinctions: the distinction between *demand* and *quantity demanded*.

The term **demand** refers to the entire relationship between the price of a good and the quantity demanded of that good. Demand is illustrated by the demand curve and the demand schedule. The term *quantity demanded* refers to a point on a demand curve—the quantity demanded at a particular price.

Figure 3.1 shows the demand curve for energy bars. A **demand curve** shows the relationship between the quantity demanded of a good and its price when all other influences on consumers' planned purchases remain the same.

The table in Fig. 3.1 is the demand schedule for energy bars. A *demand schedule* lists the quantities demanded at each price when all the other influences on consumers' planned purchases remain the same. For example, if the price of a bar is 50¢, the quantity demanded is 22 million a week. If the price is $2.50, the quantity demanded is 5 million a week. The other rows of the table show the quantities demanded at prices of $1.00, $1.50, and $2.00.

We graph the demand schedule as a demand curve with the quantity demanded on the *x*-axis and the price on the *y*-axis. The points on the demand curve labelled *A* through *E* correspond to the rows of the demand schedule. For example, point *A* on the graph shows a quantity demanded of 22 million energy bars a week at a price of 50¢ a bar.

Willingness and Ability to Pay Another way of looking at the demand curve is as a willingness-and-ability-to-pay curve. The willingness and ability to pay is a measure of *marginal benefit*.

If a small quantity is available, the highest price that someone is willing and able to pay for one more unit is high. But as the quantity available increases, the marginal benefit of each additional unit falls and the highest price that someone is willing and able to pay also falls along the demand curve.

In Fig. 3.1, if only 5 million energy bars are available each week, the highest price that someone is willing to pay for the 5 millionth bar is $2.50. But if 22 million energy bars are available each week, someone is willing to pay 50¢ for the last bar bought.

A Change in Demand

When any factor that influences buying plans other than the price of the good changes, there is a **change in demand**. Figure 3.2 illustrates an increase in demand. When demand increases, the demand curve shifts rightward and the quantity demanded at each price is greater. For example, at $2.50 a bar, the quantity demanded on the original (blue) demand curve is 5 million energy bars a week. On the new (red) demand curve, at $2.50 a bar, the quantity demanded is 15 million bars a week. Look closely at the numbers in the table and check that the quantity demanded at each price is greater.

FIGURE 3.1 The Demand Curve

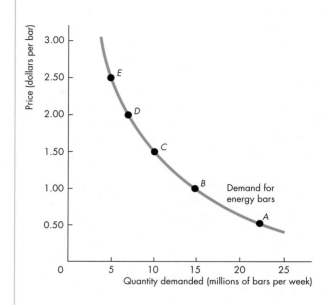

	Price (dollars per bar)	Quantity demanded (millions of bars per week)
A	0.50	22
B	1.00	15
C	1.50	10
D	2.00	7
E	2.50	5

The table shows a demand schedule for energy bars. At a price of 50¢ a bar, 22 million bars a week are demanded; at a price of $1.50 a bar, 10 million bars a week are demanded. The demand curve shows the relationship between quantity demanded and price, other things remaining the same. The demand curve slopes downward: As the price decreases, the quantity demanded increases.

The demand curve can be read in two ways. For a given price, the demand curve tells us the quantity that people plan to buy. For example, at a price of $1.50 a bar, people plan to buy 10 million bars a week. For a given quantity, the demand curve tells us the maximum price that consumers are willing and able to pay for the last bar available. For example, the maximum price that consumers will pay for the 15 millionth bar is $1.00.

FIGURE 3.2   An Increase in Demand

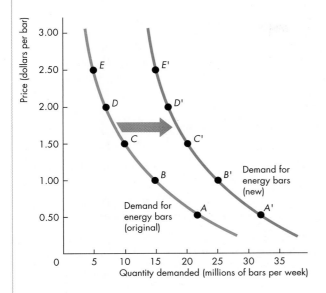

Original demand schedule		New demand schedule		
Original income		**New higher income**		
Price (dollars per bar)	**Quantity demanded** (millions of bars per week)		**Price** (dollars per bar)	**Quantity demanded** (millions of bars per week)
A	0.50	22	A'	0.50	32
B	1.00	15	B'	1.00	25
C	1.50	10	C'	1.50	20
D	2.00	7	D'	2.00	17
E	2.50	5	E'	2.50	15

A change in any influence on buyers' plans other than the price of the good itself results in a new demand schedule and a shift of the demand curve. A change in income changes the demand for energy bars. At a price of $1.50 a bar, 10 million bars a week are demanded at the original income (row C of the table) and 20 million bars a week are demanded at the new higher income (row C'). A rise in income increases the demand for energy bars. The demand curve shifts rightward, as shown by the shift arrow and the resulting red curve.

myeconlab animation

Six main factors bring changes in demand. They are changes in

- The prices of related goods
- Expected future prices
- Income
- Expected future income and credit
- Population
- Preferences

Prices of Related Goods   The quantity of energy bars that consumers plan to buy depends in part on the prices of substitutes for energy bars. A **substitute** is a good that can be used in place of another good. For example, a bus ride is a substitute for a train ride; a hamburger is a substitute for a hot dog; and an energy drink is a substitute for an energy bar. If the price of a substitute for an energy bar rises, people buy less of the substitute and more energy bars. For example, if the price of an energy drink rises, people buy fewer energy drinks and more energy bars. The demand for energy bars increases.

The quantity of energy bars that people plan to buy also depends on the prices of complements with energy bars. A **complement** is a good that is used in conjunction with another good. Hamburgers and fries are complements, and so are energy bars and exercise. If the price of an hour at the gym falls, people buy more gym time *and more* energy bars.

Expected Future Prices   If the price of a good is expected to rise in the future and if the good can be stored, the opportunity cost of obtaining the good for future use is lower today than it will be when the price has increased. So people retime their purchases—they substitute over time. They buy more of the good now before its price is expected to rise (and less afterward), so the demand for the good today increases.

For example, suppose that a Florida frost damages the season's orange crop. You expect the price of orange juice to rise, so you fill your freezer with enough frozen juice to get you through the next six months. Your current demand for frozen orange juice has increased, and your future demand has decreased.

Similarly, if the price of a good is expected to fall in the future, the opportunity cost of buying the good today is high relative to what it is expected to be in the future. So again, people retime their purchases. They buy less of the good now before its price falls, so the demand for the good decreases today and increases in the future.

Computer prices are constantly falling, and this fact poses a dilemma. Will you buy a new computer now, in time for the start of the school year, or will you wait until the price has fallen some more? Because people expect computer prices to fall, the current demand for computers is less (and the future demand is greater) than it otherwise would be.

Income   Consumers' income influences demand. When income increases, consumers buy more of most goods; and when income decreases, consumers buy less of most goods. Although an increase in income leads to an increase in the demand for *most* goods, it does not lead to an increase in the demand for *all* goods. A **normal good** is one for which demand increases as income increases. An **inferior good** is one for which demand decreases as income increases. As incomes increase, the demand for air travel (a normal good) increases and the demand for long-distance bus trips (an inferior good) decreases.

Expected Future Income and Credit   When income is expected to increase in the future, or when credit is easy to obtain, demand might increase now. For example, a salesperson gets the news that she will receive a big bonus at the end of the year, so she goes into debt and buys a new car right now.

Population   Demand also depends on the size and the age structure of the population. The larger the population, the greater is the demand for all goods and services; the smaller the population, the smaller is the demand for all goods and services.

For example, the demand for parking spaces or movies or just about anything that you can imagine is much greater in the Greater Toronto Area (population 5.6 million) than it is in Thunder Bay (population 124,000).

Also, the larger the proportion of the population in a given age group, the greater is the demand for the goods and services used by that age group.

For example, in 2007, there were 2.3 million 20- to 24-year-olds in Canada compared with 2.4 million in 1987. As a result, the demand for university places in 2007 was similar to what it was in 1987. Over this same period, the number of Canadians age 85 years and over increased by 313,000. As a result, the demand for nursing home services increased.

TABLE 3.1   The Demand for Energy Bars

The Law of Demand

The quantity of energy bars demanded

Decreases if:	Increases if:
■ The price of an energy bar rises	■ The price of an energy bar falls

Changes in Demand

The demand of energy bars

Decreases if:	Increases if:
■ The price of a substitute falls	■ The price of a substitute rises
■ The price of a complement rises	■ The price of a complement falls
■ The price of an energy bar is expected to fall	■ The price of an energy bar is expected to rise
■ Income falls*	■ Income rises*
■ Expected future income falls or credit becomes harder to get	■ Expected future income rises or credit becomes easier to get
■ The population decreases	■ The population increases

*An energy bar is a normal good.

Preferences   Demand depends on preferences. *Preferences* determine the value that people place on each good and service. Preferences depend on such things as the weather, information, and fashion. For example, greater health and fitness awareness has shifted preferences in favour of energy bars, so the demand for energy bars has increased.

Table 3.1 summarizes the influences on demand and the direction of those influences.

A Change in the Quantity Demanded Versus a Change in Demand

Changes in the influences on buyers' plans bring either a change in the quantity demanded or a change in demand. Equivalently, they bring either a movement along the demand curve or a shift of the demand curve. The distinction between a change in the quantity demanded and a change in demand is the same as that between a movement along the demand curve and a shift of the demand curve.

A point on the demand curve shows the quantity demanded at a given price. So a movement along the demand curve shows a **change in the quantity demanded**. The entire demand curve shows demand. So a shift of the demand curve shows a *change in demand*. Figure 3.3 illustrates these distinctions.

Movement Along the Demand Curve If the price of the good changes but no other influence on buying plans changes, we illustrate the effect as a movement along the demand curve.

A fall in the price of a good increases the quantity demanded of it. In Fig. 3.3, we illustrate the effect of a fall in price of the good as a movement down along the demand curve D_0.

A rise in the price of a good decreases the quantity demanded of it. In Fig. 3.3, we illustrate the effect of a rise in price of the good as a movement up along the demand curve D_0.

A Shift of the Demand Curve If the price of a good remains constant but some other influence on buyers' plans changes, there is a change in demand for that good. We illustrate a change in demand as a shift of the demand curve. For example, if more people work out at the gym, consumers buy more energy bars regardless of the price of a bar. That is what a rightward shift of the demand curve shows—more energy bars are demanded at each price.

In Fig. 3.3, there is a *change in demand* and the demand curve shifts when any influence on buyers' plans change, other than the price of the good. Demand *increases* and the demand curve *shifts rightward* (to the red demand curve D_1) if the price of a substitute rises, the price of a complement falls, the expected future price of the good rises, income increases (for a normal good), expected future income or credit increases, or the population increases. Demand *decreases* and the demand curve *shifts leftward* (to the red demand curve D_2) if the price of a substitute falls, the price of a complement rises, the expected future price of the good falls, income decreases (for a normal good), expected future income or credit decreases, or the population decreases. (For an inferior good, the effects of changes in income are in the opposite direction to those described above.)

FIGURE 3.3   A Change in the Quantity Demanded Versus a Change in Demand

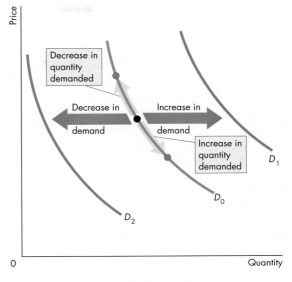

When the price of the good changes, there is a movement along the demand curve and *a change in the quantity demanded*, shown by the blue arrows on demand curve D_0. When any other influence on buyers' plans changes, there is a shift of the demand curve and a *change in demand*. An increase in demand shifts the demand curve rightward (from D_0 to D_1). A decrease in demand shifts the demand curve leftward (from D_0 to D_2).

myeconlab   animation

Review Quiz

1 Define the quantity demanded of a good or service.
2 What is the law of demand and how do we illustrate it?
3 What does the demand curve tell us about the price that consumers are willing to pay?
4 List all the influences on buying plans that change demand, and for each influence, say whether it increases or decreases demand.
5 Why does demand not change when the price of a good changes with no change in the other influences on buying plans?

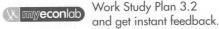
myeconlab   Work Study Plan 3.2 and get instant feedback.

◢ Supply

If a firm supplies a good or service, the firm

1. Has the resources and technology to produce it,
2. Can profit from producing it, and
3. Plans to produce it and sell it.

A supply is more than just having the *resources* and the *technology* to produce something. *Resources and technology* are the constraints that limit what is possible.

Many useful things can be produced, but they are not produced unless it is profitable to do so. Supply reflects a decision about which technologically feasible items to produce.

The **quantity supplied** of a good or service is the amount that producers plan to sell during a given time period at a particular price. The quantity supplied is not necessarily the same amount as the quantity actually sold. Sometimes the quantity supplied is greater than the quantity demanded, so the quantity sold is less than the quantity supplied.

Like the quantity demanded, the quantity supplied is measured as an amount per unit of time. For example, suppose that GM produces 1,000 cars a day. The quantity of cars supplied by GM can be expressed as 1,000 a day, 7,000 a week, or 365,000 a year. Without the time dimension, we cannot tell whether a particular quantity is large or small.

Many factors influence selling plans, and again one of them is the price of the good. We look first at the relationship between the quantity supplied of a good and its price. Just as we did when we studied demand, to isolate the relationship between the quantity supplied of a good and its price, we keep all other influences on selling plans the same and ask: How does the quantity supplied of a good change as its price changes when other things remain the same?

The law of supply provides the answer.

The Law of Supply

The **law of supply** states:

Other things remaining the same, the higher the price of a good, the greater is the quantity supplied; and the lower the price of a good, the smaller is the quantity supplied.

Why does a higher price increase the quantity supplied? It is because *marginal cost increases.* As the quantity produced of any good increases, the marginal cost of producing the good increases. (You can refresh your memory of increasing marginal cost in Chapter 2, p. 35.)

It is never worth producing a good if the price received for the good does not at least cover the marginal cost of producing it. When the price of a good rises, other things remaining the same, producers are willing to incur a higher marginal cost, so they increase production. The higher price brings forth an increase in the quantity supplied.

Let's now illustrate the law of supply with a supply curve and a supply schedule.

Supply Curve and Supply Schedule

You are now going to study the second of the two most used curves in economics: the supply curve. And you're going to learn about the critical distinction between *supply* and *quantity supplied.*

The term **supply** refers to the entire relationship between the price of a good and the quantity supplied of it. Supply is illustrated by the supply curve and the supply schedule. The term *quantity supplied* refers to a point on a supply curve—the quantity supplied at a particular price.

Figure 3.4 shows the supply curve of energy bars. A **supply curve** shows the relationship between the quantity supplied of a good and its price when all other influences on producers' planned sales remain the same. The supply curve is a graph of a supply schedule.

The table in Fig. 3.4 sets out the supply schedule for energy bars. A *supply schedule* lists the quantities supplied at each price when all the other influences on producers' planned sales remain the same. For example, if the price of a bar is 50¢, the quantity supplied is zero—in row *A* of the table. If the price of a bar is $1.00, the quantity supplied is 6 million energy bars a week—in row *B*. The other rows of the table show the quantities supplied at prices of $1.50, $2.00, and $2.50.

To make a supply curve, we graph the quantity supplied on the *x*-axis and the price on the *y*-axis, just as in the case of the demand curve. The points on the supply curve labelled *A* through *E* correspond to the rows of the supply schedule. For example, point *A* on the graph shows a quantity supplied of zero at a price of 50¢ an energy bar.

FIGURE 3.4   The Supply Curve

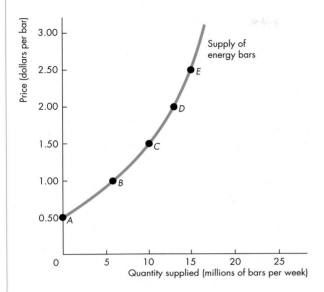

	Price (dollars per bar)	Quantity supplied (millions of bars per week)
A	0.50	0
B	1.00	6
C	1.50	10
D	2.00	13
E	2.50	15

The table shows the supply schedule of energy bars. For example, at a price of $1.00, 6 million bars a week are supplied; at a price of $2.50, 15 million bars a week are supplied. The supply curve shows the relationship between the quantity supplied and the price, other things remaining the same. The supply curve slopes upward: As the price of a good increases, the quantity supplied increases.

A supply curve can be read in two ways. For a given price, the supply curve tells us the quantity that producers plan to sell at that price. For example, at a price of $1.50 a bar, producers are willing to sell 10 million bars a week. For a given quantity, the supply curve tells us the minimum price at which producers are willing to sell one more bar. For example, if 15 million bars are produced each week, the lowest price at which a producer is willing to sell the 15 millionth bar is $2.50.

myeconlab   animation

Minimum Supply Price   The supply curve can be interpreted as a minimum-supply-price curve—a curve that shows the lowest price at which someone is willing to sell. This lowest price is the *marginal cost.*

If a small quantity is produced, the lowest price at which someone is willing to sell one more unit is low. But as the quantity produced increases, the marginal cost of each additional unit rises, so the lowest price at which someone is willing to sell one more unit rises along the supply curve.

In Fig. 3.4, if 15 million bars are produced each week, the lowest price at which someone is willing to sell the 15 millionth bar is $2.50. But if 10 million bars are produced each week, someone is willing to accept $1.50 for the last bar produced.

A Change in Supply

When any factor that influences selling plans other than the price of the good changes, there is a **change in supply**. Six main factors bring changes in supply. They are changes in

- The prices of factors of production
- The prices of related goods produced
- Expected future prices
- The number of suppliers
- Technology
- The state of nature

Prices of Factors of Production   The prices of the factors of production used to produce a good influence its supply. To see this influence, think about the supply curve as a minimum-supply-price curve. If the price of a factor of production rises, the lowest price that a producer is willing to accept for that good rises, so supply of the good decreases. For example, during 2008, as the price of jet fuel increased, the supply of air service decreased. Similarly, a rise in the minimum wage decreases the supply of hamburgers.

Prices of Related Goods Produced   The prices of related goods that firms produce influence supply. For example, if the price of energy gel rises, firms switch production from bar to gel. The supply of energy bars decreases. Energy bars and energy gel are *substitutes in production*—goods that can be produced by using the same resources. If the price of beef rises, the supply of cowhide increases. Beef and cowhide are *complements in production*—goods that must be produced together.

Expected Future Prices If the price of a good is expected to rise, the return from selling the good in the future is higher than it is today. So supply decreases today and increases in the future.

The Number of Suppliers The larger the number of firms that produce a good, the greater is the supply of the good. And as firms enter an industry, the supply in that industry increases. As firms leave an industry, the supply in that industry decreases.

Technology The term "technology" is used broadly to mean the way that factors of production are used to produce a good. A technology change occurs when a new method is discovered that lowers the cost of producing a good. For example, new methods used in the factories that produce computer chips have lowered the cost and increased the supply of chips.

The State of Nature The state of nature includes all the natural forces that influence production. It includes the state of the weather and, more broadly, the natural environment. Good weather can increase the supply of many agricultural products and bad weather can decrease their supply. Extreme natural events such as earthquakes, tornadoes, and hurricanes can also influence supply.

Figure 3.5 illustrates an increase in supply. When supply increases, the supply curve shifts rightward and the quantity supplied at each price is larger. For example, at $1.00 per bar, on the original (blue) supply curve, the quantity supplied is 6 million bars a week. On the new (red) supply curve, the quantity supplied is 15 million bars a week. Look closely at the numbers in the table in Fig. 3.5 and check that the quantity supplied is larger at each price.

Table 3.2 summarizes the influences on supply and the directions of those influences.

A Change in the Quantity Supplied Versus a Change in Supply

Changes in the influences on producers' planned sales bring either a change in the quantity supplied or a change in supply. Equivalently, they bring either a movement along the supply curve or a shift of the supply curve.

A point on the supply curve shows the quantity supplied of a good at a given price. A movement along the supply curve shows a **change in the quantity supplied**. The entire supply curve shows supply. A shift of the supply curve shows a *change in supply*.

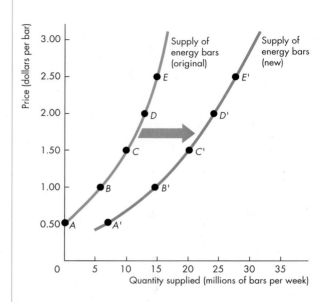

FIGURE 3.5   An Increase in Supply

Original supply schedule Old technology			New supply schedule New technology		
	Price (dollars per bar)	Quantity supplied (millions of bars per week)		Price (dollars per bar)	Quantity supplied (millions of bars per week)
A	0.50	0	A'	0.50	7
B	1.00	6	B'	1.00	15
C	1.50	10	C'	1.50	20
D	2.00	13	D'	2.00	25
E	2.50	15	E'	2.50	27

A change in any influence on sellers' plans other than the price of the good itself results in a new supply schedule and a shift of the supply curve. For example, a new, cost-saving technology for producing energy bars changes the supply of energy bars. At a price of $1.50 a bar, 10 million bars a week are supplied when producers use the old technology (row C of the table) and 20 million energy bars a week are supplied when producers use the new technology (row C'). An advance in technology *increases* the supply of energy bars. The supply curve shifts *rightward*, as shown by the shift arrow and the resulting red curve.

myeconlab animation

Figure 3.6 illustrates and summarizes these distinctions. If the price of the good falls and other things remain the same, the quantity supplied of that good decreases and there is a movement down along the supply curve S_0. If the price of the good rises and other things remain the same, the quantity supplied of that good increases and there is a movement up along the supply curve S_0. When any other influence on selling plans changes, the supply curve shifts and there is a *change in supply*. If supply increases, the supply curve shifts rightward to S_1. If supply decreases, the supply curve shifts leftward to S_2.

TABLE 3.2 The Supply of Energy Bars

The Law of Supply

The quantity of energy bars supplied

Decreases if:	*Increases if:*
■ The price of an energy bar falls	■ The price of an energy bar rises

Changes in Supply

The supply of energy bars

Decreases if:	*Increases if:*
■ The price of a factor of production used to produce energy bars rises	■ The price of a factor of production used to produce energy bars falls
■ The price of a substitute in production rises	■ The price of a substitute in production falls
■ The price of a complement in production falls	■ The price of a complement in production rises
■ The price of an energy bar is expected to rise	■ The price of an energy bar is expected to fall
■ The number of suppliers of bars decreases	■ The number of suppliers of bars increases
■ A technology change decreases energy bar production	■ A technology change increases energy bar production
■ A natural event decreases energy bar production	■ A natural event increases energy bar production

FIGURE 3.6 A Change in the Quantity Supplied Versus a Change in Supply

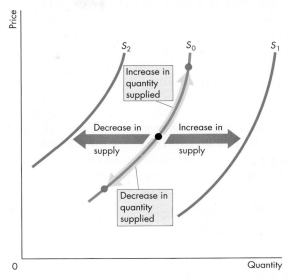

When the price of the good changes, there is a movement along the supply curve and *a change in the quantity supplied,* shown by the blue arrows on supply curve S_0. When any other influence on selling plans changes, there is a shift of the supply curve and a *change in supply.* An increase in supply shifts the supply curve rightward (from S_0 to S_1), and a decrease in supply shifts the supply curve leftward (from S_0 to S_2).

 animation

Review Quiz

1 Define the quantity supplied of a good or service.
2 What is the law of supply and how do we illustrate it?
3 What does the supply curve tell us about the producer's minimum supply price?
4 List all the influences on selling plans, and for each influence, say whether it changes supply.
5 What happens to the quantity of cell phones supplied and the supply of cell phones if the price of a cell phone falls?

 Work Study Plan 3.3 and get instant feedback.

Now we're going to combine demand and supply and see how prices and quantities are determined.

Market Equilibrium

We have seen that when the price of a good rises, the quantity demanded *decreases* and the quantity supplied *increases*. We are now going to see how the price adjusts to coordinate the plans of buyers and sellers and achieve an equilibrium in the market.

An *equilibrium* is a situation in which opposing forces balance each other. Equilibrium in a market occurs when the price balances the plans of buyers and sellers. The **equilibrium price** is the price at which the quantity demanded equals the quantity supplied. The **equilibrium quantity** is the quantity bought and sold at the equilibrium price. A market moves towards its equilibrium because

- Price regulates buying and selling plans.
- Price adjusts when plans don't match.

Price as a Regulator

The price of a good regulates the quantities demanded and supplied. If the price is too high, the quantity supplied exceeds the quantity demanded. If the price is too low, the quantity demanded exceeds the quantity supplied. There is one price at which the quantity demanded equals the quantity supplied. Let's work out what that price is.

Figure 3.7 shows the market for energy bars. The table shows the demand schedule (from Fig. 3.1) and the supply schedule (from Fig. 3.4). If the price of a bar is 50¢, the quantity demanded is 22 million bars a week but no bars are supplied. There is a shortage of 22 million bars a week. This shortage is shown in the final column of the table. At a price of $1.00 a bar, there is still a shortage, but only of 9 million bars a week. If the price of a bar is $2.50, the quantity supplied is 15 million bars a week but the quantity demanded is only 5 million. There is a surplus of 10 million bars a week. The one price at which there is neither a shortage nor a surplus is $1.50 a bar. At that price, the quantity demanded is equal to the quantity supplied: 10 million bars a week. The equilibrium price is $1.50 a bar, and the equilibrium quantity is 10 million bars a week.

Figure 3.7 shows that the demand curve and the supply curve intersect at the equilibrium price of $1.50 a bar. At each price *above* $1.50 a bar, there is a surplus of bars. For example, at $2.00 a bar, the surplus is 6 million bars a week, as shown by the blue arrow.

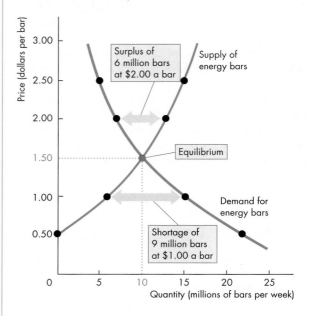

FIGURE 3.7 Equilibrium

Price (dollars per bar)	Quantity demanded	Quantity supplied	Shortage (−) or surplus (+)
	(millions of bars per week)		
0.50	22	0	−22
1.00	15	6	−9
1.50	10	10	0
2.00	7	13	+6
2.50	5	15	+10

The table lists the quantity demanded and the quantity supplied as well as the shortage or surplus of bars at each price. If the price is $1.00 a bar, 15 million bars a week are demanded and 6 million are supplied. There is a shortage of 9 million bars a week, and the price rises.

If the price is $2.00 a bar, 7 million bars a week are demanded and 13 million are supplied. There is a surplus of 6 million bars a week, and the price falls.

If the price is $1.50 a bar, 10 million bars a week are demanded and 10 million bars are supplied. There is neither a shortage nor a surplus. Neither buyers nor sellers have an incentive to change the price. The price at which the quantity demanded equals the quantity supplied is the equilibrium price. The quantity, 10 million bars a week, is the equilibrium quantity.

At each price *below* $1.50 a bar, there is a shortage of bars. For example, at $1.00 a bar, the shortage is 9 million bars a week, as shown by the red arrow.

Price Adjustments

You've seen that if the price is below equilibrium, there is a shortage and that if the price is above equilibrium, there is a surplus. But can we count on the price to change and eliminate a shortage or a surplus? We can, because such price changes are beneficial to both buyers and sellers. Let's see why the price changes when there is a shortage or a surplus.

A Shortage Forces the Price Up Suppose the price of an energy bar is $1. Consumers plan to buy 15 million bars a week, and producers plan to sell 6 million bars a week. Consumers can't force producers to sell more than they plan, so the quantity that is actually offered for sale is 6 million bars a week. In this situation, powerful forces operate to increase the price and move it towards the equilibrium price. Some producers, noticing lines of unsatisfied consumers, raise the price. Some producers increase their output. As producers push the price up, the price rises towards its equilibrium. The rising price reduces the shortage because it decreases the quantity demanded and increases the quantity supplied. When the price has increased to the point at which there is no longer a shortage, the forces moving the price stop operating and the price comes to rest at its equilibrium.

A Surplus Forces the Price Down Suppose the price of a bar is $2. Producers plan to sell 13 million bars a week, and consumers plan to buy 7 million bars a week. Producers cannot force consumers to buy more than they plan, so the quantity that is actually bought is 7 million bars a week. In this situation, powerful forces operate to lower the price and move it towards the equilibrium price. Some producers, unable to sell the quantities of bars they planned to sell, cut their prices. In addition, some producers scale back production. As producers cut the price, the price falls towards its equilibrium. The falling price decreases the surplus because the quantity demanded increases and the quantity supplied decreases. When the price has fallen to the point at which there is no longer a surplus, the forces moving the price stop operating and the price comes to rest at its equilibrium.

The Best Deal Available for Buyers and Sellers When the price is below equilibrium, it is forced upward. Why don't buyers resist the increase and refuse to buy at the higher price? Because they value the good more highly than the current price and they can't satisfy their demand at the current price. In some markets—for example, the markets that operate on eBay—the buyers might even be the ones who force the price up by offering to pay more.

When the price is above equilibrium, it is bid downward. Why don't sellers resist this decrease and refuse to sell at the lower price? Because their minimum supply price is below the current price and they cannot sell all they would like to at the current price. Normally, it is the sellers who force the price down by offering lower prices to gain market share.

At the price at which the quantity demanded and the quantity supplied are equal, neither buyers nor sellers can do business at a better price. Buyers pay the highest price they are willing to pay for the last unit bought, and sellers receive the lowest price at which they are willing to supply the last unit sold.

When people freely make offers to buy and sell and when demanders try to buy at the lowest possible price and suppliers try to sell at the highest possible price, the price at which trade takes place is the equilibrium price—the price at which the quantity demanded equals the quantity supplied. The price coordinates the plans of buyers and sellers, and no one has an incentive to change it.

Review Quiz

1 What is the equilibrium price of a good or service?

2 Over what range of prices does a shortage arise? What happens to the price when there is a shortage?

3 Over what range of prices does a surplus arise? What happens to the price when there is a surplus?

4 Why is the price at which the quantity demanded equals the quantity supplied the equilibrium price?

5 Why is the equilibrium price the best deal available for both buyers and sellers?

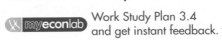 Work Study Plan 3.4 and get instant feedback.

Predicting Changes in Price and Quantity

The demand and supply model that we have just studied provides us with a powerful way of analyzing influences on prices and the quantities bought and sold. According to the model, a change in price stems from a change in demand, a change in supply, or a change in both demand and supply. Let's look first at the effects of a change in demand.

An Increase in Demand

When more and more people join health clubs, the demand for energy bars increases. The table in Fig. 3.8 shows the original and new demand schedules for energy bars (the same as those in Fig. 3.2) as well as the supply schedule of energy bars.

When demand increases, there is a shortage at the original equilibrium price of $1.50 a bar. To eliminate the shortage, the price must rise. The price that makes the quantity demanded and quantity supplied equal again is $2.50 a bar. At this price, 15 million bars are bought and sold each week. When demand increases, both the price and the quantity increase.

Figure 3.8 shows these changes. The figure shows the original demand for and supply of energy bars. The original equilibrium price is $1.50 an energy bar, and the quantity is 10 million energy bars a week. When demand increases, the demand curve shifts rightward. The equilibrium price rises to $2.50 an energy bar, and the quantity supplied increases to 15 million energy bars a week, as highlighted in the figure. There is an *increase in the quantity supplied* but *no change in supply*—a movement along, but no shift of, the supply curve.

A Decrease in Demand

We can reverse this change in demand. Start at a price of $2.50 a bar with 15 million energy bars a week being bought and sold, and then work out what happens if demand decreases to its original level. Such a decrease in demand might arise if people switch to energy gel (a substitute for energy bars). The decrease in demand shifts the demand curve leftward. The equilibrium price falls to $1.50 a bar, and the equilibrium quantity decreases to 10 million bars a week.

FIGURE 3.8 The Effects of a Change in Demand

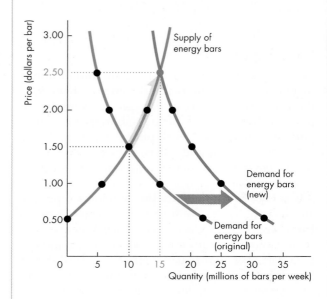

Price (dollars per bar)	Quantity demanded (millions of bars per week)		Quantity supplied (millions of bars per week)
	Original	New	
0.50	22	32	0
1.00	15	25	6
1.50	**10**	20	**10**
2.00	7	17	13
2.50	5	15	15

Initially, the demand for energy bars is the blue demand curve. The equilibrium price is $1.50 a bar, and the equilibrium quantity is 10 million bars a week. When more health-conscious people do more exercise, the demand for energy bars increases and the demand curve shifts rightward to become the red curve.

At $1.50 a bar, there is now a shortage of 10 million bars a week. The price of a bar rises to a new equilibrium of $2.50. As the price rises to $2.50, the quantity supplied increases—shown by the blue arrow on the supply curve—to the new equilibrium quantity of 15 million bars a week. Following an increase in demand, the quantity supplied increases but supply does not change—the supply curve does not shift.

 animation

We can now make our first two predictions:

1. When demand increases, both the price and the quantity increase.

2. When demand decreases, both the price and the quantity decrease.

An Increase in Supply

When Nestlé (the producer of PowerBar) and other energy bar producers switch to a new cost-saving technology, the supply of energy bars increases. The table in Fig. 3.9 shows the new supply schedule (the same one that was shown in Fig. 3.5). What are the new equilibrium price and quantity? The price falls to $1.00 a bar, and the quantity increases to 15 million bars a week. You can see why by looking at the quantities demanded and supplied at the old price of $1.50 a bar. The quantity supplied at that price is now 20 million bars a week, and there is a surplus of bars. The price falls. Only when the price is $1.00 a bar does the quantity supplied equal the quantity demanded.

Figure 3.9 illustrates the effect of an increase in supply. It shows the demand curve for energy bars and the original and new supply curves. The initial equilibrium price is $1.50 a bar, and the quantity is 10 million bars a week. When supply increases, the supply curve shifts rightward. The equilibrium price falls to $1.00 a bar, and the quantity demanded increases to 15 million bars a week, highlighted in the figure. There is an *increase in the quantity demanded* but *no change in demand*—a movement along, but no shift of, the demand curve.

A Decrease in Supply

Start out at a price of $1.00 a bar with 15 million bars a week being bought and sold. Then suppose that the cost of labour or raw materials rises and the supply of energy bars decreases. The decrease in supply shifts the supply curve leftward. The equilibrium price rises to $1.50 a bar, and the equilibrium quantity decreases to 10 million bars a week.

We can now make two more predictions:

1. When supply increases, the quantity increases and the price falls.

2. When supply decreases, the quantity decreases and the price rises.

FIGURE 3.9 The Effects of a Change in Supply

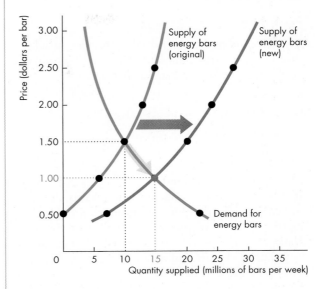

Price (dollars per bar)	Quantity demanded (millions of bars per week)	Quantity supplied (millions of bars per week)	
		Original	New
0.50	22	0	7
1.00	15	6	15
1.50	**10**	**10**	20
2.00	7	13	25
2.50	5	15	27

Initially, the supply of energy bars is shown by the blue supply curve. The equilibrium price is $1.50 a bar, and the equilibrium quantity is 10 million bars a week. When the new cost-saving technology is adopted, the supply of energy bars increases and the supply curve shifts rightward to become the red curve.

At $1.50 a bar, there is now a surplus of 10 million bars a week. The price of an energy bar falls to a new equilibrium of $1.00 a bar. As the price falls to $1.00, the quantity demanded increases—shown by the blue arrow on the demand curve—to the new equilibrium quantity of 15 million bars a week. Following an increase in supply, the quantity demanded increases but demand does not change—the demand curve does not shift.

myeconlab animation

How Markets Interact to Reallocate Resources

Fuel, Food, and Fertilizer

The demand and supply model provides insights into all competitive markets. Here, we'll apply what you've learned to the markets for

- Crude oil
- Corn
- Fertilizers

Crude Oil

Crude oil is like the life-blood of the global economy. It is used to fuel our cars, airplanes, trains, and buses, to generate electricity, and to produce a wide range of plastics. When the price of crude oil rises, the cost of transportation, power, and materials all increase.

In 2006, the price of a barrel of oil was $50. In 2008, the price reached $135. While the price of oil has been rising, the quantity of oil produced and consumed has barely changed. Since 2006, the world has produced a steady 85 million barrels of oil a day. Who or what has been raising the price of oil? Is it the fault of greedy oil producers?

Oil producers might be greedy, and some of them might be big enough to withhold supply and raise the price, but it wouldn't be in their self-interest to do so. The higher price would bring forth a greater quantity supplied from other producers and the profit of the one limiting supply would fall.

Producers could try to cooperate and jointly withhold supply. The Organization of Petroleum Exporting Countries, OPEC, is such a group of suppliers. But OPEC doesn't control the world supply and the self-interest of each of its members is to produce the quantity that gives it the maximum attainable profit.

So even though the global oil market has some big players, they don't fix the price. Instead, the actions of thousands of buyers and sellers and the forces of demand and supply determine the price of oil. So how have demand and supply changed?

Because the price has increased with an unchanged quantity, demand must have increased and supply must have decreased.

Demand has increased for two reasons. First, world production, particularly in China and India, is expanding at a rapid rate. The increased production of electricity, gasoline, plastics, and other oil-using goods has increased the demand for oil.

Second, the rapid expansion of production in China, India, and other developing economies is expected to continue. So the demand for oil is expected to keep increasing at a rapid rate. As the demand for oil keeps increasing, the price of oil will keep rising *and be expected* to keep rising.

A higher expected future price increases demand today yet further. It also decreases supply today because producers know they can get a greater return from their oil by leaving it in the ground and selling it in a later year. So an *expected* rise in price brings both an increase in demand and a decrease in supply, which in turn brings an *actual* rise in price.

Because an expected price rise brings an actual price rise, it is possible for expectations to create a process called a **speculative bubble**. In a speculative bubble, the price rises purely because it is expected to rise and events reinforce the expectation. No one knows yet whether the world oil market was in a bubble in 2008, but bubbles always burst, so eventually we will know.

Figure 1 illustrates the events that we've just described and summarizes the forces at work on demand and supply in the world market for oil.

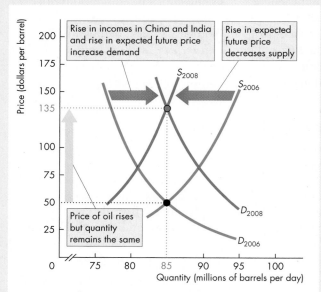

Figure 1 The Market for Crude Oil

Corn

Corn is used as food, animal feed, and a source of ethanol. Global corn production increased during the past few years, but the price also increased.

The story of the production and price of corn, like the story of the price of oil, begins in China and India. Greater production and higher incomes in these countries have increased the demand for corn.

Some of the increase in demand is for corn as food. But more of the increase is for corn as cattle feed, driven by an increased demand for beef—it takes 7 kilograms of corn to produce 1 kilogram of beef.

In addition, mandated targets for ethanol production in the United States have increased the demand for corn as a source of biofuel.

While the demand for corn has increased, the supply has decreased. Drought in several parts of the world cut production and decreased supply. Higher fertilizer prices increased the cost of growing corn, which also decreased supply.

So the demand for corn increased and the supply of corn decreased. This combination of changes in demand and supply raised the price of corn. Also, the increase in demand was greater than the decrease in supply, so the quantity of corn increased.

Figure 2 provides a summary of the events that we've just described in the market for corn.

Fertilizers

Nitrogen, potassium, and potash are not on your daily shopping list, but you consume them many times each day. They are the reason why our farms are so productive. And like the prices of oil and corn, the prices of fertilizers have gone skyward.

The increase in the global production of corn and other grains as food and sources of biofuels has increased the demand for fertilizers.

All fertilizers are costly to produce and use energy-intensive processes. Nitrogen is particularly energy intensive and uses natural gas. Potash is made from deposits of chloride and sodium chloride that are found 900 metres or deeper underground, and energy is required to bring the material to the surface and more energy is used to separate the chemicals and turn them into fertilizer.

All energy sources are substitutes, so the rise in the price of oil has increased the prices of all other energy sources. Consequently, the energy cost of producing fertilizers has risen. This higher cost of production has decreased the supply of fertilizers.

The increase in demand and the decrease in supply combine to raise the price. The increase in demand has been greater than the decrease in supply, so the quantity of fertilizer has increased. Figure 3 illustrates the market for fertilizers.

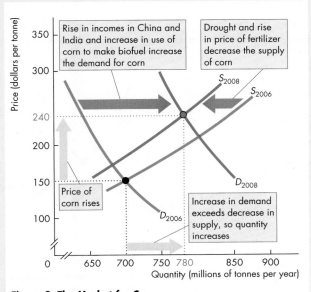

Figure 2 The Market for Corn

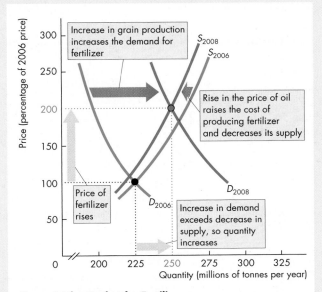

Figure 3 The Market for Fertilizer

FIGURE 3.10 The Effects of All the Possible Changes in Demand and Supply

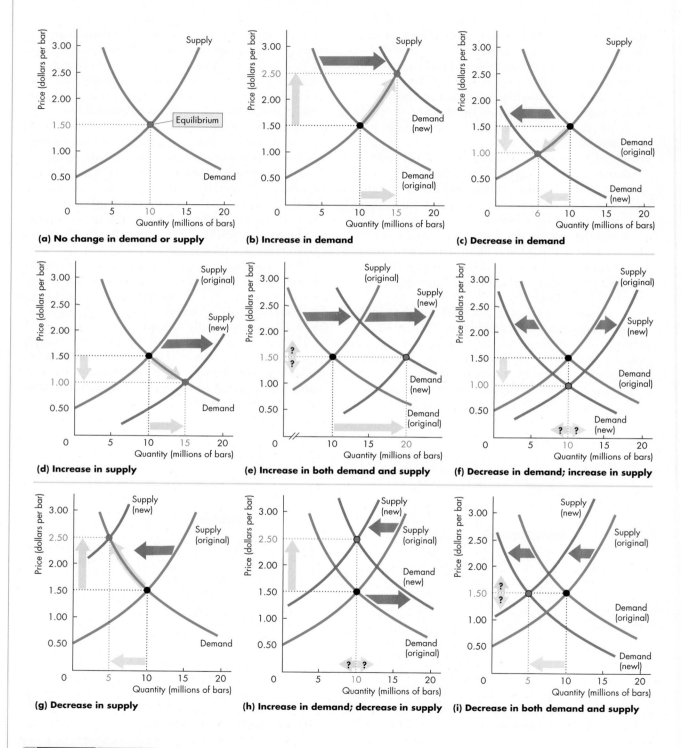

(a) No change in demand or supply

(b) Increase in demand

(c) Decrease in demand

(d) Increase in supply

(e) Increase in both demand and supply

(f) Decrease in demand; increase in supply

(g) Decrease in supply

(h) Increase in demand; decrease in supply

(i) Decrease in both demand and supply

All the Possible Changes in Demand and Supply

Figure 3.10 brings together and summarizes the effects of all the possible changes in demand and supply. With what you've learned about the effects of a change in *either* demand or supply, you can predict what happens if *both* demand and supply change together. Let's begin by reviewing what you already know.

Change in Demand with No Change in Supply   The first row of Fig. 3.10, parts (a), (b), and (c), summarizes the effects of a change in demand with no change in supply. In part (a), with no change in either demand or supply, neither the price nor the quantity changes. With an *increase* in demand and no change in supply in part (b), both the price and quantity increase. And with a *decrease* in demand and no change in supply in part (c), both the price and the quantity decrease.

Change in Supply with No Change in Demand   The first column of Fig. 3.10, parts (a), (d), and (g), summarizes the effects of a change in supply with no change in demand. With an *increase* in supply and no change in demand in part (d), the price falls and quantity increases. And with a *decrease* in supply and no change in demand in part (g), the price rises and the quantity decreases.

Increase in Both Demand and Supply   You've seen that an increase in demand raises the price and increases the quantity. And you've seen that an increase in supply lowers the price and increases the quantity. Fig. 3.10(e) combines these two changes. Because either an increase in demand or an increase in supply increases the quantity, the quantity also increases when both demand and supply increase. But the effect on the price is uncertain. An increase in demand raises the price and an increase in supply lowers the price, so we can't say whether the price will rise or fall when both demand and supply increase. We need to know the magnitudes of the changes in demand and supply to predict the effects on price. In the example in Fig. 3.10(e), the price does not change. But notice that if demand increases by slightly more than the amount shown in the figure, the price will rise. And if supply increases by slightly more than the amount shown in the figure, the price will fall.

Decrease in Both Demand and Supply   Figure 3.10(i) shows the case in which demand and supply *both decrease*. For the same reasons as those we've just reviewed, when both demand and supply decrease, the quantity decreases, and again the direction of the price change is uncertain.

Decrease in Demand and Increase in Supply   You've seen that a decrease in demand lowers the price and decreases the quantity. You've also seen that an increase in supply lowers the price and increases the quantity. Figure 3.10(f) combines these two changes. Both a decrease in demand and an increase in supply lower the price, so the price falls. But a decrease in demand decreases the quantity and an increase in supply increases the quantity, so we can't predict the direction in which the quantity will change unless we know the magnitudes of the changes in demand and supply. In Fig. 3.10(f), the quantity does not change. But notice that if demand decreases by slightly more than the amount shown in the figure, the quantity will decrease; if supply increases by slightly more than the amount shown in the figure, the quantity will increase.

Increase in Demand and Decrease in Supply   Figure 3.10(h) shows the case in which demand increases and supply decreases. Now, the price rises, but the direction of the quantity change is uncertain.

Review Quiz

What is the effect on the price of an MP3 player (such as an iPod) and the quantity of MP3 players if

1   The price of a PC falls or the price of an MP3 download rises? (Draw the diagrams!)

2   More firms produce MP3 players or electronics workers' wages rise? (Draw the diagrams!)

3   Any two of the events in questions 1 and 2 occur together? (Draw the diagrams!)

myeconlab   Work Study Plan 3.5 and get instant feedback.

Now that you understand the demand and supply model and the predictions that it makes, try to get into the habit of using it in your everyday life. To see how you might use the model, take a look at *Reading Between the Lines* on pp. 76–77, which uses the tools of demand and supply to explain the rising price of gasoline in 2008.

Demand and Supply: The Price of Gasoline

"Mass Exodus" from Roads: Surging Gas Prices May Park Millions of Cars

June 27, 2008

Gasoline prices are becoming so high that one of Canada's top banks is predicting a "mass exodus" of vehicles from U.S. highways within four years, with a slightly less dramatic drop in Canada. …

CIBC World Markets said in a report yesterday that gas prices in the U.S. will hit $7 US a gallon—the equivalent of $1.86 Canadian a litre—two summers from now. That marks a 70 percent increase over today's record levels. …

The meteoric rise in crude oil prices has been a major factor in soaring pump prices. CIBC predicts crude will hit $200 a barrel by 2010.

The average pump price in Canada yesterday was $1.38 a litre, nearly 30 cents higher than it was a year ago, according to the price-tracking website Gasbuddy.com. …

CIBC senior economist Benjamin Tal said: there will be about 700,000 fewer cars on Canadian roads by 2012 and a 10 percent decrease in average kilometres driven.

"Canada will feel the pain, but it's not going to be the same as in the U.S.," Tal said in an interview. …

"In Canada, more low-income Canadians have access to public transportation, therefore the adjustment will not come from them," he said. "The adjustment will come from middle-class families that will start giving up the second or third cars."

"With Americans abandoning their gas-guzzling SUVs and pickup trucks for small, more fuel-efficient vehicles, we estimate that the average fuel-efficiency of this year's fleet has climbed by nearly 20 percent from the previous model year," said auto industry specialist Carlos Gomes. …

The trend is less pronounced in Canada, where there has traditionally been a greater appetite for fuel-efficient vehicles, Gomes said in an interview

Reprinted courtesy of *The Hamilton Spectator.*

Essence of the Story

- The average price of gasoline in Canada on June 27, 2008 was $1.38 a litre, up 30 cents from June, 2007.

- A CIBC economist made four predictions for Canada in 2010.

- First, the price of gasoline will rise to $1.86 a litre.

- Second, the price of crude oil to rise to $200 a barrel.

- Third, there will be 700,000 fewer cars on the road and average kilometres driven will be down 10 percent.

- Fourth, low-income people will use more public transportation and middle-class families will give up the second and third cars.

Economic Analysis

- Figure 1 shows the market for gasoline in Canada in June 2008. The demand curve is D, the supply curve is S_{08}, and the market equilibrium is at 110 million litres a day and $1.38 a litre, the price reported in the news article.

- Gasoline is made from crude oil and when the price of crude oil rises, the cost of producing gasoline also rises, and the supply of gasoline decreases.

- The news article predicts that the price of crude oil will rise to $200 a barrel by 2010. This rise in price will decrease the supply of gasoline.

- We have no information about the likely change in the demand for gasoline. It is likely to change but by much less than the change in supply and we will assume no change in the demand for gasoline.

- The forecast in the news article is that the price of gasoline will rise to $1.86 a litre in 2010 and that the number of kilometres driven will decrease by 10 percent. We will assume that the quantity of gasoline used will also fall by 10 percent.

- Figure 2 shows the market for gasoline in 2010 that is consistent with these forecasts. Supply decreases and the supply curve shifts leftward from S_{08} to S_{10}.

- With no change in demand, the demand curve remains the same as in Fig. 1. The decrease in supply raises the price of gasoline to $1.86 a litre and the quantity decreases to 99 million litres a day—a decrease of 10 percent.

- The quantity of gasoline demanded decreases—shown as a movement up along the demand curve—by 10 percent.

- This decrease in the quantity demanded occurs as the higher price of gasoline induces low-income drivers to use public transport and middle-income families to operate fewer cars.

- This analysis of the market for gasoline emphasizes the distinction between a change in demand and a *change in the quantity demanded* and the distinction between a change in supply and a *change in the quantity supplied*.

- In this example, supply changes, demand remains constant, and the quantity demanded changes.

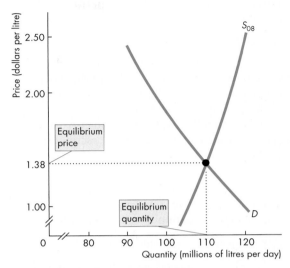

Figure 1 The gasoline market in 2008

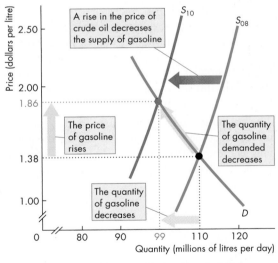

Figure 2 Forecast of the gasoline market in 2010

MATHEMATICAL NOTE

Demand, Supply, and Equilibrium

Demand Curve

The law of demand says that as the price of a good or service falls, the quantity demanded of that good or service increases. We can illustrate the law of demand by drawing a graph of the demand curve or writing down an equation. When the demand curve is a straight line, the following equation describes it:

$$P = a - bQ_D$$

where P is the price and Q_D is the quantity demanded. The a and b are positive constants.

The demand equation tells us three things:

1. The price at which no one is willing to buy the good (Q_D is zero). That is, if the price is a, then the quantity demanded is zero. You can see the price a in Fig. 1. It is the price at which the demand curve hits the y-axis—what we call the demand curve's "intercept on the y-axis."

2. As the price falls, the quantity demanded increases. If Q_D is a positive number, then the price P must be less than a. And as Q_D gets larger, the price P becomes smaller. That is, as the quantity increases, the maximum price that buyers are willing to pay for the last unit of the good falls.

3. The constant b tells us how fast the maximum price that someone is willing to pay for the good falls as the quantity increases. That is, the constant b tells us about the steepness of the demand curve. The equation tells us that the slope of the demand curve is $-b$.

Supply Curve

The law of supply says that as the price of a good or service rises, the quantity supplied of that good or service increases. We can illustrate the law of supply by drawing a graph of the supply curve or writing down an equation. When the supply curve is a straight line, the following equation describes it:

$$P = c + dQ_S$$

where P is the price and Q_S is the quantity supplied. The c and d are positive constants.

The supply equation tells us three things:

1. The price at which sellers are not willing to supply the good (Q_S is zero). That is, if the price is c, then no one is willing to sell the good. You can see the price c in Fig. 2. It is the price at which the supply curve hits the y-axis—what we call the supply curve's "intercept on the y-axis."

2. As the price rises, the quantity supplied increases. If Q_S is a positive number, then the price P must be greater than c. And as Q_S increases, the price P becomes larger. That is, as the quantity increases, the minimum price that sellers are willing to accept for the last unit rises.

3. The constant d tells us how fast the minimum price at which someone is willing to sell the good rises as the quantity increases. That is, the constant d tells us about the steepness of the supply curve. The equation tells us that the slope of the supply curve is d.

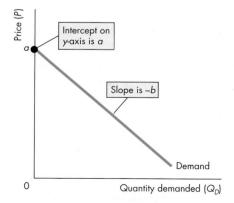

Figure 1   Demand curve

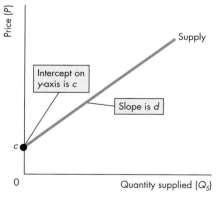

Figure 2 Supply curve

Market Equilibrium

Demand and supply determine market equilibrium. Figure 3 shows the equilibrium price (P^*) and equilibrium quantity (Q^*) at the intersection of the demand curve and the supply curve.

We can use the equations to find the equilibrium price and equilibrium quantity. The price of a good adjusts until the quantity demanded Q_D equals the quantity supplied Q_S. So at the equilibrium price (P^*) and equilibrium quantity (Q^*),

$$Q_D = Q_S = Q^*.$$

To find the equilibrium price and equilibrium quantity, substitute Q^* for Q_D in the demand equation and Q^* for Q_S in the supply equation. Then the price is the equilibrium price (P^*), which gives

$$P^* = a - bQ^*$$

$$P^* = c + dQ^*.$$

Notice that

$$a - bQ^* = c + dQ^*.$$

Now solve for Q^*:

$$a - c = bQ^* + dQ^*$$

$$a - c = (b + d)Q^*$$

$$Q^* = \frac{a - c}{b + d}.$$

To find the equilibrium price, (P^*), substitute for Q^* in either the demand equation or the supply equation.

Using the demand equation, we have

$$P^* = a - b\left(\frac{a - c}{b + d}\right)$$

$$P^* = \frac{a(b + d) - b(a - c)}{b + d}$$

$$P^* = \frac{ad + bc}{b + d}.$$

Alternatively, using the supply equation, we have

$$P^* = c + d\left(\frac{a - c}{b + d}\right)$$

$$P^* = \frac{c(b + d) - d(a - c)}{b + d}$$

$$P^* = \frac{ad + bc}{b + d}.$$

An Example

The demand for ice cream cones is

$$P = 800 - 2Q_D.$$

The supply of ice cream cones is

$$P = 200 + 1Q_S.$$

The price of a cone is expressed in cents, and the quantities are expressed in cones per day.

To find the equilibrium price (P^*) and equilibrium quantity (Q^*), substitute Q^* for Q_D and Q_S and P^* for P. That is,

$$P^* = 800 - 2Q^*$$

$$P^* = 200 + 1Q^*.$$

Now solve for Q^*:

$$800 - 2Q^* = 200 + 1Q^*$$

$$600 = 3Q^*$$

$$Q^* = 200.$$

And

$$P^* = 800 - 2(200)$$

$$= 400.$$

The equilibrium price is $4 a cone, and the equilibrium quantity is 200 cones per day.

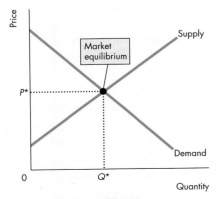

Figure 3 Market equilibrium

SUMMARY ◆

Key Points

Markets and Prices (p. 58)

- A competitive market is one that has so many buyers and sellers that no single buyer or seller can influence the price.
- Opportunity cost is a relative price.
- Demand and supply determine relative prices.

Demand (pp. 59–63)

- Demand is the relationship between the quantity demanded of a good and its price when all other influences on buying plans remain the same.
- The higher the price of a good, other things remaining the same, the smaller is the quantity demanded—the law of demand.
- Demand depends on the prices of related goods (substitutes and complements), expected future prices, income, expected future income and credit, population, and preferences.

Supply (pp. 64–67)

- Supply is the relationship between the quantity supplied of a good and its price when all other influences on selling plans remain the same.
- The higher the price of a good, other things remaining the same, the greater is the quantity supplied—the law of supply.

- Supply depends on the prices of factors of production used to produce a good, the prices of related goods produced, expected future prices, the number of suppliers, technology, and the state of nature.

Market Equilibrium (pp. 68–69)

- At the equilibrium price, the quantity demanded equals the quantity supplied.
- At any price above equilibrium, there is a surplus and the price falls.
- At any price below equilibrium, there is a shortage and the price rises.

Predicting Changes in Price and Quantity (pp. 70–75)

- An increase in demand brings a rise in the price and an increase in the quantity supplied. A decrease in demand brings a fall in the price and a decrease in the quantity supplied.
- An increase in supply brings a fall in the price and an increase in the quantity demanded. A decrease in supply brings a rise in the price and a decrease in the quantity demanded.
- An increase in demand and an increase in supply bring an increased quantity but an uncertain price change. An increase in demand and a decrease in supply bring a higher price but an uncertain change in quantity.

Key Figures

Key Terms

PROBLEMS and APPLICATIONS

 Work problems 1–13 in Chapter 3 Study Plan and get instant feedback.
Work problems 15–27 as Homework, a Quiz, or a Test if assigned by your instructor.

1. In December 1862, William Gregg, a mill owner, placed a notice in the *Edgehill Advertiser* announcing his willingness to exchange cloth for food and other items. Here is an extract:

   1 yard of cloth for 1 pound of bacon
   2 yards of cloth for 1 pound of butter
   4 yards of cloth for 1 pound of wool
   8 yards of cloth for 1 bushel of salt

   a. What is the relative price of butter in terms of wool?
   b. If the money price of bacon was 20¢ a pound, what do you predict was the money price of butter?
   c. If the money price of bacon was 20¢ a pound and the money price of salt was $2.00 a bushel, do you think anyone would accept Mr. Gregg's offer of cloth for salt?

2. The price of food increased during the past year.

   a. Explain why the law of demand applies to food just as it does to all other goods and services.
   b. Explain how the substitution effect influences food purchases and provide some examples of substitutions that people might make when the price of food rises and other things remain the same.
   c. Explain how the income effect influences food purchases and provide examples of the income effect that might occur when the price of food rises and other things remain the same.

3. Place the following goods and services into pairs of likely substitutes and pairs of likely complements. (You may use an item in more than one pair.) The goods and services are coal, oil, natural gas, wheat, corn, rye, pasta, pizza, sausage, skateboard, roller blades, video game, laptop, iPod, cell phone, text message, e-mail, phone call, and voice mail.

4. During 2008, the average income in China increased by 10 percent. Compared to 2007, how do you expect the following would change:

   a. The demand for beef? Explain your answer.
   b. The demand for rice? Explain your answer.

5. The following events occur one at a time in the market for cell phones:

   ■ The price of a cell phone falls.
   ■ Everyone believes that the price of a cell phone will fall next month.
   ■ The price of a call made from a cell phone falls.
   ■ The price of a call made from a land-line phone increases.
   ■ The introduction of camera phones makes cell phones more popular.

   a. Explain the effect of each event on the demand for cell phones.
   b. Use a graph to illustrate the effect of each event.
   c. Does any event (or events) illustrate the law of demand?

6. On July 22, 2008, the *Montreal Gazette* reported: "Pump prices have fluctuated over the past few months from the $1.20 range upwards to nearly $1.50 a litre, driving down consumption." Assume that there were no changes in average income, population, or any other influence on buying plans. How would you expect the rise in the price of gasoline to affect

   a. The demand for gasoline? Explain your answer.
   b. The quantity of gasoline demanded? Explain your answer.

7. Timber beams are made from logs and in the process of making beams the mill produces sawdust, which is made into pressed wood. In the market for timber beams, the following events occur one at a time:

   ■ The wage rate of sawmill workers rises.
   ■ The price of sawdust rises.
   ■ The price of a timber beam rises.
   ■ The price of a timber beam is expected to rise next year.
   ■ Environmentalists convince Parliament to introduce a new law that reduces the amount of forest that can be cut for timber products.
   ■ A new technology lowers the cost of producing timber beams.

a. Explain the effect of each event on the supply of timber beams.

b. Use a graph to show the effect of each event.

c. Does any event (or events) illustrate the law of supply?

8. **Air Canada Cuts Flights on High Jet Prices**
Air Canada announced June 17 it is reducing flights by about 7 percent and laying off up to 2,000 staff in the fourth quarter of 2008 and the first quarter of 2009 because of high fuel costs.

Platts Oilgram Price Report, June 18, 2008

a. How does this news clip illustrate a change in supply? Explain your answer.

b What is the influence on supply identified in the news clip? Explain your answer.

c. Explain how supply changes.

9. **Oil Soars to New Record Over $135**
The price of oil hit a record high above $135 a barrel on Thursday—more than twice what it cost a year ago ... OPEC has so far blamed price rises on speculators and says there is no shortage of oil.

BBC News, May 22, 2008

a. Explain how the price of oil can rise even though there is no shortage of oil.

b. If a shortage of oil does occur, what does that imply about price adjustments and the role of price as a regulator in the market for oil?

c. If OPEC is correct, what factors might have changed demand and/or supply and shifted the demand curve and/or the supply curve to cause the price to rise?

10. "As more people buy computers, the demand for Internet service increases and the price of Internet service decreases. The fall in the price of Internet service decreases the supply of Internet service." Is this statement true or false? Explain.

11. The following events occur one at a time:
 (i)   The price of crude oil rises.
 (ii) The price of a car rises.
 (iii) All speed limits on highways are abolished.
 (iv) Robots cut car production costs.

Which of these events will increase or decrease (state which occurs)

a. The demand for gasoline?
b. The supply of gasoline?
c. The quantity of gasoline demanded?
d. The quantity of gasoline supplied?

12. The demand and supply schedules for gum are

Price (cents per pack)	Quantity demanded	Quantity supplied
	(millions of packs a week)	
20	180	60
40	140	100
60	100	140
80	60	180
100	20	220

a. Draw a graph of the gum market, label the axes and the curves, and mark in the equilibrium price and quantity.

b. Suppose that the price of gum is 70¢ a pack. Describe the situation in the gum market and explain how the price adjusts.

c. Suppose that the price of gum is 30¢ a pack. Describe the situation in the gum market and explain how the price adjusts.

d. A fire destroys some factories that produce gum and the quantity of gum supplied decreases by 40 million packs a week at each price. Explain what happens in the market for gum and illustrate the changes on your graph.

e. If at the same time as the fire occurs in d, there is an increase in the teenage population, which increases the quantity of gum demanded by 40 million packs a week at each price, what are the new equilibrium price and quantity of gum? Illustrate these changes in your graph.

13. **Eurostar Boosted by *Da Vinci Code***
Eurostar, the train service linking London to Paris, ... said on Wednesday first-half sales rose 6 per cent, boosted by devotees of the blockbuster Da Vinci movie.

CNN, July 26, 2006

a. Explain how *Da Vinci Code* fans helped to raise Eurostar's sales.

b. What markets in Paris did these fans influence? Explain the influence on three markets.

14. Use the link on MyEconLab (Textbook Resources, Chapter 3, Web Links) to obtain data on the prices and quantities of bananas in 1985 and 2002.

a. Make a graph to illustrate the market for bananas in 1985 and 2002.

b. On the graph, show the changes in demand, supply, the quantity demanded, and the quantity supplied that are consistent with the data.

c. Why did the demand and supply change?

15. What features of the world market for crude oil make it a competitive market?

16. The money price of a textbook is $90 and the money price of the Wii game *Super Mario Galaxy* is $45.
    a. What is the opportunity cost of a textbook in terms of the Wii game?
    b. What is the relative price of the Wii game in terms of textbooks?

17. The price of gasoline increased during the past year.
    a. Explain why the law of demand applies to gasoline just as it does to all other goods and services.
    b. Explain how the substitution effect influences gasoline purchases and provide some examples of substitutions that people might make when the price of gasoline rises and other things remain the same.
    c. Explain how the income effect influences gasoline purchases and provide some examples of the income effects that might occur when the price of gasoline rises and other things remain the same.

18. Classify the following pairs of goods and services as substitutes, complements, substitutes in production, or complements in production.
    a. Bottled water and health club memberships
    b. French fries and baked potatoes
    c. Leather purses and leather shoes
    d. SUVs and compact cars
    e. Diet coke and regular coke
    f. Low-fat milk and cream

19. Think about the demand for the three popular game consoles: XBox, PS3, and Wii. Explain the effect of the following events on the demand for XBox games and the quantity of XBox games demanded, other things remaining the same.
    a. The price of an XBox falls.
    b. The prices of a PS3 and a Wii fall.
    c. The number of people writing and producing XBox games increases.
    d. Consumers' incomes increase.
    e. Programmers who write code for XBox games become more costly to hire.
    f. The price of an XBox game is expected to fall.
    g. A new game console comes onto the market, which is a close substitute for XBox.

20. **Rising Corn Prices Hit Grocery Shoppers' Pocketbooks**

    The rising demand for corn as a source of ethanol-blended fuel is largely to blame for increasing food costs. ... Food prices rose 10 per cent in 2006, "driven mainly by surging prices of corn, wheat and soybean oil in the second part of the year," the International Monetary Fund said in a report. "Looking ahead, rising demand for biofuels will likely cause the prices of corn and soybean oil to rise further," ...

    Statistics Canada says consumers in the country paid 3.8 per cent more for food in April 2007, compared to the same month last year.

    CBC News Online, May 22, 2008

    a. Explain why the demand for ethanol has influenced the price of corn.
    b. Use graphs to show why the higher price of corn affects the price of food.

21. **G.M. Cuts Production for Quarter**

    General Motors cut its fourth-quarter production schedule by 10 percent on Tuesday as a tightening credit market caused sales at the Ford Motor Company, Chrysler, and even Toyota to decline in August. ... Bob Carter, group vice president for Toyota Motor Sales USA, said ... dealerships were still seeing fewer potential customers browsing the lots.

    New York Times, September 5, 2007

    Explain whether this news clip illustrates
    a. A change in supply.
    b. A change in the quantity supplied.
    c. A change in demand.
    d. A change in the quantity demanded.

22. **"Popcorn Movie" Experience Gets Pricier**

    ... cinemas are raising ... prices. ... Demand for field corn, used for animal feed, ... corn syrup and ... ethanol, has caused its price to explode. That's caused some farmers to shift from popcorn to easier-to-grow field corn, cutting supply and pushing its price higher, too. ...

    USA Today, May 24, 2008

    Explain and illustrate graphically the events described in the news clip in the markets for

    a. Popcorn.
    b. Cinema tickets.
    c. Field corn.

23. The figure illustrates the market for pizza.

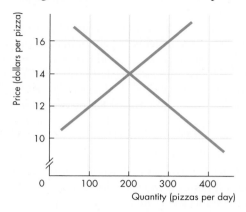

a. Label the curves. Which curve shows the willingness to pay for a pizza?
b. If the price of a pizza is $16, is there a shortage or a surplus and does the price rise or fall?
c. Sellers want to receive the highest possible price, so why would they be willing to accept less than $16 a pizza?
d. If the price of a pizza is $12, is there a shortage or a surplus and does the price rise or fall?
e. Buyers want to pay the lowest possible price, so why would they be willing to pay more than $12 for a pizza?

24. What is the effect on the equilibrium price and equilibrium quantity of orange juice if the price of apple juice decreases and the wage rate paid to orange grove workers increases?

25. The table sets out the demand and supply schedules for potato chips.

Price (cents per bag)	Quantity demanded	Quantity supplied
	(millions of bags per week)	
50	160	130
60	150	140
70	140	150
80	130	160
90	120	170
100	110	180

a. Draw a graph of the potato chip market and mark in the equilibrium price and quantity.
b. If the price is 60¢ a bag, is there a shortage or a surplus, and how does the price adjust?
c. If a new dip increases the quantity of potato chips that people want to buy by 30 million

bags per week at each price, how does the demand and/or supply of chips change?
d. If a new dip has the effect described in c, how does the price and quantity of chips change?
e. If a virus destroys potato crops and the quantity of potato chips produced decreases by 40 million bags a week at each price, how does the supply of chips change?
f. If the virus described in e hits just as the new dip in c comes onto the market, how do the price of chips and the quantity bought change?

26. **Consumer Tech: Blu-Ray Wins, but Does Anyone Care?**
Toshiba Corp. yesterday raised the white flag in the war over the next-generation home movie format, announcing the end of its HD DVD business in a victory for Sony Corp.'s Blu-ray technology.

Canadian Business Online, July 9, 2008

How would you expect the end of Toshiba's HD DVD format to influence
a. The price of a used Toshiba player on eBay? Would the outcome that you predict result from a change in demand or a change in supply or both, and in which directions?
b. The price of a Blu-ray player?
c. The demand for Blu-ray format movies?
d. The supply of Blu-ray format movies?
e. The price of Blu-ray format movies?
f. The quantity of Blu-ray format movies?

27. After you have studied *Reading Between the Lines* on pp. 76–77, answer the following questions:
a. What substitutions did drivers make to decrease the quantity of gasoline demanded?
b. What were the two main factors that influenced the demand for gasoline in 2008 and how did they change demand?
c. What was the main influence on the supply of gasoline during early 2008 and how did supply change?
d. How did the combination of the factors you have noted in c and d influence the price and quantity of gasoline?
e. Did the quantity demanded or the quantity supplied change?

UNDERSTANDING HOW MARKETS WORK

The Amazing Market

The five chapters that you've just studied explain how markets work. The market is an amazing instrument. It enables people who have never met and who know nothing about each other to interact and do business. It also enables us to allocate our scarce resources to the uses that we value most highly. Markets can be very simple or highly organized. Markets are ancient and they are modern.

A simple and ancient market is one that the American historian Daniel J. Boorstin describes in *The Discoverers* (p. 161). In the late fourteenth century,

> *The Muslim caravans that went southward from Morocco across the Atlas Mountains arrived after twenty days at the shores of the Senegal River. There the Moroccan traders laid out separate piles of salt, of beads from Ceutan coral, and cheap manufactured goods. Then they retreated out of sight. The local tribesmen, who lived in the strip mines where they dug their gold, came to the shore and put a heap of gold beside each pile of Moroccan goods. Then they, in turn, went out of view, leaving the Moroccan traders either to take the gold offered for a particular pile or to reduce the pile of their merchandise to suit the offered price in gold. Once again the Moroccan traders withdrew, and the process went on. By this system of commercial etiquette, the Moroccans collected their gold.*

An organized and modern market is an auction at which the Canadian government sells rights to broadcasters and cellular telephone companies for the use of the airwaves.

Everything and anything that can be exchanged is traded in markets—goods, services, and resources; dollars, euros, and yen; goods to be delivered now and for goods to be delivered in the future. Only the imagination places limits on what can be traded in markets.

Alfred Marshall *(1842–1924) grew up in an England that was being transformed by the railroad and by the expansion of manufacturing. Mary Paley was one of Marshall's students at Cambridge, and when Alfred and Mary married, in 1877, celibacy rules barred Alfred from continuing to teach at Cambridge. By 1884, with more liberal rules, the Marshalls returned to Cambridge, where Alfred became Professor of Political Economy.*

Many economists had a hand in refining the demand and supply model, but the first thorough and complete statement of the model as we know it today was set out by Alfred Marshall, with the help of Mary Paley Marshall. Published in 1890, this monumental treatise, The Principles of Economics, became the textbook on economics on both sides of the Atlantic for almost half a century.

"The forces to be dealt with are ... so numerous, that it is best to take a few at a time. ... Thus we begin by isolating the primary relations of supply, demand, and price."

ALFRED MARSHALL
The Principles of Economics

TALKING
WITH

Susan Athey

Susan Athey is Professor of Economics at Harvard University. Born in 1970 in Boston and growing up in Rockville, Maryland, she completed high school in three years, wrapped up three majors—in economics, mathematics, and computer science—at Duke University at 20, completed her Ph.D. at Stanford University at 24, and was voted tenure at MIT and Stanford at 29. After teaching at MIT for six years and Stanford for five, she moved to Harvard in 2006. Among her many honours and awards, the most prestigious is the John Bates Clark Medal given to the best economist under 40. She is the first woman to receive this award.

Professor Athey's research is broad in both scope and style. A government that wants to auction natural resources will turn to her fundamental discoveries (and possibly consult with her) before deciding how to organize the auction. An economist who wants to test a theory using a large data set will use her work on statistics and econometrics.

Michael Parkin and Robin Bade talked with Susan Athey about her research, the progress that economists have made in understanding and designing markets, and her advice to students.

What sparked your interest in economics?

I was studying mathematics and computer science, but I felt that the subjects were not as relevant as I would like.

I discovered economics through a research assistantship with a professor who was working on auctions. I had a summer job working for a firm that sold computers to the government through auctions. Eventually my professor, Bob Marshall, wrote two articles on the topic and testified before Congress to help reform the system for government procurement of computers. That really inspired me and showed me the power of economic ideas to change the world and to make things work more efficiently.

This original inspiration has remained and continues to drive much of your research. Can you explain how economists study auctions?

The study of the design of markets and auction-based marketplaces requires you to use all of the different tools that economics offers.

An auction is a well-defined game. You can write down the rules of the game and a formal theoretical model does a great job capturing the real problem that the players face. And theories do an excellent job predicting behaviour.

Buyers have a valuation for an object that is private information. They do not know the valuations of other bidders, and sometimes they don't even know their own valuation. For example, if they're buying oil rights, there may be uncertainty about how much oil there is in the ground. In that case, information about the amount of oil available is dispersed among the bidders, because each bidder has done their own survey. The bidders face a strategic problem of bidding, and they face an informational problem of trying to draw inferences about how valuable the object will be if they win.

Bidders need to recognize that their bid only matters when they win the auction, and they only win when they bid the most. The knowledge that they were the most optimistic of all the competitors should cause them to revise their beliefs.

From the seller's perspective, there are choices about how an auction is designed—auctions can use sealed bidding, where the seller receives bids and then opens them at a pre-determined time, or alternatively bidding may be interactive, where each bidder has an opportunity to outbid the previous high bidder. There are also different ways to use bids received by the auctioneer to determine the price. The seller may consider revenue, though governments are often most concerned about efficient allocation.

Both revenue and efficiency are affected by auction design. One key question the seller must consider is how the design will affect the participation of bidders, as this will determine how competitive bidding will be as well as whether the object gets to the potential bidder who values the item the most.

What must the designer of an auction-based marketplace take into account?

An example of an auction-based marketplace is eBay, where the market designer sets the rules for buyers and sellers to interact.

When you design an auction-based marketplace, you have a whole new set of concerns. The buyers and sellers themselves are independent agents, each acting in their own interest. The design is a two-step process: You need to design an auction that is going to achieve an efficient allocation; and you need design both the auction and the overall structure of the marketplace to attract participation.

In the case of eBay, the platform itself chooses the possible auction formats: auctions take place over time and bidders have the opportunity to outbid the standing high bidder during that time. The platform also allows sellers to use the "buy it now" option. The platform also makes certain tools and services available, such as the ability to search for items in various ways, track auctions, provide feedback, and monitor reputation. The sellers can select the level of the reserve price, whether they want to have a secret reserve price, how long the auction will last, whether to use "buy it now," what time of day the auction closes, how much information to provide, how many pictures they post.

These are all factors that impact participation of bidders and the revenue the seller will receive. The success of the platform hinges on both buyers and sellers choosing to participate.

Does auction theory enable us to predict the differences in the outcomes of an open ascending-bid English auction and a sealed-bid auction?

Sure. In some of my research, I compared open ascending auctions and pay-your-bid, sealed-bid auctions. I showed how the choice of auction format can make a big difference when you have small bidders bidding against larger, stronger bidders who usually (but not always) have higher valuations.

In an open ascending auction, it is hard for a small weaker bidder to ever win, because a stronger bidder can see their bids, respond to them, and outbid them

But in a pay-your-bid, sealed-bid auction, bidders shade their bids—they bid less than their value, assuring themselves of some profit if they win—and a large bidder doesn't have the opportunity to see and respond to an unusually high bid from a weak bidder. Strong bidders realize that their competition is weak, and they shade their bids a lot—they bid a lot less than their value. That gives a small bidder the opportunity to be aggressive and outbid a larger bidder, even if it has a lower value. So what that does is encourage entry of small bidders. I found empirically that this entry effect was important and it helps sealed-bid auctions generate larger revenue than open ascending-bid auctions.

> Sealed-bid auctions can do a better job of deterring collusion ... and raise more revenue

Does a sealed-bid auction always generate more revenue, other things equal, than an open ascending-bid auction?

Only if you have asymmetric bidders—strong large bidders and weaker small bidders—and even then the effect is ambiguous. It's an empirical question, but it tends to be true. We also showed that sealed-bid auctions can do a better job of deterring collusion. There are theoretical reasons to suggest that sealed-bid auctions are more difficult to collude at than open ascending actions, since at open ascending auctions, bidders can detect an opponent who is bidding higher than an agreement specifies and then respond to that. We found empirically in U.S. Forest Service timber auctions that the gap between sealed-bid auctions and ascending auctions was even greater than what a competitive model would predict, suggesting that some collusion may be at work.

What is the connection between auctions and the supply and demand model?

The basic laws of supply and demand can be seen in evidence in a market like eBay. The more sellers that are selling similar products, the lower the prices they can expect to achieve. Similarly the more buyers there are demanding those objects, the higher the prices the sellers can achieve.

> The basic laws of supply and demand can be seen in evidence in a market like eBay.

An important thing for an auction marketplace is to attract a good balance of buyers and sellers so that both the buyers and the sellers find it more profitable to transact on that marketplace rather than using some other mechanism. From a seller's perspective, the more bidders there are on the platform, the greater the demand and the higher the prices. And from the buyer's perspective, the more sellers there are on the platform, the greater the supply and the lower the prices.

Can we think of this thought experiment you just described as discovering demand and supply curves?

Exactly. When you study supply and demand curves, you wave your hands about how the prices actually get set. In different kinds of market settings, the actual mechanisms for setting prices are different. One way of setting prices is through auctions. But we tend to use auctions in settings where there are unique objects, so there isn't just one market price for the thing you are selling. If you were selling something that had lots of market substitutes, you can think of there being a market price in which this object can transact. An auction is a way to find a market price for something where there might not be a fixed market.

Can we think of an auction as a mechanism for finding the equilibrium price and quantity?

Exactly. We can think of the whole collection of auctions on eBay as being a mechanism to discover a market-clearing price, and individual items might sell a little higher or a little lower but overall we believe that the prices on eBay auctions will represent market-clearing (equilibrium) prices.

Is economics a good subject in which to major? What subjects work well as complements with economics?

Of course I think economics is a fabulous major and I am passionate about it. I think it's a discipline that trains you to think rigorously. And if you apply yourself you'll finish an economics major with a more disciplined mind than when you started. Whether you go into the business world or academics, you'll be able to confront and think in a logical and structured way about whether a policy makes sense, a business model makes sense, or an industry structure is likely to be sustainable. You should look for that in an undergraduate major. You should not be looking to just absorb facts, but you should be looking to train your mind and to think in a way that you will be able to apply to the rest of your career. I think that economics combines well with statistics and mathematics or with more policy-oriented disciplines.

Do you have anything special to say to women who might be making a career choice? Why is economics a good field for a woman?

On the academic side, economics is a fairly objective field, where the best ideas win, so it's a level playing field. Academics is not very family friendly before you get tenured and extremely family friendly after. Within academics or outside of it, there are a wide range of fairly high-paying jobs that still allow some autonomy over your schedule and that have a deeper and more compelling meaning. For both men and women, if you choose to have a family, you reevaluate your career choices and the tradeoff between time and money changes. And you're more likely to stick with and excel in a career if you find some meaning in it. So economics combines some of the advantages of having a strong job market and opportunities to have a large enough salary to pay for child care, and makes it economically worthwhile to stay in the workforce, without sacrificing the sense of the greater good.

20  Measuring GDP and Economic Growth

After studying this chapter, you will be able to

- Define GDP and use the circular flow model to explain why GDP equals aggregate expenditure and aggregate income

- Explain how Statistics Canada measures Canadian GDP and *real* GDP

- Describe how real GDP is used to measure economic growth and fluctuations and explain the limitations of real GDP as a measure of economic well-being

Will our economy remain weak through 2010 in a recession, or worse, a depression? Or will it begin to expand more rapidly? Many Canadian businesses wanted to know the answers to these questions in 2009. Nortel wanted to know whether to maintain its workforce or lay off some workers. Bombardier wanted to know whether to increase its capacity to build railroad engines. To assess the state of the economy and to make big decisions about business contraction or expansion, firms such as Nortel and Bombardier use forecasts of GDP. What exactly is GDP and what does it tell us about the state of the economy?

To reveal the rate of growth or shrinkage of production, we must remove the effects of inflation and assess how pro-

duction is *really* changing. How do we remove the effects of inflation to reveal *real* production?

Some countries are rich while others are poor. How do we compare economic well-being in one country with that in another? How can we make international comparisons of production?

In this chapter, you will find out how economic statisticians at Statistics Canada measure GDP and the economic growth rate. You will also learn about the uses and the limitations of these measures. In *Reading Between the Lines* at the end of the chapter, we'll look at the Canadian economy during the slowdown that began in 2008.

Gross Domestic Product

What exactly is GDP, how is it calculated, what does it mean, and why do we care about it? You are going to discover the answers to these questions in this chapter. First, what *is* GDP?

GDP Defined

GDP, or **gross domestic product**, is the market value of the final goods and services produced within a country in a given time period. This definition has four parts:

- Market value
- Final goods and services
- Produced within a country
- In a given time period

We'll examine each in turn.

Market Value To measure total production, we must add together the production of apples and oranges, computers and popcorn. Just counting the items doesn't get us very far. For example, which is the greater total production: 100 apples and 50 oranges or 50 apples and 100 oranges?

GDP answers this question by valuing items at their *market values*—the prices at which items are traded in markets. If the price of an apple is 10 cents, then the market value of 50 apples is $5. If the price of an orange is 20 cents, then the market value of 100 oranges is $20. By using market prices to value production, we can add the apples and oranges together. The market value of 50 apples and 100 oranges is $5 plus $20, or $25.

Final Goods and Services To calculate GDP, we value the *final goods and services* produced. A **final good** (or service) is an item that is bought by its final user during a specified time period. It contrasts with an **intermediate good** (or service), which is an item that is produced by one firm, bought by another firm, and used as a component of a final good or service.

For example, a Ford truck is a final good, but a Firestone tire on the truck is an intermediate good. A Dell computer is a final good, but an Intel Pentium chip inside it is an intermediate good.

If we were to add the value of intermediate goods and services produced to the value of final goods and services, we would count the same thing many times—a problem called *double counting*. The value of a truck already includes the value of the tires, and the value of a Dell PC already includes the value of the Pentium chip inside it.

Some goods can be an intermediate good in some situations and a final good in other situations. For example, the ice cream that you buy on a hot summer day is a final good, but the ice cream that a restaurant buys and uses to make sundaes is an intermediate good. The sundae is the final good. So whether a good is an intermediate good or a final good depends on what it is used for, not what it is.

Some items that people buy are neither final goods nor intermediate goods and they are not part of GDP. Examples of such items include financial assets—stocks and bonds—and secondhand goods—used cars or existing homes. A secondhand good was part of GDP in the year in which it was produced, but not part of GDP this year.

Produced Within a Country Only goods and services that are produced *within a country* count as part of that country's GDP. Roots Canada Limited, a Canadian firm, produces T-shirts in Taiwan, and the market value of those shirts is part of Taiwan's GDP, not part of Canada's GDP. Toyota, a Japanese firm, produces automobiles in Cambridge, Ontario, and the value of this production is part of Canada's GDP, not part of Japan's GDP.

In a Given Time Period GDP measures the value of production *in a given time period*—normally either a quarter of a year—called the quarterly GDP data—or a year—called the annual GDP data.

GDP measures not only the value of total production but also total income and total expenditure. The equality between the value of total production and total income is important because it shows the direct link between productivity and living standards. Our standard of living rises when our incomes rise and we can afford to buy more goods and services. But we must produce more goods and services if we are to be able to buy more goods and services.

Rising incomes and a rising value of production go together. They are two aspects of the same phenomenon: increasing productivity. To see why, we study the circular flow of expenditure and income.

GDP and the Circular Flow of Expenditure and Income

Figure 20.1 illustrates the circular flow of expenditure and income. The economy consists of households, firms, governments, and the rest of the world (the rectangles), which trade in factor markets and goods (and services) markets. We focus first on households and firms.

Households and Firms   Households sell and firms buy the services of labour, capital, and land in factor markets. For these factor services, firms pay income to households: wages for labour services, interest for the use of capital, and rent for the use of land. A fourth factor of production, entrepreneurship, receives profit.

Firms' retained earnings—profits that are not distributed to households—are part of the household sector's income. You can think of retained earnings as being income that households save and lend back to firms. Figure 20.1 shows the total income—*aggregate income*—received by households, including retained earnings, by the blue flow labelled Y.

Firms sell and households buy consumer goods and services—such as inline skates and haircuts—in the goods market. The total payment for these goods and services is **consumption expenditure**, shown by the red flow labelled C.

Firms buy and sell new capital equipment—such as computer systems, airplanes, trucks, and assembly line equipment—in the goods market. Some of what firms produce is not sold but is added to inventory. For example, if GM produces 1,000 cars and sells 950 of them, the other 50 cars remain in GM's inventory of unsold cars, which increases by 50 cars. When a firm adds unsold output to inventory, we can think of the firm as buying goods from itself. The purchase of new

FIGURE 20.1   The Circular Flow of Expenditure and Income

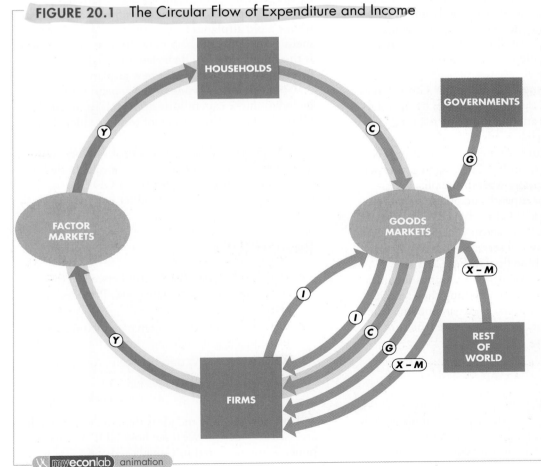

Households make consumption expenditures (C); firms make investments (I); governments buy goods and services (G); and the rest of the world buys net exports ($X - M$). Firms pay incomes (Y) to households. Aggregate income equals aggregate expenditure.

Billions of dollars in 2008

$$C = 885$$
$$I = 304$$
$$G = 357$$
$$\underline{X - M = 32}$$
$$Y = 1{,}578$$

Source of data: Statistics Canada, CANSIM Table 380-0002. (The data are for the first quarter of 2008 annual rate.)

myeconlab animation

plant, equipment, and buildings and the additions to inventories are **investment**, shown by the red flow labelled *I*.

Governments Governments buy goods and services from firms and their expenditure on goods and services is called **government expenditure**. In Fig. 20.1, government expenditure is shown as the red flow *G*.

Governments finance their expenditure with taxes. But taxes are not part of the circular flow of expenditure and income. Governments also make financial transfers to households, such as social security benefits and unemployment benefits, and pay subsidies to firms. These financial transfers, like taxes, are not part of the circular flow of expenditure and income.

Rest of the World Firms in Canada sell goods and services to the rest of the world—**exports**—and buy goods and services from the rest of the world—**imports**. The value of exports (*X*) minus the value of imports (*M*) is called **net exports**, the red flow *X − M* in Fig 20.1. If net exports are positive, the net flow of goods and services is from Canadian firms to the rest of the world. If net exports are negative, the net flow of goods and services is from the rest of the world to Canadian firms.

GDP Equals Expenditure Equals Income Gross domestic product can be measured in two ways: by the total expenditure on goods and services or by the total income earned producing goods and services.

The total expenditure—*aggregate expenditure*—is the sum of the red flows in Fig. 20.1. Aggregate expenditure equals consumption expenditure plus investment plus government expenditure plus net exports.

Aggregate income is equal to the total amount paid for the services of the factors of production used to produce final goods and services—wages, interest, rent, and profit. The blue flow in Fig. 20.1 shows aggregate income. Because firms pay out as incomes (including retained profits) everything they receive from the sale of their output, aggregate income (the blue flow) equals aggregate expenditure (the sum of the red flows). That is,

$$Y = C + I + G + X - M.$$

The table in Fig. 20.1 shows the numbers for 2008. You can see that the sum of the expenditures is $1,578 billion, which also equals aggregate income.

Because aggregate expenditure equals aggregate income, the two methods of measuring GDP give the same answer. So

GDP equals aggregate expenditure and equals aggregate income.

The circular flow model is the foundation on which the national economic accounts are built.

Why Is Domestic Product "Gross"?

"Gross" means before subtracting the depreciation of capital. The opposite of "gross" is "net," which means after subtracting the depreciation of capital.

Depreciation is the decrease in the value of a firm's capital that results from wear and tear and obsolescence. The total amount spent both buying new capital and replacing depreciated capital is called **gross investment**. The amount by which the value of capital increases is called **net investment**. Net investment equals gross investment minus depreciation.

For example, if an airline buys 5 new airplanes and retires 2 old airplanes from service, its gross investment is the value of the 5 new airplanes, depreciation is the value of the 2 old airplanes retired, and net investment is the value of 3 new airplanes.

Gross investment is one of the expenditures included in the expenditure approach to measuring GDP. So the resulting value of total product is a gross measure.

Gross profit, which is a firm's profit before subtracting depreciation, is one of the incomes included in the income approach to measuring GDP. So again, the resulting value of total product is a gross measure.

Review Quiz

1 Define GDP and distinguish between a final good and an intermediate good. Provide examples.
2 Why does GDP equal aggregate income and also equal aggregate expenditure?
3 What is the distinction between gross and net?

 Work Study Plan 20.1 and get instant feedback.

Let's now see how the ideas that you've just studied are used in practice. We'll see how GDP and its components are measured in Canada today.

Measuring Canada's GDP

Statistics Canada uses the concepts in the circular flow model to measure GDP and its components in the *National Income and Expenditure Accounts.* Because the value of aggregate production equals aggregate expenditure and aggregate income, there are two approaches available for measuring GDP, and both are used. They are

- The expenditure approach
- The income approach

The Expenditure Approach

The *expenditure approach* measures GDP as the sum of consumption expenditure (C), investment (I), government expenditure on goods and services (G), and net exports of goods and services ($X - M$), corresponding to the red flows in the circular flow model in Fig. 20.1. Table 20.1 shows the result of this approach for 2008. The table uses the terms in the *National Income and Expenditure Accounts.*

Personal expenditures on consumer goods and services are the expenditures by Canadian households on goods and services produced in Canada and in the rest of the world. They include goods such as pop and books and services such as banking and legal advice. They also include the purchase of consumer durable goods, such as TVs and microwave ovens. But they do *not* include the purchase of new homes, which Statistics Canada counts as part of investment.

Business investment is expenditure on capital equipment and buildings by firms and the additions to business inventories. It also includes expenditure on new homes by households.

Government expenditures on goods and services is the expenditure by all levels of government on goods and services, such as national defence and garbage collection. It does *not* include *transfer payments,* such as unemployment benefits, because they are not expenditures on goods and services.

Net exports of goods and services are the value of exports minus the value of imports. This item includes telephone equipment that Nortel sells to AT&T (a Canadian export), and Japanese DVD players that Sears buys from Sony (a Canadian import).

Table 20.1 shows the relative magnitudes of the four items of aggregate expenditure.

TABLE 20.1 GDP: The Expenditure Approach

Item	Symbol	Amount in 2008 (billions of dollars)	Percentage of GDP
Personal expenditures on consumer goods and services	C	885	56.1
Business investment	I	304	19.3
Government expenditures on goods and services	G	357	22.6
Net exports of goods and services	X − M	32	2.0
Gross domestic product	Y	**1,578**	**100.0**

The expenditure approach measures GDP as the sum of personal expenditures on consumer goods and services, (C), business investment (I), government expenditures on goods and services (G), and net exports (X − M).

In 2008, GDP measured by the expenditure approach was $1,578 billion. Personal expenditures on consumption goods and services is the largest expenditure item.

Source of data: Statistics Canada, CANSIM Table 380-0002.

The Income Approach

The *income approach* measures GDP by summing the incomes that firms pay households for the factors of production they hire—wages for labour, interest for capital, rent for land, and profit for entrepreneurship. The *National Income and Expenditure Accounts* divide incomes into five categories:

1. Wages, salaries, and supplementary labour income
2. Corporate profits
3. Interest and miscellaneous investment income
4. Farmers' income
5. Income from non-farm unincorporated businesses

Wages, salaries, and supplementary labour income is the payment for labour services. It includes net wages and salaries (called "take-home pay") plus taxes withheld on earnings plus benefits such as pension contributions.

Corporate profits are the profits of corporations, some of which are paid to households in the form of dividends and some of which are retained by corporations as undistributed profits. They are all income.

Interest and miscellaneous investment income is the interest households receive on loans they make minus the interest households pay on their own borrowing.

Farmers' income and *income from non-farm unincorporated businesses* are mixtures of the previous three items. They include compensation for the owner's labour, payment for the use of the owner's capital, and profit, lumped together in these two catch-all categories.

Table 20.2 shows these five incomes and their relative magnitudes. They sum to *net domestic income at factor cost*. The term "factor cost" is used because it is the cost of the factors of production used to produce final goods. When we sum the expenditures on final goods, we arrive at a total called *domestic product at market prices*. Market prices and factor cost diverge because of indirect taxes and subsidies.

An *indirect tax* is a tax paid by consumers when they buy goods and services. (In contrast, a *direct tax* is a tax on income.) Provincial sales taxes, GST, and taxes on alcohol, gasoline, and tobacco are indirect taxes. Because of indirect taxes, consumers pay more for some goods and services than producers receive. Market price exceeds factor cost. For example, if the sales tax is 7 percent, you pay $1.07 when you buy a $1 chocolate bar. The factor cost of the chocolate bar including profit is $1. The market price is $1.07.

A *subsidy* is a payment by the government to a producer. Payments made to grain growers and dairy farmers are subsidies. Because of subsidies, consumers pay less for some goods and services than producers receive. Factor cost exceeds market price.

To get from factor cost to market price, we add indirect taxes and subtract subsidies. Making this adjustment brings us to *net domestic income at market prices*. We still must get from a *net* to a *gross* measure.

Total expenditure is a *gross* number because it includes *gross* investment. Net domestic income at market prices is a net income measure because corporate profits are measured *after deducting depreciation*. They are a *net* income measure. To get from net income to gross income, we must *add depreciation*.

We've now arrived at GDP using the income approach. This number is not exactly the same as GDP using the expenditure approach. If a waiter doesn't report all his tips when he fills out his income

tax return, they get missed in the income approach but they show up in the expenditure approach when he spends his income. Also because some expenditure items are estimated rather than directly measured, the sum of expenditures might exceed the sum of incomes.

The gap between the expenditure approach and the income approach is called the **statistical discrepancy** and it is calculated as the GDP expenditure total minus the GDP income total. The discrepancy is never large. In 2008, it was 0.1 percent of GDP.

TABLE 20.2   GDP: The Income Approach

Item	Amount in 2008 (billions of dollars)	Percentage of GDP
Wages, salaries, and supplementary labour income	815	51.6
Corporate profits	226	14.3
Interest and miscellaneous investment income	75	4.7
Farmers' income	1	0.1
Income from non-farm unincorporated businesses	93	5.9
Net domestic income at factor cost	1,210	76.6
Indirect taxes *less* subsidies	165	10.5
Net domestic income at market prices	1,375	87.1
Depreciation	202	12.8
GDP (income approach)	**1,577**	**99.9**
Statistical discrepancy	1	0.1
GDP (expenditure approach)	**1,578**	**100.0**

The sum of all incomes equals *net domestic income at factor cost*. GDP equals net domestic income at factor cost plus indirect taxes less subsidies plus depreciation. In 2008, GDP measured by the income approach was $1,577 billion. This amount is $1 billion less than GDP measured by the expenditure approach—a statistical discrepancy of $1 billion or 0.1 percent of GDP.

Wages, salaries, and supplementary labour income is by far the largest part of aggregate income.

Source of data: Statistics Canada, CANSIM Table 380-0001.

Nominal GDP and Real GDP

Often, we want to *compare* GDP in two periods, say 2002 and 2008. In 2002, GDP was $1,153 billion and in 2008, it was $1,578 billion—37 percent higher than in 2002. This increase in GDP is a combination of an increase in production and a rise in prices. To isolate the increase in production from the rise in prices, we distinguish between *real* GDP and *nominal* GDP.

Real GDP is the value of final goods and services produced in a given year when *valued at the prices of a reference base year*. By comparing the value of production in the two years at the same prices, we reveal the change in production.

Currently, the reference base year is 2002 and we describe real GDP as measured in 2002 dollars—in terms of what the dollar would buy in 2002.

Nominal GDP is the value of final goods and services produced in a given year valued at the prices of that year. Nominal GDP is just a more precise name for GDP.

Economists at Statistics Canada calculate real GDP using the method described in the Mathematical Note on pp. 482–483. Here, we'll explain the basic idea but not the technical details.

Calculating Real GDP

We'll calculate real GDP for an economy that produces one consumption good, one capital good, and one government service. Net exports are zero.

Table 20.3 shows the quantities produced and the prices in 2002 (the base year) and in 2009. In part (a), we calculate nominal GDP in 2002. For each item, we multiply the quantity produced by its price to find the total expenditure on the item. We then sum the expenditures to find nominal GDP, which in 2002 is $100 million. Because 2002 is the base year, real GDP and nominal GDP both equal $100 million.

In Table 20.3(b), we calculate nominal GDP in 2009, which is $300 million. Nominal GDP in 2009 is three times its value in 2000. But by how much has production increased? Real GDP will tell us.

In Table 20.3(c), we calculate real GDP in 2009. The quantities of the goods and services produced are those of 2009, as in part (b). The prices are those in the reference base year—2002, as in part (a).

For each item, we multiply the quantity produced in 2009 by its price in 2002. We then sum these expenditures to find real GDP in 2009, which is

TABLE 20.3 Calculating Nominal GDP and Real GDP

Item		Quantity (millions)	Price (dollars)	Expenditure (millions of dollars)
(a)	**In 2002**			
C	T-shirts	10	5	50
I	Computer chips	3	10	30
G	Security services	1	20	20
Y	Real and nominal GDP in 2002			100
(b)	**In 2009**			
C	T-shirts	4	5	20
I	Computer chips	2	20	40
G	Security services	6	40	240
Y	Nominal GDP in 2009			300
(c)	**Quantities of 2009 valued at prices of 2002**			
C	T-shirts	4	5	20
I	Computer chips	2	10	20
G	Security services	6	20	120
Y	Real GDP in 2009			160

In 2002, the reference base year, real GDP equals nominal GDP and was $100 million. In 2009, nominal GDP increased to $300 million. But real GDP in 2009 in part (c), which is calculated by using the quantities of 2009 in part (b) and the prices of 2002 in part (a), was only $160 million—a 60 percent increase from 2002.

$160 million. This number is what total expenditure would have been in 2009 if prices had remained the same as they were in 2000.

Nominal GDP in 2009 is three times its value in 2002, but real GDP in 2009 is only 1.6 times its 2002 value—a 60 percent increase in production.

Review Quiz

1 What is the expenditure approach to measuring GDP?

2 What is the income approach to measuring GDP?

3 What adjustments must be made to total income to make it equal GDP?

4 What is the distinction between nominal GDP and real GDP?

5 How is real GDP calculated?

myeconlab Work Study Plan 20.2 and get instant feedback.

◆ The Uses and Limitations of Real GDP

Economists use estimates of real GDP for two main purposes:

- To compare the standard of living over time
- To compare the standard of living across countries

The Standard of Living Over Time

One method of comparing the standard of living over time is to calculate real GDP per person in different years. **Real GDP per person** is real GDP divided by the population. Real GDP per person tells us the value of goods and services that the average person can enjoy. By using *real* GDP, we remove any influence that rising prices and a rising cost of living might have had on our comparison.

We're interested in both the long-term trends and the shorter-term cycles in the standard of living.

Long-Term Trend A handy way of comparing real GDP per person over time is to express it as a ratio of some reference year. For example, in 1971, real GDP per person was $20,127, and in 2007, it was $40,070. So real GDP per person in 2007 was (approximately) double its 1971 level. Measured by real GDP per person, people were twice as well off in 2007 as their parents had been in 1971.

Figure 20.2 shows the path of Canadian real GDP per person from 1961 to 2007 and highlights two features of our expanding living standard:

- The growth of potential GDP per person
- Fluctuations of real GDP around potential GDP

The Growth of Potential GDP When all the economy's labour, capital, land, and entrepreneurial ability are fully employed, the value of real GDP is called **potential GDP**. Potential GDP per person, the smoother black line in Fig. 20.2, grows at a steady pace because the quantities of the factors of production and their productivity grow at a steady pace.

But potential GDP per person doesn't grow at a *constant* pace. During the 1960s, it grew at a rate of 3.4 percent per year. Its growth rate then slowed and the average after 1970 was only 2.4 percent per year. This slowdown in the growth of potential GDP per person might seem small, but it had big consequences, as you'll soon see.

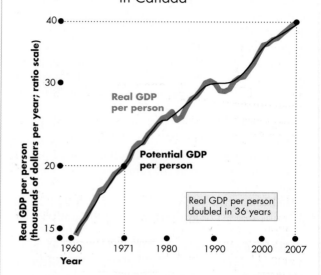

FIGURE 20.2 Rising Standard of Living in Canada

Real GDP per person in Canada doubled over the 36 years between 1971and 2007. Real GDP per person, the red line, fluctuates around potential GDP, the black line.

Sources of data: Real GDP, Statistics Canada, CANSIM Tables 380-0017 and 051-0005. Potential GDP, based on Bank of Canada output gap estimate after 1985 and authors' assumptions before 1985.

myeconlab animation

Fluctuations around Potential GDP You can see that real GDP shown by the red line in Fig. 20.2 fluctuates around potential GDP. Sometimes, real GDP is above potential; sometimes, it is below potential; and sometimes, real GDP shrinks.

Let's take a closer look at the two features of our expanding living standard that we've just outlined.

Productivity Growth Slowdown You've just seen that the growth rate of real GDP per person slowed after 1970. How costly was that slowdown? The answer is provided by a number that we'll call the **Lucas wedge**, which is the dollar value of the accumulated gap between what real GDP per person would have been if the 1960s growth rate had persisted and what real GDP per person turned out to be.

University of Chicago economist and Nobel Laureate Robert E. Lucas Jr., who drew attention to this measure, remarked that once he began to think about the benefits of faster economic growth, he found it hard to think about anything else.

Figure 20.3 illustrates the Lucas wedge. The red line is actual real GDP per person and the thin black line is the trend that real GDP per person would have followed if the 1960s growth rate of potential GDP had persisted through the years to 2007.

You can see in the figure that the gap—the wedge—had accumulated to an astonishing $316,000 per person by 2007. The gap started out small during the 1970s but in 2008, real GDP per person was $23,230 per year lower than it would have been with no growth slowdown.

Real GDP Fluctuations We call the fluctuations in the pace of expansion of real GDP the business cycle. A **business cycle** is a periodic but irregular up-and-down movement of total production and other measures of economic activity. The business cycle isn't a regular, predictable, and repeating cycle like the phases of the moon. The timing and the intensity of the business cycle vary a lot, but every cycle has two phases:

1. Expansion
2. Recession

and two turning points:

1. Peak
2. Trough

Figure 20.4 shows these features of the most recent Canadian business cycle.

An **expansion** is a period during which real GDP increases. In the early stage of an expansion real GDP returns to potential GDP and as the expansion progresses, potential GDP grows and real GDP eventually exceeds potential GDP. Canada experienced an expansion before the first quarter of 1990 and again after the first quarter of 1991.

A **recession** is a period during which real GDP decreases—its growth rate is negative—for at least two successive quarters. Canada's most recent recession occurred between the first quarter of 1990 and the first quarter of 1991.

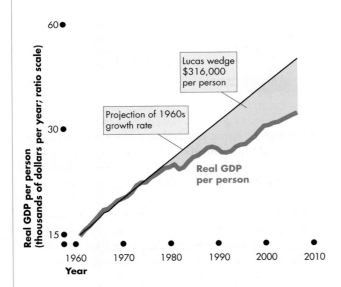

FIGURE 20.3 The Cost of Slower Growth: The Lucas Wedge

The black line projects the 1960s growth rate of real GDP per person to 2007. The Lucas wedge arises from the slowdown of productivity growth that began during the 1970s. The cost of the slowdown is $316,000 per person.

Sources of data: Statistics Canada, CANSIM Tables 380-0017 and 051-0005 and authors' calculations.

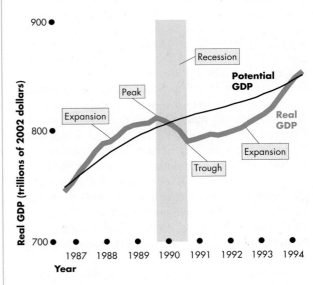

FIGURE 20.4 The Most Recent Canadian Business Cycle

The most recent business cycle peak occurred at the end of an expansion in the first quarter of 1990. A recession ran from that peak through the first quarter of 1991. A new expansion then began.

Sources of data: Statistics Canada, CANSIM Table 380-0002 and Bank of Canada estimate of the output gap.

A *peak* is the point in a business cycle at which real GDP reaches its highest level in an expansion and from which a recession begins. Canada's last business cycle peak occurred in the first quarter of 1990.

A *trough* is the point in a business cycle at the bottom of a recession when real GDP reaches a temporary low point from which the next expansion begins. Canada's last trough occurred in the first quarter of 1991.

You can see that recessions are infrequent and relatively short. Expansion is the normal state of the economy. The expansion that began in the first quarter of 1991 was still running in the second quarter of 2008, although a new recession was then predicted.

Let's now leave comparisons of the standard of living over time and look at those across countries.

The Standard of Living Across Countries

Two problems arise in using real GDP to compare living standards across countries. First, the real GDP of one country must be converted into the same currency units as the real GDP of the other country. Second, the goods and services in both countries must be valued at the same prices. We'll look at these two problems by using a striking example: a comparison of the United States and China.

China and the United States Compared   In 2008, real GDP per person in the United States was $38,422. The official Chinese statistics published in the International Monetary Fund's *World Economic Outlook* says that real GDP per person in China in 2008 was 16,400 yuan. (The yuan is the currency of China.) On average, during 2008, $1 U.S. was worth 8.3 yuan. If we use this exchange rate to convert 16,400 yuan into U.S. dollars, we get $1,976. This comparison of real GDP per person in China and the United States makes China look extremely poor. In 2008, real GDP per person in the United States was 19 times that in China, or real GDP per person in China was less than 4 percent of that in the United States.

The red line in Fig. 20.5 shows real GDP per person in China from 1980 to 2008 when the market exchange rate is used to convert yuan to U.S. dollars.

Purchasing Power Parity Comparison   Figure 20.5 shows another estimate of China's real GDP per person that is much larger than the one we've just calculated. Let's see how this alternative measurement is made.

U.S. real GDP is measured by using prices that prevail in the United States. China's real GDP is

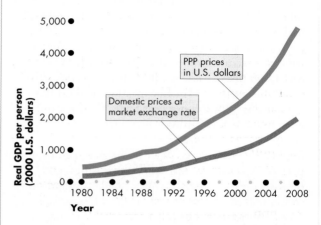

FIGURE 20.5   Two Views of Real GDP in China

Real GDP per person in China has grown rapidly. But how rapidly it has grown and to what level depends on how real GDP is valued. When GDP is valued at the market exchange rate, China is a poor developing country in which income per person in 2008 was 5 percent of the U.S. level. But when GDP is valued at purchasing power parity prices, China seems to be much less poor with real GDP per person in 2008 at 12.5 percent of the U.S. level.

Sources of data: International Monetary Fund, World Economic Outlook database, April 2008 and Alan Heston, Robert Summers, and Bettina Aten, Penn World Table Version 6.1, Center for International Comparisons at the University of Pennsylvania (CICUP), October 2002.

myeconlab   animation

measured by using prices that prevail in China. But the *relative prices* in these countries are very different.

The prices of some goods are higher in the United States than in China, so these items get a smaller weight in China's real GDP than they get in U.S. real GDP. For example, a Big Mac that costs $3.57 in Chicago costs 12.5 yuan, which is the equivalent of $1.83, in Shanghai. So in China's real GDP, a Big Mac gets about half the weight that it gets in U.S. real GDP.

At the same time, the prices of some goods are higher in China than in the United States, so these items get a bigger weight in China's real GDP than they get in U.S. real GDP. For example, a Buick LaCrosse that costs $25,000 in Chicago costs 239,800 yuan, which is the equivalent of $35,000, in Shanghai. So a Buick LaCrosse made in China gets about 40 percent more weight than the same car made in Detroit gets in U.S. real GDP.

More prices are lower in China than in the United States, so Chinese prices put a lower value on China's production than do U.S. prices.

To avoid putting a lower value on China's production, we use **purchasing power parity** or **PPP** prices, which are the same prices for both countries when converted at the market exchange rate. By using PPP prices, we make a more valid comparison of real GDP in China and the United States.

Alan Heston, Robert Summers, and Bettina Aten, economists at the Center for International Comparisons at the University of Pennsylvania, have used PPP prices to construct real GDP data for more than 100 countries. The IMF now uses a method similar to that of Heston, Summers, and Aten to calculate PPP estimates of real GDP in all countries. The PPP comparisons tell a remarkable story.

Figure 20.5 shows the PPP view of China's real GDP, the green line. According to the PPP comparisons, real GDP per person in the United States in 2008 was 8 times that of China, or real GDP per person in China was 12.5 percent of that in the United States.

You've seen how real GDP is used to make standard of living comparisons over time and across countries. But real GDP isn't a perfect measure of the standard of living and we'll now examine its limitations.

Limitations of Real GDP

Real GDP measures the value of goods and services that are bought in markets. Some of the factors that influence the standard of living and that are not part of GDP are

- Household production
- Underground economic activity
- Health and life expectancy
- Leisure time
- Environmental quality
- Political freedom and social justice

Household Production An enormous amount of production takes place every day in our homes. Preparing meals, cleaning the kitchen, changing a light bulb, cutting the grass, washing the car, and caring for a child are all examples of household production. Because these productive activities are not traded in markets, they are not included in GDP.

The omission of household production from GDP means that GDP *underestimates* total production. But it also means that the growth rate of GDP *overestimates* the growth rate of total production. The reason is that some of the growth rate of market production (included in GDP) is a replacement for home production. So part of the increase in GDP arises from a decrease in home production.

Two trends point in this direction. One is the number of women who have jobs, which increased from 58 percent in 1970 to 62 percent in 2008. The other is the trend in the market purchase of traditionally home-produced goods and services. For example, more and more families now eat in fast-food restaurants—one of the fastest-growing industries in Canada—and use day-care services. This trend means that an increasing proportion of food preparation and child care that were part of household production are now measured as part of GDP. So real GDP grows more rapidly than does real GDP plus home production.

Underground Economic Activity The *underground economy* is the part of the economy that is purposely hidden from the view of the government to avoid taxes and regulations or because the goods and services being produced are illegal. Because underground economic activity is unreported, it is omitted from GDP.

The underground economy is easy to describe, even if it is hard to measure. It includes the production and distribution of illegal drugs, production that uses illegal labour that is paid less than the minimum wage, and jobs done for cash to avoid paying income taxes. This last category might be quite large and includes tips earned by cab drivers, hairdressers, and hotel and restaurant workers.

Estimates of the scale of the underground economy in Canada range between 5 and 15 percent of GDP ($66 billion to almost $200 billion). Provided that the underground economy is a reasonably stable proportion of the total economy, the growth rate of real GDP still gives a useful estimate of changes in economic well-being and the standard of living. But sometimes production shifts from the underground economy to the rest of the economy, and sometimes it shifts the other way. The underground economy expands relative to the rest of the economy if taxes become especially high or if regulations become especially restrictive. And the underground economy shrinks relative to the rest of the economy if the burdens of taxes and regulations are eased. During the 1980s, when tax rates were cut, there was an increase in the reporting of previously hidden income and tax revenues increased. So some part (but probably a very small part) of the expansion of real GDP during the 1980s represented a shift from the underground economy rather than an increase in production.

Health and Life Expectancy Good health and a long life—the hopes of everyone—do not show up in real GDP, at least not directly. A higher real GDP enables us to spend more on medical research, health care, a good diet, and exercise equipment. And as real GDP has increased, our life expectancy has lengthened—from 70 years at the end of World War II to approaching 80 years today. Infant deaths and death in childbirth, two fearful scourges of the nineteenth century, have been greatly reduced.

But we face new health and life expectancy problems every year. AIDS and drug abuse are taking young lives at a rate that causes serious concern. When we take these negative influences into account, we see that real GDP growth overstates the improvements in the standard of living.

Leisure Time Leisure time is an economic good that adds to our economic well-being and the standard of living. Other things remaining the same, the more leisure we have, the better off we are. Our working time is valued as part of GDP, but our leisure time is not. Yet that leisure time must be at least as valuable to us as the wage that we earn for the last hour worked. If it were not, we would work instead of taking leisure. Over the years, leisure time has steadily increased. The workweek has become shorter, more people take early retirement, and the number of vacation days has increased. These improvements in economic well-being are not reflected in real GDP.

Environmental Quality Economic activity directly influences the quality of the environment. The burning of hydrocarbon fuels is the most visible activity that damages our environment, but it is not the only example. The depletion of nonrenewable natural resources, the mass clearing of forests, and the pollution of lakes and rivers are other major environmental consequences of industrial production.

Resources that are used to protect the environment are valued as part of GDP. For example, the value of catalytic converters that help to protect the atmosphere from automobile emissions is part of GDP. But if we did not use such pieces of equipment and instead polluted the atmosphere, we would not count the deteriorating air that we were breathing as a negative part of GDP.

An industrial society possibly produces more atmospheric pollution than an agricultural society does. But pollution does not always increase as we become wealthier. Wealthy people value a clean environment and are willing to pay for one. Compare the pollution in China today with pollution in Canada. China, a poor country, pollutes its rivers, lakes, and atmosphere in a way that is unimaginable in Canada.

Political Freedom and Social Justice Most people in the Western world value political freedoms such as those provided by the Canadian Constitution. And they value social justice—equality of opportunity and of access to social security safety nets that protect people from the extremes of misfortune.

A country might have a very large real GDP per person but have limited political freedom and social justice. For example, a small elite might enjoy political liberty and extreme wealth while the vast majority are effectively enslaved and live in abject poverty. Such an economy would generally be regarded as having a lower standard of living than one that had the same amount of real GDP but in which political freedoms were enjoyed by everyone. Today, China has rapid real GDP growth but limited political freedoms, while Poland and Ukraine have moderate real GDP growth but democratic political systems. Economists have no easy way to determine which of these countries is better off.

The Bottom Line Do we get the wrong message about the growth in economic well-being and the standard of living by looking at the growth of real GDP? The influences that are omitted from real GDP are probably important and could be large. Developing countries have a larger underground economy and a larger amount of household production than do developed countries. So as an economy develops and grows, part of the apparent growth of real GDP might reflect a switch from underground to regular production and from home to market production. This measurement error overstates the growth in economic well-being and the improvement in the standard of living.

A Broader Indicator of Economic Well-Being

The Human Development Index

The limitations of real GDP reviewed in this chapter affect the standard of living and general well-being of every country. So to make international comparisons of the general state of economic well-being, we must look at real GDP and other indicators.

The United Nations has constructed a broader measure called the Human Development Index (HDI), which combines real GDP, life expectancy and health, and education. Real GDP per person (measured on the PPP basis) is a major component of the HDI.

The dots in the figure show the relationship between real GDP per person and the HDI. Canada has the tenth highest real GDP per person but the fourth highest HDI. (The countries with higher HDIs and GDPs per person are named in the figure.)

The HDI of Canada is lower than that of 9 other countries because the people of those countries live longer and have better access to health care and education than do Canadians.

Five African nations have the lowest real GDP per person and Sierra Leone has the lowest HDI.

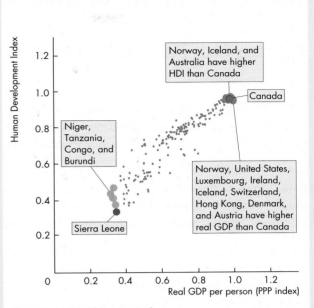

The Human Development Index

Source of data: United Nations hdr.undp.org/en/statistics/data/.

Other influences on the standard of living include the amount of leisure time available, the quality of the environment, the security of jobs and homes, and the safety of city streets.

It is possible to construct broader measures that combine the many influences that contribute to human happiness. Real GDP will be one element in those broader measures, but it will by no means be the whole of those measures.

The United Nations Human Development Index (HDI) is one example of attempts to provide broader measures of economic well-being and the standard of living. But this measure places a good deal of weight on real GDP.

Dozens of other measures have been proposed. One includes resource depletion and emissions in a "green" GDP measure. Another emphasizes the enjoyment of life rather than the production of goods in a "genuine progress index" or GPI.

Despite all the alternatives, real GDP per person remains the most widely used indicator of economic well-being.

Review Quiz

1 Distinguish between real GDP and potential GDP and describe how each grows over time.
2 How does the growth rate of real GDP contribute to an improved standard of living?
3 What is a business cycle and what are its phases and turning points?
4 What is PPP and how does it help us to make valid international comparisons of real GDP?
5 Explain why real GDP might be an unreliable indicator of the standard of living.

myeconlab Work Study Plan 20.3 and get instant feedback.

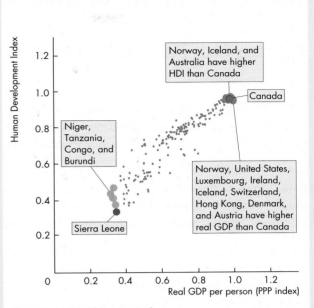 You've now studied the methods used to measure GDP and real GDP. You've also learned about the uses of real GDP and some of its limitations. *Reading Between the Lines* on pp. 480–481 looks at Canadian real GDP in 2008.

Your next task is to learn how we measure employment and unemployment and the CPI.

Real GDP in the Slowing Economy of 2008

October Still the Cruellest Month: Recession Fears

November 1, 2008

The Canadian economy shrank in August as most sectors, including mines and petroleum, gave way to the pressure of a global slowdown. The contraction was by no means good, but that snapshot of the past paled in comparison to what followed.

The tumultuous events of October, which took root in the financial upheaval of September, have convinced most economists that Canada has entered recession. Even those not predicting the two consecutive months of economic contraction required to be classed as a "technical recession" are forecasting something close to borderline.

The diagnosis is that while Canada is positioned better than most to tackle the credit crisis and global downturn, the pain is largely unavoidable. ...

GDP contracted by an annualized 0.3% in August, with six of 10 sectors of the economy shrinking, Statistics Canada figures showed yesterday. The result followed a 0.7% rise in July and a flat reading in June. ...

David Wolf, an economist at Merrill Lynch, said the manufacturing and wholesale trades were the biggest drags on the Canadian economy in August. The energy sector, which was responsible for the jump in July, fell back to earth, while construction and transportation also contracted. ...

"We expect that the decline in August will cascade into the fourth quarter and likely into the first half of next year," said Douglas Porter, deputy chief economist at BMO Capital Markets. ...

Essence of the Story

- The Canadian economy shrank in August 2008.

- Most economists say that Canada entered recession.

- Canada is positioned better than most nations to tackle global downturn but cannot avoid some pain.

- GDP contracted by an annualized rate of 0.3 percent in August 2008.

- Merrill Lynch economist David Wolf said the manufacturing and wholesale trades had the largest declines.

- BMO Capital Markets economist Douglas Porter expected the August decline to persist into the first half of 2009.

Economic Analysis

- This news article reports real GDP numbers for August 2008.

- The data for this month show a shrinking economy and had most economists predicting that Canada (with the entire world) was heading for recession.

- Figure 1 shows the real GDP growth rate (annualized) quarter to quarter from the first quarter of 2000 to the second quarter of 2008.

- The quarter-to-quarter growth rate fluctuated between a high of 5.5 percent in 2000 and a low of –0.6 percent in 2001.

- You can see slow growth in 2001 and then more rapid growth in 2004 through early 2007.

- The slow growth rate in 2007 turned slightly negative in 2008.

- Figure 2 shows the growth rates of the components of real GDP. The green bars are average growth rates from 2000 through 2007 and the orange bars are the growth rates for the first half of 2008.

- You can see that in the first half of 2008, consumption expenditure (C) grew a bit slower than average. You can also see that net exports grew rapidly—exports (X) increased by more than average and imports (M) decreased.

- Figure 2 shows that government expenditure decreased and so it contributed to the slowdown of real GDP growth.

- But Fig. 2 shows the major sign of future recession in the large decrease in investment (I).

- When investment collapses as it did in 2008, recession is usually not far away.

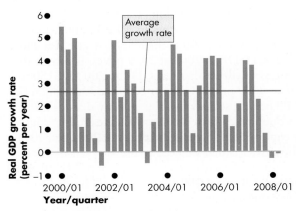

Figure 1 Real GDP growth rate: 2000–2008

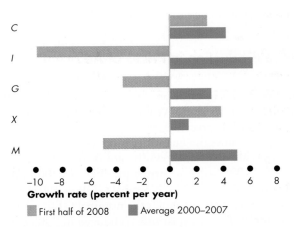

Figure 2 Real GDP components growth rate

481

MATHEMATICAL NOTE

Chained-Dollar Real GDP

In the real GDP calculation on pp. 473–474, real GDP in 2009 is three times its value in 2002. But suppose that we use 2009 as the reference base year and value real GDP in 2002 at 2009 prices. If you do the math, you will see that real GDP in 2002 is $150 million at 2009 prices. GDP in 2009 is $300 million (in 2009 prices), so now the numbers say that real GDP has doubled. Which is correct? Did real GDP double or triple? Should we use the prices of 2002 or 2009? The answer is that we need to use *both* sets of prices.

Statistics Canada uses a measure of real GDP called **chained-dollar real GDP**. Three steps are needed to calculate this measure:

- Value production in the prices of adjacent years.
- Find the average of two percentage changes.
- Link (chain) back to the reference base year.

Value Production in Prices of Adjacent Years

The first step is to value production in *adjacent* years at the prices of *both* years. We'll make these calculations for 2009 and its preceding year, 2008.

Table 1 shows the quantities produced and prices in the two years. Part (a) shows the nominal GDP calculation for 2008—the quantities produced in 2008 valued at the prices of 2008. Nominal GDP in 2008 is $145 million. Part (b) shows the nominal GDP calculation for 2009—the quantities produced in 2009 valued at the prices of 2009. Nominal GDP in 2009 is $172 million. Part (c) shows the value of the quantities produced in 2009 at the prices of 2008. This total is $160 million. Finally, part (d) shows the value of the quantities produced in 2008 at the prices of 2009. This total is $158 million.

Find the Average of Two Percentage Changes

The second step is to find the percentage change in the value of production based on the prices in the two adjacent years. Table 2 summarizes these calculations.

Part (a) shows that, valued at the prices of 2008, production increased from $145 million in 2008 to $160 million in 2009, an increase of 10.3 percent.

TABLE 1   GDP Calculation Step 1:
Value Production in Adjacent Years at Prices of Both Years

	Item	Quantity (millions)	Price (dollars)	Expenditure (millions of dollars)
(a)	**In 2008**			
C	T-shirts	3	5	15
I	Computer chips	3	10	30
G	Security services	5	20	100
Y	Real and nominal GDP in 2008			**145**
(b)	**In 2009**			
C	T-shirts	4	4	16
I	Computer chips	2	12	24
G	Security services	6	22	132
Y	Nominal GDP in 2009			**172**
(c)	**Quantities of 2009 valued at prices of 2008**			
C	T-shirts	4	5	20
I	Computer chips	2	10	20
G	Security services	6	20	120
Y	2009 production at 2008 prices			**160**
(d)	**Quantities of 2008 valued at prices of 2009**			
C	T-shirts	3	4	12
I	Computer chips	3	12	36
G	Security services	5	22	110
Y	2008 production at 2009 prices			**158**

Step 1 is to value the production of adjacent years at the prices of both years. Here, we value the production of 2008 and 2009 at the prices of both 2008 and 2009. The value of 2008 production at 2008 prices, in part (a), is nominal GDP in 2008. The value of 2009 production at 2009 prices, in part (b), is nominal GDP in 2009. Part (c) calculates the value of 2009 production at 2008 prices, and part (d) calculates the value of 2008 production at 2009 prices. We use these numbers in step 2.

Part (b) shows that, valued at the prices of 2009, production increased from $158 million in 2008 to $172 million in 2009, an increase of 8.9 percent. Part (c) shows that the average of these two percentage changes in the value of production is 9.6. That is, $(10.3 + 8.9) \div 2 = 9.6$.

By applying this average percentage change to real GDP, we can find the value of real GDP in 2009. Real GDP in 2008 is $145 million, so a 9.6 percent increase is $14 million, so real GDP in 2009 is

TABLE 2 Real GDP Calculation Step 2: Find Average of Two Percentage Changes

Value of Production	Millions of dollars
(a) At 2008 prices	
Nominal GDP in 2008	145
2009 production at 2008 prices	160
Percentage change in production at 2008 prices	10.3
(b) At 2009 prices	
2008 production at 2009 prices	158
Nominal GDP in 2009	172
Percentage change in production at 2009 prices	8.9
(c) Average of percentage change	**9.6**

Using the numbers calculated in step 1, the percentage change in production from 2008 to 2009 valued at 2008 prices is 10.3 percent, in part (a). The percentage change in production from 2008 to 2009 valued at 2009 prices is 8.9 percent, in part (b). The average of these two percentage changes is 9.6 percent, in part (c).

◆

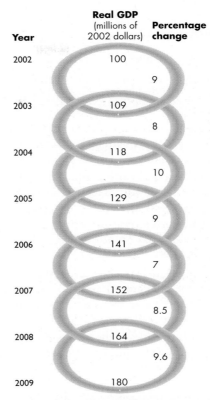

Figure 1 Real GDP calculation step 3: link (chain) back to base year

$145 million plus $14 million, which equals $159 million. Because real GDP in 2008 is in 2008 dollars, real GDP in 2009 is also in 2008 dollars.

Although the real GDP of $159 million is expressed in 2008 dollars, the calculation uses the average of the prices of the final goods and services that make up GDP in 2008 and 2009.

Link (Chain) Back to the Base Year

Today, Statistics Canada uses 2002 as the reference base year. The third step in calculating real GDP is to express it in the prices of the reference base year. To do this, Statistics Canada performs calculations like the ones that you've just worked through to find the percentage change in real GDP in each pair of years going back to 2002.

We start with nominal GDP in 2002, which equals real GDP in 2002. We then use the calculated percentage change for 2003 to find real GDP in 2003 expressed in the prices of 2002. We repeat this calculation for each year. In this way, real GDP in 2009 is linked (chained) to the base-year real GDP.

Figure 1 shows an example. Starting with real GDP in 2002 (assumed to be $100 million), we apply the

calculated percentage changes to obtain *chained-dollar real GDP* in 2002 dollars. By 2008, real GDP was $164 million (in 2002 dollars). In 2009, real GDP grew by 9.6 percent of $164 million, which is $16 million, so real GDP in 2009 was $180 million (in 2002 dollars).

Exercise

The table provides data on the economy of Tropical Republic that produces only bananas and coconuts.

Quantities	2008	2009
Bananas	1,000 bunches	1,100 bunches
Coconuts	500 bunches	525 bunches
Prices		
Bananas	$2 a bunch	$3 a bunch
Coconuts	$10 a bunch	$8 a bunch

Calculate Tropical Republic's nominal GDP in 2008 and 2009 and its chained-dollar real GDP in 2009 expressed in 2008 dollars.

SUMMARY

Key Points

Gross Domestic Product (pp. 468–470)

- GDP, or gross domestic product, is the market value of all the final goods and services produced in a country during a given period.
- A final good is an item that is bought by its final user, and it contrasts with an intermediate good, which is a component of a final good.
- GDP is calculated by using either the expenditure or income totals in the circular flow model.
- Aggregate expenditure on goods and services equals aggregate income and GDP.

Measuring Canada's GDP (pp. 471–473)

- Because aggregate expenditure, aggregate income, and the value of aggregate production are equal, we can measure GDP by using the expenditure approach or the income approach.
- The expenditure approach sums consumption expenditure, investment, government expenditure on goods and services, and net exports.

- The income approach sums wages, interest, rent, and profit (and indirect taxes less subsidies and depreciation).
- Real GDP is measured using a common set of prices to remove the effects of inflation from GDP.

The Uses and Limitations of Real GDP (pp. 474–479)

- Real GDP is used to compare the standard of living over time and across countries.
- Real GDP per person grows and fluctuates around the more smoothly growing potential GDP.
- Incomes would be much higher today if the growth rate of real GDP per person had not slowed during the 1970s.
- International real GDP comparisons use PPP prices.
- Real GDP is not a perfect measure of the standard of living because it excludes household production, the underground economy, health and life expectancy, leisure time, environmental quality, and political freedom and social justice.

Key Figures and Tables

Key Terms

PROBLEMS and APPLICATIONS ◆

 Work problems 1–11 in Chapter 20 Study Plan and get instant feedback.
Work problems 12–18 as Homework, a Quiz, or a Test if assigned by your instructor.

1. The figure below shows the flows of expenditure and income in Canada. During 2007, *B* was $852 billion, *C* was $342 billion, *D* was $311 billion, and *E* was $30 billion. Name the flows and then calculate

   a. Aggregate expenditure.
   b. Aggregate income.
   c. GDP.

2. The figure below shows the flows of expenditure and income in Canada during 2006. *B* was $803 billion, *C* was $320 billion, *D* was $291 billion, and *E* was $36 billion.

   Calculate the quantities in problem 1 during 2006.

3. The figure below shows the flows of expenditure and income in Canada during 2005. *A* was $1,373 billion, *B* was $759 billion, *D* was $264 billion, and *E* was $51 billion. Calculate

   a. Aggregate expenditure.
   b. Aggregate income.
   c. GDP.
   d. Government expenditure.

4. The firm that printed this textbook bought the paper from XYZ Paper Mills. Was this purchase of paper part of GDP? If not, how does the value of the paper get counted in GDP?

5. The table sets out some data for the United Kingdom in 2005.

Item	Billions of pounds
Wages paid to labour	685
Consumption expenditure	791
Taxes	394
Transfer payments	267
Profits	273
Investment	209
Government expenditure	267
Exports	322
Saving	38
Imports	366

   a. Calculate GDP in the United Kingdom.
   b. Explain the approach (expenditure or income) that you used to calculate GDP.

6. Tropical Republic produces only bananas and coconuts. The base year is 2008, and the tables give the quantities produced and the prices.

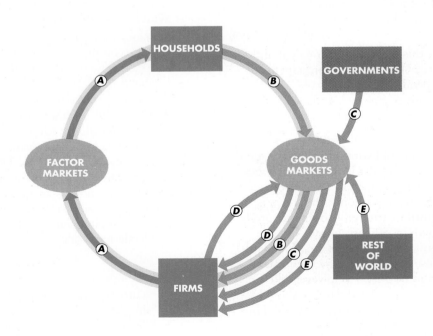

Quantities	2008	2009
Bananas	800 bunches	900 bunches
Coconuts	400 bunches	500 bunches
Prices		
Bananas	$2 a bunch	$4 a bunch
Coconuts	$10 a bunch	$5 a bunch

a. Calculate Tropical Republic's nominal GDP in 2008 and 2009.

b. Calculate real GDP in 2009 in terms of the base-year prices.

7. Use the Data Grapher in MyEconLab to answer the following questions. In 2007 in which country was

a. The growth rate of real GDP highest: Canada, Japan, or the United States?

b. The growth rate of real GDP lowest: France, China, or the United States?

8. **Honda Canada Begins Production of New 2006 Civic at its Canadian Plant**

Honda Canada today celebrated the start of production of the new Honda Civic coupe at its Honda of Canada Manufacturing facility in Alliston, Ontario. The Civic [is] Canada's best-selling passenger car the past seven years. ... All global production for the new 2-door Civic coupes will come from the Honda of Canada Manufacturing facility in Alliston and all Civic sedan models for the Canadian market will also be produced at the Honda plant ...

CNW Group, October 3, 2005

a. Explain how this change by Honda will influence Canadian GDP and the components of aggregate expenditure.

b. Explain how this change by Honda will influence factor incomes in Canada.

9. **Toting Katrina's Severe Distortions**

Hurricane Katrina could wind up being the most devastating storm to hit the U.S. Early forecasts of insured losses run as much as $26 billion. ... As far as damage to the economy, the storm is likely to drop third-quarter gross domestic product (GDP) growth by 50 basis points, figures Beth Ann Bovino, senior economist at Standard & Poor's. She also expects consumer sentiment and production to be hurt. ... However, likely repairs from hurricane-related damage should boost GDP in the following three quarters. This is largely because of rebuilding. ...

BusinessWeek, August 31, 2005

a. Explain how a devastating storm can initially decrease GDP.

b. How can a devastating storm then contribute to an increase in GDP?

c. Does the increase in GDP indicate a rise in the standard of living as a result of the storm?

10. **Poor India Makes Millionaires at Fastest Pace**

India, with the world's largest population of poor people living on less than a dollar a day, also paradoxically created millionaires at the fastest pace in the world in 2007. ... Growing them at a blistering pace of 22.7 per cent, India added another 23,000 more millionaires in 2007 to its 2006 tally of 100,000 millionaires measured in dollars. ... In contrast, developmental agencies put the number of subsistence level Indians living on less than a dollar a day at 350 million and those living on less than $2 a day at 700 million. In other words, for every millionaire, India has about 7,000 impoverished people. ...

Times of India, June 25, 2008

a. Why might a measurement of real GDP per person misrepresent the standard of living of the average Indian?

b. Why might $1 a day and $2 a day underestimate the standard of living of the poorest Indians?

11. **Canada Agency Says 2nd Quarter GDP Dip Won't Prove Recession**

Statistics Canada may not conclude the economy is in a recession even if gross domestic product contracts for a second straight quarter, according to one of the agency's top economists. ... Defining a recession as two consecutive quarterly drops in GDP "is a silly, simplistic, simplification," Cross said by telephone. ... The National Bureau of Economic Research, which chronicles business cycles in the U.S., defines a recession as "a significant decline in economic activity spread across the economy, lasting more than a few months, normally visible in real GDP, real income, employment, industrial production, and wholesale-retail sales."

Bloomberg, June 18, 2008

a. Why might defining a recession as "two consecutive quarterly drops in GDP" be too "simplistic"?

b. Why might people still be feeling the pain of recession after an expansion begins?

12. **GDP Expands 11.4 Percent, Fastest in 13 Years**

China's economy expanded at its fastest pace in 13 years in 2007. ... The country's Gross Domestic Product (GDP) grew 11.4 percent last year from 2006, to 24.66 trillion yuan ($3.42 trillion). ... That marked a fifth year of double-digit growth for the world's fourth largest economy after the U.S., Japan, and Germany. The increase was especially remarkable given the fact that the United States is experiencing a slowdown due to the sub-prime crisis and housing slump. ... According to Citigroup estimates, each one percent drop in the U.S. economy will shave 1.3 percent off China's growth, as Americans are heavy users of Chinese products. In spite of the uncertainties, the country's economy is widely expected to post its sixth year of double-digit growth in 2008 on investment and exports.

China Daily, January 24, 2008

a. Use the expenditure approach for calculating China's GDP to explain why "each one percent drop in the U.S. economy will shave 1.3 percent off China's growth."
b. Why might China's recent double-digit GDP growth rates overstate the actual increase in the level of production taking place in China?
c. Explain the complications involved with attempting to compare the economic welfare in China and the United States by using the GDP for each country.

13. **Study: Household Spending and Debt**

Canadian households have been spending more and saving less during the past two decades ... As a result almost one-half, or 47 percent of all households were spending more than their pre-tax income in 2001, up from 39 percent in 1982. ... Household deficit spending may be financed by drawing down savings or selling financial assets, but data indicate that borrowing is most closely tied to the increase in spending. Between 1982 and 2001, per capita debt doubled, stemming from dramatic increases in both mortgage and consumer debt. ...

The study suggests that a number of factors contributed to the increase in debt-financed spending. Interest rates fell dramatically over this period ... creating an "easy credit" environment.

At the same time, income taxes and Canada/Quebec Pension Plan and Employment Insurance premiums took a larger bite out of pre-tax income, squeezing the amount of income available for personal consumption and savings.

Other studies show that increasing financial wealth, particularly home equity, stimulates household spending. So the recent run-up in real estate values in many areas of the country may have helped to loosen the purse strings of homeowners.

Statistics Canada, March 22, 2005

a. How has consumer spending in relation to pre-tax income changed in Canada over the past two decades?
b. Explain the key influences on this change in consumer spending.
c. With home prices falling, as they were in 2008, how would you expect consumer spending and GDP to change in 2009?

14. **Consumer Spending a Big Factor: NBS**

When the [Chinese] National Bureau of Statistics (NBS) in October released its consumption figures for the first three quarters, people were surprised to discover that consumers are playing an ever-important role in the growth of the economy. ... Consumption contributed 37 percent of gross domestic product while foreign demand, or net exports, accounted for 21.4 percent. ... The remaining 41.6 percent was made by investment. ...

While exports are growing, imports are increasing at a faster pace, narrowing the gap and leading to shrinking net exports. ... But challenges lie ahead. Consumption will continue to grow, but only slowly, analysts said, because the public are still bothered by spending pressures like Social Security, health, education and housing. With those uncertainties, they prefer to save rather than spend.

China remains a developing country with a relatively low level of income, which cannot provide a strong back-up for consumption. ... The government has yet to provide adequate public services, such as education and health, and people prefer to save more in anticipation of rising future expenditure. ... In 2006, rural residents earned about one-third of the income earned by urban residents.

China Daily, December 11, 2007

a. Compare the relative magnitudes of consumption expenditure, net exports, and investment in China with those in Canada.

b. Why is consumption expenditure in China so low?

15. **Totally Gross**

Over the years, GNP and GDP have proved spectacularly useful in tracking economic change—both short-term fluctuations and long-run growth. Which isn't to say GDP doesn't miss some things. [Amartya] Sen, a development economist at Harvard, has long argued that health is a big part of living standards—and in 1990 he helped create the United Nations' Human Development Index, which combines health and education data with per capita GDP to give a more complete view of the wealth of nations (the United States currently comes in 12th, while on per capita GDP alone, it ranks second). [Joseph] Stiglitz, a Columbia professor and former World Bank chief economist, advocates a "green net national product" that takes into account the depletion of natural resources. Also sure to come up ... is the currently fashionable idea of trying to include happiness in the equation. The issue with these alternative benchmarks is not whether they have merit (most do) but whether they can be measured with anything like the frequency, reliability and impartiality of GDP.

Time, April 21, 2008

a. Explain the factors identified here that limit the usefulness of using GDP to measure economic welfare.

b. What are the challenges involved in trying to incorporate measurements of those factors in an effort to better measure economic welfare?

c. What does the ranking of Canada in the Human Development Index (10th) imply about the levels of health and education relative to other nations?

16. **Boeing Bets the House**

Boeing plans to produce some components of its new 787 Dreamliner in Japan. The aircraft will be assembled in the United States, and much of the first year's production will be sold to ANA (All Nippon Airways), a Japanese airline.

New York Times, May 7, 2006

a. Explain how Boeing's activities and its transactions affect U.S. and Japanese GDP.

b. Explain how ANA's activities and its transactions affect U.S. and Japanese GDP.

c. Use a circular flow diagram to illustrate your answers to a and b.

17. The United Nations Human Development Index (HDI) is based on real GDP per person, life expectancy at birth, and indicators of the quality and quantity of education.

a. Explain why the HDI might be better than real GDP as a measure of economic welfare.

b. Which items in the HDI are part of real GDP and which items are not in real GDP?

c. Do you think the HDI should be expanded to include items such as pollution, resource depletion, and political freedom? Explain.

d. What other influences on economic welfare should be included in a comprehensive measure?

18. Study *Reading Between the Lines* on pp. 480–481 and then answer the following questions:

a. Which components of aggregate expenditure increased at the fastest rate in the first half of 2008?

b. Which components of aggregate expenditure increased at the slowest rate (or decreased at the fastest rate) in the first half of 2008?

c. For how long has the Canadian economy been expanding since the last business cycle trough?

d. What is the main sign that the economy was heading for recession in 2009?

19. Use the link on MyEconLab (Chapter Resources, Chapter 20, Web links) to find the available data from Statistics Canada on GDP and the components of aggregate expenditure and aggregate income. The data are in current prices (nominal GDP) and constant prices (real GDP).

a. What are the levels of nominal GDP and real (chained-dollar) GDP in the current quarter?

b. What was the level of real GDP in the same quarter of the previous year?

c. By what percentage has real GDP changed over the past year?

21 Monitoring Jobs and Inflation

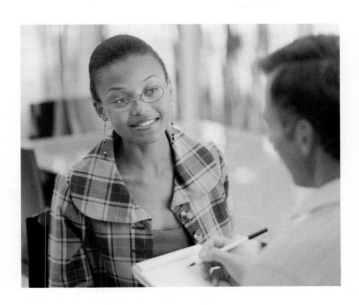

After studying this chapter, you will be able to

- Explain why unemployment is a problem, define the unemployment rate, the employment-to-population ratio, and the labour force participation rate, and describe the trends and cycles in these labour market indicators

- Explain why unemployment is an imperfect measure of underutilized labour, why it is present even at full employment, and how unemployment and real GDP fluctuate together over a business cycle

- Explain why inflation is a problem, how we measure the price level and the inflation rate, and why the CPI measure of inflation might be biased

Each month, we chart the course of employment and unemployment as measures of Canadian economic health. How do we count the number of people working and the number unemployed? What do the level of employment and the unemployment rate tell us? Are they reliable vital signs for the economy?

We always have some unemployment—we never get to a point at which no one is unemployed. So what is full employment? How many people are unemployed when there is full employment?

Having a good job that pays a decent wage is only half of the equation that translates into a good standard of living. The other half is the cost of living. We track the cost of the items that we buy with another number that is published every month: the Consumer Price Index, or CPI. What is the CPI? How is it calculated? And does it provide a reliable guide to the changes in our cost of living?

As the Canadian and global economies slowed in the wake of the financial crisis of 2007–2008, Canadian unemployment edged upward. *Reading Between the Lines* at the end of this chapter puts the spotlight on the labour market during the expansion of the years leading up to the 2008 slowdown.

We begin by looking at unemployment: What is it, why does it matter, and how do we measure it?

◆ Employment and Unemployment

What kind of job market will you enter when you graduate? Will there be plenty of good jobs to choose among, or will jobs be so hard to find that you end up taking one that doesn't use your education and pays a low wage? The answer depends, to a large degree, on the total number of jobs available and on the number of people competing for them.

The Canadian economy is an incredible job-creating machine. In 2008, 17 million people had jobs, which was 3 million more than in 1998 and 7 million more than in 1978. But not everyone who wants a job can find one. On a typical day, more than one million people are unemployed. That's equivalent to the population of Calgary. During a recession this number rises and during a boom year it falls. At its worst, during the Great Depression, one in every five workers was unemployed.

Why Unemployment Is a Problem

Unemployment is a serious personal and social economic problem for two main reasons. It results in

- Lost production and incomes
- Lost human capital

Lost Production and Incomes The loss of a job brings a loss of income for the unemployed worker and a loss of production. The loss of income is devastating for the people who bear it and makes unemployment a frightening prospect for everyone. Today, employment benefits create a safety net, but they don't fully replace lost earnings and not every person who becomes unemployed receives benefits.

Lost Human Capital Prolonged unemployment permanently damages a person's job prospects by destroying human capital. Think about a manager who loses his job when his employer downsizes. The only work

The Great Depression

What Keeps Ben Bernanke Awake at Night

The Great Depression began in October 1929, when the U.S. and global stock markets crashed. It reached its deepest point in 1933, when 25 percent of the Canadian and U.S. labour force was unemployed and production stood at less than 70 percent of its 1929 level. It was a depression that quickly spread globally to envelop most nations and lasted until 1941, when the United States entered World War II.

The 1930s were and remain the longest and worst period of high unemployment in history. Failed banks, shops, farms, and factories left millions of families all around the world without jobs, homes, and food. Without the support of governments and charities, millions would have starved.

The Great Depression was an enormous political event: It fostered the rise of the German and Japanese militarism that were to bring the most devastating war humans have ever fought. It also led to President Franklin D. Roosevelt's "New Deal," which enhanced the role of government in economic life and made government intervention in markets popular and the market economy unpopular.

The Great Depression also brought a revolution in economic ideas. In 1936, the English economist John Maynard Keynes published his *General Theory of Employment, Interest, and Money*, a book that created what we now call macroeconomics.

Many economists have studied the Great Depression and tried to determine why what started out as an ordinary recession became so devastating. Among them are Ben Bernanke, Chairman of the United States Federal Reserve (or U.S. Fed).

One of the reasons why the U.S. Fed has been so aggressive in cutting interest rates, saving Bear Stearns, and propping up Fannie Mae and Freddie Mac is because Ben Bernanke knows how financial collapse leads to broader economic collapse and is determined to avoid a repeat of the Great Depression.

he can find is driving a taxi. After a year in this work, he discovers that he can't compete with new MBA graduates. Eventually, he gets hired as a manager but in a small firm and at a lower wage than before. He has lost some of his human capital.

Governments make strenuous efforts to measure unemployment accurately and to adopt policies to moderate its level and ease its pain. Let's see how the Canadian government monitors unemployment.

Labour Force Survey

Every month, Statistics Canada conducts a *Labour Force Survey* in which it asks 54,000 households a series of questions about the age and job market status of the members of each household. Figure 21.1 shows the population categories used by Statistics Canada and the relationships among the categories.

The population divides into two broad groups: the working-age population and others who are too young to work or who live in institutions and are unable to work. The **working-age population** is the total number of people age 15 years and over. The working-age population is also divided into two groups: those in the labour force and those not in the labour force. Members of the labour force are either employed or unemployed. So the **labour force** is the sum of the employed and the unemployed. The employed are either full-time or part-time workers; and part-time workers are either want part-time work (voluntary part time) or full-time work (involuntary part time).

To be counted as employed in the Labour Force Survey, a person must have either a full-time job or a part-time job. To be counted as *un*employed, a person must be available for work and must be in one of three categories:

1. Without work but has made specific efforts to find a job within the previous four weeks
2. Laid off from a job and be waiting to be called back to work
3. Waiting to start a new job within four weeks

Anyone surveyed who satisfies one of these three criteria is counted as unemployed. People in the working-age population who are neither employed nor unemployed are classified as not in the labour force.

In 2007, the population of Canada was 32.9 million; the working-age population was 26.6 million. Of this number, 8.7 million were not in the labour

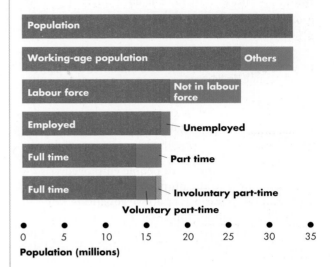

FIGURE 21.1 Population Labour Force Categories

Population (millions)

The population is divided into the working-age population and others. The working-age population is divided into those in the labour force and those not in the labour force. The labour force is divided into the employed and the unemployed. The employed are divided into the full-time and part-time employed, and the part-time employed are divided into voluntary and involuntary part-time.

Source of data: Statistics Canada, CANSIM Tables 282-0002 and 051-0001.

 myeconlab animation

force. Most of these people were in school full time or had retired from work. The remaining 17.9 million people made up the Canadian labour force. Of these, 16.9 million were employed and 1.0 million were unemployed. Of the 16.9 million employed, 3.1 million had part-time jobs, and of these, 0.7 million wanted a full-time job but couldn't find one.

Four Labour Market Indicators

Statistics Canada calculates four indicators of the state of the labour market. They are

- The unemployment rate
- The involuntary part-time rate
- The labour force participation rate
- The employment-to-population ratio

The Unemployment Rate The amount of unemployment is an indicator of the extent to which people who want jobs can't find them. The **unemployment rate** is the percentage of the people in the labour force who are unemployed. That is,

$$\text{Unemployment rate} = \frac{\text{Number of people unemployed}}{\text{Labour force}} \times 100.$$

and

$$\text{Labour force} = \frac{\text{Number of people employed}}{} + \frac{\text{Number of people unemployed}}{}$$

In 2007, the number of people employed was 16.87 million and the number unemployed was 1.08 million. By using the above equations, you can verify that the labour force was 17.95 million (16.87 million plus 1.08 million) and the unemployment rate was 6.0 percent (1.08 million divided by 17.95 million, multiplied by 100).

Figure 21.2 shows the unemployment rate from 1960 to 2007. The average unemployment rate during this period was 7.6 percent. The unemployment rate fluctuates over the business cycle: It increases as a recession deepens, reaches a peak after the recession ends, and decreases after a recovery gets going.

The Involuntary Part-Time Rate Part-time workers who want full-time work are underemployed and Statistics Canada counts their number. The involuntary part-time rate is the percentage of the people in the labour force who work part time but want full-time jobs.

$$\text{Involuntary part-time rate} = \frac{\text{Number of involuntary part-time workers}}{\text{Labour force}} \times 100.$$

In 2007, with 679,000 involuntary part-time workers and a labour force of 17.95 million, the involuntary part-time rate was 3.8 percent.

The Labour Force Participation Rate The number of people in the labour force is an indicator of the willingness of people of working age to take jobs. The **labour force participation rate** is the percentage of the working-age population who are members of the labour force. That is,

$$\text{Labour force participation rate} = \frac{\text{Labour force}}{\text{Working-age population}} \times 100.$$

In 2007, the labour force was 17.95 million and the working-age population was 26.55 million. By using the above equation, you can see that the labour

FIGURE 21.2   The Unemployment Rate: 1960–2007

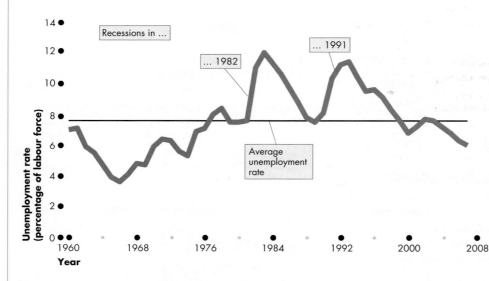

The average unemployment rate from 1960 to 2007 was 7.6 percent. The unemployment rate increases in a recession, peaks after the recession ends, and decreases in an expansion. The unemployment rate was unusually high following the recessions of 1982 and 1991.

Source of data: Statistics Canada, CANSIM Table 282-0002.

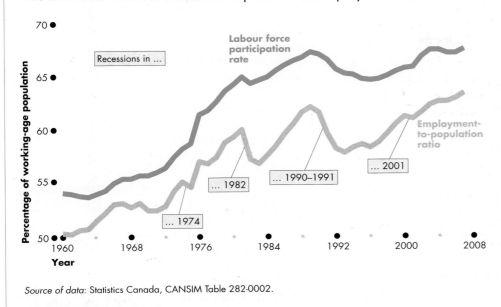

FIGURE 21.3 Labour Force Participation and Employment: 1960–2007

The labour force participation rate and the employment-to-population ratio have upward trends before 1990 and then flatten off after 1990. They fluctuate with the business cycle.

The employment-to-population ratio fluctuates more than the labour force participation rate and reflects cyclical fluctuations in the unemployment rate.

Source of data: Statistics Canada, CANSIM Table 282-0002.

myeconlab animation

force participation was 67.6 percent (17.95 million divided by 26.55 million, multiplied by 100).

The Employment-to-Population Ratio The number of people of working age who have jobs is an indicator of both the availability of jobs and the degree of match between people's skills and jobs. The **employment-to-population ratio** is the percentage of people of working age who have jobs. That is,

$$\text{Employment-to-population ratio} = \frac{\text{Number of people employed}}{\text{Working-age population}} \times 100.$$

In 2007, the number of people employed was 16.87 million and the working-age population was 26.55 million. By using the above equation, you can see that the employment-to-population ratio was 63.5 percent (16.87 million divided by 26.55 million, multiplied by 100).

Figure 21.3 shows the labour force participation rate and the employment-to-population ratio from 1960 to 2007. These indicators follows an upward trend before 1990 and then flatten off after 1990. The increase before 1990 means that the Canadian economy created jobs at a faster rate than the working-age population grew.

The employment-to-population ratio fluctuates with the business cycle: It falls in a recession and rises in an expansion. The labour force participation rate has milder business cycle swings that reflect movements into and out of the labour force.

Review Quiz

1 What determines whether a person is in the labour force?
2 What distinguishes an unemployed person from a person who is not in the labour force?
3 Describe the trends and fluctuations in the Canadian unemployment rate.
4 Describe the trends and fluctuations in the Canadian labour force participation rate and employment-to-population ratio.

 Work Study Plan 21.1 and get instant feedback.

You've seen how we measure employment and unemployment. Your next task is to see what the unemployment numbers tell us and what we mean by full employment.

◆ Unemployment and Full Employment

What does the unemployment rate seek to measure and does it provide an accurate measure?

The purpose of the unemployment rate is to measure the underutilization of labour resources, but it is an imperfect measure for two sets of reasons.

- It excludes some underutilized labour.
- Some unemployment is unavoidable—is "natural."

Underutilized Labour Excluded

Two types of underutilized labour are excluded from the official unemployment measure. They are

- Marginally attached workers
- Part-time workers who want full-time jobs

Marginally Attached Workers A **marginally attached worker** is a person who currently is neither working nor looking for work but has indicated that he or she wants and is available for a job and has looked for work sometime in the recent past. A subset of marginally attached workers is a group called discouraged workers.

A **discouraged worker** is a marginally attached worker who has stopped looking for a job because of repeated failure to find one. The numbers of marginally attached and discouraged workers is small. In 2007, when the official unemployment rate was 6.0 percent, adding the discouraged workers raised the rate to 6.1 percent of the labour force.

Part-Time Workers Who Want Full-Time Jobs Many part-time workers want to work part time. This arrangement fits in with the other demands on their time. But some part-time workers would like full-time jobs and can't find them. In the official statistics, these workers are called *involuntary part-timers* and they are partly unemployed.

A large number of workers fall into this group, and the rate fluctuates with the overall unemployment rate. In 2007, when the official unemployment rate was 6.0 percent, the involuntary part-time unemployment rate was 1.7 percent, which means that the overall unemployment rate including marginally attached workers was 7.8 percent.

"Natural" Unemployment

Unemployment arises from job search activity. There is always someone without a job who is searching for one, so there is always some unemployment. The key reason why there is always someone who is searching for a job is that the economy is a complex mechanism that is always changing—it is a churning economy.

The Churning Economy Some of the change in the churning economy comes from the transitions that people make through the stages of life—from being in school to finding a job to working, perhaps to becoming unhappy with a job and looking for a new one, and finally to retiring from full-time work.

In Canada in 2007, almost 500,000 new workers entered the labour force and around 150,000 workers retired.

Other change comes from the transitions that businesses make. Every day, new firms are born, existing firms grow or shrink, and firms fail and go out of business. This process of business creation, expansion, contraction, and failure creates and destroys jobs.

Both of these transition processes—of people and businesses—create frictions and dislocations that make unemployment unavoidable.

The Sources of Unemployment In the churning economy that we've just described, people become unemployed if they

1. Lose their jobs and search for another job.
2. Leave their jobs and search for another job.
3. Enter or reenter the labour force to search for a job.

And people end a spell of unemployment if they

1. Are hired or recalled.
2. Withdraw from the labour force.

People who are laid off from their jobs, either permanently or temporarily, are called *job losers*. Some job losers become unemployed, but some immediately withdraw from the labour force. People who voluntarily quit their jobs are called *job leavers*. Like job losers, some job leavers become unemployed and search for a better job while others either withdraw from the labour force temporarily or permanently retire from work. People who enter or reenter the labour force are called *entrants* and *reentrants*.

Entrants are mainly people who have just left school. Some entrants get a job right away and are never unemployed, but many spend time searching for their first job, and during this period, they are unemployed. Reentrants are people who have previously withdrawn from the labour force. Most of these people are formerly discouraged workers.

Job losers are the biggest source of unemployment. On the average, they account for more than half of total unemployment. Also, their number fluctuates a great deal. At the troughs of the recessions of 1982 and 1991, on any given day, around 800,000 of the 1.4 million unemployed were job losers. In contrast, at the business cycle peaks of 1987 and 2001, around half a million of the 1 million unemployed were job losers.

Entrants and reentrants also make up a large component of the unemployed. Their number fluctuates but more mildly than the fluctuations in the number of job losers.

Job leavers are the smallest and most stable source of unemployment. On any given day, fewer than 1 million people are unemployed because they are job leavers. The number of job leavers is remarkably constant. To the extent that this number fluctuates, it does so in line with the business cycle: A slightly larger number of people leave their jobs in good times than in bad times.

Frictions, Structural Change, and Cycles The unemployment that arises from normal labour turnover—from people entering and leaving the labour force and from the ongoing creation and destruction of jobs—is **frictional unemployment**. Frictional unemployment is a permanent and healthy phenomenon in a dynamic, growing economy.

The flow of people into and out of the labour force and the processes of job creation and job destruction means that people must search for jobs and businesses must search for workers. There are always businesses with unfilled jobs and people seeking jobs. Businesses don't usually hire the first person who applies for a job, and unemployed people don't usually take the first job that comes their way. Both firms and workers spend time searching for what they believe will be the best available match. By this process of search, people match their skills and interests with the available jobs and find a satisfying job and a good income. While these unemployed people are searching, their unemployment is frictional.

The unemployment that arises when changes in technology or international competition change the skills needed to perform jobs or change the locations of jobs is called **structural unemployment**. Structural unemployment usually lasts longer than frictional unemployment because workers must usually retrain and possibly relocate to find a job. When a steel plant in Hamilton, Ontario, is automated, some jobs in that city disappear. Meanwhile, in the Ottawa valley and Vancouver, new jobs for security guards, retail clerks, and life-insurance salespeople are created. The unemployed former steelworkers remain unemployed for several months until they move, retrain, and get one of these jobs. Structural unemployment is painful, especially for older workers for whom the

Structural Unemployment in Canada

The Maritime Provinces

Unemployment rates across Canada's provinces range from almost 14 percent in Newfoundland and Labrador to less than 4 percent in Alberta. This range of unemployment rates arises from structural features of the Canadian economy. Alberta and the West in general are growing rapidly. The Maritimes and to a lesser extent Quebec are growing more slowly. People must leave the eastern provinces and move westward to find work. A reluctance to uproot keeps the unemployment rates widely dispersed.

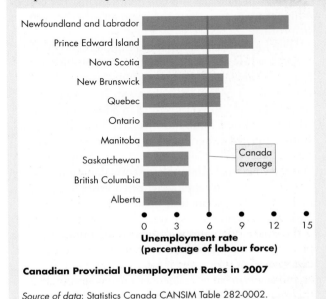

Canadian Provincial Unemployment Rates in 2007

Source of data: Statistics Canada CANSIM Table 282-0002.

best available option might be to retire early or take a lower-skilled, lower-paying job. At some times, the amount of structural unemployment is modest. At other times, it is large, and at such times, structural unemployment can become a serious long-term problem. It was especially large during the late 1970s and early 1980s. During those years, oil price hikes and an increasingly competitive international environment destroyed jobs in traditional Canadian industries, such as auto and steel, and created jobs in new industries, such as electronics and bioengineering, as well as in banking and insurance. Structural unemployment was also present during the early 1990s as many businesses and governments "downsized."

Two other structural sources of higher unemployment are a *minimum wage* and an *efficiency wage*. Chapter 6 (see pp. 133–135) explains how the minimum wage creates unemployment.

An **efficiency wage** is a wage set above the going market wage, and it creates unemployment just like the minimum wage does.

A firm might choose to pay an efficiency wage for four reasons. First, it enables the firm to face a steady stream of available new workers. Second, it attracts the most productive workers. Third, the fear of losing a well-paid job stimulates greater work effort. Fourth, workers are less likely to quit their jobs, so the firm faces a lower rate of labour turnover and lower recruiting and training costs.

The firm balances these benefits against the cost of a higher wage and offers the wage rate that maximizes its profit.

The higher-than-normal unemployment that arises at a business cycle trough and the unusually low unemployment that exists at a business cycle peak is called **cyclical unemployment**. A worker who is laid off because the economy is in a recession and who gets rehired some months later when the expansion begins has experienced cyclical unemployment.

What Is "Natural" Unemployment? Natural unemployment is the unemployment that arises from normal frictions and structural change when there is no cyclical unemployment—when all the unemployment is frictional and structural. Natural unemployment as a percentage of the labour force is called the **natural unemployment rate**.

Full employment is defined as a situation in which the unemployment rate equals the natural unemployment rate.

There can be a lot of unemployment at full employment, and the term "full employment" is an example of a technical economic term that does not correspond with everyday language. The term "natural unemployment rate" is another technical economic term whose meaning does not correspond with everyday language. For most people—especially for unemployed workers—there is nothing natural about unemployment. But if you think for a moment, you will come up with many other natural phenomena that are unpleasant. Floods, hurricanes, ice storms, and the feeding frenzy of sharks are just three examples.

So when economists call a situation with a lot of unemployment one of "full employment" and describe the unemployment rate at full employment as the "natural rate," they are talking about the unemployment that results from natural physical constraints on the ease with which the labour market can match workers with jobs.

There is not much controversy about the existence of a natural unemployment rate. Nor is there much disagreement that it changes. The natural unemployment rate arises from the existence of labour market frictions and structural change, and it fluctuates because the frictions and the amount of structural change fluctuate. But economists don't agree about the size of the natural unemployment rate and the extent to which it fluctuates. Some economists believe that the natural unemployment rate fluctuates frequently and that at times of rapid demographic and technological change, the natural unemployment rate can be high. Others think that the natural unemployment rate changes slowly.

Real GDP and Unemployment Over the Cycle

The quantity of real GDP at full employment is *potential GDP* (p. 474). Over the business cycle, real GDP fluctuates around potential GDP. The gap between real GDP and potential GDP is called the **output gap**. As the output gap fluctuates over the business cycle, the unemployment rate fluctuates around the natural unemployment rate.

Figure 21.4 illustrates these fluctuations in Canada between 1985 and 2007—the output gap in part (a) and the unemployment rate and natural unemployment rate in part (b).

FIGURE 21.4   The Output Gap and the Unemployment Rate

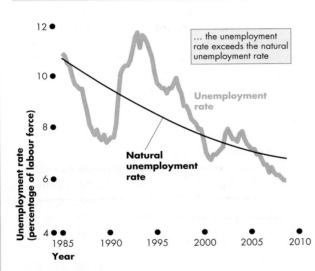

(a) Output gap

(b) Unemployment rate

As real GDP fluctuates around potential GDP in part (a), the unemployment rate fluctuates around the natural unemployment rate in part (b). At the end of the deep 1991 recession, the unemployment rate reached almost 12 percent. The natural unemployment rate decreased during the 1980s, 1990s, and 2000s. Fluctuations in unemployment and output do not exactly line up: The unemployment rate lags the output gap.

Sources of data: Bank of Canada output gap estimate and Statistics Canada, CANSIM Table 282-0002. Natural unemployment is the authors' assumption.

myeconlab animation

When the economy is at full employment, the unemployment rate equals the natural unemployment rate and real GDP equals potential GDP so the output gap is zero. When the unemployment rate is less than the natural unemployment rate, real GDP is greater than potential GDP and the output gap is positive. And when the unemployment rate is greater than the natural unemployment rate, real GDP is less than potential GDP and the output gap is negative.

Figure 21.4(b) shows one view of the natural unemployment rate. Keep in mind that economists do not know the magnitude of the natural unemployment rate and that shown in the figure is only one estimate. In Fig. 21.4(b), the natural unemployment rate was close to 11 percent in 1985 and it fell steadily through the 1980s, 1990s, and 2000s to about 6.5 percent by 2007. This estimate of the natural unemployment rate in Canada is one that many, but not all, economists would agree with.

The fluctuations in unemployment tend to lag behind the output gap fluctuations.

Review Quiz

1 What is the unemployment rate supposed to measure and why is it an imperfect measure?
2 Why might the official unemployment rate underestimate the underutilization of labour resources?
3 Why does unemployment arise and what makes some unemployment unavoidable?
4 Define frictional unemployment, structural unemployment, and cyclical unemployment. Give examples of each type of unemployment.
5 What is the natural unemployment rate?
6 How does the natural unemployment rate change and what factors might make it change?
7 How does the unemployment rate fluctuate over the business cycle?

myeconlab Work Study Plan 21.2 and get instant feedback.

Your next task in this chapter is to see how we monitor the price level and the inflation rate. You will learn about the Consumer Price Index (CPI), a vital sign that gets monitored every month. You will also learn about other measures of the price level and inflation rate.

The Price Level and Inflation

What will it *really* cost you to pay off your student loan? What will your parents' life savings buy when they retire? The answers depend on what happens to the **price level**, the average level of prices, and the value of money.

We are interested in the price level for two main reasons. First, we want to measure the **inflation rate**, which is the annual percentage change of the price level. Second, we want to distinguish between the money values and real values of economic variables such as your student loan and your parents' savings.

We will begin by explaining why we're interested in the inflation rate—why inflation is a problem. We'll then look at the ways in which we measure the price level and the inflation rate. Finally, we'll return to the task of separating real values from money values of economic variables.

Why Inflation Is a Problem

Inflation is a problem for several reasons, but the main one is that once it takes hold, its rate is unpredictable. Unpredictable inflation brings serious social and personal problems because it

- Redistributes income and wealth
- Diverts resources from production

Redistributes Income and Wealth Inflation makes the economy behave like a casino in which some people gain and some lose and no one can predict where the gains and losses will fall. Gains and losses occur because of unpredictable changes in the value of money. Money is used as a measuring rod of value in the transactions that we undertake. Borrowers and lenders, workers and employers all make contracts in terms of money. If the value of money varies unpredictably over time, then the amounts *really* paid and received—the quantities of goods that the money will buy—also fluctuate unpredictably. Measuring value with a measuring rod whose units vary is a bit like trying to measure a piece of cloth with an elastic tape measure. The size of the cloth depends on how tightly the elastic is stretched.

Diverts Resources from Production In a period of rapid, unpredictable inflation, resources get diverted from productive activities to forecasting inflation. It

can even become more profitable to forecast the inflation rate correctly than to invent a new product. Doctors, lawyers, accountants, farmers—just about everyone—can make themselves better off, not by specializing in the profession for which they have been trained but by spending more of their time dabbling as amateur economists and inflation forecasters and managing their investments.

From a social perspective, this diversion of talent resulting from inflation is like throwing scarce resources onto the garbage heap. This waste of resources is a cost of inflation.

At its worst, inflation becomes **hyperinflation**, an inflation rate so rapid that workers are paid twice a day because money loses its value so quickly. As soon as workers are paid, they rush out to spend their wages before the money loses too much value. In this situation, the economy grinds to a halt and society collapses. Hyperinflation is rare, but Zimbabwe has it today and several European and Latin American countries have experienced it.

It is to avoid the consequences of inflation that we pay close attention to it, even when its rate is low. We monitor inflation every month and devote considerable resources to measuring it accurately. You're now going to see how we do this.

The Consumer Price Index

Every month, Statistics Canada measures the price level by calculating the **Consumer Price Index (CPI)**, which is a measure of the average of the prices paid by urban consumers for a fixed basket of consumer goods and services. What you learn here will help you to make sense of the CPI and relate it to your own economic life. The CPI tells you what has happened to the value of the money in your pocket.

Reading the CPI Numbers

The CPI is defined to equal 100 for a period called the **reference base period**. Currently, the reference base period is 2002. That is, for the average of the 12 months of 2002, the CPI equals 100.

In September 2008, the CPI was 115.7. This number tells us that the average of the prices paid by urban consumers for a fixed market basket of consumer goods and services was 15.7 percent higher in September 2008 than it was on the average during 2002.

Constructing the CPI

Constructing the CPI is a huge operation that involves three stages:

- Selecting the CPI basket
- Conducting the monthly price survey
- Calculating the CPI

The CPI Basket The first stage in constructing the CPI is to select what is called the *CPI basket*. This basket contains the goods and services represented in the index and the relative importance attached to each of them. The idea is to make the relative importance of the items in the CPI basket the same as that in the budget of an average urban household. For example, because people spend more on housing than on bus rides, the CPI places more weight on the price of housing than on the price of bus rides.

To determine the CPI basket, Statistics Canada conducts a survey of consumer expenditure. Today's basket is based on data gathered in a 2005 survey.

Figure 21.5 shows the CPI basket. It contains thousands of individual goods and services arranged in the eight large groups shown in the figure. The most important item in a household's budget is shelter, which accounts for 27 percent of total expenditure. Transportation comes next at 20 percent. Third in relative importance is food at 17 percent. These three groups account for almost two-thirds of the average household budget. Recreation, education, and reading take 12 percent. Another 11 percent is spent on household operations and furnishings, 5 percent on clothing and footwear, 5 percent on health and personal care, and 3 percent on alcoholic beverages and tobacco products.

Statistics Canada breaks down each of these categories into smaller ones. For example, the recreation, education, and reading category breaks down into textbooks and supplies, telephone services, and personal computer services.

As you look at the relative importance of the items in the CPI basket, remember that they apply to the *average* household. *Individual* households are spread around the average. Think about your own expenditure and compare the basket of goods and services you buy with the CPI basket.

The Monthly Price Survey Each month, Statistics Canada employees check the prices of the 80,000 goods and services in the CPI basket in 30 metropolitan areas. Because the CPI aims to measure price

FIGURE 21.5 The CPI Basket

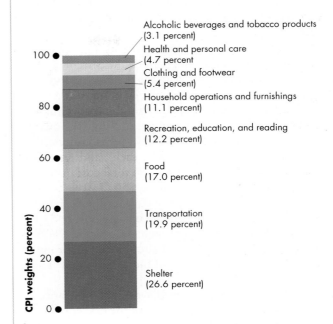

The CPI basket consists of the items that an average urban household buys. It consists mainly of shelter (27 percent), transportation (20 percent), and food (17 percent). All other items add up to 36 percent of the total.

Source of data: Statistics Canada, CANSIM CPI Report, September 2008.

myeconlab animation

changes, it is important that the prices recorded each month refer to exactly the same item. For example, suppose the price of a box of jelly beans has increased but a box now contains more beans. Has the price of jelly beans increased? Statistics Canada employees must record the details of changes in quality or packaging so that price changes can be isolated from other changes.

Once the raw price data are in hand, the next task is to calculate the CPI.

Calculating the CPI To calculate the CPI, we

1. Find the cost of the CPI basket at base-period prices.
2. Find the cost of the CPI basket at current-period prices.
3. Calculate the CPI for the base period and the current period.

We'll work through these three steps for a simple example. Suppose the CPI basket contains only two goods and services: oranges and haircuts. We'll construct an annual CPI rather than a monthly CPI with the reference base period 2008 and the current period 2009.

Table 21.1 shows the quantities in the CPI basket and the prices in the base period and current period.

Part (a) contains the data for the base period. In that period, consumers bought 10 oranges at $1 each and 5 haircuts at $8 each. To find the cost of the CPI basket in the base-period prices, multiply the quantities in the CPI basket by the base-period prices. The cost of oranges is $10 (10 at $1 each), and the cost of haircuts is $40 (5 at $8 each). So total cost in the base period of the CPI basket is $50 ($10 + $40).

Part (b) contains the price data for the current period. The price of an orange increased from $1 to $2, which is a 100 percent increase—($1 ÷ $1) × 100 = 100. The price of a haircut increased from $8 to $10, which is a 25 percent increase—($2 ÷ $8) × 100 = 25.

The CPI provides a way of averaging these price increases by comparing the cost of the basket rather than the price of each item. To find the cost of the CPI basket in the current period, 2009, multiply the quantities in the basket by their 2009 prices. The cost of oranges is $20 (10 at $2 each), and the cost of haircuts is $50 (5 at $10 each). So total cost of the fixed CPI basket at current-period prices is $70 ($20 + $50).

TABLE 21.1   The CPI:
A Simplified Calculation

(a) The cost of the CPI basket at base-period prices: 2008

CPI basket			Cost of
Item	Quantity	Price	CPI Basket
Oranges	10	$1.00	$10
Haircuts	5	$8.00	$40
Cost of CPI basket at base-period prices			$50

(b) The cost of the CPI basket at current-period prices: 2009

CPI basket			Cost of
Item	Quantity	Price	CPI Basket
Oranges	10	$2.00	$20
Haircuts	5	$10.00	$50
Cost of CPI basket at current-period prices			$70

You've now taken the first two steps towards calculating the CPI: calculating the cost of the CPI basket in the base period and the current period. The third step uses the numbers you've just calculated to find the CPI for 2008 and 2009.

The formula for the CPI is

$$CPI = \frac{\text{Cost of CPI basket at current-period prices}}{\text{Cost of CPI basket at base-period prices}} \times 100.$$

In Table 21.1, you established that in 2008 (the base period), the cost of the CPI basket was $50 and in 2009, it was $70. If we use these numbers in the CPI formula, we can find the CPI for 2008 and 2009. For 2008, the CPI is

$$CPI \text{ in } 2008 = \frac{\$50}{\$50} \times 100 = 100.$$

For 2009, the CPI is

$$CPI \text{ in } 2009 = \frac{\$70}{\$50} \times 100 = 140.$$

The principles that you've applied in this simplified CPI calculation apply to the more complex calculations performed every month by Statistics Canada.

Measuring the Inflation Rate

A major purpose of the CPI is to measure changes in the cost of living and in the value of money. To measure these changes, we calculate the *inflation rate* as the annual percentage change in the price level. To calculate the inflation rate, we use the formula:

$$\frac{\text{Inflation}}{\text{rate}} = \frac{\text{CPI this year} - \text{CPI last year}}{\text{CPI last year}} \times 100.$$

We can use this formula to calculate the inflation rate in 2008. The CPI in September 2008 was 115.7, and the CPI in September 2007 was 111.9. So the inflation rate during the year to September 2008 was

$$\frac{\text{Inflation}}{\text{rate}} = \frac{(115.7 - 111.9)}{111.9} \times 100 = 3.4\%.$$

Distinguishing High Inflation from a High Price Level

Figure 21.6 shows the CPI and the inflation rate in Canada during the 36 years between 1972 and 2008. The two parts of the figure are related and emphasize the distinction between high inflation and high prices.

Figure 21.6 shows that when the price level in part (a) *rises rapidly*, as it did during the 1970s and through 1982, the inflation rate in part (b) is *high*. When the price level in part (a) *rises slowly*, as it did after 1982, the inflation rate in part (b) is *low*.

A high inflation rate means that the price level is rising rapidly. A high price level means that there has been a sustained period of rising prices like that shown in Fig. 21.6(a).

The CPI is not a perfect measure of the price level and changes in the CPI probably overstate the inflation rate. Let's look at the sources of bias.

The Biased CPI

The main sources of bias in the CPI are

- New goods bias
- Quality change bias
- Commodity substitution bias
- Outlet substitution bias

New Goods Bias   If you want to compare the price level in 2009 with that in 1969, you must somehow compare the price of a computer today with that of a typewriter in 1969. Because a PC is more expensive than a typewriter was, the arrival of the PC puts an upward bias into the CPI and its inflation rate.

Quality Change Bias   Cars, CD players, and many other items get better every year. Part of the rise in the prices of these items is a payment for improved quality and is not inflation. But the CPI counts the entire price rise as inflation and so overstates inflation.

Commodity Substitution Bias   Changes in relative prices lead consumers to change the items they buy. For example, if the price of beef rises and the price of chicken remains unchanged, people buy more chicken and less beef. This switch from beef to chicken might provide the same amount of protein and the same enjoyment as before and expenditure is the same as before. The price of protein has not changed. But because the CPI ignores the substitution of chicken for beef, it says the price of protein has increased.

FIGURE 21.6   The CPI and the Inflation Rate

(a) CPI

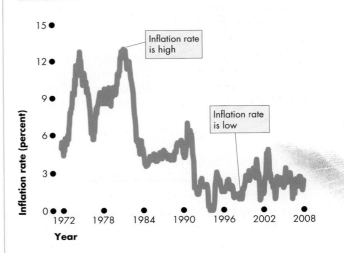

(b) Inflation rate

When the price level rises rapidly, the inflation rate is high, and when the price level rises slowly, the inflation rate is low.

During the 1970s and through 1982, the price level increased rapidly in part (a) and the inflation rate was high in part (b). The inflation rate averaged a bit more than 5 percent a year and sometimes exceeded 10 percent a year.

After 1982, the price level rose slowly in part (a) and the inflation rate was low in part (b). The inflation rate averaged 3 percent a year.

Source of data: Statistics Canada, CANSIM Table 326-0002.

myeconlab animation

Outlet Substitution Bias When confronted with higher prices, people use discount stores more frequently and convenience stores less frequently. This phenomenon is called *outlet substitution*. The CPI surveys do not monitor outlet substitutions.

The Magnitude of the Bias

You've reviewed the sources of bias in the CPI. But how big is the bias? This question is addressed periodically and the most recent estimate is provided in a study by Bank of Canada economist James Rossiter at about 0.6 percent per year.

Some Consequences of the Bias

The bias in the CPI distorts private contracts and increases government outlays. Many private agreements, such as wage contracts, are linked to the CPI. For example, a firm and its workers might agree to a three-year wage deal that increases the wage rate by 2 percent a year *plus* the percentage increase in the CPI. Such a deal ends up giving the workers more real income than the firm intended.

Close to a third of federal government outlays are linked directly to the CPI. And while a bias of 0.6 percent a year seems small, accumulated over a decade it adds up to several billion dollars of additional expenditures.

Alternative Price Indexes

The CPI is just one of many alternative price level index numbers and because of the bias in the CPI, other measures are used for some purposes. We'll describe two alternatives to the CPI and explain when and why they might be preferred to the CPI. The alternatives are

- GDP deflator
- Chained price index for consumption

GDP Deflator The **GDP deflator** is an index of the prices of all the items included in GDP and is the ratio of nominal GDP to real GDP. That is, to calculate the GDP deflator, we divide nominal GDP by real GDP and multiply by 100.

Because real GDP includes consumption expenditure, investment, government expenditure, and net exports, the GDP deflator is an index of the prices of all these items.

Real GDP is calculated using the *chained-dollar method* (see pp. 482–483), which means that the weights attached to each item in the GDP deflator are the components of GDP in both the current year and the preceding year.

Because it uses current period and previous period quantities rather than fixed quantities from an earlier period, a *chained-dollar* price index incorporates substitution effects and new goods and overcomes the sources of bias in the CPI.

Since 2000, the GDP deflator has increased at an average rate of 2.4 percent per year, which is 0.3 percentage points above the CPI inflation rate.

The GDP deflator is appropriate for macroeconomics because, like GDP, it is a comprehensive measure of the cost of the real GDP basket of goods and services. But as a measure of the cost of living, it is too broad—it includes items that people don't buy.

Chained Price Index for Consumption The **chained price index for consumption (CPIC)** is an index of the prices of all the items included in consumption expenditure in GDP and is the ratio of nominal consumption expenditure to real consumption expenditure. That is, to calculate the CPIC, we divide nominal consumption expenditure by real consumption expenditure and multiply by 100.

Like the GDP deflator, because the CPIC uses current period and previous period quantities rather than fixed quantities from an earlier period, it incorporates substitution effects and new goods and overcomes the sources of bias in the CPI.

Since 2000, the CPIC has increased at an average rate of 1.6 percent per year, which is 0.5 percentage points below the CPI inflation rate.

Core Inflation

No matter whether we calculate the inflation rate using the CPI, the GDP deflator, or the CPIC, the number bounces around a good deal from month to month or quarter to quarter. To determine whether the inflation rate is trending upward or downward, we need to strip the raw numbers of their volatility. The **core inflation rate**, which is the inflation rate excluding volatile elements, attempts to do just that and reveal the underlying inflation trend.

The most commonly used measure of core inflation is the *core CPI inflation rate* and as a practical matter, the core CPI inflation rate is calculated as the percentage change in the CPI *excluding food and fuel*.

The prices of these two items are among the most volatile.

While the core CPI inflation rate removes the volatile elements in inflation, it can give a misleading view of the true underlying inflation rate. If the relative prices of the excluded items are changing, the core inflation rate will give a biased measure of the true underlying inflation rate.

Such a misleading account was given during the years between 2000 and 2008 when the relative prices of food and fuel were rising. The result was a core CPI inflation rate that was systematically below the CPI rate by an average of 0.5 percentage points.

Figure 21.7 shows the two series since 1993. More refined measures of core inflation have been suggested that eliminate the bias but are not in common use.

The Real Variables in Macroeconomics

You saw in Chapter 3 the distinction between a *money price* and a *relative price* (see p. 58). Another name for a *money* price is a *nominal* price. In macroeconomics, we often want to distinguish between a real variable and its corresponding nominal variable. We want to distinguish a real price from its corresponding nominal price because a real price is an opportunity cost that influences choices. And we want to distinguish a real quantity (like real GDP) from a nominal quantity (like nominal GDP) because we want to see what is "really" happening to variables that influence the standard of living.

You've seen in this chapter how we view real GDP as nominal GDP deflated by the *GDP deflator*. Viewing real GDP in this way opens up the idea of using the same method to calculate other real variables. Using the GDP deflator, we can deflate any nominal variable and find its corresponding real value.

An important example is the wage rate, which is the price of labour. We measure the *real wage rate* as the nominal wage rate divided by the GDP deflator.

There is one variable that is a bit different—an interest rate. A real interest rate is *not* a nominal interest rate divided by the price level. You'll learn how to adjust interest rates for inflation to find a real interest rate in Chapter 23. But all the other real variables of macroeconomics are calculated by dividing a nominal variable by the price level.

FIGURE 21.7 CPI and Core CPI Inflation

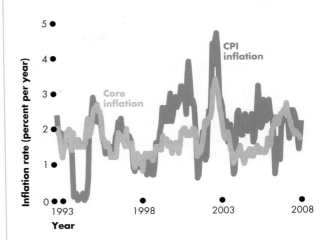

The core CPI inflation rate excludes price changes of food and fuel. Since 2000, the core inflation rate has been 0.5 percentage points below the CPI inflation rate because the relative prices of food and fuel have been rising.

Sources of data: Statistics Canada, CANSIM Table 380-0002.

myeconlab animation

Review Quiz

1 What is the price level?
2 What is the CPI and how is it calculated?
3 How do we calculate the inflation rate and what is the relationship between the CPI and the inflation rate?
4 What are the four main ways in which the CPI is an upward-biased measure of the price level?
5 What problems arise from the CPI bias?
6 What are the alternative measures of the price level and how do they address the problem of bias in the CPI?

myeconlab Work Study Plan 21.3 and get instant feedback.

You've now completed your study of the measurement of macroeconomic performance. Your task in the following chapters is to learn what determines that performance and how policy actions might improve it. But first, take a close-up look at the labour market in the slowdown of 2008 in *Reading Between the Lines* on pp. 504–505.

Jobs in the Slowdown of 2008

Canada adds 9,500 jobs, U.S. loses 240,000

November 7, 2008

The Canadian jobless rate held up remarkably well compared to the United States in October, as one country managed to add jobs while the other suffered yet another steep decline, new data showed on Friday.

Canadian employment rolls remained largely unchanged in October after September's surprising gains, however, a federal election that briefly added more than 40,000 jobs may have veiled mounting weakness elsewhere.

In stark contrast, the American economy shed more than 240,000 jobs last month, as the world's largest economy cooled further. The worse-than-expected results catapulted the jobless rate to 6.5 percent from 6.1 percent—a level last touched in 1994.

In Canada, the unemployment rate edged up to 6.2 percent in October, an increase of 0.1 percent from the previous month, Statistics Canada said. October witnessed an increase of 9,500 new jobs to add to September's surge of more than 107,000, even as the global credit crisis roiled on.

The figure was in line with what economists had expected. Employment increased in Alberta as that province added 15,000 more jobs and the unemployment rate remained the lowest in the country, at 3.7 percent. "There was little employment change in the other provinces," the federal agency said. ...

Material reprinted with the express permission of "The National Post Company", a Canwest Partnership.

Essence of the Story

- Canadian employment increased by 107,000 in September 2008 and by 9,500 in October 2008.

- The unemployment rate increased from 6.1 percent in September to 6.2 percent in October.

- In the United States, employment decreased by 240,000 jobs in October 2008 and the unemployment rate increased from 6.1 percent in September to 6.5 percent in October, its highest level since 1994.

- Employment in Alberta increased by 15,000 and the unemployment rate remained at 3.7 percent, the lowest in Canada.

Economic Analysis

- This news article reports some labour market data for both Canada and the United States in 2008.

- The credit crisis that began in August 2007 and intensified through 2008 had a bigger effect on the U.S. economy than on the Canadian economy.

- The three figures compare the labour markets of United States and Canada during 2008.

- Figure 1 shows that the employment-to-population ratio in Canada is higher than in the United States.

- This figure also shows that although the employment-to-population ratio fell in both countries, the fall in the United States was large and Canadian employment held steady with only a very slight fall.

- Figure 2 shows the unemployment rates. Normally, Canada has a higher unemployment rate than the United States.

- At the beginning of 2008, the normal state of affairs prevailed, but during 2008, the U.S. unemployment rate climbed steeply and by July, it equalled the Canadian rate. In October, the U.S. rate pulled ahead of the Canadian rate.

- Figure 3 shows that most of the job growth during 2008 was in part-time work. In both Canada and the United States, the part-time employment rate increased by about half a percentage point.

- Figure 3 also shows that Canada has more part-time employment than the United States—about a full percentage point more.

- Canada's relatively strong performance through October 2008 is also reflected in estimates of the output gaps in the two countries. Canada's output gap was estimated at –0.6 percent of potential GDP while the U.S. gap was estimated to be –2.7 percent of potential GDP.

- The reasons for Canada's relatively strong performance through October 2008 are not well understood, but if the United States goes into a long and deep recession, it is unlikely that Canada will continue to perform as well as it did during the first 10 months of 2008.

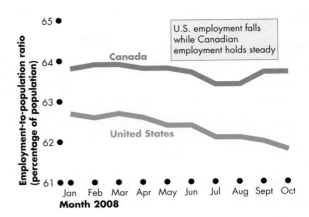

Figure 1 Employment

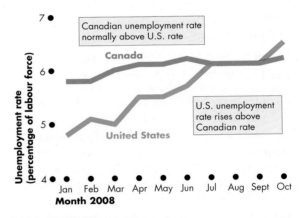

Figure 2 Unemployment

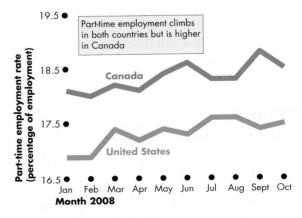

Figure 3 Part-time employment

SUMMARY ◆

Key Points

Employment and Unemployment (pp. 490–493)

- Unemployment is a serious personal, social, and economic problem because it results in lost output and income and a loss of human capital.

- The unemployment rate averaged 7.6 percent between 1960 and 2007. It increases in recessions and decreases in expansions.

- The labour force participation rate and the employment-to-population ratio have an upward trend and fluctuate with the business cycle.

Unemployment and Full Employment (pp. 494–497)

- The unemployment rate is an imperfect measure of the underutilization of labour resources because it excludes some underutilized labour and some unemployment is unavoidable.

- The unemployment rate underestimates the underutilization of labour resources because it excludes marginally attached workers and part-time workers who want full-time jobs.

- Some unemployment is unavoidable because people are constantly entering and leaving the labour force and losing or quitting jobs; also firms that create jobs are constantly being born, expanding, contracting, and dying.

- Unemployment can be frictional, structural, or cyclical.

- When all unemployment is frictional and structural, the unemployment rate equals the natural unemployment rate, the economy is at full employment, and real GDP equals potential GDP.

- Over the business cycle, real GDP fluctuates around potential GDP and the unemployment rate fluctuates around the natural unemployment rate.

The Price Level and Inflation (pp. 498–503)

- Inflation is a problem because it redistributes income and wealth and diverts resources from production.

- The Consumer Price Index (CPI) is a measure of the average of the prices paid by urban consumers for a fixed basket of consumer goods and services.

- The CPI is defined to equal 100 for a reference base period—currently 2002.

- The inflation rate is the percentage change in the CPI from one period to the next.

- Changes in the CPI probably overstate the inflation rate because of the bias that arises from new goods, quality changes, commodity substitution, and outlet substitution.

- The bias in the CPI distorts private contracts and increases government outlays.

- Alternative price level measures avoid the bias of the CPI but do not make a large difference to the measured inflation rate.

- Real economic variables are calculated by dividing nominal variables by the price level.

Key Figures

Key Terms

PROBLEMS and APPLICATIONS

myeconlab Work problems 1–9 in Chapter 21 Study Plan and get instant feedback.
Work problems 10–18 as Homework, a Quiz, or a Test if assigned by your instructor.

1. Statistics Canada reported the following data for October 2008:
   Labour force: 18,345,500
   Employment: 17,215,800
   Working-age population: 27,044,100.
   Calculate for that month the

   a. Unemployment rate.
   b. Labour force participation rate.
   c. Employment-to-population ratio.

2. The Canadian unemployment rate was 6.4 percent in August 2006 and 6.1 percent in August 2008. Use this information to predict what happened between August 2006 and August 2008 to the numbers of

   a. Job losers and job leavers.
   b. Entrants and reentrants into the labour force.

3. In July 2009, on Sandy Island, 10,000 people were employed, 1,000 were unemployed, and 5,000 were not in the labour force. During August 2009, 80 people lost their jobs and didn't look for new ones, 20 people quit their jobs and retired, 150 people were hired or recalled, 50 people withdrew from the labour force, and 40 people entered or reentered the labour force to look for work. Calculate for July 2009

   a. The unemployment rate.
   b. The employment-to-population ratio.

   Calculate for the end of August 2009

   c. The number of people unemployed.
   d. The number of people employed.
   e. The unemployment rate.

4. Statistics Canada reported the following data:
   CPI in June 2006: 109.5
   CPI in June 2007: 111.9
   CPI in June 2008: 114.6

   a. What do these numbers tell you about the price level in these three years?
   b. Calculate the inflation rates for the years ending in June 2007 and June 2008.
   c. How did the inflation rate change in 2008?
   d. Why might these CPI numbers be biased?

   e. How do alternative price indexes help to avoid the bias in the CPI numbers?

5. The IMF *World Economic Outlook* reports the following price level data (2000 = 100):

Region	2006	2007	2008
United States	117.1	120.4	124.0
Euro area	113.6	117.1	119.6
Japan	98.1	98.1	98.8

   a. Which region had the highest inflation rate in 2007 and which had the highest inflation rate in 2008?
   b. Describe the path of the price level in Japan.

6. **September Job Gains Defy "Wisdom"**
   The Canadian economy produced a record number of new jobs in September, a perplexing development given the onset of a global recession in the midst of a horrendous financial crisis. A whopping 107,000 new jobs were created last month, a gain that not only defied "conventional wisdom but gravity as well," Douglas Porter, deputy chief economist at BMO Capital Markets said. ... But scrape below the surface and the details were not as impressive as the headline, Mr. Porter said. A large part of the gain—which predates the worst of the financial crisis—was in part-time youth employment, not necessarily the underpinnings of a sustainable economy. ...

   National Post, October 11, 2008

   a. Why did Douglas Porter say the September 2008 job numbers defied gravity and conventional wisdom?
   b. Why might the September job numbers overstate the rise in employment?
   c. Given the information in the news article, what do you predict happened to the gap between real GDP and potential GDP during September 2008?

7. **GM, Ford Cuts Show Difficult Times Far f**
   Over
   A pink slip is a nasty thing. In fact, next to and divorce, it's the most devastating expe in one's lifetime. Sadly, workers at GM a know it all too well. On top of the 2,6(coming next year in Oshawa when G

truck plant, now 500 workers at the car plant face layoff early next year ... In total, another 3,600 in North America could be getting pink slips just before Christmas. And the number doesn't include the 1,400 workers who'll lose their jobs in 2010, when GM closes a Windsor transmission plant. ... Ford is also bleeding red ink, ... [and] announced a further 10-per-cent cut in white-collar, salaried positions, with 2,260 more layoffs. This is chilling news for Ontario, now a have-not province, where layoffs are piling high. ... Bottom line is that for every job in an assembly plant, there are 7.5 jobs with auto-parts suppliers and other companies, meaning the auto industry accounts for millions of jobs in North America. The Centre for Automotive Research estimates if the U.S. auto industry shrinks by 50 per cent, 2.5 million jobs will be lost. Now the question is will GM survive?

Timmins Daily Press, November 11, 2008

a. How will the events described in this news article change the employment rate, the labour force participation rate, and the unemployment rate in Ontario?
b. Will the change in Ontario's unemployment rate arise from a change in frictional, structural, or cyclical unemployment? Explain.
c. How will the events described in the news article change the natural unemployment rate? Explain.

8. **Canada Inflation Rate Rises More than Forecast on Gas**

Canada's annual inflation accelerated for the second straight month in May as gasoline prices surged, lending support to the Bank of Canada's prediction last week that prices may keep rising all year. Consumer prices rose 2.2 percent from a year earlier, the fastest pace since January, Statistics Canada said today. ... Gasoline prices spurred May's acceleration, soaring 15 percent from a year ago. Excluding gasoline, consumer prices would have gained 1.6 percent in April, the agency said. ... "It's no surprise that gasoline prices are leading the charge," said Pascal Gauthier, an economist with Toronto-Dominion Bank. ... Month-over-month inflation accelerated in May in part because of a 2.9 percent gain in transportation costs and a 1 percent gain in food prices, Statistics Canada said. The core inflation rate was unchanged from a year earlier

at 1.5 percent and the monthly core inflation rate stayed at 0.3 percent, in both cases matching economists' median forecast. The core rate, used by policy makers as a guide to future trends, excludes volatile items such as gasoline and fresh fruit and discounts tax changes such as a reduction in the federal sales tax earlier this year. An 8.1 percent drop in car prices kept the core index from rising in May, Statistics Canada said.

Bloomberg, June 13, 2008

a. How do the inflation rates described in this article compare to average inflation since 1993? How do they compare to average inflation during the 1970s and early 1980s?
b. Which components of the CPI basket are experiencing price increases faster than the average and which have price increases below the average?
c. What is the difference between the CPI and the core CPI? Why might the core CPI be a useful measurement and why might it be misleading?

9. **Dress for Less**

Since 1998, the price of a "Speedy" handbag— the entry-level style at Louis Vuitton—has more than doubled, to $685, indicative of a precipitous price increase throughout the luxury goods market. The price of Joe Boxer's "licky face" underwear, meanwhile, has dropped by nearly half, to $8.99, representing just as seismic a shift at the other end of the fashion continuum, where the majority of ... consumers do their shopping.

As luxury fashion has become more expensive, mainstream apparel has become markedly less so. ... Clothing is one of the few categories in the federal Consumer Price Index in which overall prices have declined—about 10 percent—since 1998 (the cost of communication is another). That news may be of solace to anyone whose budget has been stretched just to drive to work or to stop at the supermarket; in fashion, at least, there are still deals to be had. ...

New York Times, May 29, 2008

a. What percentage of the CPI basket does clothing and footware comprise?
b. If luxury clothing prices have increased dramatically since the late 1990s, why has the clothing category of the CPI actually declined by about 10 percent?

10. In the New Orleans metropolitan area in August 2005, the labour force was 634,512 and 35,222 people were unemployed. In September 2005 following Hurricane Katrina, the labour force fell by 156,498 and the number employed fell by 206,024. Calculate the unemployment rate in August 2005 and in September 2005.

11. The IMF *World Economic Outlook* reports the following unemployment rates:

Region	2007	2008
United States	4.6	5.4
Euro area	7.4	7.3
Japan	3.9	3.9

   a. What do these numbers tell you about the phase of the business cycle in the United States, the Euro area, and Japan in 2008?
   b. What do you think these numbers tell us about the relative size of the natural unemployment rates in the United States, the Euro area, and Japan?
   c. Do these numbers tell us anything about the relative size of the labour force participation rates and employment-to-population ratios in the three regions?
   d. Why might these unemployment numbers understate or overstate the true amount of unemployment?

12. A typical family on Sandy Island consumes only juice and cloth. Last year, which was the base year, the family spent $40 on juice and $25 on cloth. In the base year, juice was $4 a bottle and cloth was $5 a length. This year, juice is $4 a bottle and cloth is $6 a length. Calculate

   a. The CPI basket.
   b. The CPI in the current year.
   c. The inflation rate in the current year.

13. **A Half-Year of Job Losses**
   Employers trimmed jobs from their payrolls in June for the sixth straight month, as the government's closely watched report Thursday showed continued weakness in the labour market. ... The June number brought to 438,000 the number of jobs lost by the U.S. economy so far this year. ... The job losses in the monthly report were concentrated in manufacturing and construction, two sectors that have been badly battered in the current economic downturn. ...

   CNN, July 3, 2008

   a. How do the job losses for the first half of 2008 compare to the total number of people employed (as seen in this chapter)?
   b. Based on the news clip, what might be the main source of increased unemployment?
   c. Based on the news clip, what might be the main type of increased unemployment?

14. **Out of a Job and Out of Luck at 54**
   Too young to retire, too old to get a new job. That's how many older workers are feeling these days. ... Older job seekers are discovering the search is even rougher as many employers shy away from hiring those closer to retirement than to the start of their careers. ... After they get the pink slip, older workers spend more time on the unemployment line. Many lack the skills to search for jobs in today's online world and to craft resumes and cover letters, experts say. ... It took those age 55 and older an average of 21.1 weeks to land a new job in 2007, about five weeks longer than their younger counterparts, according to AARP. "Clearly older workers will be more adversely affected because of the time it takes to transition into another job," said Deborah Russell, AARP's director of workforce issues.

   CNN, May 21, 2008

   a. What type of unemployment might older workers be more prone to experience?
   b. Explain how the unemployment rate of older workers would be influenced by the business cycle.
   c. Why might older unemployed workers become marginally attached or discouraged workers during a recession?

15. **Unemployment Up, Even as Economy Sprouts New Jobs**
   Canada's unemployment rate edged up to 6.2 per cent in October from 6.1 per cent the previous month, Statistics Canada said Friday, even as the economy unexpectedly added thousands of new positions despite struggling to avoid a recession amid a global economic slowdown.

   There were 9,500 jobs created during the month, compared to a gain of 107,000 positions in September, the federal agency said. ... Alberta's unemployment rate remained the lowest in the country at 3.7 per cent, which added 15,000 jobs in October. "There was little employment change in the other provinces." Statistics Canada said.

Newfoundland and Labrador had the highest jobless rate at 13.7 per cent, followed by Prince Edward Island at 11.5 per cent. ...

Windsor Star, November 7, 2008

a. How can the unemployment rate increase when employment increases?
b. How would you explain the large difference in the unemployment rates in Alberta, Newfoundland and Labrador, and Prince Edward Island?
c. Explain why most of the difference in the unemployment rates in Alberta, Newfoundland and Labrador, and Prince Edward Island is a difference in the natural unemployment rate in each province.

16. **Economic "Misery" More Widespread**

Unemployment and inflation are typically added together to come up with a so-called "Misery Index." The "Misery Index" was often cited during periods of high unemployment and inflation, such as the mid 1970s and late 1970s to early 1980s.

And some fear the economy may be approaching those levels again. The official numbers produce a current Misery Index of only 8.9—inflation of 3.9% plus unemployment of 5%. That's not far from the Misery Index's low of 6.1 seen in 1998. ... Some worry it could even approach the post-World War II record of 20.6 in 1980. ...

CNN, May 13, 2008

a. Explain how the "Misery Index" might serve as a gauge of how the economy is performing.
b. How does the most current "Misery Index" compare to the high and low given in this article? (You may find it useful to use the link of MyEconLab—Chapter Resources, Chapter 21, Web links—to visit the Bureau of Labour Statistics Web site for the current unemployment rate and the most recent 12-month change in the CPI.)

17. **The Great Inflation Cover-Up**

The 1996 Boskin Commission ... was established to determine the accuracy of the [U.S.] CPI. The commission concluded that the CPI overstated inflation by 1.1%, and methodologies were adjusted to reflect that. Critics of the Boskin Commission suggest that the basis upon which the CPI was revised doesn't account for the way people actually purchase and consume products. The commission pointed to four biases inherent in the way the CPI was determined that supposedly contribute to overstatement. ... But the Boskin critics note several reasonable exceptions to those biases. The Boskin Commission suggests that when customers substitute one good for another, the CPI should treat those goods equally. If [someone] orders a hanger steak instead of his beloved filet mignon because the hanger steak is cheaper, Boskin argues that the hanger steak prices should be compared with previous filet mignon prices. It's all beef, right? But critics of the Boskin report point to areas where substitution is so price-driven that consumers are pushed out of the category altogether. What happens when the consumer gives up steak entirely and switches to chicken? ... Boskin also says that whatever you're paying in price increases is offset by the additional pleasure you get from better goods. To put it another way, you adjust for improvement in quality over time. ... So, for example, energy price increases due to federally mandated environmental measures are offset by how much we all sit around enjoying the cleaner environment.

Fortune, April 3, 2008

a. What are the main sources of bias that are generally believed to make the CPI overstate the inflation rate?
b. Is the U.S. or Canadian CPI more biased?
c. Do the substitutions among different kinds of meat make the CPI biased up or down?
d. Why does it matter if the CPI overstates or understates the inflation rate?

18. Study *Reading Between the Lines* on pp. 504–505 and then answer the following questions:

a. What are the key differences in performance of the U.S. and Canadian job markets during 2008?
b. How do the part-time employment rates of the two countries compare?
c. Why might the United States job market have been so much weaker than the Canadian job market during 2008?
d. Are the differences between the U.S. and Canadian job markets in 2008 seasonal, frictional, structural, or cyclical unemployment?

PART 7

UNDERSTANDING MACROECONOMIC TRENDS AND FLUCTUATIONS

The Big Picture

Macroeconomics is a large and controversial subject that is interlaced with political ideological disputes. And it is a field in which charlatans as well as serious thinkers have much to say.

You have just learned in Chapters 20 and 21 how we monitor and measure the main macroeconomic variables. We use real GDP to calculate the rate of economic growth and business cycle fluctuations. And we use the CPI and other measures of the price level to calculate the inflation rate and to "deflate" nominal values to find *real* values.

In the chapters that lie ahead, you will learn the theories that economists have developed to explain economic growth, fluctuations, and inflation.

First, in Chapters 22 through 25, you will study the long-term trends. This material is central to the oldest question in macroeconomics that Adam Smith tried to answer: What are the causes of the wealth of nations? You will also study three other old questions that Adam Smith's contemporary and friend David Hume first addressed: What causes inflation? What causes international deficits and surpluses? And why do exchange rates fluctuate?

In Chapters 26 through 28, you will study macroeconomic fluctuations.

Finally, in Chapters 29 and 30, you will study the policies that the federal government and the Bank of Canada might adopt to make the economy perform well.

David Hume, *a Scot who lived from 1711 to 1776, did not call himself an economist. "Philosophy and general learning" is how he described the subject of his life's work. Hume was an extraordinary thinker and writer. Published in 1742, his* Essays, Moral and Political, *range across economics, political science, moral philosophy, history, literature, ethics, and religion and explore such topics as love, marriage, divorce, suicide, death, and the immortality of the soul!*

His economic essays provide astonishing insights into the forces that cause inflation, business cycle fluctuations, balance of payments deficits, and interest rate fluctuations; and they explain the effects of taxes and government deficits and debts.

Data were scarce in Hume's day, so he was not able to draw on detailed evidence to support his analysis. But he was empirical. He repeatedly appealed to experience and evidence as the ultimate judge of the validity of an argument. Hume's fundamentally empirical approach dominates macroeconomics today.

"... in every kingdom into which money begins to flow in greater abundance than formerly, everything takes a new face: labour and industry gain life; the merchant becomes more enterprising, the manufacturer more diligent and skillful, and even the farmer follows his plow with greater alacrity and attention."

DAVID HUME
Essays, Moral and Political

TALKING
WITH

Peter Howitt

Peter Howitt is Lyn Crost Professor of Social Sciences in the Department of Economics at Brown University. Born in 1946 in Toronto, he was an undergraduate at McGill University and a graduate student at Northwestern University. He began his research and teaching career at the University of Western Ontario in 1972, where he spent many productive years before moving to the United States in 1996. Professor Howitt is a past president of the Canadian Economics Association and is one of the world's leading macroeconomists. He has done research on all aspect of macroeconomics, with a focus in recent years on economic growth.

Michael Parkin and Robin Bade talked with Peter Howitt about his work and the major macroeconomic problems facing Canada today.

Peter, what attracted you to economics?

When I was in high school I had a part-time job as office boy with a small company that imported wool from around the world and sold it to textile mills in Ontario and Quebec. I was fascinated by the way wool prices went up and down all the time, and this curiosity led me to enroll in an honours economics course. My interests soon switched to macroeconomics, but I was always driven by curiosity to find out more about the workings of the human anthill.

You have made outstanding contributions to our understanding of all the major problems of macroeconomics, notably unemployment, economic growth, and inflation. Which of these issues do you believe is the most serious one for Canada today? Can they be separated?

Right now [November 2008], we are in the midst of a global financial crisis. I hope that the attempts by governments and central banks around the world to stabilize financial markets will succeed, but I fear the worst. The financial situation has led to a contraction of new credit and a drop in global aggregate demand. If aggregate demand continues to fall, as many are predicting, our biggest economic problem will soon be unemployment.

I am also concerned that long-term economic growth will be set back by the crisis. Financial markets are likely to remain in their current state for several years, and as long as they do, many of the investments, in plant and equipment and in research and development, that are needed for long-term economic growth will be choked off for lack of credit. In this sense the problems of unemployment and growth are closely linked. As for inflation, I am confident that the Bank of Canada's inflation-targeting policy will probably keep it under control. I also think that inflation-targeting will help to dampen the downturn of aggregate demand and thus to mitigate the potential problems of unemployment and economic growth.

Of course, all of these problems are interrelated. Learning about all the interrelationships is one of the things that makes economics so interesting. Take the relationship between growth and unemployment, for example. If you take a short-run perspective, then these two variables would appear to be negatively related. If the economy grows faster, there will be more jobs, and better paying jobs, which will draw people out of unemployment. But in the long run it looks quite different. You can't maintain a high growth rate indefinitely by continuing to put idle people to work, because at some point you will have everyone in the economy working. Instead, to keep the economy growing at a high rate you have to keep finding ways to make people more productive. You get this from having technological progress, from innovations that improve the efficiency of production processes and that allow people to produce new goods that contribute to our material welfare in ways that previous generations never have imagined.

> ... industrial innovations that underlie economic growth in the long run usually come at a cost. This is what Schumpeter meant by the term "creative destruction."

Now the industrial innovations that underlie economic growth in the long run usually come at a cost. This is what Schumpeter meant by the term "creative destruction." For example, if I invent a new good this will create new jobs for people to produce the good, but it will also destroy the jobs of people who produce the goods that mine will replace. So an economy that is going through a period of rapid technological change is likely to have good growth prospects, but it may also have a high rate of unemployment. The people whose jobs are destroyed may eventually find even better jobs but it will take time, so there will be a lot of people in a temporary situation of unemployment. To make a long story short, even though a short burst of growth from one quarter to the next is likely to reduce the rate of unemployment, a sustained rise in the rate of growth from one decade to the next will create a rise in the rate of unemployment.

What does your research tell us about the main sources of Canada's persistently high unemployment rate during the 1980s and 1990s?

I think a lot of what has taken place in Canada is an example of the effects of creative destruction that I talked about. A lot of technological change destroys low-skill jobs, and also destroys the value of old skills. In particular, a lot of clerical and middle management jobs have been made redundant by computers. Computers open up new jobs for people able to master the technology, but a lot of people don't have the skills or the knowledge to profit from these opportunities.

This is a global phenomenon, not just limited to Canada. Computers are having a revolutionary effect on economic life all over the world. In the United States it hasn't appeared to produce much unemployment. Instead what you see is a growing gap between the wages of skilled and unskilled workers. In Canada that gap isn't as visible, largely because we have more generous minimum wages and unemployment insurance benefits, which means that a fall in the demand for low-skill workers shows up more in a rise in unemployment and less in a fall in their wages than in the United States.

Why did our economic growth rate slow during the 1980s?

The short answer is that no one knows. But I think the answer probably lies in the computer revolution that I have talked about. Ultimately I think this revolution is going to give us a higher growth rate. But we have to accumulate a lot of knowledge in order to profit from it. We have been going through a collective learning experience that has been enormously costly, and this has been a continual drag on productivity, even though in the end I expect it will greatly enhance productivity.

Also, I think we are underestimating growth rates nowadays. This is because we are investing a lot in knowledge—knowledge of how to harness the power of the computer and to exploit the opportunities that it presents. Investment in knowledge is like investment in machinery in that it entails the sacrifice of resources now in return for the promise of more income sometime in the future. But while the national income accountant measures investment in machines as part of the economy's output of final goods and services, investment in knowledge is just treated as wasted resources.

Was the pursuit of low inflation worthwhile? Have we now got too low an inflation rate?

I think the pursuit of low inflation was definitely worthwhile, although in retrospect we maybe should have been more patient. Inflation impairs one of the most useful devices in the economic system—the conventional measure of value. Now that we have almost eliminated inflation we have a much healthier economic system. I don't think we should go much further, however, because you may have to raise unemployment even higher in order to get inflation all the way down to zero, and once you have it down to 2 percent you have little more to gain by reducing it even further. Also, further reductions in inflation may impair the working of the labour market. That is, people whose real wages are falling for whatever reason may be more inclined to continue working if they can at least avoid having to submit to a nominal wage cut, but can instead take the real-wage cut through the back door of inflation. With 2 percent inflation there is still lots of room for this sort of real-wage flexibility, but with no inflation there is none at all.

Some economists say that the Bank of Canada can speed up the economic growth rate by forgetting about low inflation and keeping interest rates low. Others say the best hope for increasing the growth rate is low inflation. Who is right?

The first group is certainly now right, except perhaps in a very short-run sense. You can't sustain a high growth rate for long by printing more money. Before long you'll end up with a higher rate of inflation and even higher interest rates as lenders seek compensation for the fall in the value of money. A lot of recent econometric evidence has been produced by various writers studying the experience of different countries that

> ... one of the great things about economics is that you can be paid well for spending your time satisfying your curiosity.

shows over long periods of time that inflation and growth are negatively correlated. More inflation from one decade to the next is likely to produce a fall in the growth rate rather than a rise. The effect doesn't appear to be numerically very large, but even a small drop in the growth rate can have a significant depressing effect on the level of real income if sustained for a decade or two.

What advice would you give to a student who wants to become a professional economist today?

My first advice for anyone interested in doing economics is to give full reign to your curiosity. The greatest satisfaction that I have received as an economist has been from discovering things about how the world works, from seeing a little more clearly some of the complex interactions between the different parts of the economy. I can still remember the excitement I felt when I started to see how demand and supply work, and when I learned about the circular flow of economic activity and how it can be affected by saving and investment decisions. I am happy to say that this sense of excitement has never left me. Furthermore, one of the great things about economics is that you can be paid well for spending your time satisfying your curiosity. Satisfying your curiosity is enjoyable, but if you want to accomplish something you can't let yourself be satisfied easily. You have to keep asking questions, and trying to answer them. It's easy to think you have solved a problem when you haven't explored things deeply enough. The best way for a student to do this is to do lots of exercises, and to discuss what you are doing with others. The same applies throughout one's career.

22 ◆ Economic Growth

After studying this chapter, you will be able to

- Define and calculate the economic growth rate and explain the implications of sustained growth

- Describe the economic growth trends in Canada and other countries and regions

- Explain how population growth and labour productivity growth make potential GDP grow

- Explain and measure the sources of labour productivity growth

- Explain the theories of economic growth and policies designed to increase the growth rate

Real GDP *per person* in Canada tripled between 1958 and 2008. If you live in a dorm that was built during the 1960s, it is likely to have just two power outlets: one for a desk lamp and one for a bedside lamp. Today, with the help of a power bar (or two), your room bulges with a personal computer, television and DVD player, microwave, refrigerator, coffeemaker, and toaster—and the list goes on. What has brought about this growth in production, incomes, and living standards?

We see even greater economic growth in modern Asia. At the mouth of the Yangtze River in one of the world's great cities, Shanghai, people are creating businesses, investing in new technologies, developing local and global markets, and transforming their lives. Incomes have tripled in the short 13 years since 1995. Why are incomes in China growing so rapidly?

In this chapter, we study the forces that make real GDP grow, that make some countries grow faster than others, and that make growth rates sometimes slow down and sometimes speed up.

In *Reading Between the Lines* at the end of the chapter we return to the economic growth of China and see how it compares with that of the much richer United States.

The Basics of Economic Growth

Economic growth is a sustained expansion of production possibilities measured as the increase in real GDP over a given period. Rapid economic growth maintained over a number of years can transform a poor nation into a rich one. Such have been the stories of Hong Kong, South Korea, Taiwan, and some other Asian economies. Slow economic growth or the absence of growth can condemn a nation to devastating poverty. Such has been the fate of Sierra Leone, Somalia, Zambia, and much of the rest of Africa.

The goal of this chapter is to help you to understand why some economies expand rapidly and others stagnate. We'll begin by learning how to calculate the economic growth rate and by discovering the magic of sustained growth.

Calculating Growth Rates

We express the **economic growth rate** as the annual percentage change of real GDP. To calculate this growth rate, we use the formula:

$$\text{Real GDP growth rate} = \frac{\text{Real GDP in current year} - \text{Real GDP in previous year}}{\text{Real GDP in previous year}} \times 100.$$

For example, if real GDP in the current year is $11 trillion and if real GDP in the previous year was $10 trillion, then the economic growth rate is 10 percent.

The growth rate of real GDP tells us how rapidly the *total* economy is expanding. This measure is useful for telling us about potential changes in the balance of economic power among nations. But it does not tell us about changes in the standard of living.

The standard of living depends on **real GDP per person** (also called *per capita* real GDP), which is real GDP divided by the population. So the contribution of real GDP growth to the change in the standard of living depends on the growth rate of real GDP per person. We use the above formula to calculate this growth rate, replacing real GDP with real GDP per person.

Suppose, for example, that in the current year, when real GDP is $1,100 billion, the population is 20.2 million. Then real GDP per person is $1,100 billion divided by 20.2 million, which equals $54,455. And suppose that in the previous year, when real GDP was $1 billion, the population was 20 million. Then real GDP per person in that year was $1 billion divided by 20 million, which equals $50,000.

Use these two values of real GDP per person with the growth formula above to calculate the growth rate of real GDP per person. That is,

$$\text{Real GDP per person growth rate} = \frac{\$54,455 - \$50,000}{\$50,000} \times 100 = 8.9 \text{ percent.}$$

The growth rate of real GDP per person can also be calculated (approximately) by subtracting the population growth rate from the real GDP growth rate. In the example you've just worked through, the growth rate of real GDP is 10 percent. The population changes from 20 million to 20.2 million, so the population growth rate is 1 percent. The growth rate of real GDP per person is approximately equal to 10 percent minus 1 percent, which equals 9 percent.

Real GDP per person grows only if real GDP grows faster than the population grows. If the growth rate of the population exceeds the growth of real GDP, then real GDP per person falls.

The Magic of Sustained Growth

Sustained growth of real GDP per person can transform a poor society into a wealthy one. The reason is that economic growth is like compound interest.

Compound Interest   Suppose that you put $100 in the bank and earn 5 percent a year interest on it. After one year, you have $105. If you leave that $105 in the bank for another year, you earn 5 percent interest on the original $100 *and on the $5 interest that you earned last year*. You are now earning interest on interest! The next year, things get even better. Then you earn 5 percent on the original $100 and on the interest earned in the first year and the second year. You are even earning interest on the interest that you earned on the interest of the first year.

Your money in the bank is growing at a rate of 5 percent a year. Before too many years have passed, your initial deposit of $100 will have grown to $200. But after how many years?

The answer is provided by a formula called the **Rule of 70**, which states that the number of years it

FIGURE 22.1   The Rule of 70

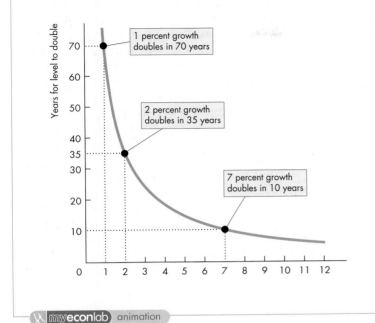

Growth rate (percent per year)	Years for level to double
1	70.0
2	35.0
3	23.3
4	17.5
5	14.0
6	11.7
7	10.0
8	8.8
9	7.8
10	7.0
11	6.4
12	5.8

The number of years it takes for the level of a variable to double is approximately 70 divided by the annual percentage growth rate of the variable.

 myeconlab animation

takes for the level of any variable to double is approximately 70 divided by the annual percentage growth rate of the variable. Using the Rule of 70, you can now calculate how many years it takes your $100 to become $200. It is 70 divided by 5, which is 14 years.

Applying the Rule of 70

The Rule of 70 applies to any variable, so it applies to real GDP per person. Figure 22.1 shows the doubling time for growth rates of 1 percent per year to 12 percent per year.

You can see that real GDP per person doubles in 70 years (70 divided by 1)—an average human life span—if the growth rate is 1 percent a year. It doubles in 35 years if the growth rate is 2 percent a year and in just 10 years if the growth rate is 7 percent a year.

We can use the Rule of 70 to answer other questions about economic growth. For example, in 2000, real GDP per person in the United States was approximately 8 times that of China. China's recent growth rate of real GDP per person was 7 percent a year. If this growth rate were maintained, how long would it take China's real GDP per person to reach that of the

United States in 2000? The answer, provided by the Rule of 70, is 30 years. China's real GDP per person doubles in 10 years (70 divided by 7). It doubles again to 4 times its current level in another 10 years. And it doubles yet again to 8 times its current level in another 10 years. So after 30 years of growth at 7 percent a year, China's real GDP per person is 8 times its current level and equals that of the United States in 2000. Of course, after 30 years, real GDP per person in the United States would have increased, so China would still not have caught up to the United States.

Review Quiz

1   What is economic growth and how do we calculate its rate?
2   What is the relationship between the growth rate of real GDP and the growth rate of real GDP per person?
3   Use the Rule of 70 to calculate the growth rate that leads to a doubling of real GDP per person in 20 years.

myeconlab   Work Study Plan 22.1 and get instant feedback.

◆ Economic Growth Trends

You have just seen the power of economic growth to increase incomes. At a 1 percent growth rate, it takes a human life span to double the standard of living. But at a 7 percent growth rate, the standard of living doubles every decade. How fast is our economy growing? How fast are other economies growing? Are poor countries catching up to rich ones, or do the gaps between the rich and poor persist or even widen? Let's answer these questions.

Growth in the Canadian Economy

Figure 22.2 shows real GDP *per person* in Canada for the 81 years from 1926 to 2007. The average growth rate over this period was 2.1 percent a year.

The earliest years in the graph are dominated by two extraordinary events: the Great Depression of the 1930s and World War II of the 1940s. The fall in real GDP during the depression and the bulge during the

war obscure the changes in the long-term growth trend that occurred within these years. Averaging out the depression and the war, the long-term growth rate was close to its 81-year average of 2.1 percent a year.

The 1950s had slow growth but then the growth rate increased and during the 1960s, it averaged 3.3 percent a year. During the 1970s, the growth slowed to 2.1 percent a year and in the 1980s it slowed to a crawl of 0.7 percent a year. After 1996, the growth rate increased again and for the 11 years between 1996 and 2007, the growth rate was back at its 81-year average.

A major goal of this chapter is to explain why our economy grows and why the long-term growth rate varies. Why did growth speed up during the 1960s, slow through the 1970s and 1980s, and then speed up again during the late 1990s? Another goal is to explain variations in the growth rates across countries.

Let's look at some facts about the growth rates of other nations and compare them with Canada's growth rate.

FIGURE 22.2 Economic Growth in Canada: 1926–2007

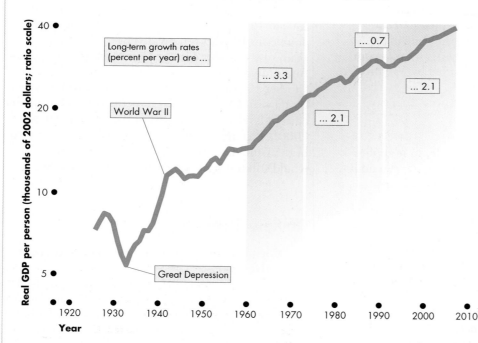

During the 81 years from 1926 to 2007, real GDP per person in Canada grew by 2.1 percent a year, on the average. Growth was the most rapid during the 1960s and slowest during the 1980s.

Sources of data: F.H. Leacy (ed.), *Historical Statistics of Canada*, 2nd ed., catalogue 11-516, series A1, F32, F55, Statistics Canada, Ottawa, 1983; and Statistics Canada, Tables 380-0002 and 051-0005.

myeconlab animation

Real GDP Growth in the World Economy

Figure 22.3 shows real GDP per person in Canada and in other countries between 1960 and 2008. Part (a) looks at the seven richest countries—known as the G7 nations. Among these nations, the United States has the highest real GDP per person. In 2008, Canada had the second-highest real GDP per person, ahead of Japan and France, Germany, Italy, and the United Kingdom (collectively the Europe Big 4).

During the 48 years shown here, the gaps between the United States, Canada, and the Europe Big 4 have been almost constant. But starting from a long way below, Japan grew fastest. It caught up to Europe in 1982 and to Canada in 1990. But during the 1990s, Japan's economy stagnated.

Many other countries are growing more slowly than, and falling farther behind, Canada. Figure 22.3(b) looks at some of these countries.

Real GDP per person in Central and South America was 34 percent of the Canadian level in 1960. It grew more quickly than Canada and reached 36 percent of the Canadian level by 1970. Growth slowed through 2004, then increased and by 2008, real GDP per person in these countries was 40 percent of the Canadian level.

In Central and Eastern Europe, real GDP per person has grown more slowly than anywhere except Africa, and has fallen from 32 percent of the Canadian level in 1980 to 26 percent in 2008.

Real GDP per person in Africa, the world's poorest continent, has fallen from 11 percent of the Canadian level in 1960 to 6 percent in 2008.

FIGURE 22.3 Economic Growth Around the World

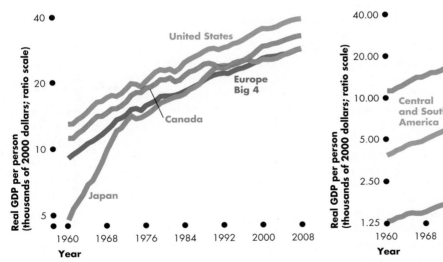

(a) Growth in the rich G7

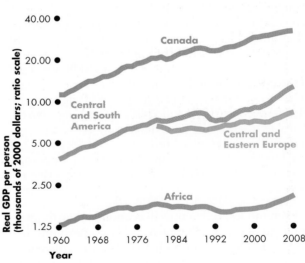

(b) Persistent gaps between rich and poor

Real GDP per person has grown throughout the world. Among the rich industrial countries in part (a), real GDP per person has grown slightly faster in the United States than in Canada and the four big countries of Europe (France, Germany, Italy, and the United Kingdom). Japan had the fastest growth rate before 1973 but then growth slowed and Japan's economy stagnated during the 1990s.

Part (b) shows real GDP per person in a wider range of countries. Central and South America was growing more quickly than Canada during the 1960s but slumped during the early 2000s before increasing again. Growth in Central and Eastern Europe and in Africa has been slower than in Canada, so the gaps between the real GDP per person in Canada and these countries have widened.

Sources of data: (1960–2004) Alan Heston, Robert Summers, and Bettina Aten, Penn World Table Version 6.2, Center for International Comparisons at the University of Pennsylvania (CICUP), September 2006; and (2005–2008) International Monetary Fund, *World Economic Outlook*, April 2008.

myeconlab animation

Catch-Up in Asia

Fast Trains on the Same Track

Five Asian economies, Hong Kong, Korea, Singapore, Taiwan, and China have experienced spectacular growth, which you can see in the figure. During the 1960s, real GDP per person in these economies ranged from 2.6 to 25 percent of that in Canada. But by 1993, real GDP per person in Singapore surpassed that of Canada. By 2005, real GDP per person in Hong Kong had overtaken that of Canada, and Taiwan and Korea were only a short distance behind.

The figure also shows that China is catching up but from a long way behind. China's real GDP per person increased from 2.6 percent of the Canadian level in 1960 to 15 percent in 2008.

The Asian economies shown here are like fast trains running on the same track at similar speeds and with a roughly constant gap between them. Singapore and Hong Kong are hooked together as the lead train, which runs about 15 years in front of Taiwan and Korea and about 40 years in front of the rest of China, which is the last train.

Real GDP per person in Korea in 2008 was similar to that in Hong Kong in 1988, and real GDP in China in 2008 was similar to that of Hong Kong in 1968. Between 1968 and 2008, Hong Kong transformed itself from a poor developing economy into one of the richest economies in the world.

The rest of China is now doing what Hong Kong has done. China has a population 200 times that of

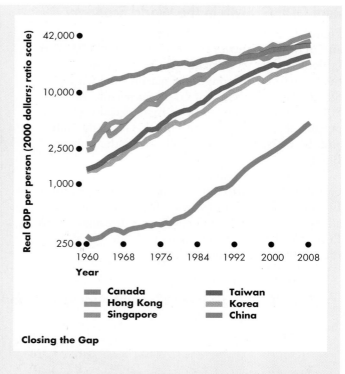

Closing the Gap

Hong Kong and more than 40 times that of Canada. So if China continues its rapid growth, the world economy will change dramatically.

As these fast-growing Asian economies catch up with Canada, we can expect their growth rates to slow. But it will be surprising if China's growth rate slows much before it has closed the gap on Canada (and the United States).

Even modest differences in economic growth rates sustained over a number of years bring enormous differences in the standard of living. And the differences that you've just seen are enormous. So the facts about economic growth in Canada and around the world raise some big questions.

What are the preconditions for economic growth? What sustains economic growth once it gets going? How can we identify the sources of economic growth and measure the contribution that each source makes? What can we do to increase the sustainable rate of economic growth?

We're now going to address these questions and discover the causes of economic growth. We start by seeing how potential GDP is determined and what makes it grow. We'll discover that labour productivity growth is the key to a rising living standard and go on to explore the sources of this growth.

Review Quiz

1 What has been the average growth rate of Canadian real GDP per person over the past 81 years? In which periods was growth the most rapid and in which periods was it the slowest?

2 Describe the gaps between real GDP per person across countries. For which countries is the gap narrowing? For which is it widening? And for which is it remaining the same?

3 Compare the growth rates and levels of real GDP per person in Hong Kong, Korea, Singapore, Taiwan, China, and Canada. How far is China's real GDP per person behind that of the other Asian economies?

 Work Study Plan 22.2 and get instant feedback.

How Potential GDP Grows

Economic growth occurs when real GDP increases. But a one-shot rise in real GDP or a recovery from recession isn't economic growth. Economic growth is a sustained, year-after-year increase in *potential GDP*.

We'll begin our study of the process of economic growth by looking at potential GDP. We'll see how it is determined and what forces make it grow.

How Potential GDP Is Determined

Labour, capital, land, and entrepreneurship produce real GDP, and the productivity of the factors of production determines the quantity of real GDP that can be produced.

The quantity of land is fixed and on any given day, the quantities of entrepreneurial ability and capital are also fixed and their productivities are given. The quantity of labour employed is the only *variable* factor of production. Potential GDP is the level of real GDP when the quantity of labour employed is the full-employment quantity.

To determine potential GDP, we use a model with two components:

- The aggregate production function
- The aggregate labour market

The Aggregate Production Function When you studied the limits to production in Chapter 2 (see p. 32), you learned that the *production possibilities frontier* is the boundary between the combinations of goods and services that can be produced and those that cannot. Let's think about the production possibilities frontier for two "goods": real GDP and the quantity of leisure time.

Think of real GDP as a number of big shopping carts. Each cart contains some of each kind of different goods and services produced, and one cartload of items costs $1 billion. To say that real GDP is $1,200 billion means that you can think of real GDP as 1,200 very big shopping carts of goods and services.

The quantity of leisure time is the number of hours spent not working. Each leisure hour could have been spent working. If we spent all our time taking leisure, we would do no work and produce nothing. Real GDP would be zero. The more leisure we forgo, the greater is the quantity of labour and the greater is the quantity of real GDP produced.

But labour hours are not all equally productive. We use our most productive hours first and as more hours are worked less and less productive hours are used. So for each additional hour of leisure forgone (each additional hour of labour), real GDP increases but by successively smaller amounts.

The **aggregate production function** is the relationship that tell us how real GDP changes as the quantity of labour changes when all other influences on production remain the same. Figure 22.4 shows this relationship—the curve labelled *PF*. An increase in the quantity of labour (and a corresponding decrease in leisure hours) brings a movement along the production function and an increase in real GDP.

The Aggregate Labour Market The aggregate labour market determines the quantity of labour hours employed and the quantity of real GDP supplied. To see how the labour market works, we need to study the demand for labour, the supply of labour, and labour market equilibrium.

The Demand for Labour The demand for labour is the relationship between the quantity of labour demanded and the real wage rate. The quantity of labour demanded is the number of labour hours hired by all the firms in the economy during a given period. This

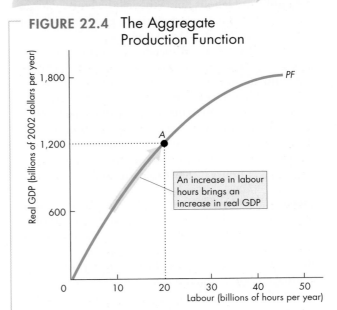

FIGURE 22.4 The Aggregate Production Function

At point *A* on the aggregate production function *PF*, 20 billion hours of labour produce $1,200 billion of real GDP.

myeconlab animation

quantity depends on the price of labour, which is the real wage rate.

The **real wage rate** is the money (or nominal) wage rate divided by the price level. The *real wage rate* is the quantity of goods and services that an hour of labour earns. It contrasts with the money wage rate, which is the number of dollars that an hour of labour earns.

The *real* wage rate influences the quantity of labour demanded because what matters to firms is not the number of dollars they pay (money wage rate) but how much output they must sell to earn those dollars.

The quantity of labour demanded *increases* as the real wage rate *decreases*—the demand for labour curve slopes downward. Why? The answer lies in the shape of the production function.

You've seen that along the production function, each additional hour of labour increases real GDP by successively smaller amounts. This tendency has a name: the *law of diminishing returns.* Because of diminishing returns, firms will hire more labour only if the real wage rate falls to match the fall in the extra output produced by that labour.

The Supply of Labour The *supply of labour* is the relationship between the quantity of labour supplied and the real wage rate. The quantity of labour supplied is the number of labour hours that all the households in the economy plan to work during a given period. This quantity depends on the real wage rate.

The *real* wage rate influences the quantity of labour supplied because what matters to households is not the number of dollars they earn (money wage rate) but what they can buy with those dollars.

The quantity of labour supplied *increases* as the real wage rate *increases*—the supply of labour curve slopes upward. At a higher real wage rate, more people choose to work and more people choose to work longer hours if they can earn more per hour.

Labour Market Equilibrium The price of labour is the real wage rate. The forces of supply and demand operate in labour markets just as they do in the markets for goods and services to eliminate a shortage or a surplus. But a shortage or a surplus of labour brings only a gradual change in the real wage rate. If there is a shortage of labour, the real wage rate rises to eliminate it; and if there is a surplus of labour, the real wage rate eventually falls to eliminate it. When there is neither a shortage nor a surplus, the labour market is in equilibrium—a full-employment equilibrium.

FIGURE 22.5 Labour Market Equilibrium

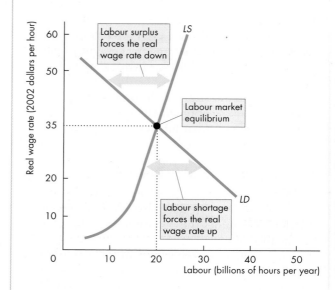

Labour market equilibrium occurs when the quantity of labour demanded equals the quantity of labour supplied. The equilibrium real wage rate is $35 an hour, and equilibrium employment is 20 billion hours per year.

At a wage rate above $35 an hour, there is a surplus of labour and the real wage rate falls to eliminate the surplus. At a wage rate below $35 an hour, there is a shortage of labour and the real wage rate rises to eliminate the shortage.

myeconlab animation

Figure 22.5 illustrates labour market equilibrium. The demand for labour curve is *LD* and the supply of labour curve *LS*. This labour market is in equilibrium at a real wage rate of $35 an hour and 20 billion hours a year are employed.

If the real wage rate exceeds $35 an hour, the quantity of labour supplied exceeds the quantity demanded and there is a surplus of labour. When there is a surplus of labour, the real wage rate falls towards the equilibrium real wage rate where the surplus is eliminated.

If the real wage rate is less than $35 an hour, the quantity of labour demanded exceeds the quantity supplied and there is a shortage of labour. When there is a shortage of labour, the real wage rate rises towards the equilibrium real wage rate where the shortage is eliminated.

If the real wage rate is $35 an hour, the quantity of labour demanded equals the quantity supplied and there is neither a shortage nor a surplus of labour. In this situation, there is no pressure in either direction on the real wage rate. So the real wage rate remains constant and the market is in equilibrium. At this equilibrium real wage rate and level of employment, the economy is at *full employment*.

Potential GDP You've seen that the production function tells us the quantity of real GDP that a given amount of labour can produce—see Fig. 22.4. The quantity of real GDP produced increases as the quantity of labour increases. At the equilibrium quantity of labour, the economy is at full employment, and the quantity of real GDP at full employment is potential GDP. So the full-employment quantity of labour produces potential GDP.

Figure 22.6 illustrates the determination of potential GDP. Part (a) shows labour market equilibrium. At the equilibrium real wage rate, equilibrium employment is 20 billion hours. Part(b) shows the production function. With 20 billion hours of labour, the economy can produce a real GDP of $1,200 billion. The amount is potential GDP.

What Makes Potential GDP Grow?

We can divide all the forces that make potential GDP grow into two categories:

- Growth of the supply of labour
- Growth of labour productivity

Growth of the Supply of Labour When the supply of labour grows, the supply of labour curve shifts rightward. The quantity of labour at a given real wage rate increases.

The quantity of labour is the number of workers employed multiplied by average hours per worker; and the number employed equals the employment-to-population ratio multiplied by the working-age population (see Chapter 21, p. 492). So the quantity of labour changes as a result of changes in

1. Average hours per worker
2. The employment-to-population ratio
3. The working-age population

Average hours per worker have decreased as the workweek has become shorter and the employment-to-population ratio has increased as more women have entered the labour force. The combined effects

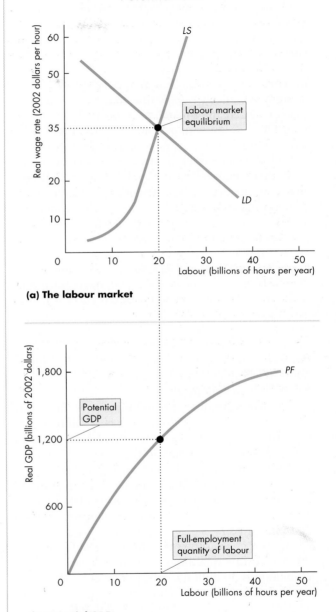

FIGURE 22.6 The Labour Market and Potential GDP

(a) The labour market

(b) Potential GDP

The economy is at full employment when the quantity of labour demanded equals the quantity of labour supplied, in part (a). The real wage rate is $35 an hour, and employment is 20 billion hours a year. Part (b) shows potential GDP. It is the quantity of real GDP determined by the production function at the full-employment quantity of labour.

of these two factors have kept average hours per working-age person (approximately) constant.

Growth in the supply of labour has come from growth in the working-age population. In the long run, the working-age population grows at the same rate as the total population.

The Effects of Population Growth Population growth brings growth in the supply of labour, but it does not change the demand for labour or the production function. The economy can produce more output by using more labour, but there is no change in the quantity of real GDP that a given quantity of labour can produce.

With an increase in the supply of labour and no change in the demand for labour, the real wage rate falls and the equilibrium quantity of labour increases. The increased quantity of labour produces more output and potential GDP increases.

Illustrating the Effects of Population Growth Figure 22.7 illustrates the effects of an increase in the population. In Fig. 22.7(a), the demand for labour curve is *LD* and initially the supply of labour curve is *LS₀*. The equilibrium real wage rate is $35 an hour and the quantity of labour is 20 billion hours a year. In Fig. 22.7(b), the production function (*PF*) shows that with 20 billion hours of labour employed, potential GDP is $1,200 billion at point *A*.

An increase in the population increases the supply of labour and the supply of labour curve shifts rightward to *LS₁*. At a real wage rate of $35 an hour, there is now a surplus of labour. So the real wage rate falls. In this example, the real wage rate will fall until it reaches $25 an hour. At $25 an hour, the quantity of labour demanded equals the quantity of labour supplied. The equilibrium quantity of labour increases to 30 billion a year.

Figure 22.7(b) shows the effect on real GDP. As the equilibrium quantity of labour increases from 20 billion to 30 billion hours, potential GDP increases along the production function from $1,200 billion to $1,500 billion at point *B*.

So an increase in the population increases the full-employment quantity of labour, increases potential GDP, and lowers the real wage rate. But the population increase *decreases* potential GDP per hour of labour. Initially, it was $60 ($1,200 billion divided by 20 billion). With the population increase, potential GDP per hour of labour is $50 ($1,500 billion divided by 30 billion). Diminishing returns are the source of the decrease in potential GDP per hour of labour.

FIGURE 22.7 The Effects of an Increase in Population

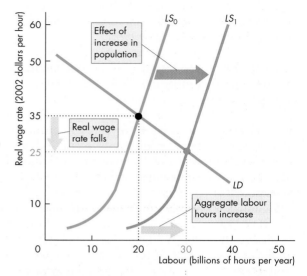

(a) The labour market

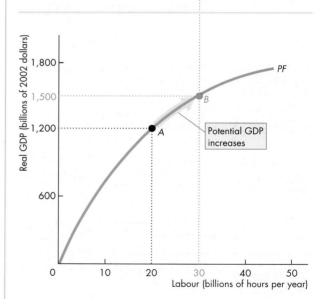

(b) Potential GDP

An increase in the population increases the supply of labour. In part (a), the supply of labour curve shifts rightward. The real wage rate falls and aggregate labour hours increase. In part (b), the increase in aggregate labour hours brings an increase in potential GDP. But diminishing returns bring a decrease in potential GDP per hour of labour.

Growth of Labour Productivity **Labour productivity** is the quantity of real GDP produced by an hour of labour. It is calculated by dividing real GDP by aggregate labour hours. For example, if real GDP is $1,200 billion and aggregate hours are 20 billion, labour productivity is $60 per hour.

When labour productivity grows, real GDP per person grows and brings a rising standard of living. Let's see how an increase in labour productivity changes potential GDP.

Effects of an Increase in Labour Productivity If labour productivity increases, production possibilities expand. The quantity of real GDP that any given quantity of labour can produce increases. If labour is more productive, firms are willing to pay more for a given number of hours of labour so the demand for labour also increases.

With an increase in the demand for labour and *no change in the supply of labour*, the real wage rate rises and the quantity of labour supplied increases. The equilibrium quantity of labour also increases.

So an increase in labour productivity increases potential GDP for two reasons: Labour is more productive and more labour is employed.

Illustrating the Effects of an Increase in Labour Productivity Figure 22.8 illustrates the effects of an increase in labour productivity.

In part (a), the production function initially is PF_0. With 20 billion hours of labour employed, potential GDP is $1,200 billion at point A.

In part (b), the demand for labour curve is LD_0 and the supply of labour curve is LS. The real wage rate is $35 an hour, and the equilibrium quantity of labour is 20 billion hours a year.

Now labour productivity increases. In Fig. 22.8(a), the increase in labour productivity shifts the production function upward to PF_1. At each quantity of labour, more real GDP can be produced. For example, at 20 billion hours, the economy can now produce $1,700 billion of real GDP at point B.

In Fig. 22.8(b), the increase in labour productivity increases the demand for labour and the demand for labour curve shifts rightward to LD_1. At the initial real wage rate of $35 an hour, there is now a shortage of labour. The real wage rate rises. In this example, the real wage rate will rise until it reaches $45 an hour. At $45 an hour, the quantity of labour demanded equals the quantity of labour supplied and the equilibrium quantity of labour is 22.5 billion a year.

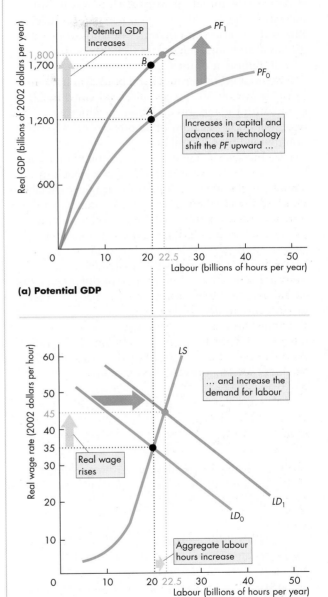

FIGURE 22.8 The Effects of an Increase in Labour Productivity

(a) Potential GDP

(b) The labour market

An increase in labour productivity shifts the production function upward from PF_0 to PF_1 in part (a) and shifts the demand for labour curve rightward from LD_0 to LD_1 in part (b). The real wage rate rises to $45 an hour, and aggregate labour hours increase to 22.5 billion. Potential GDP increases from $1,200 billion to $1,800 billion.

 animation

Figure 22.8(a) shows the effects of the increase in labour productivity on potential GDP. There are two effects. At the initial quantity of labour, real GDP increases to point *B* on the new production function. But as the equilibrium quantity of labour increases to 22.5 billion hours, potential GDP increases to $1,800 billion at point *C.*

Potential GDP per hour of labour also increases. Initially, it was $60 ($1,200 billion divided by 20 billion). With the increase in labour productivity, potential GDP per hour of labour is $80 ($1,800 billion divided by 22.5 billion).

The increase in aggregate labour hours that you have just seen is a consequence of an increase in labour productivity. This increase in aggregate labour hours and labour productivity is an example of the interaction effects that economists seek to identify in their search for the ultimate *causes* of economic growth. In the case that we've just studied, aggregate labour hours increase but that increase is a *consequence*, not a cause, of the growth of potential GDP. The source of the increase in potential GDP is an increase in labour productivity.

Labour productivity is the key to increasing output per hour of labour and rising living standards. But what brings an increase in labour productivity? The next section answers this question.

Review Quiz

1 What is the aggregate production function?
2 What determines the demand for labour, the supply of labour, and labour market equilibrium?
3 What determines potential GDP?
4 What are the two broad sources of potential GDP growth?
5 What are the effects of an increase in the population on potential GDP, the quantity of labour, the real wage rate, and potential GDP per hour of labour?
6 What are the effects of an increase in labour productivity on potential GDP, the quantity of labour, the real wage rate, and potential GDP per hour of labour?

 Work Study Plan 22.3 and get instant feedback.

Why Labour Productivity Grows

You've seen that labour productivity growth makes potential GDP grow; and you've seen that labour productivity growth is essential if real GDP per person and the standard of living are to grow. But *why* does labour productivity grow? What are the preconditions that make labour productivity growth possible and what are the forces that make it grow? Why does labour productivity grow faster at some times and in some places than others?

Preconditions for Labour Productivity Growth

The fundamental precondition for labour productivity growth is the *incentive* system created by firms, markets, property rights, and money. These four social institutions are the same as those described in Chapter 2 (see pp. 43–44) that enable people to gain by specializing and trading.

It was the presence of secure property rights in Britain in the middle 1700s that got the Industrial Revolution going, and it is their absence in some parts of Africa today that is keeping labour productivity stagnant.

With the preconditions for labour productivity growth in place, three things influence its pace:

■ Physical capital growth
■ Human capital growth
■ Technological advances

Physical Capital Growth

As the amount of capital per worker increases, labour productivity also increases. Production processes that use hand tools can create beautiful objects, but production methods that use large amounts of capital per worker are much more productive. The accumulation of capital on farms, in textile factories, in iron foundries and steel mills, in coal mines, on building sites, in chemical plants, in auto plants, in banks and insurance companies, and in shopping malls has added incredibly to labour productivity of our economy. The next time you see a movie that is set in the Old West or colonial times, look carefully at the small amount of capital around. Try to imagine how productive you would be in such circumstances compared with your productivity today.

Human Capital Growth

Human capital—the accumulated skill and knowledge of human beings—is the most fundamental source of labour productivity growth. Human capital grows when a new discovery is made and it grows when more and more people learn how to use past discoveries.

The development of one of the most basic human skills—writing—was the source of some of the earliest major gains in productivity. The ability to keep written records made it possible to reap ever-larger gains from specialization and trade. Imagine how hard it would be to do any kind of business if all the accounts, invoices, and agreements existed only in people's memories.

Later, the development of mathematics laid the foundation for the eventual extension of knowledge about physical forces and chemical and biological processes. This base of scientific knowledge was the foundation for the technological advances of the Industrial Revolution and of today's information revolution.

But a lot of human capital that is extremely productive is much more humble. It takes the form of millions of individuals learning and becoming remarkably more productive by repetitively doing simple production tasks. One much studied example of this type of human capital growth occurred in World War II. With no change in physical capital, thousands of workers and managers in U.S. shipyards learned from experience and accumulated human capital that more than doubled their productivity in less than two years.

Technological Advances

The accumulation of physical capital and human capital have made a large contribution to labour productivity growth. But technological change—the discovery and the application of new technologies—has made an even greater contribution.

Labour is many times more productive today than it was a hundred years ago but not because we have more steam engines and more horse-drawn carriages per person. Rather, it is because we have transportation equipment that uses technologies that were unknown a hundred years ago and that are more productive than the old technologies were.

Technological advance arises from formal research and development programs and from informal trial and error, and it involves discovering new ways of getting more out of our resources.

To reap the benefits of technological change, capital must increase. Some of the most powerful and far-reaching fundamental technologies are embodied in human capital—for example, language, writing, and mathematics. But most technologies are embodied in physical capital. For example, to reap the benefits of the internal combustion engine, millions of horse-drawn carriages had to be replaced with automobiles; and to reap the benefits of digital music, millions of Discmans had to be replaced by iPods.

Figure 22.9 summarizes the sources of labour productivity growth and more broadly of real GDP growth. The figure also emphasizes that for real GDP per person to grow, real GDP growth must exceed the population growth rate.

FIGURE 22.9 The Sources of Economic Growth

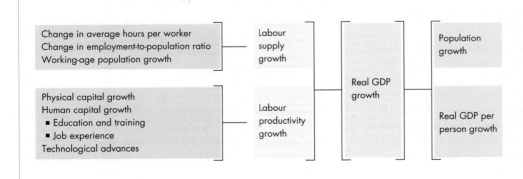

Labour supply growth and labour productivity growth combine to determine real GDP growth. Real GDP per person growth depends on real GDP growth and population growth.

Growth Accounting

The accumulation of physical capital and human capital and the discovery of new technologies bring increased labour productivity. But how much does each source of labour productivity growth contribute? Edward F. Denison, an economist at the Brookings Institution, provided the answer by developing **growth accounting**, a tool that calculates the quantitative contribution to labour productivity growth of each of its sources.

To make these calculations, we use information about the Canadian production function.

The Canadian Production Function Using data on capital, labour hours, and real GDP in Canada, economists at the Centre for the Study of Living Standards (CSLS) in Ottawa has estimated the effect of capital on labour productivity. They have discovered that on average, with no change in technology, a 1 percent increase in capital per hour of labour brings a 0.49 percent increase in labour productivity. We can use this rule to calculate the contributions of capital growth and technological change to the growth of labour productivity.

Suppose that capital per hour of labour grows by 3 percent a year and labour productivity grows by 2.5 percent a year. The 0.49 percent rule tells us that capital growth contributed 0.49 of 3 percent, which is 1.47 percent, to the growth of labour productivity. The rest of the 2.5 percent growth of labour productivity comes from technological change. That is, technological change contributed 1.03 percent, which is the 2.5 percent growth of labour productivity minus the estimated 1.47 percent contribution of capital growth.

Accounting for the Productivity Growth Slowdown and Speedup We can use Canada's production function to measure the contributions to Canadian productivity growth. Figure 22.10 shows the results for the years 1961 through 2007.

Between 1960 and 1973, labour productivity grew by 3 percent a year and capital growth contributed about one-third of this growth.

Between 1973 and 1985, labour productivity growth slowed to 1.5 percent a year and between 1985 and 1991, it slowed even more to 0.5 percent a year. A collapse of the contributions of technological change and human capital brought this slowdown. Technological change and capital accumulation didn't stop during the productivity growth slowdown, but its focus changed from increasing labour productivity

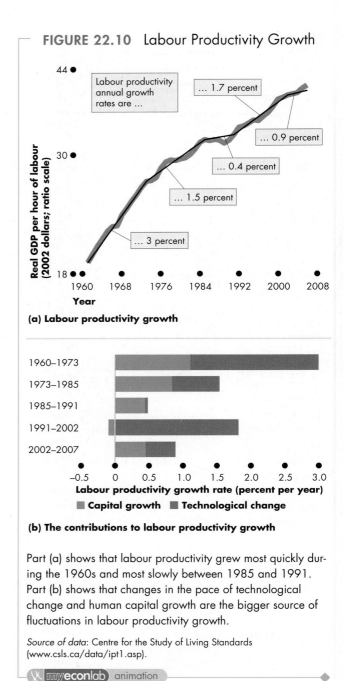

FIGURE 22.10 Labour Productivity Growth

(a) Labour productivity growth

(b) The contributions to labour productivity growth

Part (a) shows that labour productivity grew most quickly during the 1960s and most slowly between 1985 and 1991. Part (b) shows that changes in the pace of technological change and human capital growth are the bigger source of fluctuations in labour productivity growth.

Source of data: Centre for the Study of Living Standards (www.csls.ca/data/ipt1.asp).

myeconlab animation

to coping with energy price shocks and learning how to use the new information technologies.

Between 1991 and 2002, labour productivity growth sped to 2 percent a year and this growth came entirely from technological change. Finally, between 2002 and 2007, labour productivity growth slowed again.

Accounting for Faster Growth in Asia You saw earlier in this chapter that some Asian economies are growing at much faster rates than Canada and other rich economies. Growth accounting can be used to quantify the sources of this more rapid growth. We don't have enough data to replicate the calculations that we have made for Canada, but we can use the general idea to see why these economies grow so fast.

The fast-growing Asian economies are starting from a long way behind Canada. In many industries in these economies, the technologies in use are not the latest and most productive. As a result, just by adopting more productive technologies that have already been developed elsewhere, these economies can grow faster than the rich economies.

In some cases, a developing economy can leapfrog over technologies still in use in developed economies. Telecommunication is a striking example. Developing economies are bypassing old technology land lines and installing cell phone networks.

To benefit from new technologies, developing economies must invest in new capital. The scale of investment influences how fast the new technologies spread. Table 22.1 shows some numbers. Most of the fast-growing Asian economies invest a larger percentage of their incomes in new capital than Canada invests. Because they invest such a large percentage of income, capital per hour of labour increases more rapidly, and so does labour productivity.

TABLE 22.1 Investment in Seven Economies

Economy	Investment (percentage of GDP)
China	28
Hong Kong	26
Korea	36
Singapore	44
Taiwan	19
Canada	25
United States	21

Source of data: (1960–2004) Alan Heston, Robert Summers, and Bettina Aten, Penn World Table Version 6.2, Center for International Comparisons at the University of Pennsylvania (CICUP), September 2006.

Microloans Boost Growth

Women Are the Better Borrowers

Microloans are very small loans made to poor and unemployed potential entrepreneurs, who are often women. These people have no credit history that enables them to borrow from a bank.

Microloans originated in Bangladesh but have now spread throughout the developing world. They have become so successful that some regular banks are beginning to get into the business. These loans enable poor people to start a small business, employ a few people, and start to earn an income. As their incomes grow, they can pay off their microloans, and begin to save and accumulate more capital.

Kiva.org and MicroPlace.com (owned by eBay) are Web sites that enable people to lend money that is used to make microloans in developing economies.

Throughout the developing world, microloans are helping women to feed and cloth their families and to grow their small businesses, often in agriculture.

Review Quiz

1 What are the preconditions for and sources of labour productivity growth?
2 What is growth accounting and how is it used?
3 What brought about the slower labour productivity growth between 1973 and 1991?

 Work Study Plan 22.4 and get instant feedback

Canadian Economic Growth Since 1987

Productivity and Population Growth

We're going to look at the process that made Canadian real GDP grow between 1987 and 2007.

In 1987, employment was 29 billion labour hours, the real wage rate was $16.50 an hour, and real GDP and potential GDP were $933 billion. (We are measuring in 2002 dollars.)

By 2007, labour hours had increased to 32 billion, the real wage rate had risen to $21 an hour, and real GDP and potential GDP had increased to $1,320 billion (in 2002 dollars).

You can use the model that you've just studied to understand the process of growth that increased employment, the real wage rate, and potential GDP.

First, advances in technology and the investment in capital that brought us the Internet, the cell phone, MP3 audio, and MP4 video also brought us robots in factories and warehouses and more productive equipment in offices, shops, farms, and mines. As a result, labour productivity increased. The Centre for the Study of Living Standards estimates that the increase in labour productivity was 23 percent. These same advances in technology and growth of capital increased the demand for labour.

Second, the population grew. In 1987, the working-age population was 20.3 million. By 2007, that number was 26.6 million—a 31 percent increase. This increase in the working-age population increased the supply of labour.

Although the percentage increase in labour productivity was smaller than the percentage increase in population, labour demand is more responsive to the real wage rate than labour supply and the combined effects of these changes increased employment and potential GDP and raised the real wage rate.

The figures illustrate these outcomes. Figure 1 shows the Canadian production function in 1987 as PF_{1987}. Figure 2 shows the demand for labour in 1987 as LD_{1987} and the supply of labour as LS_{1987}. In 1987, the equilibrium real wage rate was $16.50 an hour, and 29 billion hours of labour were employed. On the production function PF_{1987}, this equilibrium quantity of labour produced a potential GDP of $933 billion.

By 2007, advances in technology and capital accumulation had increased labour productivity, which shifted the production function upward to PF_{2007} and shifted the demand for labour curve to LD_{2007}. The increase in the working-age population had increased

the supply of labour and shifted the supply of labour curve to LS_{2007}.

At the 2007 full-employment equilibrium, the real wage rate had increased to $21 an hour, employment had increased to 32 billion hours, and potential GDP had increased to $1,320 billion.

The process described here is the source of rising living standards in Canada.

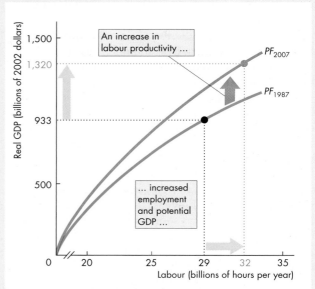

Figure 1 Canadian Production Function

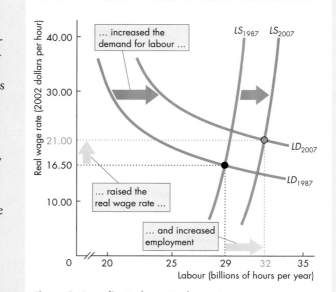

Figure 2 Canadian Labour Market

◆ Growth Theories and Policies

You've seen how population growth and labour productivity growth make potential GDP grow. You've also seen that the growth of physical capital and human capital and technological advances make labour productivity grow. How do all these factors interact? Growth theory addresses this question.

You're going to study three theories of economic growth, each of which gives some insights into the process of economic growth. But none provides a complete and definite answer to the basic questions: What causes economic growth and why do growth rates vary? Economics has some way to go before it can provide a definite answer to these questions. We study the three theories of growth:

- Classical growth theory
- Neoclassical growth theory
- New growth theory

Classical Growth Theory

Classical growth theory is the view that the growth of real GDP per person is temporary and that when it rises above the subsistence level, a population explosion eventually brings it back to the subsistence level. Adam Smith, Thomas Robert Malthus, and David Ricardo—the leading economists of the late eighteenth century and early nineteenth century—proposed this theory, but the view is most closely associated with the name of Malthus and is sometimes called the *Malthusian theory*.

Modern-Day Malthusians Many people today are Malthusians. They say that if today's global population of 6.7 billion explodes to 11 billion by 2050 and perhaps to 35 billion by 2300, we will run out of resources, real GDP per person will decline, and we will return to a primitive standard of living. We must act, say the Malthusians, to contain the population growth.

Modern-day Malthusians also point to global warming and climate change as reasons to believe that eventually, real GDP per person will decrease. Doomsday conditions, they believe, will arise as a direct consequence of today's economic growth and the vast and growing amounts of activity that are increasing the amount of carbon dioxide in Earth's atmosphere.

Classical Theory of Population Growth When the classical economists were developing their ideas about population growth, an unprecedented population explosion was under way. In Britain and other Western European countries, improvements in diet and hygiene had lowered the death rate while the birth rate remained high. For several decades, population growth was extremely rapid. After being stable for several centuries, the population of Britain increased by 40 percent between 1750 and 1800 and by a further 50 percent between 1800 and 1830. Meanwhile, an estimated 1 million people (about 20 percent of the 1750 population) left Britain for America and Australia before 1800, and outward migration continued on a similar scale through the nineteenth century. These facts are the empirical basis for the classical theory of population growth.

To explain the high rate of population growth, the classical economists used the idea of a **subsistence real wage rate**, which is the minimum real wage rate needed to maintain life. If the actual real wage rate is less than the subsistence real wage rate, some people cannot survive and the population decreases. In classical theory, when the real wage rate exceeds the subsistence real wage rate, the population grows. But an increasing population brings diminishing returns to labour, so labour productivity eventually decreases. This dismal implication led to economics being called the *dismal science*. The dismal implication is that no matter how much technological change occurs, the real wage rate is always pushed back towards the subsistence level.

The dismal conclusion of classical growth theory is a direct consequence of the assumption that the population explodes if real GDP per hour of labour exceeds the subsistence real wage rate. To avoid this conclusion, we need a different view of population growth. Neoclassical growth theory provides a different view.

Neoclassical Growth Theory

Neoclassical growth theory is the proposition that real GDP per person grows because technological change induces an amount of saving and investment that makes capital per hour of labour grow. Growth ends only if technological change stops. Robert Solow of MIT suggested the most popular version of neoclassical growth theory in the 1950s.

Neoclassical growth theory's break with its classical predecessor is its view about population growth.

The Neoclassical Economics of Population Growth

The population explosion of eighteenth century Europe that created the classical theory of population eventually ended. The birth rate fell, and while the population continued to increase, its rate of increase became moderate. This slowdown in population growth seemed to make the classical theory less relevant. It also eventually led to the development of a modern economic theory of population growth.

The modern view is that although the population growth rate is influenced by economic factors, the influence is not a simple and mechanical one like that proposed by the classical economists. Key among the economic influences on population growth is the opportunity cost of a woman's time. As women's wage rates increase and their job opportunities expand, the opportunity cost of having children increases. Faced with a higher opportunity cost, families choose to have fewer children and the birth rate falls.

A second economic influence works on the death rate. The technological advance that brings increased labour productivity and increased incomes brings advances in health care that extend lives.

These two opposing economic forces influence the population growth rate. As incomes increase, both the birth rate and the death rate decrease. It turns out that these opposing forces almost offset each other, so the rate of population growth is independent of the economic growth rate.

This modern view of population growth and the historical trends that support it contradict the views of the classical economists. They also call into question the modern doomsday conclusion that the planet will one day be swamped with more people than it can support. Neoclassical growth theory adopts this modern view of population growth. Forces other than real GDP and its growth rate determine population growth.

Technological Change

In neoclassical growth theory, the pace of technological change influences the economic growth rate but economic growth does not influence the pace of technological change. It is assumed that technological change results from chance. When we're lucky, we have rapid technological change, and when bad luck strikes, the pace of technological advance slows.

The Basic Neoclassical Idea

To understand neoclassical growth theory, imagine the world of the mid-1950s, when Robert Solow is explaining his idea.

Americans are enjoying post–World War II prosperity. Income per person is around $12,000 a year in today's money. The population is growing at about 1 percent a year. Saving and investment are about 18 percent of GDP, enough to keep the quantity of capital per hour of labour constant. Income per person is growing but not by much.

Then technology begins to advance at a more rapid pace across a range of activities. The transistor revolutionizes an emerging electronics industry. New plastics revolutionize the manufacture of household appliances. The interstate highway system revolutionizes road transportation. Jet airliners start to replace piston-engine airplanes and speed air transportation.

These technological advances bring new profit opportunities. Businesses expand, and new businesses are created to exploit the newly available profitable technologies. Investment and saving increase. The economy enjoys new levels of prosperity and growth. But will the prosperity last? And will the growth last? Neoclassical growth theory says that the *prosperity* will last but the *growth* will not last unless technology keeps advancing.

According to neoclassical growth theory, the prosperity will persist because there is no classical population growth to induce the wage rate to fall.

But growth will eventually stop if technology stops advancing, for two related reasons. First, the high profit rates that result from technological change bring increased saving and capital accumulation. But second, as more capital is accumulated, more and more projects are undertaken that have lower rates of return. The return on capital falls and the incentive to keep investing weakens. With weaker incentives to save and invest, saving decreases and the rate of capital accumulation slows.

A Problem with Neoclassical Growth Theory

All economies have access to the same technologies, and capital is free to roam the globe, seeking the highest available real interest rate. Given these facts, neoclassical growth theory implies that growth rates and income levels per person around the world will converge. While there is some sign of convergence among the rich countries, as Fig. 22.3(a) shows, convergence is slow, and it does not appear to be imminent for all countries, as Fig. 22.3(b) shows.

New growth theory overcomes this shortcoming of neoclassical growth theory. It also explains what determines the pace of technological change.

New Growth Theory

New growth theory holds that real GDP per person grows because of the choices people make in the pursuit of profit and that growth will persist indefinitely. Paul Romer of Stanford University developed this theory during the 1980s based on the ideas of Joseph Schumpeter during the 1930s and 1940s.

The theory begins with two facts about market economies:

- Discoveries result from choices.
- Discoveries bring profit, and competition destroys profit.

Discoveries and Choices When people discover a new product or technique, they think of themselves as being lucky. They are right. But the pace at which new discoveries are made—and at which technology advances—is not determined by chance. It depends on how many people are looking for a new technology and how intensively they are looking.

Discoveries and Profits Profit is the spur to technological change. The forces of competition squeeze profits, so to increase profit, people constantly seek either lower-cost methods of production or new and better products for which people are willing to pay a higher price. Inventors can maintain a profit for several years by taking out a patent or a copyright, but eventually, a new discovery is copied, and profits disappear.

Two further facts play a key role in the new growth theory:

- Discoveries are a public capital good.
- Knowledge is capital that is not subject to the law of diminishing returns.

Discoveries Are a Public Capital Good Economists call a good a *public good* when no one can be excluded from using it and when one person's use does not prevent others from using it. National defence is one example of a public good. Knowledge is another.

In 1992, Marc Andreesen and his friend Eric Bina developed a browser they called Mosaic. This browser laid the foundation for today's Web browsers that have increased productivity by an unimaginably large amount.

While patents and copyrights protect the inventors or creators of new products and production processes and enable them to profit from their innovative ideas, once a new discovery has been made, everyone can benefit from its use. And one person's use of a new discovery does not prevent others from using it. Your use of a Web browser doesn't prevent someone else from using that same code simultaneously.

Because knowledge is a public good, as the benefits of a new discovery spread, free resources become available. These resources are free because nothing is given up when they are used. They have a zero opportunity cost. Knowledge is even more special because it is not subject to diminishing returns.

Knowledge Capital Is Not Subject to Diminishing Returns Production is subject to diminishing returns when one resource is fixed and the quantity of another resource changes. Adding labour to a fixed amount of capital or adding capital to a fixed amount of labour both bring diminishing marginal product—diminishing returns.

But increasing the stock of knowledge makes both labour and machines more productive. Knowledge capital does not bring diminishing returns.

The fact that knowledge capital does *not* experience diminishing returns is the central novel proposition of new growth theory. And the implication of this simple and appealing idea is astonishing. Unlike the other two theories, new growth theory has no growth-stopping mechanism. As physical capital accumulates, the return to capital—the real interest rate—falls. But the incentive to innovate and earn a higher profit becomes stronger. So innovation occurs, capital becomes more productive, the demand for capital increases, and the real interest rate rises again.

Labour productivity grows indefinitely as people discover new technologies that yield a higher real interest rate. This growth rate depends on people's ability to innovate.

Over the years, the ability to innovate has changed. The invention of language and writing (the two most basic human capital tools) and later the development of the scientific method and the establishment of universities and research institutions brought huge increases in the pace of innovation. Today, a deeper understanding of genes is bringing profit in a growing biotechnology industry. And advances in computer technology are creating an explosion of profit opportunities in a wide range of information-age industries.

A Perpetual Motion Economy New growth theory sees the economy as a perpetual motion machine, which Fig. 22.11 illustrates.

No matter how rich we become, our wants will always exceed our ability to satisfy them. We will always want a higher standard of living. In the pursuit of a higher standard of living, human societies have developed incentive systems—markets, property rights, and money—that enable people to profit from innovation. Innovation leads to the development of new and better techniques of production and new and better products. To take advantage of new techniques and to produce new products, new firms start up and old firms go out of business—firms are born and die. As old firms die and new firms are born, some jobs are destroyed and others are created. The new jobs created are better than the old ones and they pay higher real wage rates. Also, with higher wage rates and more productive techniques, leisure increases. New and better jobs and new and better products lead to more consumption goods and

services and, combined with increased leisure, bring a higher standard of living.

But our insatiable wants are still there, so the process continues, going round and round a circle of wants, incentives, innovation, and new and better products, and a yet higher standard of living.

New Growth Theory Versus Malthusian Theory

The contrast between the Malthusian theory and new growth theory couldn't be more sharp. Malthusians see the end of prosperity as we know it today and new growth theorists see unending plenty. The contrast becomes clearest by thinking about the differing views about population growth.

To a Malthusian, population growth is part of the problem. To a new growth theorist, population growth is part of the solution. People are the ultimate economic resource. A larger population brings forth

---

FIGURE 22.11 A Perpetual Motion Machine

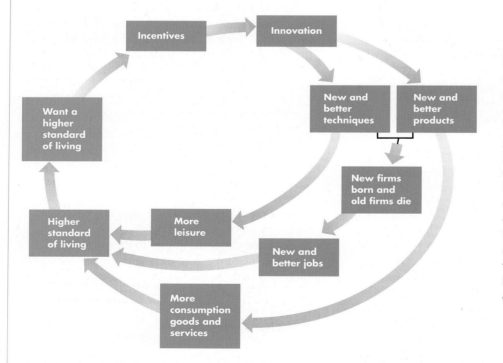

People want a higher standard of living and are spurred by profit incentives to make the innovations that lead to new and better techniques and new and better products. These new and better techniques and products, in turn, lead to the birth of new firms and the death of some old firms, new and better jobs, and more leisure and more consumption goods and services. The result is a higher standard of living. But people want a still higher standard of living, and the growth process continues.

Source: Based on a similar figure in *These Are the Good Old Days: A Report on U.S. Living Standards*, Federal Reserve Bank of Dallas 1993 Annual Report.

myeconlab animation

more wants, but it also brings a greater amount of scientific discovery and technological advance. So rather than being the source of falling real GDP per person, population growth generates faster labour productivity growth and rising real GDP per person. Resources are limited, but the human imagination and ability to increase productivity are unlimited.

Sorting Out the Theories

Which theory is correct? None of them tells us the whole story, but they all teach us something of value.

Classical growth theory reminds us that our physical resources are limited and that without advances in technology, we must eventually hit diminishing returns.

Neoclassical growth theory reaches the same conclusion but not because of a population explosion. Instead, it emphasizes diminishing returns to capital and reminds us that we cannot keep growth going just by accumulating physical capital. We must also advance technology and accumulate human capital. We must become more creative in our use of scarce resources.

New growth theory emphasizes the capacity of human resources to innovate at a pace that offsets diminishing returns. New growth theory fits the facts of today's world more closely than do either of the other two theories. But that doesn't make it correct.

Achieving Faster Growth

Growth theory tells us that to achieve faster economic growth, we must increase the growth rate of physical capital, the pace of technological advance, or the growth rate of human capital.

The main suggestions for achieving these objectives are

- Stimulate saving
- Stimulate research and development
- Encourage international trade
- Improve the quality of education

Stimulate Saving Saving finances investment, which brings capital accumulation. So stimulating saving can increase economic growth. The East Asian economies have the highest growth rates and the highest saving rates. Some African economies have the lowest growth rates and the lowest saving rates.

Tax incentives can increase saving. Registered Retirement Savings Plans (RRSPs) are a tax incentive to save. Economists claim that a tax on consumption rather than income provides the best saving incentive.

Stimulate Research and Development Everyone can use the fruits of *basic* research and development efforts. For example, all biotechnology firms can use advances in gene-splicing technology. Because basic inventions can be copied, the inventor's profit is limited and the market allocates too few resources to this activity.

Governments can direct public funds towards financing basic research, but this solution is not foolproof. It requires a mechanism for allocating the public funds to their highest-valued use. The National Science and Engineering Research Council is one possibly efficient channel for allocating public funds to universities to finance and stimulate basic research.

Encourage International Trade Free international trade stimulates growth by extracting all the available gains from specialization and trade. The fastest-growing nations today are those with the fastest-growing exports and imports.

Improve the Quality of Education The free market produces too little education because it brings benefits beyond those valued by the people who receive the education. By funding basic education and by ensuring high standards in basic skills such as language, mathematics, and science, governments can contribute to a nation's growth potential. Education can also be stimulated and improved by using tax incentives to encourage improved private provision.

Review Quiz

1 What is the key idea of classical growth theory that leads to the dismal outcome?
2 What, according to neoclassical growth theory, is the fundamental cause of economic growth?
3 What is the key proposition of new growth theory that makes economic growth persist?

myeconlab Work Study Plan 22.5 and get instant feedback.

To complete your study of economic growth, take a look at *Reading Between the Lines* on pp. 536–537 to see how economic growth is transforming the economy of China.

Economic Growth in China

China Industrial-Output Growth Is Slowest in 6 Years

September 12, 2008

China's industrial production grew at the slowest pace in six years on weaker export demand and factory shutdowns for the Olympics, increasing the likelihood the government will stimulate the economy.

Output rose 12.8 percent in August from a year earlier, the statistics bureau said today, after gaining 14.7 percent in July. That was less than the 14.5 percent median estimate of 22 economists surveyed by Bloomberg News. …

China's economic expansion slowed for a fourth quarter to 10.1 percent in the three months through June. Its growth remained the fastest of the world's 20 biggest economies. …

Power shortages are also restraining output. Aluminum Corp. of China Ltd. and 19 of its peers signed an accord in July to reduce production by as much as 10 percent until the end of the year to ease the shortages. Electricity output growth slowed in August for the fifth straight month to 5.1 percent. …

Still, the signs aren't all negative. Retail sales grew 23.2 percent last month, close to the fastest pace in nine years, the statistics bureau said today. While export growth slowed, the 21.1 percent increase was more than economists estimated.

Last month's industrial-output growth was the slowest since August 2002 after excluding the distortions in January and February each year caused by China's Lunar New Year holiday.

Essence of the Story

- China's industrial production grew by 12.8 percent in the year to August 2008, its slowest pace since 2002.

- China's real GDP growth slowed to 10.1 percent in the second quarter—the fourth successive quarter of slower growth.

- China's real GDP growth is the fastest of the world's 20 biggest economies.

- Power shortages limited production.

- Retail sales grew 23.2 percent in August 2008, close to the fastest pace in nine years.

- Export growth slowed to 21.1 percent.

Economic Analysis

- In 1978, under the leadership of Deng Xiaoping, China embarked on a program of economic reform.

- Gradually, state-owned monopolies were replaced by private competitive businesses, often financed with foreign capital and operated as joint ventures with foreign firms.

- By the early 1980s, China's real GDP was growing at one of the fastest rates in the world and the fastest ever known. We compare China's growth with that of the largest economy—the United States.

- In 2008, China's real GDP was more than $9 trillion (using U.S. dollars and PPP prices in 2000—see Chapter 20, p. 477).

- U.S. real GDP in 2008 was almost $12 trillion (2000 dollars).

- Although China's real GDP was not far behind U.S. real GDP in 2008, China used much more labour than the United States used.

- Aggregate labour hours in the United States in 2008 were about 250 billion.

- We don't know what China's aggregate labour hours were. But employment was 790 million and with an average workweek of 40 hours (an assumption), aggregate hours would be around 1,650 billion—more than 6 times the U.S. labour hours.

- So real GDP per hour of labour in China in 2008 was around $5 compared to about $48 in the United States.

- But China's real GDP is growing at about 10 percent a year. In contrast, U.S. real GDP is growing at about 2.5 percent a year.

- If these growth rates persist, China's real GDP will surpass that of the United States within the next decade.

- But China's real GDP per hour of labour will continue to lag well behind that of the United States.

- The figure shows the situation in China and the United States in 2008.

- The U.S. production function is PF_{US08}, and China's production function is PF_{C08}.

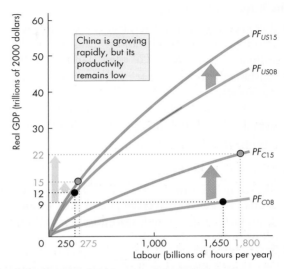

Figure 1 Growth in China and the United States

- With employment of 250 billion hours, the United States produces $12 trillion of real GDP, and with employment of 1,650 billion hours, China produces $9 trillion of real GDP.

- That is, an hour of labour in the United States produces around 10 times as much as an hour of labour in China produces.

- The figure also shows the situation in the United States and China in 2015 if current growth rates persist.

- The U.S. production function will be PF_{US15}, and China's production function will be PF_{C15}.

- With population growth at about 1 percent a year in both countries, labour hours will increase and so will real GDP.

- In 2015, China will be producing a larger real GDP than the United States but real GDP per hour of labour in China will still lag that in the United States.

SUMMARY ◆

Key Points

The Basics of Economic Growth (pp. 516–517)

- Economic growth is the sustained expansion of production possibilities and is measured as the annual percentage rate of change of real GDP.
- Sustained growth transforms poor nations into rich ones.
- The Rule of 70 tells us the number of years in which real GDP doubles—70 divided by the annual percentage growth rate.

Economic Growth Trends (pp. 518–520)

- Between 1926 and 2007, real GDP per person in Canada grew at an average rate of 2.1 percent a year. Growth was most rapid during the 1960s and slowest during the 1980s.
- Real GDP per person has grown slightly faster in the United States than in Canada and the four big countries of Europe.
- The gap in real GDP per person between Canada and Central and South America has narrowed. The gaps between Canada and Africa and Central Europe have widened.

How Potential GDP Grows (pp. 521–526)

- The aggregate production function and equilibrium in the aggregate labour market determine potential GDP.
- Potential GDP grows if the labour supply grows or if labour productivity grows.

- Only labour productivity growth makes real GDP per person and the standard of living grow.

Why Labour Productivity Grows (pp. 526–530)

- Labour productivity growth requires an incentive system created by firms, markets, property rights, and money.
- The sources of labour productivity growth are growth of physical capital and human capital and advances in technology.
- Growth accounting measures the contributions of capital accumulation and technological change to the growth of labour productivity.
- During the productivity growth slowdown of the 1970s, technological change did not stop growing but its focus changed to coping with energy price shocks and environmental protection.

Growth Theories and Policies (pp. 531–535)

- In classical theory, real GDP per person keeps returning to the subsistence level.
- In neoclassical growth theory, without further technological change, diminishing returns to capital bring economic growth to a halt.
- In new growth theory, economic growth persists indefinitely at a rate determined by decisions that lead to innovation and technological change.
- Policies for achieving faster growth include stimulating saving and research and development, encouraging international trade, and improving the quality of education.

Key Figures

Key Terms

PROBLEMS and APPLICATIONS

 Work problems 1–9 in Chapter 22 Study Plan and get instant feedback.
Work problems 10–18 as Homework, a Quiz, or a Test if assigned by your instructor.

1. Japan's real GDP was 561 trillion yen in 2007 and 569 trillion yen in 2008. Japan's population was 127.7 million in 2007 and 127.8 million in 2008. Calculate

   a. The economic growth rate.
   b. The growth rate of real GDP per person.
   c. The approximate number of years it takes for real GDP per person in Japan to double if the 2008 economic growth rate and population growth rate are maintained.

2. For three years, there was no technological change in Longland but capital per hour of labour increased from $10 to $20 to $30 and real GDP per hour of labour increased from $3.80 to $5.70 to $7.13. Then, in the fourth year, capital per hour of labour remained constant but real GDP per hour of labour increased to $10.

   a. Does Longland experience diminishing returns? Explain why or why not.
   b. In Longland, use growth accounting to calculate the effect on labour productivity of a 1 percent increase in capital.
   c. Explain how you would do the growth accounting for Longland and calculate the effect of technological change on growth in the fourth year described above.

3. If Canada cracks down on illegal immigrants and returns millions of workers to their home countries, explain what happens to

   a. Canadian potential GDP.
   b. Canadian employment.
   c. The real wage rate in Canada.

   In the countries to which the immigrants return, explain what happens to

   d. Potential GDP.
   e. Employment.
   f. The real wage rate.

4. In the economy of Cape Despair, the subsistence real wage rate is $15 an hour. Whenever real GDP per hour rises above $15, the population grows, and whenever real GDP per hour of labour falls below this level, the population falls. The table shows Cape Despair's production function:

Labour (billions of hours per year)	Real GDP (billions of 2002 dollars)
0.5	8
1.0	15
1.5	21
2.0	26
2.5	30
3.0	33
3.5	35

Initially, the population of Cape Despair is constant and real GDP per hour of labour is at the subsistence level of $15. Then a technological advance shifts the production function upward by 50 percent at each level of labour.

   a. What are the initial levels of real GDP and labour productivity?
   b. What happens to labour productivity immediately following the technological advance?
   c. What happens to the population growth rate following the technological advance?
   d. What are the eventual levels of real GDP and real GDP per hour of labour?

5. Explain the processes that will bring the growth of real GDP per person to a stop according to

   a. Classical growth theory.
   b. Neoclassical growth theory.
   c. New growth theory.

6. **U.S. Workers World's Most Productive**
   American workers stay longer in the office, at the factory, or on the farm than their counterparts in Europe and most other rich nations, and they produce more per person over the year. ... Productivity ... is found by dividing the country's gross domestic product by the number of people employed. ... Only part of the U.S. productivity growth ... can be explained by the longer hours Americans are putting in. ... [The U.S.] also beats all 27 nations in the European Union, Japan, and Switzerland in the amount of wealth created per hour of work. ... The U.S. employee put in an average 1,804 hours of work in 2006 ... compared with 1,407.1 hours for the Norwegian worker and 1,564.4 for the French. It pales,

however, in comparison with the annual hours worked per person in Asia, where seven economies—South Korea, Bangladesh, Sri Lanka, Hong Kong, China, Malaysia and Thailand—surpassed 2,200 average hours per worker. But those countries had lower productivity rates. ...

CBS News, September 3, 2007

a. What is the difference between productivity in this article and per capita real GDP?
b. Identify and correct a confusion between levels and growth rates of productivity in the news article.
c. If workers in developing Asian economies work more hours than Americans, why are they not the world's most productive?

7. **You Have Seven Years to Learn Mandarin**
A recent study by the economist Angus Maddison projects that China will become the world's dominant economic superpower ... in 2015. ... If that happens, America will close out a 125-year run as the No. 1 economy. [The United States] assumed the title in 1890. ... China was the largest economy for centuries because everyone had the same type of economy —subsistence—and so the country with the most people would be economically biggest. Then the Industrial Revolution sent the West on a more prosperous path. Now the world is returning to a common economy, this time technology- and information-based, so once again population triumphs.

Fortune, May 12, 2008

a. Why was China the world's largest economy until 1890?
b. Why did the United States surpass China in 1890 to become the world's largest economy?
c. Explain why China is predicted to become the world's largest economy again.
d. When China becomes the world's largest economy, does that mean that the standard of living in China will be higher than that in the United States? Explain.

8. **Dodge's Successor Too Optimistic About Globalization**
Mark Carney, our new governor of the Bank of Canada, chose to use his first speech to extol the benefits of globalization, as well as to highlight some of the challenges ... "While it is true that

this [globalization] adjustment process can be, and has been, difficult for certain individuals and firms, the overall picture is quite positive," he said, suggesting that Canada, with flexible labour markets, has made it possible for workers to re-skill or retrain and, on balance, "find more productive employment" ... Carney's prescription focuses on promoting "flexibility," especially in labour markets, by helping workers to relocate, maintaining social safety nets that don't discourage employment, and investing in lifelong learning and retraining. But while investing in education and skills for lifelong learning is important, it will take more than this to prepare Canada for the next wave of globalization. Canada urgently needs ... increased public and private investment in research and development, more spending on infrastructure including high-speed broadband, more public-private risk-sharing to commercialize new knowledge and more incentives for entrepreneurial growth companies or gazelles.

Toronto Star, February 24, 2008

a. Explain which growth theory most closely describes the arguments made in this article.
b. Explain the suggestions in this article that can help Canada achieve faster economic growth.

9. **Aptera: Road Runner**
Steve Fambro was sick of people whizzing past him in the carpool lane, so he ... set out to design a three-wheeled vehicle—technically a motorcycle—that would make it legal for him to drive alone in that lane and be cozy enough for daily commuting. While researching designs, he realized something important about fuel efficiency: It's all about aerodynamics. By tearing up the rule book, he found a shape that would nearly eliminate wind resistance, thereby reducing by two thirds the energy needed to move a car. With ... $20 million from Idealab ... Fambro's company, Aptera, is scheduled to begin production later this year. The vehicle gets an average of 300 miles per gallon. ... Priced at around $30,000, Aptera's cars are already sold out.

Fortune, April 28, 2008

a. Explain which growth theory best describes the news article.
b. Use the model explained in this chapter to illustrate your answer in a.

10. If China's real GDP grows at 9 percent a year, its population grows at 1 percent a year, and these growth rates continue, in what year will China's real GDP per person be twice its 2008 level?

11. If a large increase in investment increases labour productivity, explain what will happen to

a. Potential GDP.
b. Employment.
c. The real wage rate.

If a severe drought decreases labour productivity, explain what will happen to

d. Potential GDP.
e. Employment.
f. The real wage rate.

12. **The New New World Order**

"If you're a consumer sitting in Paris and you're ... watching TV, it looks like the world is coming to an end," says [international grocery store chain] Carrefour executive David Shriver. "But consumers in places like China and Brazil simply don't see it that way." Welcome to the new, precariously bipolar world. While gross domestic product growth is cooling a bit in emerging markets, the results are still tremendous compared with the U.S. and much of Western Europe. The 54 developing markets surveyed by Global Insight will post a 6.7% jump in real GDP this year, down from 7.5% last year. The 31 developed countries will grow an estimated 1.6%. The difference in growth rates represents the largest spread between developed and developing markets in the 37-year history of the survey.

Fortune, July 14, 2008

a. Explain the "bipolar world" that is revealed by recent economic growth rates.
b. Do growth rates over the past few decades indicate that gaps in per capita real GDP around the world are shrinking, growing, or staying the same? Explain.

13. **Underinvesting in the Future**

South Korea, Hong Kong, Taiwan, and Singapore have over 40 years averaged roughly the highest consistent economic growth rates in the world. ... But change the national accounting principles behind these rosy numbers and a different picture emerges, one that the societies concerned have barely begun to grapple with. In one vital respect these countries (soon to be joined by China) collectively may have the worst record of

investment in the future since homo sapiens evolved: Investment in the next generation. They have the lowest fertility rates in the world. ... Economists forget that people as well as buildings depreciate at a roughly predictable rate. Child-rearing is at least as essential as building roads. Imagine if these four economies had invested less in infrastructure and ... more in people. ... They would not be facing a situation in which their workforces—unless replaced by immigrants—will decline dramatically within 20 years as the population over 65 continues to grow. The payback for years of what may well have been the misallocation of resources is not far in the future.

International Herald Tribune, July 7, 2008

a. Explain why the rapid growth rates of these Asian economies might be masking a "misallocation of resources" that will result in lower income per person in the future.
b. Explain the difficulties in balancing goals for immediate economic growth and future economic growth.

14. **India's Economy Hits the Wall**

Just six months ago, India was looking good. Annual growth was 9%, corporate profits were surging 20%, the stock market had risen 50% in 2007, consumer demand was huge, local companies were making ambitious international acquisitions, and foreign investment was growing. Nothing, it seemed, could stop the forward march of this Asian nation. But stop it has. ... The country is reeling from 11.4% inflation, large government deficits, and rising interest rates. Foreign investment in India's stock market is fleeing, the rupee is falling, and the stock market is down over 40% from the year's highs. Most economic forecasts expect growth to slow to 7%—a big drop for a country that needs to accelerate growth, not reduce it. ... India needs urgently to spend $500 billion on new infrastructure and more on upgrading education and health-care facilities. ... A plan to build 30 Special Economic Zones is virtually suspended because New Delhi has not sorted out how to acquire the necessary land, a major issue in both urban and rural India, without a major social and political upheaval. Agriculture [is] ... technologically laggard ... [and] woefully unproductive. Simple and non-political reforms, like strengthening the legal system and adding more judges, have been ignored. ... A June 16 report by Goldman Sachs' Jim O'Neill and Tushar Poddar ... urges India to improve governance, raise educational achievement, and control inflation. It also advises reining in profligate expenditures, liberalizing its financial markets, increasing agricultural productivity, and improving infrastructure, the environment, and energy use.

Business Week, July 1, 2008

Explain five potential sources for faster economic growth in India suggested in this news clip.

15. **Makani Power: A Mighty Wind**

Makani Power aims to generate energy from what are known as high-altitude wind-extraction technologies. And that's about all its 34-year-old Aussie founder, Saul Griffith, wants to say about it. ... But Makani can't hide entirely, not when its marquee investor is Google.org, the tech company's philanthropic arm. Makani's plan is to capture that high-altitude wind ... with a very old tool: kites. Harnessing higher-altitude wind, at least in theory, has greater potential than the existing wind industry ... a thousand feet above ground, wind is stronger and more consistent.

Fortune, April 28, 2008

Explain which growth theory best describes the news article.

16. **Canadians Win Japan's Kyoto Prize**

Two Canadians have been honoured with Japan's equivalent of the Nobel Prize. Toronto-based biologist Anthony Pawson ... was picked in the basic sciences for research that deepened understanding of how cells communicate. [Pawson's] discoveries have spurred progress in a wide range of biomedical research and the development of anti-cancer drugs. ... American computer scientist Richard Karp ... was also honoured. He won the prize in advanced technology for his work in measuring how difficult certain computational problems are to solve—a fundamental step in designing computer algorithms. ... Each received a gold medal and 50 million yen, worth about US$500,000. ... Founded in 1985, the Kyoto Prize is given to people for their contribution in the scientific, cultural and spiritual betterment of humankind.

Toronto Star, November 10, 2008

a. Explain how the Kyoto Prize helps fuel the perpetual motion economic growth machine.
b. How does Japan benefit from awarding researchers in other countries?

17. **Make Way for India—The Next China**

... China ... [is] growing at around 9 percent a year. ... [China's] one-child policy will start to reduce the size of China's working population within the next 10 years. India, by contrast, will have an increasing working population for another generation at least.

The Independent, March 1, 2006

a. Given the expected population changes, do you think China or India will have the greater economic growth rate? Why?
b. Would China's growth rate remain at 9 percent a year without the restriction on its population growth rate?
c. India's population growth rate is 1.6 percent a year, and in 2005 its economic growth rate was 8 percent a year. China's population growth rate is 0.6 percent a year, and in 2005 its economic growth rate was 9 percent a year. In what year will real GDP per person double in each country?

18. After studying *Reading Between the Lines* on pp. 536–537, answer the following questions:

a. What was the growth rate of real GDP in China in the year ending in August 2008?
b. Is real GDP per hour of labour in China growing because labour productivity is increasing or only because the population is increasing? How would you determine the contribution of each factor?
c. With the population growth in both countries at about 1 percent a year, is China narrowing the gap in real GDP per person between China and the United States?
d. At the current rate of convergence in c, how long will it take for real GDP per person in China to equal that in the United States?

19. Use the link on MyEconLab (Chapter Resources, Chapter 22, Web links) to obtain data on real GDP per person for the United States, China, South Africa, and Mexico since 1960.

a. Draw a graph of the data.
b. Which country has the lowest real GDP per person and which has the highest?
c. Which country has experienced the fastest growth rate since 1960 and which the slowest?
d. Explain why the growth rates in these four countries are ranked in the order you have discovered.

23

Finance, Saving, and Investment

After studying this chapter, you will be able to

- Describe the financial markets and financial institutions and the flows of funds that finance investment
- Explain how investment and saving decisions and borrowing and lending decisions are made and how these decisions interact in the market for loanable funds
- Explain how a government deficit (or surplus) influences the real interest rate, saving, and investment in the market for loanable funds
- Explain how international borrowing or lending influences the real interest rate, saving, and investment in the global market for loanable funds

During normal times, financial markets play their quiet unseen role of funnelling funds from savers and lenders to investors and borrowers. But 2008 was not a normal time. Beginning in August 2007 and running through 2008, global financial markets were in crisis. The epicentre of the crisis was a collapse of house prices in the United States and a crash in the values of securities held by banks and other institutions that finance house purchases. Banks around the world took big losses and venerable Wall Street investment banks Bear Stearns and Lehman Brothers disappeared.

The strains spread to Canada and all the big Canadian banks sustained heavy losses. But the crisis was less severe here than in the United States and Europe.

This chapter explains how financial markets work and their place in the economy. We look mainly at the normal functioning of these markets. But at various points in the chapter and in *Reading Between the Lines* at the end of the chapter, we examine the unusual and fearful events of the 2008 financial crisis.

◆ Financial Institutions and Financial Markets

The financial institutions and markets that we study in this chapter play a crucial role in the economy. They provide the channels through which saving flows to finance the investment in new capital that makes the economy grow.

In studying the economics of financial institutions and markets, we distinguish between

- Finance and money
- Physical capital and financial capital

Finance and Money

In economics, we use the term *finance* to describe the activity of providing the funds that finance expenditures on capital. The study of finance looks at how households and firms obtain and use financial resources and how they cope with the risks that arise in this activity.

Money is what we use to pay for goods and services and factors of production and to make financial transactions. The study of money looks at how households and firms use it, how much of it they hold, how banks create and manage it, and how its quantity influences the economy.

In the economic lives of individuals and businesses, finance and money are closely interrelated. And some of the main financial institutions, such as banks, provide both financial services and monetary services. Nevertheless, by distinguishing between *finance* and *money* and studying them separately, we will better understand our financial and monetary markets and institutions.

For the rest of this chapter, we study finance. Money is the topic of the next chapter.

Physical Capital and Financial Capital

Economists distinguish between physical capital and financial capital. *Physical capital* is the tools, instruments, machines, buildings, and other items that have been produced in the past and that are used today to produce goods and services. Inventories of raw materials, semifinished goods, and components are part of physical capital. When economists use the term capital, they mean *physical* capital. The funds that firms use to buy physical capital are called **financial capital**.

Along the *aggregate production function* in Chapter 22, the quantity of capital is fixed. An increase in the quantity of capital increases production possibilities and shifts the aggregate production function upward. You're going to see, in this chapter, how investment, saving, borrowing, and lending decisions influence the quantity of capital and make it grow, and as a consequence, make real GDP grow.

We begin by describing the links between capital and investment and between wealth and saving.

Capital and Investment

The quantity of capital changes because of investment and depreciation. *Investment* (Chapter 20, p. 470) increases the quantity of capital and *depreciation* (Chapter 20, p. 470) decreases it. The total amount spent on new capital is called **gross investment**. The change in the value of capital is called **net investment**. Net investment equals gross investment minus depreciation.

Figure 23.1 illustrates these terms. On January 1, 2008, Ace Bottling Inc. had machines worth $30,000—Ace's initial capital. During 2008, the market value of Ace's machines fell by 67 percent— $20,000. After this depreciation, Ace's machines were valued at $10,000. During 2008, Ace spent $30,000 on new machines. This amount is Ace's gross investment. By December 31, 2008, Ace Bottling had capital valued at $40,000, so its capital had increased by $10,000. This amount is Ace's net investment. Ace's net investment equals its gross investment of $30,000 minus depreciation of its initial capital of $20,000.

Wealth and Saving

Wealth is the value of all the things that people own. What people own is related to what they earn, but it is not the same thing. People earn an *income*, which is the amount they receive during a given time period from supplying the services of the resources they own. **Saving** is the amount of income that is not paid in taxes or spent on consumption goods and services. Saving increases wealth. Wealth also increases when the market value of assets rises— called *capital gains*—and decreases when the market value of assets falls—called *capital losses*.

For example, at the end of the school year you have $250 in the bank and a coin collection worth

FIGURE 23.1 Capital and Investment

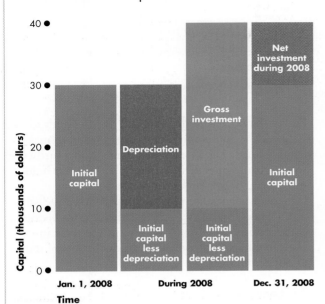

On January 1, 2008, Ace Bottling had capital worth $30,000. During the year, the value of Ace's capital fell by $20,000—depreciation—and Ace spent $30,000 on new capital—gross investment. Ace's net investment was $10,000 ($30,000 gross investment minus $20,000 depreciation) so at the end of 2008, Ace had capital worth $40,000.

myeconlab animation

$300, so your wealth is $550. During the summer, you earn $5,000 (net of taxes) and spend $1,000 on consumption goods and services, so your saving is $4,000. Your bank account increases to $4,250 and your wealth becomes $4,550. The $4,000 increase in wealth equals saving. If coins rise in value and your coin collection is now worth $500, you have a capital gain of $200, which is also added to your wealth.

National wealth and national saving work like this personal example. The wealth of a nation at the end of a year equals its wealth at the start of the year plus its saving during the year, which equals income minus consumption expenditure.

To make real GDP grow, saving and wealth must be transformed into investment and capital. This transformation takes place in the markets for financial capital and through the activities of financial institutions. We're now going to describe these markets and institutions.

Markets for Financial Capital

Saving is the source of the funds that are used to finance investment, and these funds are supplied and demanded in three types of financial markets:

- Loan markets
- Bond markets
- Stock markets

Loan Markets Businesses often want short-term finance to buy inventories or to extend credit to their customers. Sometimes they get this finance in the form of a loan from a bank. Households often want finance to purchase big-ticket items, such as automobiles or household furnishings and appliances. They get this finance as bank loans, often in the form of outstanding credit card balances.

Households also get finance to buy new homes. (Expenditure on new homes is counted as part of investment.) These funds are usually obtained as a loan that is secured by a **mortgage**—a legal contract that gives ownership of a home to the lender in the event that the borrower fails to meet the agreed loan payments (repayments and interest). Mortgage loans were at the centre of the 2007–2008 U.S. credit crisis that engulfed the global economy.

All of these types of financing take place in loan markets.

Bond Markets When Bombardier expands its airplane production plant, it gets the finance it needs by selling bonds. Governments—federal, provincial, and municipal—also raise finance by issuing bonds.

A **bond** is a promise to make specified payments on specified dates. For example, you can buy a Bombardier bond that promises to pay $7.35 every year and then to make a final payment of $100 in December 2026.

The buyer of a bond from Bombardier makes a loan to the company and is entitled to the payments promised by the bond. When a person buys a newly issued bond, he or she may hold the bond until the borrower has repaid the amount borrowed or sell it to someone else. Bonds issued by firms and governments are traded in the **bond market**.

The term of a bond might be long (decades) or short (just a month or two). Firms often issue very short-term bonds as a way of getting paid for their sales before the buyer is able to pay. For example, when Bombardier sells $100 million of airplanes to

Air Canada, Bombardier wants to be paid when the items are shipped. But Air Canada doesn't want to pay until the airplanes are earning an income. In this situation, Air Canada might promise to pay Bombardier $101 million three months in the future. TD Bank might be willing to buy this promise for (say) $100 million. Bombardier gets $100 million immediately and the bank gets $101 million in three months when Air Canada honours its promise. The government of Canada issues promises of this type, called Treasury bills.

Another type of bond is a **mortgage-backed security**, which entitles its holder to the income from a package of mortgages. Mortgage lenders create mortgage-backed securities. They make mortgage loans to home buyers and then create securities that they sell to obtain more funds to make more mortgage loans. The holder of a mortgage-backed security is entitled to receive payments that derive from the payments received by the mortgage lender from the home buyer–borrower.

Mortgage-backed securities were at the centre of the storm in the financial markets in 2007–2008.

Stock Markets When Petro-Canada wants finance to expand its oilsands operation in Alberta, it might issue stock. A **stock** is a certificate of ownership and claim to the firm's profits. Petro-Canada has issued 484 million shares of its stock. So if you owned 484 Petro-Canada shares, you would own one-millionth of the company and be entitled to receive one-millionth of its profits.

Unlike a stockholder, a bondholder does not own part of the firm that issued the bond.

A **stock market** is a financial market in which shares of stocks of corporations are traded. The Toronto Stock Exchange, the New York Stock Exchange, and the London Stock Exchange (in England) are all examples of stock markets.

Financial Institutions

Financial markets are highly competitive because of the role played by financial institutions in those markets. A **financial institution** is a firm that operates on both sides of the markets for financial capital. It is a borrower in one market and a lender in another.

Financial institutions also stand ready to trade so that households with funds to lend and firms or households seeking funds can always find someone on the other side of the market with whom to trade.

The key Canadian financial institutions are

- Banks
- Trust and loan companies
- Credit unions and caisses populaires
- Pension funds
- Insurance companies

Banks Banks accept deposits and use the funds to buy government bonds and other securities and to make loans. Canada has 14 domestic banks, and a further 33 foreign banks operate in Canada. These banks hold more than 70 percent of the total assets of the Canadian financial services sector. Economists distinguish banks from other financial institutions because bank deposits are money. We'll return to these institutions in Chapter 24, where we study the role of money in our economy.

Trust and Loan Companies Trust and loan companies provide similar services to banks and the largest of them are owned by banks. They accept deposits and make personal loans and mortgage loans. They also administer estates, trusts, and pension plans.

Credit Unions and Caisses Populaires Credit unions and caisses populaires are banks that are owned and controlled by their depositors and borrowers, are regulated by provincial rules, and operate only inside their own provincial boundaries. These institutions are large in number but small in size.

Pension Funds Pension funds are financial institutions that receive the pension contributions of firms and workers. They use these funds to buy a diversified portfolio of bonds and stocks that they expect to generate an income that balances risk and return. The income is used to pay pension benefits.

Some pension funds invest in mortgage-backed securities of the type that collapsed in value during the 2008 financial crisis.

Pension funds can be very large and play an active role in the firms whose stock they hold.

Insurance Companies Insurance companies provide risk-sharing services. They enter into agreements with households and firms to provide compensation in the event of accident, theft, fire, ill-health, and a host of other misfortunes. They receive premiums from their customers and make payments against claims.

Financial Failures

The Institutions at the Centre of the Storm

Bear Stearns: absorbed by JPMorgan Chase with help from the U.S. Federal Reserve. Lehman Brothers: gone. Fannie Mae and Freddie Mac: taken into government oversight with U.S. taxpayer guarantees. Merrill Lynch: absorbed by Bank of America. AIG: given an $85 billion lifeline by the Federal Reserve and sold off in parcels to financial institutions around the world. Wachovia: taken over by Citigroup. Washington Mutual: taken over by JPMorgan. Morgan Stanley: 20 percent bought by Mitsubishi, a large Japanese bank. These are some of the events in the financial crisis of 2008. What was going on?

Between 2002 and 2005, mortgage lending exploded and home prices rose. Mortgage lenders bundled their loans into *mortgage-backed securities* and sold them to eager buyers around the world.

In 2006, interest rates began to rise and the values of financial assets fell. With lower asset values, financial institutions took big losses. Some losses of some institutions were too big to bear and these institutions became insolvent.

Insurance companies use the funds they have received but not paid out as claims to buy bonds and stocks on which they earn an interest income.

Some insurance companies also insure corporate bonds and other risky financial assets. They provide insurance that pays out if a firm fails and cannot meet its bond obligations. Some insurance companies insure other insurers in a complex network of reinsurance.

In normal times, insurance companies have a steady flow of funds coming in from premiums and interest on the financial assets they hold and a steady, but smaller, flow of funds paying claims. Their profit is the gap between the two flows. But in unusual times, when large and widespread losses are being incurred, insurance companies can run into difficulty in meeting their obligations. Such a situation arose in 2008 for one of the world's biggest insurers, AIG, and the firm was taken into public ownership.

Canadian insurance companies have very large international operations and earn 70 percent of their income outside Canada.

All financial institutions face risk and this risk poses two problems: a solvency problem and a liquidity problem.

Solvency and Liquidity

A financial institution's **net worth** is the total market value of what it has lent minus the market value of what it has borrowed. If net worth is positive, the institution is *solvent* and can remain in business. But if net worth is negative, the institution is *insolvent* and goes out of business. The owners of an insolvent financial institution—usually its stockholders—bear the loss when the assets are sold and debts paid.

A financial institution both borrows and lends, so it is exposed to the risk that its net worth might become negative. To limit that risk, financial institutions are regulated and a minimum amount of their lending must be backed by their net worth.

Sometimes a financial institution is solvent but illiquid. A firm is *illiquid* if it has made long-term loans with borrowed funds and is faced with a sudden demand to repay more of what it has borrowed than its available cash. In normal times, a financial institution that is illiquid can borrow from another institution. But if all financial institutions are short of cash, the market for loans among financial institutions dries up.

Insolvency and illiquidity were at the core of the financial meltdown of 2007–2008.

Interest Rates and Asset Prices

Stocks, bonds, short-term securities, and loans are collectively called *financial assets*. The interest rate on a financial asset is the interest received expressed as a percentage of the price of the asset.

Because the interest rate is a percentage of the price of an asset, if the asset price rises, other things remaining the same, the interest rate falls. Conversely, if the asset price falls, other things remaining the same, the interest rate rises.

To see this inverse relationship between an asset price and the interest rate, look at the example of a Petro-Canada share. In November 2008, the price of a Petro-Canada share was $20 and each share entitled its owner to 80 cents of Petro-Canada profit. The interest rate on a Petro-Canada share was

Interest rate = ($0.80 ÷ $20) × 100 = 4 percent.

If the price of a Petro-Canada share increased to $40 and each share still entitled its owner to 80 cents of Petro-Canada profit, the interest rate on a Petro-Canada share would become

Interest rate = ($0.80 ÷ $40) × 100 = 2 percent.

This relationship means that the price of an asset and the interest rate on that asset are determined simultaneously—one implies the other.

This relationship also means that if the interest rate on the asset rises, the price of the asset falls, debts become harder to pay, and the net worth of the financial institution falls. Insolvency can arise from previously unexpected large rises in the interest rate.

In the next part of this chapter, we learn how interest rates and asset prices are determined in the financial markets.

Review Quiz

1 Distinguish between physical capital and financial capital and give two examples of each.
2 What is the distinction between gross investment and net investment?
3 What are the three main types of markets for financial capital?
4 Explain the connection between the price of a financial asset and its interest rate.

 Work Study Plan 23.1 and get instant feedback.

The Market for Loanable Funds

In macroeconomics, we group all the financial markets that we described in the previous section into a single market for loanable funds. The **market for loanable funds** is the aggregate of all the individual financial markets.

The circular flow model of Chapter 20 (see p. 469) can be extended to include flows in the market for loanable funds that finance investment.

Funds that Finance Investment

Figure 23.2 shows the flows of funds that finance investment. They come from three sources:

1. Household saving
2. Government budget surplus
3. Borrowing from the rest of the world

Households' income, Y, is spent on consumption goods and services, C, saved, S, or paid in net taxes, T. **Net taxes** are the taxes paid to governments minus the cash transfers received from governments (such as social insurance and unemployment benefits). So income is equal to the sum of consumption expenditure, saving, and net taxes:

$$Y = C + S + T.$$

You saw in Chapter 20 (p. 470) that Y also equals the sum of the items of aggregate expenditure: consumption expenditure, C, investment, I, government expenditure, G, and exports, X, minus imports, M. That is,

$$Y = C + I + G + X - M.$$

By using these two equations, you can see that

$$I + G + X = M + S + T.$$

Subtract G and X from both sides of the last equation to obtain

$$I = S + (T - G) + (M - X).$$

This equation tells us the investment, I, is financed by household saving, S, the government budget surplus, $(T - G)$, and borrowing from the rest of the world, $(M - X)$.

A government budget surplus $(T > G)$ contributes funds to finance investment, but a government budget deficit $(T < G)$, competes with investment for funds.

FIGURE 23.2   Financial Flows and the Circular Flow of Expenditure and Income

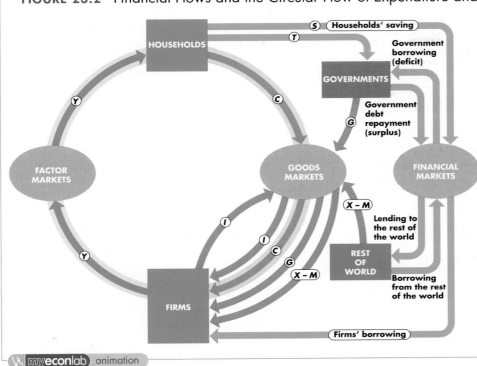

Households use their income for consumption expenditure (C), saving (S), and net taxes (T). Firms borrow to finance their investment expenditure. Governments borrow to finance a budget deficit or repay debt if they have a budget surplus. The rest of the world borrows to finance its deficit or lends its surplus.

myeconlab animation

If we export less than we import, we borrow (M – X) from the rest of the world to finance some of our investment. If we export more than we import, we lend (X – M) to the rest of the world and part of Canadian saving finances investment in other countries.

The sum of private saving, S, and government saving, (T – G), is called **national saving**. National saving and foreign borrowing finance investment.

In 2008, Canadian investment was $304 billion and lending to the rest of the world (positive net exports) was $32 billion. This total of $336 billion was financed by private saving of $296 billion and a government (federal, provincial, and local combined) budget surplus of $40 billion.

You're going to see how investment and saving and the flows of loanable funds—all measured in constant 2002 dollars—are determined. The price in the market for loanable funds that achieves equilibrium is an interest rate, which we also measure in real terms as the *real* interest rate. In the market for loanable funds, there is just one interest rate, which is an average of the interest rates on all the different types of financial securities that we described earlier. Let's see what we mean by the real interest rate.

The Real Interest Rate

The **nominal interest rate** is the number of dollars that a borrower pays and a lender receives in interest in a year expressed as a percentage of the number of dollars borrowed and lent. For example, if the annual interest paid on a $500 loan is $25, the nominal interest rate is 5 percent per year ($25 ÷ $500 × 100).

The **real interest rate** is the nominal interest rate adjusted to remove the effects of inflation on the buying power of money. The real interest rate is approximately equal to the nominal interest rate minus the inflation rate.

You can see why if you suppose that you have put $500 in a savings account that earns 5 percent a year. At the end of a year, you have $525 in your savings account. Suppose that the inflation rate is 2 percent per year—during the year, all prices increased by 2 percent. You need $510 to buy what a year earlier cost $500. So you can buy $15 more worth of goods and services than you could have bought a year earlier. You've earned goods and services worth $15, which is a real interest rate of 3 percent a year. And the bank has paid a real interest rate of 3 percent a year. So the real interest rate is the 5 percent nominal interest rate minus the 2 percent inflation rate.[1]

The real interest rate is the opportunity cost of loanable funds. The real interest *paid* on borrowed funds is the opportunity cost of borrowing. And the real interest rate *forgone* when funds are used either to buy consumption goods and services or to invest in new capital goods is the opportunity cost of not saving or not lending those funds.

We're now going to see how the loanable funds market determines the real interest rate, the quantity of funds loaned, saving, and investment. In the rest of this section, we will ignore the government and the rest of the world and focus on households and firms in the market for loanable funds. We will study

- The demand for loanable funds
- The supply of loanable funds
- Equilibrium in the market for loanable funds

The Demand for Loanable Funds

The *quantity of loanable funds demanded* is the total quantity of funds demanded to finance investment, the government budget deficit, and international investment or lending during a given period. Our focus here is on investment. We'll bring the other two items into the picture in later sections of this chapter.

What determines investment and the demand for loanable funds to finance it? Many details influence this decision, but we can summarize them in two factors:

1. The real interest rate
2. Expected profit

Firms invest in capital only if they expect to earn a profit, and fewer projects are profitable at a high real interest rate than at a low real interest rate, so

Other things remaining the same, the higher the real interest rate, the smaller is the quantity of loanable funds demanded; and the lower the real interest rate, the greater is the quantity of loanable funds demanded.

_____
[1]The *exact* real interest rate formula, which allows for the change in the purchasing power of both the interest and the loan, is Real interest rate = (Nominal interest rate − Inflation rate) ÷ (1 + Inflation rate/100). If the nominal interest rate is 5 percent a year and the inflation rate is 2 percent a year, the real interest rate is (5 − 2) ÷ (1 + 0.02) = 2.94 percent a year.

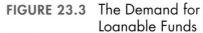

FIGURE 23.3 The Demand for Loanable Funds

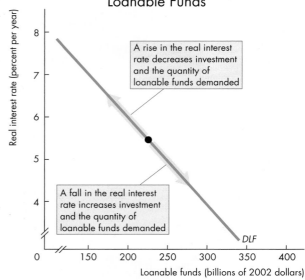

A rise in the real interest rate decreases investment and the quantity of loanable funds demanded

A fall in the real interest rate increases investment and the quantity of loanable funds demanded

A change in the real interest rate changes the quantity of loanable funds demanded and brings a movement along the demand curve.

Demand for Loanable Funds Curve The **demand for loanable funds** is the relationship between the quantity of loanable funds demanded and the real interest rate, when all other influences on borrowing plans remain the same. The demand curve *DLF* in Fig. 23.3 is a demand for loanable funds curve.

To understand the demand for loanable funds, think about Bell Canada's decision to borrow $100 million to buy some new phone mail servers. If Bell expects to get a return of $5 million a year from this investment before paying interest costs and the interest rate is less than 5 percent a year, Bell would make a profit, so it buys the servers. But if the interest rate is more than 5 percent a year, Bell would incur a loss, so it doesn't buy the servers. The quantity of loanable funds demanded is greater, the lower is the real interest rate.

Changes in the Demand for Loanable Funds When the expected profit changes, the demand for loanable funds changes. Other things remaining the same, the greater the expected profit from new capital, the greater is the amount of investment and the greater is the demand for loanable funds.

Expected profit rises during a business cycle expansion and falls during a recession; rises when technological change creates profitable new products; rises as a growing population brings increased demand for goods and services; and fluctuates with contagious swings of optimism and pessimism, called "animal spirits" by Keynes and "irrational exuberance" by Alan Greenspan.

When expected profit changes, the demand for loanable funds curve shifts.

The Supply of Loanable Funds

The *quantity of loanable funds supplied* is the total funds available from private saving, a government budget surplus, and international borrowing during a given period. Our focus here is on saving. We'll bring the other two items into the picture later.

How do you decide how much of your income to save and supply in the market for loanable funds? Your decision is influenced by many factors, but chief among them are

1. The real interest rate
2. Disposable income
3. Expected future income
4. Wealth
5. Default risk

We begin by focusing on the real interest rate.

Other things remaining the same, the higher the real interest rate, the greater is the quantity of loanable funds supplied; and the lower the real interest rate, the smaller is the quantity of loanable funds supplied.

The Supply of Loanable Funds Curve The **supply of loanable funds** is the relationship between the quantity of loanable funds supplied and the real interest rate when all other influences on lending plans remain the same. The curve *SLF* in Fig. 23.4 is a supply of loanable funds curve.

Think about a student's decision to save some of what she earns from her summer job. With a real interest rate of 2 percent a year, she decides that it is not worth saving much—better to spend the income and take a student loan if funds run out during the semester. But if the real interest rate jumped to 10 percent a year, the payoff from saving would be high enough to encourage her to cut back on spending and increase the amount she saves.

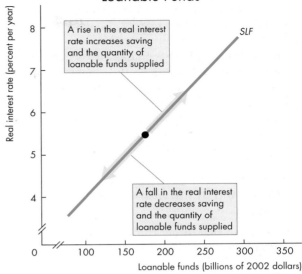

FIGURE 23.4 The Supply of Loanable Funds

A rise in the real interest rate increases saving and the quantity of loanable funds supplied

A fall in the real interest rate decreases saving and the quantity of loanable funds supplied

A change in the real interest rate changes the quantity of loanable funds supplied and brings a movement along the supply curve.

myeconlab animation

Changes in the Supply of Loanable Funds A change in disposable income, expected future income, wealth, or default risk changes the supply of loanable funds.

Disposable Income A household's *disposable income* is the income earned minus net taxes. When disposable income increases, other things remaining the same, consumption expenditure increases but by less than the increase in income. Some of the increase in income is saved. So the greater a household's disposable income, other things remaining the same, the greater is its saving.

Expected Future Income The higher a household's expected future income, other things remaining the same, the smaller is its saving today.

Wealth The higher a household's wealth, other things remaining the same, the smaller is its saving. If a person's wealth increases because of a capital gain, the person sees less need to save. For example, from 2002 to 2006, when house prices were rising at more than 10 percent a year, wealth increased despite the fact that personal saving dropped to less than 34 percent.

Default Risk Default risk is the risk that a loan will not be repaid. The greater that risk, the higher is the interest rate needed to induce a person to lend and the smaller is the supply of loanable funds.

Shifts of the Supply of Loanable Funds Curve When any of the four influences on the supply of loanable funds changes, the supply of loanable funds changes and the supply curve shifts. An increase in disposable income, a decrease in expected future income, a decrease in wealth, or a fall in default risk increases the supply of loanable funds.

Equilibrium in the Market for Loanable Funds

You've seen that, other things remaining the same, the higher the real interest rate, the greater is the quantity of loanable funds supplied and the smaller is the quantity of loanable funds demanded. There is one real interest rate at which the quantities of loanable funds demanded and supplied are equal, and that interest rate is the equilibrium real interest rate.

Figure 23.5 shows how the demand for and supply of loanable funds determine the real interest rate. The *DLF* curve is the demand curve and the *SLF* curve is the supply curve. If the real interest rate exceeds 6 percent a year, the quantity of loanable funds supplied exceeds the quantity demanded. Borrowers find it easy to get funds, but lenders are unable to lend all the funds they have available. The real interest rate falls until the quantity of funds supplied equals quantity of funds demanded.

If the real interest rate is less than 6 percent a year, the quantity of loanable funds supplied is less than the quantity demanded. Borrowers can't get the funds they want, but lenders are able to lend all the funds they have available. So the real interest rate rises and continues to rise until the quantity of funds supplied equals the quantity demanded.

Regardless of whether there is a surplus or a shortage of loanable funds, the real interest rate changes and is pulled towards an equilibrium level. In Fig. 23.5, the equilibrium real interest rate is 6 percent a year. At this interest rate, there is neither a surplus nor a shortage of loanable funds. Borrowers can get the funds they want, and lenders can lend all the funds they have available. The investment plans of borrowers and the saving plans of lenders are consistent with each other.

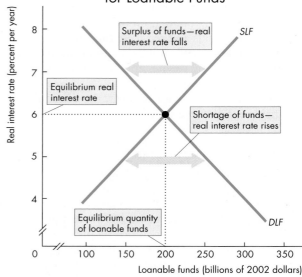

FIGURE 23.5 Equilibrium in the Market for Loanable Funds

A surplus of funds lowers the real interest rate and a shortage of funds raises it. At a real interest rate of 6 percent a year, the quantity of funds demanded equals the quantity supplied and the market is in equilibrium.

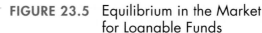

Changes in Demand and Supply

Financial markets are highly volatile in the short run but remarkably stable in the long run. Volatility in the market comes from fluctuations in either the demand for loanable funds or the supply of loanable funds. These fluctuations bring fluctuations in the real interest rate and in the equilibrium quantity of funds lent and borrowed. They also bring fluctuations in asset prices.

Here we'll illustrate the effects of *increases* in demand and supply in the market for loanable funds.

An Increase in Demand If the profits that firms expect to earn increase, firms increase their planned investment and increase their demand for loanable funds to finance that investment. With an increase in the demand for loanable funds, but no change in the supply of loanable funds, there is a shortage of funds. As borrowers compete for funds, the interest rate rises and lenders increase the quantity of funds supplied.

Figure 23.6(a) illustrates these changes. An increase in the demand for loanable funds shifts the demand curve rightward from DLF_0 to DLF_1. With

FIGURE 23.6   Changes in Demand and Supply

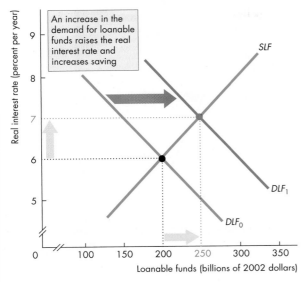

An increase in the demand for loanable funds raises the real interest rate and increases saving

(a) An increase in demand

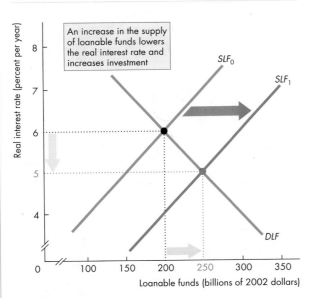

An increase in the supply of loanable funds lowers the real interest rate and increases investment

(b) An increase in supply

In part (a), the demand for loanable funds increases and supply doesn't change. The real interest rate rises (financial asset prices fall) and the quantity of funds increases.

In part (b), the supply of loanable funds increases and demand doesn't change. The real interest rate falls (financial asset prices rise) and the quantity of funds increases.

myeconlab animation

no change in the supply of loanable funds, there is a shortage of funds at a real interest rate of 6 percent a year. The real interest rate rises until it is 7 percent a year. Equilibrium is restored and the equilibrium quantity of funds has increased.

An Increase in Supply If one of the influences on saving plans changes and increases saving, the supply of loanable funds increases. With no change in the demand for loanable funds, the market is flush with loanable funds. Borrowers find bargains and lenders find themselves accepting a lower interest rate. At the lower interest rate, borrowers find additional investment projects profitable and increase the quantity of loanable funds that they borrow.

Figure 23.6(b) illustrates these changes. An increase in supply shifts the supply curve rightward from SLF_0 to SLF_1. With no change in demand, there is a surplus of funds at a real interest rate of 6 percent a year. The real interest rate falls until it is 5 percent a year. Equilibrium is restored and the equilibrium quantity of funds has increased.

Long-Run Growth of Demand and Supply Over time, both demand and supply in the market for loanable funds fluctuate and the real interest rate rises and falls. Both the supply of loanable funds and the demand for loanable funds tend to increase over time. On average, they increase at a similar pace, so although demand and supply trend upward, the real interest rate has no trend. It fluctuates around a constant average level.

Review Quiz

1 What is the market for loanable funds?
2 Why is the real interest rate the opportunity cost of loanable funds?
3 How do firms make investment decisions?
4 What determines the demand for loanable funds and what makes it change?
5 How do households make saving decisions?
6 What determines the supply of loanable funds and what makes it change?
7 How do changes in the demand for and supply of loanable funds change the real interest rate and the quantity of loanable funds?

myeconlab   Work Study Plan 23.2 and get instant feedback.

The Origins of the 2007–2008 Financial Crisis

Loanable Funds Fuel U.S. Home-Price Bubble

The financial crisis that gripped the U.S. and global economies in 2007 and cascaded through the financial markets in 2008 had its origins much earlier in events taking place in the market for loanable funds.

Between 2001 and 2005, a massive injection of loanable funds occurred in the United States. Some funds came from the rest of the world, but that source of supply has been stable. The U.S. Federal Reserve (the Fed) provided funds to keep interest rates low and that was a major source of the increase in the supply of funds. (The next chapter explains how a central bank does this.)

Figure 1 illustrates the U.S. loanable funds market starting in 2001. In that year, the demand for loanable funds was DLF_{01} and the supply of loanable funds was SLF_{01}. The equilibrium real interest rate was 4 percent a year and the equilibrium quantity of loanable funds was $29 trillion (in 2000 dollars).

During the ensuing four years, a massive increase in the supply of loanable funds shifted the supply curve rightward to SLF_{05}. A smaller increase in demand shifted the demand for loanable funds curve to DLF_{05}. The real interest rate fell to 1 percent a year and the quantity of loanable funds increased to $36 trillion—a 24 percent increase in just four years.

With this large increase in available funds, much of it in the form of mortgage loans to home buyers, the demand for homes increased by more than the increase in the supply of homes. Home prices rose and the expectation of further increases fuelled the demand for loanable funds.

By 2006, the expectation of continued rapidly rising home prices brought a very large increase in the demand for loanable funds. At the same time, the Fed began to tighten credit. (Again, you'll learn how this is done in the next chapter.) The result of the tighter credit policy was a slowdown in the pace of increase in the supply of loanable funds.

Figure 2 illustrates these events. In 2006, the demand for loanable funds increased from DLF_{05} to DLF_{06} and the supply of loanable funds increased by a smaller amount from SLF_{05} to SLF_{06}. The real interest rate increased to 3 percent a year.

The rise in the real interest rate (and a much higher rise in the nominal interest rate) put many homeowners in financial difficulty. Mortgage

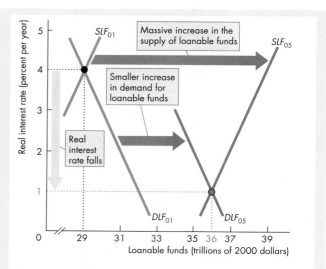

Figure 1 The Foundation of the Crisis: 2001–2005

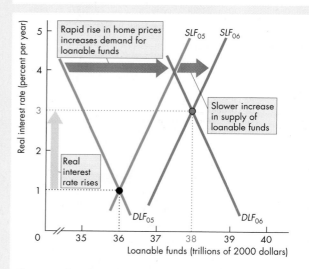

Figure 2 The Start of the Crisis: 2005–2006

repayments increased and some borrowers stopped repaying their loans. By August 2007, the damage from mortgage default and foreclosure was so large that the credit market began to dry up. A large decrease in both demand and supply kept interest rates roughly constant but decreased the quantity of new business.

The total quantity of loanable funds didn't decrease, but the rate of increase slowed to a snail's pace and the financial institutions most exposed to the bad mortgage debts and the securities that they backed (described on p. 546) began to fail.

These events illustrate the crucial role played by the loanable funds market in our economy.

Government in the Market for Loanable Funds

Government enters the market for loanable funds when it has a budget surplus or budget deficit. A government budget surplus increases the supply of loanable funds and contributes to financing investment; a government budget deficit increases the demand for loanable funds and competes with businesses for funds. Let's study the effects of government on the market for loanable funds.

A Government Budget Surplus

A government budget surplus increases the supply of loanable funds. The real interest rate falls, which decreases household saving and decreases the quantity of private funds supplied. The lower real interest rate increases the quantity of loanable funds demanded, and as a result investment increases.

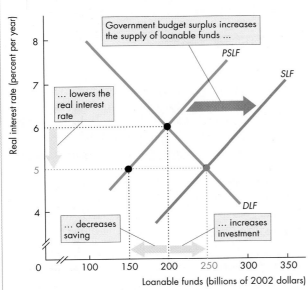

FIGURE 23.7   A Government
Budget Surplus

A government budget surplus of $100 billion is added to private saving and the private supply of loanable funds (PSLF) to determine the supply of loanable funds, SLF. The real interest rate falls to 5 percent a year, private saving decreases, but investment increases to $250 billion.

myeconlab animation

Figure 23.7 shows these effects of a government budget surplus. The private supply of loanable funds curve is PSLF. The supply of loanable funds curve, SLF, shows the sum of private supply and the government budget surplus. Here, the government budget surplus is $100 billion, so at each real interest rate the SLF curve lies $100 billion to the right of the PSLF curve. That is, the horizontal distance between the PSLF curve and the SLF curve equals the government budget surplus.

With no government surplus, the real interest rate is 6 percent a year, the quantity of loanable funds is $200 billion a year, and investment is $200 billion a year. But with the government surplus of $100 billion a year, the equilibrium real interest rate falls to 5 percent a year and the quantity of loanable funds increases to $250 billion a year.

The fall in the interest rate decreases private saving to $150 billion, but investment increases to $250 billion, which is financed by private saving plus the government budget surplus (government saving).

A Government Budget Deficit

A government budget deficit increases the demand for loanable funds. The real interest rate rises, which increases household saving and increases the quantity of private funds supplied. But the higher real interest rate decreases investment and the quantity of loanable funds demanded by firms to finance investment.

Figure 23.8 shows these effects of a government budget deficit. The private demand for loanable funds curve is PDLF. The demand for loanable funds curve, DLF, shows the sum of private demand and the government budget deficit. Here, the government budget deficit is $100 billion, so at each real interest rate the DLF curve lies $100 billion to the right of the PDLF curve. That is, the horizontal distance between the PDLF curve and the DLF curve equals the government budget deficit.

With no government deficit, the real interest rate is 6 percent a year, the quantity of loanable funds is $200 billion a year, and investment is $200 billion a year. But with the government budget deficit of $100 billion a year, the equilibrium real interest rate rises to 7 percent a year and the quantity of loanable funds increases to $250 billion a year.

The rise in the real interest rate increases private saving to $250 billion, but investment decreases to $150 billion because $100 billion of private saving must finance the government budget deficit.

FIGURE 23.8 A Government Budget Deficit

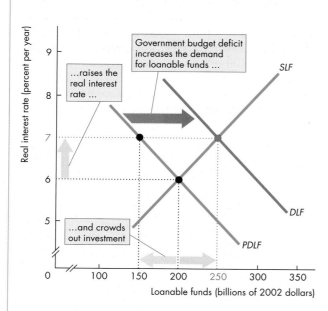

A government budget deficit adds to the private demand for loanable funds (*PDLF*) to determine the demand for loanable funds, *DLF*. The real interest rate rises, saving increases, but investment decreases—a crowding-out effect.

FIGURE 23.9 The Ricardo-Barro Effect

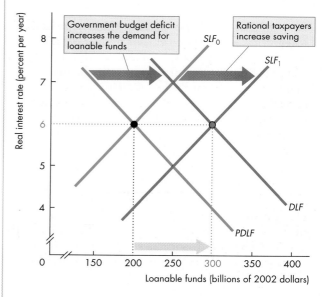

A budget deficit increases the demand for loanable funds to *DLF*. Rational taxpayers increase saving, which increases the supply of loanable funds from SLF_0 to SLF_1. Crowding out is avoided: Increased saving finances the budget deficit.

The Crowding-Out Effect The tendency for a government budget deficit to raise the real interest rate and decrease investment is called the **crowding-out effect**. The budget deficit crowds out investment by competing with businesses for scarce financial capital.

The crowding-out effect does not decrease investment by the full amount of the government budget deficit because the higher real interest rate induces an increase in private saving that partly contributes to financing the deficit.

The Ricardo-Barro Effect First suggested by the English economist David Ricardo in the nineteenth century and refined by Robert J. Barro of Harvard University, the Ricardo-Barro effect holds that both of the effects we've just shown are wrong and that the government budget, whether in surplus or deficit, has no effect on either the real interest rate or investment.

Barro says that taxpayers are rational. They can see that a budget deficit today means that future taxes will be higher and future disposable incomes will be smaller. With smaller expected future disposable incomes, saving increases today. Private saving and the private supply of loanable funds increase to match the quantity of loanable funds demanded by the government. So the budget deficit has no effect on either the real interest rate or investment. Figure 23.9 shows this outcome.

Most economists regard the Ricardo-Barro view as extreme. But there might be some change in private saving that goes in the direction suggested by the Ricardo-Barro effect that lessens the crowding-out effect.

Review Quiz

1 How does a government budget surplus or deficit influence the market for loanable funds?

2 What is the crowding-out effect and how does it work?

3 What is the Ricardo-Barro effect and how does it modify the crowding-out effect?

myeconlab Work Study Plan 23.3 and get instant feedback.

The Global Loanable Funds Market

The loanable funds market is global, not national. Lenders on the supply side of the market want to earn the highest possible real interest rate and they will seek it by looking everywhere in the world. Borrowers on the demand side of the market want to pay the lowest possible real interest rate and they will seek it by looking everywhere in the world. Financial capital is mobile: It moves to the best advantage of lenders and borrowers.

International Capital Mobility

If a Canadian supplier of loanable funds can earn a higher interest rate in Tokyo than in Toronto, funds supplied in Japan will increase and funds supplied in Canada will decrease—funds will flow from Canada to Japan.

If a Canadian demander of loanable funds can pay a lower interest rate in Paris than in Toronto, the demand for funds in France will increase and the demand for funds in Canada will decrease—funds will flow from France to Canada.

Because lenders are free to seek the highest real interest rate and borrowers are free to seek the lowest real interest rate, the loanable funds market is a single, integrated, global market. Funds flow into the country in which the interest rate is highest and out of the country in which the interest rate is lowest.

When funds leave the country with the lowest interest rate, a shortage of funds raises the real interest rate in that country. When funds move into the country with the highest interest rate, a surplus of funds lowers the real interest rate in that country. The free international mobility of financial capital pulls real interest rates around the world towards equality.

Only when the real interest rates in Toronto, Tokyo, and Paris are equal does the incentive to move funds from one country to another stop.

Equality of real interest rates does not mean that if you calculate the average real interest rate in Toronto, Tokyo, and Paris, you'll get the same number. To compare real interest rates, we must compare financial assets of equal risk.

Lending is risky. A loan might not be repaid. Or the price of a stock or bond might fall. Interest rates include a risk premium—the riskier the loan, other things remaining the same, the higher is the interest rate. The interest rate on a risky loan minus that on a safe loan is called the *risk premium*.

International capital mobility brings *real* interest rates in all parts of the world to equality except for differences that reflect differences in risk—differences in the risk premium.

International Borrowing and Lending

A country's loanable funds market connects with the global market through net exports. If a country's net exports are negative ($X < M$), the rest of the world supplies funds to that country and the quantity of loanable funds in that country is greater than national saving. If a country's net exports are positive ($X > M$), the country is a net supplier of funds to the rest of the world and the quantity of loanable funds in that country is less than national saving.

Demand and Supply in the Global and National Markets

The demand for and supply of funds in the global loanable funds market determines the world equilibrium real interest rate. This interest rate makes the quantity of loanable funds demanded equal the quantity supplied in the world economy. But it does not make the quantity of funds demanded and supplied equal in each national economy. The demand for and supply of funds in a national economy determine whether the country is a lender to or a borrower from the rest of the world.

The Global Loanable Funds Market   Figure 23.10(a) illustrates the global market. The demand for loanable funds, DLF_W, is the sum of the demands in all countries. Similarly, the supply of loanable funds, SLF_W, is the sum of the supplies in all countries. The world equilibrium real interest rate makes the quantity of funds supplied in the world as a whole equal to the quantity demanded. In this example, the equilibrium real interest rate is 5 percent a year and the quantity of funds is $10 trillion.

An International Borrower   Figure 23.10(b) shows the market for loanable funds in a country that borrows from the rest of the world. The country's demand for loanable funds, DLF, is part of the world demand in Fig. 23.10(a). The country's supply of loanable funds, SLF_D, is part of the world supply.

FIGURE 23.10   Borrowing and Lending in the Global Loanable Funds Market

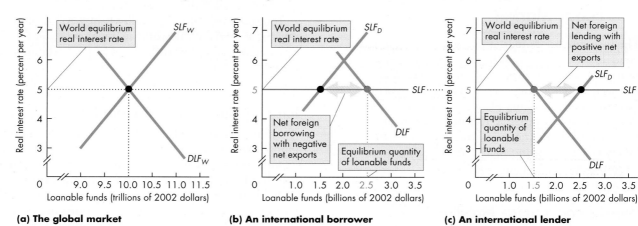

(a) The global market   **(b) An international borrower**   **(c) An international lender**

In part (a), the demand for loanable funds, *DLF*, and the supply of funds, *SLF*, determine the equilibrium real interest rate in the global loanable funds market.

The country in part (b) has a shortage of funds at the

world equilibrium real interest rate. The country borrows from the rest of the world and has negative net exports.

The country in part (c) has a surplus of funds at the world equilibrium real interest rate. The country lends to the rest of the world and has positive net exports.

myeconlab animation

If this country were isolated from the global market, the real interest rate would be 6 percent a year (where the *DLF* and *SLF*$_D$ curves intersect). But if the country is integrated into the global economy, with a real interest rate of 6 percent a year, funds would flood into it. With a real interest rate of 5 percent a year in the rest of the world, suppliers of loanable funds would seek the higher return in this country. In effect, the country faces the supply of loanable funds curve *SLF*, which is horizontal at the world equilibrium real interest rate.

The country's demand for loanable funds and the world interest rate determine the equilibrium quantity of loanable funds—$2.5 billion in Fig. 23.10(b).

An International Lender Figure 23.10(c) shows the situation in a country that lends to the rest of the world. As before, the country's demand for loanable funds, *DLF*, is part of the world demand and the country's supply of loanable funds, *SLF*$_D$, is part of the world supply in Fig. 23.10(a).

If this country were isolated from the global economy, the real interest rate would be 4 percent a year (where the *DLF* and *SLF*$_D$ curves intersect). But if this country is integrated into the global economy, with a real interest rate of 4 percent a year, funds

would quickly flow out of it. With a real interest rate of 5 percent a year in the rest of the world, suppliers of loanable funds would seek the higher return in other countries. Again, the country faces the supply of loanable funds curve *SLF*, which is horizontal at the world equilibrium real interest rate.

The country's demand for loanable funds and the world interest rate determine the equilibrium quantity of loanable funds—$1.5 billion in Fig. 23.10(c).

Changes in Demand and Supply   A change in the demand or supply in the global market of loanable funds changes the real interest rate in the way shown in Fig. 23.6 (see p. 553). The effect of a change in demand or supply in a national market depends on the size of the country. A change in demand or supply in a small country has no significant effect on global demand or supply, so it leaves the world real interest rate unchanged and changes only the country's net exports and international borrowing or lending. A change in demand or supply in a large country has a significant effect on global demand or supply, so it changes the world real interest rate as well as the country's net exports and international borrowing or lending. Every country feels some of the effect of a large country's change in demand or supply.

Greenspan's Interest Rate Puzzle

The Role of the Global Market

The real interest rate paid by big U.S. corporations fell from 5.5 percent a year in 2001 to 2.5 percent a year in 2005. Alan Greenspan, then the chairman of the U.S. Federal Reserve, said he was puzzled that the real interest rate was falling at a time when the U.S. government budget deficit was increasing.

Why did the real interest rate fall?

The answer lies in the global loanable funds market. Rapid economic growth in Asia and Europe brought a large increase in global saving, which in turn increased the global supply of loanable funds. The supply of loanable funds increased because Asian and European saving increased strongly.

The U.S. government budget deficit increased the U.S. and global demand for loanable funds. But this increase was very small compared to the increase in supply.

The result of a large increase in supply and a small increase in demand was a fall in the world average real interest rate and an increase in the equilibrium quantity of loanable funds.

The figure illustrates these events. The supply of loanable funds increased from SLF_{01} in 2001 to SLF_{05} in 2005. (In the figure, we ignore the change in the global demand for loanable funds because it was very small relative to the increase in supply.)

With the increase in supply, the real interest rate fell from 5.5 percent to 2.5 percent a year and the quantity of loanable funds increased.

In the United States, borrowing from the rest of the world increased to finance the increased government budget deficit.

The interest rate puzzle illustrates the important fact that the loanable funds market is a global market, not a national market.

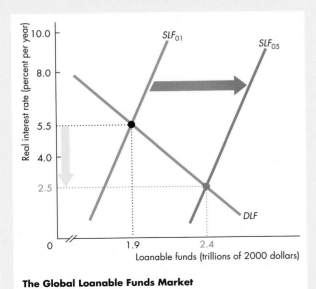

The Global Loanable Funds Market

Review Quiz

1 Why do loanable funds flow among countries?
2 What determines the demand for and supply of loanable funds in an individual economy?
3 What happens if a country has a shortage of loanable funds at the world real interest rate?
4 What happens if a country has a surplus of loanable funds at the world real interest rate?
5 How is a government budget deficit financed in an open economy?

 Work Study Plan 23.4 and get instant feedback.

◆ To complete your study of financial markets, take a look at *Reading Between the Lines* on pp. 560–561 and see how you can use the model of the loanable funds market to understand the events in the financial market crisis of 2008.

Bailing Out Troubled U.S. Financial Markets

Bailout Plan Wins Approval

October 3, 2008

After the House reversed course and gave final approval to the $700 billion economic bailout package, President Bush quickly signed it into law on Friday, authorizing the Treasury to undertake what could become the most expensive government intervention in history.

But even as Mr. Bush declared that the measure would "help prevent the crisis on Wall Street from becoming a crisis in communities across our country," Congressional Democrats said that it was only a first step and pledged to carry out a sweeping overhaul of the nation's financial regulatory system. ...

Some measures of the credit markets improved after the bill was approved, but only modestly. Analysts said it was too soon to tell whether borrowing rates—the interest rates banks charge each other for loans, and a key indicator of the flow of credit—would fall. ...

Supporters said the bailout was needed to prevent economic collapse; opponents said it was hasty, ill conceived and risked too much taxpayer money to help Wall Street tycoons, while providing no guarantees of success. The rescue plan allows the Treasury to buy troubled securities from financial firms in an effort to ease a deepening credit crisis that is choking off business and consumer loans, the lifeblood of the economy, and contributing to a string of bank failures. ...

Essence of the Story

- In October 2008, the U.S. Congress passed a $700 billion economic bailout package for troubled financial institutions.

- The plan allows the U.S. Treasury to buy troubled securities from financial firms.

- The goal was to unfreeze credit and make loan markets work normally.

- Analysts said it was too soon to tell whether interest rates would fall.

- Supporters of the bailout said it was needed to prevent economic collapse.

Economic Analysis

- In the fall of 2008, the U.S. loanable funds market was in a distressed state.

- The spread in interest rates between safe U.S. government Treasury bills and risky commercial loans was unusually high and the quantity of loans was unusually low.

- Banks and other financial institutions were holding financial assets that they could sell only at a large loss—referred to as *toxic assets*.

- The financial markets were operating at an equilibrium that was hampering continued economic growth.

- The U.S. Congress hoped to inject life into the markets by creating a $700 billion fund to buy toxic assets and enable financial institutions to start lending again. (In the event, the Treasury used the funds to buy bank stocks.)

- It was feared that without the $700 billion of funds, financial institutions would not only fail to provide the funds required to make the economy grow but also slide into a deeper state of stress with the quantity of funds available decreasing further.

- The figures illustrate the hope and the fear.

- In 2008 (both figures), the demand for loanable funds was DLF_{08} and the supply was SLF_{08}. The real interest rate was 3 percent a year and quantity of funds was $40 trillion (2000 dollars).

- Figure 1 shows the hope. A rescue package increases the supply of loanable funds and increases optimism about the future. Increased optimism increases profit expectations and increases the demand for funds. The demand and supply curve shift rightward to DLF_{09} and SLF_{09}. The quantity of funds increases and the economy begins to expand again.

- Figure 2 shows the fear. With no rescue package, the supply of loanable funds decreases and pessimism about the future increases. The increased pessimism decreases profit expectations and decreases the demand for funds. The demand and supply curve shift leftward to DLF_{09} and SLF_{09}. The quantity of funds decreases and the economy goes into recession or worse.

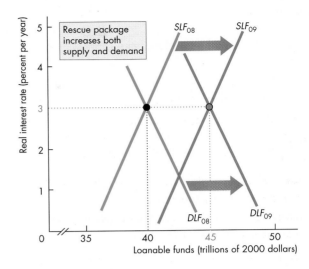

Figure 1 The hope

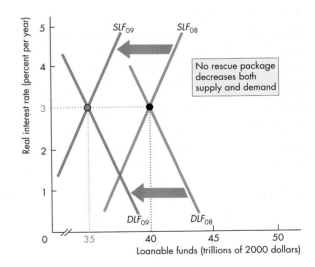

Figure 2 The fear

- Whether a rescue would work as hoped or whether the dire consequences of no rescue would occur as feared is not known. We have no direct experience of events like the ones described here on which to base solid predictions.

561

SUMMARY ◆

Key Points

Financial Institutions and Financial Markets
(pp. 544–548)

- Capital (*physical capital*) is a real productive resource; financial capital is the funds used to buy capital.
- Gross investment increases the quantity of capital and depreciation decreases it. Saving increases wealth.
- The markets for financial capital are the markets for loans, bonds, and stocks.
- Financial institutions ensure that borrowers and lenders can always find someone with whom to trade.

The Market for Loanable Funds (pp. 548–554)

- Investment in capital is financed by household saving, a government budget surplus, and funds from the rest of the world.
- The quantity of loanable funds demanded depends negatively on the real interest rate and the demand for loanable funds changes when profit expectations change.
- The quantity of loanable funds supplied depends positively on the real interest rate and the supply of loanable funds changes when disposable income, expected future income, wealth, and default risk change.
- Equilibrium in the loanable funds market determines the real interest rate and quantity of funds.

Government in the Market for Loanable Funds
(pp. 555–556)

- A government budget surplus increases the supply of loanable funds, lowers the real interest rate, and increases investment and the equilibrium quantity of loanable funds.
- A government budget deficit increases the demand for loanable funds, raises the real interest rate, decreases investment in a crowding-out effect, and decreases the equilibrium quantity of loanable funds.
- The Ricardo-Barro effect is the response of rational taxpayers to a budget deficit: Private saving increases to finance the budget deficit. The real interest rate remains constant and the crowding-out effect is avoided.

The Global Loanable Funds Market (pp. 557–559)

- The loanable funds market is a global market.
- The equilibrium real interest rate is determined in the global loanable funds market and national demand and supply determine the quantity of international borrowing or lending.

Key Figures

Key Terms

PROBLEMS and APPLICATIONS ◆

Work problems 1–10 in Chapter 23 Study Plan and get instant feedback.
Work problems 11–19 as Homework, a Quiz, or a Test if assigned by your instructor.

1. Michael is an Internet service provider. On December 31, 2007, he bought an existing business with servers and a building worth $400,000. During his first year of operation, his business grew and he bought new servers for $500,000. The market value of some of his older servers fell by $100,000.

   a. What was Michael's gross investment, depreciation, and net investment during 2008?
   b. What was the value of Michael's capital at the end of 2008?

2. Lori is a student who teaches golf on the weekend and in a year earns $20,000 after paying her taxes. At the beginning of 2007, Lori owned $1,000 worth of books, CDs, and golf clubs and she had $5,000 in a savings account at the bank. During 2007, the interest on her savings account was $300 and she spent a total of $15,300 on consumption goods and services. There was no change in the market values of her books, CDs, and golf clubs.

   a. How much did Lori save in 2007?
   b. What was her wealth at the end of 2007?

3. First Call is a cellular phone company. It plans to build an assembly plant that costs $10 million if the real interest rate is 6 percent a year. If the real interest rate is 5 percent a year, First Call will build a larger plant that costs $12 million. And if the real interest rate is 7 percent a year, First Call will build a smaller plant that costs $8 million.

   a. Draw a graph of First Call's demand for loanable funds curve.
   b. First Call expects its profit from the sale of cellular phones to double next year. If other things remain the same, explain how this increase in expected profit influences First Call's demand for loanable funds.

4. Draw a graph to illustrate how an increase in the supply of loanable funds and a decrease in the demand for loanable funds can lower the real interest rate and leave the equilibrium quantity of loanable funds unchanged.

5. The table shows an economy's demand for loanable funds and supply of loanable funds schedules when the government's budget is balanced.

Real interest rate (percent per year)	Loanable funds demanded	Loanable funds supplied
	(trillions of 2002 dollars)	
4	8.5	5.5
5	8.0	6.0
6	7.5	6.5
7	7.0	7.0
8	6.5	7.5
9	6.0	8.0
10	5.5	8.5

   a. If the government has a budget surplus of $1 trillion, what are the real interest rate, the quantity of investment, and the quantity of private saving? Is there any crowding out in this situation?
   b. If the government has a budget deficit of $1 trillion, what are the real interest rate, the quantity of investment, and the quantity of private saving? Is there any crowding out in this situation?
   c. If the government has a budget deficit of $1 trillion and the Ricardo-Barro effect occurs, what are the real interest rate and the quantity of investment?

6. In the loanable funds market in problem 5, the quantity of loanable funds demanded increases by $1 trillion at each real interest rate and the quantity of loanable funds supplied increases by $2 trillion at each real interest rate.

   a. If the government budget is balanced, what are the real interest rate, the quantity of loanable funds, investment, and private saving? Does any crowding out occur?
   b. If the government budget becomes a deficit of $1 trillion, what are the real interest rate, the quantity of loanable funds, investment, and private saving? Does any crowding out occur?
   c. If the government wants to stimulate the quantity of investment and increase it to $9 trillion, what must they do?

7. **Household Debt Now Rising Faster than Wealth**

   The debt of Canadian households is now rising faster than their wealth in the wake of the stock market correction and a housing market slow-down. ... The mortgage market is still expanding ... although it will likely slow by more than half ... due to the correction in the formerly overheated markets in western Canadian cities and the tightening up of federal mortgage lending restrictions. There are also early signs that the pace of growth in non-mortgage consumer credit is slowing. ... And that's a good thing, said CIBC economist and author of the report Benjamin Tal. "If household credit were to continue to rise by 13% a year at some point I would become concerned because you would have too much credit and not enough wealth to support it ... "During the first quarter of the year, overall household debt rose by almost 3%, while personal disposable income rose by 2%. ...

Financial Post Magazine, August 19, 2008

a. Explain why the growth of household wealth has slowed in Canada.
b. When a household buys stocks, does that represent consumption, saving, or investment? Explain.
c. When a household buys a new house, does that represent consumption, saving, or investment? Explain.
d. What factors may influence a household when deciding between buying stocks, bonds, or a house?

8. **The Global Saving Glut and the U.S. Current Account,** remarks by Ben Bernanke (then a governor of the U.S. Federal Reserve) on March 10, 2005:

On most dimensions the U.S. economy appears to be performing well. Output growth has returned to healthy levels, the labor market is firming, and inflation appears to be well controlled. However, one aspect of U.S. economic performance still evokes concern among economists and policy-makers: the nation's large and growing current account deficit [negative net exports]. ... Most forecasters expect the nation's current account imbalance to decline slowly at best, implying a continued need for foreign credit and a concomitant decline in the U.S. net foreign asset position. Bernanke went on to ask the following questions. What are *your* answers to his questions:

a. Why is the United States, with the world's largest economy, borrowing heavily on international capital markets—rather than lending, as would seem more natural?
b. What implications do the U.S. current account deficit (negative net exports) and the U.S. consequent reliance on foreign credit have for U.S. economic performance?
c. What policies, if any, should be used to address this situation?

9. **The New New World Order**

... While gross domestic product growth is cooling a bit in emerging markets, the results are still tremendous compared with the United States and much of Western Europe. The 54 developing markets surveyed by Global Insight will post a 6.7% jump in real GDP this year, down from 7.5% last year. The 31 developed countries will grow an estimated 1.6%. The difference in growth rates represents the largest spread between developed and developing markets in the 37-year history of the survey.

Fortune, July 14, 2008

a. Do growth rates of real GDP over the past few decades indicate that world saving is shrinking, growing, or staying the same? Explain.
b. If the world demand for loanable funds remains the same, will the world real interest rate rise, fall, or remain the same? Explain.

10. **IMF Warning Over Slowing Growth**

The global economy may face a marked slowdown next year as a result of the turmoil in financial markets, the International Monetary Fund has warned. The IMF said the global credit squeeze would test the ability of the economy to continue expanding at recent rates. While future economic stability could not be taken for granted, there was plenty of evidence that the global economy remained durable, it added.

BBC News, October 10, 2007

a. Explain how turmoil in global financial markets might affect the demand for loanable funds, investment, and global economic growth in the future.
b. What might be the evidence that the global economy will continue to grow?

11. Annie runs a fitness centre. On December 31, 2008, she bought an existing business with exercise equipment and a building worth $300,000. During 2009, business improved and she bought some new equipment for $50,000. At the end of 2009, her equipment and buildings were worth $325,000. Calculate Annie's gross investment, depreciation, and net investment during 2009.

12. Karrie is a golf pro, and after she paid taxes, her income from golf and interest from financial assets was $1,500,000 in 2008. At the beginning of 2008, she owned $900,000 worth of financial assets. At the end of 2008, Karrie's financial assets were worth $1,900,000.

    a. How much did Karrie save during 2008?
    b. How much did she spend on consumption goods and services?

13. In 2008, the Lee family had disposable income of $80,000, wealth of $140,000, and an expected future income of $80,000 a year. At a real interest rate of 4 percent a year, the Lee family saves $15,000 a year; at a real interest rate of 6 percent a year, they save $20,000 a year; and at a real interest rate of 8 percent, they save $25,000 a year.

    a. Draw a graph of the Lee family's supply of loanable funds curve.
    b. In 2009, suppose that the stock market crashes and the default risk increases. Explain how this increase in default risk influences the Lee family's supply of loanable funds curve.

14. Draw a graph that illustrates the effect of an increase in the demand for loanable funds and an even larger increase in the supply of loanable funds on the real interest rate and the equilibrium quantity of loanable funds.

15. **India's Economy Hits the Wall**

    Just six months ago, India was looking good. Annual growth was 9%, corporate profits were surging 20%, the stock market had risen 50% in 2007, consumer demand was huge, local companies were making ambitious international acquisitions, and foreign investment was growing. Nothing, it seemed, could stop the forward march of this Asian nation. But stop it has. ... The country is reeling from 11.4% inflation, large government deficits, and rising interest rates. ... Most economic forecasts expect growth to slow to 7%—a big drop for a country that needs to accelerate growth, not reduce it. ... A June 16 report by Goldman Sachs' Jim O'Neill and Tushar Poddar ... urges India to improve governance, raise educational achievement, and control inflation. It also advises ... liberalizing its financial markets. ...

    BusinessWeek, July 1, 2008

    a. Suppose that the Indian government reduces its deficit and returns to a balanced budget. If other things remain the same, how will the demand or supply of loanable funds in India change?
    b. With economic growth forecasted to slow, future incomes are expected to fall. If other things remain the same, how will the demand or supply of loanable funds in India change?

16. **The Global Savings Glut and Its Consequences**

    The world is experiencing an unprecedented glut of savings, driving down real interest rates. It is a good time to borrow rather than lend. ... Several developing countries are running large current account surpluses (representing an excess of savings over investment). ... China has the biggest surplus of $1.2 trillion, but other developing countries put together have accumulated almost as much. ... Rapid growth leads to high saving rates: people save a large fraction of additional income. In India, GDP growth has accelerated from 6% to 9%, lifting the saving rate from 23% a decade ago to 33% today. China's saving rate is a dizzy 55%. Not even the investment boom in Asia can absorb these huge savings, which are therefore put into U.S. bonds. When a poor country buys U.S. bonds, it is in effect lending to the United States.

    Cato Institute, June 8, 2007

    a. Graphically illustrate and explain the impact of the "unprecedented glut of savings" on the real interest rate and the quantity of loanable funds.
    b. How do the high saving rates in China and India impact investment in the United States? How does this investment influence the production function and potential GDP in the United States?

17. **China's Integration Into the Global Financial System**

China's global economic significance is growing. Its gross domestic product (GDP) is the world's second largest when measured in terms of purchasing-power parities, and its share in world exports is exceeded only by Germany's and that of the United States. China is Canada's second-largest trading partner, and trade between the two countries is continuing to grow rapidly. ... Yet China has only a minor role in the global financial system. Its banks, some of which are the largest in the world by market capitalization and the size of their balance sheets, have only a modest international presence. ... China's currency ... is virtually not used outside the country and, with a few exceptions, Chinese capital markets are not a source of financing for foreign borrowers. China's lack of integration into the global financial system needs to be understood primarily in the context of China's own interests and domestic policy priorities. The central economic goal of the Chinese authorities has been to achieve growth with stability while radically restructuring the industrial sector and creating enough jobs each year to absorb layoffs and large numbers of new entrants into the labour force. ... As the Chinese economy matures, however, and as reforms strengthen the domestic financial system, China will become more important in global financial markets. Changes are already occurring as China's financial might is being channeled towards overseas investments. ...

Bank of Canada Review, Summer 2008

a. Explain the effects of increased integration of China into the global loanable funds market. Will the world equilibrium real interest rate rise or fall as China becomes more integrated? Draw a graph to illustrate your answer.
b. Explain the potential effect on Canada of an increased Chinese presence in global financial markets.
c. What are the advantages and disadvantages to China of isolating itself from the global loanable funds market?

18. **Greenspan's Conundrum Spells Confusion for Us All**

... At the beginning of the year, the consensus was that ... bond yields would rise. ... Gradually, over February, the consensus has started to reassert itself. ... Ten-year Treasury bond yields were hovering below 4 percent in the early part of the month but now they are around 4.3 percent.

Because the consensus was that bond yields should be 5 percent by the end of the year, most commentators have focused, not on why bond yields have suddenly risen, but on why they were so low before.

A number of explanations for this "conundrum" have been advanced. First, bond yields are being held artificially low by unusual buying. ... Another [is] ... bond yields reflect investors' expectations for an economic slowdown in 2005.

Financial Times, February 26, 2005

a. Explain how "unusual buying" might lead to a low real interest rate.
b. Explain how "investors' expectations for an economic slowdown" might lead to a lower real interest rate.

19. Study *Reading Between the Lines* on pp. 560–561 and then answer the following questions.

a. What was the financial rescue package passed by U.S. Congress and what was it supposed to do?
b. What did the U.S. Congress hope would occur after the rescue package was passed?
c. Based on what happened in the stock market, in the weeks after the package was passed, do you think we can conclude that suppliers of loanable funds believed that the rescue package was working? Explain your answer.
d. What did people fear would occur if the rescue package didn't work as intended?
e. Based on what happened in the stock market, do you think we can conclude that suppliers of loanable funds shared the fears? Explain your answer.
f. What other measures might the government take if it wants to boost supply and demand in the market for loanable funds?
g. How do you think the global nature of the loanable funds markets influences how the U.S. market would respond to no rescue?

24 Money, the Price Level, and Inflation

After studying this chapter, you will be able to

- Define money and describe its functions
- Describe the banking system and explain the economic functions of banks, the Bank of Canada, and the payments system
- Explain how the banking system creates money
- Explain what determines the demand for money, the supply of money, and the nominal interest rate
- Explain how the quantity of money influences the price level and the inflation rate in the long run

Money, like fire and the wheel, has been around for a long time, and it has taken many forms. Money was wampum (beads made from shells) for North American Indians, whale's teeth for Fijians, and tobacco for early American colonists. Cakes of salt served as money in Ethiopia and Tibet. Today, when we want to buy something, we use coins or dollar bills, write a cheque, or swipe a card. Soon, we'll be using a "smart card" that keeps track of spending and that our pocket computer can read. Are all these things money?

When we deposit some coins or notes into a bank, is that still money? And what happens when the bank lends the money we've deposited to someone else? How can we get our money back if it has been lent out?

The Bank of Canada regulates the quantity of money in our economy. How does the Bank of Canada influence the quantity of money and what happens if it creates too much money or too little money?

In this chapter, we study the functions of money; the banks that create it; the Bank of Canada, which influences the quantity of money; and the long-run consequences of changes in the quantity of money. In *Reading Between the Lines* at the end of the chapter, we look at a spectacular example of money, inflation, and economic collapse in the African nation, Zimbabwe.

What Is Money?

What do wampum, tobacco, and nickels and dimes have in common? They are all examples of **money**, which is defined as any commodity or token that is generally acceptable as a means of payment. A **means of payment** is a method of settling a debt. When a payment has been made, there is no remaining obligation between the parties to a transaction. So what wampum, tobacco, and nickels and dimes have in common is that they have served (or still do serve) as the means of payment. Money serves three other functions:

- Medium of exchange
- Unit of account
- Store of value

Medium of Exchange

A *medium of exchange* is any object that is generally accepted in exchange for goods and services. Without a medium of exchange, goods and services must be exchanged directly for other goods and services—an exchange called **barter**. Barter requires a *double coincidence of wants*, a situation that rarely occurs. For example, if you want a hamburger, you might offer a CD in exchange for it. But you must find someone who is selling hamburgers and wants your CD.

A medium of exchange overcomes the need for a double coincidence of wants. Money acts as a medium of exchange because people with something to sell will always accept money in exchange for it. But money isn't the only medium of exchange. You can buy with a credit card, but a credit card isn't money. It doesn't make a final payment, and the debt it creates must eventually be settled by using money.

Unit of Account

A *unit of account* is an agreed measure for stating the prices of goods and services. To get the most out of your budget, you have to figure out whether seeing one more movie is worth its opportunity cost. But that cost is not dollars and cents. It is the number of ice cream cones, cases of pop, or cups of coffee that you must give up. It's easy to do such calculations when all these goods have prices in terms of dollars and cents (see Table 24.1). If the price of a movie is $8 and the price of a case of pop is $4, you know

TABLE 24.1 The Unit of Account Function of Money Simplifies Price Comparisons

Good	Price in money units	Price in units of another good
Movie	$8.00 each	2 cases of pop
Pop	$4.00 per case	2 ice cream cones
Ice cream	$2 per cone	4 packs of jelly beans
Jelly beans	$0.50 per pack	2 sticks of gum
Gum	$0.25 per stick	

Money as a unit of account: The price of a movie is $8 and the price of a stick of gum is 25¢, so the opportunity cost of a movie is 32 sticks of gum ($8.00 ÷ 25¢ = 32).

No unit of account: You go to a movie theatre and learn that the price of a movie is 2 cases of pop. You go to a candy store and learn that a pack of jelly beans costs 2 sticks of gum. But how many sticks of gum does seeing a movie cost you? To answer that question, you go to the convenience store and find that a case of pop costs 2 ice cream cones. Now you head for the ice cream shop, where an ice cream cone costs 4 packs of jelly beans. Now you get out your pocket calculator: 1 movie costs 2 cases of pop, or 4 ice cream cones, or 16 packs of jelly beans, or 32 sticks of gum!

right away that seeing one movie costs you 2 cases of pop. If jelly beans are $0.50 a pack, 1 movie costs 16 packs of jelly beans. You need only one calculation to figure out the opportunity cost of any pair of goods and services.

Imagine how troublesome it would be if your local movie theatre posted its price as 2 cases of pop, the convenience store posted the price of a case of pop as 2 ice cream cones, the ice cream shop posted the price of an ice cream cone as 4 packs of jelly beans, and the candy store priced a pack of jelly beans as 2 sticks of gum! Now how much running around and calculating will you have to do to find out how much that movie is going to cost you in terms of the pop, ice cream, jelly beans, or gum that you must give up to see it? You get the answer for pop right away from the sign posted at the movie theatre. But for all the other goods, you're going to have to visit many different stores to establish the price of each commodity in terms of another and then calculate the prices in units that are relevant for your own decision. The hassle of doing all this research might be enough to make a person swear off movies! You can see how much simpler it is if all the prices are expressed in dollars and cents.

Store of Value

Money is a *store of value* in the sense that it can be held and exchanged later for goods and services. If money were not a store of value, it could not serve as a means of payment.

Money is not alone in acting as a store of value. A house, a car, and a work of art are other examples.

The more stable the value of a commodity or token, the better it can act as a store of value and the more useful it is as money. No store of value has a completely stable value. The value of a house, a car, or a work of art fluctuates over time. The value of the commodities and tokens that are used as money also fluctuate over time.

Inflation lowers the value of money and the values of other commodities and tokens that are used as money. To make money as useful as possible as a store of value, a low inflation rate is needed.

Money in Canada Today

In Canada today, money consists of

- Currency
- Deposits at banks and other depository institutions

Currency The notes and coins held by individuals and businesses are known as **currency**. Notes are money because the government declares them so. Look at a Bank of Canada note and notice the words "Ce billet a cours légal–this note is legal tender." Currency is the most convenient type of money for settling small debts and buying low-priced items.

Deposits Deposits of individuals and businesses at banks and other depository institutions, such as trust and mortgage companies, credit unions, and caisses populaires, are also counted as money. Deposits are money because the owners of the deposits can use them to make payments.

Official Measures of Money in Canada
Currency a Small Part of the Total

The figure shows the relative magnitudes of the items that make up M1 and M2. Notice that M2 is a bit more than double M1 and that currency is a small part of our money.

	$ billions in November 2008
M2	838
Comprises all in M1, plus...	
Fixed term deposits	317
Non-chequable deposits, non-personal	11
Non-chequable deposits, personal	103
M1	407
Chequable deposits, non-personal	212
Chequable deposits, personal	145
Currency outside banks	50

Two Official Measures of Money

M1
- Currency outside banks
- Personal chequable deposits
- Non-personal chequable deposits

M2
- M1
- Personal non-chequable deposits
- Non-personal non-chequable deposits
- Fixed term deposits

Source of data: Statistics Canada CANSIM Table 176-0020.

Official Measures of Money Two official measures of money* in Canada today are known as M1 and M2. **M1** consists of currency and chequable deposits of individuals and businesses. M1 does *not* include currency held by banks, or currency and chequable deposits of the government of Canada. **M2** consists of M1 plus all other deposits.

---

* In the Bank of Canada's official statistics, M1 is called M1+ (gross) and M2 is is called M2 (gross).

Are M1 and M2 Really Money? Money is the means of payment. So the test of whether an asset is money is whether it serves as a means of payment. Currency passes the test. But what about deposits? Chequable deposits are money because they can be transferred from one person to another by writing a cheque or using a debit card. Such a transfer of ownership is equivalent to handing over currency. Because M1 consists of currency plus chequable deposits and each of these is a means of payment, *M1 is money*.

But what about M2? Some of the savings deposits in M2 are just as much a means of payment as the chequable deposits in M1. You can use the ATM at the grocery store checkout or gas station and transfer funds directly from your savings account to pay for your purchase. But some savings deposits are not means of payment. These deposits are known as liquid assets. *Liquidity* is the property of being easily convertible into a means of payment without loss in value. Because the deposits in M2 that are not means of payment are quickly and easily converted into a means of payment—into currency or chequable deposits—they are counted as money.

Deposits Are Money but Cheques Are Not In defining money, we include, along with currency, deposits at banks and other depository institutions. But we do not count the cheques that people write as money. Why are deposits money and cheques not?

To see why deposits are money but cheques are not, think about what happens when Colleen buys some roller blades for $200 from Rocky's Rollers. When Colleen goes to Rocky's shop, she has $500 in her deposit account at the Laser Bank. Rocky has $1,000 in his deposit account—at the same bank, as it happens. The total deposits of these two people are $1,500. Colleen writes a cheque for $200. Rocky takes the cheque to the bank right away and deposits it. Rocky's bank balance rises from $1,000 to $1,200, and Colleen's balance falls from $500 to $300. The total deposits of Colleen and Rocky are still the same as before: $1,500. Rocky now has $200 more than before, and Colleen has $200 less.

This transaction has transferred money from Colleen to Rocky, but the cheque itself was never money. There wasn't an extra $200 of money while the cheque was in circulation. The cheque instructs the bank to transfer money from Colleen to Rocky.

If Colleen and Rocky use different banks, there is an extra step. Rocky's bank credits $200 to Rocky's account and then takes the cheque to a cheque-clearing centre. The cheque is then sent to Colleen's bank, which pays Rocky's bank $200 and then debits Colleen's account $200. This process can take a few days, but the principles are the same as when two people use the same bank.

Credit Cards Are Not Money You've just seen that cheques are not money. What about credit cards? Isn't having a credit card in your wallet and presenting the card to pay for your roller blades the same thing as using money? Why aren't credit cards somehow valued and counted as part of the quantity of money?

When you pay by cheque, you are frequently asked to prove your identity by showing your driver's licence. It would never occur to you to think of your driver's licence as money. It's just an ID card. A credit card is also an ID card, but one that lets you take out a loan at the instant you buy something. When you sign a credit card sales slip, you are saying, "I agree to pay for these goods when the credit card company bills me." Once you get your statement from the credit card company, you must make at least the minimum payment due. To make that payment, you need money—you need to have currency or a chequable deposit to pay the credit card company. So although you use a credit card when you buy something, the credit card is not the *means of payment* and it is not money.

Review Quiz

1 What makes something money? What functions does money perform? Why do you think packs of chewing gum don't serve as money?

2 What are the problems that arise when a commodity is used as money?

3 What are the main components of money in Canada today?

4 What are the official measures of money? Are all the measures really money?

5 Why are cheques and credit cards not money?

 Work Study Plan 24.1 and get instant feedback.

We've seen that the main component of money in Canada is deposits at banks and other depository institutions. Let's take a closer look at these institutions.

◆ The Banking System

The banking system consists of private and public institutions that create money and manage the nation's monetary and payments systems. These institutions play a crucial role in financial markets and have profound effects on overall economic performance. To describe these institutions and explain their functions, we'll divide them into three groups:

- Depository institutions
- The Bank of Canada
- The payments system

Depository Institutions

A **depository institution** is a private firm that takes deposits from households and firms and makes loans to other households and firms. The deposits of three types of depository institution make up the nations money. They are

- Chartered banks
- Credit unions and caisses populaires
- Trust and mortgage loan companies

Chartered Banks A **chartered bank** is a private firm, chartered under the Bank Act of 1992 to receive deposits and make loans. The chartered banks are by far the largest institutions in the banking system and conduct all types of banking and financial business. In 2008, 14 Canadian-owned banks (including the Royal Bank of Canada, CIBC, Bank of Montreal, Bank of Nova Scotia, National Bank of Canada, and TD Canada Trust) and 33 foreign-owned banks had the bulk of the deposits in M1 and M2.

Credit Unions and Caisses Populaires A **credit union** is a cooperative organization that operates under the Co-operative Credit Association Act of 1992 and that receives deposits from and makes loans to its members. A caisse populaire is a similar type of institution that operates in Quebec.

Trust and Mortgage Loan Companies A **trust and mortgage loan company** is a privately owned depository institution that operates under the Trust and Loan Companies Act of 1992. These institutions receive deposits, make loans, and act as trustee for pension funds and for estates.

All Banks Now Historically, Canada made a sharp legal distinction between banks and other depository institutions. But the economic functions of all depository institutions have grown increasingly similar. This fact is recognized in laws governing these institutions that became effective in 1992. Because they all perform the same essential economic functions, we'll call all these institutions banks unless we need to distinguish among them.

What Depository Institutions Do Depository institutions provide services such as cheque clearing, account management, credit cards, and Internet banking, all of which provide an income from service fees. But depository institutions earn most of their income by using the funds they receive from depositors to make loans and buy securities that earn a higher interest rate than that paid to depositors. In this activity, a depository institution must perform a balancing act weighing return against risk. To see this balancing act, we'll focus on the chartered banks.

A chartered bank puts the funds it receives from depositors and other funds that it borrows into four types of assets:

1. Reserves Reserves are notes and coins in a bank's vault or in a deposit account at the Bank of Canada. (We'll study the Bank of Canada later in this chapter.) These funds are used to meet depositors' currency withdrawals and to make payments to other banks. In normal times, a bank keeps about a half of one percent of deposits as reserves.

2. Liquid Assets Liquid assets are government of Canada Treasury bills and commercial bills. These assets are the banks' first line of defence if they need reserves. Liquid assets can be sold and instantly converted into reserves with virtually no risk of loss. Because they have a low risk, they earn a low interest rate.

3. Securities Securities are government of Canada bonds and other bonds such as mortgage-backed securities. These assets can be converted into reserves but at prices that fluctuate. Because their prices fluctuate, these assets are riskier than liquid assets, but they also have a higher interest rate.

4. Loans Loans are commitments of funds for an agreed-upon period of time. Banks make loans to corporations to finance the purchase of capital. They also make mortgage loans to finance the purchase of homes, and personal loans to finance consumer durable goods, such as cars or boats. The outstanding balances on credit card accounts are also bank loans. Loans are the riskiest assets of a bank. They cannot be converted into reserves until they are due to be repaid. And some borrowers default and never repay. These assets earn the highest interest rate.

Table 24.2 provides a snapshot of the sources and uses of funds of all the chartered banks in 2008.

Economic Benefits Provided by Depository Institutions

You've seen that a depository institution earns part of its profit because it pays a lower interest rate on deposits than what it earns on loans. What benefits do these institutions provide that make depositors willing to put up with a low interest rate and borrowers willing to pay a higher one? They provide four benefits:

- Create liquidity
- Pool risk
- Lower the cost of borrowing
- Lower the cost of monitoring borrowers

Create Liquidity Depository institutions create liquidity by *borrowing short and lending long*—taking deposits and standing ready to repay them on short notice or on demand and making loan commitments that run for terms of many years.

TABLE 24.2 Chartered Banks: Sources and Uses of Funds

	$ billion September 2008	Percentage of deposits
Total funds	1,762.5	159.0
Sources		
Deposits	1,108.4	100.0
Borrowing and own capital	654.1	59.0
Uses		
Reserves	4.7	0.4
Liquid assets	216.0	19.5
Securities and other assets	194.7	17.6
Loans	1,347.1	121.5

Chartered banks get two-thirds of their funds from depositors and use the funds to make loans. Banks hold a very small amount of reserves—less than a half of one percent of deposits. They hold about 20 percent of deposits as liquid assets.

Source of data: Statistics Canada, CANSIM Table 176-0011.

Pool Risk A loan might not be repaid—a default. If you lend to one person who defaults, you lose the entire amount loaned. If you lend to 1,000 people (through a bank) and one person defaults, you lose almost nothing. Depository institutions pool risk.

Lower the Cost of Borrowing Imagine there are no depository institutions and a firm is looking for $1 million to buy a new factory. It hunts around for several dozen people from whom to borrow the funds. Depository institutions lower the cost of this search. The firm gets its $1 million from a single institution that gets deposits from a large number of people but spreads the cost of this activity over many borrowers.

Lower the Cost of Monitoring Borrowers By monitoring borrowers, a lender can encourage good decisions that prevent defaults. But this activity is costly. Imagine how costly it would be if each household that lent money to a firm incurred the costs of monitoring that firm directly. Depository institutions can perform this task at a much lower cost.

You now know what money is and that the bulk of the nation's money is deposits in banks and other institutions. Your next task is to learn about the Bank of Canada and the ways in which it can influence the quantity of money.

The Bank of Canada

The Bank of Canada is Canada's **central bank**, a public authority that supervises other banks and financial institutions, financial markets, and the payments system, and conducts monetary policy.

The Bank of Canada is a bank. And like all banks, it accepts deposits, makes loans, and holds investment securities. But the Bank of Canada is special in three important ways. It is the

- Banker to banks and government
- Lender of last resort
- Sole issuer of bank notes

Banker to Banks and Government The Bank of Canada has a restricted list of customers. They are the chartered banks, credit unions and caisses populaires, and trust and mortgage loan companies that make up the banking system; the government of Canada; and the central banks of other countries. The Bank of Canada accepts deposits from these customers, and these deposits are part of the reserves of the banks.

Lender of Last Resort The Bank of Canada makes loans to banks. And it is the **lender of last resort**, which means that it stands ready to make loans when the banking system as a whole is short of reserves. If some banks are short of reserves while others have surplus reserves, the overnight loan market moves the funds from one bank to another.

Sole Issuer of Bank Notes The Bank of Canada is the only bank that is permitted to issue bank notes. You might think that such a monopoly is natural, but it isn't. In some banking systems—those of Ireland and Scotland are examples—private banks also issue bank notes. But in Canada and most other countries, the central bank has a monopoly on this activity.

The Bank of Canada's Balance Sheet The Bank of Canada influences the economy by changing interest rates. You'll learn the details of the Bank's monetary policy strategy in Chapter 30 when you've studied all the tools needed to understand monetary policy. But to influence interest rates, the Bank must change the quantity of money in the economy. And this quantity depends on the size and composition of its balance sheet—its assets and the liabilities. Lets look at the Bank of Canada's balance sheet starting with its assets.

The Bank of Canada's Assets The Bank of Canada has two main assets:

1. Government securities
2. Loans to depository institutions

The Bank of Canada holds government of Canada securities—Treasury bills—that it buys in the bills market. The Bank of Canada makes loans to depository institutions. When these institutions in aggregate are short of reserves, they can borrow from the Bank of Canada. In normal times this item is small, but during 2008, it grew as the Bank provided increasing amounts of relief from the sub-prime mortgage crisis. In September 2008, loans to depository institutions almost equalled government securities in the Bank of Canada's balance sheet (see Table 24.3).

The Bank of Canada's Liabilities The Bank of Canada has two liabilities:

1. Bank of Canada notes
2. Depository institution deposits

Bank of Canada notes are the dollar bills that we use in our daily transactions. Some of these notes are held by individuals and businesses; others are in the tills and vaults of banks and other depository institutions. Depository institution deposits at the Bank of Canada are part of the reserves of these institutions (see p. 571).

The Monetary Base The Bank of Canada's liabilities together with coins issued by the Royal Canadian Mint (coins are not liabilities of the Bank of Canada) make up the monetary base. That is, the **monetary base** is the sum of Bank of Canada notes, coins, and depository institution deposits at the Bank of Canada. The monetary base is so named because it acts like a base that supports the nation's money. Table 24.3 provides a snapshot of the sources and uses of the monetary base in September 2008.

To change the monetary base, the Bank of Canada conducts an **open market operation**, which is the purchase or sale of government of Canada securities—Treasury bills and bonds—by the Bank of Canada in the open market. When the Bank of Canada conducts an open market operation, it makes a transaction with a bank or some other business but it does not transact with the federal government.

We explain how open market operations work and their effects in Chapter 30 (pp. 736–737).

The Payments System

The **payments system** is the system through which banks make payments to each other to settle transactions by their customers. You saw why we need such a system when you thought about Colleen buying some new roller blades from Rocky. If Colleen banks at TD Canada Trust and Rocky's bank is CIBC, when

---

TABLE 24.3 The Sources and Uses of the Monetary Base

Sources (billions of dollars)		Uses (billions of dollars)	
Government of Canada securities	26.6	Currency	51.2
Loans to depository institutions	25.0	Reserves of depository institutions	0.4
Monetary base	51.6	Monetary base	51.6

Source of data: Statistics Canada, CANSIM Table 176-0011. The data are for September 2008.

Central Banks in a Credit Crisis

The Striking Contrast Between Canada and the United States

The balance sheets of central banks underwent some remarkable changes from mid-2007 to late 2008. The United States was at the epicentre of the financial tsunami, and its central bank, the Federal Reserve (the U.S. Fed), took steps to lower interest rates and boost the reserves of banks. The world's other major central banks, the Bank of Canada, the European Central Bank, and the Bank of Japan took steps to coordinate their actions with the U.S. Fed.

In normal times, a central bank's holding of its country's government securities are almost as large as the monetary base (currency and depository institution reserves). But during the 2007–2008 sub-prime crisis, central banks swapped a large volume of safe government securities for riskier loans to depository institutions.

The Bank of Canada, see Fig. 1(a), halved its holding of government securities and replaced them with loans to banks. The U.S. Fed, see Fig. 2(a), almost halved its holdings of government securities and increased its loans to depository institutions from zero to $1 trillion—an amount close to equalling the size of the entire Canadian economy.

Changes also occurred on the liabilities side of the central banks' balance sheets. But these changes were small in Canada and dramatic in the United States.

In Canada, see Fig. 1(b), currency increased somewhat but the reserves of depository institutions barely changed. In contrast, in the United States, see Fig. 2(b), the reserves of the banks increased a staggering *fifteenfold* from $44 billion to $650 billion.

The difference in the increase in reserves might, in part, arise from the fact that Canada has a small number of very large banks while the United States has a large number of very small banks. The Canadian banks are more willing to lend to each other, so small reserves are adequate. The U.S. banks are extremely reluctant to lend to each other, so much larger reserves are wanted.

When the credit crisis finally ends and banks' desired reserves decrease, the U.S. Fed will need to act swiftly to mop up the vast quantity of reserves to prevent the banks from creating an unprecedented quantity of money. The Bank of Canada doesn't face this problem.

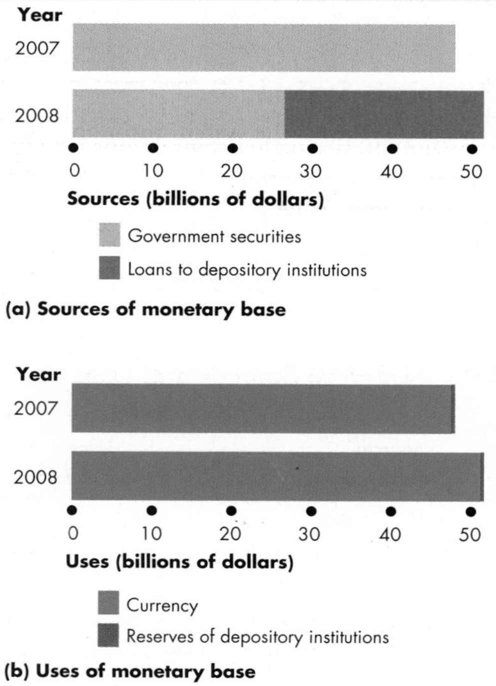

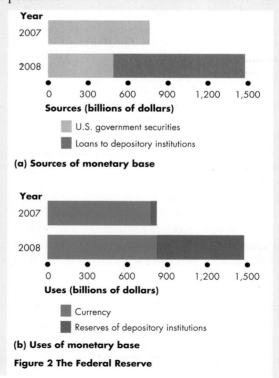

(a) Sources of monetary base

(b) Uses of monetary base

Figure 1 The Bank of Canada

(a) Sources of monetary base

(b) Uses of monetary base

Figure 2 The Federal Reserve

Sources of data: Statistics Canada, CANSIM Table 176-0011 and Board of Governors of the Federal Reserve System.

Colleen writes her cheque to buy the roller blades, TD Canada Trust must take $200 from Colleen and pay that amount to CIBC, and CIBC must put the $200 into Rocky's account.

Most transactions between two parties involve two banks and so require one bank to pay another. Think about what happens when Jack, who banks at CIBC, gets $50 cash from an Interac ABM. Interac gives Jack the $50 in cash and his CIBC deposit balance goes down by $50. But now, CIBC owes Interac $50. The payments system enables banks to make payments to each other. This system in Canada is operated by the Canadian Payments Association (CPA). The CPA owns and operates the two national payments systems:

- Large Value Transfer System
- Automated Clearing Settlement System

Large Value Transfer System The **Large Value Transfer System (LVTS)** is an electronic payments system that enables financial institutions and their customers to make large payments instantly and with the sure knowledge that the payment has been made. On an average day, the LVTS handles more than 18,000 payments worth an astonishing $140 billion.

Automated Clearing Settlement System The **Automated Clearing Settlement System (ACSS)** is the system through which all payments not processed by the LVTS are handled. These payments include cheques and small-value electronic payments. On an average day, the ACSS handles more than 20 million payments worth around $17 billion.

Next, we're going to see how the banking system—the banks and the Bank of Canada—creates money.

Review Quiz

1 What are Canada's depository institutions?
2 What are the economic functions of banks?
3 How do banks balance risk and return?
4 How do banks create liquidity and pool risks?
5 How does the Bank of Canada differ from other banks?
6 What is the payments system?

 Work Study Plan 24.2 and get instant feedback.

How Banks Create Money

Banks create money. But this doesn't mean that they have smoke-filled back rooms in which counterfeiters are busily working. Remember, most money is bank deposits, not currency. What banks create is deposits, and they do so by making loans.

Creating Deposits by Making Loans

The easiest way to see that banks create deposits is to think about what happens when Andy, who has a Visa card issued by CIBC, uses his card to buy a tank of gas from Petro-Canada. When Andy signs the card sales slip, he takes a loan from CIBC and obligates himself to repay the loan at a later date. At the end of the business day, a Petro-Canada clerk takes a pile of signed credit card sales slips, including Andy's, to Petro-Canada's bank. For now, let's assume that Petro-Canada also banks at CIBC. The bank immediately credits Petro-Canada's account with the value of the slips (minus the bank's commission).

You can see that these transactions have created a bank deposit and a loan. Andy has increased the size of his loan (his credit card balance) and Petro-Canada has increased the size of its bank deposit. Because bank deposits are money, CIBC has created money.

If Andy and Petro-Canada use the same bank (as we just assumed), no further transactions take place. But the outcome is essentially the same when they use different banks. If Petro-Canada's bank is the Bank of Nova Scotia, then CIBC uses its reserves to pay the Bank of Nova Scotia. CIBC has an increase in loans and a decrease in reserves; the Bank of Nova Scotia has an increase in reserves and an increase in deposits. The banking system has an increase in loans and deposits but no change in reserves.

If Andy had swiped his card at an automatic payment pump, all these transactions would have occurred at the time he filled his tank, and the quantity of money would have increased by the amount of his purchase (minus the bank's commission for conducting the transactions).

The quantity of deposits that the banking system can create is limited by three factors:

- The monetary base
- Desired reserves
- Desired currency holdings

The Monetary Base You've seen that the *monetary base* is the sum of Bank of Canada notes, coins, and banks' deposits at the Bank of Canada. The size of the monetary base limits the total quantity of money that the banking system can create. The reason is that banks have a desired level of reserves, households and firms have a desired holding of currency, and both of these desired holdings of the monetary base depend on the quantity of money.

Desired Reserves A bank's *actual* **reserves** consist of the notes and coins in its vaults and its deposit at the Bank of Canada. A bank uses its reserves to meet depositors' demand for currency and to make payments to other banks.

You've also seen that banks don't have $100 of reserves for every $100 that people have deposited with them. If the banks did behave that way, they wouldn't make a profit.

In September 2008, banks had reserves of $1.20 for every $100 of M1 deposits and $0.60 for every $100 of M2 deposits. Most of these reserves are currency. You saw in the previous section that reserves in the form of deposits at the Bank of Canada are tiny. But there's no need for panic. Each bank holds the quantity of reserves that is adequate for its ordinary business needs.

The fraction of a bank's total deposits that are held in reserves is called the **reserve ratio**. So with reserves of $1.20 for every $100 of M1 deposits, the M1 reserve ratio is 0.012 or 1.2 percent, and with reserves of $0.60 for every $100 of M2 deposits, the M2 reserve ratio is 0.006 or 0.6 percent.

A bank's desired reserves are the reserves that it wishes to hold. Banks choose to hold reserves so that they can make payments—just as households and firms hold money to enable them to make payments. The quantity of reserves that a bank plans to hold is its *desired reserves*, and desired reserves expressed as a percentage of total deposits is called the **desired reserve ratio**. In Canada, with its highly efficient Large Value Transfer System that banks use to make payments, the desired reserve ratio is very small.

A bank's reserve ratio changes when its customers make a deposit or a withdrawal. If a bank's customer makes a deposit, reserves and deposits increase by the same amount, so the bank's reserve ratio increases. Similarly, if a bank's customer makes a withdrawal, reserves and deposits decrease by the same amount, so the bank's reserve ratio decreases.

A bank's **excess reserves** are its actual reserves minus its desired reserves. When a bank has excess reserves, it makes loans and creates money; when it is short of reserves—when desired reserves exceed actual reserves—its loans and deposits shrink.

When the entire banking system has excess reserves, banks make loans and deposits increase; when the banking system is short of reserves, banks decrease loans and deposits decrease.

The greater the desired reserve ratio, the smaller is the quantity of money that the banking system can create from a given monetary base.

Desired Currency Holding We hold our money in the form of currency and bank deposits. The proportion of money held as currency isn't constant but at any given time, people have a definite view as to how much they want to hold in each form of money.

In 2008, for every dollar of M1 deposits held, we held 12.3 cents of currency and for every dollar of M2 deposits, we held 6 cents of currency.

Because households and firms want to hold some proportion of their money in the form of currency, when the total quantity of bank deposits increases, so does the quantity of currency that they want to hold. Because desired currency holding increases when deposits increase, currency leaves the banks when loans are made and deposits increase. We call the leakage of currency from the banking system the *currency drain*, and we call the ratio of currency to deposits the **currency drain ratio**.

The greater the currency drain ratio, the smaller is the quantity of deposits and money that the banking system can create from a given amount of monetary base.

The Money Creation Process

The money creation process begins when the monetary base increases and the banking system has excess reserves. These excess reserves come from a purchase of securities by the Bank of Canada from a bank. (Chapter 30, pp. 736–737, explains exactly how the Bank of Canada conducts such a purchase—open market operation.)

When the Bank of Canada buys securities from a bank, the bank's reserves increase but its deposits do not change. So the bank has excess reserves. It lends those excess reserves and a sequence of events then plays out.

The sequence, which keeps repeating until all the reserves held are desired and banks have no excess reserves, has eight steps:

1. Banks have excess reserves.
2. Banks lend excess reserves.
3. The quantity of money increases.
4. New money is used to make payments.
5. Some of the new money remains on deposit.
6. Some of the new money is a *currency drain.*
7. Desired reserves increase because deposits have increased.
8. Excess reserves decrease but remain positive.

The sequence repeats in a series of rounds, but excess reserves shrink at each round. The process of money creation continues until excess reserves have been eliminated.

Figure 24.1 illustrates the first round in this process.

The Money Multiplier

The **money multiplier** is the ratio of the change in the quantity of money to the change in monetary base. For example, if an increase in the monetary base by $100,000 increases the quantity of money by $250,000, then the money multiplier is 2.5.

The Mathematical Note on pp. 586–587 explains how the size of the money multiplier depends on the reserve ratio and the currency drain ratio.

Review Quiz

1 How do banks create money?
2 What limits the quantity of money that the banking system can create?
3 A bank manager tells you that she doesn't create money: She just lends what people deposit. Explain why she is wrong.

myeconlab Work Study Plan 24.3 and get instant feedback.

FIGURE 24.1   How the Banking System Creates Money by Making Loans

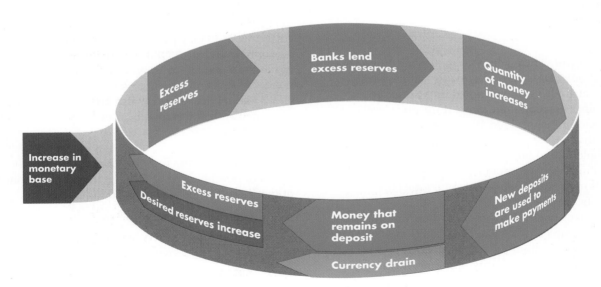

The Bank of Canada increases the monetary base, which increases bank reserves and creates excess reserves. Banks lend the excess reserves and create new deposits. The quantity of money increases. New deposits are used to make payments. Some of the new money remains on deposit at banks and some leaves the banks in a currency drain. The increase in bank deposits increases banks' desired reserves. But the banks still have excess reserves, though less than before. The process repeats until excess reserves have been eliminated.

myeconlab animation

The Market for Money

There is no limit to the amount of money we would like to *receive* in payment for our labour or as interest on our savings. But there *is* a limit to how big an inventory of money we would like to *hold* and neither spend nor use to buy assets that generate an income. The *quantity of money demanded* is the inventory of money that people plan to hold on any given day. It is the quantity of money in our wallets and in our deposit accounts at banks. The quantity of money held must equal the quantity supplied, and the forces that bring about this equality in the money market have powerful effects on the economy, as you will see in the rest of this chapter.

But first, we need to explain what determines the amount of money that people plan to hold.

The Influences on Money Holding

The quantity of money that people plan to hold depends on four main factors:

- The price level
- The *nominal* interest rate
- Real GDP
- Financial innovation

The Price Level The quantity of money measured in dollars is *nominal money*. The quantity of nominal money demanded is proportional to the price level, other things remaining the same. If the price level rises by 10 percent, people hold 10 percent more nominal money than before, other things remaining the same. If you hold $20 to buy your weekly movies and pop, you will increase your money holding to $22 if the prices of movies and pop—and your wage rate—increase by 10 percent.

The quantity of money measured in constant dollars (for example, in 2000 dollars) is real money. *Real money* is equal to nominal money divided by the price level and is the quantity of money measured in terms of what it will buy. In the above example, when the price level rises by 10 percent and you increase your money holding by 10 percent, your *real* money holding is constant. Your $22 at the new price level buys the same quantity of goods and is the same quantity of *real money* as your $20 at the original price level. The quantity of real money demanded is independent of the price level.

The Nominal Interest Rate A fundamental principle of economics is that as the opportunity cost of something increases, people try to find substitutes for it. Money is no exception. The higher the opportunity cost of holding money, other things remaining the same, the smaller is the quantity of real money demanded. The nominal interest rate on other assets minus the nominal interest rate on money is the opportunity cost of holding money.

The interest rate that you earn on currency and chequable deposits is zero. So the opportunity cost of holding these items is the nominal interest rate on other assets such as a savings bond or a Treasury bill. By holding money instead, you forgo the interest that you otherwise would have received.

Money loses value because of inflation, so why isn't the inflation rate part of the cost of holding money? It is. Other things remaining the same, the higher the expected inflation rate, the higher is the nominal interest rate.

Real GDP The quantity of money that households and firms plan to hold depends on the amount they are spending, and the quantity of money demanded in the economy as a whole depends on aggregate expenditure—real GDP.

Again, suppose that you hold an average of $20 to finance your weekly purchases of movies and pop. Now imagine that the prices of these goods and of all other goods remain constant but that your income increases. As a consequence, you now buy more goods and services and you also keep a larger amount of money on hand to finance your higher volume of expenditure.

Financial Innovation Technological change and the arrival of new financial products influence the quantity of money held. Financial innovations include

1. Daily interest chequable deposits
2. Automatic transfers between chequable deposits and saving deposits
3. Automatic teller machines
4. Credit cards and debit cards
5. Internet banking and bill paying

These innovations have occurred because of the development of computing power that has lowered the cost of calculations and record keeping.

We summarize the effects of the influences on money holding by using a demand for money curve.

The Demand for Money

The **demand for money** is the relationship between the quantity of real money demanded and the nominal interest rate when all other influences on the amount of money that people wish to hold remain the same.

Figure 24.2 shows a demand for money curve, *MD*. When the interest rate rises, other things remaining the same, the opportunity cost of holding money rises and the quantity of real money demanded decreases—there is a movement up along the demand for money curve. Similarly, when the interest rate falls, the opportunity cost of holding money falls, and the quantity of real money demanded increases—there is a movement down along the demand for money curve.

When any influence on money holding other than the interest rate changes, there is a change in the demand for money and the demand for money curve shifts. Let's study these shifts.

Shifts in the Demand for Money Curve

A change in real GDP or financial innovation changes the demand for money and shifts the demand for money curve.

Figure 24.3 illustrates the change in the demand for money. A decrease in real GDP decreases the demand for money and shifts the demand for money curve leftward from MD_0 to MD_1. An increase in real GDP has the opposite effect: It increases the demand for money and shifts the demand for money curve rightward from MD_0 to MD_2.

The influence of financial innovation on the demand for money curve is more complicated. It decreases the demand for currency and might increase the demand for some types of deposits and decrease the demand for others. But generally, financial innovation decreases the demand for money.

You can see the effects of changes in real GDP and financial innovation by looking at the demand for money in Canada on the next page.

FIGURE 24.2 The Demand for Money

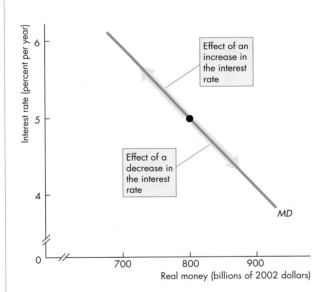

The demand for money curve, *MD*, shows the relationship between the quantity of real money that people plan to hold and the nominal interest rate, other things remaining the same. The interest rate is the opportunity cost of holding money. A change in the interest rate brings a movement along the demand for money curve.

FIGURE 24.3 Changes in the Demand for Money

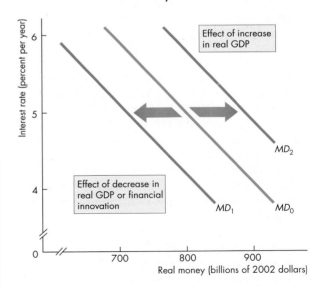

A decrease in real GDP decreases the demand for money. The demand for money curve shifts leftward from MD_0 to MD_1. An increase in real GDP increases the demand for money. The demand for money curve shifts rightward from MD_0 to MD_2. Financial innovation generally decreases the demand for money.

Demand for Money in Canada

How Money Holding Bounces Around

The growth of real GDP brings sustained growth in the demand for money. If real GDP were the only influence on the demand for money, the demand for money curve would shift rightward whenever real GDP increased, which is most of the time.

But financial innovation also influences the demand for money. During the early 1970s, the spread of credit cards decreased the demand for currency and chequable deposits (M1).

A continued increase in the use of credit cards and the spread of ATMs further decreased the demand for M1 during the 1990s and 2000s. But debit cards and the payment of interest on chequable account balances increased the demand for M1 during the 1990s.

Similarly, financial innovation has changed the demand for the non-chequable deposits that make up M2. New interest-bearing deposits increased the demand for M2 during the 1970s. But during the 1990s, the interest-bearing chequable deposits that increased the demand for M1 had the opposite effect on M2. Also, innovations in financial products that compete with deposits of all kinds occurred and the demand for M2 decreased.

The figures illustrate the effects of financial innovation on the demand for M1 in part (a) and M2 in part (b). The effects of real GDP growth are removed by measuring money as a percentage of GDP.

Each dot represents the quantity of real money as a percentage of real GDP and the interest rate in each year between 1971 and 2007. In 1971, the demand for M1 curve was MD_0 in part (a). The demand for M1 decreased during the 1980s and the demand curve shifted leftward to MD_1. But the demand for M1 increased during the 1990s and the demand curve had shifted rightward to MD_2.

In 1971, the demand for M2 curve was MD_0 in part (b). During the 1970s, the demand for M2 increased and the demand curve shifted rightward to MD_1. During the 1990s, new substitutes for M2 decreased the demand for M2 and the demand curve shifted leftward to MD_2.

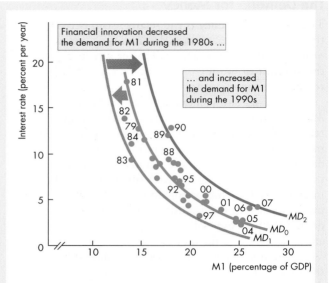

(a) Demand for M1+ gross

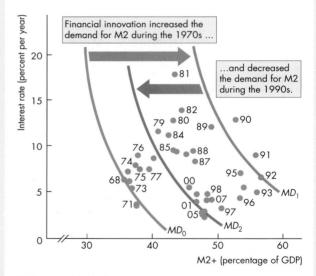

(b) Demand for M2+ gross

The Canadian Demand for Money

Sources of data: Statistics Canada, CANSIM Tables 176-0020, 176-0043, and 380-0002.

You now know what determines the demand for money, and you've seen how the banking system creates money.

Your next task is to bring the two sides of the money market together and see how the money market reaches an equilibrium. This matter is a bit complicated and we study it in two time frames, the short run and the long run.

Money Market Equilibrium

Money market equilibrium occurs when the quantity of money demanded equals the quantity of money supplied. The adjustments that bring about money market equilibrium are fundamentally different in the short run and the long run. Here, we explore the short run only briefly. We study the short run at length in Chapters 26–30, which explain the transmission of monetary policy through the economy.

Short-Run Equilibrium The quantity of money supplied is determined by the actions of the banks and the Bank of Canada. Each day, the Bank of Canada adjusts the quantity of money to hit its interest rate target. In Fig. 24.4, with the demand for money curve *MD*, if the Bank of Canada wants the interest rate to be 5 per-

cent a year, the Bank of Canada adjusts the quantity of money so that the quantity of real money supplied is $800 billion and the supply of money curve is *MS*.

The equilibrium interest rate is 5 percent a year. If the interest rate were 4 percent a year, people would want to hold more money than is available. They would sell bonds, bid down their price, and the interest rate would rise. If the interest rate were 6 percent a year, people would want to hold less money than is available. They would buy bonds, bid up their price, and the interest rate would fall.

Long-Run Equilibrium In the long run, supply and demand in the loanable funds market determines the real interest rate. The nominal interest rate equals the equilibrium real interest rate plus the expected inflation rate. Real GDP, which influences the demand for money, equals potential GDP. So the *only* variable that is left to adjust in the long run is the price level. The price level adjusts to make the quantity of real money supplied equal to the quantity demanded. If the Bank of Canada changes the nominal quantity of money, the price level changes (in the long run) by a percentage equal to the percentage change in the quantity of nominal money. In the long run, the change in the price level is proportional to the change in the quantity of money.

FIGURE 24.4 Money Market Equilibrium

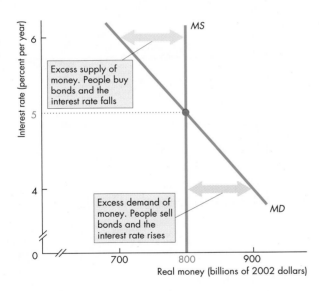

Money market equilibrium occurs when the quantity of money demanded equals the quantity supplied.

   Short run: In the short run, the quantity of real money and real GDP are given and the interest rate adjusts to achieve equilibrium, here 5 percent a year.

   Long run: In the long run, supply and demand in the loanable funds market determines the interest rate, real GDP equals potential GDP, and the price level adjusts to make the quantity of real money supplied equal the quantity demanded, here $800 billion.

 animation

Review Quiz

1 What are the main influences on the quantity of real money that people and businesses plan to hold?

2 How does a change in the nominal interest rate change the quantity of money demanded? Illustrate the effect by using the demand for money curve.

3 How does a change in real GDP change the demand for money? Illustrate the effect by using the demand for money curve.

4 How has financial innovation changed the demand for M1 and the demand for M2?

5 How is money market equilibrium determined in the short run and in the long run?

myeconlab Work Study Plan 24.4 and get instant feedback.

Let's explore the long-run link between money and the price level more thoroughly.

◆ The Quantity Theory of Money

In the long run, the price level adjusts to make the quantity of real money demanded equal the quantity supplied. A special theory of the price level and inflation—the quantity theory of money—explains this long-run adjustment of the price level.

The **quantity theory of money** is the proposition that in the long run, an increase in the quantity of money brings an equal percentage increase in the price level. To explain the quantity theory of money, we first need to define *the velocity of circulation*.

The **velocity of circulation** is the average number of times a dollar of money is used annually to buy the goods and services that make up GDP. But GDP equals the price level (P) multiplied by *real* GDP (Y). That is,

$$GDP = PY.$$

Call the quantity of money M. The velocity of circulation, V, is determined by the equation

$$V = PY/M.$$

For example, if GDP is \$1,000 billion (PY is \$1,000 billion) and the quantity of money is \$250 billion, then the velocity of circulation is 4.

From the definition of the velocity of circulation, the *equation of exchange* tells us how M, V, P, and Y are connected. This equation is

$$MV = PY.$$

Given the definition of the velocity of circulation, the equation of exchange is always true—it is true by definition. It becomes the quantity theory of money if the quantity of money does not influence the velocity of circulation or real GDP. In this case, the equation of exchange tells us that in the long run, the price level is determined by the quantity of money. That is,

$$P = M(V/Y),$$

where (V/Y) is independent of M. So a change in M brings a proportional change in P.

We can also express the equation of exchange in growth rates[1] in which form it states that

$$\text{Money growth rate} + \text{Rate of velocity change} = \text{Inflation rate} + \text{Real GDP growth rate}$$

Does the Quantity Theory Work?

Yes, on Average

On average, as predicted by the quantity theory of money, the inflation rate fluctuates in line with fluctuations in the money growth rate minus the real GDP growth rate. Figure 1 shows the relationship between money growth (M2 definition) and inflation in Canada. You can see a clear relationship between the two variables.

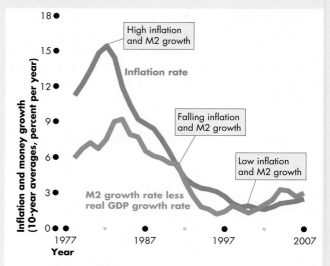

Figure 1 Canadian Money Growth and Inflation

Sources of data: Statistics Canada, CANSIM Tables 176-0020 and 380-0002.

Solving this equation for the inflation rate gives

$$\text{Inflation rate} = \text{Money growth rate} + \text{Rate of velocity change} - \text{Real GDP growth rate}$$

In the long run, the rate of velocity change is not influenced by the money growth rate. More strongly, in the long run, the rate of velocity change is approxi-

---

[1] To obtain this equation, begin with
$$MV = PY,$$
and then changes in these variables are related by the equation
$$\Delta MV + M\Delta V = \Delta PY + P\Delta Y.$$
Divide this equation by the equation of exchange to obtain
$$\Delta M/M + \Delta V/V = \Delta P/P + \Delta Y/Y.$$
The term $\Delta M/M$ is the money growth rate, $\Delta V/V$ is the rate of velocity change, $\Delta P/P$ is the inflation rate, and $\Delta Y/Y$ is the real GDP growth rate.

International data also support the quantity theory. Figure 2 shows a scatter diagram of the inflation rate and the money growth rate in 134 countries and Fig. 3 shows the inflation rate and money growth rate in countries with inflation rates below 20 percent a year. You can see a general tendency for money growth and inflation to be correlated but the quantity theory (the red line) does not predict inflation precisely.

The correlation between money growth and inflation isn't perfect, and the correlation does not tell us that money growth *causes* inflation. Money growth might cause inflation; inflation might cause money growth; or some third variable might cause both inflation and money growth. Other evidence does confirm, though, that causation runs from money growth to inflation.

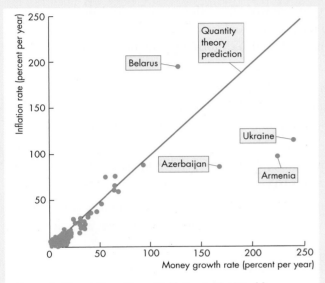

Figure 2 Money Growth and Inflation in the World

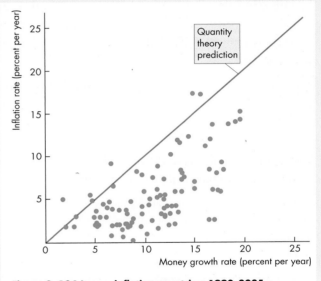

Figure 3 104 Lower-inflation countries: 1990–2005

Sources of data: International Financial Statistics Yearbook, 2008, and International Monetary Fund, *World Economic Outlook*, October 2008.

mately zero. With this assumption, the inflation rate in the long run is determined as

$$\text{Inflation rate} = \text{Money growth rate} - \text{Real GDP growth rate}$$

In the long run, fluctuations in the money growth rate minus the real GDP growth rate bring equal fluctuations in the inflation rate.

Also in the long run, with the economy at full employment, real GDP equals potential GDP, so the real GDP growth rate equals the potential GDP growth rate. This growth rate might be influenced by inflation, but the influence is most likely small and the quantity theory assumes that it is zero. So the real GDP growth rate is given and doesn't change when the money growth rate changes—inflation is correlated with money growth.

Review Quiz

1 What is the quantity theory of money?
2 How is the velocity of circulation calculated?
3 What is the equation of exchange? Can it be wrong?
4 Does the quantity theory correctly predict the effects of money growth on inflation?

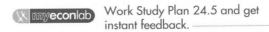 Work Study Plan 24.5 and get instant feedback.

You now know what money is, how the banks create it, and how the quantity of money influences the nominal interest rate in the short run and the price level in the long run. *Reading Between the Lines* rounds out the chapter by looking at the quantity theory of money in action in Zimbabwe today.

The Quantity Theory of Money in Zimbabwe

Life in Zimbabwe: Wait for Useless Money, Then Scour for Food

October 2, 2008

Harare, Zimbabwe—Long before the rooster in their dirt yard crowed, Rose Moyo and her husband rolled out of bed ... and took their daily moonlit stroll to the bank ... hoping for a chance to withdraw the maximum amount of Zimbabwean currency the government allowed last month—the equivalent of just a dollar or two.

Zimbabwe is in the grip of one of the great hyperinflations in world history. The people of this once proud capital have been plunged into a Darwinian struggle to get by. Many have been reduced to peddlers and paupers, hawkers and black-market hustlers, eating just a meal or two a day, their hollowed cheeks a testament to their hunger. ...

Mrs. Moyo has calculated the price of goods by the number of days she had to spend in line at the bank to withdraw cash to buy them: a day for a bar of soap; another for a bag of salt; and four for a sack of cornmeal.

The withdrawal limit rose on Monday, but with inflation surpassing what independent economists say is an almost unimaginable 40 million percent, she said the value of the new amount would quickly be a pittance, too.

"It's survival of the fittest," said Mrs. Moyo, 29, a hair braider who sells the greens she grows in her yard for a dime a bunch. "If you're not fit, you will starve."

Economists here and abroad say Zimbabwe's economic collapse is gaining velocity, radiating instability into the heart of southern Africa. As the bankrupt government prints ever more money, inflation has gone wild, rising from 1,000 percent in 2006 to 12,000 percent in 2007 to a figure so high the government had to lop 10 zeros off the currency in August to keep the nation's calculators from being overwhelmed. (Had it left the currency alone, $1 would now be worth about 10 trillion Zimbabwean dollars.) ...

Essence of the Story

- Hyperinflation in Zimbabwe is the worst in world history—40 million percent a year.

- $1 U.S. was heading towards $10 trillion Zimbabwean before 10 zeros were lopped off the currency unit.

- People get up in the middle of the night to stand in line for cash at the bank because the government limits cash withdrawals.

- Prices of goods are measured in the number of days spent in line to withdraw the cash to buy them: a day for a bar of soap or a bag of salt; four days for a sack of cornmeal.

- The people of Harare (the capital city) are on the edge of survival.

- The government fuels the inflation by printing ever more money.

Economic Analysis

- Zimbabwe has the highest inflation rate in world history, so it provides a good example of the quantity theory of money in action.

- The Zimbabwe economy is in a state of total collapse, so this case study also provides a graphic example of the devastating costs of high inflation.

- During 2008, the inflation rate in Zimbabwe was so high, it could not be measured accurately but it was reputed to be 231 million percent a year.

- To appreciate an inflation rate of 231 million percent a year, translate it into a monthly inflation rate. Every month, on average, prices rise by 239 percent. A cup of coffee that costs $3 in January costs $10 in February, $117 in April and $4,560 in July!

- Figure 1 shows Zimbabwe's reported inflation rate and money growth rate record from 2000 to 2007.

- The money growth rate increased from 52 percent a year in 2000 to 66,700 percent a year in 2007.

- The reported inflation rate increased slowly at first, from 56 percent a year in 2000 to 303 percent a year in 2005. In 2006, the inflation rate took off and climbed to a reported 1,100 percent in 2006 and 24,000 percent in 2007.

- The quantity theory predicts that inflation will outpace the money growth rate, not fall behind it as these reported inflation rates show.

- The reported inflation rate is almost certainly far lower than the true inflation rate.

- When people expect rapid inflation, they expect the money they hold to lose value rapidly, so they spend and hold goods rather than money.

- The velocity of circulation rises. The velocity of circulation is independent of the quantity of money but not independent of the money growth rate.

- We can measure the velocity of circulation in Zimbabwe by using the equation of exchange

$$MV = PY$$

along with data on M, P, and Y.

- Real GDP, Y, has fallen every year since 2000, and in 2007 it stood at 70 percent of its 2000 level.

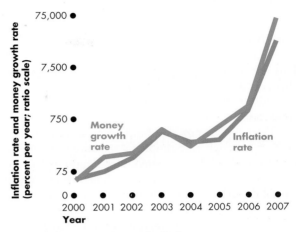

Figure 1 Money growth and inflation

- The velocity of circulation, based on the reported data, *fell* from 6.7 in 2000 to 0.6 in 2007.

- The true velocity of circulation could not have fallen. A lower velocity implies that people are hoarding more money.

- The explanation for the fall in the calculated velocity of circulation is that the true inflation rate is much higher than the reported rate.

- The unofficial reported inflation of 40 million percent a year in 2008 might be close to the truth. The inflation rate during the years 2003 through 2007 was almost certainly greater than the money growth rate.

- The reported change in the currency unit, lopping off 10 zeroes, has no effect on the inflation rate. It only changes the units in which prices are measured.

- To lower its inflation rate, the government of Zimbabwe must stop printing money to finance its expenditures.

MATHEMATICAL NOTE

The Money Multiplier

This note explains the basic math of the money multiplier and shows how the value of the multiplier depends on the banks' reserve ratio and the currency drain ratio.

To make the process of money creation concrete, we work through an example for a banking system in which each bank has a desired reserve ratio of 10 percent of deposits and the currency drain ratio is 50 percent of deposits or 0.5. (Although these ratios are larger than the ones in the Canadian economy, they make the process end more quickly and enable you to see more clearly the principles at work.)

The figure keeps track of the numbers. Before the process begins, the banks have no excess reserves. Then the monetary base increases by $100,000 and a bank has excess reserves of this amount.

The bank lends the $100,000 of excess reserves. When this loan is made, new money increases by $100,000.

With a currency drain ratio of 50 percent of deposits, $33,333 drains out of the banks as currency and $66,667 remains in the banks as deposits. The quantity of money has increased by $100,000—the increase in deposits plus the increase in currency holding.

The increased bank deposits of $66,667 generate an increase in desired reserves of 10 percent of that amount, which is $6,667. Actual reserves have increased by the same amount as the increase in deposits: $66,667. So the banks now have excess reserves of $60,000.

The process we've just described repeats but begins with excess reserves of $60,000. The figure shows the next two rounds. At the end of the process, the quantity of money has increased by a multiple of the increase in the monetary base. In this case, the increase is $250,000, which is 2.5 times the increase in the monetary base.

The sequence in the figure is the first stage of the process that finally reaches the total shown in the final row of the "money" column.

To calculate what happens at the later stages in the process and the final increase in the quantity of money,

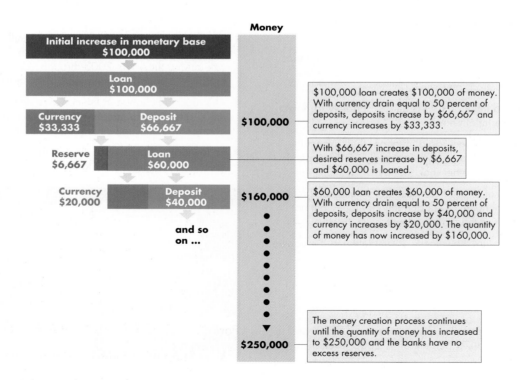

Figure 1 The money creation process

look closely at the numbers in the figure. The initial increase in reserves is $100,000 (call it A). At each stage, the loan is 60 percent (0.6) of the previous loan and the quantity of money increases by 0.6 of the previous increase. Call that proportion L ($L = 0.6$). We can write down the complete sequence for the increase in the quantity of money as

$$A + AL + AL^2 + AL^3 + AL^4 + AL^5 + \dots .$$

Remember, L is a fraction, so at each stage in this sequence, the amount of new loans and new money gets smaller. The total value of loans made and money created at the end of the process is the sum of the sequence, which is[2]

$$A/(1 - L).$$

If we use the numbers from the example, the total increase in the quantity of money is

$$\$100,000 + 60,000 + 36,000 + \dots$$

$$= \$100,000 \, (1 + 0.6 + 0.36 + \dots)$$

$$= \$100,000 \, (1 + 0.6 + 0.6^2 + \dots)$$

$$= \$100,000 \times 1/(1 - 0.6)$$

$$= \$100,000 \times 1/(0.4)$$

$$= \$100,000 \times 2.5$$

$$= \$250,000.$$

The magnitude of the money multiplier depends on the desired reserve ratio and the currency drain ratio. Call the monetary base MB and the quantity of money M. When there are no excess reserves,

$$MB = \text{Desired currency holding} + \text{Desired reserves.}$$

$$M = \text{Deposits} + \text{Desired currency holding.}$$

Call the currency drain ratio a and the desired reserve ratio b. Then

$$\text{Desired currency holding} = a \times \text{Deposits}$$

$$\text{Desired reserves} = b \times \text{Deposits}$$

$$MB = (a + b) \times \text{Deposits}$$

$$M = (1 + a) \times \text{Deposits.}$$

Call the change in monetary base ΔMB and the change in the quantity of money ΔM. Then

$$\Delta MB = (a + b) \times \text{Change in deposits}$$

$$\Delta M = (1 + a) \times \text{Change in deposits.}$$

The money multiplier is the ratio of ΔM to ΔMB, so divide the above equation for ΔM by the one for ΔMB. That is,

$$\text{Money multiplier} = (1 + a)/(a + b).$$

If we use the values of the example summarized in the figure, $a = 0.5$ and $b = 0.1$, the

$$\text{Money multiplier} = (1 + 0.5)/(0.5 + 0.1)$$

$$= 1.5/0.6 = 2.5.$$

The Canadian Money Multiplier

The money multiplier in Canada can be found by using the formula above along with the values of a and b in the Canadian economy.

Because we have two definitions of money, M1 and M2, we have two money multipliers. The numbers for M1 in 2008 are $a = 0.14$ and $b = 0.0004$. So

$$\text{M1 multiplier} = (1 + 0.14)/(0.14 + 0.0004)$$

$$= 1.14/0.1404 = 8.1.$$

For M2 in 2008, $a = 0.063$ and $b = 0.0002$, so

$$\text{M2 multiplier} = (1 + 0.063)/(0.063 + 0.0002)$$

$$= 1.063/0.0632 = 16.8.$$

---

[2] The sequence of values is called a convergent geometric series. To find the sum of a series such as this, begin by calling the sum S. Then write the sum as

$$S = A + AL + AL^2 + AL^3 + AL^4 + AL^5 + \dots .$$

Multiply by L to get

$$LS = AL + AL^2 + AL^3 + AL^4 + AL^5 + . \dots$$

Then subtract the second equation from the first to get

$$S(1 - L) = A$$

or

$$S = A/(1 - L).$$

SUMMARY ◆

Key Points

What Is Money? (pp. 568–570)

- Money is the means of payment. It functions as a medium of exchange, a unit of account, and a store of value.
- Today, money consists of currency and deposits.

The Banking System (pp. 571–575)

- The banking system consists of the depository institutions (chartered banks, credit unions and caisses populaires, and trust and mortgage loan companies), the Bank of Canada, and the payments system.
- Depository institutions provide four main economic services: They create liquidity, minimize the cost of obtaining funds, minimize the cost of monitoring borrowers, and pool risks.
- The Bank of Canada is the central bank of Canada.

How Banks Create Money (pp. 575–577)

- Banks create money by making loans.
- The total quantity of money that can be created depends on the monetary base, the desired reserve ratio, and the currency drain ratio.

The Market for Money (pp. 578–581)

- The quantity of money demanded is the amount of money that people plan to hold.
- The quantity of real money equals the quantity of nominal money divided by the price level.
- The quantity of real money demanded depends on the nominal interest rate, real GDP, and financial innovation. A rise in the nominal interest rate brings a decrease in the quantity of real money demanded.
- In the short run, the Bank of Canada sets the quantity of money to hit a target nominal interest rate.
- In the long run, the loanable funds market determines the real interest rate and the quantity of money determines the price level.

The Quantity Theory of Money (pp. 582–583)

- The quantity theory of money is the proposition that money growth and inflation move up and down together in the long run.
- The Canadian and international evidence is consistent with the quantity theory, on average.

Key Figures

Key Terms

PROBLEMS and APPLICATIONS

 Work problems 1–12 in Chapter 24 Study Plan and get instant feedback.
Work problems 13–22 as Homework, a Quiz, or a Test if assigned by your instructor.

1. In Canada today, money includes which of the following items?
   a. Bank of Canada bank notes in CIBC's ATMs
   b. Your Visa card
   c. Coins inside a vending machine
   d. Bank of Canada bank notes in your wallet
   e. The cheque you have just written to pay for your rent
   f. The student loan you took out last August

2. The chartered banks in Zap have

Reserves	$250 million
Loans	$1,000 million
Deposits	$2,000 million
Total assets	$2,500 million

   If banks have no excess reserves, calculate the banks' desired reserve ratio.

3. You are given the following information about the economy of Nocoin: The banks have deposits of $300 billion. Their reserves are $15 billion, two-thirds of which is in deposits with the central bank. Households and firms hold $30 billion in bank notes. There are no coins! Calculate

   a. The monetary base.
   b. The quantity of money.
   c. The banks' reserve ratio (as a percentage).
   d. The currency drain ratio (as a percentage).

4. [Study the Mathematical Note on pp. 586–587 to work this problem.] In problem 3, the banks have no excess reserves. Suppose that the Bank of Nocoin, the central bank, increases bank reserves by $0.5 billion.

   a. What happens to the quantity of money?
   b. Explain why the change in the quantity of money is not equal to the change in the monetary base.
   c. Calculate the money multiplier.

5. [Study the Mathematical Note on pp. 586–587 to work this problem.] In problem 3, the banks have no excess reserves. Suppose that the Bank of Nocoin, the central bank, decreases bank reserves by $0.5 billion.

   a. Calculate the money multiplier.
   b. What happens to the quantity of money?

   c. What happens to the quantity of deposits?
   d. What happens to the quantity of currency?

6. The spreadsheet provides information about the demand for money in Minland. Column A is the nominal interest rate, r. Columns B and C show the quantity of money demanded at two different levels of real GDP: Y_0 is $10 billion and Y_1 is $20 billion.

	A	B	C
	r	Y_0	Y_1
1			
2	7	1.0	1.5
3	6	1.5	2.0
4	5	2.0	2.5
5	4	2.5	3.0
6	3	3.0	3.5
7	2	3.5	4.0
8	1	4.0	4.5

   The quantity of money is $3 billion and, initially, real GDP is $20 billion. What happens in Minland if the interest rate

   a. Exceeds 4 percent a year?
   b. Is less than 4 percent a year?
   c. Equals 4 percent a year?

7. The Minland economy in problem 6 experiences a severe recession. Real GDP decreases to $10 billion. If the quantity of money supplied does not change,

   a. What happens in Minland if the interest rate is 4 percent a year?
   b. Do people buy bonds or sell bonds?
   c. Will the interest rate rise or fall? Why?

8. Quantecon is a country in which the quantity theory of money operates. The country has a constant population, capital stock, and technology. In year 1, real GDP was $400 million, the price level was 200, and the velocity of circulation was 20. In year 2, the quantity of money was 20 percent higher than in year 1. What was

   a. The quantity of money in year 1?
   b. The quantity of money in year 2?
   c. The price level in year 2?
   d. The level of real GDP in year 2?
   e. The velocity of circulation in year 2?

9. In Quantecon described in problem 8, in year 3, the quantity of money falls to one-fifth of its level in year 2.

   a. What is the quantity of money in year 3?
   b. What is the price level in year 3?
   c. What is the level of real GDP in year 3?
   d. What is the velocity of circulation in year 3?
   e. If it takes more than one year for the full quantity theory effect to occur, what do you predict happens to real GDP in Quantecon in year 3? Why?

10. **Financial System Review** The key risk to the [Canadian] financial system is that the downturn in the U.S. economy may be deeper than currently anticipated. ... The direct exposure of Canadian banks to the United States represents about 16 per cent of total bank assets, more than the combined exposure to any other group of foreign countries. ... In the mid-1990s, exposure to U.S. securities and loans represented roughly 3 per cent and 10 per cent of total Canadian bank assets, respectively. By 2007, these figures had converged, each representing just under 8 per cent of total Canadian bank assets. This shift towards increased holdings of U.S. securities, all else being equal, implies that the return on U.S. exposures has become more dependent on the performance of financial markets. ...

   Bank of Canada, June 2008

   a. Explain a bank's "balancing act."
   b. How and why have Canadian banks' holdings of U.S. assets changed?
   c. How might the over-pursuit of profit or underestimation of risk create problems for Canadian banks?

11. **"Boring" Canada's Financial Tips for the World**

   The financial crisis that began 14 months ago in the U.S. has intensified and spread around the world. ... Few countries are as dependent on trade or as integrated into the global financial system as Canada. Yet our financial sector continues to weather the turbulence better than many other countries. This did not happen by chance. Canadians by nature are prudent and our financial system has been characterized as unexciting. Canada's regulatory regime ensures that stability and efficiency are balanced. As a result, Canadian taxpayers have not had their money put at risk in response to this crisis. If Canada's financial system is boring, perhaps the world needs to be more like Canada ... capital and liquidity buffers need to be large enough to handle big shocks ... Some have criticized high Canadian capital requirements for banks as being too conservative. But the strong balance sheets of Canada's banks through this period speak for themselves ... The open market system did not fail in this crisis. However, some forgot Adam Smith's maxim that the invisible hand needs to be supported by an appropriate legal and regulatory framework.

   Financial Times, November 12, 2008

   a. Explain how Canada's financial system might be considered "boring."
   b. What are the advantages and disadvantages of a "boring" financial system?
   c. Explain how the last sentence of the news clip can be applied to organizing a country's financial system.

12. **Banks Drop on Higher Reserve Requirement**
    China's central bank will raise its reserve ratio requirement by a percentage point to a record 17.5 percent by June 25, stepping up a battle to contain lending growth. ... The increase will freeze up about 422 billion yuan of funds, equivalent to 91 percent of the value of new yuan-denominated loans extended in April. ... The latest move adds to the 614.7 billion yuan removed from the financial system through reserve ratio increases since January. China's banks had an average excess reserve deposit ratio of 2 percent as of March 31, down from 3.3 percent in December. The rate that banks charge each other for seven-day loans ... rose to 4.93 percent in Shanghai, the highest since Jan 24, according to China Bond Interbank Market. The gain suggests banks are hoarding cash in anticipation of further reserve ratio requirement increases. ... Every half-point increase in the reserve ratio requirement cuts banks' profits by as much as 1.5 percent, assuming they reduce lending to comply with it, said Li Qing, an analyst at CSC Securities HK Ltd.

    People's Daily Online, June 11, 2008

    a. Compare the reserve ratios in China and Canada.
    b. Explain how the reserve ratio influences China's money multiplier.
    c. Why would a higher reserve ratio decrease bank profits?

13. Sara withdraws $1,000 from her savings account at the Lucky Credit Union, keeps $50 in cash, and deposits the balance in her chequable account at the Royal Bank of Canada. What is the immediate change in M1 and M2?

14. Banks in New Transylvania have a desired reserve ratio of 10 percent and no excess reserves. The currency drain ratio is 50 percent. Then the central bank increases bank reserves by $1,200.

    a. What is the initial increase in the monetary base?
    b. How much do the banks lend in the first round of the money creation process?
    c. How much of the amount initially lent does not return to the banks but is held as currency?
    d. Set out the transactions that take place and calculate the amount of deposits created and the increase in the amount of currency held after the second round of the money creation process.

15. [Study the Mathematical Note on pp. 586–587 to work this problem.] In the United Kingdom, the currency drain ratio is 0.38 of deposits and the desired reserve ratio is 0.002. In Australia, the quantity of money is $150 billion, the currency drain ratio is 33 percent of deposits, and the desired reserve ratio is 8 percent.

    a. Calculate the U.K. money multiplier.
    b. Calculate the monetary base in Australia.

16. The table provides some data for the United States in the first decade following the Civil War.

	1869	1879
Quantity of money	$1.3 billion	$1.7 billion
Real GDP (1929 dollars)	$7.4 billion	Z
Price level (1929 = 100)	X	54
Velocity of circulation	4.50	4.61

Source: Milton Friedman and Anna J. Schwartz, *A Monetary History of the United States 1867–1960.*

    a. Calculate the value of X in 1869.
    b. Calculate the value of Z in 1879.
    c. Are the data consistent with the quantity theory of money? Explain your answer.

17. **Canada Backs Its Banks' Borrowing**

Canada guaranteed borrowing by its banks yesterday in a move that could find the government responsible for up to C$218bn in debt. ... The government this month [also] offered to buy as much as C$25bn in mortgages. ... The government offered to back any debt issued by Canadian banks with terms greater than three months and will charge a premium to those who opt into the guarantee. Laurence Booth, an economist at the University of Toronto, said: "I don't think [the guarantee] will be relied on heavily. It sounds like a fig leaf. It is not really needed but it shows concern for the banks."

Financial Times, October 24, 2008

    a. Explain how the government guaranteeing bank borrowing and buying up risky mortgages can change the risk-return balancing act by banks. How does charging a premium to banks who opt into the guarantee alter that balancing act?
    b. What is the government trying to accomplish by guaranteeing borrowing? How might this policy be successful even if few banks opt into the guarantee?

18. **U.S. Proposals to Increase Deposit Protection May Push Canada to Raise CDIC Limits**

Canada can bolster confidence in its financial institutions by insuring bank deposits beyond $100,000. ... Wilfrid Laurier finance professor Brian Smith said U.S. proposals to increase the federal deposit insurance on bank accounts will put pressure on Canada to also act. "It could be a useful measure to assure some Canadians that in fact that they're monies are protected and would instill some more confidence in the system," Smith said. ... Parliament increased coverage by the Canada Deposit Insurance Corp. for the first time in more than 20 years in 2005 by raising insurance for eligible deposits to $100,000 from $60,000. ... More than $512 billion of individual deposits in Canada are currently insured if financial institutions fail. ... [An increase in deposit insurance] would allow all members to increase their deposits at a time when the cost of interbanking borrowing is increasing. It could also help them to capture the growing liquidity that is available as Canadians extricate themselves from the stock market. ... Since the CDIC was created in 1967, 43 member financial institutions have failed.

Canoe Money, September 30, 2008

a. Explain how bank attempts to maximize profits can sometimes lead to bank failures.

b. How does CDIC insurance help minimize bank failures and bring more stability to the banking system?

c. How might CDIC insurance create a moral hazard situation for banks?

d. Explain how increasing CDIC deposit protection could improve liquidity for the banking system.

e. Even in the absence of a financial crisis, why might it be necessary to raise deposit protection limits over time?

19. **Fed at Odds with ECB over Value of Policy Tool**

Financial innovation and the spread of U.S. currency throughout the world has broken down relationships between money, inflation and growth, making monetary gauges a less useful tool for policy makers, the U.S. Federal Reserve chairman, Ben Bernanke, said. ... The European Central Bank, Bank of Japan and Bank of England all use growth in the supply of money in formulating policy. "Heavy reliance on monetary aggregates as a guide to policy would seem to be unwise in the U.S. context," Bernanke said. ... "The empirical relationship between money growth and variables such as inflation and nominal output growth has continued to be unstable." ... He said the Fed had "philosophical" and economic differences with European central bankers regarding the role of money and that debate between institutions was healthy. ... "Unfortunately, forecast errors for money growth are often significant," reducing their effectiveness as a tool for policy, Bernanke said. "There are differences between the U.S. and Europe in terms of the stability of money demand and financial innovation," Bernanke said. ... [Ultimately,] the risk of bad policy through a devoted following of money growth led the Fed to downgrade the importance of money measures.

International Herald Tribune, November 10, 2006

a. Explain how the debate surrounding the quantity theory of money could make "monetary gauges a less useful tool for policy makers."

b. What do Bernanke's statements reveal about his stance on the accuracy of the quantity theory of money?

20. Rapid inflation in Brazil in the early 1990s caused the cruzeiro to lose its ability to function as money. Which of the following commodities do you think would most likely have taken the place of the cruzeiro in the Brazilian economy? Explain why.

a. Tractor parts
b. Packs of cigarettes
c. Loaves of bread
d. Impressionist paintings
e. Baseball trading cards

21. **From Paper-Clip to House, in 14 Trades**

A 26-year-old Montreal man appears to have succeeded in his quest to barter a single, red paper-clip all the way up to a house. It took almost a year and 14 trades. ...

CBC News, 7 July 2006

a. Is barter a means of payment?
b. Is barter just as efficient as money when trading on eBay? Explain.

22. Study *Reading Between the Lines* on pp. 584–585 and then

a. Describe the money growth rate and the inflation rate in Zimbabwe since 2000.

b. How do we know that Zimbabwe's reported inflation between 2003 and 2007 is almost certainly below the true inflation rate?

c. What feature of Zimbabwe's economy provides a view of the cost of hyperinflation?

d. What must be done to stop Zimbabwe's inflation?

e. Why will knocking 10 zeroes off all prices not stop Zimbabwe's inflation?

23. Use the link on MyEconLab (Textbook Resources, Chapter 24, Web links) to visit "Money—Past, Present, and Future" and study the section on e-money.

a. What is e-money and what are the alternative forms that it takes?

b. Do you think that the widespread use of e-money will limit the ability of the Bank of Canada to control the quantity of money? Why or why not?

c. When you buy an item on the Internet and pay for it using PayPal, are you using money? Explain why or why not.

d. Why might e-money be superior to cash as a means of payment?

25

The Exchange Rate and the Balance of Payments

After studying this chapter, you will be able to

- Describe the foreign exchange market and distinguish between the nominal exchange rate and the real exchange rate
- Explain how the exchange rate is determined day by day
- Explain the long-run trends in the exchange rate and explain interest rate parity and purchasing power parity
- Describe the balance of payments accounts and explain what causes an international deficit
- Describe the alternative exchange rate policies and explain their long-run effects

The Canadian dollar—the loonie—is just one of more than a hundred different monies that circulate in the global economy. The loonie is an important money, but it isn't in the truly big league. The world's three big monies are the U.S. dollar ($), the euro (€), and the yen (¥). Most international payments are made using one of these monies.

In February 2007, one Canadian dollar bought 85 U.S. cents. By November 2007, the Canadian dollar had soared to $1.09 U.S. But for the next year, the Canadian dollar sank against the U.S. dollar to only 77 U.S cents. Why did our dollar rise and then fall against the U.S. dollar? Can or should Canada do anything to stabilize the value of the dollar?

From the early 1980s until 1999, the value of Canadian imports exceeded the value of Canadian exports and we borrowed a total of $223 billion from the rest of the world. During the 2000s, this situation reversed: The value of exports exceeded the value of imports and we repaid $178 billion of our earlier borrowing. Why do we sometimes have to borrow from foreigners and at other times repay our international debts?

In this chapter, you're going to discover why our dollar fluctuates against other currencies and what determines the amount of international borrowing and lending. In *Reading Between the Lines* at the end of the chapter, we'll look at China's foreign exchange rate policy and see why it troubles many people, especially Americans.

Currencies and Exchange Rates

When Canadian Tire imports snow blowers from China, it pays for them using Chinese yuan. And when China Airlines buys an airplane from Bombardier, it pays using Canadian dollars. Whenever people buy things from another country, they use the currency of that country to make the transaction. It doesn't make any difference what the item is that is being traded internationally. It might be a snow blower, an airplane, insurance or banking services, real estate, the stocks and bonds of a government or corporation, or even an entire business.

Foreign money is just like Canadian money. It consists of notes and coins issued by a central bank and mint and deposits in banks and other depository institutions. When we described Canadian money in Chapter 24, we distinguished between currency (notes and coins) and deposits. But when we talk about foreign money, we refer to it as foreign currency. **Foreign currency** is the money of other countries regardless of whether that money is in the form of notes, coins, or bank deposits.

We buy these foreign currencies and foreigners buy Canadian dollars in the foreign exchange market.

The Foreign Exchange Market

The **foreign exchange market** is the market in which the currency of one country is exchanged for the currency of another. The foreign exchange market is not a place like a downtown flea market or a fruit and vegetable market. The foreign exchange market is made up of thousands of people—importers and exporters, banks, international travellers, and specialist traders called *foreign exchange brokers*.

The foreign exchange market opens on Monday morning in Sydney, Australia, and Hong Kong, which is still Sunday evening in Toronto. As the day advances, markets open in Singapore, Tokyo, Bahrain, Frankfurt, London, New York, Toronto, and San Francisco. As the West Coast markets close, Sydney is only an hour away from opening for the next day of business. The sun barely sets on the foreign exchange market. Dealers around the world are in continual contact by telephone and computer, and on a typical day in 2008, around $2 trillion (of all currencies) were traded in the foreign exchange market—or more than $400 trillion in a year.

Exchange Rates

An **exchange rate** is the price at which one currency exchanges for another currency in the foreign exchange market. For example, on December 1, 2008, one Canadian dollar would buy 80 U.S. cents—the exchange rate was $0.80 U.S per Canadian dollar.

The exchange rate fluctuates. A rise in the exchange rate is called an *appreciation* of the dollar, and a fall in the exchange rate is called a *depreciation* of the dollar. For example, when the exchange rate rises from 77 U.S. cents to 80 U.S. cents per dollar, the Canadian dollar appreciates, and when the exchange rate falls from 80 U.S. cents to 77 U.S. cents per dollar, the Canadian dollar depreciates.

The quantity of foreign money that we can buy with our dollar changes when the dollar appreciates or depreciates. But a change in the value of the dollar might not change what we *really* pay for our imports and earn from our exports. The reason is that prices of goods and services might change to offset the change in the value of the dollar and leave the terms on which we trade with other countries unchanged.

To determine whether a change in the exchange rate changes what we earn from exports and pay for imports, we need to distinguish between the *nominal* exchange rate and the *real* exchange rate.

Nominal and Real Exchange Rates

The **nominal exchange rate** is the value of the Canadian dollar expressed in units of foreign currency per Canadian dollar. It measures how much of one money exchanges for a unit of another money.

The **real exchange rate** is the relative price of Canadian-produced goods and services to foreign-produced goods and services. It is a measure of the quantity of the real GDP of other countries that a unit of Canadian real GDP buys.

The exchange rates that we've just discussed are *nominal* exchange rates. To understand the real exchange rate, suppose that China produces only snow blowers and Canada produces only airplanes. The price of a snow blower is 8,000 yuan, and the price of an airplane is $8 million. Also suppose that the exchange rate—the *nominal* exchange rate—is 10 yuan per dollar. With this information, we can calculate the *real* exchange rate, which is the number of snow blowers that one airplane buys. Let's do this calculation.

The Fluctuating Canadian Dollar

A Volatile Market

The figure shows the Canadian dollar exchange rate against the three big currencies that feature most prominently in global trade—the U.S. dollar, the Japanese yen, and the European euro—between 1988 and 2008.

The Canadian dollar has fluctuated most against the yen and least against the euro. The dollar depreciated sharply against the yen from 1990 to 1995 and appreciated from 2000 to 2007. The dollar depreciated against the U.S. dollar before 2002 and appreciated from 2002 to 2007. The dollar fluctuated around a constant 65 euro cents. In 2008, the dollar depreciated against these three currencies.

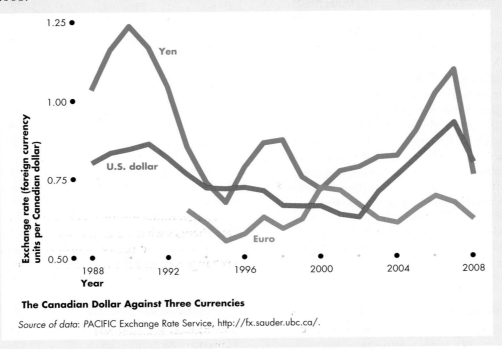

The Canadian Dollar Against Three Currencies

Source of data: PACIFIC Exchange Rate Service, http://fx.sauder.ubc.ca/.

At a price of 8,000 yuan and an exchange rate of 10 yuan per dollar, the price of a snow blower is $800. At a price of $8 million per airplane and $800 per snow blower, one airplane buys 10,000 snow blowers. The real exchange rate is 10,000 snow blowers per airplane.

Airplanes represent Canadian real GDP, and snow blowers represent Chinese real GDP. The price of a snow blower in China and the price of an airplane in Canada represent the price levels (GDP deflators) in the two countries. Call the Canadian price level P, the Chinese price level P^*, the nominal exchange rate E (yuan per dollar) and the real exchange rate RER (Chinese real GDP per unit of Canadian real GDP). Then the real exchange rate is

$$RER = E \times (P/P^*).$$

In words, the real exchange rate equals the nominal exchange rate multiplied by the ratio of the Canadian price level to the foreign price level.

The real exchange rate changes if the nominal exchange rate changes and prices remain constant. But if the dollar appreciates (E rises) and foreign prices rise (P^* rises) by the same percentage, the real exchange rate doesn't change. In the above example, if the exchange rate rises to 12 yuan per dollar and the price of a snow blower rises to 9,600 yuan, one airplane still buys 10,000 snow blowers.

How has the real exchange rate changed over time? Has it changed in the same way as the nominal exchange rate? We could answer these questions by calculating a real exchange rate in terms of each of the individual currencies of the countries with which we trade. But there is a more efficient way of measuring the real exchange rate. Instead of looking at the exchange rates between many different currencies, we look at an average of the exchange rates against all the currencies in which Canada trades.

Canadian-Dollar Effective Exchange Rate Index

The **Canadian-dollar effective exchange rate index (CERI)** is an average of the exchange rates of the Canadian dollar against the U.S. dollar, the European Union euro, the Japanese yen, the U.K. pound, the Chinese yuan, and the Mexican peso. In the CERI, each currency gets a weight that represents the importance of the currency in Canada's international trade.

The blue line in Fig. 25.1 shows the nominal CERI since 1997. We have defined the value of this index to be 100 in 1997. So the index tells us the value of the Canadian dollar against the other six currencies as a percentage of its value in 1997.

The index shows that the dollar depreciated on the average through 2002 and then appreciated through 2007 before depreciating again. The red line in Fig. 25.1 shows the real CERI. You can see that the nominal and real exchange rates moved in the same direction, but the nominal exchange rate appreciated by less and depreciated by more than the real exchange rate. The absence of a gap between the real exchange rate and the nominal exchange rate results from the fact that the inflation rates in Canada and the other countries were similar.

Questions About the Exchange Rate

The performance of the Canadian dollar in the foreign exchange market raises a number of questions that we address in the rest of this chapter.

First, how are the nominal exchange rate and real exchange rate determined? Why did the dollar appreciate from 2002 through 2007 and then depreciate?

Second, how do exchange rate fluctuations influence our international trade and international payments? In particular, could we use the exchange rate to maintain our international surplus?

Third, how do the Bank of Canada and other central banks operate in the foreign exchange market to change the value of the exchange rate? In some economies, the exchange rate is fixed, usually against the U.S. dollar. How did China fix the value of the yuan and keep it constant for many years? Could an appreciation of the yuan against the U.S. dollar change the balance of trade and payments between the United States (in deficit) and China (in surplus)?

We begin by learning how trading in the foreign exchange market determines the exchange rate.

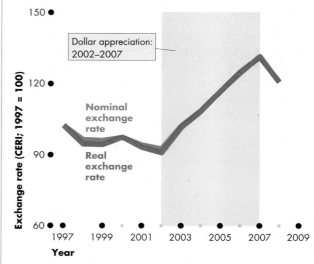

FIGURE 25.1 The Canadian-Dollar Effective Exchange Rate Index

The nominal CERI (blue line) and the real CERI (red line) depreciated slightly through 2002, appreciated through 2007, and then depreciated in 2008. The nominal CERI and real CERI are very similar because the inflation rates in the countries were similar.

Sources of data: PACIFIC Exchange Rate Service, http://fx.sauder.ubc.ca/, World Economic Outlook database, and Bank of Canada formula at www.bankofcanada.ca/en/rates/ceri.html. CERI calculated by authors with 1997 = 100.

 animation

Review Quiz

1 What is the foreign exchange market and what prices are determined in this market?
2 Distinguish between appreciation and depreciation of the dollar.
3 What are the world's major currencies?
4 Against which currencies and during which years has the Canadian dollar appreciated since 1998?
5 Against which currencies and during which years has the Canadian dollar depreciated since 1998?
6 What is the distinction between a nominal exchange rate and the real exchange rate?
7 What does the CERI measure?

 Work Study Plan 25.1 and get instant feedback.

◆ The Foreign Exchange Market

An exchange rate is a price—the price of one currency in terms of another. And like all prices, an exchange rate is determined in a market—the *foreign exchange market*.

The Canadian dollar trades in the foreign exchange market and is supplied and demanded by tens of thousands of traders every hour of every business day. Because the foreign exchange market has many traders and no restrictions on who may trade, it is a *competitive market*.

In a competitive market, demand and supply determine the price. So to understand the forces that determine the exchange rate, we need to study the factors that influence demand and supply in the foreign exchange market. But there is a feature of the foreign exchange market that makes it special.

The Demand for One Money Is the Supply of Another Money

When people want to exchange a foreign currency for Canadian dollars, they demand Canadian dollars and supply that other currency. And when people want to exchange Canadian dollars for a foreign currency, they supply Canadian dollars and demand that other currency.

Dealers in the foreign exchange market.

So the factors that influence the demand for Canadian dollars also influence the supply of European Union euros, U.S. dollars, or Japanese yen. And the factors that influence the demand for that other country's money also influence the supply of Canadian dollars.

We'll first look at the influences on the demand for Canadian dollars in the foreign exchange market.

Demand in the Foreign Exchange Market

People buy Canadian dollars in the foreign exchange market so that they can buy Canadian-produced goods and services—Canadian exports. They also buy Canadian dollars so that they can buy Canadian assets such as bonds, stocks, businesses, and real estate or so that they can keep part of their money in a Canadian dollar bank account.

The quantity of Canadian dollars demanded in the foreign exchange market is the amount that traders plan to buy during a given time period at a given exchange rate. This quantity depends on many factors, but the main ones are

1. The exchange rate
2. World demand for Canadian exports
3. Interest rates in Canada and other countries
4. The expected future exchange rate

To see how the exchange rate is determined, we'll look first at the relationship between the quantity of Canadian dollars demanded in the foreign exchange market and the exchange rate when the other three influences remain the same. This relationship is called the law of demand in the foreign exchange market. Then in the next section, we'll consider what happens when these other influences change.

The Law of Demand for Foreign Exchange

The law of demand applies to Canadian dollars just as it does to anything else that people value. Other things remaining the same, the higher the exchange rate, the smaller is the quantity of Canadian dollars demanded in the foreign exchange market. For example, if the price of the Canadian dollar rises from 70 U.S. cents to 80 U.S. cents but nothing else changes, the quantity of Canadian dollars that people plan to buy in the foreign exchange market decreases. The exchange rate influences the quantity of Canadian dollars demanded for two reasons:

- Exports effect
- Expected profit effect

Exports Effect The larger the value of Canadian exports, the larger is the quantity of Canadian dollars demanded in the foreign exchange market. But the value of Canadian exports depends on the prices of Canadian-produced goods and services *expressed in the currency of the foreign buyer*. And these prices depend on the exchange rate. The lower the exchange rate, other things remaining the same, the lower are the prices of Canadian-produced goods and services to foreigners and the greater is the volume of Canadian exports. So if the exchange rate falls (and other influences remain the same), the quantity of Canadian dollars demanded in the foreign exchange market increases.

To see the exports effect at work, think about orders for Bombardier regional jets. If the price of a plane is $8 million and the exchange rate is 75 euro cents per Canadian dollar, the price of this airplane to KLM, a European airline, is €6 million. KLM decides that this price is too high, so it doesn't buy a new Bombardier airplane. If the exchange rate falls to 60 euro cents per Canadian dollar and other things remain the same, the price of a Bombardier plan falls to €4.8 million. KLM now decides to buy the airplane and buys Canadian dollars in the foreign exchange market.

Expected Profit Effect The larger the expected profit from holding Canadian dollars, the greater is the quantity of Canadian dollars demanded in the foreign exchange market. But expected profit depends on the exchange rate. For a given expected future exchange rate, the lower the exchange rate today, the larger is the expected profit from buying Canadian dollars today and holding them, so the greater is the quantity of Canadian dollars demanded in the foreign exchange market today. Let's look at an example.

Suppose that Mizuho Bank, a Japanese bank, expects the exchange rate to be 110 yen per Canadian dollar at the end of the year. If today's exchange rate is also 110 yen per Canadian dollar, Mizuho Bank expects no profit from buying Canadian dollars and holding them until the end of the year. But if today's exchange rate is 100 yen per Canadian dollar and Mizuho Bank buys Canadian dollars, it expects to sell them at the end of the year for 110 yen per dollar and make a profit of 10 yen per Canadian dollar.

The lower the exchange rate today, other things remaining the same, the greater is the expected profit from holding Canadian dollars and the greater is the quantity of Canadian dollars demanded in the foreign exchange market today.

Demand Curve for Canadian Dollars

Figure 25.2 shows the demand curve for Canadian dollars in the foreign exchange market. A change in the exchange rate, other things remaining the same, brings a change in the quantity of Canadian dollars demanded and a movement along the demand curve. The arrows show such movements.

We will look at the factors that change demand in the next section of this chapter. But first, let's see what determines the supply of Canadian dollars.

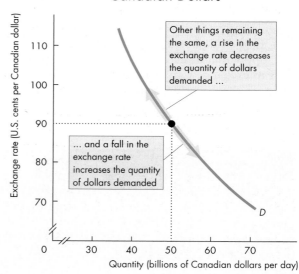

FIGURE 25.2 The Demand for Canadian Dollars

The quantity of Canadian dollars demanded depends on the exchange rate. Other things remaining the same, if the exchange rate rises, the quantity of Canadian dollars demanded decreases and there is a movement up along the demand curve for Canadian dollars. If the exchange rate falls, the quantity of Canadian dollars demanded increases and there is a movement down along the demand curve for Canadian dollars.

Supply in the Foreign Exchange Market

People sell Canadian dollars and buy other currencies so that they can buy foreign-produced goods and services—Canadian imports. People also sell Canadian dollars and buy foreign currencies so that they can buy foreign assets such as bonds, stocks, businesses, and real estate or so that they can hold part of their money in bank deposits denominated in a foreign currency.

The quantity of Canadian dollars supplied in the foreign exchange market is the amount that traders plan to sell during a given time period at a given exchange rate. This quantity depends on many factors, but the main ones are

1. The exchange rate
2. Canadian demand for imports
3. Interest rates in Canada and other countries
4. The expected future exchange rate

Let's look at the law of supply in the foreign exchange market—the relationship between the quantity of Canadian dollars supplied in the foreign exchange market and the exchange rate when the other three influences remain the same.

The Law of Supply of Foreign Exchange

Other things remaining the same, the higher the exchange rate, the greater is the quantity of Canadian dollars supplied in the foreign exchange market. For example, if the exchange rate rises from 70 U.S. cents to 80 U.S. cents per Canadian dollar and other things remain the same, the quantity of Canadian dollars that people plan to sell in the foreign exchange market increases.

The exchange rate influences the quantity of dollars supplied for two reasons:

- Imports effect
- Expected profit effect

Imports Effect The larger the value of Canadian imports, the larger is the quantity of Canadian dollars supplied in the foreign exchange market. But the value of Canadian imports depends on the prices of foreign-produced goods and services *expressed in Canadian dollars*. These prices depend on the exchange rate. The higher the exchange rate, other things remaining the same, the lower are the prices of foreign-produced goods and services to Canadians and the greater are

Canadian imports. So if the exchange rate rises (and other influences remain the same), the quantity of Canadian dollars supplied in the foreign exchange market increases.

Expected Profit Effect This effect works just like that on the demand for the Canadian dollar but in the opposite direction. The higher the exchange rate today, other things remaining the same, the larger is the expected profit from selling Canadian dollars today and holding foreign currencies, so the greater is the quantity of Canadian dollars supplied.

Supply Curve for Canadian Dollars

Figure 25.3 shows the supply curve of Canadian dollars in the foreign exchange market. A change in the exchange rate, other things remaining the same, brings a change in the quantity of Canadian dollars supplied and a movement along the supply curve. The arrows show such movements.

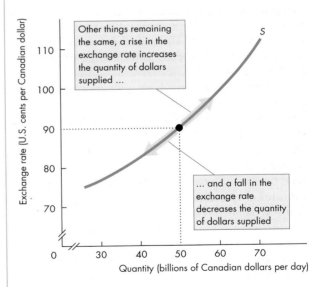

FIGURE 25.3   The Supply of Canadian Dollars

Other things remaining the same, a rise in the exchange rate increases the quantity of dollars supplied ...

... and a fall in the exchange rate decreases the quantity of dollars supplied

The quantity of Canadian dollars supplied depends on the exchange rate. Other things remaining the same, if the exchange rate rises, the quantity of Canadian dollars supplied increases and there is a movement up along the supply curve of Canadian dollars. If the exchange rate falls, the quantity of Canadian dollars supplied decreases and there is a movement down along the supply curve of Canadian dollars.

myeconlab animation

Market Equilibrium

Equilibrium in the foreign exchange market depends on how the Bank of Canada and other central banks operate. Here, we will study equilibrium when central banks keep out of this market. (We examine the effects of intervention in the foreign exchange market on pp. 611–613).

Figure 25.4 shows the demand curve for Canadian dollars, *D*, from Fig. 25.2, the supply curve of Canadian dollars, *S*, from Fig. 25.3, and the equilibrium exchange rate.

The exchange rate acts as a regulator of the quantities demanded and supplied. If the exchange rate is too high, there is a surplus—the quantity supplied exceeds the quantity demanded. For example, in Fig. 25.4, if the exchange rate is 100 U.S. cents per Canadian dollar, there is a surplus of Canadian dollars. If the exchange rate is too low, there is a shortage—the quantity supplied is less than the quantity demanded. For example, if the exchange rate is 80 U.S. cents per Canadian dollar, there is a shortage of Canadian dollars.

At the equilibrium exchange rate, there is neither a shortage nor a surplus—the quantity supplied equals the quantity demanded. In Fig. 25.4, the equilibrium exchange rate is 90 U.S. cents per Canadian dollar. At this exchange rate, the quantity demanded and the quantity supplied are each $50 billion a day.

The foreign exchange market is constantly pulled to its equilibrium by the forces of supply and demand. Foreign exchange traders are constantly looking for the best price they can get. If they are selling, they want the highest price available. If they are buying, they want the lowest price available. Information flows from trader to trader through the worldwide computer network, and the price adjusts minute by minute to keep buying plans and selling plans in balance. That is, the price adjusts minute by minute to keep the exchange rate at its equilibrium.

Figure 25.4 shows how the exchange rate between the Canadian dollar and U.S. dollar is determined. The exchange rates between the Canadian dollar and all other currencies are determined in a similar way. So are the exchange rates among the other currencies. Exchange rates are tied together so that no profit can be made by buying one currency, selling it for a second one, and then buying back the first one. If such a profit were available, traders would spot it, demand and supply would change, and the exchange rates would snap into alignment.

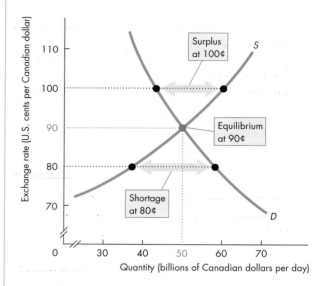

FIGURE 25.4 Equilibrium Exchange Rate

The demand curve for Canadian dollars is *D*, and the supply curve of Canadian dollars is *S*. If the exchange rate is 100 U.S cents per Canadian dollar, there is a surplus of Canadian dollars and the exchange rate falls. If the exchange rate is 80 U.S. cents per Canadian dollar, there is a shortage of Canadian dollars and the exchange rate rises. If the exchange rate is 90 U.S. cents per Canadian dollar, there is neither a shortage nor a surplus of Canadian dollars and the exchange rate remains constant. The foreign exchange market is in equilibrium.

 animation

Review Quiz

1 What are the influences on the demand for and supply of Canadian dollars in the foreign exchange market?

2 Provide an example of the exports effect on the demand for Canadian dollars and the imports effect on the supply of Canadian dollars.

3 How is the equilibrium exchange rate determined?

4 What happens if there is a shortage or a surplus of Canadian dollars in the foreign exchange market?

 Work Study Plan 25.2 and get instant feedback.

Changes in Demand and Supply: Exchange Rate Fluctuations

When the demand for Canadian dollars or the supply of Canadian dollars changes, the exchange rate changes. We'll now look at the factors that make demand and supply change, starting with the demand side of the market.

A Change in Demand for Canadian Dollars

The demand for Canadian dollars in the foreign exchange market changes when there is a change in

- World demand for Canadian exports
- Canadian and foreign interest rates
- The expected future exchange rate

World Demand for Canadian Exports An increase in world demand for Canadian exports increases the demand for Canadian dollars. For example, an increase in demand for air travel in Australia sends that country's airlines on a global shopping spree. They decide that the Bombardier regional jet is the ideal product, so they order 50 airplanes. The demand for Canadian dollars now increases.

Canadian and Foreign Interest Rates People buy financial assets to make a return. The higher the interest rate that people can earn on Canadian assets compared with foreign assets, the more Canadian assets they buy.

What matters is not the *level* of the Canadian interest rate, but the Canadian interest rate minus the foreign interest rate—a gap called the **Canadian interest rate differential**. If the Canadian interest rate rises and the foreign interest rate remains constant, the Canadian interest rate differential increases. The larger the Canadian interest rate differential, the greater is the demand for both Canadian assets and Canadian dollars.

The Expected Future Exchange Rate For a given current exchange rate, other things remaining the same, a rise in the expected future exchange rate increases the profit that people expect to make by holding Canadian dollars and the demand for Canadian dollars increases today.

Figure 25.5 summarizes the influences on the demand for Canadian dollars. An increase in the demand for Canadian exports, a rise in the Canadian interest rate differential, or a rise in the expected future exchange rate increases the demand for Canadian dollars and shifts the demand curve rightward from D_0 to D_1. A decrease in the demand for Canadian exports, a fall in the Canadian interest rate differential, or a fall in the expected future exchange rate decreases the demand for Canadian dollars and shifts the demand curve leftward from D_0 to D_2.

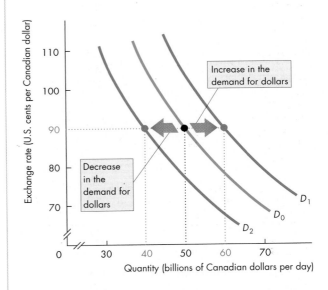

FIGURE 25.5 Changes in the Demand for Canadian Dollars

A change in any influence on the quantity of Canadian dollars that people plan to buy, other than the exchange rate, brings a change in the demand for Canadian dollars.

The demand for Canadian dollars

Increases if:	*Decreases if:*
■ World demand for Canadian exports increases	■ World demand for Canadian exports decreases
■ The Canadian interest rate differential rises	■ The Canadian interest rate differential falls
■ The expected future exchange rate rises	■ The expected future exchange rate falls

myeconlab animation

Changes in the Supply of Canadian Dollars

The supply of Canadian dollars in the foreign exchange market changes when there is a change in

- Canadian demand for imports
- Canadian and foreign interest rates
- The expected future exchange rate

Canadian Demand for Imports An increase in the Canadian demand for imports increases the supply of Canadian dollars in the foreign exchange market. For example, an increase in the demand for snow blowers sends Canadian Tire shopping in China. The supply of Canadian dollars increases as Canadian Tire goes to the foreign exchange market for Chinese yuan to pay for the snow blowers that it imports.

Canadian and Foreign Interest Rates The effect of the Canadian interest rate differential on the supply of Canadian dollars is the opposite of its effect on the demand for Canadian dollars. The larger the Canadian interest rate differential, the *smaller* is the supply of Canadian dollars in the foreign exchange market. The supply of Canadian dollars is smaller because the demand for *foreign* assets is smaller. If people spend less on foreign assets, the quantity of Canadian dollars they supply in the foreign exchange market decreases. So, a rise in the Canadian interest rate, other things remaining the same, increases the Canadian interest rate differential and decreases the supply of Canadian dollars in the foreign exchange market.

The Expected Future Exchange Rate For a given current exchange rate, other things remaining the same, a fall in the expected future exchange rate decreases the profit that can be made by holding Canadian dollars and decreases the quantity of Canadian dollars that people want to hold. To reduce their holdings of Canadian dollar assets, people must sell Canadian dollars. When they do so, the supply of Canadian dollars in the foreign exchange market increases.

Figure 25.6 summarizes the influences on the supply of Canadian dollars. If the supply of Canadian dollars decreases, the supply curve shifts leftward from S_0 to S_1. And if the supply of Canadian dollars increases, the supply curve shifts rightward from S_0 to S_2.

Changes in the Exchange Rate

If the demand for Canadian dollars increases and the supply does not change, the exchange rate rises.

FIGURE 25.6 Changes in the Supply of Canadian Dollars

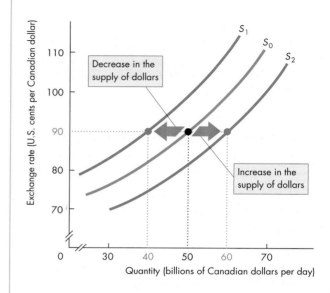

A change in any influence on the quantity of Canadian dollars that people plan to sell, other than the exchange rate, brings a change in the supply of dollars.

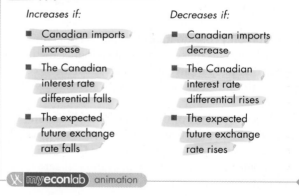

The supply of Canadian dollars

Increases if:	Decreases if:
■ Canadian imports increase	■ Canadian imports decrease
■ The Canadian interest rate differential falls	■ The Canadian interest rate differential rises
■ The expected future exchange rate falls	■ The expected future exchange rate rises

myeconlab   animation

If the demand for Canadian dollars decreases and the supply does not change, the exchange rate falls. Similarly, if the supply of Canadian dollars decreases and the demand does not change, the exchange rate rises. If the supply of Canadian dollars increases and the demand does not change, the exchange rate falls.

These predictions are the same as those for any other market and two episodes in the life of the Canadian dollar (next page) illustrate them.

Two Episodes in the Life of the Dollar

A Currency on a Roller Coaster

The foreign exchange market is a striking example of a competitive market. The expectations of thousands of traders around the world influence this market minute by minute throughout the 24-hour global trading day.

Demand and supply rarely stand still and their fluctuations bring a fluctuating exchange rate. Two episodes in the life of the dollar illustrate these fluctuations: 2005–2007, when the dollar appreciated, and 2007–2008, when the dollar depreciated.

An Appreciating Canadian Dollar: 2005–2007

Between 2005 and July 2007, the Canadian dollar appreciated against the U.S. dollar. It rose from 79 U.S. cents to 109 U.S. cents per Canadian dollar. Part (a) of the figure provides an explanation for this appreciation.

In 2005, the demand and supply curves were those labelled D_{05} and S_{05}. The exchange rate was 79 U.S. cents per Canadian dollar.

During 2005 and 2006, the global demand for resources increased the demand for Canadian exports. The increase in demand for Canadian exports increased the demand for the Canadian dollar. Also, currency traders, anticipating the increased demand, expected the dollar to appreciate against the U.S.

dollar. The demand for Canadian dollars increased, and the supply of Canadian dollars decreased.

In the figure, the demand curve shifted rightward from D_{05} to D_{07} and the supply curve shifted leftward from S_{05} to S_{07}. The exchange rate rose to 109 U.S. cents per Canadian dollar. In the figure, the equilibrium quantity remained unchanged—an assumption.

A Depreciating Canadian Dollar: 2007–2008

Between July 2007 and November 2008, the Canadian dollar depreciated against the U.S. dollar. It fell from 109 U.S. cents to 77 U.S. cents per Canadian dollar. Part (b) of the figure provides a possible explanation for this depreciation. The demand and supply curves labelled D_{07} and S_{07} are the same as in part (a).

During the last quarter of 2007 and the first three quarters of 2008, the U.S. economy entered a severe credit crisis and global demand for resources collapsed. A decrease in the demand for Canadian exports decreased the demand for Canadian dollars. Also, currency traders expected the Canadian dollar to depreciate against the U.S. dollar. The demand for Canadian dollars decreased and the supply of Canadian dollars increased.

In part (b) of the figure, the demand curve shifted leftward from D_{07} to D_{08}, the supply curve shifted rightward from S_{07} to S_{08}, and the exchange rate fell to 77 U.S. cents per Canadian dollar.

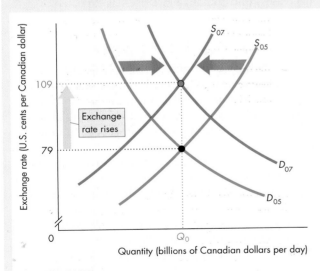

(a) 2005–2007

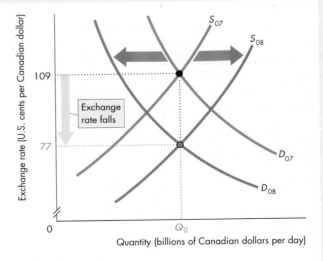

(b) 2007–2008

The Rising and Falling Canadian Dollar

Exchange Rate Expectations

The changes in the exchange rate that we've just examined occurred in part because the exchange rate was *expected to change.* This explanation sounds a bit like a self-fulfilling prophecy. So what makes expectations change? The answer is new information about the deeper forces that influence the value of one money relative to the value of another money. There are two such forces:

- Interest rate parity
- Purchasing power parity

Interest Rate Parity One definition of what money is worth is what it can earn. Two kinds of money—Canadian dollars and Japanese yen, for example—might earn different amounts. Suppose that the interest rate on a yen bank deposit in Tokyo is 1 percent a year and on a Canadian dollar bank deposit in Toronto is 3 percent a year. In this situation, why does anyone deposit money in Tokyo? Why doesn't all the money flow to Toronto? The answer is because of exchange rate expectations. Suppose that people expect the yen to appreciate by 2 percent a year. Canadian investors expect that if they buy and hold yen for a year, they will earn 1 percent interest and 2 percent from the higher yen (lower dollar) to give a total return of 3 percent. So the interest rate in terms of Canadian dollars is the same in Tokyo and Toronto. This situation is one of **interest rate parity**, which means equal rates of return.

Adjusted for risk, interest rate parity always prevails. Funds move to get the highest return available. If for a few seconds a higher return is available in Toronto than in Tokyo, the demand for Canadian dollars increases and the exchange rate rises until the expected rates of return are equal.

Purchasing Power Parity Another definition of what money is worth is what it will buy. But two kinds of money—Canadian dollars and Japanese yen, for example—might buy different amounts of goods and services. Suppose a memory stick costs 5,000 yen in Tokyo and $50 in Vancouver. If the exchange rate is 100 yen per dollar, the two monies have the same value. You can buy a memory stick in either Tokyo or Vancouver for the same price. You can express that price as either 5,000 yen or $50, but the price is the same in the two currencies.

The situation we've just described is called **purchasing power parity**, which means *equal value of money.* If purchasing power parity does not prevail, some powerful forces go to work. To understand these forces, let's suppose that the price of a memory stick in Vancouver rises to $60, but in Tokyo it remains at 5,000 yen. Further, suppose the exchange rate remains at 100 yen per dollar. In this case, a memory stick in Tokyo still costs 5,000 yen or $50, but in Vancouver, it costs $60 or 6,000 yen. Money buys more in Japan than in Canada. Money is not of equal value in the two countries.

If all (or most) prices have increased in Canada and not increased in Japan, then people will generally expect that the value of the Canadian dollar in the foreign exchange market must fall. In this situation, the exchange rate is expected to fall. The demand for Canadian dollars decreases, and the supply of Canadian dollars increases. The exchange rate falls, as expected. If the exchange rate falls to 83.33 yen per dollar and there are no further price changes, purchasing power parity is restored. A memory stick that costs $60 in Vancouver also costs the equivalent of $60 ($60 \times 83.33 = 5,000$) in Tokyo.

If prices increase in Japan and other countries but remain constant in Canada, then people will generally expect that the value of the Canadian dollar in the foreign exchange market is too low and that it is going to rise. In this situation, the exchange rate is expected to rise. The demand for Canadian dollars increases, and the supply of Canadian dollars decreases. The exchange rate rises, as expected.

Instant Exchange Rate Response

The exchange rate responds instantly to news about changes in the variables that influence demand and supply in the foreign exchange market. You can see why the response is immediate by thinking about the expected profit opportunities that such news creates.

Suppose that the Bank of Japan is reported to be considering raising the interest rate next week. If this move is regarded as likely, then traders expect the demand for yen to increase and the demand for dollars to decrease. They also expect the yen to appreciate and the dollar to depreciate.

But to benefit from a yen appreciation and to avoid the loss from a dollar depreciation, yen must be bought and dollars must be sold *before* the exchange rate changes. Each trader knows that all the other traders share the same information and have similar expectations. And each trader knows that when people begin to sell dollars and buy yen, the exchange rate will change. To transact before the exchange rate changes means transacting right away, as soon as the information that changes expectations is received.

The Nominal and Real Exchange Rates in the Short Run and in the Long Run

Earlier in this chapter, we distinguished between the nominal exchange rate and the real exchange rate. So far we've explained only how the nominal exchange rate is determined and we've focused on the day-to-day fluctuations in the nominal exchange rate. We're going to turn now to the real exchange rate and explain how it is determined. We're also going to distinguish between the short run and the long run.

Continuing with the Canada–Japan example, the equation that links the nominal and real exchange rates is

$$RER = E \times (P^*/P).$$

where P is the Canadian price level, P^* is the Japanese price level, E is the nominal exchange rate (yen per Canadian dollar), and RER is the real exchange rate (the quantity of Japanese real GDP per unit of Canadian real GDP).

In the short run, this equation determines the real exchange rate. The price levels in Canada and Japan don't change every time the nominal exchange rate changes. So a change in E brings an equivalent change in RER.

But in the long run, demand and supply in the markets for goods and services determine the real exchange rate. If Japan and Canada produced identical goods (if GDP in both countries consisted only of memory sticks, for example), purchasing power parity would make the real exchange rate equal 1. One Japanese memory stick would exchange for one Canadian memory stick. In reality, although there is overlap in what each country produces, Canadian real GDP is a different bundle of goods and services from Japanese real GDP. So the relative price of Japanese and Canadian real GDP—the real exchange rate—is not 1 and it fluctuates. The forces of demand and supply in the markets for the millions of goods and services that make up real GDP determine the relative prices of Japanese and Canadian real GDP.

In the long run, with the real exchange rate determined by the real forces of demand and supply in markets for goods and services, the above equation must be turned around to determine the nominal exchange rate. That is, the nominal exchange rate is

$$E = RER \times (P^*/P).$$

This equation tells us that in the long run, the nominal exchange rate is determined by the equilibrium real exchange rate and the price levels in the two countries. A rise in the Japanese price level, P^*, brings a rise in E and dollar appreciation; and a rise in the Canadian price level, P, brings a fall in E and dollar depreciation.

You learned in Chapter 24 (see pp. 582–583) that in the long run, the quantity of money determines the price level. But the quantity theory of money applies to all countries. So the quantity of money in Japan determines the price level in Japan, and the quantity of money in Canada determines the price level in Canada.

A nominal exchange rate, then, in the long run, is a monetary phenomenon. It is determined by the quantities of money in two countries.

The long-run forces that we've just described explain the broad trends in exchange rates. For example, the Canadian dollar has generally depreciated against the Japanese yen because Japan has created money at a slower pace than has Canada and the price level in Japan has risen more slowly than the Canadian price level. The Canadian dollar has been constant, on average, against the European euro because inflation rates have been similar in Canada and Europe.

Review Quiz

1 Why do the demand for and supply of Canadian dollars change?
2 What makes the Canadian dollar exchange rate fluctuate?
3 What is interest rate parity and what happens when this condition doesn't hold?
4 What is purchasing power parity and what happens when this condition doesn't hold?
5 What determines the real exchange rate and the nominal exchange rate in the short run?
6 What determines the real exchange rate and the nominal exchange rate in the long run?

 Work Study Plan 25.3 and get instant feedback.

Financing International Trade

You now know how the exchange rate is determined. What is the effect of the exchange rate? How does currency depreciation or currency appreciation influence our international trade and payments? We're going to lay the foundation for addressing these questions by looking at the scale of international trading, borrowing, and lending and at the way in which we keep our records of international transactions. These records are called the balance of payments accounts.

Balance of Payments Accounts

A country's **balance of payments accounts** records its international trading, borrowing, and lending in three accounts:

1. Current account
2. Capital account
3. Official settlements account

The **current account** records receipts from exports of goods and services sold abroad, payments for imports of goods and services from abroad, net interest income paid abroad, and net transfers abroad (such as foreign aid payments). The *current account balance* equals the sum of exports minus imports, net interest income, and net transfers.

The **capital account** records foreign investment in Canada minus Canadian investment abroad. (This account also has a statistical discrepancy that arises from errors and omissions in measuring international capital transactions.)

The **official settlements account** records the change in **official reserves**, which are the government's holdings of foreign currency. If official reserves *increase*, the official settlements account balance is *negative*. The reason is that holding foreign money is like investing abroad. Canadian investment abroad is a minus item in the capital account and in the official settlements account.

The sum of the balances on the three accounts *always* equals zero. If a country has a current account deficit, it either borrows more from abroad than it lends abroad or it uses its official reserves to cover the shortfall. A country with a current account surplus must lend more abroad than it borrows or increase its official reserves.

Table 25.1 shows the Canadian balance of payments accounts in 2007. Items in the current account and the capital account that provide foreign currency to Canada have a plus sign; items that cost Canada foreign currency have a minus sign. The table shows that in 2007, Canadian exports exceeded Canadian imports and the current account had a surplus of $14 billion. What do we do with our surplus of exports over imports? That is, how do we use our current account surplus?

We use our surplus by lending to the rest of the world. The capital account tells us how much we lend. We made loans of $167 billion (Canadian investment abroad) and borrowed $153 billion (foreign investment in Canada). Our *net* foreign lending was $167 billion minus $153 billion, which equals $14 billion. There is almost always a statistical discrepancy between our capital account and current account transactions, and in 2007, the discrepancy was $4 billion. Combining the discrepancy with the measured net foreign borrowing gives a capital account balance of –$10 billion.

TABLE 25.1   Canadian Balance of Payments Accounts in 2007

Current account	Billions of dollars
Exports of goods and services	+530
Imports of goods and services	−501
Net interest income	−14
Net transfers	−1
Current account balance	14

Capital account	
Foreign investment in Canada	+153
Canadian investment abroad	−167
Statistical discrepancy	4
Capital account balance	−10

Official settlements account	
Official settlements account balance	−4

Source of data: Statistics Canada, CANSIM Tables 376-0001 and 376-0002.

Our capital account balance plus our current account balance equals the change in Canadian official reserves. In 2007, our capital account balance of –$10 billion plus our current account balance of $14 billion equalled $4 billion. Our official reserves *increased* in 2007 by $4 billion. Holding more foreign reserves is like lending to the rest of the world, so this amount appears in the official settlements account in Table 25.1 as –$4 billion. The sum of the current account balance, the capital account balance. and the official settlements balance equals zero.

To see more clearly what the nation's balance of payments accounts mean, think about your own balance of payments accounts. They are similar to the nation's accounts.

An Individual's Balance of Payments Accounts An individual's current account records the individual's income from supplying the services of factors of production and expenditure on goods and services.

Consider Jackie, for example. She worked in 2005 and earned an income of $25,000. Jackie has $10,000 worth of investments that earned her an interest income of $1,000. Jackie's current account shows an income of $26,000. Jackie spent $18,000 buying consumption goods and services. She also bought a new house, which cost her $60,000. So Jackie's total expenditure was $78,000. Jackie's expenditure minus her income is $52,000 ($78,000 minus $26,000). This amount is Jackie's current account deficit.

The Canadian Balance of Payments Since 1984

From Deficit to Surplus

The numbers that you reviewed in Table 25.1 give a snapshot of the Canadian balance of payments accounts in 2007. The figure puts that snapshot into perspective by showing the balance of payments between 1984 and 2007.

Because the economy grows and the price level rises, changes in the dollar value of the balance of payments do not convey much information. To remove the influences of economic growth and inflation, the figure shows the balance of payments expressed as a percentage of nominal GDP.

As you can see, the current account was in deficit before 2000 (except for a brief and small surplus in 1996). After 2000, the current account was in surplus.

The capital account balance is almost a mirror image of the current account balance because the official settlements balance is very small in comparison with the balances of the other two accounts.

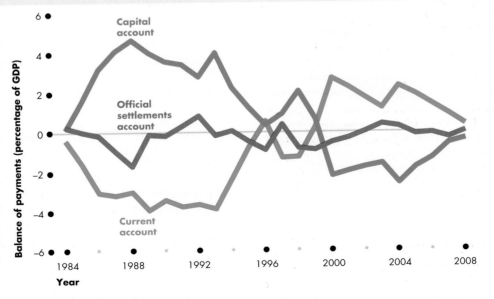

The Canadian Balance of Payments

Source of data: Statistics Canada, CANSIM Tables 376-0001 and 376-0002.

To pay for an expenditure of $52,000 in excess of her income, Jackie must either use the money that she has in the bank or take out a loan. Suppose that Jackie took out a loan of $50,000 to help buy her house and that this loan was the only borrowing that she did. Borrowing is an *inflow* in the capital account, so Jackie's capital account *surplus* was $50,000. With a current account deficit of $52,000 and a capital account surplus of $50,000, Jackie was still $2,000 short. She got that $2,000 from her own bank account. Her cash holdings fell by $2,000.

Jackie's income from her work is like a country's income from its exports. Her income from her investments is like a country's interest income from foreigners. Her purchases of goods and services, including her purchase of a house, are like a country's imports. Jackie's loan—borrowing from someone else—is like a country's borrowing from the rest of the world. The change in Jackie's bank account is like the change in the country's official reserves.

Borrowers and Lenders

A country that is borrowing more from the rest of the world than it is lending to the rest of the world is called a **net borrower**. Similarly, a **net lender** is a country that is lending more to the rest of the world than it is borrowing from the rest of the world.

Since 2000, Canada has been a net lender. But in most years before 2000, Canada was a net borrower.

The United States is the world's largest net borrower. Since the early 1980s, with the exception of only a single year, 1991, the United States has been a net borrower from the rest of the world. And during the years since 1992, the scale of U.S. borrowing has mushroomed.

Most countries are net borrowers like the United States. But a few countries, including China, Japan, and oil-rich Saudi Arabia, are net lenders. When the United States borrowed more than $700 billion from the rest of the world in 2008, these three countries lent $700 billion. China alone lent $380 billion.

Debtors and Creditors

A net borrower might be decreasing its net assets held in the rest of the world, or it might be going deeper into debt. A nation's total stock of foreign investment determines whether it is a debtor or a creditor. A **debtor nation** is a country that during its entire history has borrowed more from the rest of the world than it has lent to other countries. It has a stock of outstanding debt to the rest of the world that exceeds the stock of its own claims on the rest of the world. A **creditor nation** is a country that during its entire history has invested more in the rest of the world than other countries have invested in it.

Canada is a debtor nation. Throughout the nineteenth century we borrowed from Europe to finance our westward expansion, railroads, and industrialization. The capital-hungry developing countries (like Canada during the nineteenth century) are among the largest debtor nations. The international debt of these countries grew from less than a third to more than a half of their gross domestic product during the 1980s and created what was called the "Third World debt crisis."

But the United States is the world's largest debtor nation. Since 1984, the total stock of U.S. borrowing from the rest of the world has exceeded U.S. lending to the rest of the world by $7.4 trillion (almost as much as Canada's gross domestic product).

Should the world be concerned that the United States is the largest net borrower and debtor? The answer to this question depends mainly on what the net borrower is doing with the borrowed money. If borrowing is financing investment that in turn is generating economic growth and higher income, borrowing is not a problem. It earns a return that more than pays the interest. But if borrowed money is used to finance consumption, to pay the interest and repay the loan, consumption will eventually have to be reduced. In this case, the greater the borrowing and the longer it goes on, the greater is the reduction in consumption that will eventually be necessary.

Is the United States Borrowing for Consumption?

In 2008, the United States borrowed $700 billion from abroad. In that year, U.S. private investment in buildings, plant, and equipment was $1,980 billion and government investment in defence equipment and social projects was $480 billion. All this investment added to U.S. capital, and much of it increased productivity. Government also spends on education and health care services, which increase *human capital*. So U.S. international borrowing is financing private and public investment, not consumption. The same is true for most other international borrowers.

Current Account Balance

What determines a country's current account balance and net foreign borrowing? You've seen that net exports (*NX*) is the main item in the current account. We can define the current account balance (*CAB*) as

$$CAB = NX + \text{Net interest income} + \text{Net transfers.}$$

We can study the current account balance by looking at what determines net exports because the other two items are small and do not fluctuate much.

Net Exports

Net exports are determined by the government budget and private saving and investment. To see how net exports are determined, we need to recall some of the things that we learned in Chapter 23 about the flows of funds that finance investment. Table 25.2 refreshes your memory and summarizes some calculations.

Part (a) lists the national income variables that are needed, with their symbols. Part (b) defines three balances. **Net exports** are exports of goods and services minus imports of goods and services.

The **government sector balance** is equal to net taxes minus government expenditure on goods and services. If that number is positive, a government sector surplus is lent to other sectors; if that number is negative, a government deficit must be financed by borrowing from other sectors. The government sector deficit is the sum of the deficits of the federal, provincial, and local governments.

The **private sector balance** is saving minus investment. If saving exceeds investment, a private sector surplus is lent to other sectors. If investment exceeds saving, a private sector deficit is financed by borrowing from other sectors.

Part (b) also shows the values of these balances for Canada in 2007. As you can see, net exports were $31 billion, a surplus of $31 billion. The government sector's revenue from net taxes was $383 billion and its expenditure was $342 billion, so the government sector balance was $41 billion—a surplus of $41 billion. The private sector saved $301 billion and invested $311 billion, so the private sector balance was –$10 billion. The private sector had a deficit of $10 billion.

Part (c) shows the relationship among the three balances. From the national income accounts, we

TABLE 25.2 Net Exports, the Government Budget, Saving, and Investment

	Symbols and equations	Canada in 2007 (billions of dollars)
(a) Variables		
Exports*	X	532
Imports*	M	501
Government expenditure	G	342
Net taxes	T	383
Investment	I	311
Saving	S	301
(b) Balances		
Net exports	$X - M$	$532 - 501 = 31$
Government sector	$T - G$	$383 - 342 = 41$
Private sector	$S - I$	$301 - 311 = -10$
(c) Relationship among balances		
National accounts	$Y = C + I + G + X - M$	
	$= C + S + T$	
Rearranging:	$(X - M) = (T - G) + (S - I)$	
Net exports	$X - M$	31
equals:		
Government sector	$T - G$	41
plus		
Private sector	$S - I$	-10

Source of data: Statistics Canada, CANSIM Tables 380-0002 and 380-0017.

*The national income accounts measures of exports and imports are slightly different from the balance of payments accounts measures in Table 25.1 on p. 606.

know that real GDP, *Y*, is the sum of consumption expenditure (*C*), investment, government expenditure, and net exports. Real GDP also equals the sum of consumption expenditure, saving, and net taxes. Rearranging these equations tells us that net exports (*X* – *M*) equals the sum of the government sector balance (*T* – *G*) and the private sector balance (*S* – *I*). In Canada in 2007, the government sector balance was $41 billion and the private sector balance was –$10 billion. The government sector balance plus the private sector balance equalled net exports of $31 billion.

The Three Sector Balances

Deficits and Surpluses

You've seen that net exports equal the sum of the government sector balance and the private sector balance. How do these three sector balances fluctuate over time?

The figure answers this question. It shows the government sector balance (the red line), net exports (the blue line), and the private sector balance (the green line).

The private sector balance and the government sector balance move in opposite directions. When the government sector deficit was large during the 1980s and the first half of the 1990s, the private sector surplus was large. And when the government sector deficit was turned around to become a surplus during the second half of the 1990s and the 2000s, the private sector surplus decreased and eventually became a deficit.

Net exports are somewhat correlated with the government balance and are sometimes called twins. But the net exports balance does not follow the government sector balance closely. Rather, net exports respond to the *sum* of the government sector and private sector balances. When both the private sector and the government sector have a deficit, net exports

are negative and the combined private and government deficit is financed by borrowing from the rest of the world.

The trend in Canada's net exports is slightly positive.

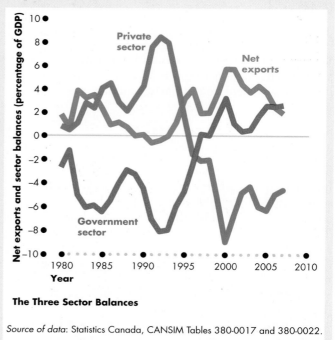

The Three Sector Balances

Source of data: Statistics Canada, CANSIM Tables 380-0017 and 380-0022.

Where Is the Exchange Rate?

In explaining the current account balance, we have not mentioned the exchange rate. Doesn't the exchange rate play a role?

In the short run, a fall in the nominal exchange rate lowers the real exchange rate, which makes our imports more costly and our exports more competitive. A higher price of imported consumption goods and services might induce a decrease in consumption expenditure and an increase in saving. A higher price of imported capital goods might induce a decrease in investment. Other things remaining the same, an increase in saving or a decrease in investment decreases the private sector deficit and decreases the current account deficit.

But in the long run, a change in the nominal exchange rate leaves the real exchange rate and all other real variables unchanged. So in the long run,

the nominal exchange rate plays no role in influencing the current account balance.

Review Quiz

1 What are the transactions that the current account records?

2 What are the transactions that the capital account records?

3 What are the transactions that the official settlements account records?

4 What are the biggest net borrower and debtor nations and do they borrow to consume?

5 How are net exports and the government sector budget balance linked?

 Work Study Plan 25.4 and get instant feedback.

Exchange Rate Policy

Because the exchange rate is the price of a country's money in terms of another country's money, governments and central banks must have a policy towards the exchange rate. Three possible exchange rate policies are

- Flexible exchange rate
- Fixed exchange rate
- Crawling peg

Flexible Exchange Rate

A **flexible exchange rate** policy is one that permits the exchange rate to be determined by demand and supply with no direct intervention in the foreign exchange market by the central bank. Most countries —and Canada is prominent among them—operate a flexible exchange rate, and the foreign exchange market that we have studied so far in this chapter is an example of a flexible exchange rate regime.

But even a flexible exchange rate is influenced by central bank actions. If the Bank of Canada raises the Canadian interest rate and other countries keep their interest rates unchanged, the demand for Canadian dollars increases, the supply of Canadian dollars decreases, and the exchange rate rises. (Similarly, if the Bank of Canada lowers the Canadian interest rate, the demand for Canadian dollars decreases, the supply increases, and the exchange rate falls.)

In a flexible exchange rate regime, when the central bank changes the interest rate, its purpose is not to influence the exchange rate, but to achieve some other monetary policy objective. (We return to this topic at length in Chapter 30.)

Fixed Exchange Rate

A **fixed exchange rate** policy is one that pegs the exchange rate at a value decided by the government or central bank and that blocks the unregulated forces of demand and supply by direct intervention in the foreign exchange market. The world economy operated a fixed exchange rate regime from the end of World War II to the early 1970s. China had a fixed exchange rate against the U.S. dollar until recently. Hong Kong has had a fixed exchange rate for many years and continues with that policy today.

A fixed exchange rate requires active intervention in the foreign exchange market.

If the Bank of Canada wanted to fix the Canadian dollar exchange rate against the U.S. dollar, it would sell Canadian dollars to prevent the exchange rate from rising above the target value and buy Canadian dollars to prevent the exchange rate from falling below the target value.

There is no limit to the quantity of Canadian dollars that the Bank of Canada can *sell*. The Bank of Canada creates Canadian dollars and can create any quantity it chooses. But there is a limit to the quantity of Canadian dollars the Bank of Canada can *buy*. That limit is set by Canadian official foreign currency reserves because to buy Canadian dollars the Bank of Canada must sell foreign currency. Intervention to buy Canadian dollars stops when Canadian official foreign currency reserves run out.

Let's look at the foreign exchange interventions that the Bank of Canada can make.

Suppose the Bank of Canada wants the exchange rate to be steady at 90 U.S. cents per Canadian dollar. If the exchange rate rises above that level, the Bank of Canada sells dollars. If the exchange rate falls below 90 U.S. cents, the Bank of Canada buys dollars. By these actions, the Bank of Canada keeps the exchange rate close to its target rate.

Figure 25.7 shows the Bank of Canada's intervention in the foreign exchange market. The supply of dollars is S and initially the demand for dollars is D_0. The equilibrium exchange rate is 90 U.S. cents per dollar. This exchange rate is also the target exchange rate, shown by the horizontal red line.

When the demand for Canadian dollars increases and the demand curve shifts rightward to D_1, the Bank of Canada sells \$10 billion. This action prevents the exchange rate from rising. When the demand for Canadian dollars decreases and the demand curve shifts leftward to D_2, the Bank of Canada buys \$10 billion. This action prevents the exchange rate from falling.

If the demand for Canadian dollars fluctuates between D_1 and D_2 and on average is D_0, the Bank of Canada can repeatedly intervene in the way we've just seen. Sometimes it buys and sometimes it sells, but on average, it neither buys nor sells.

But suppose the demand for Canadian dollars *increases permanently* from D_0 to D_1. To maintain the exchange rate at 90 U.S. cents per Canadian dollar, the Bank of Canada must sell dollars and buy foreign currency, so Canadian official foreign currency reserves would be increasing. At some point, the

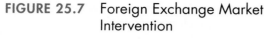

FIGURE 25.7   Foreign Exchange Market Intervention

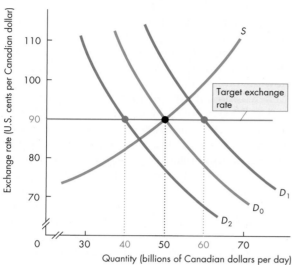

Initially, the demand for Canadian dollars is D_0, the supply of Canadian dollars is S, and the exchange rate is 90 U.S. cents per Canadian dollar. The Bank of Canada can intervene in the foreign exchange market to keep the exchange rate close to its target rate. If demand increases from D_0 to D_1, the Bank of Canada sells dollars. If demand decreases from D_0 to D_2, the Bank of Canada buys dollars. Persistent intervention on one side of the market cannot be sustained.

myeconlab   animation

Bank would abandon the exchange rate target to stop piling up foreign currency reserves.

Now suppose the demand for Canadian dollars *decreases permanently* from D_0 to D_2. In this situation, the Bank of Canada *cannot* maintain the exchange rate target indefinitely. To do so, it must *buy* Canadian dollars using the official foreign currency reserves. Eventually, the Bank would run out of foreign currency and have to abandon the target exchange rate.

Crawling Peg

A **crawling peg** exchange rate policy is one that selects a target for the exchange rate that changes periodically, with intervention in the foreign exchange market to achieve the target.

A crawling peg works like a fixed exchange rate except that the target value changes. Sometimes the

The People's Bank of China in the Foreign Exchange Market

Fixed Rate Followed by Crawling Peg

For several years, the exchange rate between the Chinese yuan and the U.S. dollar was constant. The reason for this near constant exchange rate is that China's central bank, the People's Bank of China, intervened to operate a fixed exchange rate policy. From 1997 until 2005, the yuan was pegged at 8.28 yuan per U.S. dollar. Since 2005, the yuan has appreciated slightly, but it has not been permitted to fluctuate freely. Since 2005, the yuan has been on a crawling peg.

The immediate consequence of the fixed yuan exchange rate (and crawling exchange rate) is that since 2000, China has piled up U.S dollar reserves on a huge scale. By mid-2006, China's official foreign currency reserves approached $1 trillion and by the end of 2007, they were fast approaching $2 trillion!

Part (a) of the figure shows the increase in China's official foreign currency reserves, some of which are euros and yen, but most of which are U.S. dollars. You can see that China's reserves increased by $200 billion in 2004 and 2005, by a bit more than $200 billion in 2006, and by $460 billion in 2007.

The demand and supply curves in part (b) of the figure illustrate what is happening in the market for U.S. dollars priced in terms of the yuan and explains why China's reserves have increased. The demand curve D and supply curve S intersect at 5 yuan per U.S. dollar. If the People's Bank of China takes no actions in the market, this exchange rate is the equilibrium rate (an assumed value).

By intervening in the foreign exchange market and buying U.S. dollars, the People's Bank pegs the yuan

target changes once a month, and sometimes it changes every day.

The Bank of Canada has never operated a crawling peg. But some prominent countries do use this system. When China abandoned its fixed exchange rate, it replaced it with a crawling peg. China and some other developing countries use a crawling peg as a method of trying to control inflation—a policy that we examine in Chapter 30, p. 748.

The ideal crawling peg sets a target for the exchange rate equal to the equilibrium exchange rate

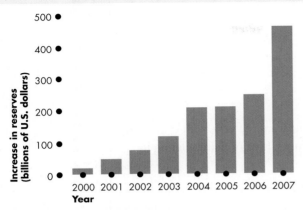

(a) Increase in U.S. Dollar Reserves

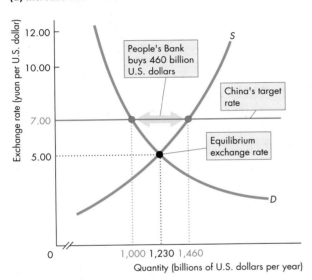

(b) Pegging the Yuan

China's Foreign Exchange Market Intervention

at 7 yuan per U.S. dollar. But to do so, it must pile up U.S. dollars. To hold the exchange rate at 7 yuan per dollar, the People's Bank bought $460 billion in 2007.

If the People's Bank stopped buying U.S. dollars, the U.S. dollar would depreciate, the yuan would appreciate, and China would stop piling up U.S. dollar reserves.

Why Does China Manage Its Exchange Rate? The popular story is that China manages its exchange rate to keep its export prices low and to make it easier to compete in world markets. You've seen that this story is correct in the short run. Given the prices in China and the rest of the world, a low yuan–U.S. dollar exchange rate brings lower U.S. dollar prices for China's exports. But the yuan–U.S. dollar exchange rate was fixed for almost 10 years and has been managed for 3 more years. This long period of a fixed exchange rate has long-run, not short-run, effects. In the long run, the exchange rate has no effect on competitiveness. The reason is that prices adjust to reflect the exchange rate and the real exchange rate is unaffected by the nominal exchange rate.

So why does China fix its exchange rate? The more convincing answer is that China sees a fixed exchange rate as a way of controlling its inflation rate. By making the yuan crawl against the U.S. dollar, China's inflation rate is anchored to the U.S. inflation rate and will not stray too far from that rate (see Chapter 30, p. 747).

The bottom line is that in the long run, exchange rate policy is monetary policy, not balance of payments policy. To change its balance of payments, a country must change its saving and investment.

on average. The peg seeks only to prevent large swings in the expected future exchange rate that change demand and supply and make the exchange rate fluctuate too wildly.

A crawling peg departs from the ideal if, as often happens with a fixed exchange rate, the target rate departs from the equilibrium exchange rate for too long. When this happens, the country either runs out of reserves or piles up reserves.

Reading Between the Lines on pp. 614–615 looks further at China's crawling peg exchange rate policy.

Review Quiz

1 What is a flexible exchange rate and how does it work?
2 What is a fixed exchange rate and how is its value fixed?
3 What is a crawling peg and how does it work?
4 How has China operated in the foreign exchange market, why, and with what effect?

 Work Study Plan 25.5 and get instant feedback.

The Rising Chinese Yuan

Bush Aides Struggling with Yuan

May 10, 2006

After nearly three years of pushing China to let its currency float more freely, with only modest results, the Bush administration still appears reluctant to accuse China of manipulating its exchange rate. ...

American manufacturers and many members of Congress have complained for years that China has kept its currency, the yuan, at an artificially low exchange rate to the dollar as a way of selling its exports at cheap prices.

Treasury Secretary John W. Snow has resisted demands to threaten Beijing, arguing that Chinese leaders are making "progress" towards a more flexible exchange rate and a more open financial system.

This week, a Treasury official again emphasized China's steps towards openness.

"If you look at what China is doing in exercising their commitment on putting in place a foreign-exchange regime that has greater flexibility," Mr. Snow's principal spokesman, Tony Fratto, told reporters on Monday, "you see some evidence that they're doing that."

But changes in the yuan's value have been relatively minor. Chinese leaders let the yuan climb about 2 percent against the dollar last July, and another similarly small amount more recently.

When President Hu Jintao visited President Bush in Washington last month, top Chinese officials re-emphasized a need for "stability" and offered no hint of when they might let the yuan move more freely. ...

The United States' trade deficit with China ballooned to $202 billion in 2005, an imbalance that might ordinarily have pushed up the value of the yuan in relation to the dollar. China has prevented the yuan from rising by buying hundreds of billions in dollar-denominated reserves. ...

Essence of the Story

- U.S. producers and members of Congress complain that China has kept the yuan artificially low to sell exports at low prices.

- Treasury Secretary John W. Snow says that China is moving towards a more flexible exchange rate.

- Changes in the yuan–dollar exchange rate have been small.

- The yuan appreciated in July 2005 and by small amounts more recently.

- The U.S. trade deficit with China was $202 billion in 2005.

- This imbalance should have pushed up the value of the yuan, but China prevented that from happening and increased its U.S. dollar reserves.

Economic Analysis

- China's exchange rate was pegged at 8.28 yuan per U.S. dollar until July 2005.

- In July 2005, the yuan appreciated against the U.S. dollar (the U.S. dollar depreciated) by 2.1 percent.

- Since July 2005, the yuan has slowly but persistently appreciated against the dollar (the dollar has depreciated against the yuan).

- Figure 1 shows the path of the depreciating dollar against the yuan.

- To peg the yuan before July 2005 and since then to keep the exchange rate from rising more than it wants, the People's Bank of China buys U.S. dollars in the foreign exchange market.

- The result of these foreign exchange market transactions has been a strong growth in China's foreign reserves.

- Figure 2 shows the buildup of China's reserves, which, by 2008, were approaching $2 trillion.

- Americans are concerned about the yuan–U.S. dollar exchange rate because China has a large trade surplus with the United States.

- But China's overall current account surplus is not large and is a fraction of the large U.S. current account deficit.

- Figure 3 shows the U.S. current account deficit and China's current account surplus.

- The analysis in this chapter explains that a current account deficit results from too little private and government saving relative to investment.

- China saves more than it invests, and the United States invests more than it saves.

- A change in the nominal exchange rate between the U.S. dollar and the Chinese yuan cannot make a large contribution to changing these imbalances.

- The main effect of the appreciation of the yuan against the U.S. dollar will be to slow China's inflation rate relative to the U.S. inflation rate.

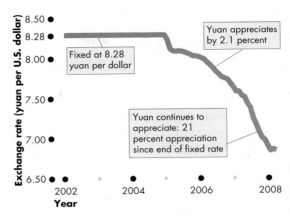

Figure 1 The yuan–U.S. dollar exchange rate

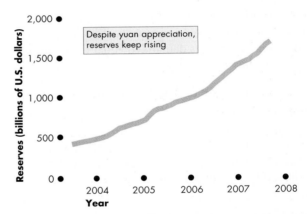

Figure 2 China's reserves pile up

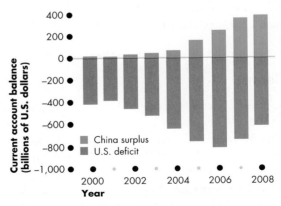

Figure 3 Current account balances

SUMMARY ◆

Key Points

Currencies and Exchange Rates (pp. 594–596)

- Foreign currency is obtained in exchange for domestic currency in the foreign exchange market.
- The nominal exchange rate is the value of one currency in terms of another currency.
- The real exchange rate is the price of one country's real GDP in terms of another country's real GDP.

The Foreign Exchange Market (pp. 597–600)

- Demand and supply in the foreign exchange market determine the exchange rate.
- The higher the exchange rate, the smaller is the quantity of Canadian dollars demanded and the greater is the quantity of Canadian dollars supplied.
- The equilibrium exchange rate makes the quantity of Canadian dollars demanded equal the quantity of Canadian dollars supplied.

Changes in Demand and Supply: Exchange Rate Fluctuations (pp. 601–605)

- Changes in the world demand for Canadian exports, the Canadian interest rate differential, or the expected future exchange rate change the demand for Canadian dollars.

- Changes in the Canadian demand for imports, the Canadian interest rate differential, or the expected future exchange rate change the supply of Canadian dollars.
- Exchange rate expectations are influenced by purchasing power parity and interest rate parity.
- In the long run, the nominal exchange rate is a monetary phenomenon and the real exchange rate is independent of the nominal exchange rate.

Financing International Trade (pp. 606–610)

- International trade, borrowing, and lending are financed by using foreign currency.
- A country's international transactions are recorded in its current account, capital account, and official settlements account.
- The current account balance is similar to net exports and is determined by the government sector balance plus the private sector balance.

Exchange Rate Policy (pp. 611–613)

- An exchange rate can be flexible, fixed, or a crawling peg.
- To achieve a fixed or a crawling exchange rate, a central bank must intervene in the foreign exchange market and either buy or sell foreign currency.

Key Figures and Table

Key Terms

PROBLEMS and APPLICATIONS

 Work problems 1–14 in Chapter 25 Study Plan and get instant feedback.
Work problems 15–21 as Homework, a Quiz, or a Test if assigned by your instructor.

1. The U.S. dollar exchange rate increased from $0.97 Canadian in 2007 to $1.06 Canadian in 2008, and it decreased from 115 Japanese yen in 2007 to 107 Japanese yen in 2008.
   a. Did the U.S. dollar appreciate or depreciate against the Canadian dollar?
   b. Did the U.S. dollar appreciate or depreciate against the Japanese yen?
   c. What was the value of the Canadian dollar in terms of U.S. dollars in 2007 and 2008?
   d. What was the value of 100 Japanese yen in terms of U.S. dollars in 2007 and 2008?
   e. Did the Canadian dollar appreciate or depreciate against the U.S. dollar in 2008?
   f. Did the Japanese yen appreciate or depreciate against the U.S. dollar in 2008?

2. In 2004, the price level in the Eurozone was 112.4, the price level in the United States was 109.1, and the nominal exchange rate was 80 euro cents per U.S. dollar. What was the real exchange rate expressed as Eurozone real GDP per unit of U.S. real GDP?

3. In 2003, the price level in the United States was 106.3, the price level in Japan was 95.4, and the real exchange rate expressed as Japanese real GDP per unit of U.S. real GDP was 103.6. What was the nominal exchange rate?

4. There is a large increase in the global demand for roses and Colombia is the biggest producer of roses. At the same time, the central bank of Colombia increases the interest rate. What happens in the foreign exchange market for Colombian pesos to
   a. The demand for pesos?
   b. The supply of pesos?
   c. The quantity of pesos demanded?
   d. The quantity of pesos supplied?
   e. The exchange rate of the pesos against the U.S. dollar?

5. If a euro deposit in a bank in Paris, France, earns interest of 4 percent a year and a yen deposit in Tokyo, Japan, earns 0.5 percent a year, everything else remaining the same and adjusted for risk, what is the exchange rate expectation of the Japanese yen?

6. The U.K. pound is trading at 1.82 U.S. dollars per U.K. pound. There is purchasing power parity at this exchange rate. The interest rate in the United States is 2 percent a year and the interest rate in the United Kingdom is 4 percent a year.
   a. Calculate the U.S. interest rate differential.
   b. What is the U.K. pound expected to be worth in terms of U.S. dollars one year from now?
   c. Which country more likely has the lower inflation rate? How can you tell?

7. You can purchase a laptop in Mexico City for 12,960 Mexican pesos. If the exchange rate is 10.8 Mexican pesos per Canadian dollar and if purchasing power parity prevails, at what price can you buy an identical computer in Vancouver?

8. The table gives some information about a country's international transactions in 2008.

Item	Millions of dollars
Imports of goods and services	1,487
Foreign investment in the country	1,051
Exports of goods and services	990
Investment abroad	456
Net interest income	7
Net transfers	−68
Statistical discrepancy	−36

   a. Calculate the current account balance.
   b. Calculate the capital account balance.
   c. Did the country's official reserves increase or decrease?
   d. Was the country a net borrower or a net lender in 2008? Explain your answer.

9. A country has a lower inflation rate than all other countries. It has more rapid economic growth. The central bank does not intervene in the foreign exchange market. What can you say (and why) about
   a. The exchange rate?
   b. The current account balance?
   c. The expected exchange rate?
   d. The interest rate differential?
   e. Interest rate parity?
   f. Purchasing power parity?

10. **The Lesson: Buy Ruffles in Myanmar**

    ... A small bag of cheese-flavored Ruffles potato chips is $1.69 in Japan and only 8 cents in Myanmar. ... The price of spending 1 hour at an Internet cafe in Vietnam is $0.62 U.S., in China is $1.48 U.S., and in South Africa is $3.40 U.S.

    Los Angeles Times, April 23, 2006

    Do these prices indicate that purchasing power parity does not prevail? Why or why not?

11. **Peso's Party**

    It was bad enough when Canada's Loonie surpassed the U.S. dollar, but now the Mexican peso is gaining on the greenback, too. In April, the peso hit 10.44 to the U.S. dollar, its best rate in two years. Mexico's 4.2 percent GDP growth in January and February ... finally convinced currency investors that the peso shouldn't be tethered to the dollar, as it has been in recent years.

    ... At current levels, exports might soon become more expensive for gringos. In other words, time to stock up on Coronas.

    Fortune, May 12, 2008

    a. Is the news clip about the real exchange rate or the nominal exchange rate? Explain.
    b. Explain why "the Mexican peso is gaining on the greenback."
    c. Draw a graph to illustrate why "the Mexican peso is gaining on the greenback."
    d. Explain why Mexican goods might become more expensive for U.S. consumers.

12. **Canada's Experience with Flexible Exchange Rate in the 1950s: Valuable Lessons Learned**

    Canada's experience with a flexible exchange rate regime in the twentieth and twenty-first centuries is remarkable not only for sheer length, but also for its impact on macroeconomic theory and policy in open economies. ... Canada had a flexible exchange rate regime over the periods 1933–39 and 1950–62, and has maintained one since 1970 ... [There are] benefits of a flexible exchange rate regime: namely, its ability to insulate the domestic economy from external shocks by facilitating a smoother and thus less costly macroeconomic adjustment, and the fact that it permits the operation of an independent national monetary policy. ... Canada's experience led to a

    better understanding of the impact of monetary and fiscal policies in an open economy with a high degree of capital mobility ... Canada's floating-rate experience contributed to the postwar debate on exchange rate regimes by providing evidence to support the case for a flexible rate as a viable alternative to ... pegged exchange rates.

    Bank of Canada Review, Spring 2008

    a. Explain the difference between the flexible exchange rate policy that Canada pioneered and a fixed exchange rate policy.
    b. Explain the advantages of a flexible exchange rate policy over a fixed exchange rate policy.
    c. If a fixed exchange rate does not influence competitiveness in the long run, why might a country adopt this policy?

13. **The United States, Debtor Nation**

    The United States is a debtor nation, just like the poorest states in Africa, Latin America and Asia. ... For most of the past 30 years the United States has been piling up large trade deficits. The current account ... has now reached a deficit of 6 percent of GDP, and must be financed by capital inflows. Foreigners must purchase large amounts of US property, stocks, bonds, bank deposits and currency, or the current-account deficit cannot be financed. ...

    Asia Times, September 28, 2006

    a. Explain why a current account deficit "must be financed by capital inflows."
    b. Under what circumstances should the debtor nation status of the United States be a concern?

14. The *Economist* magazine uses the price of a Big Mac to determine whether a currency is undervalued or overvalued. In May 2006, the price of a Big Mac was $3.10 in New York, 10.5 yuan in Beijing, and 6.30 Swiss francs in Geneva. The exchange rates were 8.03 yuan per U.S. dollar and 1.21 Swiss francs per U.S. dollar.

    a. Was the yuan undervalued or overvalued relative to purchasing power parity?
    b. Was the Swiss franc undervalued or overvalued relative to purchasing power parity?
    c. Do you think the price of a Big Mac in different countries provides a valid test of purchasing power parity?

15. The table gives some information about the U.K. economy in 2003:

Item	Billions of U.K. pounds
Consumption expenditure	721
Exports of goods and services	277
Government expenditure	230
Net taxes	217
Investment	181
Saving	162

   a. Calculate the private sector balance.
   b. Calculate the government sector balance.
   c. Calculate net exports.
   d. What is the relationship between the government sector balance and net exports?

16. A country's currency appreciates, and its official holdings of foreign currency increase. What can you say about

   a. The central bank's intervention in the foreign exchange market?
   b. The country's current account balance?
   c. The country's official settlements account?

17. **Top U.S. Real Estate Markets for Investment**
   Rahul Reddy ... has been investing in commercial properties in Western Australia for the last two years. Now, with the Australian dollar growing in strength and the American housing market strained, he's got his eye on residential and commercial properties in Florida and California, areas he believes will recover over the long term. He's not alone. Encouraged by a weak dollar and a belief in the resiliency of the U.S. economy, individuals like Reddy, along with institutional investors such as pension funds and private equity groups, are seeking investment properties and development opportunities in the United States. ... "The U.S. is good for speculative higher-risk investments from our perspective because the strong Australian dollar will enable us to gain hold of properties at prices we will probably not see for a long time," says Reddy. "The U.S. is an economic powerhouse that I think will recover, and if the exchange rate goes back to figures from a few years ago, that will benefit us. ..."
   Forbes, July 10, 2008

   a. Explain why foreign individuals and institutions are "seeking investment properties and development opportunities in the United States."
   b. Explain what would happen if the speculation made by Reddy became widespread. Would expectations become self-fulfilling?
   c. Draw a graph of the foreign exchange market to illustrate your explanation in b.

18. **Canada's Dollar Depreciates as Stock Indexes in the U.S. Fall**
   Canada's currency depreciated as U.S. stocks fell, signaling an increase in risk aversion.
   The Canadian dollar has weakened 11 percent this quarter. ... The U.S. is Canada's largest trading partner. "The direction of the Canadian dollar is very much a function of how risk is seen in the global landscape," said Jack Spitz, managing director of foreign exchange at National Bank of Canada in Toronto. "Equities are off their highs, so the Canadian dollar gets swept up in this environment." ... Bank of Canada Governor Mark Carney signalled his country may slide into a recession like other industrialized nations, adding weight to economists' forecasts that he may pare interest rates to the lowest since 1960. ... Carney cut his key interest rate to 2.25 percent last month and said the world's eighth-largest economy would shrink this quarter and stall in the first three months of 2009. Three of the country's biggest banks predict a recession. ... The Canadian dollar will plunge 10 percent over the next three months ... as global growth slows, according to Barclays Capital.
   Bloomberg, November 10, 2008

   Explain and draw a graph to illustrate the individual effect of each of the following events on the exchange rate of the Canadian dollar against the U.S. dollar.

   a. The Bank of Canada cuts the interest rate while foreign interest rates remain unchanged.
   b. The Bank of Canada cuts the interest rate and foreign central banks cut their interest rates by the same amount and at the same time.
   c. Expectations that the Bank of Canada will cut interest rates in the future increase.
   d. A recession occurs in Canada but not in the United States.
   e. A recession occurs in both the United States and Canada.

19. **U.S. Declines to Cite China as Currency Manipulator**

The Bush administration has declined to cite China for manipulating its currency to gain unfair trade advantages against the United States ... despite pressure in Congress for penalties. America's growing trade deficit with China, which last year hit an all-time high of $256.3 billion, [is] the largest deficit ever recorded with a single country. ... Chinese currency, the yuan, has risen in value by 18.4 percent against the dollar since the Chinese government loosened its currency system in July 2005. However, American manufacturers contend the yuan is still undervalued by as much as 40 percent, making Chinese products more competitive in this country and U.S. goods more expensive in China. ... China is a major holder of dollar-denominated investments such as U.S. Treasury securities, which it buys to keep the dollar from falling in value against the yuan.

MSN, May 15, 2008

a. Explain how China was able to maintain a fixed exchange rate with the dollar until July 2005.
b. Draw a graph to illustrate how China kept the exchange rate fixed.
c. Has China used a flexible exchange rate policy since July 2005?
d. Explain how fixed and crawling peg exchange rates can be used to manipulate trade balances in the short run, but not in the long run.
e. What is the long-run rationale behind a fixed or crawling peg exchange rate?

20. **Inside the Mind of a Debtor Nation**

Year after year, I am stunned by the decisions people make that get them into financial trouble. I've seen monthly car notes the size of mortgage payments. People take vacations or buy big-screen televisions and expensive jewelry while ignoring huge federal tax obligations. ... Why do they continue to use credit even though they are already weighed down by so much debt? ... What has made us into a nation of people who spend more than we earn? ... Part of the problem is our economy's reliance on personal consumption. On some level, we all know our buying is out of control, but we are constantly bombarded with messages encouraging us to shop. The steady stream blunts our reasoning power. ... Much of the difficulty stems from new retail technologies that make it easy to act without thinking. ... What's the long-term effect of our overspending?

Washington Post, March 2, 2008

a. Explain the effect on the dollar of "out of control" consumer spending and draw a graph of the foreign exchange market to illustrate your explanation.
b. How can "out of control" spending be used to explain the trends in balance of payments since the 1990s?
c. Explain whether or not Americans should be concerned that the United States is a net borrower and debtor nation.

21. Study *Reading Between the Lines* on pp. 614–615 and then answer the following questions.

a. Do you think the yuan–U.S. dollar exchange rate is a problem for Americans or the source of the U.S. current account deficit?
b. Do you think that appreciation of the yuan against the U.S. dollar can help the United States to eliminate its current account deficit?
c. What do you predict would be the main effects of an increase in the yuan–U.S. dollar exchange rate?
d. What, if anything, could U.S. policy do to reduce the U.S. current account deficit?

22. Use the link in MyEconLab (Textbook resources, Chapter 25, Weblinks) to visit PACIFIC, an exchange rate service, and read the page on purchasing power parity.

a. What is purchasing power parity?
b. Which currencies are the most overvalued relative to the U.S. dollar today?
c. Which currencies are the most undervalued relative to the U.S. dollar today?
d. Give some suggestions as to why some currencies are overvalued and some undervalued.
e. Do you think that the information on overvaluation and undervaluation is useful to currency speculators? Why or why not?

Expanding the Frontier

Economics is about how we cope with scarcity. We cope as individuals by making choices that balance marginal benefits and marginal costs so that we use our scarce resources efficiently. We cope as societies by creating incentive systems and social institutions that encourage specialization and exchange.

These choices and the incentive systems that guide them determine what we specialize in; how much work we do; how hard we work at school to learn the mental skills that form our human capital and that determine the kinds of jobs we get and the incomes we earn; how much we save for future big-ticket expenditures; how much businesses and governments spend on new capital—on auto assembly lines, computers and fibre cables for improved Internet services, shopping malls, highways, bridges, and tunnels; how intensively existing capital and natural resources are used and how quickly they wear out or are used up; and the problems that scientists, engineers, and other inventors work on to develop new technologies.

All the choices we've just described combine to determine the standard of living and the rate at which it improves—the economic growth rate.

Money that makes specialization and exchange in markets possible is a huge contributor to economic growth. But too much money brings a rising cost of living with no improvement in the standard of living.

Joseph Schumpeter, *the son of a textile factory owner, was born in Austria in 1883. He moved from Austria to Germany during the tumultuous 1920s when those two countries experienced hyperinflation. In 1932, in the depths of the Great Depression, he went to the United States and became a professor of economics at Harvard University.*

This creative economic thinker wrote about economic growth and development, business cycles, political systems, and economic biography. He was a person of strong opinions who expressed them forcefully and delighted in verbal battles.

Schumpeter saw the development and diffusion of new technologies by profit-seeking entrepreneurs as the source of economic progress. But he saw economic progress as a process of creative destruction—the creation of new profit opportunities and the destruction of currently profitable businesses. For Schumpeter, economic growth and the business cycle were a single phenomenon.

"Economic progress, in capitalist society, means turmoil."

JOSEPH SCHUMPETER
Capitalism, Socialism, and Democracy

TALKING
WITH

Xavier Sala-i-Martin

Xavier Sala-i-Martin is Professor of Economics at Columbia University. He is also a Research Associate at the National Bureau of Economic Research, Senior Economic Advisor to the World Economic Forum, Associate Editor of the *Journal of Economic Growth*, founder and CEO of Umbele Foundation: A Future for Africa, and President of the Economic Commission of the Barcelona Football Club.

Professor Sala-i-Martin was an undergraduate at Universitat Autonoma de Barcelona and a graduate student at Harvard University, where he obtained his Ph.D. in 1990.

In 2004, he was awarded the Premio Juan Carlos I de Economía, a biannual prize given by the Bank of Spain to the best economist in Spain and Latin America.

With Robert Barro, he is the author of *Economic Growth Second Edition* (MIT Press, 2003), the definitive graduate level text on this topic.

Michael Parkin and Robin Bade talked with Xavier Sala-i-Martin about his work and the progress that economists have made in understanding economic growth.

What attracted you to economics?

It was a random event. I wanted to be rich, so I asked my mom, "In my family, who is the richest guy?" She said, "Your uncle John." And I asked, "What did he study?" And she said, "Economics." So I went into economics!

In Spain, there are no liberal arts colleges where you can study lots of things. At age 18, you must decide what career you will follow. If you choose economics, you go to economics school and take economics five years in a row. So you have to make a decision in a crazy way, like I did.

How did economic growth become your major field of research?

I studied economics. I liked it. I studied mathematical economics. I liked it too, and I went to graduate school. In my second year at Harvard, Jeffrey Sachs hired me to go to Bolivia. I saw poor people for the first time in my life. I was shocked. I decided I should try to answer the question "Why are these people so poor and why are we so rich, and what can we do to turn their state into our state?" We live in a bubble world in the United States and Europe, and we don't realize how poor people really are. When you see poverty at first hand, it is very hard to think about something else. So I decided to study economic growth. Coincidentally, when I returned from Bolivia, I was assigned to be Robert Barro's teaching assistant. He was teaching economic growth, so I studied with him and eventually wrote books and articles with him.

In your first research on economic growth, you tested the neoclassical growth model using data for a number of countries and for the states of the United States. What did you discover?

Neoclassical theory was criticized on two grounds. First, its source of growth, technological change, is exogenous—not explained. Second, its assumption of diminishing marginal returns to capital seems to imply that income per person should converge to the same level in every country. If you are poor, your marginal product should be high. Every cookie that you save should

622

generate huge growth. If you are rich, your marginal product should be low. Every cookie you save should generate very little growth. Therefore poor countries should grow faster than rich countries, and convergence of income levels should occur. Convergence doesn't occur, so, said its critics, neoclassical theory must be wrong.

It turned out that it was this criticism that was wrong. Growth depends on the productivity of your cookies and on how many cookies you save. If you don't save any cookies, you don't grow, even if your marginal product is large.

Conditional convergence is the idea that income per person will converge only if countries have similar savings rates, similar technologies, and similar everything. That's what I tested. To hold every relevant factor equal, I tested the hypothesis using regions: states within the United States or countries that are similar. And once you're careful to hold other things equal, you see a perfect negative relationship between growth rates and income levels.

As predicted by neoclassical theory, poor countries grow faster than rich countries if they are similar. So my research shows that it is not so easy to reject neoclassical theory. The law of diminishing returns that comes from Adam Smith and Malthus and Ricardo is very powerful. Growth through capital accumulation is very, very hard. Growth has to come from other things, such as technological change.

What do we know today about the nature and causes of the wealth of nations that Adam Smith didn't know?

Actually, even though over the last two hundred years some of the best minds have looked at the question, we know surprisingly little. We have some general principles that are not very easy to apply in practice. We know, for example, that markets are good. We know that for the economy to work, we need property rights to be guaranteed. If there are thieves—government or private thieves—that can steal the proceeds of the

investment, there's no investment and there's no growth. We know that the incentives are very important.

These are general principles. Because we know these principles we should ask: How come Africa is still poor? The answer is, it is very hard to translate "Markets are good" and "Property rights work" into practical actions. We know that Zimbabwe has to guarantee property rights. With the government it has, that's not going to work. The U.S. Constitution works in the United States. If you try to copy the U.S. Constitution and impose the system in Zimbabwe, it's not going to work.

> Growth through capital accumulation is very, very hard. Growth has to come from other things, such as technological change.

You've done a lot of work on distribution of income, and you say we've made a lot of progress. What is the evidence to support this conclusion?

There are two issues: poverty and inequality. When in 2001 I said poverty is going down, everyone said I was crazy. The United Nations Development Report, which uses World Bank data, was saying the exact opposite. I said the World Bank methodology was flawed. After a big public argument that you can see in the *Economist*, the World Bank revised their poverty numbers and they now agree with me that poverty rates are falling.

Now why is poverty falling? In 1970, 80 percent of the world's poor were in Asia—in China, India, Bangladesh, and Indonesia. China's "Great Leap Forward" was a great leap backward. People were starving to death. Now, the growth of these countries has been spectacular and the global poverty rate has fallen. Yes, if you look at Africa, Africa is going backwards. But Africa has 700 million people. China has 1.3 billion. India has 1.1 billion. Indonesia has 300 million. Asia has 4 billion of the world's 6 billion people. These big guys are growing. It's impossible that global poverty is not going down.

But what we care about is poverty in different regions of the world. Asia has been doing very well, but Africa has not. Unfortunately, Africa is still going in the wrong direction.

You've made a big personal commitment to Africa. What is the Africa problem? Why does this continent lag behind Asia? Why, as you've just put it, is Africa going in the wrong direction?

Number one, Africa is a very violent continent. There are 22 wars in Africa as we speak. Two, nobody will invest in Africa. Three, we in the rich world—the United States, Europe, and Japan—won't let them trade. Because we have agricultural subsidies, trade barriers, and tariffs for their products, they can't sell to us.

Africans should globalize themselves. They should open, and we should let them open. They should introduce markets. But to get markets, you need legal systems, police, transparency, less red tape. You need a lot of the things we have now. They have corrupt economies, very bureaucratic, with no property rights, the judiciary is corrupt. All of that has to change.

They need female education. One of the biggest rates of return that we have is educating girls. To educate girls, they'll need to build schools, they need to pay teachers, they need to buy uniforms, they need to provide the incentives for girls to go to school, which usually is like a string. You pull it, you don't push it. Pushing education doesn't work. What you need is: Let the girls know that the rate of return on education is very high by providing jobs after they leave school. So you need to change the incentives of the girls to go to school and educate themselves. That's going to increase the national product, but it will also increase health, and it will also reduce fertility.

> Question!
> Question everything!

Returning to the problems of poverty and inequality, how can inequality be increasing within countries but decreasing globally—across countries?

Because most inequality comes from the fact that some people live in rich countries and some people live in poor countries. The big difference across people is not that there are rich Americans and poor Americans. Americans are very close to each other relative to the difference between Americans and people from Senegal.

What is closing today is the gap *across* countries—and for the first time in history. Before the Industrial Revolution, everybody was equal. Equal and poor. Equally poor. People were living at subsistence levels, which means you eat, you're clothed, you have a house, you die. No movies, no travel, no music, no toothbrush. Just subsist. And if the weather is not good, one-third of the population dies. That was the history of the world between 10,000 B.C. and today.

Yes, there was a king, there was Caesar, but the majority of the population were peasants.

All of a sudden, the Industrial Revolution means that one small country, England, takes off and there is 2 percent growth every year. The living standard of the workers of England goes up and up and up. Then the United States, then France, then the rest of Europe, then Canada all begin to grow.

In terms of today's population, 1 billion people become rich and 5 billion remain poor. Now for the first time in history, the majority of these 5 billion people are growing more rapidly than the rich guys. They're catching up quickly. The incomes of the majority of poor citizens of the world are growing faster than those of Americans.

What advice do you have for someone who is just beginning to study economics?

Question! Question everything! Take some courses in history and math. And read my latest favourite book, Bill Easterly's *White Man's Burden.* * It shows why we have not been doing the right thing in the aid business. I'm a little bit less dramatic than he is. He says that nothing has worked. I think some things have worked, and we have to take advantage of what has worked to build on it. But I agree with the general principle that being nice, being good, doesn't necessarily mean doing good. Lots of people with good intentions do harm. Economic science teaches us that incentives are the key.

---

*William Easterly, The White Man's Burden: Why the West's Efforts to Aid the Rest Have Done So Much Ill and So Little Good. New York, Penguin Books, 2006.

26

Aggregate Supply and Aggregate Demand

After studying this chapter, you will be able to

- Explain what determines aggregate supply in the long run and in the short run

- Explain what determines aggregate demand

- Explain how real GDP and the price level are determined and how changes in aggregate supply and aggregate demand bring economic growth, inflation, and the business cycle

- Describe the main schools of thought in macroeconomics today

Production grows and prices rise. But the pace at which production grows and prices rise is uneven. In 2006, real GDP grew by 3 percent, but in 2008, growth slowed to snail pace and was expected to shrink in in the last quarter of 2008 and the whole of 2009.

Similarly, during recent years, prices have increased at rates ranging from a barely perceptible 1 percent to a disturbing 4 percent a year.

The uneven pace of economic growth and inflation—the business cycle—is the subject of this chapter and the two that follow it. Here, you will discover the forces that bring fluctuations in the pace of real GDP growth and inflation and the associated fluctuations in employment and unemployment.

This chapter explains a *model* of real GDP and the price level—the *aggregate supply–aggregate demand model* or *AS–AD model*. This model represents the consensus view of macroeconomists on how real GDP and the price level are determined. The model provides a framework for understanding the forces that make our economy expand, that bring inflation, and that cause business cycle fluctuations. The *AS–AD* model also provides a framework within which we can see the range of views of macroeconomists in different schools of thought.

In *Reading Between the Lines* at the end of the chapter, we use the *AS–AD* model to interpret the course of Canadian real GDP and the price level in 2008.

## Aggregate Supply

The purpose of the aggregate supply–aggregate demand model that you study in this chapter is to explain how real GDP and the price level are determined and how they interact. The model uses similar ideas to those that you encountered in Chapter 3 when you learned how the quantity and price in a competitive market are determined. But the *aggregate* supply–*aggregate* demand model (*AS–AD* model) isn't just an application of the competitive market model. Some differences arise because the *AS–AD* model is a model of an imaginary market for the total of all the final goods and services that make up real GDP. The quantity in this "market" is real GDP and the price is the price level measured by the GDP deflator.

One thing that the *AS–AD* model shares with the competitive market model is that both distinguish between *supply* and the *quantity supplied*. We begin by explaining what we mean by the quantity of real GDP supplied.

Quantity Supplied and Supply

The *quantity of real GDP supplied* is the total quantity of goods and services, valued in constant base-year (2002) dollars, that firms plan to produce during a given period. This quantity depends on the quantity of labour employed; the quantity of physical and human capital; and the state of technology.

At any given time, the quantity of capital and the state of technology are fixed. They depend on decisions that were made in the past. The population is also fixed. But the quantity of labour is not fixed. It depends on decisions made by households and firms about the supply of and demand for labour.

The labour market can be in any one of three states: at full employment, above full employment, or below full employment. At full employment, the quantity of real GDP supplied is *potential GDP*, which depends on the full-employment quantity of labour (see Chapter 22, pp. 521–523). Over the business cycle, employment fluctuates around full employment and the quantity of real GDP supplied fluctuates around potential GDP.

Aggregate supply is the relationship between the quantity of real GDP supplied and the price level. This relationship is different in the long run than in the short run and to study aggregate supply, we distinguish between two time frames:

- Long-run aggregate supply
- Short-run aggregate supply

Long-Run Aggregate Supply

Long-run aggregate supply is the relationship between the quantity of real GDP supplied and the price level when the money wage rate changes in step with the price level to achieve full employment. The quantity of real GDP supplied at full employment equals potential GDP and this quantity is the same regardless of the price level.

The long-run aggregate supply curve in Fig. 26.1 illustrates long-run aggregate supply as the vertical line at potential GDP labelled *LAS*. Along the long-run aggregate supply curve, as the price level changes, the money wage rate also changes so the real wage rate is constant and real GDP remains at potential GDP. The long-run aggregate supply curve is always vertical and is always located at potential GDP.

The long-run aggregate supply curve is vertical because potential GDP is independent of the price level. The reason for this independence is that a movement along the *LAS* curve is accompanied by a change in *two* sets of prices: the prices of goods and services—the price level—and the prices of the factors of production, most notably, the money wage rate. A 10 percent increase in the prices of goods and services is matched by a 10 percent increase in the money wage rate. Because the price level and the money wage rate change by the same percentage, the *real wage rate* remains constant at its full-employment equilibrium level. So when the price level changes and the real wage rate remains constant, employment remains constant and real GDP remains constant at potential GDP.

Production at a Pepsi Plant You can see more clearly why real GDP remains constant when all prices change by the same percentage by thinking about production decisions at a Pepsi bottling plant. How does the quantity of Pepsi supplied change if the price of Pepsi changes and the wage rate of the workers and prices of all the other resources used vary by the same percentage? The answer is that the quantity supplied doesn't change. The firm produces the quantity that maximizes profit. That quantity depends on the price of Pepsi relative to the cost of producing it. With no change in price *relative to cost*, production doesn't change.

Short-Run Aggregate Supply

Short-run aggregate supply is the relationship between the quantity of real GDP supplied and the price level *when the money wage rate, the prices of other resources, and potential GDP remain constant.* Figure 26.1 illustrates this relationship as the short-run aggregate supply curve *SAS* and the short-run aggregate supply schedule. Each point on the *SAS* curve corresponds to a row of the short-run aggregate supply schedule. For example, point *A* on the *SAS* curve and row *A* of the schedule tell us that if the price level is 100, the quantity of real GDP supplied is $1,100 billion. In the short run, a rise in the price level brings an increase in the quantity of real GDP supplied. The short-run aggregate supply curve slopes upward.

With a given money wage rate, there is one price level at which the real wage rate is at its full-employment equilibrium level. At this price level, the quantity of real GDP supplied equals potential GDP and the *SAS* curve intersects the *LAS* curve. In this example, that price level is 110. If the price level rises above 110, the quantity of real GDP supplied increases along the *SAS* curve and exceeds potential GDP; if the price level falls below 110, the quantity of real GDP supplied decreases along the *SAS* curve and is less than potential GDP.

Back at the Pepsi Plant You can see why the short-run aggregate supply curve slopes upward by returning to the Pepsi bottling plant. If production increases, marginal cost rises; if production decreases, marginal cost falls (see Chapter 2, p. 35).

If the price of Pepsi rises with no change in the money wage rate and other costs, Pepsi can increase profit by increasing production. Pepsi is in business to maximize its profit, so it increases production.

Similarly, if the price of Pepsi falls while the money wage rate and other costs remain constant, Pepsi can avoid a loss by decreasing production. The lower price weakens the incentive to produce, so Pepsi decreases production.

What's true for Pepsi bottlers is true for the producers of all goods and services. When all prices rise, the *price level rises.* If the price level rises and the money wage rate and other factor prices remain constant, all firms increase production and the quantity of real GDP supplied increases. A fall in the price level has the opposite effect and decreases the quantity of real GDP supplied.

FIGURE 26.1   Long-Run and Short-Run Aggregate Supply

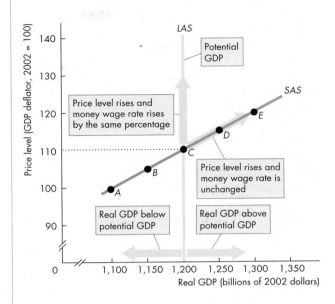

	Price level (GDP deflator)	Real GDP supplied (billions of 2002 dollars)
A	100	1,100
B	105	1,150
C	**110**	**1,200**
D	115	1,250
E	120	1,300

In the long run, the quantity of real GDP supplied is potential GDP and the *LAS* curve is vertical at potential GDP. In the short run, the quantity of real GDP supplied increases if the price level rises, while all other influences on supply plans remain the same.

The short-run aggregate supply curve, *SAS*, slopes upward. The short-run aggregate supply curve is based on the aggregate supply schedule in the table. Each point *A* through *E* on the curve corresponds to the row in the table identified by the same letter.

When the price level is 110, the quantity of real GDP supplied is $1,200 billion, which is potential GDP. If the price level rises above 110, the quantity of real GDP supplied increases and exceeds potential GDP; if the price level falls below 110, the quantity of real GDP supplied decreases below potential GDP.

myeconlab animation

Changes in Aggregate Supply

You've just seen that a change in the price level brings a movement along the aggregate supply curves, but it does not change aggregate supply. Aggregate supply changes when an influence on production plans other than the price level changes. These other influences include a change in potential GDP and the money wage rate and other factor prices. Let's begin by looking at factors that change potential GDP.

Changes in Potential GDP When potential GDP changes, aggregate supply changes. An increase in potential GDP increases both long-run aggregate supply and short-run aggregate supply.

Figure 26.2 shows the effects of an increase in potential GDP. Initially, the long-run aggregate supply curve is LAS_0 and the short-run aggregate supply curve is SAS_0. If potential GDP increases to $1,300 billion, long-run aggregate supply increases and the long-run aggregate supply curve shifts rightward to LAS_1. Short-run aggregate supply also increases, and the short-run aggregate supply curve shifts rightward to SAS_1. The two supply curves shift by the same amount only if the full-employment price level remains constant, which we will assume to be the case.

Potential GDP can increase for any of three reasons:

- An increase in the full-employment quantity of labour
- An increase in the quantity of capital
- An advance in technology

Let's look at these influences on potential GDP and the aggregate supply curves.

An Increase in the Full-Employment Quantity of Labour A Pepsi bottling plant that employs 100 workers bottles more Pepsi than does an otherwise identical plant that employs 10 workers. The same is true for the economy as a whole. The larger the quantity of labour employed, the greater is real GDP.

Over time, potential GDP increases because the labour force increases. But, with constant capital and technology, *potential* GDP increases only if the full-employment quantity of labour increases.

Fluctuations in employment over the business cycle bring fluctuations in real GDP. But these changes in real GDP are fluctuations *around* potential GDP. They are not changes in potential GDP and long-run aggregate supply.

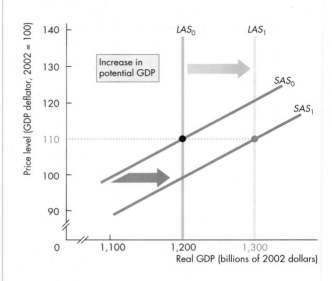

FIGURE 26.2   A Change in Potential GDP

An increase in potential GDP increases both long-run aggregate supply and short-run aggregate supply and shifts both aggregate supply curves rightward from LAS_0 to LAS_1 and from SAS_0 to SAS_1.

myeconlab animation

An Increase in the Quantity of Capital A Pepsi bottling plant with two production lines bottles more Pepsi than does an otherwise identical plant that has only one production line. For the economy, the larger the quantity of capital, the more productive is the labour force and the greater is its potential GDP. Potential GDP per person in capital-rich Canada is vastly greater than that in capital-poor China and Russia.

Capital includes *human capital*. One Pepsi plant is managed by an economics major with an MBA and has a labour force with an average of 10 years of experience. This plant produces a larger output than does an otherwise identical plant that is managed by someone with no business training or experience and that has a young labour force that is new to bottling. The first plant has a greater amount of human capital than the second. For the economy as a whole, the larger the quantity of *human capital*—the skills that people have acquired in school and through on-the-job training—the greater is potential GDP.

An Advance in Technology A Pepsi plant that has pre-computer age machines produces less than one that uses the latest robot technology. Technological change enables firms to produce more from any given amount of factors of production. So even with fixed quantities of labour and capital, improvements in technology increase potential GDP.

Technological advances are by far the most important source of increased production over the past two centuries. As a result of technological advances, one farmer in Canada today can feed 100 people and in a year one autoworker can produce almost 14 cars and trucks.

Let's now look at the effects of changes in the money wage rate.

Changes in the Money Wage Rate and Other Factor Prices

When the money wage rate (or the money price of any other factor of production such as oil) changes, short-run aggregate supply changes but long-run aggregate supply does not change.

Figure 26.3 shows the effect of an increase in the money wage rate. Initially, the short-run aggregate supply curve is SAS_0. A rise in the money wage rate *decreases* short-run aggregate supply and shifts the short-run aggregate supply curve leftward to SAS_2.

A rise in the money wage rate decreases short-run aggregate supply because it increases firms' costs. With increased costs, the quantity that firms are willing to supply at each price level decreases, which is shown by a leftward shift of the *SAS* curve.

A change in the money wage rate does not change long-run aggregate supply because on the *LAS* curve, the change in the money wage rate is accompanied by an equal percentage change in the price level. With no change in *relative* prices, firms have no incentive to change production and real GDP remains constant at potential GDP. With no change in potential GDP, the long-run aggregate supply curve *LAS* does not shift.

What Makes the Money Wage Rate Change?

The money wage rate can change for two reasons: departures from full employment and expectations about inflation. Unemployment above the natural rate puts downward pressure on the money wage rate, and unemployment below the natural rate puts upward pressure on it. An expected rise in the inflation rate makes the money wage rate rise faster, and an expected fall in the inflation rate slows the rate at which the money wage rate rises.

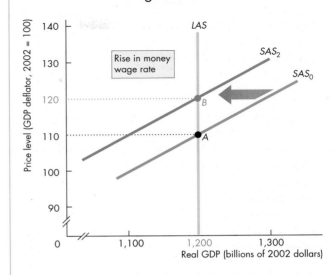

FIGURE 26.3   A Change in the Money Wage Rate

A rise in the money wage rate decreases short-run aggregate supply and shifts the short-run aggregate supply curve leftward from SAS_0 to SAS_2. A rise in the money wage rate does not change potential GDP, so the long-run aggregate supply curve does not shift.

myeconlab animation

Review Quiz

1 If the price level and the money wage rate rise by the same percentage, what happens to the quantity of real GDP supplied? Along which aggregate supply curve does the economy move?

2 If the price level rises and the money wage rate remains constant, what happens to the quantity of real GDP supplied? Along which aggregate supply curve does the economy move?

3 If potential GDP increases, what happens to aggregate supply? Does the *LAS* curve shift or is there a movement along the *LAS* curve? Does the *SAS* curve shift or is there a movement along the *SAS* curve?

4 If the money wage rate rises and potential GDP remains the same, does the *LAS* curve or the *SAS* curve shift or is there a movement along the *LAS* curve or the *SAS* curve?

myeconlab   Work Study Plan 26.1 and get instant feedback.

Aggregate Demand

The quantity of real GDP demanded (Y) is the sum of real consumption expenditure (C), investment (I), government expenditure (G), and exports (X) minus imports (M). That is,

$$Y = C + I + G + X - M.$$

The *quantity of real GDP demanded* is the total amount of final goods and services produced in Canada that people, businesses, governments, and foreigners plan to buy. These buying plans depend on many factors. Some of the main ones are

- The price level
- Expectations
- Fiscal policy and monetary policy
- The world economy

We first focus on the relationship between the quantity of real GDP demanded and the price level. To study this relationship, we keep all other influences on buying plans the same and ask: How does the quantity of real GDP demanded vary as the price level varies?

The Aggregate Demand Curve

Other things remaining the same, the higher the price level, the smaller is the quantity of real GDP demanded. This relationship between the quantity of real GDP demanded and the price level is called **aggregate demand**. Aggregate demand is described by an *aggregate demand schedule* and an *aggregate demand curve*.

Figure 26.4 shows an aggregate demand curve (AD) and an aggregate demand schedule. Each point on the AD curve corresponds to a row of the schedule. For example, point C' on the AD curve and row C' of the schedule tell us that if the price level is 110, the quantity of real GDP demanded is $1,200 billion.

The aggregate demand curve slopes downward for two reasons:

- Wealth effect
- Substitution effects

Wealth Effect When the price level rises but other things remain the same, *real* wealth decreases. Real

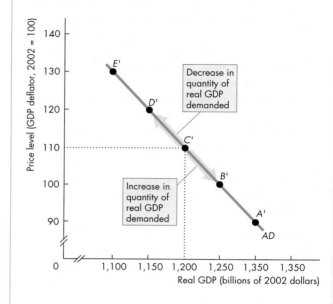

FIGURE 26.4 Aggregate Demand

	Price level (GDP deflator)	Real GDP demanded (billions of 2002 dollars)
A'	90	1,300
B'	100	1,250
C'	110	1,200
D'	120	1,150
E'	130	1,100

The aggregate demand curve (AD) shows the relationship between the quantity of real GDP demanded and the price level. The aggregate demand curve is based on the aggregate demand schedule in the table. Each point A' through E' on the curve corresponds to the row in the table identified by the same letter. When the price level is 110, the quantity of real GDP demanded is $1,200 billion, as shown by point C' in the figure. A change in the price level, when all other influences on aggregate buying plans remain the same, brings a change in the quantity of real GDP demanded and a movement along the AD curve.

 animation

wealth is the amount of money in the bank, bonds, stocks, and other assets that people own, measured not in dollars but in terms of the goods and services that the money, bonds, and stock will buy.

People save and hold money, bonds, and stocks for many reasons. One reason is to build up funds for education expenses. Another reason is to build up enough funds to meet possible medical expenses or other big bills. But the biggest reason is to build up enough funds to provide a retirement income.

If the price level rises, real wealth decreases. People then try to restore their wealth. To do so, they must increase saving and, equivalently, decrease current consumption. Such a decrease in consumption is a decrease in aggregate demand.

Maria's Wealth Effect You can see how the wealth effect works by thinking about Maria's buying plans. Maria lives in Moscow, Russia. She has worked hard all summer and saved 20,000 rubles (the ruble is the currency of Russia), which she plans to spend attending graduate school when she has finished her economics degree. So Maria's wealth is 20,000 rubles. Maria has a part-time job, and her income from this job pays her current expenses. The price level in Russia rises by 100 percent, and now Maria needs 40,000 rubles to buy what 20,000 once bought. To try to make up some of the fall in value of her savings, Maria saves even more and cuts her current spending to the bare minimum.

Substitution Effects When the price level rises and other things remain the same, interest rates rise. The reason is related to the wealth effect that you've just studied. A rise in the price level decreases the real value of the money in people's pockets and bank accounts. With a smaller amount of real money around, banks and other lenders can get a higher interest rate on loans. But faced with a higher interest rate, people and businesses delay plans to buy new capital and consumer durable goods and cut back on spending.

This substitution effect involves substituting goods in the future for goods in the present and is called an *intertemporal* substitution effect—a substitution across time. Saving increases to increase future consumption.

To see this intertemporal substitution effect more clearly, think about your own plan to buy a new computer. At an interest rate of 5 percent a year, you might borrow $1,000 and buy the new computer. But at an interest rate of 10 percent a year, you might decide that the payments would be too high. You don't abandon your plan to buy the computer, but you decide to delay your purchase.

A second substitution effect works through international prices. When the Canadian price level rises and other things remain the same, Canadian-made goods and services become more expensive relative to foreign-made goods and services. This change in *relative prices* encourages people to spend less on Canadian-made items and more on foreign-made items. For example, if the Canadian price level rises relative to the Japanese price level, Japanese buy fewer Canadian-made cars (Canadian exports decrease) and Canadians buy more Japanese-made cars (Canadian imports increase). Canadian GDP decreases.

Maria's Substitution Effect In Moscow, Russia, Maria makes some substitutions. She was planning to trade in her old motor scooter and get a new one. But with a higher price level and a higher interest rate, she decides to make her old scooter last one more year. Also, with the prices of Russian goods sharply increasing, Maria substitutes a low-cost dress made in Malaysia for the Russian-made dress she had originally planned to buy.

Changes in the Quantity of Real GDP Demanded
When the price level rises and other things remain the same, the quantity of real GDP demanded decreases—a movement up along the *AD* curve as shown by the arrow in Fig. 26.4. When the price level falls and other things remain the same, the quantity of real GDP demanded increases—a movement down along the *AD* curve.

We've now seen how the quantity of real GDP demanded changes when the price level changes. How do other influences on buying plans affect aggregate demand?

Changes in Aggregate Demand

A change in any factor that influences buying plans other than the price level brings a change in aggregate demand. The main factors are

- Expectations
- Fiscal policy and monetary policy
- The world economy

Expectations An increase in expected future income increases the amount of consumption goods (especially big-ticket items such as cars) that people plan to buy today and increases aggregate demand.

An increase in the expected future inflation rate increases aggregate demand today because people decide to buy more goods and services at today's relatively lower prices.

An increase in expected future profits increases the investment that firms plan to undertake today and increases aggregate demand.

Fiscal Policy and Monetary Policy The government's attempt to influence the economy by setting and changing taxes, making transfer payments, and purchasing goods and services is called **fiscal policy**. A tax cut or an increase in transfer payments—for example, unemployment benefits or welfare payments—increases aggregate demand. Both of these influences operate by increasing households' *disposable* income. **Disposable income** is aggregate income minus taxes plus transfer payments. The greater the disposable income, the greater is the quantity of consumption goods and services that households plan to buy and the greater is aggregate demand.

Government expenditure on goods and services is one component of aggregate demand. So if the government spends more on hospitals, schools, and highways, aggregate demand increases.

Monetary policy consists of changes in the interest rate and in the quantity of money in the economy. The quantity of money is determined by the Bank of Canada and the banks (in a process described in Chapters 24 and 30). An increase in the quantity of money in the economy increases aggregate demand. To see why money affects aggregate demand, imagine that the Bank of Canada borrows the army's helicopters, loads them with millions of new $10 bills, and sprinkles them like confetti across the nation. People gather the newly available money and plan to spend some of it. So the quantity of goods and services demanded increases. But people don't plan to spend all the new money. They plan to save some of it and lend it to others through the banks. The interest rate falls, and with a lower interest rate, people plan to buy more consumer durables and firms plan to increase their investment.

The World Economy Two main influences that the world economy has on aggregate demand are the exchange rate and foreign income. The *exchange rate* is the amount of a foreign currency that you can buy with a Canadian dollar. Other things remaining the same, a rise in the exchange rate decreases aggregate

Fiscal Policy to Fight Recession

Relying on Automatic Stabilizers

In the slowing economy of 2008, the U.S. government used fiscal policy to stimulate business investment and consumption expenditure and increase aggregate demand.

In Canada, the government relied on the automatic tendency for tax revenues to fall and spending on unemployment benefits to rise as the economy slowed.

But by the end of 2008, a lively debate was underway between the government and the opposition parties on how much fiscal stimulus is needed.

Jim Flaherty versus John McCallum on fiscal stimulus

Monetary Policy to Fight Recession

Concerted Interest Rate Cuts

In the fall of 2008, the Bank of Canada, in concert with the U.S. Federal Reserve, the European Central Bank, and the Bank of England, cut the interest rate and took other measures to ease credit and encourage banks and others to increase their lending. The U.S. interest rate was the lowest (see below).

Like the earlier fiscal stimulus package, the idea of these interest rate cuts and easier credit was to stimulate business investment and consumption expenditure and increase aggregate demand.

 0.5%   **2.5%**

Ben Bernanke
Federal Reserve

Jean-Claude Trichet
ECB

 **2.0%**   **1.5%**

Mervyn King
Bank of England

Mark Carney
Bank of Canada

FIGURE 26.5 Changes in Aggregate Demand

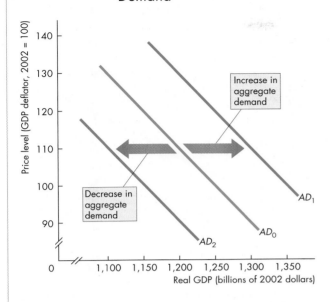

Aggregate demand

Decreases if:

- Expected future income, inflation, or profits decrease

- Fiscal policy decreases government expenditure, increases taxes, or decreases transfer payments

- Monetary policy decreases the quantity of money and increases interest rates

- The exchange rate increases or foreign income decreases

Increases if:

- Expected future income, inflation, or profits increase

- Fiscal policy increases government expenditure, decreases taxes, or increases transfer payments

- Monetary policy increases the quantity of money and decreases interest rates

- The exchange rate decreases or foreign income increases

myeconlab animation

demand. To see how the exchange rate influences aggregate demand, suppose that the exchange rate is 80 euro cents per Canadian dollar. A Nokia cell phone from Finland costs 160 euros. An equivalent BlackBerry from Canada costs $220. In Canadian dollars, the Nokia phone costs $200, so people around the world buy the cheaper phone from

Finland. Now suppose the exchange rate falls to 70 euro cents per Canadian dollar. The Nokia phone now costs almost $230 and is more expensive than the BlackBerry. People will switch from the Nokia phone to the BlackBerry. Canadian exports increase and Canadian imports decrease, so Canadian aggregate demand increases.

An increase in foreign income increases Canadian exports and increases Canadian aggregate demand. For example, an increase in income in Japan and Germany increases Japanese and German consumers' and producers' planned expenditures on Canadian-produced goods and services.

Shifts of the Aggregate Demand Curve When aggregate demand changes, the aggregate demand curve shifts. Figure 26.5 shows two changes in aggregate demand and summarizes the factors that bring about such changes.

Aggregate demand increases and the *AD* curve shifts rightward from AD_0 to AD_1 when expected future income, inflation, or profit increases; government expenditure on goods and services increases; taxes are cut; transfer payments increase; the quantity of money increases and the interest rate falls; the exchange rate falls; or foreign income increases.

Aggregate demand decreases and the *AD* curve shifts leftward from AD_0 to AD_2 when expected future income, inflation, or profit decreases; government expenditure on goods and services decreases; taxes increase; transfer payments decrease; the quantity of money decreases and the interest rate rises; the exchange rate rises; or foreign income decreases.

Review Quiz

1 What does the aggregate demand curve show? What factors change and what factors remain the same when there is a movement along the aggregate demand curve?

2 Why does the aggregate demand curve slope downward?

3 How do changes in expectations, fiscal policy and monetary policy, and the world economy change aggregate demand and the aggregate demand curve?

myeconlab Work Study Plan 26.2 and get instant feedback.

Explaining Macroeconomic Fluctuations

The purpose of the *AS–AD* model is to explain changes in real GDP and the price level. The model's main purpose is to explain business cycle fluctuations in these variables. But the model also aids our understanding of economic growth and inflation trends. We begin by combining aggregate supply and aggregate demand to determine real GDP and the price level in equilibrium. Just as there are two time frames for aggregate supply, there are two time frames for macroeconomic equilibrium: a long-run equilibrium and a short-run equilibrium. We'll first look at short-run equilibrium.

Short-Run Macroeconomic Equilibrium

The aggregate demand curve tells us the quantity of real GDP demanded at each price level, and the short-run aggregate supply curve tells us the quantity of real GDP supplied at each price level. **Short-run macroeconomic equilibrium** occurs when the quantity of real GDP demanded equals the quantity of real GDP supplied. That is, short-run macroeconomic equilibrium occurs at the point of intersection of the *AD* curve and the *SAS* curve. Figure 26.6 shows such an equilibrium at a price level of 110 and real GDP of $1,200 billion (points *C* and *C'*).

To see why this position is the equilibrium, think about what happens if the price level is something other than 110. Suppose, for example, that the price level is 125 and that real GDP is $1,300 billion (at point *E* on the *SAS* curve). The quantity of real GDP demanded is less than $1,300 billion, so firms are unable to sell all their output. Unwanted inventories pile up, and firms cut both production and prices. Production and prices are cut until firms can sell all their output. This situation occurs only when real GDP is $1,200 billion and the price level is 110.

Now suppose the price level is 100 and real GDP is $1,100 billion (at point *A* on the *SAS* curve). The quantity of real GDP demanded exceeds $1,100 billion, so firms are unable to meet the demand for their output. Inventories decrease, and customers clamour for goods and services, so firms increase production and raise prices. Production and prices increase until firms can meet the demand for their output. This situation

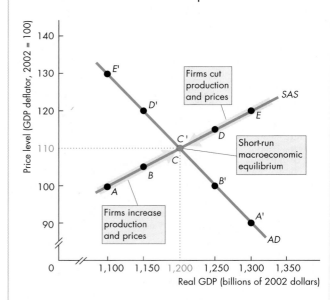

FIGURE 26.6 Short-Run Equilibrium

Short-run macroeconomic equilibrium occurs when real GDP demanded equals real GDP supplied—at the intersection of the aggregate demand curve (*AD*) and the short-run aggregate supply curve (*SAS*). Here, such an equilibrium occurs at points *C* and *C'*, where the price level is 110 and real GDP is $1,200 billion.

If the price level is 120 and real GDP is $1,300 billion (point *E*), firms will not be able to sell all their output. They will decrease production and cut prices. If the price level is 100 and real GDP is $1,100 billion (point *A*), people will not be able to buy all the goods and services they demand. Firms will increase production and raise their prices.

Only when the price level is 110 and real GDP is $1,200 billion can firms sell all that they produce and can people buy all the goods and services they demand. This is the short-run macroeconomic equilibrium.

myeconlab animation

occurs only when real GDP is $1,200 billion and the price level is 110.

In the short run, the money wage rate is fixed. It does not adjust to move the economy to full employment. So in the short run, real GDP can be greater than or less than potential GDP. But in the long run, the money wage rate does adjust and real GDP moves towards potential GDP. We are going to study this adjustment process. But first, let's look at the economy in long-run equilibrium.

Long-Run Macroeconomic Equilibrium

Long-run macroeconomic equilibrium occurs when real GDP equals potential GDP—equivalently, when the economy is on its *LAS* curve. Figure 26.7 shows the long-run macroeconomic equilibrium, which occurs at the intersection of the *AD* curve and the *LAS* curve (the blue curves). Long-run macroeconomic equilibrium comes about because the money wage rate adjusts. Potential GDP and aggregate demand determine the price level, and the price level influences the money wage rate. In long-run equilibrium, the money wage rate has adjusted to put the *SAS* curve through the long-run equilibrium point.

We'll look at this money wage adjustment process later in this chapter. But first, let's see how the *AS–AD* model helps us to understand economic growth and inflation.

Economic Growth in the *AS–AD* Model

Economic growth occurs because the quantity of labour and labour productivity grow. Population growth is the source of labour growth, and capital accumulation and technological change are the sources of labour productivity growth. Chapter 22 explains the effects of population growth and an increase in the supply of labour. That chapter also explains and illustrates the effects of labour productivity growth on the aggregate production function and on the demand for labour. These changes increase potential GDP.

The *AS–AD* model explains and illustrates potential GDP growth as a rightward shift of the *LAS* curve. For example, in Fig. 26.8, potential GDP grows from $1,200 billion to $1,300 billion and the *LAS* curve shifts rightward from LAS_0 to LAS_1.

FIGURE 26.7 Long-Run Equilibrium

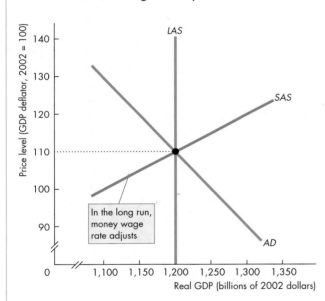

In long-run macroeconomic equilibrium, real GDP equals potential GDP. So long-run equilibrium occurs where the aggregate demand curve, *AD*, intersects the long-run aggregate supply curve, *LAS*. In the long run, aggregate demand determines the price level and has no effect on real GDP. The money wage rate adjusts in the long run, so that the *SAS* curve intersects the *LAS* curve at the long-run equilibrium price level.

FIGURE 26.8 Economic Growth and Inflation

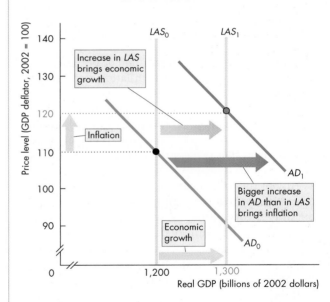

Economic growth is the persistent increase in potential GDP. Economic growth is shown as an ongoing rightward shift of the *LAS* curve. The pace at which the *LAS* curve shifts rightward depends on the growth rate of the labour force and the growth rate of labour productivity.

Inflation is a persistently rising price level and it occurs when the quantity of money grows to make the *AD* curve shift rightward at a faster pace than that of the *LAS* curve.

Inflation in the *AS–AD* Model

Inflation occurs because the quantity of money grows more rapidly than potential GDP. In Chapter 24, the quantity theory of money, derived from the equation of exchange, explains inflation. With a constant velocity of circulation of money, the inflation rate equals the growth rate of the quantity of money minus the growth rate of real GDP. At full employment (in the macroeconomic long run), real GDP grows at the growth rate of potential GDP. So the inflation rate equals the growth rate of the quantity of money minus the growth rate of potential GDP.

We can explain and illustrate this inflation process using the *AS–AD* model. Inflation occurs when aggregate demand increases at a faster rate than the growth rate of potential GDP. That is, inflation occurs if the *AD* curve shifts rightward at a faster rate than the rate of rightward shift of the *LAS* curve. Figure 26.8 shows shifts of the *AD* and *LAS* curves that bring inflation.

If aggregate demand increases at the same rate as long-run aggregate supply, we experience real GDP growth with no inflation.

You've seen that the growth rate of potential GDP doesn't change much, but the inflation rate varies a great deal. During the 1970s, it reached a double-digit level and then during the 1980s, its rate fell to the low levels maintained through the 1990s and into the 2000s. It is changes in the growth rate of aggregate demand that explain the changes in the inflation rate.

Any of the influences on aggregate demand can change its growth rate. Using the ideas from the quantity theory of money, we can summarize those influences as the quantity of money and the velocity of circulation. Although either one can change, only the growth rate of the quantity of money can change by enough to explain the large and persistent changes in the inflation rate that we experience. When the quantity of money grows rapidly, aggregate demand grows rapidly and the inflation rate is high. When the growth rate of the quantity of money slows, the inflation rate eventually slows.

Our economy experiences periods of growth and inflation, like those shown in Fig. 26.8, but it does not experience *steady* growth and *steady* inflation. Real GDP fluctuates around potential GDP in a business cycle, and inflation fluctuates. When we study the business cycle, we ignore economic growth. By doing so, we see the business cycle more clearly.

The Business Cycle in the *AS–AD* Model

The business cycle occurs because aggregate demand and short-run aggregate supply fluctuate but the money wage rate does not adjust quickly enough to keep real GDP at potential GDP. Figure 26.9 shows three types of short-run equilibrium.

Figure 26.9(a) shows a below full-employment equilibrium. A **below full-employment equilibrium** is an equilibrium in which potential GDP exceeds real GDP. The gap between real GDP and potential GDP is the **output gap**. When potential GDP exceeds real GDP, the output gap is called a **recessionary gap**.

The below full-employment equilibrium in Fig. 26.9(a) occurs where the aggregate demand curve AD_0 intersects the short-run aggregate supply curve SAS_0 at a real GDP of $1,180 billion. Potential GDP is $1,200 billion. The recessionary gap is $20 billion.

The Canadian Business Cycle

The Fluctuating Output Gap

The Canadian economy had a recessionary gap in 2003 (at *A* in the figure), full employment in 2004 (at *B*), and an inflationary gap in 2007 (at *C*). The fluctuating output gap below is the real-world version of Fig. 26.9(d) and is generated by fluctuations in aggregate demand and short-run aggregate supply.

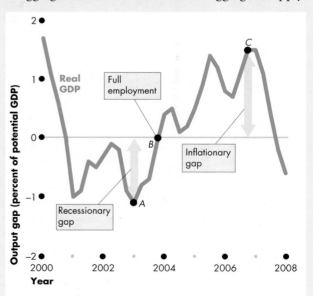

The Canadian Output Gap

Source of data: Bank of Canada output gap, www.bankofcanada.ca/en/rates/indinf/product_data_en.html.

Figure 26.9(b) is an example of **full-employment equilibrium**, in which real GDP equals potential GDP. In this example, the equilibrium occurs where the aggregate demand curve AD_1 intersects the short-run aggregate supply curve SAS_1 at an actual and potential GDP of $1,200 billion.

In part (c), there is an above full-employment equilibrium. An **above full-employment equilibrium** is an equilibrium in which real GDP exceeds potential GDP. When real GDP exceeds potential GDP, the output gap is called an **inflationary gap**.

The above full-employment equilibrium in Fig.

26.9(c) occurs where the aggregate demand curve AD_2 intersects the short-run aggregate supply curve SAS_2 at a real GDP of $1,220 billion. Potential GDP is $1,200 billion. The inflationary gap is $20 billion.

The economy moves from one type of macroeconomic equilibrium to another as a result of fluctuations in aggregate demand and in short-run aggregate supply. These fluctuations produce fluctuations in real GDP. Figure 26.9(d) shows how real GDP fluctuates around potential GDP.

Let's now look at some of the sources of these fluctuations around potential GDP.

FIGURE 26.9   The Business Cycle

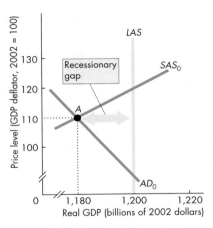

(a) Below full-employment equilibrium

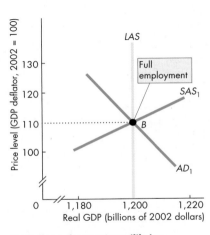

(b) Full-employment equilibrium

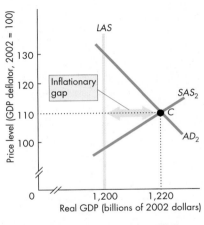

(c) Above full-employment equilibrium

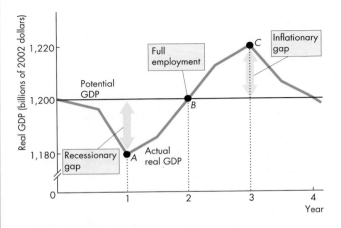

(d) Fluctuations in real GDP

Part (a) shows a below full-employment equilibrium in year 1; part (b) shows a full-employment equilibrium in year 2; and part (c) shows an above full-employment equilibrium in year 3. Part (d) shows how real GDP fluctuates around potential GDP in a business cycle.

In year 1, a recessionary gap exists and the economy is at point A in parts (a) and (d). In year 2, the economy is at full employment and the economy is at point B in parts (b) and (d). In year 3, an inflationary gap exists and the economy is at point C in parts (c) and (d).

Fluctuations in Aggregate Demand

One reason real GDP fluctuates around potential GDP is that aggregate demand fluctuates. Let's see what happens when aggregate demand increases.

Figure 26.10(a) shows an economy at full employment. The aggregate demand curve is AD_0, the short-run aggregate supply curve is SAS_0, and the long-run aggregate supply curve is LAS. Real GDP equals potential GDP at $1,200 billion, and the price level is 110.

Now suppose that the world economy expands and that the demand for Canadian-produced goods increases in Japan and Europe. The increase in Canadian exports increases aggregate demand in Canada, and the aggregate demand curve shifts rightward from AD_0 to AD_1 in Fig. 26.10(a).

Faced with an increase in demand, firms increase production and raise prices. Real GDP increases to $1,250 billion, and the price level rises to 115. The economy is now in an above full-employment equilibrium. Real GDP exceeds potential GDP, and there is an inflationary gap.

The increase in aggregate demand has increased the prices of all goods and services. Faced with higher prices, firms have increased their output rates. At this stage, prices of goods and services have increased but the money wage rate has not changed. (Recall that as we move along the SAS curve, the money wage rate is constant.)

The economy cannot produce in excess of potential GDP forever. Why not? What are the forces at work that bring real GDP back to potential GDP?

Because the price level has increased and the money wage rate is unchanged, workers have experienced a fall in the buying power of their wages and firms' profits have increased. Under these circumstances, workers demand higher wages, and firms, anxious to maintain their employment and output levels, meet those demands. If firms do not raise the money wage rate, they will either lose workers or have to hire less productive ones.

As the money wage rate rises, the short-run aggregate supply begins to decrease. In Fig. 26.10(b), the short-run aggregate supply curve begins to shift from

---

FIGURE 26.10   An Increase in Aggregate Demand

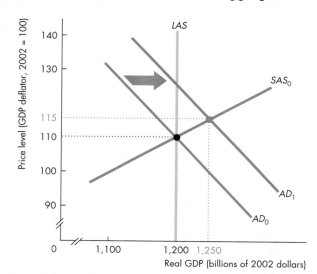

(a) Short-run effect

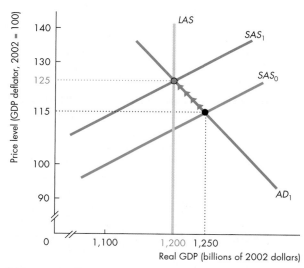

(b) Long-run effect

An increase in aggregate demand shifts the aggregate demand curve from AD_0 to AD_1. In short-run equilibrium, real GDP increases to $1,250 billion and the price level rises to 115. In this situation, an inflationary gap exists. In the long run in part (b), the money wage rate rises and the

short-run aggregate supply curve shifts leftward. As short-run aggregate supply decreases, the SAS curve shifts from SAS_0 to SAS_1 and intersects the aggregate demand curve AD_1 at higher price levels and real GDP decreases. Eventually, the price level rises to 125 and real GDP decreases to $1,200 billion—potential GDP.

SAS_0 towards SAS_1. The rise in the money wage rate and the shift in the SAS curve produce a sequence of new equilibrium positions. Along the adjustment path, real GDP decreases and the price level rises. The economy moves up along its aggregate demand curve as shown by the arrows in the figure.

Eventually, the money wage rate rises by the same percentage as the price level. At this time, the aggregate demand curve AD_1 intersects SAS_1 at a new full-employment equilibrium. The price level has risen to 125, and real GDP is back where it started, at potential GDP.

A decrease in aggregate demand has effects similar but opposite to those of an increase in aggregate demand. That is, a decrease in aggregate demand shifts the aggregate demand curve leftward. Real GDP decreases to less than potential GDP, and a recessionary gap emerges. Firms cut prices. The lower price level increases the purchasing power of wages and increases firms' costs relative to their output prices because the money wage rate is unchanged. Eventually, the money wage rate falls and the short-run aggregate supply increases.

Let's now work out how real GDP and the price level change when aggregate supply changes.

Fluctuations in Aggregate Supply

Fluctuations in short-run aggregate supply can bring fluctuations in real GDP around potential GDP. Suppose that initially real GDP equals potential GDP. Then there is a large but temporary rise in the price of oil. What happens to real GDP and the price level?

Figure 26.11 answers this question. The aggregate demand curve is AD_0, the short-run aggregate supply curve is SAS_0, and the long-run aggregate supply curve is LAS. Real GDP is $1,200 billion, which equals potential GDP, and the price level is 110. Then the price of oil rises. Faced with higher energy and transportation costs, firms decrease production. Short-run aggregate supply decreases, and the short-run aggregate supply curve shifts leftward to SAS_1. The price level rises to 120, and real GDP decreases to $1,150 billion. We call the combination of falling real GDP and a rising inflation rate **stagflation**. Canada has not experienced stagflation, but the United States and several other countries experienced it during the 1970s and early 1980s.

When the aggregate supply shock ends (in our example, when the price of oil returns to its original level), the economy returns to full employment.

FIGURE 26.11   A Decrease in Aggregate Supply

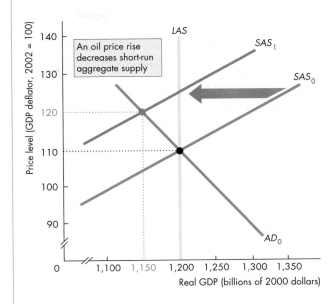

An increase in the price of oil decreases short-run aggregate supply and shifts the short-run aggregate supply curve from SAS_0 to SAS_1. Real GDP falls from $1,200 billion to $1,150 billion, and the price level rises from 110 to 120. The economy experiences stagflation.

 animation

Review Quiz

1   Does economic growth result from increases in aggregate demand, short-run aggregate supply, or long-run aggregate supply?

2   Does inflation result from increases in aggregate demand, short-run aggregate supply, or long-run aggregate supply?

3   Describe three types of short-run macroeconomic equilibrium.

4   How do fluctuations in aggregate demand and short-run aggregate supply bring fluctuations in real GDP around potential GDP?

myeconlab   Work Study Plan 26.3 and get instant feedback.

We can use the *AS–AD* model to explain and illustrate the views of the alternative schools of thought in macroeconomics. That is your next task.

◆ Macroeconomic Schools of Thought

Macroeconomics is an active field of research, and much remains to be learned about the forces that make our economy grow and fluctuate. There is a greater degree of consensus and certainty about economic growth and inflation—the longer-term trends in real GDP and the price level—than there is about the business cycle—the short-term fluctuations in these variables. Here, we'll look only at differences of view about short-term fluctuations.

The *AS–AD* model that you've studied in this chapter provides a good foundation for understanding the range of views that macroeconomists hold about this topic. But what you will learn here is just a first glimpse at the scientific controversy and debate. We'll return to these issues at various points later in the text and deepen your appreciation of the alternative views.

Classification usually requires simplification, and classifying macroeconomists is no exception to this general rule. The classification that we'll use here is simple, but it is not misleading. We're going to divide macroeconomists into three broad schools of thought and examine the views of each group in turn. The groups are

- Classical
- Keynesian
- Monetarist

The Classical View

A **classical** macroeconomist believes that the economy is self-regulating and always at full employment. The term "classical" derives from the name of the founding school of economics that includes Adam Smith, David Ricardo, and John Stuart Mill.

A **new classical** view is that business cycle fluctuations are the efficient responses of a well-functioning market economy that is bombarded by shocks that arise from the uneven pace of technological change.

The classical view can be understood in terms of beliefs about aggregate demand and aggregate supply.

Aggregate Demand Fluctuations In the classical view, technological change is the most significant influence on both aggregate demand and aggregate supply. For this reason, classical macroeconomists don't use the

AS–AD framework. But their views can be interpreted in this framework. A technological change that increases the productivity of capital brings an increase in aggregate demand because firms increase their expenditure on new plant and equipment. A technological change that lengthens the useful life of existing capital decreases the demand for new capital, which decreases aggregate demand.

Aggregate Supply Response In the classical view, the money wage rate that lies behind the short-run aggregate supply curve is instantly and completely flexible. The money wage rate adjusts so quickly to maintain equilibrium in the labour market that real GDP always adjusts to equal potential GDP.

Potential GDP itself fluctuates for the same reasons that aggregate demand fluctuates: technological change. When the pace of technological change is rapid, potential GDP increases quickly and so does real GDP. And when the pace of technological change slows, so does the growth rate of potential GDP.

Classical Policy The classical view of policy emphasizes the potential for taxes to stunt incentives and create inefficiency. By minimizing the disincentive effects of taxes, employment, investment, and technological advance are at their efficient levels and the economy expands at an appropriate and rapid pace.

The Keynesian View

A **Keynesian** macroeconomist believes that left alone, the economy would rarely operate at full employment and that to achieve and maintain full employment, active help from fiscal policy and monetary policy is required.

The term "Keynesian" derives from the name of one of the twentieth century's most famous economists, John Maynard Keynes (see p. 703).

The Keynesian view is based on beliefs about the forces that determine aggregate demand and short-run aggregate supply.

Aggregate Demand Fluctuations In the Keynesian view, *expectations* are the most significant influence on aggregate demand. Those expectations are based on herd instinct, or what Keynes himself called "animal spirits." A wave of pessimism about future profit prospects can lead to a fall in aggregate demand and plunge the economy into recession.

Aggregate Supply Response In the Keynesian view, the money wage rate that lies behind the short-run aggregate supply curve is extremely sticky in the downward direction. Basically, the money wage rate doesn't fall. So if there is a recessionary gap, there is no automatic mechanism for getting rid of it. If it were to happen, a fall in the money wage rate would increase short-run aggregate supply and restore full employment. But the money wage rate doesn't fall, so the economy remains stuck in recession.

A modern version of the Keynesian view, known as the **new Keynesian** view, holds not only that the money wage rate is sticky but also that prices of goods and services are sticky. With a sticky price level, the short-run aggregate supply curve is horizontal at a fixed price level.

Policy Response Needed The Keynesian view calls for fiscal policy and monetary policy to actively offset changes in aggregate demand that bring recession.

By stimulating aggregate demand in a recession, full employment can be restored.

The Monetarist View

A **monetarist** is a macroeconomist who believes that the economy is self-regulating and that it will normally operate at full employment, provided that monetary policy is not erratic and that the pace of money growth is kept steady.

The term "monetarist" was coined by an outstanding twentieth-century economist, Karl Brunner, to describe his own views and those of Milton Friedman (see p. 757).

The monetarist view can be interpreted in terms of beliefs about the forces that determine aggregate demand and short-run aggregate supply.

Aggregate Demand Fluctuations In the monetarist view, *the quantity of money* is the most significant influence on aggregate demand. The quantity of money is determined by the Bank of Canada. If the Bank of Canada keeps money growing at a steady pace, aggregate demand fluctuations will be minimized and the economy will operate close to full employment. But if the Bank of Canada decreases the quantity of money or even just slows its growth rate too abruptly, the economy will go into recession. In the monetarist view, all recessions result from inappropriate monetary policy.

Aggregate Supply Response The monetarist view of short-run aggregate supply is the same as the Keynesian view: The money wage rate is sticky. If the economy is in recession, it will take an unnecessarily long time for it to return unaided to full employment.

Monetarist Policy The monetarist view of policy is the same as the classical view on fiscal policy. Taxes should be kept low to avoid disincentive effects that decrease potential GDP. Provided that the quantity of money is kept on a steady growth path, no active stabilization is needed to offset changes in aggregate demand.

The Way Ahead

In the chapters that follow, you're going to encounter Keynesian, classical, and monetarist views again. In the next chapter, we study the original Keynesian model of aggregate demand. This model remains useful today because it explains how expenditure fluctuations are magnified and bring changes in aggregate demand that are larger than the changes in expenditure. We then go on to apply the *AS–AD* model to a deeper look at Canadian inflation and business cycles. Our attention then turns to short-run macroeconomic policy—the fiscal policy of the government and the monetary policy of the Bank of Canada.

Review Quiz

1 What are the defining features of classical macroeconomics and what policies do classical macroeconomists recommend?
2 What are the defining features of Keynesian macroeconomics and what policies do Keynesian macroeconomists recommend?
3 What are the defining features of monetarist macroeconomics and what policies do monetarist macroeconomists recommend?

Work Study Plan 26.4
myeconlab and get instant feedback.

To complete your study of the *AS–AD* model, take a look at the Canadian economy in 2008 through the eyes of this model in *Reading Between the Lines* on pp. 642–643.

Aggregate Supply and Aggregate Demand in Action

Canadians Shopped 'til Economy Dropped

November 25, 2008

Canadians shopped right up until the economy dropped, reports Tuesday suggest.

Consumers went on an unexpected shopping spree in September, just prior to the economy sliding into what a major international think-tank is projecting was the start of a prolonged recession that will linger right through to the middle of next year.

The Canadian economy is projected to contract 1.6 percent in the current quarter, reducing growth for the year to 0.5 percent, the Paris-based Organization for Economic Co-operation and Development said in a downwardly revised forecast for the Canadian and the global economy. Economic output will fall a further 1.4 percent in the first quarter of 2009 and by 0.3 percent in the second quarter and despite a slow recovery in the second half of the year output for the year as a whole will fall 0.5 percent. ...

Statistics Canada reported that retail sales jumped 1.1 percent in September, the largest gain since January, thanks to what was also the first increase in new car sales since January. ...

"Part of the explanation of the resilience in retailing activity is the fact that the Canadian job market has not cratered like in the U.S. and other domestic fundamentals, such as the housing market, have exhibited an orderly correction," said TD Securities analyst Charmain Buskas.

However, she and other analysts cautioned that it's in the fourth quarter where they expect sales and the overall economy to stumble, a view reinforced by the forecast by the OECD. ...

Essence of the Story

- Statistics Canada reported that retail sales increased by 1.1 percent in September 2008.

- A TD Securities analyst said that retail sales were strong because Canadian employment had not fallen and house price falls were moderate.

- The Organization for Economic Co-operation and Development (OECD) forecasted that the Canadian economy would contract at a 1.6 percent (annual) rate during the fourth quarter of 2008.

- The OECD forecasted that the economy would continue to contract through 2009.

- Analysts predicted that retail sales would fall in the fourth quarter of 2008 in line with the OECD forecast.

Economic Analysis

- Forecasters predicted that the Canadian economy would sink into recession at the end of 2008 and through 2009.

- The OECD predicted falling real GDP during the fourth quarter of 2008 and through 2009.

- The Bank of Canada estimate of potential GDP implied that an inflationary gap in 2007 and early 2008 became a widening recessionary gap in the second half of 2008.

- Figure 1 illustrates the path of real GDP and the estimate of potential GDP implied by the Bank of Canada's output gap estimates from the last quarter of 2006 through the last quarter of 2008.

- Real GDP grew faster than potential GDP from the last quarter of 2006 until the third quarter of 2007, so the inflationary gap widened.

- Real GDP stopped growing after the last quarter of 2007 and a recessionary gap opened up in the second quarter of 2008.

- In the third quarter of 2007, real GDP was $1,326 billion and the price level (GDP deflator) was 117. Potential GDP was $1,306 billion, so the inflationary gap was $20 billion (1.5 percent of potential GDP).

- Figure 2 illustrates the economy in the third quarter of 2007.

- Aggregate demand, AD_{07}, and short-run aggregate supply, SAS_{07}, intersect at a real GDP of $1,326 billion and a price level of 117.

- The Bank of Canada's implicit estimate of potential GDP of $1,306 billion provides the location of the LAS_{07} curve.

- Figure 3 illustrates the economy in the third quarter of 2008.

- Aggregate demand, AD_{08}, and short-run aggregate supply, SAS_{08}, intersect at a real GDP of $1,325 billion and a price level of 120.

- The Bank of Canada's implicit estimate of potential GDP of $1,346 billion provides the location of the LAS_{08} curve.

- Comparing Fig. 2 and Fig. 3, you can see that real GDP barely changed but potential GDP increased.

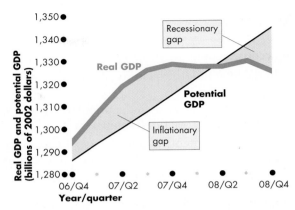

Figure 1 Actual and potential real GDP

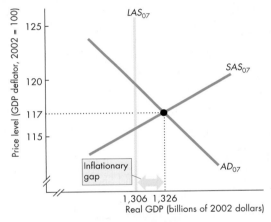

Figure 2 Aggregate supply and aggregate demand in 2007

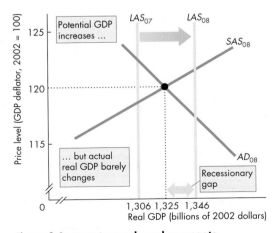

Figure 3 Aggregate supply and aggregate demand in 2008

SUMMARY ▸

Key Points

Aggregate Supply (pp. 626–629)

- In the long run, the quantity of real GDP supplied is potential GDP.
- In the short run, a rise in the price level increases the quantity of real GDP supplied.
- A change in potential GDP changes long-run and short-run aggregate supply. A change in the money wage rate changes only short-run aggregate supply.

Aggregate Demand (pp. 630–633)

- A rise in the price level decreases the quantity of real GDP demanded.
- Changes in expected future income, inflation, and profits; in fiscal policy and monetary policy; and in world real GDP and the exchange rate change aggregate demand.

Explaining Macroeconomic Fluctuations (pp. 634–639)

- Aggregate demand and short-run aggregate supply determine real GDP and the price level.
- In the long run, real GDP equals potential GDP and aggregate demand determines the price level.
- The business cycle occurs because aggregate demand and aggregate supply fluctuate.

Macroeconomic Schools of Thought (pp. 640–641)

- Classical economists believe that the economy is self-regulating and always at full employment.
- Keynesian economists believe that full employment can be achieved only with active policy.
- Monetarist economists believe that recessions result from inappropriate monetary policy.

Key Figures

Key Terms

PROBLEMS and APPLICATIONS

 Work problems 1–7 in Chapter 26 Study Plan and get instant feedback.
Work problems 8–15 as Homework, a Quiz, or a Test if assigned by your instructor.

1. The following events occur at times in the history of Canada:

   - A deep recession hits the world economy.
   - The world oil price rises sharply.
   - Canadian firms expect future profits to fall.

   a. Explain for each event whether it changes short-run aggregate supply, long-run aggregate supply, aggregate demand, or some combination of them.
   b. Explain the separate effects of each event on real GDP and the price level, starting from a position of long-run equilibrium.
   c. Explain the combined effects of these events on real GDP and the price level, starting from a position of long-run equilibrium.
   d. Describe what a classical macroeconomist, a Keynesian, and a monetarist would want to do in response to each of the above events.

2. The table shows aggregate demand and short-run aggregate supply in Virtual Kingdom. Potential GDP is 1,100 billion (2007 pounds).

Price level	Real GDP demanded	Real GDP supplied in the short run
	(billions of 2007 pounds)	
100	1,250	1,050
110	1,200	1,100
120	1,150	1,150
130	1,100	1,200
140	1,050	1,250
150	1,000	1,300
160	950	1,350

   a. What is the short-run equilibrium real GDP and price level?
   b. What is the output gap and is it an inflationary gap or a recessionary gap?
   c. What is the long-run equilibrium price level?

3. U.S. real GDP during the second quarter of 2008 was $11,727 billion compared to $11,491 billion in the same quarter of 2007. The GDP deflator was 121.9, up from 119.5 in the second quarter of 2007. The Congressional Budget Office estimated potential GDP to be $11,888 billion in the second quarter of 2008 and $11,568 billion a year earlier.

   a. Draw a graph of the U.S. aggregate demand curve, the short-run aggregate supply curve, and the long-run aggregate supply curve in 2007 that is consistent with these numbers.
   b. On the graph, show how the aggregate demand curve, the short-run aggregate supply curve, and the long-run aggregate supply curve shifted during the year to the second quarter of 2008.

4. Initially, short-run aggregate supply is SAS_0 and aggregate demand is AD_0. Some events change aggregate demand, and later, some other events change aggregate supply.

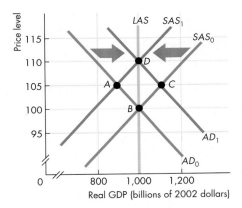

   a. What is the equilibrium after the change in aggregate demand?
   b. What is the equilibrium after the change in aggregate supply?
   c. Describe two events that could have changed aggregate demand from AD_0 to AD_1.
   d. Describe two events that could have changed aggregate supply from SAS_0 to SAS_1.

5. **Business Confidence Sinking**

   Business confidence in the economy has plunged to a near record low, suggesting that a fall in investment in new plants and equipment will follow, the Conference Board of Canada reported yesterday. ... The latest survey, conducted in the first three weeks of October, found that business leaders were much more concerned about the economy and their future financial situations than they had been in the summer survey. Expectations about future profitability also fell. "The ongoing financial and equity market mayhem is having a significant impact on business leaders' views about near-term economic prospects," it said, noting the survey found that nearly 70 percent believed that the economy would be in worse shape in six months. Only 12 percent, and probably those that benefit from a weaker loonie, believed conditions would improve, it said, adding that ratio is the "worst" since the final quarter of 1990.

Gazette (Montreal), November 11, 2008

a. Explain and draw a graph to illustrate how declining business confidence can change the short-run equilibrium real GDP and price level.
b. If the economy was operating at full-employment equilibrium, describe the state of equilibrium after the fall in business confidence. In what way might business expectations have a self-fulfilling prophecy?
c. Explain how the economy can adjust in the long run to restore full-employment equilibrium and draw a graph to illustrate this adjustment process.
d. Explain the author's statement that those businesses who "believed conditions would improve" are "probably those that benefit from a weaker loonie."

6. **Canadian Dollar Provides Needed Relief to Quebec Exports in 2009, says EDC**

Quebec's international exports are expected to rise a modest 1 percent in 2009 after declining 4 percent in 2008, according to a provincial export outlook by Export Development Canada (EDC). "The slight rise in Quebec's exports in 2009 is possible thanks to an expected 10 percent depreciation of the Canadian dollar. Remove the exchange rate impact, and the province's export outlook is considerably weaker," said Peter Hall, Vice-President and Chief Economist. The industrial goods sector accounts for approximately 37 percent of Quebec's international exports. The outlook for this sector is defined by volatile ... commodity price movements. ... Lumber export volumes are unlikely to gain much of the ground lost since 2005, as existing home inven-

tories in the U.S. remain near all-time highs. ... In the aerospace sector, weak demand out of the United States, the destination for nearly half of total Canadian aerospace exports, will adversely impact the bottom line going forward. ...

Canadian Business, November 6, 2008

a. Explain the competing forces on exports for 2009 that are identified in this article.
b. Based upon the predictions made in this article for 2009, draw a graph to illustrate how these forces can change the short-run equilibrium real GDP and price level for Quebec.

7. **Harper to Canadian Consumers: "Keep Spending"**

Conservative Leader Stephen Harper reassured Canadian consumers amid economic turmoil in the United States that there will be no federal bailout of Canada's big banks. ...

He said the Canadian financial system is strong and its banks and insurance companies don't need any financial aid. ... While money is tighter these days, Harper said, consumers shouldn't panic and stop spending since they're the reason for the Canadian economy's strength. The Conservative Leader said this robust consumer spending is what has helped protect Canada from the same type of trouble currently affixing itself to the United States, and says his party's policies should be credited for encouraging this spending. "Some of the things we've done, in particular the tax changes we did ... the lowering of the GST, the lowering of the lowest personal income tax rate, the raising of the basic personal exemption," Harper said. "These have been important in sustaining strong consumer spending in this country. ... Canadian consumer spending has been a rock that has sustained the economy and we anticipate that that will continue," Harper said.

CTV News, September 19, 2008

a. Explain and draw a graph to illustrate the effects of the policy actions described by Stephen Harper.
b. Based upon his statements in this article, what macroeconomic school of thought does Stephen Harper most likely agree with?

8. The following events occur at times in the history of Canada:

   - The world economy goes into an expansion.
   - Canadian businesses expect future profits to rise.
   - The government increases its expenditure on goods and services in a time of war or increased international tension.

   a. Explain for each event whether it changes short-run aggregate supply, long-run aggregate supply, aggregate demand, or some combination of them.
   b. Explain the separate effects of each event on real GDP and the price level, starting from a position of long-run equilibrium.
   c. Explain the combined effects of these events on real GDP and the price level, starting from a position of long-run equilibrium.

9. In Japan, potential GDP is 600 trillion yen and the table shows the aggregate demand and short-run aggregate supply schedules.

Price level	Real GDP demanded	Real GDP supplied in the short run
	(trillions of 2000 yen)	
75	600	400
85	550	450
95	500	500
105	450	550
115	400	600
125	350	650
135	300	700

   a. Draw a graph of the aggregate demand curve and the short-run aggregate supply curve.
   b. What is the short-run equilibrium real GDP and price level?
   c. Does Japan have an inflationary gap or a recessionary gap and what is its magnitude?

10. **Fearful Consumers Reining in Spending**

   Canadian consumer confidence took a nosedive ... amid continuing economic uncertainty, sparking fears that shoppers are already reining in their spending. Consumer confidence plunged to levels last seen in the 1982 recession. ... The findings suggest consumers are becoming especially leery about making big-ticket purchases such as appliances, cars and homes ahead of the all-important Christmas shopping season. ... "All we are hearing is doom and gloom and people seeking advice on how they may be able to protect themselves and save money," said Bruce Cran, spokesperson for the Consumers' Association of Canada. ... Perhaps most striking is the parallels some Canadians are starting to draw between America's housing market meltdown and rapidly deflating home prices in this country. ... "The global credit crunch and major stock market declines clearly had an effect on consumer confidence in October," said Pedro Antunes, the [Conference] Board's director of national and provincial forecast. ... Respondents are increasingly worried about ... job prospects, the report found. ... The Conference Board says Canada will feel the knock-on effects of the global financial crisis but avoid a recession.

   Toronto Star, October 18, 2008

   a. Explain the various factors that are weighing down consumer confidence.
   b. Explain and draw a graph to illustrate how declining consumer confidence can change real GDP and the price level in the short run.
   c. If the economy was operating at full-employment equilibrium, describe the state of equilibrium after the fall in consumer confidence. In what way might consumer expectations have a self-fulfilling prophecy? How does this complicate economic forecasting (such as the prediction offered by the Conference Board)?
   d. Why do changes in consumer spending play such a large role in the business cycle?
   e. Explain how the economy can adjust in the long run to restore full-employment equilibrium and draw a graph to illustrate this adjustment process.

11 **It's Pinching Everyone**

   The rate of inflation [in India] has now touched a mind-boggling 11 percent. ... No one can predict when the process of spiraling prices will come to an end. ... [T]he current inflationary process is a global phenomenon and practically every country is suffering. ...

   Emerging and developing countries have been growing significantly faster than the rest of the world, and there has been a steep surge in demand in these countries. ... Since there is no reason to believe that world production will rise miraculously at least in the immediate future, many people expect that prices will keep on rising. These expectations in turn exacerbate the inflationary process. Households buy more of non-perishable goods than they need for their immediate consumption because they expect prices to go up even further. What is worse is that traders withhold stocks from the market in the hope of being able to sell these at higher prices later on. In other words, expectations of higher prices become self-fulfilling.

Times of India, June 24, 2008

Explain and use a graph to show how inflation and inflation expectations "become self-fulfilling."

12. **Shoppers Stimulate Discount Stores**

Consumers sought the biggest bang for their economic stimulus bucks in June, sending the sales of discount merchants such as Wal-Mart and Costco surging. ... As the economy remains weak ... shoppers—rich and poor—are flocking to discounters for low-cost goods. ... Wal-Mart Stores Inc. trounced analyst expectations Thursday with a 5.8 percent jump in June sales ... attributing the increase to the government's economic stimulus payments. ... The retailer said sales jumped across the board. But the most dramatic increases were in entertainment, particularly for flat-screen televisions, and apparel, especially in swimwear and sportswear. ... Another major retailer, the warehouse club Costco Wholesale, beat analyst expectations with a 9 percent increase in same-store sales for June. ... Target, a top competitor to Wal-Mart, said that its same-store sales edged up 0.4 percent, well above the 0.5 percent decline projected by analyst consensus. ...

CNN, July 10, 2008

a. Explain and draw a graph to illustrate the effect of the fiscal stimulus payments on real GDP and the price level in the short run.
b. At which type of short-run equilibrium would the government want to use this policy?
c. Which macroeconomic school of thought would justify this policy?
d. If the government used this policy when the economy was at full employment, explain what would happen in the long run.
e. Draw a graph to illustrate your answer to d.

13. **Conditions Right for Stagflation**

Soaring energy prices are casting a long shadow over the economy, increasing the risk that Canadians face a period of low growth and high inflation, economists say. ... Monday saw a smattering of reports suggesting conditions are

right for stagflation. ... [T]he toxic brew of high oil prices and a deepening slump in the United States is increasing the risks to both growth and inflation this year, economists said. ... "Consumers are becoming increasingly wary about making major purchases," said the Conference Board.

Winnipeg Free Press, July 8, 2008

a. What is stagflation?
b. Explain how the rise in oil prices, the slump in the United States, and a decrease in purchases by consumers can cause stagflation. Draw a graph to illustrate this outcome.

14. The International Monetary Fund's World Economic Outlook database provides the following data for India.

	2004	2005	2006
	(percent per year)		
Real GDP growth rate	8.1	8.3	7.3
Inflation rate	4.2	4.7	4.6

a. What changes in aggregate demand and in long-run and short-run aggregate supply are consistent with these numbers?
b. Draw a graph to illustrate your answer to a.
c. List the main factors that might have produced the changes that you have described in your answer to a.
d. From the above data, do you think India has an inflationary gap, a recessionary gap, or is at full employment?

15. Study *Reading Between the Lines* on pp. 642–643 and then answer the following questions:

a. Did Canada have a recessionary gap or an inflationary gap in 2008? How do you know?
b. Use the *AS–AD* model to show the *changes* in aggregate demand and aggregate supply that brought the standstill in real GDP and rise in the price level between the third quarter of 2007 and the third quarter of 2008.
c. Use the *AS–AD* model to show the changes that would occur if monetary policy cut the interest rate and increased the quantity of money.
d. Use the *AS–AD* model to show the changes that would occur if the government increased its expenditure on goods and services or cut taxes.

27

Expenditure Multipliers: The Keynesian Model

After studying this chapter, you will be able to

- Explain how expenditure plans are determined when the price level is fixed
- Explain how real GDP is determined when the price level is fixed
- Explain the expenditure multiplier when the price level is fixed
- Explain the relationship between aggregate expenditure and aggregate demand and explain the multiplier when the price level changes

Céline Dion sings into a microphone in a barely audible whisper. Increasing in volume, through the magic of electronic amplification, her voice fills Toronto's Molson Amphitheatre.

Ed Stelmach, the premier of Alberta, and an assistant are being driven to a business meeting along one of Edmonton's less well-repaired streets. The car's wheels bounce and vibrate over the uneven road, but its passengers are undisturbed and the assistant's notes are written without a ripple, thanks to the car's efficient shock absorbers.

Investment and exports fluctuate like the volume of Céline Dion's voice and the uneven surface of an Edmonton street. How does the economy react to those fluctuations? Does it behave like an amplifier, blowing up the fluctuations and spreading them out to affect the many millions of participants in an economic rock concert? Or does it react like a limousine, absorbing the shocks and providing a smooth ride for the economy's passengers?

You will explore these questions in this chapter. You will learn how a recession or an expansion begins when a change in investment or exports induces an amplified change in aggregate expenditure and real GDP. *Reading Between the Lines* at the end of the chapter looks at the role played by consumption expenditure during 2008 as the economy began to shrink.

Fixed Prices and Expenditure Plans

In the Keynesian model that we study in this chapter, all the firms are like your grocery store: They set their prices and sell the quantities their customers are willing to buy. If they persistently sell a greater quantity than they plan to and are constantly running out of inventory, they eventually raise their prices. And if they persistently sell a smaller quantity than they plan to and have inventories piling up, they eventually cut their prices. But on any given day, their prices are fixed and the quantities they sell depend on demand, not supply.

Because each firm's prices are fixed, for the economy as a whole

1. The *price level* is fixed, and
2. *Aggregate demand* determines real GDP.

The Keynesian model explains fluctuations in aggregate demand at a fixed price level by identifying the forces that determine expenditure plans.

Expenditure Plans

Aggregate expenditure has four components: consumption expenditure, investment, government expenditure on goods and services, and net exports (exports *minus* imports). These four components of aggregate expenditure sum to real GDP (see Chapter 20, pp. 469–470).

Aggregate planned expenditure is equal to the sum of the *planned* levels of consumption expenditure, investment, government expenditure on goods and services, and exports minus imports. Two of these components of planned expenditure, consumption expenditure and imports, change when income changes and so they depend on real GDP.

A Two-Way Link Between Aggregate Expenditure and Real GDP
There is a two-way link between aggregate expenditure and real GDP. Other things remaining the same,

- An increase in real GDP increases aggregate expenditure, and
- An increase in aggregate expenditure increases real GDP.

You are now going to study this two-way link.

Consumption and Saving Plans

Several factors influence consumption expenditure and saving plans. The more important ones are

- Disposable income
- Real interest rate
- Wealth
- Expected future income

Disposable income is aggregate income minus taxes plus transfer payments. Aggregate income equals real GDP, so disposable income depends on real GDP. To explore the two-way link between real GDP and planned consumption expenditure, we focus on the relationship between consumption expenditure and disposable income when the other three factors listed above are constant.

Consumption Expenditure and Saving   The table in Fig. 27.1 lists the consumption expenditure and the saving that people plan at each level of disposable income. Households can only spend their disposable income on consumption or save it, so planned consumption expenditure plus planned saving *always* equals disposable income.

The relationship between consumption expenditure and disposable income, other things remaining the same, is called the **consumption function**. The relationship between saving and disposable income, other things remaining the same, is called the **saving function**.

Consumption Function   Figure 27.1(a) shows a consumption function. The *y*-axis measures consumption expenditure, and the *x*-axis measures disposable income. Along the consumption function, the points labelled *A* through *F* correspond to the rows of the table. For example, point *E* shows that when disposable income is $800 billion, consumption expenditure is $750 billion. As disposable income increases, consumption expenditure also increases.

At point *A* on the consumption function, consumption expenditure is $150 billion even though disposable income is zero. This consumption expenditure is called *autonomous consumption*, and it is the amount of consumption expenditure that would take place in the short run even if people had no current income. Consumption expenditure in excess of this amount is called *induced consumption*, which is the consumption expenditure that is induced by an increase in disposable income.

45° Line Figure 27.1(a) also contains a 45° line, the height of which measures disposable income. At each point on this line, consumption expenditure equals disposable income. Between A and D, consumption expenditure exceeds disposable income, between D and F, consumption expenditure is less than disposable income, and at point D, consumption expenditure equals disposable income.

Saving Function Figure 27.1(b) shows a saving function. Again, the points A through F correspond to the rows of the table. For example, point E shows that when disposable income is $800 billion, saving is $50 billion. As disposable income increases, saving increases. Notice that when consumption expenditure exceeds disposable income in part (a), saving is negative, called *dissaving,* in part (b).

FIGURE 27.1   Consumption Function and Saving Function

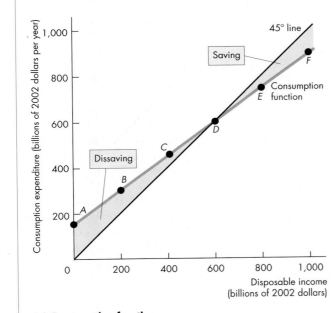

(a) Consumption function

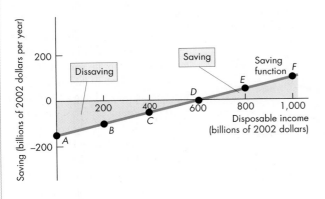

(b) Saving function

	Disposable income	Planned consumption expenditure	Planned saving
		(billions of 2002 dollars)	
A	0	150	−150
B	200	300	−100
C	400	450	−50
D	600	600	0
E	800	750	50
F	1,000	900	100

The table shows consumption expenditure and saving plans at various levels of disposable income. Part (a) of the figure shows the relationship between consumption expenditure and disposable income (the consumption function). The height of the consumption function measures consumption expenditure at each level of disposable income. Part (b) shows the relationship between saving and disposable income (the saving function). The height of the saving function measures saving at each level of disposable income. Points A through F on the consumption and saving functions correspond to the rows in the table.

The height of the 45° line in part (a) measures disposable income. So along the 45° line, consumption expenditure equals disposable income. Consumption expenditure plus saving equals disposable income. When the consumption function is above the 45° line, saving is negative (dissaving occurs). When the consumption function is below the 45° line, saving is positive. At the point where the consumption function intersects the 45° line, all disposable income is spent on consumption and saving is zero.

Marginal Propensities to Consume and Save

The **marginal propensity to consume** (*MPC*) is the fraction of a *change* in disposable income that is spent on consumption. It is calculated as the *change* in consumption expenditure (ΔC) divided by the *change* in disposable income (ΔYD). The formula is

$$MPC = \frac{\Delta C}{\Delta YD}.$$

In the table in Fig. 27.1, when disposable income increases by $200 billion, consumption expenditure increases by $150 billion. The *MPC* is $150 billion divided by $200 billion, which equals 0.75.

The **marginal propensity to save** (*MPS*) is the fraction of a *change* in disposable income that is saved. It is calculated as the *change* in saving (ΔS) divided by the *change* in disposable income (ΔYD). The formula is

$$MPS = \frac{\Delta S}{\Delta YD}.$$

In the table in Fig. 27.1, when disposable income increases by $200 billion, saving increases by $50 billion. The *MPS* is $50 billion divided by $200 billion, which equals 0.25.

Because an increase in disposable income is either spent on consumption or saved, the marginal propensity to consume plus the marginal propensity to save equals 1. You can see why by using the equation:

$$\Delta C + \Delta S = \Delta YD.$$

Divide both sides of the equation by the change in disposable income to obtain

$$\frac{\Delta C}{\Delta YD} + \frac{\Delta S}{\Delta YD} = 1.$$

$\Delta C/\Delta YD$ is the marginal propensity to consume (*MPC*), and $\Delta S/\Delta YD$ is the marginal propensity to save (*MPS*), so

$$MPC + MPS = 1.$$

Slopes and Marginal Propensities

The slope of the consumption function is the marginal propensity to consume, and the slope of the saving function is the marginal propensity to save.

Figure 27.2(a) shows the *MPC* as the slope of the consumption function. An increase in disposable income of $200 billion is the base of the red triangle. The increase in consumption expenditure that results from this increase in disposable income is $150 billion and is the height of the triangle. The slope of the consumption function is given by the formula "slope equals rise over run" and is $150 billion divided by $200 billion, which equals 0.75—the *MPC*.

Figure 27.2(b) shows the *MPS* as the slope of the saving function. An increase in disposable income of $200 billion (the base of the red triangle) increases saving by $50 billion (the height of the triangle). The slope of the saving function is $50 billion divided by $200 billion, which equals 0.25—the *MPS*.

FIGURE 27.2 The Marginal Propensities to Consume and Save

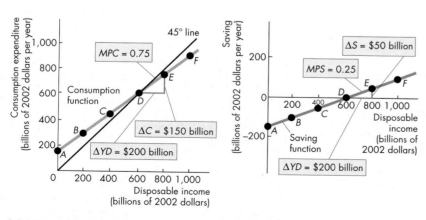

(a) Consumption function

(b) Saving function

The marginal propensity to consume, *MPC*, is equal to the change in consumption expenditure divided by the change in disposable income, other things remaining the same. It is measured by the slope of the consumption function. In part (a), the *MPC* is 0.75.

The marginal propensity to save, *MPS*, is equal to the change in saving divided by the change in disposable income, other things remaining the same. It is measured by the slope of the saving function. In part (b), the *MPS* is 0.25.

myeconlab animation

The Canadian Consumption Function

Other Things Not Always Equal

The figure shows the Canadian consumption function. Each point identified by a blue dot represents consumption expenditure and disposable income for a particular year. (The dots are for the years 1961 to 2007, and the dots of six of the years are identified in the figure.)

The Canadian consumption function is CF_0 in 1961 and CF_1 in 2007.

The slope of the consumption function in the figure is 0.85, which means that a \$1 increase in disposable income brings an increase in consumption expenditure of 85 cents. This slope, which is an estimate of the marginal propensity to consume, is an assumption that is at the upper end of the range of values that economists have estimated for the marginal propensity to consume.

The consumption function shifts upward over time as other influences on consumption expenditure change. Of these other influences, the real interest rate and wealth fluctuate and bring upward and downward shifts in the consumption function.

But rising wealth and rising expected future income bring a steady upward shift in the consumption function. As the consumption function shifts upward, autonomous consumption increases.

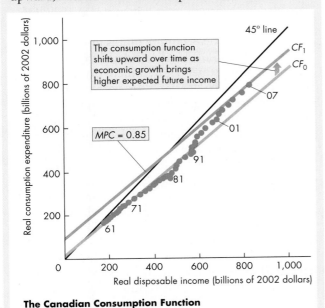

The Canadian Consumption Function

Source of data: Statistics Canada, CANSIM Tables 380-0002 and 380-0004.

Consumption as a Function of Real GDP

Consumption expenditure changes when disposable income changes and disposable income changes when real GDP changes. So consumption expenditure depends not only on disposable income but also on real GDP. We use this link between consumption expenditure and real GDP to determine equilibrium expenditure. But before we do so, we need to look at one further component of aggregate expenditure: imports. Like consumption expenditure, imports are influenced by real GDP.

Import Function

Of the many influences on Canadian imports in the short run, Canadian real GDP is the main influence. Other things remaining the same, an increase in Canadian real GDP increases the quantity of Canadian imports.

The effect of real GDP on imports is determined by the **marginal propensity to import**, which is the fraction of an increase in real GDP that is spent on imports. It is calculated as the change in imports divided by the change in real GDP, other things remaining the same. For example, if a \$100 billion increase in real GDP increases imports by \$250 billion, the marginal propensity to import is 0.25.

Review Quiz

1 Which components of aggregate expenditure are influenced by real GDP?

2 Define and explain how we calculate the marginal propensity to consume and the marginal propensity to save.

3 How do we calculate the effects of real GDP on consumption expenditure and imports by using the marginal propensity to consume and the marginal propensity to import?

myeconlab Work Study Plan 27.1 and get instant feedback.

Real GDP influences consumption expenditure and imports, which in turn influence real GDP. Your next task is to study this second piece of the two-way link between aggregate expenditure and real GDP and see how all the components of aggregate planned expenditure interact to determine real GDP.

◆ Real GDP with a Fixed Price Level

You are now going to see how, at a given price level, aggregate expenditure plans determine real GDP. We start by looking at the relationship between aggregate planned expenditure and real GDP. This relationship can be described by an aggregate expenditure schedule or an aggregate expenditure curve. The *aggregate expenditure schedule* lists aggregate planned expenditure generated at each level of real GDP. The *aggregate expenditure curve* is a graph of the aggregate expenditure schedule.

Aggregate Planned Expenditure

The table in Fig. 27.3 sets out an aggregate expenditure schedule. To calculate aggregate planned expenditure at a given real GDP, we add the expenditure components together. The first column of the table shows real GDP, and the second column shows the planned consumption at each level of real GDP. A $100 billion increase in real GDP increases consumption expenditure by $70 billion—the *MPC* is 0.7.

The next two columns show investment and government expenditure on goods and services, both of which are independent of the level of real GDP. Investment depends on the real interest rate and the expected profit (see Chapter 23, p. 550). At a given point in time, these factors generate a given level of investment. Suppose this level of investment is $200 billion. Also, suppose that government expenditure is $220 billion.

The next two columns show exports and imports. Exports are influenced by events in the rest of the world, prices of foreign-produced goods and services relative to the prices of similar Canadian-produced goods and services, and exchange rates. But they are not directly affected by Canadian real GDP. Exports are a constant $180 billion. Imports increase as Canadian real GDP increases. A $100 billion increase in Canadian real GDP generates a $20 billion increase in imports—the marginal propensity to import is 0.2.

The final column shows aggregate planned expenditure—the sum of planned consumption expenditure, investment, government expenditure on goods and services, and exports minus imports.

Figure 27.3 plots an aggregate expenditure curve. Real GDP is shown on the *x*-axis, and aggregate planned expenditure is shown on the *y*-axis. The

aggregate expenditure curve is the red line *AE*. Points *A* through *F* on that curve correspond to the rows of the table. The *AE* curve is a graph of aggregate planned expenditure (the last column) plotted against real GDP (the first column).

Figure 27.3 also shows the components of aggregate expenditure. The constant components—investment (*I*), government expenditure on goods and services (*G*), and exports (*X*)—are shown by the horizontal lines in the figure. Consumption expenditure (*C*) is the vertical gap between the lines labelled *I* + *G* + *X* and *I* + *G* + *X* + *C*.

To construct the *AE* curve, subtract imports (*M*) from the *I* + *G* + *X* + *C* line. Aggregate expenditure is expenditure on Canadian-produced goods and services. But the components of aggregate expenditure—*C*, *I*, and *G*—include expenditure on imported goods and services. For example, if you buy a new cell phone, your expenditure is part of consumption expenditure. But if the cell phone is an LG made in Korea, your expenditure on it must be subtracted from consumption expenditure to find out how much is spent on goods and services produced in Canada—on Canadian real GDP. Money paid to LG for cell phones imported from Korea does not add to aggregate expenditure in Canada.

Because imports are only a part of aggregate expenditure, when we subtract imports from the other components of aggregate expenditure, aggregate planned expenditure still increases as real GDP increases, as you can see in Fig. 27.3.

Consumption expenditure minus imports, which varies with real GDP, is called **induced expenditure**. The sum of investment, government expenditure, and exports, which does not vary with real GDP, is called **autonomous expenditure**. Consumption expenditure and imports can also have an autonomous component—a component that does not vary with real GDP. Another way to think about autonomous expenditure is that it would be the level of aggregate planned expenditure if real GDP were zero.

In Fig. 27.3, autonomous expenditure is $600 billion—aggregate planned expenditure when real GDP is zero. For each $100 billion increase in real GDP, induced expenditure increases by $50 billion.

The aggregate expenditure curve summarizes the relationship between aggregate *planned* expenditure and real GDP. But what determines the point on the aggregate expenditure curve at which the economy operates? What determines *actual* aggregate expenditure?

FIGURE 27.3   Aggregate Planned Expenditure: The *AE* Curve

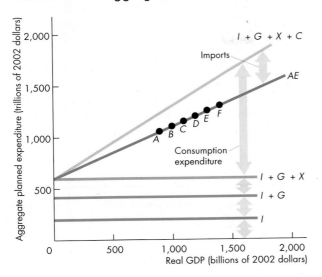

Aggregate planned expenditure is the sum of planned consumption expenditure, investment, government expenditure on goods and services, and exports minus imports. For example, in row *B* of the table, when real GDP is $1,000 billion, planned consumption expenditure is $700 billion, planned investment is $200 billion, planned government expenditure is $220 billion, planned exports are $180 billion, and planned imports are $200 billion. So when real GDP is $1,000 billion, aggregate planned expenditure is $1,100 billion ($700 + $200 + $220 + $180 − $200). The schedule shows that aggregate planned expenditure increases as real GDP increases. This relationship is graphed as the aggregate expenditure curve *AE*. The components of aggregate expenditure that increase with real GDP are consumption expenditure and imports. The other components—investment, government expenditure, and exports—do not vary with real GDP.

	Real GDP (Y)	Planned expenditure						Aggregate planned expenditure (AE = C + I + G + X − M)
		Consumption expenditure (C)	Investment (I)	Government expenditure (G)	Exports (X)	Imports (M)		
		(billions of 2002 dollars)						
	0	0	200	220	180	0		600
A	900	630	200	220	180	180		1,050
B	1,000	700	200	220	180	200		1,100
C	1,100	770	200	220	180	220		1,150
D	1,200	840	200	220	180	240		1,200
E	1,300	910	200	220	180	260		1,250
F	1,400	980	200	220	180	280		1,300

myeconlab animation

Actual Expenditure, Planned Expenditure, and Real GDP

Actual aggregate expenditure is always equal to real GDP, as we saw in Chapter 20 (p. 470). But aggregate *planned* expenditure is not always equal to actual aggregate expenditure and therefore is not always equal to real GDP. How can actual expenditure and planned expenditure differ? The answer is that firms can end up with inventories that are greater or smaller than planned. People carry out their consumption expenditure plans, the govern-

ment implements its planned expenditure on goods and services, and net exports are as planned. Firms carry out their plans to purchase new buildings, plant, and equipment. But one component of investment is the change in firms' inventories. If aggregate planned expenditure is less than real GDP, firms sell less than they planned to sell and end up with unplanned inventories. If aggregate planned expenditure exceeds real GDP, firms sell more than they planned to sell and end up with inventories being too low.

Equilibrium Expenditure

Equilibrium expenditure is the level of aggregate expenditure that occurs when aggregate *planned* expenditure equals real GDP. Equilibrium expenditure is a level of aggregate expenditure and real GDP at which spending plans are fulfilled. At a given price level, equilibrium expenditure determines real GDP. When aggregate planned expenditure and actual aggregate expenditure are unequal, a process of convergence towards equilibrium expenditure occurs. Throughout this process, real GDP adjusts. Let's examine equilibrium expenditure and the process that brings it about.

Figure 27.4(a) illustrates equilibrium expenditure. The table sets out aggregate planned expenditure at various levels of real GDP. These values are plotted as points *A* through *F* along the *AE* curve. The 45° line

FIGURE 27.4   Equilibrium Expenditure

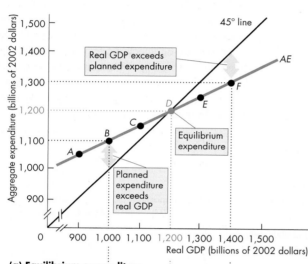

(a) Equilibrium expenditure

	Real GDP (Y)	Aggregate planned expenditure (AE)	Unplanned inventory change (Y − AE)
		(billions of 2002 dollars)	
A	900	1,050	−150
B	1,000	1,100	−100
C	1,100	1,150	−50
D	1,200	1,200	0
E	1,300	1,250	50
F	1,400	1,300	100

(b) Unplanned inventory changes

The table shows expenditure plans at different levels of real GDP. When real GDP is $1,200 billion, aggregate planned expenditure equals real GDP.

Part (a) of the figure illustrates equilibrium expenditure, which occurs when aggregate planned expenditure equals real GDP at the intersection of the 45° line and the *AE* curve. Part (b) of the figure shows the forces that bring about equilibrium expenditure. When aggregate planned expenditure exceeds real GDP, inventories decrease—for example, at point *B* in both parts of the figure. Firms increase production, and real GDP increases.

When aggregate planned expenditure is less than real GDP, inventories increase—for example, at point *F* in both parts of the figure. Firms decrease production, and real GDP decreases. When aggregate planned expenditure equals real GDP, there are no unplanned inventory changes and real GDP remains constant at equilibrium expenditure.

shows all the points at which aggregate planned expenditure equals real GDP. So where the *AE* curve lies above the 45° line, aggregate planned expenditure exceeds real GDP; where the *AE* curve lies below the 45° line, aggregate planned expenditure is less than real GDP; and where the *AE* curve intersects the 45° line, aggregate planned expenditure equals real GDP. Point *D* illustrates equilibrium expenditure. At this point, real GDP is $1,200 billion.

Convergence to Equilibrium

What are the forces that move aggregate expenditure towards its equilibrium level? To answer this question, we must look at a situation in which aggregate expenditure is away from its equilibrium level.

From Below Equilibrium Suppose that in Fig. 27.4, real GDP is $1,000 billion. Real GDP and actual aggregate expenditure are always equal, so actual aggregate expenditure is $1,000 billion. But aggregate *planned* expenditure is $1,100 billion, point *B* in Fig. 27.4(a). Aggregate planned expenditure exceeds *actual* expenditure. When people spend $1,100 billion and firms produce goods and services worth $1,000 billion, firms' inventories fall by $100 billion, point *B* in Fig. 27.4(b). Because the change in inventories is part of investment, *actual* investment is $100 billion less than *planned* investment.

Real GDP doesn't remain at $1,000 billion for very long. Firms have inventory targets based on their sales. When inventories fall below target, firms increase production to restore inventories to the target level. To increase inventories, firms hire additional labour and increase production.

Suppose that firms increase production in the next period by $100 billion. Real GDP increases by $100 billion to $1,100 billion. But again, aggregate planned expenditure exceeds real GDP. When real GDP is $1,100 billion, aggregate planned expenditure is $1,150 billion, point *C* in Fig. 27.4(a). Again, inventories decrease, but this time by less than before. With real GDP of $1,100 billion and aggregate planned expenditure of $1,150 billion, inventories decrease by $50 billion, point *C* in Fig. 27.4(b). Again, firms hire additional labour and production increases; real GDP increases yet further.

The process that we've just described—planned expenditure exceeds real GDP, inventories decrease, and production increases to restore inventories—ends when real GDP has reached $1,200 billion. At this real GDP, there is equilibrium. Unplanned inventory changes are zero. Firms do not change their production.

From Above Equilibrium If, in Fig. 27.4, real GDP is $1,400 billion, the process that we've just described works in reverse. With real GDP at $1,400 billion, actual aggregate expenditure is also $1,400 billion. But aggregate planned expenditure is $1,300 billion, point *F* in Fig. 27.4(a). Actual expenditure exceeds planned expenditure. When people spend $1,300 billion and firms produce goods and services worth $1,400 billion, firms' inventories rise by $100 billion, point *F* in Fig. 27.4(b). Now, real GDP begins to fall. As long as actual expenditure exceeds planned expenditure, inventories rise and production decreases. Again, the process ends when real GDP has reached $1,200 billion, the equilibrium at which unplanned inventory changes are zero and firms do not change their production.

Review Quiz

1 What is the relationship between aggregate planned expenditure and real GDP at equilibrium expenditure?

2 How does equilibrium expenditure come about? What adjusts to achieve equilibrium?

3 If real GDP and aggregate expenditure are less than equilibrium expenditure, what happens to firms' inventories? How do firms change their production? And what happens to real GDP?

4 If real GDP and aggregate expenditure are greater than equilibrium expenditure, what happens to firms' inventories? How do firms change their production? And what happens to real GDP?

 Work Study Plan 27.2 and get instant feedback.

We've learned that when the price level is fixed, real GDP is determined by equilibrium expenditure. And we have seen how unplanned changes in inventories and the production response they generate bring a convergence towards equilibrium expenditure. We're now going to study *changes* in equilibrium expenditure and discover an economic amplifier called the *multiplier*.

◆ The Multiplier

Investment and exports can change for many reasons. A fall in the real interest rate might induce firms to increase their planned investment. A wave of innovation, such as occurred with the spread of multimedia computers in the 1990s, might increase expected future profits and lead firms to increase their planned investment. An economic boom in Western Europe and Japan might lead to a large increase in their expenditure on Canadian-produced goods and services—on Canadian exports. These are all examples of increases in autonomous expenditure.

When autonomous expenditure increases, aggregate expenditure increases and so does equilibrium expenditure and real GDP. But the increase in real GDP is *larger* than the change in autonomous expenditure. The **multiplier** is the amount by which a change in autonomous expenditure is magnified or multiplied to determine the change in equilibrium expenditure and real GDP.

To get the basic idea of the multiplier, we'll work with an example economy in which there are no income taxes and no imports. So we'll first assume that these factors are absent. Then, when you understand the basic idea, we'll bring these factors back into play and see what difference they make to the multiplier.

The Basic Idea of the Multiplier

Suppose that investment increases. The additional expenditure by businesses means that aggregate expenditure and real GDP increase. The increase in real GDP increases disposable income, and with no income taxes, real GDP and disposable income increase by the same amount. The increase in disposable income brings an increase in consumption expenditure. And the increased consumption expenditure adds even more to aggregate expenditure. Real GDP and disposable income increase further, and so does consumption expenditure. The initial increase in investment brings an even bigger increase in aggregate expenditure because it induces an increase in consumption expenditure. The magnitude of the increase in aggregate expenditure that results from an increase in autonomous expenditure is determined by the *multiplier*.

The table in Fig. 27.5 sets out an aggregate planned expenditure schedule. Initially, when real GDP is $1,100 billion, aggregate planned expenditure

is $1,125 billion. For each $100 billion increase in real GDP, aggregate planned expenditure increases by $75 billion. This aggregate expenditure schedule is shown in the figure as the aggregate expenditure curve AE_0. Initially, equilibrium expenditure is $1,200 billion. You can see this equilibrium in row B of the table and in the figure where the curve AE_0 intersects the 45° line at the point marked B.

Now suppose that autonomous expenditure increases by $50 billion. What happens to equilibrium expenditure? You can see the answer in Fig. 27.5. When this increase in autonomous expenditure is added to the original aggregate planned expenditure, aggregate planned expenditure increases by $50 billion at each level of real GDP. The new aggregate expenditure curve is AE_1. The new equilibrium expenditure, highlighted in the table (row D), occurs where AE_1 intersects the 45° line and is $1,400 billion (point D'). At this real GDP, aggregate planned expenditure equals real GDP.

The Multiplier Effect

In Fig. 27.5, the increase in autonomous expenditure of $50 billion increases equilibrium expenditure by $200 billion. That is, the change in autonomous expenditure leads, like Céline Dion's electronic equipment, to an amplified change in equilibrium expenditure. This amplified change is the *multiplier effect*—equilibrium expenditure increases by *more than* the increase in autonomous expenditure. The multiplier is greater than 1.

Initially, when autonomous expenditure increases, aggregate planned expenditure exceeds real GDP. As a result, inventories decrease. Firms respond by increasing production so as to restore their inventories to the target level. As production increases, so does real GDP. With a higher level of real GDP, *induced expenditure* increases. Thus equilibrium expenditure increases by the sum of the initial increase in autonomous expenditure and the increase in induced expenditure. In this example, equilibrium expenditure increases by $200 billion and autonomous expenditure increases by $50 billion, so induced expenditure increases by $150 billion.

Although we have just analyzed the effects of an *increase* in autonomous expenditure, this analysis also applies to a decrease in autonomous expenditure. If initially the aggregate expenditure curve is AE_1, equilibrium expenditure and real GDP are $1,400 billion. A decrease in autonomous expenditure of $50 billion

FIGURE 27.5   The Multiplier

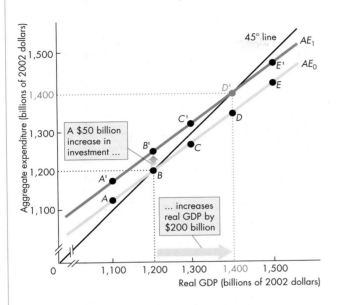

Real GDP	Aggregate planned expenditure			
(Y)	Original **(AE₀)**		New **(AE₁)**	
	(billions of 2002 dollars)			
1,100	A	1,125	A'	1,175
1,200	**B**	**1,200**	B'	1,250
1,300	C	1,275	C'	1,325
1,400	D	1,350	D'	1,400
1,500	E	1,425	E'	1,475

A $50 billion increase in autonomous expenditure shifts the AE curve upward by $50 billion from AE_0 to AE_1. Equilibrium expenditure increases by $200 billion from $1,200 billion to $1,400 billion. The increase in equilibrium expenditure is 4 times the increase in autonomous expenditure, so the multiplier is 4.

  myeconlab animation

shifts the aggregate expenditure curve downward by $50 billion to AE_0. Equilibrium expenditure decreases from $1,400 billion to $1,200 billion. The decrease in equilibrium expenditure ($200 billion) is larger than the decrease in autonomous expenditure that brought it about ($50 billion).

Why Is the Multiplier Greater Than 1?

We've seen that equilibrium expenditure increases by more than the increase in autonomous expenditure. This makes the multiplier greater than 1. How come? Why does equilibrium expenditure increase by more than the increase in autonomous expenditure?

The multiplier is greater than 1 because induced expenditure increases—an increase in autonomous expenditure *induces* further increases in expenditure. If Rogers Cablesystems spends $10 million on a new pay-per-view system, real GDP increases by $10 million. But that is not the end of the story. Video systems designers now have more income, and they spend part of the extra income on goods and services. Real GDP now rises by the initial $10 million plus the extra consumption expenditure induced by the $10 million increase in income. The producers of automobiles, vacations, and other goods and services now have increased incomes, and they, in turn, spend part of the increase in their incomes on consumption goods and services. Additional income induces additional expenditure, which creates additional income.

How big is the multiplier effect?

The Size of the Multiplier

Suppose that the economy is in a recession. Now profit prospects start to look better, and firms are planning a large increase in investment. The world economy is heading towards expansion. The question on everyone's lips is: How strong will the expansion be? This is a hard question to answer, but an important ingredient in the answer is the size of the multiplier.

The *multiplier* is the amount by which a change in autonomous expenditure is multiplied to determine the change in equilibrium expenditure that it generates. To calculate the multiplier, we divide the change in equilibrium expenditure by the change in autonomous expenditure.

Let's calculate the multiplier for the example in Fig. 27.5. Initially, equilibrium expenditure is $1,200 billion. Then autonomous expenditure increases by $50 billion, and equilibrium expenditure increases by $200 billion, to $1,400 billion. Then

$$\text{Multiplier} = \frac{\text{Change in equilibrium expenditure}}{\text{Change in autonomous expenditure}}$$

$$\text{Multiplier} = \frac{\$200 \text{ billion}}{\$50 \text{ billion}} = 4.$$

The Multiplier and the Slope of the *AE* Curve

The magnitude of the multiplier depends on the slope of the *AE* curve. In Fig. 27.6, the *AE* curve in part (a) is steeper than the *AE* curve in part (b), and the multiplier is larger in part (a) than in part (b). To see why, let's do a calculation.

Aggregate expenditure and real GDP change because induced expenditure and autonomous expenditure change. The change in real GDP (ΔY) equals the change in induced expenditure (ΔN) plus the change in autonomous expenditure (ΔA). That is,

$$\Delta Y = \Delta N + \Delta A.$$

But the change in induced expenditure is determined by the change in real GDP and the slope of the *AE* curve. To see why, begin with the fact that the slope of the *AE* curve equals the "rise," ΔN, divided by the "run," ΔY. That is

$$\text{Slope of } AE \text{ curve } = \Delta N \div \Delta Y.$$

So

$$\Delta N = \text{Slope of } AE \text{ curve} \times \Delta Y.$$

Now, use this equation to replace ΔN in the first equation above to give

$$\Delta Y = \text{Slope of } AE \text{ curve} \times \Delta Y + \Delta A.$$

Now, solve for ΔY as

$$(1 - \text{Slope of } AE \text{ curve}) \times \Delta Y = \Delta A$$

and rearrange to give

$$\Delta Y = \frac{\Delta A}{1 - \text{Slope of } AE \text{ curve}}.$$

Finally, divide both sides of this equation by ΔA to give

$$\text{Multiplier} = \frac{\Delta Y}{\Delta A} = \frac{1}{1 - \text{Slope of } AE \text{ curve}}.$$

If we use the example in Fig. 27.5, the slope of the *AE* curve is 0.75, so

$$\text{Multiplier} = \frac{1}{1 - 0.75} = \frac{1}{0.25} = 4.$$

Where there are no income taxes and no imports, the slope of the *AE* curve equals the marginal propensity to consume (*MPC*). So

$$\text{Multiplier} = \frac{1}{1 - MPC}.$$

But $(1 - MPC)$ equals *MPS*. So another formula is

$$\text{Multiplier} = \frac{1}{MPS}.$$

Again using the numbers in Fig. 27.5, we have

$$\text{Multiplier} = \frac{1}{0.25} = 4.$$

Because the marginal propensity to save (*MPS*) is a fraction—a number between 0 and 1—the multiplier is greater than 1.

FIGURE 27.6   The Multiplier and the Slope of the *AE* Curve

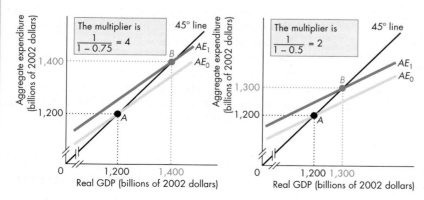

(a) Multiplier is 4

(b) Multiplier is 2

Imports and income taxes make the *AE* curve less steep and reduce the value of the multiplier. In part (a), with no imports and income taxes, the slope of the *AE* curve is 0.75 (the marginal propensity to consume) and the multiplier is 4. But with imports and income taxes, the slope of the *AE* curve is less than the marginal propensity to consume. In part (b), the slope of the *AE* curve is 0.5. In this case, the multiplier is 2.

myeconlab animation

Imports and Income Taxes

Imports and income taxes influence the size of the multiplier and make it smaller than it otherwise would be.

To see why imports make the multiplier smaller, think about what happens following an increase in investment. The increase in investment increases real GDP, which in turn increases consumption expenditure. But part of the increase in expenditure is on imported goods and services. Only expenditure on Canadian-produced goods and services increases Canadian real GDP. The larger the marginal propensity to import, the smaller is the change in Canadian real GDP.*

Income taxes also make the multiplier smaller than it otherwise would be. Again, think about what happens following an increase in investment. The increase in investment increases real GDP. Income tax payments increase so disposable income increases by less than the increase in real GDP and consumption expenditure increases by less than it would if taxes had not changed. The larger the income tax rate, the smaller is the change in real GDP.

The marginal propensity to import, the income tax rate, and the marginal propensity to consume determine the slope of the *AE* curve and the multiplier.

Over time, the value of the multiplier changes as tax rates change and as the marginal propensity to consume and the marginal propensity to import change. These ongoing changes make the multiplier hard to predict. But they do not change the fundamental fact that an initial change in autonomous expenditure leads to a magnified change in aggregate expenditure and real GDP.

The Multiplier Process

The multiplier effect isn't a one-shot event. It is a process that plays out over a few months. Figure 27.7 illustrates the multiplier process. Autonomous expenditure increases by $50 billion and real GDP increases by $50 billion (the green bar in round 1). This increase in real GDP increases induced expenditure in round 2. With the slope of the *AE* curve equal to 0.75, induced expenditure increases by 0.75 times the increase in real GDP, so the increase in real GDP of $50 billion induces a further increase in expenditure of $37.5 billion. This

*The Mathematical Note on pp. 670–671 shows the effects of imports and income taxes on the multiplier.

change in induced expenditure (the green bar in round 2) when added to the previous increase in expenditure (the blue bar in round 2) increases real GDP by $87.5 billion. The round 2 increase in real GDP induces a round 3 increase in induced expenditure. The process repeats through successive rounds. Each increase in real GDP is 0.75 times the previous increase and eventually real GDP increases by $200 billion.

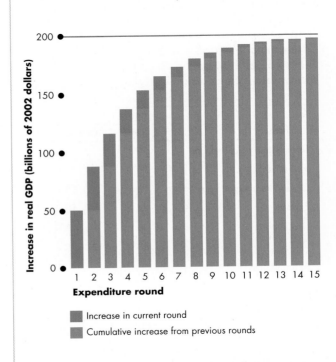

FIGURE 27.7 The Multiplier Process

Autonomous expenditure increases by $50 billion. In round 1, real GDP increases by the same amount. With the slope of the *AE* curve equal to 0.75, each additional dollar of real GDP induces an additional 0.75 of a dollar of induced expenditure. The round 1 increase in real GDP brings an increase in induced expenditure of $37.5 billion in round 2. At the end of round 2, real GDP has increased by $87.5 billion. The extra $37.5 billion of real GDP in round 2 brings a further increase in induced expenditure of $28.1 billion in round 3. Real GDP increases yet further to $115.6 billion. This process continues with real GDP increasing by ever-smaller amounts. When the process comes to an end, real GDP has increased by a total of $200 billion.

myeconlab animation

The Multiplier in the Great Depression

Investment Collapse Kills the Economy

The aggregate expenditure model and its multiplier were developed during the 1930s by John Maynard Keynes to understand the most traumatic event in economic history, the *Great Depression*.

In 1929, the Canadian and global economies were booming. Canadian real GDP and real GDP per person had never been higher. By 1933, real GDP had fallen to 69 percent of its 1929 level and more than a quarter of the labour force was unemployed.

The table shows the GDP numbers and components of aggregate expenditure in 1929 and 1933. Investment collapsed with a decrease from $16 billion to $1 billion. Exports fell by $4 billion. Government expenditure held steady.

If we assume that the marginal propensity to consume is 0.7 and the marginal propensity to import is 0.2, the slope of the *AE* curve is 0.5.

Autonomous expenditure and induced expenditure are each equal to a half of real GDP—$40 billion in 1929 and $27.5 billion in 1933.

The figure shows the *AE* curve in 1929 as AE_{29}. Equilibrium expenditure and real GDP were $80 billion. By 1933, autonomous expenditure had fallen by $12.5 billion to $27.5 billion and the *AE* curve had shifted downward to AE_{33}. Equilibrium expenditure and real GDP had fallen to $55 billion.

The decrease in autonomous expenditure of $12.5 billion brought a decrease in real GDP of $25 billion. The multiplier was $25/$12.5 = 2.

Item	1929	1933
	(billions of 2002 dollars)	
Consumption expenditure	50	40
Imvestment	16	1
Government expenditure	13	12
Exports	14	10
Less imports	−13	−8
GDP	80	55
Assumptions		
Induced expenditure	40	27.5
Autonomous expenditure	40	27.5
GDP	80	55.0

Source of data: Statistics Canada, *Historical Statistics of Canada,* Second Edition, F. H. Leacy (ed.), Ottawa, 1939, series F33, F34, F35, F51, F52, and F55 re-based to 2002 dollars.

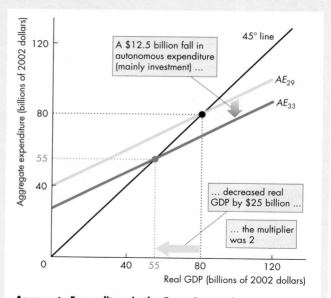

Aggregate Expenditure in the Great Depression

Business Cycle Turning Points

At business cycle turning points, the economy moves from expansion to recession or from recession to expansion. Economists understand these turning points as seismologists understand earthquakes. They know quite a lot about the forces and mechanisms that produce them, but they can't predict them. The forces that bring business cycle turning points are the swings in autonomous expenditure, such as investment and exports. The multiplier that you've just studied is the mechanism that gives momentum to the economy's new direction.

Review Quiz

1 What is the multiplier? What does it determine? Why does it matter?

2 How do the marginal propensity to consume, the marginal propensity to import, and the income tax rate influence the multiplier?

3 How do fluctuations in autonomous expenditure influence real GDP?

 Work Study Plan 27.3 and get instant feedback.

The Multiplier and the Price Level

We have just considered adjustments in spending that occur in the very short run when the price level is fixed. In this time frame, the economy's cobblestones, which are changes in investment and exports, are not smoothed by shock absorbers like those on Ed Stelmach's car. Instead, they are amplified like Céline Dion's voice. But these outcomes occur only when the price level is fixed. We now investigate what happens after a long enough time lapse for the price level to change.

Adjusting Quantities and Prices

When firms can't keep up with sales and their inventories fall below target, they increase production, but at some point, they raise their prices. Similarly, when firms find unwanted inventories piling up, they decrease production, but eventually they cut their prices. So far, we've studied the macroeconomic consequences of firms changing their production levels when their sales change, but we haven't looked at the effects of price changes. When individual firms change their prices, the economy's price level changes.

To study the simultaneous determination of real GDP and the price level, we use the *AS–AD model*, which is explained in Chapter 26. But to understand how aggregate demand adjusts, we need to work out the connection between the *AS–AD* model and the aggregate expenditure model that we've used in this chapter. The key to understanding the relationship between these two models is the distinction between the aggregate *expenditure* and aggregate *demand* and the related distinction between the aggregate *expenditure curve* and the aggregate *demand* curve.

Aggregate Expenditure and Aggregate Demand

The aggregate expenditure curve is the relationship between the aggregate planned expenditure and real GDP, all other influences on aggregate planned expenditure remaining the same. The aggregate demand curve is the relationship between the aggregate quantity of goods and services demanded and the price level, all other influences on aggregate demand remaining the same. Let's explore the links between these two relationships.

Deriving the Aggregate Demand Curve

When the price level changes, aggregate planned expenditure changes and the quantity of real GDP demanded changes. The aggregate demand curve slopes downward. Why? There are two main reasons:

- Wealth effect
- Substitution effects

Wealth Effect Other things remaining the same, the higher the price level, the smaller is the purchasing power of wealth. For example, suppose you have $100 in the bank and the price level is 105. If the price level rises to 125, your $100 buys fewer goods and services. You are less wealthy. With less wealth, you will probably want to try to spend a bit less and save a bit more. The higher the price level, other things remaining the same, the lower is aggregate planned expenditure.

Substitution Effects For a given expected future price level, a rise in the price level today makes current goods and services more expensive relative to future goods and services and results in a delay in purchases—an *intertemporal substitution*. A rise in the Canadian price level, other things remaining the same, makes Canadian-produced goods and services more expensive relative to foreign-produced goods and services. As a result, Canadian imports increase and Canadian exports decrease—an *international substitution*.

When the price level rises, each of these effects reduces aggregate planned expenditure at each level of real GDP. As a result, when the price level *rises*, the aggregate expenditure curve shifts *downward*. A fall in the price level has the opposite effect. When the price level *falls*, the aggregate expenditure curve shifts *upward*.

Figure 27.8(a) shows the shifts of the *AE* curve. When the price level is 110, the aggregate expenditure curve is AE_0, which intersects the 45° line at point B. Equilibrium expenditure is $1,200 billion. If the price level increases to 130, the aggregate expenditure curve shifts downward to AE_1, which intersects the 45° line at point A. Equilibrium expenditure decreases to $1,100 billion. If the price level decreases to 90, the aggregate expenditure curve shifts upward to AE_2, which intersects the 45° line at point C. Equilibrium expenditure increases to $1,300 billion.

We've just seen that when the price level changes, other things remaining the same, the aggregate expenditure curve shifts and the equilibrium expenditure changes. But when the price level changes, other things remaining the same, there is a movement along the aggregate demand curve.

Figure 27.8(b) shows the movements along the aggregate demand curve. At a price level of 110, the aggregate quantity of goods and services demanded is $1,200 billion—point B on the AD curve. If the price level rises to 130, the aggregate quantity of goods and services demanded decreases to $1,100 billion. There is a movement up along the aggregate demand curve to point A. If the price level falls to 90, the aggregate quantity of goods and services demanded increases to $1,300 billion. There is a movement down along the aggregate demand curve to point C.

Each point on the aggregate demand curve corresponds to a point of equilibrium expenditure. The equilibrium expenditure points A, B, and C in Fig. 27.8(a) correspond to the points A, B, and C on the aggregate demand curve in Fig. 27.8(b).

Changes in Aggregate Expenditure and Aggregate Demand

When any influence on aggregate planned expenditure other than the price level changes, both the aggregate expenditure curve and the aggregate demand curve shift. For example, an increase in investment or exports increases both aggregate planned expenditure and aggregate demand and shifts both the AE curve and the AD curve. Figure 27.9 illustrates the effect of such an increase.

Initially, the aggregate expenditure curve is AE_0 in part (a) and the aggregate demand curve is AD_0 in part (b). The price level is 110, real GDP is $1,200 billion, and the economy is at point A in both parts of Fig. 27.9. Now suppose that investment increases by $100 billion. At a constant price level of 110, the aggregate expenditure curve shifts upward to AE_1. This curve intersects the 45° line at an equilibrium expenditure of $1,400 billion (point B). This equilibrium expenditure of $1,400 billion is the aggregate quantity of goods and services demanded at a price level of 110, as shown by point B in part (b). Point B lies on a new aggregate demand curve. The aggregate demand curve has shifted rightward to AD_1.

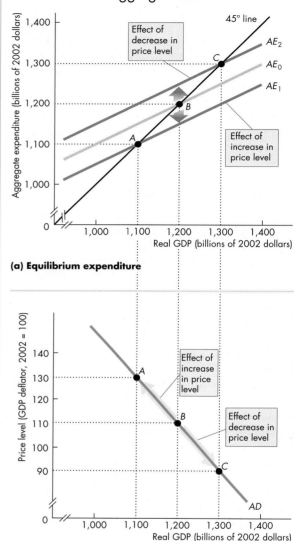

FIGURE 27.8 Equilibrium Expenditure and Aggregate Demand

(a) Equilibrium expenditure

(b) Aggregate demand

A change in the price level *shifts* the AE curve and results in a *movement along* the AD curve. When the price level is 110, the AE curve is AE_0 and equilibrium expenditure is $1,200 billion at point B. When the price level rises to 130, the AE curve is AE_1 and equilibrium expenditure is $1,100 billion at point A. When the price level falls to 90, the AE curve is AE_2 and equilibrium expenditure is $1,300 billion at point C. Points A, B, and C on the AD curve in part (b) correspond to the equilibrium expenditure points A, B, and C in part (a).

 animation

FIGURE 27.9   A Change in Aggregate Demand

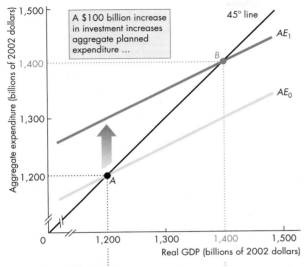

A $100 billion increase in investment increases aggregate planned expenditure ...

(a) Aggregate expenditure

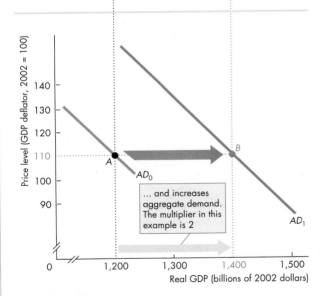

... and increases aggregate demand. The multiplier in this example is 2

(b) Aggregate demand

The price level is 110. When the aggregate expenditure curve is AE_0 in part (a), the aggregate demand curve is AD_0 in part (b). An increase in autonomous expenditure shifts the AE curve upward to AE_1. In the new equilibrium, real GDP is $1,400 billion (at point B). Because the quantity of real GDP demanded at a price level of 110 increases to $1,400 billion, the AD curve shifts rightward to AD_1.

myeconlab animation

But how do we know by how much the AD curve shifts? The multiplier determines the answer. The larger the multiplier, the larger is the shift in the aggregate demand curve that results from a given change in autonomous expenditure. In this example, the multiplier is 2. A $100 billion increase in investment produces a $200 billion increase in the aggregate quantity of goods and services demanded at each price level. That is, a $100 billion increase in autonomous expenditure shifts the aggregate demand curve rightward by $200 billion.

A decrease in autonomous expenditure shifts the aggregate expenditure curve downward and shifts the aggregate demand curve leftward. You can see these effects by reversing the change that we've just described. If the economy is initially at point B on the aggregate expenditure curve AE_1 and on the aggregate demand curve AD_1, a decrease in autonomous expenditure shifts the aggregate expenditure curve downward to AE_0. The aggregate quantity of goods and services demanded decreases from $1,400 billion to $1,200 billion, and the aggregate demand curve shifts leftward to AD_0.

Let's summarize what we have just discovered:

If some factor other than a change in the price level increases autonomous expenditure, the AE curve shifts upward and the AD curve shifts rightward. The size of the AD curve shift equals the change in autonomous expenditure multiplied by the multiplier.

Equilibrium Real GDP and the Price Level

In Chapter 26, we learned that aggregate demand and short-run aggregate supply determine equilibrium real GDP and the price level. We've now put aggregate demand under a more powerful microscope and have discovered that a change in investment (or in any component of autonomous expenditure) changes aggregate demand and shifts the aggregate demand curve. The magnitude of the shift depends on the multiplier. But whether a change in autonomous expenditure results ultimately in a change in real GDP, a change in the price level, or a combination of the two depends on aggregate supply. There are two time frames to consider: the short run and the long run. First we'll see what happens in the short run.

An Increase in Aggregate Demand in the Short Run

Figure 27.10 describes the economy. Initially, in part (a), the aggregate expenditure curve is AE_0 and equilibrium expenditure is $1,200 billion—point A. In part (b), aggregate demand is AD_0 and the short-run aggregate supply curve is SAS. (Chapter 26, pp. 627–629 explains the SAS curve.) Equilibrium is at point A in part (b), where the aggregate demand and short-run aggregate supply curves intersect. The price level is 110, and real GDP is $1,200 billion.

Now suppose that investment increases by $100 billion. With the price level fixed at 110, the aggregate expenditure curve shifts upward to AE_1. Equilibrium expenditure increases to $1,400 billion—point B in part (a). In part (b), the aggregate demand curve shifts rightward by $200 billion, from AD_0 to AD_1. How far the aggregate demand curve shifts is determined by the multiplier when the price level is fixed.

But with this new aggregate demand curve, the price level does not remain fixed. The price level rises, and as it does, the aggregate expenditure curve shifts downward. The short-run equilibrium occurs when the aggregate expenditure curve has shifted downward to AE_2 and the new aggregate demand curve, AD_1, intersects the short-run aggregate supply curve at point C in both part (a) and part (b). Real GDP is $1,330 billion, and the price level is 123.

When price level effects are taken into account, the increase in investment still has a multiplier effect on real GDP, but the multiplier is smaller than it would be if the price level were fixed. The steeper the slope of the short-run aggregate supply curve, the larger is the increase in the price level and the smaller is the multiplier effect on real GDP.

An Increase in Aggregate Demand in the Long Run

Figure 27.11 illustrates the long-run effect of an increase in aggregate demand. In the long run, real GDP equals potential GDP and there is full employment. Potential GDP is $1,200 billion, and the long-run aggregate supply curve is LAS. Initially, the economy is at point A in parts (a) and (b).

Investment increases by $100 billion. In Fig. 27.11, the aggregate expenditure curve shifts to AE_1 and the aggregate demand curve shifts to AD_1. With no change in the price level, the economy would move to point B and real GDP would increase to $1,400 billion. But in the short run, the price level rises to 123 and real GDP increases to only $1,330 billion. With the higher price level, the AE curve

FIGURE 27.10   The Multiplier in the Short Run

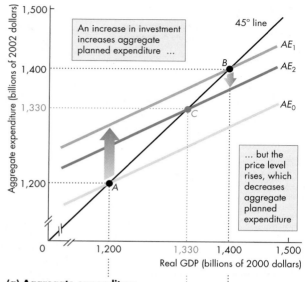

(a) Aggregate expenditure

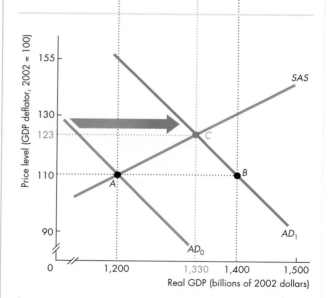

(b) Aggregate demand

An increase in investment shifts the AE curve from AE_0 to AE_1 and the AD curve from AD_0 to AD_1. The price level rises, and the higher price level shifts the AE curve downward from AE_1 to AE_2. The economy moves to point C in both parts. In the short run, when prices are flexible, the multiplier effect is smaller than when the price level is fixed.

myeconlab   animation

FIGURE 27.11   The Multiplier in the Long Run

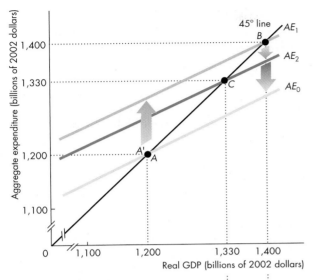

(a) Aggregate expenditure

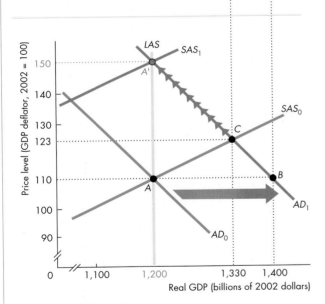

(b) Aggregate demand

Starting from point A, an increase in investment shifts the AE curve to AE_1 and the AD curve to AD_1. In the short run, the economy moves to point C. In the long run, the money wage rate rises and the SAS curve shifts to SAS_1. As the price level rises, the AE curve shifts back to AE_0 and the economy moves to point A'. In the long run, the multiplier is zero.

myeconlab animation

shifts from AE_1 to AE_2. The economy is now in a short-run equilibrium at point C in both part (a) and part (b).

Real GDP now exceeds potential GDP. The labour force is more than fully employed, and in the long run, shortages of labour increase the money wage rate. The higher money wage rate increases firms' costs, which decreases short-run aggregate supply and shifts the SAS curve leftward towards SAS_1. The price level rises further, and real GDP decreases. There is a movement along AD_1, and the AE curve shifts downward from AE_2 towards AE_0. When the money wage rate and the price level have increased by the same percentage, real GDP is again equal to potential GDP and the economy is at point A'. In the long run, the multiplier is zero.

Review Quiz

1 How does a change in the price level influence the AE curve and the AD curve?

2 If autonomous expenditure increases with no change in the price level, what happens to the AE curve and the AD curve? Which shift is determined by the multiplier and why?

3 How does an increase in autonomous expenditure change real GDP in the short run? Does real GDP change by the same amount as the change in aggregate demand? Why or why not?

4 How does real GDP change in the long run when autonomous expenditure increases? Does real GDP change by the same amount as the change in aggregate demand? Why or why not?

myeconlab   Work Study Plan 27.4 and get instant feedback.

◆ You are now ready to build on what you've learned about aggregate expenditure fluctuations. We'll study the business cycle and the roles of fiscal policy and monetary policy in smoothing the cycle while achieving price stability and sustained economic growth. In Chapter 28, we study the Canadian business cycle and inflation, and in Chapters 29 and 30, we study fiscal policy and monetary policy respectively. But before you leave the current topic, look at *Reading Between the Lines* on pp. 668–669 to see the aggregate expenditure model in action in the Canadian economy during 2008.

Recession Coming

GDP Rise in Q3 Masks Layoffs, Recession to Come

December 1, 2008

Climbing inventories from producers and manufacturers helped spark an unexpected burst of economic growth in Canada last quarter. But excess product will drive unemployment higher as the country moves into recession, economists warned Monday.

"Inventories are building in the auto sector [and] much of the manufacturing sector, and that means factories will have to cut back production over the next while," said Sal Guatieri, a senior economist at BMO Capital Markets.

Warehouses brimming with unsold goods contributed to a stronger-than-expected 1.3 percent rise in real gross domestic product in the third quarter, as producers logged a robust level of output.

It does not mean they sold it.

Final domestic demand, which encompasses corporate and consumer spending, fell to its slowest pace in a dozen years in the three-month period, while exports declined for the fifth consecutive quarter.

Idle inventory combined with still-falling demand is a recipe for layoffs, Mr. Guatieri said. "We will likely see a wave of job losses because of that."...

"You could anticipate anywhere from 100 [thousand] to 200 thousand job losses over the next year," he said, adding BMO expects the unemployment rate to jump above 7 percent from 6.2 percent by this time next year. ...

Essence of the Story

- Real GDP grew by 1.3 percent (annual rate) in the third quarter of 2008.

- Unwanted rising inventories were a large component of the increase in real GDP.

- Unwanted rising inventories will bring a cut in production.

- Final domestic demand in the three-month period fell to its slowest pace in a dozen years.

- Exports decreased for the fifth consecutive quarter.

- Economists say the economy is heading towards recession.

- BMO economists expect between 100,000 and 200,000 people to lose jobs and the unemployment rate to increase above 7 percent by the end of 2009.

Economic Analysis

- We can interpret this news article by using the analysis of convergence to equilibrium on p. 656 and in Fig. 27.4.

- The article reports that although real GDP increased during the third quarter of 2008, the main source of the increase was a rise in unplanned inventories.

- The table shows the real GDP and aggregate expenditure numbers for the second quarter and third quarter of 2008.

- Figure 1 illustrates the situation in the third quarter of 2008 and its implications for future quarters.

- Real GDP was $1,333 billion. Assuming that the $12 billion increase in inventories was unplanned, aggregate planned expenditure was $1,321 billion. These two numbers provide one point on the AE curve in part (a).

- The slope of the AE curve depends on the marginal propensity to consume, the marginal propensity to import, and the marginal tax rate (see the Mathematical Note on p. 670) and we'll assume that slope to be 0.2.

- Using this information and these assumptions, the aggregate expenditure curve in the third quarter of 2008 was AE and equilibrium real GDP was $1,318 billion.

- Part (b) shows the increase in unplanned inventories, which also equals the gap between the AE curve and the 45° line in part (a).

- With no further change in aggregate planned expenditure, real GDP can be expected to fall during the fourth quarter of 2008 (as predicted in the news article).

- With further cuts in aggregate planned expenditure, real GDP will fall by even more during the fourth quarter of 2008 and through 2009.

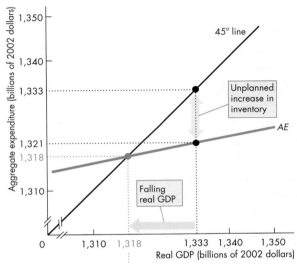

(a) Aggregate expenditure

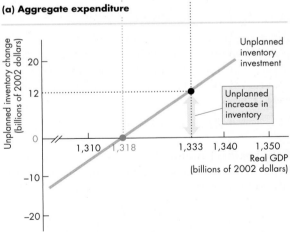

(b) Unplanned inventory changes

Figure 1 Convergence to equilibrium expenditure in onset of recession

The Components of Aggregate Expenditure

	2008 Q2	2008 Q3	Change
	(billions of 2002 dollars)		
Consumption expenditure	815	816	1
Investment expenditure	329	332	3
Government expenditure	267	268	1
Exports	489	482	−7
Imports	583	575	−8
Residual*	12	10	−2
Real GDP	1,329	1,333	4
Change in inventories	10	12	2

*The residual arises because chain-linked real variables are calculated for each expenditure component independently of chain-linked real GDP and the components don't exactly sum to real GDP.

MATHEMATICAL NOTE

The Algebra of the Keynesian Model

This mathematical note derives formulas for equilibrium expenditure and the multipliers. We begin by defining the symbols we need:

- Aggregate planned expenditure, AE
- Real GDP, Y
- Consumption expenditure, C
- Disposable income, YD
- Investment, I
- Government expenditure, G
- Exports, X
- Imports, M
- Net taxes, T
- Autonomous consumption expenditure, a
- Autonomous taxes, T_a
- Marginal propensity to consume, b
- Marginal propensity to import, m
- Marginal tax rate, t
- Autonomous expenditure, A

Aggregate Expenditure

Aggregate planned expenditure (AE) is the sum of the planned amounts of consumption expenditure (C), investment (I), government expenditure (G), and exports (X) minus the planned amount of imports (M). That is,

$$AE = C + I + G + X - M.$$

Consumption Function Consumption expenditure (C) depends on disposable income (YD), and we write the consumption function as

$$C = a + bYD.$$

Disposable income (YD) equals real GDP minus net taxes ($Y - T$). So if we replace YD with ($Y - T$), the consumption function becomes

$$C = a + b(Y - T).$$

Net taxes, T, equal autonomous taxes (that are independent of income), T_a, plus induced taxes (that vary with income), tY.

So we can write net taxes as

$$T = T_a + tY.$$

Use this last equation to replace T in the consumption function. The consumption function becomes

$$C = a - bT_a + b(1 - t)Y.$$

This equation describes consumption expenditure as a function of real GDP.

Import Function Imports depend on real GDP, and the import function is

$$M = mY.$$

Aggregate Expenditure Curve Use the consumption function and the import function to replace C and M in the AE equation. That is,

$$AE = a - bT_a + b(1 - t)Y + I + G + X - mY.$$

Collect the terms that involve Y on the right side of the equation to obtain

$$AE = (a - bT_a + I + G + X) + [b(1 - t) - m]Y.$$

Autonomous expenditure (A) is ($a - bT_a + I + G + X$), and the slope of the AE curve is $[b(1 - t) - m]$. So the equation for the AE curve, which is shown in Fig. 1, is

$$AE = A + [b(1 - t) - m]Y.$$

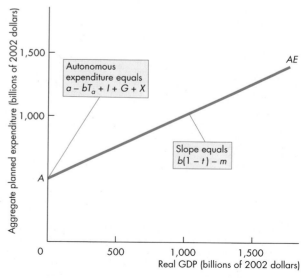

Figure 1 The AE curve

Equilibrium Expenditure

Equilibrium expenditure occurs when aggregate planned expenditure (*AE*) equals real GDP (*Y*). That is,

$$AE = Y.$$

In Fig. 2, the scales of the *x*-axis (real GDP) and the *y*-axis (aggregate planned expenditure) are identical, so the 45° line shows the points at which aggregate planned expenditure equals real GDP.

Figure 2 shows the point of equilibrium expenditure at the intersection of the *AE* curve and the 45° line.

To calculate equilibrium expenditure, solve the equations for the *AE* curve and the 45° line for the two unknown quantities *AE* and *Y*. So starting with

$$AE = A + [b(1 - t) - m]Y$$

$$AE = Y,$$

replace *AE* with *Y* in the *AE* equation to obtain

$$Y = A + [b(1 - t) - m]Y.$$

The solution for *Y* is

$$Y = \frac{1}{1 - [b(1 - t) - m]}A.$$

The Multiplier

The multiplier equals the change in equilibrium expenditure and real GDP (*Y*) that results from a change in autonomous expenditure (*A*) divided by the change in autonomous expenditure.

A change in autonomous expenditure (Δ*A*) changes equilibrium expenditure and real GDP by

$$\Delta Y = \frac{1}{1 - [b(1 - t) - m]}\Delta A.$$

$$\text{Multiplier} = \frac{1}{1 - [b(1 - t) - m]}.$$

The size of the multiplier depends on the slope of the *AE* curve, $b(1 - t) - m$. The larger the slope, the larger is the multiplier. So the multiplier is larger,

- The greater the marginal propensity to consume (*b*)
- The smaller the marginal tax rate (*t*)
- The smaller the marginal propensity to import (*m*)

An economy with no imports and no income taxes has $m = 0$ and $t = 0$. In this special case, the multiplier equals $1/(1 - b)$. If *b* is 0.75, then the multiplier is 4, as shown in Fig. 3.

In an economy with imports and income taxes, if $b = 0.75$, $t = 0.2$, and $m = 0.1$, the multiplier equals 1 divided by $[1 - 0.75(1 - 0.2) - 0.1]$, which equals 2. Make up some more examples to show the effects of *b*, *t*, and *m* on the multiplier.

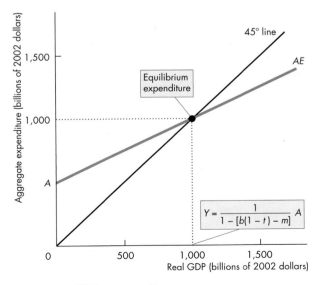

Figure 2 Equilibrium expenditure

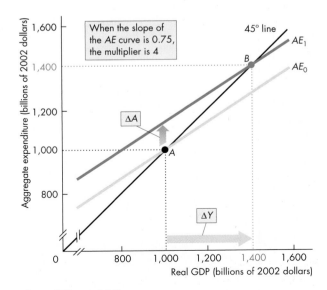

Figure 3 The multiplier

Government Expenditure Multiplier

The **government expenditure multiplier** equals the change in equilibrium expenditure (Y) that results from a change in government expenditure (G) divided by the change in government expenditure. Because autonomous expenditure is equal to

$$A = a - bT_a + I + G + X,$$

the change in autonomous expenditure equals the change in government expenditure. That is,

$$\Delta A = \Delta G.$$

You can see from the solution for equilibrium expenditure Y that

$$\Delta Y = \frac{1}{1 - [b(1 - t) - m]}\Delta G.$$

The government expenditure multiplier equals

$$\frac{1}{1 - [b(1 - t) - m]}.$$

In an economy in which $t = 0$ and $m = 0$, the government expenditure multiplier is $1/(1 - b)$. With $b = 0.75$, the government expenditure multiplier is 4, as Fig. 4 shows. Make up some examples and use the above formula to show how b, m, and t influence the government expenditure multiplier.

Autonomous Tax Multiplier

The **autonomous tax multiplier** equals the change in equilibrium expenditure (Y) that results from a change in autonomous taxes (T_a) divided by the change in autonomous taxes. Because autonomous expenditure is equal to

$$A - a - bT_a + I + G + X,$$

the change in autonomous expenditure equals minus b multiplied by the change in autonomous taxes. That is,

$$\Delta A = -b\Delta T_a.$$

You can see from the solution for equilibrium expenditure Y that

$$\Delta Y = \frac{-b}{1 - [b(1 - t) - m]}\Delta T_a.$$

The autonomous tax multiplier equals

$$\frac{-b}{1 - [b(1 - t) - m]}.$$

In an economy in which $t = 0$ and $m = 0$, the autonomous tax multiplier is $-b/(1 - b)$. In this special case, with $b = 0.75$, the autonomous tax multiplier equals -3, as Fig. 5 shows. Make up some examples and use the above formula to show how b, m, and t influence the autonomous tax multiplier.

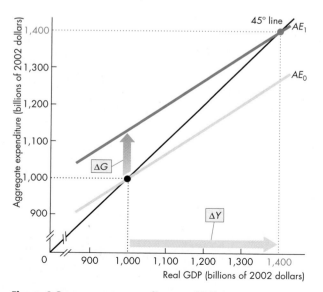

Figure 4 Government expenditure multiplier

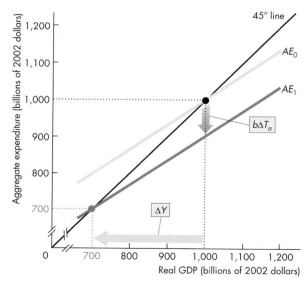

Figure 5 Autonomous tax multiplier

Balanced Budget Multiplier

The **balanced budget multiplier** equals the change in equilibrium expenditure (Y) that results from equal changes in government expenditure and autonomous taxes divided by the change in government expenditure. Because government expenditure and autonomous taxes change by the same amount, the budget balance does not change.

The change in equilibrium expenditure that results from the change in government expenditure is

$$\Delta Y = \frac{1}{1 - [b(1 - t) - m]} \Delta G.$$

And the change in equilibrium expenditure that results from the change in autonomous taxes is

$$\Delta Y = \frac{-b}{1 - [b(1 - t) - m]} \Delta T_a.$$

So the change in equilibrium expenditure resulting from the changes in government expenditure and autonomous taxes is

$$\Delta Y = \frac{1}{1 - [b(1 - t) - m]} \Delta G +$$

$$\frac{-b}{1 - [b(1 - t) - m]} \Delta T_a.$$

Notice that

$$\frac{1}{1 - [b(1 - t) - m]}$$

is common to both terms on the right side. So we can rewrite the equation as

$$\Delta Y = \frac{1}{1 - [b(1 - t) - m]} (\Delta G - b \Delta T_a)$$

The *AE* curve shifts upward by $\Delta G - b \Delta T_a$, as shown in Fig. 6.

But the change in government expenditure equals the change in autonomous taxes. That is,

$$\Delta G = \Delta T_a.$$

And

$$\Delta Y = \frac{1 - b}{1 - [b(1 - t) - m]} \Delta G.$$

The balanced budget multiplier equals

$$\frac{1 - b}{1 - [b(1 - t) - m]}.$$

In an economy in which $t = 0$ and $m = 0$, the balanced budget multiplier is $(1 - b)/(1 - b)$, which equals 1, as Fig. 6 shows. Make up some examples and use the above formula to show how b, m, and t influence the balanced budget multiplier.

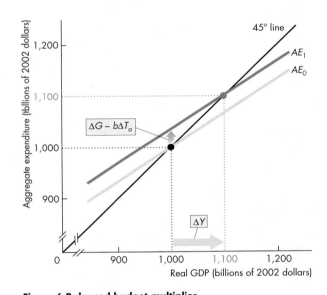

Figure 6 Balanced budget multiplier

SUMMARY ◆

Key Points

Fixed Prices and Expenditure Plans (pp. 650–653)

- When the price level is fixed, expenditure plans determine real GDP.
- Consumption expenditure is determined by disposable income, and the marginal propensity to consume (MPC) determines the change in consumption expenditure brought about by a change in disposable income. Real GDP determines disposable income.
- Imports are determined by real GDP, and the marginal propensity to import determines the change in imports brought about by a change in real GDP.

Real GDP with a Fixed Price Level (pp. 654–657)

- Aggregate *planned* expenditure depends on real GDP.
- Equilibrium expenditure occurs when aggregate planned expenditure equals actual expenditure and real GDP.

The Multiplier (pp. 658–662)

- The multiplier is the magnified effect of a change in autonomous expenditure on equilibrium expenditure and real GDP.

- The multiplier is determined by the slope of the AE curve.
- The slope of the AE curve is influenced by the marginal propensity to consume, the marginal propensity to import, and the income tax rate.

The Multiplier and the Price Leve (pp. 663–667)

- The AD curve is the relationship between the quantity of real GDP demanded and the price level, other things remaining the same.
- The AE curve is the relationship between aggregate planned expenditure and real GDP, other things remaining the same.
- At a given price level, there is a given AE curve. A change in the price level changes aggregate planned expenditure and shifts the AE curve. A change in the price level also creates a movement along the AD curve.
- A change in autonomous expenditure that is not caused by a change in the price level shifts the AE curve and shifts the AD curve. The magnitude of the shift of the AD curve depends on the multiplier and on the change in autonomous expenditure.
- The multiplier decreases as the price level changes, and the multiplier in the long run is zero.

Key Figures

Key Terms

PROBLEMS and APPLICATIONS

 Work problems 1–8 in Chapter 27 Study Plan and get instant feedback.
Work problems 9–14 as Homework, a Quiz, or a Test if assigned by your instructor.

1. You are given the following information about the economy of the United Kingdom.

Disposable income	Consumption expenditure
(billions of pounds per year)	
300	340
400	420
500	500
600	580
700	660

   a. Calculate the marginal propensity to consume.
   b. Calculate saving at each level of disposable income.
   c. Calculate the marginal propensity to save.

2. The figure illustrates the components of aggregate planned expenditure on Turtle Island. Turtle Island has no imports or exports, the people pay no incomes taxes, and the price level is fixed.

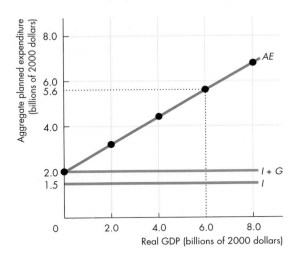

   a. Calculate autonomous expenditure and the marginal propensity to consume.
   b. What is aggregate planned expenditure when real GDP is $6 billion?
   c. If real GDP is $4 billion, what is happening to inventories?
   d. If real GDP is $6 billion, what is happening to inventories?
   e. Calculate the multiplier.

3. You are given the following information about the Canadian economy: Autonomous consumption expenditure is $50 billion, investment is $200 billion, and government expenditure is $250 billion. The marginal propensity to consume is 0.7 and net taxes are $250 billion—net taxes are assumed to be constant and not vary with income. Exports are $500 billion and imports are $450 billion.

   a. What is the consumption function?
   b. What is the equation of the *AE* curve?
   c. Calculate equilibrium expenditure.
   d. Calculate the multiplier.
   e. If investment decreases to $150 billion, what is the change in equilibrium expenditure?
   f. Describe the process in e that moves the economy to its new equilibrium expenditure.

4. Suppose that the economy is at full employment, the price level is 100, and the multiplier is 2. Investment increases by $100 billion.

   a. What is the change in equilibrium expenditure if the price level remains at 100?
   b. What is the immediate change in the quantity of real GDP demanded?
   c. Compare the increase in real GDP in the short run with the increase in the quantity of real GDP demanded in b.
   d. In the short run, does the price level remain at 100? Explain why or why not.
   e. Compare the increase in real GDP in the long run with the increase in the quantity of real GDP demanded in b.
   f. Explain how the price level changes in the long run.
   g. Are the values of the multipliers in the short run and the long run larger or smaller than 2?

5. **Canada's Harper Says Sales Tax Cut Likely the Last**
   Canadian Prime Minister Stephen Harper said on Monday that a New Year's Day cut to the country's sales tax will likely be the last. The one percentage point cut to the federal goods and services tax (GST) will ... [cut] the much-hated tax down to 5 percent ... Harper said the cut will

bring $6 billion in tax relief for Canadians in 2008. The GST ... was at 7 percent before Harper's government took power in 2006... the move has proved popular with voters, and the Canadian Federation of Independent Business said on Monday the tax reduction will "provide a much-needed boost to the Canadian economy ... at a time when sales are traditionally sluggish in many sectors."

Reuters, December 31, 2007

a. Will the effect on aggregate expenditure of a cut in GST of $6 billion likely be larger or smaller than $6 billion? Explain.
b. Explain and draw graphs to illustrate how the GST cut will influence aggregate expenditure and aggregate demand in both the short run and the long run.

6. **The U.S. and China's Savings Problems**

Last year China saved about half of its gross domestic product. ... At the same time, the U.S. saved only 13 percent of its national income. ... And that's just looking at national averages that include saving by consumers, businesses, and governments. The contrast is even starker at the household level—a personal saving rate in China of about 30 percent of household income, compared with a U.S. rate that dipped into negative territory last year (–0.4% of after-tax household income). ... Similar extremes show up in the consumption shares of the two economies. ...

Fortune, March 8, 2006

Compare the *MPC* and *MPS* in China and the United States. Why might they differ?

7. **The Debt Demon**

... [T]he Conference Board predicts decent 2.2% growth for Canada—thanks to Canadians who love to spend and are undaunted about the misery their American cousins are suffering as families lose homes and life savings. "Canada's household sector seems oblivious to the concerns that the slowdown will spread north," said [economist Pedro] Antunes. ... Now, here's a warning: South of the border, our American cousins are learning a brutal lesson, after living high off the hog to let personal savings rates plunge to lows not seen since the Great Depression, while total household debt skyrocketed to trillions. ... Here in Canada, we're going down the same dark path

of overspending with household debt now at a record $1.1 trillion, which equates to more than 110% of personal disposable income. So far, rising real estate prices have kept many families afloat, especially for those who've borrowed against home equity to prop up their lifestyles. Now is the time to shed debt and set up an emergency fund. Not spend more.

Canoe Money, April 8, 2008

a. Explain and draw a graph to illustrate how the U.S. slowdown can "spread north" and influence aggregate planned expenditure.
b. Starting from equilibrium expenditure, why might aggregate planned expenditure and actual aggregate expenditure become unequal in this situation?
c. If actual aggregate expenditure and aggregate planned expenditure become unequal, how will they return to equilibrium expenditure?
d. Explain and draw a graph to illustrate the process by which Canada could be driven into a recession if consumers follow the advice offered at the end of this article. Explain the role that the multiplier would play in this process.
e. How might years of "overspending" and "living high off the hog" increase the likelihood that an initial decrease in aggregate expenditure would push the economy all the way into a recession?
f. Explain and draw a graph to illustrate how real GDP will eventually return to potential GDP.
g. Why is the multiplier only a short-run influence on GDP?

8. You are given the following information about the economy of Australia.

Disposable income	Saving
(billions of dollars per year)	
0	–5
100	20
200	45
300	70
400	95

a. Calculate the marginal propensity to save.
b. Calculate consumption at each level of disposable income.
c. Calculate the marginal propensity to consume.

9. The spreadsheet lists the components of aggregate planned expenditure in the United Kingdom. The numbers are in billions of pounds.

	A	B	C	D	E	F	G
1		Y	C	I	G	X	M
2	A	100	110	50	60	60	15
3	B	200	170	50	60	60	30
4	C	300	230	50	60	60	45
5	D	400	290	50	60	60	60
6	E	500	350	50	60	60	75
7	F	600	410	50	60	60	90

a. Calculate autonomous expenditure.
b. Calculate the marginal propensity to consume.
c. What is aggregate planned expenditure when real GDP is 200 billion pounds?
d. If real GDP is 200 billion pounds, what is happening to inventories?
e. If real GDP is 500 billion pounds, what is happening to inventories?
f. Calculate the multiplier.

10 **Does Canada Have a Household Debt Problem?**

Household spending has been rising at a significantly faster rate than household income ever since 1990. ... Canada's personal saving rate is now a negligible 1%, having steadily declined from 10% in 1990. ... Households have taken on a lot of debt, increasing their consumption through credit despite generally stagnant real incomes. Roughly the bottom 80% of households experienced little or no growth of real income from 1992 to 2002.

Progressive Economics Forum, February 14, 2008

a. What do the facts reported in this article imply about changes in the *MPC* and *MPS*?
b. Explain and use graphs to illustrate how the consumption function and saving function have changed in Canada since the early 1990s.
c. Is it possible for the personal saving rate to become negative?
d. Is a negative personal saving rate sustainable in the long run?

11. **Housing Prices and Consumer Spending**

The likely adverse effects on consumer spending and the aggregate economy of a significant downturn in house prices are an ongoing concern for policymakers.

Movements in house prices can affect consumer spending in two ways: through a direct wealth effect ... or through a collateral effect, by allowing greater access to credit. ... Households perceive their houses as wealth, and base their spending decisions in part on movements in net wealth positions. As well, if access to credit for some consumers is contingent on their housing wealth or equity, these credit-constrained households will be able to borrow and spend more, based on an increase in the collateral value of their homes. ... The effect of housing wealth on consumption may be larger than the effect from other forms of wealth. ... Households may view some forms of wealth as more uncertain and since house prices are typically less volatile than stock prices, households may view gains in housing wealth as more permanent. ...

Bank of Canada Review, Summer 2008

a. Explain and draw a graph to illustrate how increasing housing values can impact the consumption function and saving function.
b. Explain and draw aggregate expenditure and aggregate demand models to illustrate why a significant downturn in housing values would be a concern for an economy in the short run.
c. Explain and draw a graph to illustrate the long-run impact from b.
d. Why might the *MPC* depend upon the actual source of income and wealth changes, as opposed to being identical for all influences on income and wealth?

12. **We're Juggling Record Household Debt**

Canadians are juggling record debt loads averaging $80,000 per household including mortgage debt, says the author [Roger Sauvé] of a new report, and he warns job losses would push many families over a fiscal cliff. ... [Sauvé] describes a perfect storm of flat earnings, increased spending and plummeting savings. ... Total accumulated debt was 131 per cent of Canadian household income last year after income tax and transfers such as child benefits. That's up from 91 per cent in 1990, Sauvé says. Many consumers borrowed cash at lower interest rates to buy more expensive homes as real estate prices steadily rose. But many Canadians, especially those earning net middle incomes of about $60,000 a year, have racked up consumer debt that's almost doubled since 1990 to $22,500 from $12,000 on average, Sauvé says. "They've continued spending with more debt and less savings."

Toronto Star, February 12, 2008

a. Explain how lower interest rates and rising home values may have influenced the *MPC* and *MPS* in Canada and contributed to rising household debt.

b. Explain and use a graph to illustrate how combining job losses with the "perfect storm of flat earnings, increased spending and plummeting savings" has the potential to "push many families over a fiscal cliff" and ultimately cause a recession.

c. Why might consistently higher household saving rates make an economy less susceptible to being pushed into a recession by job losses?

13. **Survey Says Canadians Eager to Spend**

A new survey suggests Canadians could spend more money this holiday season than they did last year, despite recent widespread indications that consumer confidence has been rattled ... But Bruce Cran of the Consumers' Association of Canada said the bad economic news just keeps piling up and he has a hard time believing Canadians will be spending their way through the holiday season. ... A recent survey by the Conference Board of Canada found that consumer confidence fell in October to its lowest level in more than 25 years on dire global economic news. ... Deloitte said lower gas prices will mean a little more money in pockets. ... And the sagging loonie will mean more shopping at home, the survey suggested. ... "Compared to last year, when the Canadian dollar was at or above par leading up to the holiday season, we expect to see a significantly lower number of Canadians spending their holiday budget south of the border this year, which will help out our Canadian retailers," said [Deloitte's Bruce] Houlden. ...

According to the survey, shoppers in Toronto and Vancouver are the most likely to decrease their holiday spending this year.

CNEWS, November 11, 2008

a. What is induced consumption expenditure and what is autonomous consumption expenditure? Why isn't all consumption expenditure induced expenditure? What does the survey imply about how Canadian consumers view holiday expenditures?

b. Explain and draw a graph to illustrate Cran's predictions about how declining confidence will influence aggregate expenditure and aggregate demand in the short run.

c. Explain and draw a graph to illustrate the long-run effect on aggregate expenditure and aggregate demand of the decline in consumer confidence.

d. Explain and draw a graph to illustrate how the falling gas prices may impact aggregate expenditure and aggregate demand in the short run.

e. Explain how the depreciation of the Canadian dollar may impact the marginal propensity to import. How will this impact the multiplier effect from consumption expenditure?

f. Identify potential influences on consumption expenditure decisions that may be prompting the different spending patterns of Toronto and Vancouver consumers.

14. Study *Reading Between the Lines* on pp. 668–669 and then answer the following questions:

a. If the 2008 third quarter changes in inventories were mainly of planned changes, what role did they play in shifting the *AE* curve and changing equilibrium expenditure? Use a figure similar to that on p. 656 to answer this question.

b. If, as the news article reports, the world economy is slowing and Canadian exports stop growing, what will happen to the *AE* curve in future quarters and how will real GDP change?

c. What do you think will happen to real GDP, aggregate expenditure, and inventory investment in 2009? What clues do you get from the news article?

28  Canadian Inflation, Unemployment, and Business Cycle

After studying this chapter, you will be able to

- Explain how demand-pull and cost-push forces bring cycles in inflation and output

- Explain the short-run and long-run tradeoff between inflation and unemployment

- Explain how the mainstream business cycle theory and real businesses cycle theory account for fluctuations in output and employment

The 1920s were years of unprecedented prosperity for Canadians. After the horrors of the first World War (1914–1918), the economic machine was back at work producing such technological marvels as automobiles, airplanes, telephones, and vacuum cleaners. Houses were being built at a frantic pace. Then, in October 1929, the stock market crashed. Overnight, stock prices fell by 30 percent. The Great Depression had begun: By 1933, real GDP had fallen by 30 percent, the price level had fallen by 20 percent, and one person in five was unemployed.

The 1990s and 2000s were also years of unprecedented prosperity. Again, our lives were transformed by technological miracles: this time laptop computers, cell phones, large-format flat-panel video screens, and the Internet. Again,

homes, and especially city apartments, were built at a rapid pace. Then, in October 2008, stock prices tumbled, real GDP growth and inflation slowed, and the unemployment rate began to edge upward. People began to ask if we were on the verge of a new Great Depression.

We're going to use the *AS–AD* model that you studied in Chapter 26 and a related model, the Phillips curve, to explain the patterns in output, inflation, and unemployment. We then use the model of potential GDP that you studied in Chapter 22 to explain how business cycle fluctuations can arise without cost-push or aggregate demand forces.

In *Reading Between the Lines* at the end of the chapter, we examine the state of the Canadian economy in 2008 as the U.S economy slid into deeper recession.

Inflation Cycles

In the long run, inflation is a monetary phenomenon. It occurs if the quantity of money grows faster than potential GDP. But in the short run, many factors can start an inflation, and real GDP and the price level interact. To study these interactions, we distinguish between two sources of inflation:

- Demand-pull inflation
- Cost-push inflation

Demand-Pull Inflation

An inflation that starts because aggregate demand increases is called **demand-pull inflation**. Demand-pull inflation can be kicked off by *any* of the factors that change aggregate demand. Examples are a cut in the interest rate, an increase in the quantity of money, an increase in government expenditure, a tax cut, an increase in exports, or an increase in investment stimulated by an increase in expected future profits.

Initial Effect of an Increase in Aggregate Demand

Suppose that last year the price level was 110 and real GDP was $1,200 billion. Potential GDP was also $1,200 billion. Figure 28.1(a) illustrates this situation. The aggregate demand curve is AD_0, the short-run aggregate supply curve is SAS_0, and the long-run aggregate supply curve is LAS.

The Bank of Canada cuts the interest rate and increases the quantity of money and aggregate demand increases to AD_1. With no change in potential GDP and no change in the money wage rate, the long-run aggregate supply curve and the short-run aggregate supply curve remain at LAS and SAS_0, respectively.

The price level and real GDP are determined at the point where the aggregate demand curve AD_1 intersects the short-run aggregate supply curve. The price level rises to 113, and real GDP increases above potential GDP to $1,250 billion. Unemployment falls below its natural rate. The economy is at an above full-employment equilibrium and there is an inflationary gap. The next step in the unfolding story is a rise in the money wage rate.

FIGURE 28.1   A Demand-Pull Rise in the Price Level

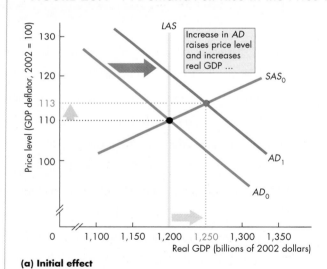

(a) Initial effect

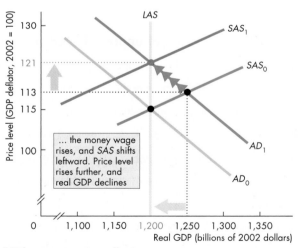

(b) The money wage adjusts

In part (a), the aggregate demand curve is AD_0, the short-run aggregate supply curve is SAS_0, and the long-run aggregate supply curve is LAS. The price level is 110, and real GDP is $1,200 billion, which equals potential GDP. Aggregate demand increases to AD_1. The price level rises to 113, and real GDP increases to $1,250 billion.

In part (b), starting from the above full-employment equilibrium, the money wage rate begins to rise and the short-run aggregate supply curve shifts leftward towards SAS_1. The price level rises further, and real GDP returns to potential GDP.

myeconlab animation

Money Wage Rate Response Real GDP cannot remain above potential GDP forever. With unemployment below its natural rate, there is a shortage of labour. In this situation, the money wage rate begins to rise. As it does so, short-run aggregate supply decreases and the *SAS* curve starts to shift leftward. The price level rises further, and real GDP begins to decrease.

With no further change in aggregate demand—that is, the aggregate demand curve remains at AD_1—this process ends when the short-run aggregate supply curve has shifted to SAS_1 in Fig. 28.1(b). At this time, the price level has increased to 121 and real GDP has returned to potential GDP of $1,200 billion, the level at which it started.

A Demand-Pull Inflation Process The events that we've just described bring a *one-time rise in the price level*, not an inflation. For inflation to proceed, aggregate demand must *persistently* increase.

The only way in which aggregate demand can persistently increase is if the quantity of money persistently increases. Suppose the government has a budget deficit that it finances by selling bonds. Also suppose that the Bank of Canada buys some of these bonds in the open market and creates more money. In this situation, aggregate demand increases year after year. The aggregate demand curve keeps shifting rightward. This persistent increase in aggregate demand puts continual upward pressure on the price level. The economy now experiences demand-pull inflation.

Figure 28.2 illustrates the process of demand-pull inflation. The starting point is the same as that shown in Fig. 28.1. The aggregate demand curve is AD_0, the short-run aggregate supply curve is SAS_0, and the long-run aggregate supply curve is *LAS*. Real GDP is $1,200 billion, and the price level is 110. Aggregate demand increases, shifting the aggregate demand curve to AD_1. Real GDP increases to $1,250 billion, and the price level rises to 113. The economy is at an above full-employment equilibrium. There is a shortage of labour, and the money wage rate rises. The short-run aggregate supply curve shifts to SAS_1. The price level rises to 121, and real GDP returns to potential GDP.

But the Bank of Canada increases the quantity of money again, and aggregate demand continues to increase. The aggregate demand curve shifts rightward to AD_2. The price level rises further to 125, and real GDP again exceeds potential GDP at

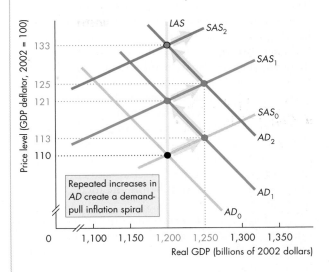

FIGURE 28.2   A Demand-Pull Inflation Spiral

Each time the quantity of money increases, aggregate demand increases and the aggregate demand curve shifts rightward from AD_0 to AD_1 to AD_2, and so on. Each time real GDP increases above potential GDP, the money wage rate rises and the short-run aggregate supply curve shifts leftward from SAS_0 to SAS_1 to SAS_2, and so on. The price level rises from 110 to 113, 121, 125, 133, and so on. There is a demand-pull inflation spiral. Real GDP fluctuates between $1,200 billion and $1,250 billion.

$1,250 billion. Yet again, the money wage rate rises and decreases short-run aggregate supply. The *SAS* curve shifts to SAS_2, and the price level rises further, to 133. As the quantity of money continues to grow, aggregate demand increases and the price level rises in an ongoing demand-pull inflation process.

The process you have just studied generates inflation—an ongoing process of a rising price level.

Demand-Pull Inflation in Chatham You may better understand the inflation process that we've just described by considering what is going on in an individual part of the economy, such as a Chatham ketchup-bottling plant. Initially, when aggregate demand increases, the demand for ketchup increases and the price of ketchup rises. Faced with a higher price, the ketchup plant works overtime and increases production. Conditions are good for workers in Chatham, and the ketchup factory finds it hard to hang on to its best people. To do so, it offers a higher money wage rate. As the wage rate rises, so do the ketchup factory's costs.

What happens next depends on aggregate demand. If aggregate demand remains constant, the firm's costs increase but the price of ketchup does not increase as quickly as its costs. In this case, the firm cuts production. Eventually, the money wage rate and costs increase by the same percentage as the rise in the price of ketchup. In real terms, the ketchup factory is in the same situation as it was initially. It produces the same amount of ketchup and employs the same amount of labour as before the increase in demand.

But if aggregate demand continues to increase, so does the demand for ketchup, and the price of ketchup rises at the same rate as wages. The ketchup factory continues to operate at above full employment and there is a persistent shortage of labour. Prices and wages chase each other upward in a demand-pull inflation spiral.

Demand-Pull Inflation in Canada A demand-pull inflation like the one you've just studied occurred in Canada during the late 1960s and early 1970s. In 1960, inflation was a moderate 2 percent a year, but its rate increased slowly through the mid-1960s. Then, between 1966 and 1969, the inflation rate surged upward. Inflation then decreased slightly during 1970 and 1971, but it took off again in 1972. By 1973, the inflation rate was almost 10 percent a year.

These increases in inflation resulted from increases in aggregate demand that had two main sources. The first was the large increase in U.S. government expenditures and in the quantity of money in the United States, which increased aggregate demand in the entire world economy. The second source was an increase in Canadian government expenditures and the quantity of money.

With the economy above full employment, the money wage rate started to rise more quickly and the *SAS* curve shifted leftward. The Bank of Canada responded with a further increase in the money growth rate, and a demand-pull inflation spiral unfolded. By 1974, the inflation rate had reached double digits.

Next, let's see how shocks to aggregate supply can create cost-push inflation.

Cost-Push Inflation

An inflation that is kicked off by an increase in costs is called **cost-push inflation**. The two main sources of cost increases are

1. An increase in the money wage rate
2. An increase in the money prices of raw materials

At a given price level, the higher the cost of production, the smaller is the amount that firms are willing to produce. So if the money wage rate rises or if the prices of raw materials (for example, oil) rise, firms decrease their supply of goods and services. Aggregate supply decreases, and the short-run aggregate supply curve shifts leftward.[1] Let's trace the effects of such a decrease in short-run aggregate supply on the price level and real GDP.

Initial Effect of a Decrease in Aggregate Supply

Suppose that last year the price level was 110 and real GDP was $1,200 billion. Potential real GDP was also $1,200 billion. Figure 28.3(a) illustrates this situation. The aggregate demand curve was AD_0, the short-run aggregate supply curve was SAS_0, and the long-run aggregate supply curve was *LAS*. In the current year, the world's oil producers form a price-fixing organization that strengthens their market power and increases the relative price of oil. They raise the price of oil, and this action decreases short-run aggregate supply. The short-run aggregate supply curve shifts leftward to SAS_1. The price level rises to 117, and real GDP decreases to $1,150 billion. The economy is at a below full-employment equilibrium and there is a recessionary gap.

This event is a *one-time rise in the price level*. It is not inflation. In fact, a supply shock on its own cannot cause inflation. Something more must happen to enable a one-time supply shock, which causes a one-time rise in the price level, to be converted into a process of ongoing inflation. The quantity of money must persistently increase. And it sometimes does increase, as you will now see.

---

[1] Some cost-push forces, such as an increase in the price of oil accompanied by a decrease in the availability of oil, can also decrease long-run aggregate supply. We'll ignore such effects here and examine cost-push factors that change only short-run aggregate supply. Later in the chapter, we study the effects of shocks to long-run aggregate supply.

FIGURE 28.3   A Cost-Push Rise in the Price Level

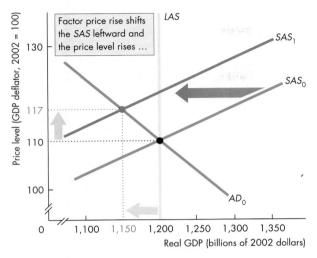

(a) Initial cost push

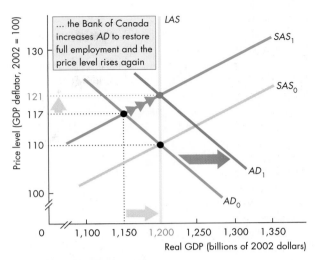

(b) The Bank of Canada responds

Initially, the aggregate demand curve is AD_0, the short-run aggregate supply curve is SAS_0, and the long-run aggregate supply curve is LAS. A decrease in aggregate supply (for example, resulting from a rise in the world price of oil) shifts the short-run aggregate supply curve to SAS_1. The economy moves to the point where the short-run aggregate supply curve SAS_1 intersects the aggregate demand curve

AD_0. The price level rises to 117, and real GDP decreases to $1,150 billion.

In part (b), if the Bank of Canada responds by increasing aggregate demand to restore full employment, the aggregate demand curve shifts rightward to AD_1. The economy returns to full employment, but the price level rises further to 121.

Aggregate Demand Response When real GDP decreases, unemployment rises above its natural rate. In such a situation, there is often an outcry of concern and a call for action to restore full employment. Suppose that the Bank of Canada cuts the interest rate and increases the quantity of money. Aggregate demand increases. In Fig. 28.3(b), the aggregate demand curve shifts rightward to AD_1 and full employment is restored. But the price level rises further to 121.

A Cost-Push Inflation Process The oil producers now see the prices of everything they buy increasing, so oil producers increase the price of oil again to restore its new high relative price. Figure 28.4 continues the story. The short-run aggregate supply curve now shifts to SAS_2. The price level rises and real GDP decreases.

The price level rises further, to 129, and real GDP decreases to $1,150 billion. Unemployment increases above its natural rate. If the Bank of Canada

responds yet again with an increase in the quantity of money, aggregate demand increases and the aggregate demand curve shifts to AD_2. The price level rises even higher—to 133—and full employment is again restored. A cost-push inflation spiral results. The combination of rising inflation and decreasing real GDP is **stagflation.**

You can see that the Bank of Canada has a dilemma. If it does not respond when producers raise the price of oil, the economy remains below full employment. If the Bank of Canada increases the quantity of money to restore full employment, it invites another oil price hike that will call forth yet a further increase in the quantity of money.

If the Bank of Canada responds to each oil price hike by increasing the quantity of money, inflation will rage along at a rate decided by oil producers. But if the Bank of Canada keeps the lid on money growth, the economy remains below full employment.

FIGURE 28.4   A Cost-Push Inflation Spiral

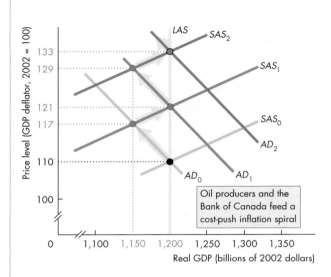

Oil producers and the Bank of Canada feed a cost-push inflation spiral

Each time a cost increase occurs, the short-run aggregate supply curve shifts leftward from SAS_0 to SAS_1 to SAS_2, and so on. Each time real GDP decreases below potential GDP, the Bank of Canada increases the quantity of money and the aggregate demand curve shifts rightward from AD_0 to AD_1 to AD_2, and so on. The price level rises from 110 to 117, 121, 129, 133, and so on. There is a cost-push inflation spiral. Real GDP fluctuates between $1,200 billion and $1,150 billion.

Cost-Push Inflation in Chatham What is going on in the Chatham ketchup-bottling plant when the economy is experiencing cost-push inflation?

When the oil price increases, so do the costs of bottling ketchup. These higher costs decrease the supply of ketchup, increasing its price and decreasing the quantity produced. The ketchup plant lays off some workers.

This situation persists until either the Bank of Canada increases aggregate demand or the price of oil falls. If the Bank of Canada increases aggregate demand, the demand for ketchup increases and so does its price. The higher price of ketchup brings higher profits, and the bottling plant increases its production. The ketchup factory rehires the laid-off workers.

Cost-Push Inflation in Canada A cost-push inflation like the one you've just studied occurred in Canada during the 1970s. It began in 1974 when the Organization of the Petroleum Exporting Countries (OPEC) pushed up the price of oil. The higher oil price decreased aggregate supply, which made the price level rise more quickly and made real GDP shrink. The Bank of Canada faced a dilemma: Would it accommodate the cost-push forces with money growth, or would it limit money growth to keep aggregate demand in check? From 1975 through 1977, the Bank of Canada allowed the quantity of money to grow quickly and inflation proceeded at a rapid rate. In 1979 and 1980, OPEC was again able to push oil prices higher. On that occasion, the Bank of Canada decided *not* to respond to the oil price hike with an increase in the quantity of money. The result was recession and, eventually, a fall in inflation.

Expected Inflation

If inflation is expected, the fluctuations in real GDP that accompany demand-pull and cost-push inflation that you've just studied don't occur. Instead, inflation proceeds with real GDP at potential GDP and unemployment at its natural rate. Figure 28.5 shows why.

Suppose that last year the aggregate demand curve was AD_0, the aggregate supply curve was SAS_0, and the long-run aggregate supply curve was LAS. The price level was 110, and real GDP was $1,200 billion, which is also potential GDP.

To keep things simple, suppose that potential GDP does not change, so the LAS curve doesn't shift. Also suppose that aggregate demand is *expected to increase* to AD_1.

In anticipation of this increase in aggregate demand, the money wage rate rises and the short-run aggregate supply curve shifts leftward. If the money wage rate rises by the same percentage as the price level is expected to rise, the short-run aggregate supply curve for next year is SAS_1.

If aggregate demand turns out to be the same as expected, the aggregate demand curve is AD_1. The short-run aggregate supply curve, SAS_1, and AD_1 determine the actual price level at 121. Between last year and this year, the price level increased from 110 to 121 and the economy experienced an inflation rate equal to that expected. If this inflation is ongoing, aggregate demand increases (as expected) in the

FIGURE 28.5 Expected Inflation

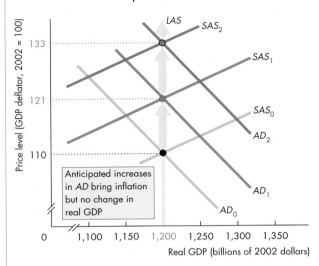

Potential real GDP is $1,200 billion. Last year, aggregate demand was AD_0 and the short-run aggregate supply curve was SAS_0. The actual price level was the same as the expected price level: 110. This year, aggregate demand is expected to increase to AD_1 and the price level is expected to rise from 110 to 121. As a result, the money wage rate rises and the short-run aggregate supply curve shifts to SAS_1.

If aggregate demand actually increases as expected, the actual aggregate demand curve AD_1 is the same as the expected aggregate demand curve. Real GDP is $1,200 billion, and the actual price level rises to 121. The inflation is expected.

Next year, the process continues with aggregate demand increasing as expected to AD_2 and the money wage rate rising to shift the short-run aggregate supply curve to SAS_2. Again, real GDP remains at $1,200 billion, and the price level rises, as expected, to 133.

[W] myeconlab animation

following year and the aggregate demand curve shifts to AD_2. The money wage rate rises to reflect the expected inflation, and the short-run aggregate supply curve shifts to SAS_2. The price level rises, as expected, to 133.

What caused this inflation? The immediate answer is that because people expected inflation, the money wage rate increased and the price level increased. But the expectation was correct. Aggregate demand was expected to increase, and it did increase. The actual and expected increase in aggregate demand caused the inflation.

An expected inflation at full employment is exactly the process that the quantity theory of money

predicts. To review the quantity theory of money, see Chapter 24, pp. 582–583. This broader *AS–AD* model of inflation shows why the quantity theory of money doesn't explain the *fluctuations* in inflation. The economy follows the course described in Fig. 28.5, and as predicted by the quantity theory, only if aggregate demand growth is forecasted correctly.

Forecasting Inflation

To anticipate inflation, people must forecast it. Some economists who work for macroeconomic forecasting agencies, banks, insurance companies, labour unions, and large corporations specialize in inflation forecasting. The best forecast available is one that is based on all the relevant information and is called a **rational expectation**. A rational expectation is not necessarily a correct forecast. It is simply the best forecast with the information available. It will often turn out to be wrong, but no other forecast that could have been made with the information available could do better.

Inflation and the Business Cycle

When the inflation forecast is correct, the economy operates at full employment. If aggregate demand grows faster than expected, real GDP rises above potential GDP, the inflation rate exceeds its expected rate, and the economy behaves like it does in a demand-pull inflation. If aggregate demand grows more slowly than expected, real GDP falls below potential GDP and the inflation rate slows.

Review Quiz

1 How does demand-pull inflation begin?
2 What must happen to create a demand-pull inflation spiral?
3 How does cost-push inflation begin?
4 What must happen to create a cost-push inflation spiral?
5 What is stagflation and why does cost-push inflation cause stagflation?
6 How does expected inflation occur?
7 How do real GDP and the price level change if the forecast of inflation is incorrect?

[W] myeconlab   Work Study Plan 28.1
and get instant feedback.

◆ Inflation and Unemployment: The Phillips Curve

Another way of studying inflation cycles focuses on the relationship and the short-run tradeoff between inflation and unemployment, a relationship called the **Phillips curve**—so named because it was first suggested by New Zealand economist A.W. Phillips.

Why do we need another way of studying inflation? What is wrong with the *AS–AD* explanation of the fluctuations in inflation and real GDP? The first answer to both questions is that we often want to study changes in both the expected and actual inflation rates, and for this purpose, the Phillips curve provides a simpler tool and clearer insights than the *AS–AD* model provides. The second answer to both questions is that we often want to study changes in the short-run tradeoff between inflation and real economic activity (real GDP and unemployment) and again, the Phillips curve serves this purpose well.

To begin our explanation of the Phillips curve, we distinguish between two time frames (similar to the two aggregate supply time frames). We study

- The short-run Phillips curve
- The long-run Phillips curve

The Short-Run Phillips Curve

The **short-run Phillips curve** shows the relationship between inflation and unemployment, holding constant

1. The expected inflation rate
2. The natural unemployment rate

You've just seen what determines the expected inflation rate. The natural unemployment rate and the factors that influence it are explained in Chapter 21, pp. 494–496.

Figure 28.6 shows a short-run Phillips curve, *SRPC*. Suppose that the expected inflation rate is 10 percent a year and the natural unemployment rate is 6 percent, point *A* in the figure. A short-run Phillips curve passes through this point. If inflation rises above its expected rate, unemployment falls below its natural rate. This joint movement in the inflation rate and the unemployment rate is illustrated as a movement up along the short-run Phillips curve from point *A* to point *B*. Similarly, if inflation falls below its expected rate, unemployment rises above its natural

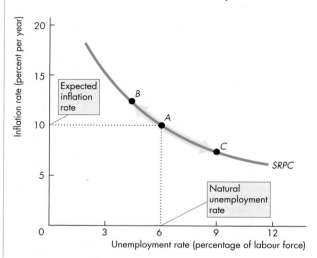

FIGURE 28.6   A Short-Run Phillips Curve

The short-run Phillips curve (*SRPC*) shows the relationship between inflation and unemployment at a given expected inflation rate and a given natural unemployment rate. With an expected inflation rate of 10 percent a year and a natural unemployment rate of 6 percent, the short-run Phillips curve passes through point *A*.

With a given short-run aggregate supply curve, and starting at full employment, an increase in aggregate demand lowers unemployment and increases the inflation rate—a movement up along the short-run Phillips curve to point *B*; and a decrease in aggregate demand increases unemployment and lowers the inflation rate—a movement down along the short-run Phillips curve to point *C*.

rate. In this case, there is movement down along the short-run Phillips curve from point *A* to point *C*.

The short-run Phillips curve is like the short-run aggregate supply curve. A movement along the *SAS* curve that brings a higher price level and an increase in real GDP is equivalent to a movement along the short-run Phillips curve from *A* to *B* that brings an increase in the inflation rate and a decrease in the unemployment rate.

Similarly, a movement along the *SAS* curve that brings a lower price level and a decrease in real GDP is equivalent to a movement along the short-run Phillips curve from *A* to *C* that brings a decrease in the inflation rate and an increase in the unemployment rate.

The Long-Run Phillips Curve

The **long-run Phillips curve** shows the relationship between inflation and unemployment when the actual inflation rate equals the expected inflation rate. The long-run Phillips curve is vertical at the natural unemployment rate. In Fig. 28.7, it is the vertical line *LRPC*.

The long-run Phillips curve tells us that any expected inflation rate is possible at the natural unemployment rate. This proposition is consistent with the *AS–AD* model, which predicts (and which Fig. 28.5 illustrates) that when inflation is expected, real GDP equals potential GDP and unemployment is at its natural rate.

The short-run Phillips curve intersects the long-run Phillips curve at the expected inflation rate. A change in the expected inflation rate shifts the short-run Phillips curve but it does not shift the long-run Phillips curve.

In Fig. 28.7, if the expected inflation rate is 10 percent a year, the short-run Phillips curve is $SRPC_0$.

If the expected inflation rate falls to 6 percent a year, the short-run Phillips curve shifts downward to $SRPC_1$. The vertical distance by which the short-run Phillips curve shifts from point *A* to point *D* is equal to the change in the expected inflation rate. If the actual inflation rate also falls from 10 percent to 6 percent, there is a movement down the long-run Phillips curve from *A* to *D*. An increase in the expected inflation rate has the opposite effect to that shown in Fig. 28.7.

The other source of a shift in the Phillips curve is a change in the natural unemployment rate.

Changes in the Natural Unemployment Rate

The natural unemployment rate changes for many reasons (see Chapter 21, pp. 494–496). A change in the natural unemployment rate shifts both the short-run and long-run Phillips curves. Figure 28.8 illustrates such shifts.

FIGURE 28.7 Short-Run and Long-Run Phillips Curve

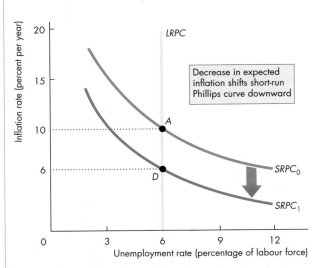

The long-run Phillips curve is *LRPC*. A fall in expected inflation from 10 percent a year to 6 percent a year shifts the short-run Phillips curve downward from $SRPC_0$ to $SRPC_1$. The long-run Phillips curve does not shift. The new short-run Phillips curve intersects the long-run Phillips curve at the new expected inflation rate — point *D*.

FIGURE 28.8 A Change in the Natural Unemployment Rate

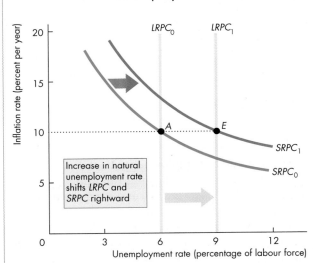

A change in the natural unemployment rate shifts both the short-run and long-run Phillips curves. An increase in the natural unemployment rate from 6 percent to 9 percent shifts the Phillips curves rightward to $SRPC_1$ and $LRPC_1$. The new long-run Phillips curve intersects the new short-run Phillips curve at the expected inflation rate — point *E*.

The Canadian Phillips Curve

The Shifting Short-Run Tradeoff

Figure 1 is a scatter diagram of the Canadian inflation rate (measured by the GDP deflator) and the unemployment rate since 1962. We can interpret the data in terms of the shifting short-run Phillips curve in Fig. 2.

During the 1960s, the short-run Phillips curve was $SRPC_0$, with a natural unemployment rate of 5 percent and an expected inflation rate of 2 percent a year (point A).

During the early 1970s, the short-run Phillips curve was $SRPC_1$, with a natural unemployment rate of 6 percent and an expected inflation rate of 10 percent a year (point B).

During the 1980s, the natural unemployment rate increased to 10 percent, the expected inflation rate fell to 8 percent (point C), and the short-run Phillips curve shifted to $SRPC_2$.

During the 1990s and 2000s, the expected inflation rate fell to 2 percent a year and and the natural unemployment rate decreased to 6 percent. The short-run Phillips curve shifted leftward to $SRPC_3$ and was almost back to $SRPC_0$, where it had been during the 1960s.

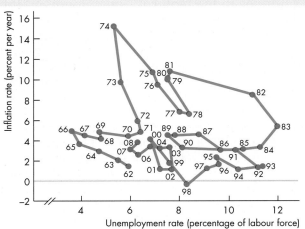

Figure 1 Phillips Curve Data in Canada: The Time Sequence

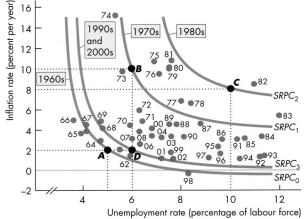

Figure 2 The Shifting Phillips Curves

Source of data: Statistics Canada, CANSIM Tables 380-0002 and 380-0056.

If the natural unemployment rate increases from 6 percent to 9 percent, the long-run Phillips curve shifts from $LRPC_0$ to $LRPC_1$, and if expected inflation is constant at 10 percent a year, the short-run Phillips curve shifts from $SRPC_0$ to $SRPC_1$. Because the expected inflation rate is constant, the short-run Phillips curve $SRPC_1$ intersects the long-run curve $LRPC_1$ (point E) at the same inflation rate at which the short-run Phillips curve $SRPC_0$ intersects the long-run curve $LRPC_0$ (point A).

Changes in both the expected inflation rate and the natural unemployment rate have shifted the Canadian Phillips curve but the expected inflation rate has had the greater effect.

Review Quiz

1 How would you use the Phillips curve to illustrate an unexpected change in inflation?

2 If the expected inflation rate increases by 10 percentage points, how do the short-run Phillips curve and the long-run Phillips curve change?

3 If the natural unemployment rate increases, what happens to the short-run Phillips curve and the long-run Phillips curve?

4 Does Canada have a stable short-run Phillips curve? Explain why or why not.

 Work Study Plan 28.2 and get instant feedback.

◆ The Business Cycle

The business cycle is easy to describe but hard to explain and business cycle theory remains unsettled and a source of controversy. We'll look at two approaches to understanding the business cycle:

- Mainstream business cycle theory
- Real business cycle theory

Mainstream Business Cycle Theory

The mainstream business cycle theory is that potential GDP grows at a steady rate while aggregate demand grows at a fluctuating rate. Because the money wage rate is sticky, if aggregate demand grows faster than potential GDP, real GDP moves above potential GDP and an inflationary gap emerges. And if aggregate demand grows slower than potential GDP, real GDP moves below potential GDP and a recessionary gap emerges. If aggregate demand decreases, real GDP also decreases in a recession.

Figure 28.9 illustrates this business cycle theory. Initially, actual and potential GDP are $900 billion. The long-run aggregate supply curve is LAS_0, the aggregate demand curve is AD_0, and the price level is 110. The economy is at full employment at point A.

An expansion occurs when potential GDP increases and the LAS curve shifts rightward to LAS_1. During an expansion, aggregate demand also increases, and usually by more than potential GDP, so the price level rises. Assume that in the current expansion, the price level is expected to rise to 120 and that the money wage rate has been set on that expectation. The short-run aggregate supply curve is SAS_1.

If aggregate demand increases to AD_1, real GDP increases to $1,200 billion, the new level of potential GDP, and the price level rises, as expected, to 120. The economy remains at full employment but now at point B.

If aggregate demand increases more slowly to AD_2, real GDP grows by less than potential GDP and the economy moves to point C, with real GDP at $1,150 billion and the price level at 117. Real GDP growth is slower and inflation is lower than expected.

If aggregate demand increases more quickly to AD_3, real GDP grows by more than potential GDP and the economy moves to point D, with real GDP at $1,250 billion and the price level at 123. Real GDP growth is faster and inflation is higher than expected.

Growth, inflation, and the business cycle arise from the relentless increases in potential GDP, faster (on average) increases in aggregate demand, and fluctuations in the pace of aggregate demand growth.

FIGURE 28.9 The Mainstream Business Cycle Theory

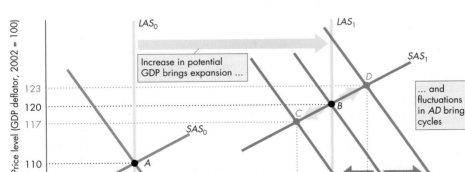

In a business cycle expansion, potential GDP increases and the LAS curve shifts rightward from LAS_0 to LAS_1. A greater-than-expected increase in aggregate demand brings inflation.

If the aggregate demand curve shifts to AD_1, the economy remains at full employment. If the aggregate demand curve shifts to AD_2, a recessionary gap arises. If the aggregate demand curve shifts to AD_3, an inflationary gap arises.

This mainstream theory comes in a number of special forms that differ regarding the source of fluctuations in aggregate demand growth and the source of money wage stickiness.

Keynesian Cycle Theory In **Keynesian cycle theory**, fluctuations in investment driven by fluctuations in business confidence—summarized by the phrase "animal spirits"—are the main source of fluctuations in aggregate demand.

Monetarist Cycle Theory In **monetarist cycle theory**, fluctuations in both investment and consumption expenditure, driven by fluctuations in the growth rate of the quantity of money, are the main source of fluctuations in aggregate demand.

Both the Keynesian and monetarist cycle theories simply assume that the money wage rate is rigid and don't explain that rigidity.

Two newer theories seek to explain money wage rate rigidity and to be more careful about working out its consequences.

New Classical Cycle Theory In **new classical cycle theory**, the rational expectation of the price level, which is determined by potential GDP and *expected* aggregate demand, determines the money wage rate and the position of the *SAS* curve. In this theory, only *unexpected* fluctuations in aggregate demand bring fluctuations in real GDP around potential GDP.

New Keynesian Cycle Theory The **new Keynesian cycle theory** emphasizes the fact that today's money wage rates were negotiated at many past dates, which means that *past* rational expectations of the current price level influence the money wage rate and the position of the *SAS* curve. In this theory, both unexpected and currently expected fluctuations in aggregate demand bring fluctuations in real GDP around potential GDP.

The mainstream cycle theories don't rule out the possibility that occasionally an aggregate supply shock might occur. An oil price rise, a widespread drought, a major hurricane, or another natural disaster could, for example, bring a recession. But supply shocks are not the normal source of fluctuations in the mainstream theories. In contrast, real business cycle theory puts supply shocks at centre stage.

Real Business Cycle Theory

The newest theory of the business cycle, known as **real business cycle theory** (or RBC theory), regards random fluctuations in productivity as the main source of economic fluctuations. These productivity fluctuations are assumed to result mainly from fluctuations in the pace of technological change, but they might also have other sources, such as international disturbances, climate fluctuations, or natural disasters. The origins of RBC theory can be traced to the rational expectations revolution set off by Robert E. Lucas, Jr., but the first demonstrations of the power of this theory were given by Edward Prescott and Finn Kydland and by John Long and Charles Plosser. Today, RBC theory is part of a broad research agenda called dynamic general equilibrium analysis, and hundreds of young macroeconomists do research on this topic.

We'll explore RBC theory by looking first at its impulse and then at the mechanism that converts that impulse into a cycle in real GDP.

The RBC Impulse The impulse in RBC theory is the growth rate of productivity that results from technological change. RBC theorists believe this impulse to be generated mainly by the process of research and development that leads to the creation and use of new technologies.

To isolate the RBC theory impulse, economists use growth accounting, which is explained in Chapter 22, p. 528. Figure 28.10 shows the RBC impulse for Canada from 1962 through 2007. You can see that fluctuations in productivity growth are correlated with real GDP fluctuations.

Most of the time, technological change is steady and productivity grows at a moderate pace. But sometimes productivity growth speeds up, and occasionally productivity *decreases*—labour becomes less productive, on average. A period of rapid productivity growth brings a business cycle expansion, and a *decrease* in productivity triggers a recession.

It is easy to understand why technological change brings productivity growth. But how does it *decrease* productivity? All technological change eventually increases productivity. But if initially, technological change makes a sufficient amount of existing capital—especially human capital—obsolete, productivity temporarily decreases. At such a time, more jobs are destroyed than created and more businesses fail than start up.

FIGURE 28.10 The Real Business Cycle Impulse

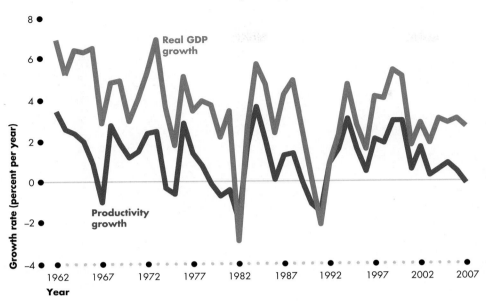

The real business cycle is caused by changes in technology that bring fluctuations in the growth rate of productivity. The fluctuations in productivity growth shown here are calculated by using growth accounting to remove the contribution of capital accumulation to productivity growth. Productivity fluctuations are correlated with real GDP fluctuations. Economists are not sure what the productivity variable actually measures or what causes it to fluctuate.

Sources of data: Statistics Canada, CANSIM Table 380-0002 and Centre for the Study of Living Standards (www.csls.ca/data/ipt1.asp).

The RBC Mechanism Two effects follow from a change in productivity that gets an expansion or a contraction going:

1. Investment demand changes.
2. The demand for labour changes.

We'll study these effects and their consequences during a recession. In an expansion, they work in the direction opposite to what is described here.

Technological change makes some existing capital obsolete and temporarily decreases productivity. Firms expect their future profits to fall and see their labour productivity falling. With lower profit expectations, they cut back their purchases of new capital, and with lower labour productivity, they plan to lay off some workers. So the initial effect of a temporary fall in productivity is a decrease in investment demand and a decrease in the demand for labour.

Figure 28.11 illustrates these two initial effects of a decrease in productivity. Part (a) shows the effects of a decrease in investment demand in the loanable funds market. The demand for loanable funds is DLF and the supply of loanable funds is SLF (both of which are explained in Chapter 23, pp. 548–554). Initially, the demand for loanable funds is DLF_0 and the equilibrium quantity of funds is $200 billion at a real interest rate of 6 percent a year. A decrease in productivity decreases investment demand, and the demand for loanable funds curve DLF shifts leftward to DLF_1. The real interest rate falls to 4 percent a year, and the equilibrium quantity of loanable funds decreases to $170 billion.

Figure 28.11(b) shows the demand for labour curve LD and the supply of labour curve LS (which are explained in Chapter 22, pp. 521–522). Initially, the demand for labour curve is LD_0, and equilibrium employment is 20 billion hours a year at a real wage rate of $35 an hour. The decrease in productivity decreases the demand for labour, and the LD curve shifts leftward to LD_1.

Before we can determine the new level of employment and real wage rate, we need to take a ripple effect into account—the key effect in RBC theory.

The Key Decision: When to Work? According to RBC theory, people decide *when* to work by doing a cost-benefit calculation. They compare the return from

FIGURE 28.11 Loanable Funds and Labour Markets in a Real Business Cycle

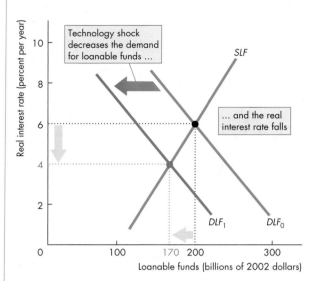

(a) Loanable funds and interest rate

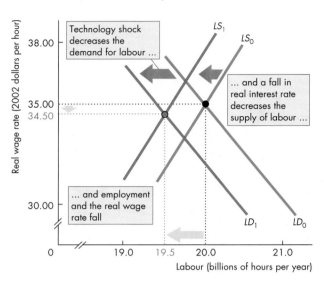

(b) Labour and wage rate

In part (a), the supply of loanable funds *SLF* and initial demand for loanable funds *DLF*$_0$ determine the real interest rate at 6 percent a year. In part (b), the initial demand for labour, *LD*$_0$, and supply of labour, *LS*$_0$, determine the real wage rate at $35 an hour and employment at 20 billion hours. A technological change temporarily decreases productivity, and both the demand for loanable funds and the

demand for labour decrease. The two demand curves shift leftward to *DLF*$_1$ and *LD*$_1$. In part (a), the real interest rate falls to 4 percent a year. In part (b), the fall in the real interest rate decreases the supply of labour (the when-to-work decision) and the supply of labour curve shifts leftward to *LS*$_1$. Employment decreases to 19.5 billion hours, and the real wage rate falls to $34.50 an hour. A recession is underway.

working in the current period with the *expected* return from working in a later period. You make such a comparison every day in school. Suppose your goal in this course is to get an A. To achieve this goal, you work hard most of the time. But during the few days before the midterm and final exams, you work especially hard. Why? Because you believe that the return from studying close to the exam is greater than the return from studying when the exam is a long time away. So during the term, you take time off for movies and other leisure pursuits, but at exam time, you study every evening and weekend.

RBC theory says that workers behave like you. They work fewer hours, sometimes zero hours, when the real wage rate is temporarily low, and they work more hours when the real wage rate is temporarily high. But to properly compare the current wage rate with the expected future wage rate, workers must use

the real interest rate. If the real interest rate is 6 percent a year, a real wage of $1 an hour earned this week will become $1.06 a year from now. If the real wage rate is expected to be $1.05 an hour next year, today's real wage of $1 looks good. By working longer hours now and shorter hours a year from now, a person can get a 1 percent higher real wage. But suppose the real interest rate is 4 percent a year. In this case, $1 earned now is worth $1.04 next year. Working fewer hours now and more next year is the way to get a 1 percent higher real wage.

So the when-to-work decision depends on the real interest rate. The lower the real interest rate, other things remaining the same, the smaller is the supply of labour today. Many economists believe this *intertemporal substitution* effect to be of negligible size. RBC theorists believe that the effect is large, and it is the key feature of the RBC mechanism.

You saw in Fig. 28.11(a) that the decrease in the demand for loanable funds lowers the real interest rate. This fall in the real interest rate lowers the return from current work and decreases the supply of labour.

In Fig. 28.11(b), the labour supply curve shifts leftward to LS_1. The effect of the decrease in productivity on the demand for labour is larger than the effect of the fall in the real interest rate on the supply of labour. That is, the LD curve shifts farther leftward than does the LS curve. As a result, the real wage rate falls to $34.50 an hour and employment decreases to 19.5 billion hours. A recession has begun and is intensifying.

What Happened to Money?   The name *real* business cycle theory is no accident. It reflects the central prediction of the theory. Real things, not nominal or monetary things, cause the business cycle. If the quantity of money changes, aggregate demand changes. But if there is no real change—with no change in the use of resources and no change in potential GDP—the change in the quantity of money changes only the price level. In RBC theory, this outcome occurs because the aggregate supply curve is the *LAS* curve, which pins real GDP down at potential GDP, so when aggregate demand changes, only the price level changes.

Cycles and Growth   The shock that drives the business cycle of RBC theory is the same as the force that generates economic growth: technological change. On average, as technology advances, productivity grows. But it grows at an uneven pace. You saw this fact when you studied growth accounting in Chapter 22, p. 528. There, we focused on slow-changing trends in productivity growth. RBC theory uses the same idea but says that there are frequent shocks to productivity that are mostly positive but that are occasionally negative.

Criticisms and Defences of RBC Theory   The three main criticisms of RBC theory are that (1) the money wage rate *is* sticky, and to assume otherwise is at odds with a clear fact; (2) intertemporal substitution is too weak a force to account for large fluctuations in labour supply and employment with small real wage rate changes; and (3) productivity shocks are as likely to be caused by *changes in aggregate demand* as by technological change.

If aggregate demand fluctuations cause the fluctuations in productivity, then the traditional aggregate demand theories are needed to explain them. Fluctuations in productivity do not cause the business cycle but are caused by it!

Building on this theme, the critics point out that the so-called productivity fluctuations that growth accounting measures are correlated with changes in the growth rate of money and other indicators of changes in aggregate demand.

The defenders of RBC theory claim that the theory explains the macroeconomic facts about the business cycle and is consistent with the facts about economic growth. In effect, a single theory explains *both growth and the business cycle*. The growth accounting exercise that explains the slowly changing trends also explains the more frequent business cycle swings. Its defenders also claim that RBC theory is consistent with a wide range of *micro*economic evidence about labour supply decisions, labour demand and investment demand decisions, and information on the distribution of income between labour and capital.

Review Quiz

1   Explain the mainstream theory of the business cycle.
2   What are the four versions of the mainstream theory and how do they differ?
3   What, according to RBC theory, is the source of the business cycle?
4   According to RBC theory, how does a fall in productivity growth influence investment demand, the market for loanable funds, the real interest rate, the demand for labour, the supply of labour, employment, and the real wage rate?
5   What are the main criticisms of RBC theory and how do its supporters defend it?

 Work Study Plan 28.3 and get instant feedback.

◆   To complete your study of economic fluctuations, take a look at the next two pages, where you will find an account of the Great Depression and an assessment of its possible return. Also, study *Reading Between the Lines* on pp. 696–697, which compares job losses in Canada and the United States during the 2007–2008 financial crisis and slowdown.

The Great Depression

From Recession to Deep Depression

The late 1920s were years of economic boom. New houses and apartments were built on an unprecedented scale, new firms were created, and the capital stock expanded. At the beginning of 1929, Canadian real GDP exceeded potential GDP and the unemployment rate was a low 2.9 percent. But the four years that followed saw a monstrous depression.

In a normal recession, the economy remains below full employment for a year or so and then starts to expand. But the recession of 1930 was not a normal one. In 1930 and the following two years, the economy was bombarded with huge negative aggregate demand shocks.

Why the Great Depression Happened

The late 1920s were years of economic boom, but they were also years of change and uncertainty. On the international scene, the patterns of world trade were changing, with Britain, the traditional economic powerhouse, in decline, and new powers, notably the United States and Japan, on the rise. Exchange rates fluctuated widely and some countries embarked on protectionist trade policies. On the domestic scene, uncertainty arose from the knowledge that the investment and housing boom couldn't last forever.

This environment of uncertainty led to a slowdown in consumer spending, especially on new homes and household appliances. By the fall of 1929, the uncertainty had reached a critical level and contributed to a major stock market crash. The stock market crash, in turn, heightened people's fears about economic prospects in the foreseeable future. Fear fed fear. Investment collapsed. The building industry almost disappeared. An industry that had been operating flat out just two years earlier was now building virtually no new houses and apartments. It was this drop in investment and the drop in consumer spending on durables that led to the initial decrease in aggregate demand.

At this stage, what became the Great Depression was no worse than many previous recessions had been. What distinguished the Great Depression from previous recessions were the events that occurred in the United States between 1930 and 1933. But economists, even to this day, have not come to agreement on how to interpret those events.

Nobel Laureate Milton Friedman and his co-researcher Anna J. Schwartz have argued that the contraction that turned recession into depression resulted from the worsening of financial and monetary conditions. Bank failures and a severe cut in the money supply lowered aggregate demand, prolonged the contraction, and deepened the depression.

Peter Temin has argued that spending continued to fall for a wide variety of reasons, including a continuation of increasing pessimism and uncertainty, but not from a collapse in the quantity of money.

It is a fact that the quantity of money fell: Between 1930 and 1933, it fell by 20 percent. This decrease in the quantity of money was not directly induced by the U.S. Fed's actions. The monetary base (currency in circulation and bank reserves) hardly fell at all, but the bank-deposits component of the money supply suffered an enormous collapse. It did so primarily because a large number of banks failed. Before the Great Depression, fuelled by increasing stock prices and booming business conditions, bank loans expanded. But after the stock market crash and the downturn, many borrowers found themselves in hard economic times. They could not pay the interest on their loans, and they could not meet their agreed repayment schedules. Bank deposits exceeded the value of the loans that the banks had made. When depositors withdrew funds from the banks, the banks lost reserves. Many of them simply couldn't meet their depositors' demands to be repaid.

Bank failures feed on themselves and create additional failures. Seeing banks fail, people become anxious to protect themselves and so take their money out of the bank. Such were the events of 1930. The quantity of notes and coins in circulation increased, and the volume of bank deposits declined. But the very action of taking money out of the bank to protect one's wealth accentuated the process of banking failure. Banks were increasingly short of cash and unable to meet their obligations.

What role did the stock market crash of 1929 play in producing the Great Depression? The crash certainly created an atmosphere of fear and panic and probably also contributed to the overall air of uncertainty that dampened investment spending. The crash also reduced the wealth of shareholders, encouraging them to cut back on their consumption spending. But the direct effect of the stock market crash on consumption, although a contributory factor to the Great Depression, was not the major source of the drop in aggregate demand. The collapse of investment arising from increased uncertainty brought the 1930 decline in aggregate demand.

The stock market crash was a predictor of severe recession. It reflected the expectations of shareholders concerning future profit prospects. As those expectations became pessimistic, people sold their shares. There were more sellers than buyers, and the share prices were bid lower and lower. That is, the behaviour of the stock market was a consequence of expectations about future profitability, and those expectations were lowered as a result of increased uncertainty.

Can It Happen Again?

Because we have an incomplete understanding of the causes of the Great Depression, we cannot be sure whether such an event will happen again. The economic turmoil of the 1920s that preceded the depression could certainly happen again. And the financial turmoil of 2007 and 2008 has an eerie similarity to the years leading into the Great Depression.

But there are significant differences between the economy of the 2000s and that of the 1930s that make a depression less likely today than it was 80 years ago. The most significant features of the economy that make severe depression less likely today are

- Bank deposit insurance
- Central banks as lenders of last resort
- Taxes and government spending
- Multi-income families

Bank Deposit Insurance As a direct result of the Great Depression, governments around the world, including in Canada, established institutions that insure bank deposits in the event of bank failure. If bank deposits had been insured before the Great Depression, the key event that turned an ordinary recession into the Great Depression is unlikely to have occurred. It was the fear of bank failure that caused people to withdraw their deposits from banks. The aggregate consequence of these individually rational acts was to cause the very bank failures that were feared. With deposit insurance, most depositors have nothing to lose if a bank fails and so have no incentive to take actions that are likely to give rise to that failure. But despite deposit insurance, the U.K. bank Northern Rock experienced a severe loss of deposits in the current financial crisis.

Lender of Last Resort Central banks today are making billions of dollars of both reserves and capital available to banks. It is generally agreed that the U.S. Federal Reserve made a serious mistake in its handling of monetary policy during the Great Depression by not being aggressive in keeping banks afloat. With an eye on the international situation, the Federal Reserve actually increased the overnight rate just when the banks needed to borrow more. Today, central banks are cutting interest rates.

Taxes and Government Spending The government sector was a much smaller part of the economy in 1929 than it is today. On the eve of that earlier recession, government purchases of goods and services were less than 11 percent of GDP. Today, they exceed 20 percent of GDP. Government transfer payments were less than 5 percent of GDP in 1929. Today, they too exceed 20 percent of GDP.

A larger level of government purchases of goods and services and transfer payments means that today we have a much more sensitive automatic stabilizer than the one available in 1929.

Multi-Income Families At the time of the Great Depression, families with more than one wage earner were much less common than they are today.

For the four reasons we have just reviewed, it appears that the economy has better shock-absorbing characteristics today than it had in the 1920s and 1930s. Even if there is a collapse of confidence, leading to a fall in investment, today's shock absorbers will not translate that initial shock into the large and prolonged fall in real GDP and rise in unemployment that occurred more than 70 years ago.

Because economies are now more immune to severe recession than they were in the 1930s, even a stock market crash of the magnitude that occurred in the United States in 2007 and 2008 had a small effect on spending. A crash of a similar magnitude in 1929 resulted in the near collapse of housing investment and consumer durable purchases. In the months following the current stock market crash, U.S. investment and spending on durable goods remained remarkably high.

None of this is to say that there might not be a deep recession or even a great depression in the 2010s (or beyond). But it would take a very severe shock to trigger one.

Onset of Recession in Canada and the United States

Massive Job Losses Hit Canada, U.S.

December 5, 2008

The Canadian economy lost a much greater than feared 71,000 jobs in November, the worst monthly loss in more than a quarter century, and a taste of what's to come, while the U.S. lost more than half a million more jobs, bringing the losses since the recession there began a year ago to nearly 1.9 million.

"With today's dismal employment reports, there is no doubt that the Canadian economy is in recession and the U.S. contraction is accelerating," said BMO Capital Markets chief economist Sherry Cooper. ...

... [T]he much worse than expected job losses were the most since the early-1980s recession, ending three straight months of gains and nudging the unemployment rate up a notch to a two-year high of 6.3 percent. ...

"Today's labour market report is further evidence that Canada's economy—particularly its manufacturing sector—is facing enormous challenges as a result of the global slowdown," said Finance Minister Jim Flaherty, adding that new measures needed to stimulate the economy will be included in his Jan. 27 budget. ...

The Canadian job market, however, is in a lot better shape than the U.S. labour market, having created 133,000 jobs during the first 11 months of the year, compared with the loss of nearly 2 million jobs there.

"For the 11th month in a row, U.S. employment shrank, and in November, shrank it did," BMO Capital Markets economist Jennifer Lee observed in the wake of news of the loss of a further 533,000 jobs, the worst in a third of a century. ...

Essence of the Story

- Canadian employment decreased by 71,000 in November 2008, the worst monthly loss since the early 1980s recession.

- The unemployment rate reached a two-year high of 6.3 percent.

- Canadian employment increased by 133,000 during the first 11 months of 2008.

- U.S. employment decreased by 533,000 in November 2008.

- U.S. employment decreased every month in 2008 and the decrease totalled 1.9 million by November.

Economic Analysis

- The most recent phase of the Canadian business cycle is very different from that in the United States.

- The news article provides one indicator of the business cycle: employment numbers during 2008 for Canada and the United States.

- The data graphed in the figures put the 2008 employment numbers in a longer perspective.

- In 2001, the United States had a mild recession and Canada had a growth rate slowdown.

- Figure 1 shows that following the 2001 recession, the labour force participation rate in Canada surged upward from 66 percent to 68 percent. At the same time, the U.S. labour force participation rate sagged from 67 percent to 66 percent.

- Figure 2 shows that following the 2001 recession, the employment rate (the employment-to-population ratio) in the United States kept falling. It did not turn upward until late 2003 and it stopped rising at the end of 2006. Through 2007 and 2008, the U.S. employment rate plunged from 63 percent to 61 percent.

- Figure 2 also shows that Canadian employment surged upward from around 61 percent to 64 percent and kept on rising through 2007 when U.S. employment was falling. Canadian employment fell only slightly during 2008.

- Figure 3 shows that the Canadian unemployment rate has been higher than the U.S. rate. But the Canadian unemployment rate kept falling through 2007 while the U.S. rate was rising. The rapid rise in the U.S. unemployment rate during 2008 is not matched by the Canadian rate.

- Why did Canada escape the severe fall in employment and rise in unemployment that the United States experienced?

- The trigger that sent the U.S. economy crashing was a collapse in house prices and its effects on the credit markets. This problem was much less severe in Canada.

- Canada produces more resources (oil, natural gas, and minerals) than the United States and all of these items were still booming through 2007.

- The Canadian dollar depreciated, which helped to keep Canadian exports high and imports low and prevent aggregate demand from falling.

Figure 1 Labour force participation rates

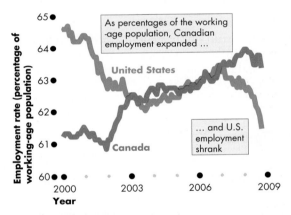

Figure 2 Employment rates

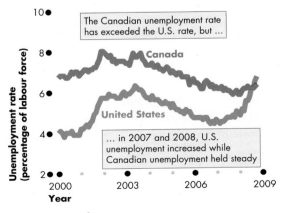

Figure 3 Unemployment rates

SUMMARY

Key Points

Inflation Cycles (pp. 680–685)

- Demand-pull inflation is triggered by an increase in aggregate demand and fuelled by ongoing money growth. Real GDP cycles above full employment.
- Cost-push inflation is triggered by an increase in the money wage rate or raw material prices and is fuelled by ongoing money growth. Real GDP cycles below full employment in a stagflation.
- When the forecast of inflation is correct, real GDP remains at potential GDP.

Inflation and Unemployment: The Phillips Curve (pp. 686–688)

- The short-run Phillips curve shows the tradeoff between inflation and unemployment when the expected inflation rate and the natural unemployment rate are constant.

- The long-run Phillips curve, which is vertical, shows that when the actual inflation rate equals the expected inflation rate, the unemployment rate equals the natural unemployment rate.

The Business Cycle (pp. 689–695)

- The mainstream business cycle theory explains the business cycle as fluctuations of real GDP around potential GDP and as arising from a steady expansion of potential GDP combined with an expansion of aggregate demand at a fluctuating rate.
- Real business cycle theory explains the business cycle as fluctuations of potential GDP, which arise from fluctuations in the influence of technological change on productivity growth.

Key Figures

Key Terms

PROBLEMS and APPLICATIONS ◆

 Work problems 1–9 in Chapter 28 Study Plan and get instant feedback.
Work problems 10–17 as Homework, a Quiz, or a Test if assigned by your instructor.

1. The spreadsheet provides information about the economy in Argentina. Column A is the year, Column B is real GDP in billions of 2000 pesos, and Column C is the price level.

	A	B	C
1	1997	277	105.6
2	1998	288	103.8
3	1999	278	101.9
4	2000	276	102.9
5	2001	264	101.8
6	2002	235	132.9
7	2003	256	146.8
8	2004	279	160.4
9	2005	305	174.5
10	2006	331	198.0
11	2007	359	226.1
12	2008	384	267.7

  a. In which years did Argentina experience inflation? In which years did it experience deflation (a falling price level)?
  b. In which years did recessions occur? In which years did expansions occur?
  c. In which years do you expect the unemployment rate was highest? Why?
  d. Do these data show a relationship between unemployment and inflation in Argentina?

Use the following figure to answer problems 2, 3, 4, and 5. In each question the economy starts out on the curves AD_0 and SAS_0.

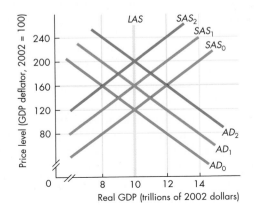

2. Some events occur and the economy experiences a demand-pull inflation.

  a. List the events that might cause a demand-pull inflation.
  b. Describe the initial effects of a demand-pull inflation.
  c. Describe what happens as a demand-pull inflation spiral proceeds.

3. Some events occur and the economy experiences a cost-push inflation.

  a. List the events that might cause a cost-push inflation.
  b. Describe the initial effects of a cost-push inflation.
  c. Describe what happens as a cost-push inflation spiral proceeds.

4. Some events occur and the economy is expected to experience inflation.

  a. List the events that might cause an expected inflation.
  b. Describe the initial effects of an expected inflation.
  c. Describe what happens as an expected inflation proceeds.

5. Suppose that people expect deflation (a falling price level), but aggregate demand remains at AD_0.

  a. What happens to the short-run and long-run aggregate supply curves? (Draw some new curves if you need to.)
  b. Describe the initial effects of an expected deflation.
  c. Describe what happens as it becomes obvious to everyone that the expected deflation is not going to occur.

6. **The Right Way to Beat Chinese Inflation**
  High inflation is threatening social stability in China, soaring from 3.3 percent in March 2007 to 8.3 percent in March 2008. ... China's accelerating inflation reflects a similar climb in its GDP growth rate, from the already high 11 percent in 2006 to 11.5 percent in 2007. The proximate cause of price growth since mid-2007 is the

appearance of production bottlenecks as domestic demand exceeds supply in an increasing number of sectors, such as power generation, transportation, and intermediate-goods industries. ... [T]he prolonged rapid increase in Chinese aggregate demand has been fueled by an investment boom, as well as a growing trade surplus. ...

Brookings Institution, July 2, 2008

a. Is China experiencing demand-pull or cost-push inflation? Explain.
b. Draw a graph to illustrate the initial rise in the price level and the money wage rate response to a one-time rise in the price level.
c. Draw a graph to illustrate and explain how China might experience an inflation spiral.

7. Recession? Maybe. Depression? Get Real.

The [U.S.] unemployment rate skyrocketed during the Depression, peaking at nearly 25 percent in 1933. The current [U.S.] unemployment rate is just 5 percent. And that's only up from 4.5 percent a year ago. Contrast that with the " far more explosive spike at the beginning of the Great Depression—from about 3 percent in 1929 to nearly 8.7 percent in 1930. ... Another hallmark of the Depression was deflation, which is obviously not happening today. ...

CNN, May 28, 2008

a. Can the inflation and unemployment trends during the Great Depression be explained by a movement along a short-run Phillips curve?
b. Can the inflation and unemployment trends during 2008 be explained by a movement along a short-run Phillips curve?

8. Energy Power Inflation to 3.5%

Canada's inflation rate last month was the highest in more than five years ... but economists say they're not overly concerned because the pace of increases appears to be slowing. Statistics Canada's consumer price index ... rose 3.5 percent between August 2007 and last month. ... "There are some grounds for optimism," said Dale Orr of the forecasting firm Global Insight Canada. "This inflation reading continues to support our forecast for a 2.7 percent increase in the over-all CPI this year, with the pace of inflation falling to the two percent level about mid-2009."... The Statistics Canada report Tuesday showed just how much inflation is tied to the price of oil. Overall, energy prices have risen 20.2

percent over the past 12 months, accounting for about half of the overall inflation run-up. ...

CNEWS, September 23, 2008

a. Explain the difference between demand-pull and cost-push inflation and use graphs to illustrate.
b. Which source more accurately describes the high inflation Canada was experiencing according to this article? Will this lead to an inflation spiral? Explain.
c. What factors may lead to a lower future inflation rate?

9. Economy on Verge of Recession, Central Bank Warns

The Canadian economy will be on the verge of recession until the spring, the Bank of Canada warned Thursday, slashing its forecast for growth to an anemic 0.6 percent this year and again next year, the weakest performance since the previous recession in the early 1990s. But the "sky is not falling," governor Mark Carney said. ... [H]e refused to label the downwardly revised forecast performance a recession, preferring instead to call it "sluggish." ... [Carney] projects strong growth of 3.4 percent in 2010. ... Statistics Canada in its report noted that in recent months growth and employment in Canada have been strong. ... Canadian employment last month and overall economic output earlier in the summer posted "large gains," Statistics Canada said, suggesting that the abrupt turnaround in both after months of weakness suggest that the earlier slack in output and employment growth was due to a shortfall in supply not in domestic demand. ... Meanwhile, the central bank said the sharp drop in the Canadian dollar will provide the economy with some cushion for domestic exporters against the impact of the current U.S. recession and what it expects will be a mild global recession.

Vancouver Sun, October 23, 2008

a. Does Carney predict a recession for Canada in 2008 or 2009? Explain.
b. Is the analysis of macroeconomic fluctuations provided by Statistics Canada most closely following the mainstream business cycle theory or real business cycle theory? Explain.
c. Explain how the weaker Canadian dollar will provide some support for the Canadian economy in the face of a mild global recession.

10. The Reserve Bank of New Zealand signed an agreement with the New Zealand government in which the Bank agreed to maintain inflation inside a low target range. Failure to achieve the target would result in the governor of the Bank of Canada losing his job.

   a. Explain how this arrangement might have influenced New Zealand's short-run Phillips curve.
   b. Explain how this arrangement might have influenced New Zealand's long-run Phillips curve.

11. An economy has an unemployment rate of 4 percent and an inflation rate of 5 percent a year at point *A* in the figure.

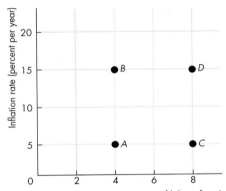

   Some events occur that move the economy in a clockwise loop from *A* to *B* to *D* to *C* and back to *A*.

   a. Describe the events that could create this sequence.
   b. Draw in the figure the sequence of the economy's short-run and long-run Phillips curves.
   c. Has the economy experienced demand-pull inflation, cost-push inflation, expected inflation, or none of these?

12. Suppose that the business cycle in Canada is best described by RBC theory. An advance in technology increases productivity.

   a. Draw a diagram to show the effect of the advance in technology in the market for loanable funds.
   b. Draw a diagram to show the effect of the advance in technology in the labour market.
   c. Explain the when-to-work decision when technology advances.

13. **Report Says Canadian Recession Is Here**

   Canadians are in store for a harsh winter of economic news with substantial job losses mounting in the next few months as recessionary times take hold, the Global Insight forecasting firm says. Managing director Dale Orr ... believes Canada has already entered the first recession in 17 years. ... Orr says the current October–December period will see the economy shrink 1.4 percent on an annualized basis, with a further 1.2 percent retreat occurring in the first quarter of 2009. For the next year as [a] whole, Orr says the economy will average zero growth. "That's quite a stretch of miserable growth," he said. Unlike the slowdown earlier this year, which was mainly been concentrated in the business community and the stock markets, this "will feel more like a recession" because of the significant job losses. ... Orr said Canada's jobless rate will rise from the current 6.2 percent to 7.2 percent at the end of next year.

   CNEWS, November 11, 2008

   a. What evidence does Orr present to support the view that Canada had entered a recession?
   b. Explain why Orr predicts that the end of 2008 and 2009 "will feel more like a recession" than the slowdown at the beginning of 2008.
   c. Use a short-run Phillips curve to explain why the inflation rate may decrease over the course of 2009.
   d. Under what circumstances might the inflation rate not decrease during 2009?

14. **Economy Facing Dual Threat—Slow Growth, High Inflation, says Bank of Canada**

   "I am not using the word stagflation," said Global Insight managing director Dale Orr. "But it's a very awkward trend when you have weak output and yet you have high inflation." He said traditionally the term stagflation—a word coined to reflect stagnant growth and price inflation—implies a prolonged condition in the economy, whereas the [central] bank's statement suggests the problem may only last a few months. Inflation had been a dead issue in Canada for months. ... But now that the central bank, and particularly record oil prices, has put inflation back on the table, future policy decisions have been made more problematic. ... Signs that Canada's economy continues to slow have been steadily building over the past month, from the recent report that gross domestic product shrank 0.3 percent in the first quarter, to last week's employment release showing job creation stalled in May, with full-time employment actually tumbling by 32,000. ... "Canada's job market has clearly weakened over the past two months because of the high Canadian dollar and its effect on the manufacturing and forestry sectors," [Canadian Labour Congress head Ken Georgetti] said. "Jobs are getting very hard to find for those entering the labour force and for those who are losing their current jobs."

CNEWS, June 10, 2008

a. Draw a graph to illustrate and explain how high oil prices might create cost-push inflation in Canada.
b. Explain why Orr refused to use the label "stagflation" to describe the situation.
c. Draw a graph to illustrate and explain how high oil prices could lead to a cost-push inflation spiral.
d. Explain why this situation makes the central bank's future monetary policy decisions "more problematic."
e. Explain and use a graph to illustrate Georgetti's claims about how the "high Canadian dollar" has weakened the job market. How might this also help to reduce inflationary pressure?

15. **Stagflation Is Back. Here's How to Beat It**

Three decades ago, in a bleak stretch of the 1970s, an economic phenomenon emerged that was as ugly as its name: stagflation. ... It created an existential crisis for the global economy, leading many to argue that the world had reached its limits of growth and prosperity. ... Fortunately, there is a better way forward than we took after 1974. We need to adopt coherent national and global technology policies to address critical needs in energy, food, water, and climate change. ... There is certainly no shortage of promising ideas, merely a lack of federal commitment to support their timely development, demonstration, and diffusion. Solar power ... high-mileage automobiles (like plug-in hybrids with advanced batteries), green buildings, carbon capture, cellulose-based ethanol, safe nuclear power, and countless other technologies on the horizon can reconcile a world of growing energy demands with increasingly scarce fossil fuels and rising

threats of human-made climate change. As for food supplies, new drought-resistant crop varieties have the potential to bolster global food security in the face of an already changing climate. New irrigation technologies can help impoverished farmers move from one subsistence crop to several high-value crops year round. Yet as promising as these alternatives are, we have not been investing enough to bring them to fruition. ...

Fortune, May 28, 2008

Does this analysis of macroeconomic performance reflect the mainstream business cycle theory or real business cycle theory? Explain.

16. **Real Wages Fail to Match a Rise in Productivity**

For most of the last century, wages and productivity—the key measure of the economy's efficiency—have risen together, increasing rapidly through the 1950s and 60s and far more slowly in the 1970s and 80s. But in recent years, the productivity gains have continued while the pay increases have not kept up.

New York Times, August 28, 2006

Explain the relationship between wages and productivity in this news article in terms of real business cycle theory.

17. Study the account of the Canadian and U.S. labour markets in *Reading Between the Lines* on pp. 696–697, then answer the following questions.

a. What are the main features of the labour force participation rate in Canada and the United States since 2000?
b. What are the main features of the employment rate (employment-to-population ratio) in Canada and the United States since 2000?
c. What are the main features of the unemployment rate in Canada and the United States since 2000?
d. Use the *AS–AD* model to show the changes in aggregate demand and aggregate supply that are consistent with the paths followed by employment in Canada and the United States from 2000 to 2006.
e. Use the *AS–AD* model to show the changes in aggregate demand and aggregate supply that are consistent with the paths followed by employment in Canada and the United States in 2007 and 2008.

UNDERSTANDING MACROECONOMIC FLUCTUATIONS

Boom and Bust

To cure a disease, doctors must first understand how the disease responds to different treatments. It helps to understand the mechanisms that operate to cause the disease, but sometimes a workable cure can be found even before the full story of the causes has been told.

Curing economic ills is similar to curing medical ills. We need to understand how the economy responds to the treatments we might prescribe for it. And sometimes we want to try a cure even though we don't fully understand the reasons for the problem we're trying to control.

You've seen how the pace of capital accumulation and technological change determine the long-term growth trend. You've learned how fluctuations around the long-term trend can be generated by changes in aggregate demand and aggregate supply. And you've learned about the key sources of fluctuations in aggregate demand and aggregate supply.

The *AS–AD* model explains the forces that determine real GDP and the price level in the short run. The model also enables us to see the big picture or grand vision of the different schools of macroeconomic thought concerning the sources of aggregate fluctuations. The Keynesian aggregate expenditure model provides an account of the factors that determine aggregate demand and make it fluctuate.

An alternative real business cycle theory puts all the emphasis on fluctuations in long-run aggregate supply. According to this theory, money changes aggregate demand and the price level but leaves the real economy untouched. The events of 2008 and 2009 will provide a powerful test of this theory.

John Maynard Keynes, *born in England in 1883, was one of the outstanding minds of the twentieth century. He represented Britain at the Versailles peace conference at the end of World War I, was a master speculator on international financial markets (an activity he conducted from bed every morning and which made and lost him several fortunes), and played a prominent role in creating the International Monetary Fund.*

He was a member of the Bloomsbury Group, a circle of outstanding artists and writers that included E. M. Forster, Bertrand Russell, and Virginia Woolf.

Keynes was a controversial and quick-witted figure. A critic once complained that Keynes had changed his opinion on some matter, to which Keynes retorted: "When I discover I am wrong, I change my mind. What do you do?"

Keynes' book, The General Theory of Employment, Interest, and Money, *written during the Great Depression and published in 1936, revolutionanized macroeconomics.*

"The ideas of economists and political philosophers, both when they are right and when they are wrong, are more powerful than is commonly understood. Indeed the world is ruled by little else."

JOHN MAYNARD KEYNES
The General Theory of Employment, Interest, and Money

TALKING
WITH

Ricardo J. Caballero

Ricardo J. Caballero is Ford Professor of International Economics at MIT. He has received many honours, the most notable of which are the Frisch Medal of the Econometric Society (2002) and being named Chile's Economist of the Year (2001). A highly regarded teacher, he is much sought as a special lecturer and in 2005 gave the prestigious Yrjo Jahnsson Lecture at the University of Helsinki.

Professor Caballero earned his B.S. degree in 1982 and M.A. in 1983 at Pontificia Universidad Católica de Chile. He then moved to the United States and obtained his Ph.D. at MIT in 1988.

Michael Parkin and Robin Bade talked with Ricardo Caballero about his work and the progress that economists have made in understanding economic fluctuations.

Professor Caballero, why did you decide to become an economist?

Did I decide? I'm convinced that one is either born an economist or not. I began studying business, but as soon as I took the first course in economics, I was captivated by the simple but elegant logic of (good) economic reasoning. Given the complexity of the real world, economic analysis is necessarily abstract. But at the same time, economics is mostly about concrete and important issues that affect the lives of millions of people. Abstraction and relevance—this is a wonderful but strange combination. Not everybody feels comfortable with it, but if you do, economics is for you.

Most of your work has been on business cycles and other high-frequency phenomena. Can we begin by reviewing the costs of recessions? Robert Lucas says that post-war U.S. recessions have cost very little. Do you agree?

No ... but I'm not sure Robert Lucas was really trying to say that. My sense is that he was trying to push the profession to focus a bit more on long-run growth issues. Putting down the costs of recessions was a useful debating device to make his important point.

I believe that the statement that recessions are not costly is incorrect. First, I think his calculation of this magnitude reflects some fundamental flaw in the way the workhorse models we use in economics fail to account for the costs of risk and volatility. This flaw shows up in many different puzzles in economics, including the well-known equity premium puzzle. Economic models underestimate, by an order of magnitude, how unhappy agents are about facing uncertainty. Second, it is highly unlikely that recessions and medium-term growth are completely separable. In particular, the ongoing process of restructuring, which is central to productivity growth, is severely hampered by deep recessions.

Recessions are costly because they waste enormous resources, affect physical and human investment decisions, have large negative distributional consequences, influence political outcomes, and so on.

What about the costs of recessions in other parts of the world, especially Latin America?

The cost of recessions grows exponentially with their size and the country's inability to soften the impact on the most affected. Less developed economies suffer much larger shocks because their economies are not well diversified, and they experience capital outflows that exacerbate the impact of recessionary shocks. Their domestic financial sectors are small and often become strained during recessions, making it difficult to reallocate scarce resources towards those who need them the most. To make matters worse, the government's ability to use fiscal policy becomes impaired by the capital outflows, and monetary policy is also out of the question when the currency is in free fall and liabilities are dollarized. There are many things that we take for granted in Canada and the United States that simply are not feasible for emerging markets in distress. One has to be careful with extrapolating too directly the countercyclical recipes used for developed economies to these countries.

Your first work, in your M.A. dissertation, was to build a macroeconomic model of the economy of Chile. What do we learn by comparing economies? Does the Chilean economy behave essentially like the U.S. economy or are there fundamental differences?

Chile is a special economy among emerging markets. It began pro-market reforms many years before the rest and has had very prudent macroeconomic management for several decades by now. For that reason, it is a bit more "like the U.S. economy" than most other emerging market economies. However, there are still important differences, of the sort described in my answer to the previous question.

Beyond the specifics of Chile, at some deep level, macroeconomic principles, and economic principles more generally, are the same everywhere. It is all about incentives, tradeoffs, effort, commitment, discipline, transparency, insurance, and so on. But different economies hurt in

> Recessions are costly because they waste enormous resources [and] affect physical and human investment decisions ...

> The most basic lesson for emerging markets is that capital flows are volatile.

different places, and hence the practice of economics has plenty of diversity.

During the most recent U.S. expansion, some asset prices—especially house prices—have looked as if they might be experiencing a speculative bubble, and you've done some recent work on bubbles. How can we tell whether we're seeing a bubble or just a rapid increase that is being driven by fundamental market forces?

First things first. I think we need to get used to the presence of speculative bubbles. The reason is that the world today has a massive shortage of financial assets that savers can use to store value. Because of this shortage, "artificial" assets are ready to emerge at all times. Specific bubbles come and go—from the NASDAQ, to real estate, to commodities—but the total is much more stable.

I do not think the distinction between bubbles and fundamentals is as clear-cut as people describe. Probably outside periods of liquidity crises, all assets have some bubble component in them. The question is how much.

You've studied situations in which capital suddenly stops flowing into an economy from abroad. What are the lessons you've learned from this research?

The most basic lesson for emerging markets is that capital flows are volatile. Sometimes they simply magnify domestic problems, but in many other cases, they are the direct source of volatility. However, the conclusion from this observation is not that capital flows should be limited, just as we do not close the banks in Canada and the United States to eliminate the possibility of bank runs. On the contrary, much of the volatility comes from insufficient integration with international capital markets, which makes emerging markets illiquid and the target of specialists and speculators. For the short and medium run, the main policy lesson is that sudden stops to the inflow of capital must be put at the centre of macroeconomic policy design in emerging markets. This has deep implications for the design of monetary and fiscal policy, as well as for international reserves management practices and domestic financial markets regulation.

> Good growth potential in the United States over that of Europe and Japan and the much better quality of its financial assets over those of emerging Asian and oil-producing countries make the United States very attractive to international private and public investors.

The U.S. current account deficit has been large and increasing for many years, and dollar debt levels around the world have increased. Do you see any danger in this process for either the United States or the rest of the world?

I believe the persistent current account deficits in the United States are not the result of an anomaly that, as such, must go away in a sudden crash, as the conventional view has it. Instead, my view is that these deficits are just the counterpart of large capital inflows resulting from the global shortage of financial assets that I mentioned earlier. Good growth potential in the United States over that of Europe and Japan and the much better quality of its financial assets over those of emerging Asian and oil-producing countries make the United States very attractive to international private and public investors.

Absent major shocks, this process may still last for quite some time. But

> Almost everything in life has an economic angle to it—look for it ...

of course shocks do happen, and in that sense, leverage is dangerous. However, there isn't much we can or should do, short of implementing structural reforms around the world aimed at improving growth potential in some cases and domestic financial development in others.

What advice do you have for someone who is just beginning to study economics but who wants to become an economist? If they are not in the United States, should they come here for graduate work as you did?

There is no other place in the world like the United States to pursue a Ph.D. and do research in economics. However, this is only the last stage in the process of becoming an economist. There are many superb economists, especially applied ones, all around the world.

I believe the most important step is to learn to think like an economist. I heard Milton Friedman say that he knows many economists who have never gone through a Ph.D. program, and equally many who have completed their Ph.D. but are not really economists. I agree with him on this one. A good undergraduate program and talking about economics is a great first step. Almost everything in life has an economic angle to it—look for it and discuss it with your friends. It will not improve your social life, but it will make you a better economist.

29 Fiscal Policy

After studying this chapter, you will be able to

- Describe how federal and provincial budgets are created and describe their recent history
- Explain the supply-side effects of fiscal policy
- Explain how fiscal policy is used to stabilize the business cycle

In 2007, the federal government spent 15 cents of every dollar that Canadians earned and collected 16 cents of every dollar earned in taxes. What are the effects of government spending and taxes on the economy? Does a dollar spent by the government have the same effect as a dollar spent by someone else? Does it create jobs, or does it destroy them? Do taxes harm employment and economic growth?

For many years during the 1980s and 1990s, the government had a large budget deficit and ran up a debt. During the late 1990s, spending cuts brought the deficit under control and created a surplus that is still in place today.

Despite recent budget surpluses, your share of government debt is $15,200. Does it matter if the government

doesn't balance its books? What are the effects of an ongoing government deficit and accumulating debt?

These are the fiscal policy issues that you will study in this chapter. At the end of the chapter, in *Reading Between the Lines*, we'll look at fiscal stimulus in the 2008–2009 global growth slowdown.

◆ Government Budgets

The annual statement of the outlays and revenues of the government of Canada, together with the laws and regulations that approve and support those outlays and revenues, make up the **federal budget**. Similarly, a **provincial budget** is an annual statement of the revenues and outlays of a provincial government, together with the laws and regulations that approve or support those revenues and outlays.

Before World War II, the federal budget had no purpose other than to finance the business of government. But since the late 1940s, the federal budget has assumed a second purpose, which is to pursue the government's fiscal policy. **Fiscal policy** is the use of the federal budget to achieve macroeconomic objectives such as full employment, sustained long-term economic growth, and price level stability. Our focus is this second purpose.

Budget Making

The federal government and Parliament make fiscal policy. The process begins with long, drawn-out consultations between the Minister of Finance and Department of Finance officials and their counterparts in the provincial governments. These discussions deal with programs that are funded and operated jointly by the two levels of government. The Minister also consults with business and consumer groups on a wide range of issues.

After all these consultations, and using economic projections made by Department of Finance economists, the Minister develops a set of proposals, which are discussed in Cabinet and which become government policy. The Minister finally presents a budget plan to Parliament, which debates the plan and enacts the laws necessary to implement it.

Highlights of the 2008 Budget

Table 29.1 shows the main items in the federal budget. The numbers are projected amounts for the fiscal year beginning on April 1, 2008. The three main items shown are

- Revenues
- Outlays
- Budget balance

TABLE 29.1 The Federal Budget in 2008–09

Item	Projections (billions of dollars)
Revenues	**242**
Personal income taxes	119
Corporate income taxes	37
Indirect and other taxes	64
Investment income	22
Outlays	**240**
Transfer payments	146
Expenditure on goods and services	62
Debt interest	32
Surplus	**2**

Sources of data: Department of Finance, Budget Plant 2008 and Statistics Canada, CANSIM Table 183-0004.

Revenues Revenues are the federal government's receipts, which in the 2008–09 budget were projected at $242 billion. These revenues come from four sources:

1. Personal income taxes
2. Corporate income taxes
3. Indirect and other taxes
4. Investment income

The largest revenue source is *personal income taxes*. In 2008–09, personal income taxes were projected to be $119 billion. These are the taxes paid by individuals on their incomes. The second largest source of revenue is *indirect taxes*, which in 2008–09 were projected to be $64 billion. These taxes include the Goods and Services Tax (GST) and taxes on the sale of gasoline, alcoholic drinks, and a few other items. The smallest revenue sources are *corporate income taxes*, which are the taxes paid by companies on their profits, and *investment income*, which is the income from government enterprises and investments. In 2008–09, corporate income taxes were projected to raise $37 billion and investment income was projected at $22 billion.

Outlays Total federal government outlays in 2008–09 were projected at $240 billion. Outlays are classified in three categories:

1. Transfer payments
2. Expenditures on goods and services
3. Debt interest

The largest outlay, and by a big margin, is *transfer payments*. Transfer payments are payments to individuals, businesses, other levels of government, and the rest of the world. In 2008–09, this item was $146 billion. It includes unemployment cheques and welfare payments to individuals, farm subsidies, grants to provincial and local governments, aid to developing countries, and dues to international organizations such as the United Nations.

Expenditures on goods and services are expenditures on final goods and services, and in 2008–09 this item totalled $62 billion. These expenditures include those on national defence, computers for the Canada Revenue Agency, government cars, and highways. This component of the federal budget is the government expenditure on goods and services that appears in the circular flow of expenditure and income and in the national income and product accounts (see Chapter 20, pp. 469–470).

Debt interest is the interest on the government debt. In 2008–09, this item was $32 billion. At its peak percentage of GDP in 1990, it exceeded govern-

ment expenditures on goods and services. This interest payment is large because the government has a large debt—$524 billion. This large debt has arisen because from 1994 to 1997 the federal government had a large and persistent budget deficit.

Budget Balance The government's budget balance is equal to its revenues minus its outlays. That is,

$$\text{Budget balance} = \text{Revenues} - \text{Outlays}.$$

If revenues exceed outlays, the government has a **budget surplus**. If outlays exceed revenues, the government has a **budget deficit**. If revenues equal outlays, the government has a **balanced budget**.

In 2008–09, with projected outlays of $240 billion and revenues of $242 billion, the government projected a budget surplus of $2 billion.

How typical is the federal budget of 2008–09? Let's look at its recent history.

The Budget in Historical Perspective

Figure 29.1 shows the government's revenues, outlays, and budget balance from 1961 to 2007. To get a better sense of the magnitudes of these items, they are shown as percentages of GDP. Expressing them in this way lets us see how large the government is relative to the size of the economy, and also helps us to study changes in the scale of government over

FIGURE 29.1 The Budget Surplus and Deficit

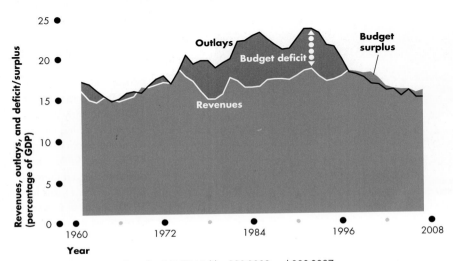

The figure records the federal government's revenues, outlays, and budget balance as percentages of GDP from 1961 to 2007. During the 1960s, outlays and revenues increased. During the late 1970s and through the 1980s, outlays continued to rise but revenues fell, so a budget deficit arose. During the 1990s, spending cuts eliminated the budget deficit, and after 1997, the federal government had a budget surplus.

Source of data: Statistics Canada, CANSIM Tables 380-0002 and 380-0007.

myeconlab animation

time. You can think of the percentages of GDP as telling you how many cents of each dollar that Canadians earn get paid to and are spent by the government.

During the 1960s, government expanded but taxes and revenues kept pace with each other. But from 1971 through 1996, the federal budget was in deficit, and the average deficit over these years was 4.2 percent of GDP. The deficit climbed to a peak of 6.6 percent of GDP in 1985. It then decreased through the rest of the 1980s. During the recession of 1990–1991, the deficit increased again. The deficit remained above 4 percent of GDP for most of the 1980s and early 1990s.

Only in 1997 did the federal government finally eradicate its deficit. And it did so by cutting outlays, especially transfer payments to provincial governments.

Why did the government deficit grow during the early 1980s and remain high through the early 1990s? The immediate answer is that outlays increased while revenues remained relatively constant. But which components of outlays increased? And did all the sources of revenues remain constant?

To answer these questions, we need to examine each of the sources of revenues and outlays in detail. We'll begin by looking at the sources of revenues.

Revenues Figure 29.2 shows the components of government revenues since 1961. Total revenues have no strong trends. They increased through the 1960s and again through the 1980s. But they decreased during the 1970s and the first half of the 2000s. The main source of the fluctuations in revenues was personal income taxes. Indirect taxes also fluctuated but corporate income taxes and investment income were more stable than the other two revenue components.

The increase in personal income taxes during the 1980s resulted from increases in tax rates in successive budgets.

Indirect taxes decreased during the 1990s mainly because an old federal sales tax was replaced by the Goods and Services Tax or GST. Initially, this switch maintained revenues at a constant level, but gradually, the revenue from indirect taxes (as a percentage of GDP) fell.

Outlays Figure 29.3 shows the components of government outlays since 1961. Total outlays increased steadily from 1971 through 1985, were relatively flat through 1993, and then decreased sharply after 1993. The main source of the changing trends in outlays is transfer payments to provincial governments. These payments swelled during the 1980s and were cut drastically during the late 1990s.

FIGURE 29.2 Federal Government Revenues

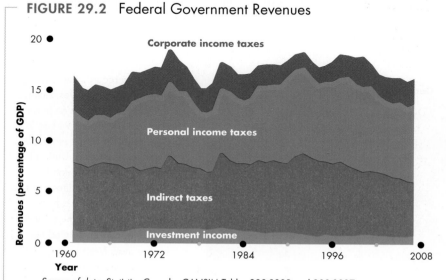

Source of data: Statistics Canada, CANSIM Tables 380-0002 and 380-0007.

The figure shows four main components of government revenues (as percentages of GDP): personal income taxes, corporate income taxes, indirect taxes, and investment income. Revenues from personal income taxes fluctuated most. They increased during the 1960s and early 1970s, decreased during the late 1970s, increased again during the 1980s and 1990s, and then decreased again during the 2000s. Indirect taxes fell after 1990. The other two components of revenues remained steady.

myeconlab animation

FIGURE 29.3   Federal Government Outlays

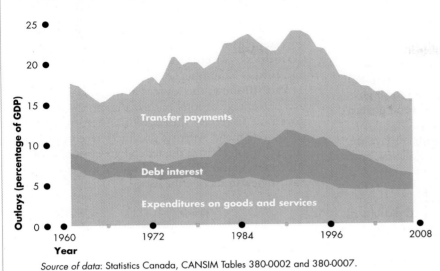

Source of data: Statistics Canada, CANSIM Tables 380-0002 and 380-0007.

The figure shows three components of government outlays (as percentages of GDP): expenditures on goods and services, debt interest, and transfer payments. Expenditures on goods and services have had a downward trend. Transfer payments increased from 1965 to 1990 but decreased sharply during the 1990s. Debt interest increased steadily during the 1980s as the budget deficit fed on itself, but decreased during the late 1990s as surpluses began to lower the government's debt.

myeconlab animation

To understand the changes in debt interest, we need to see the connection between the budget deficit and government debt.

Deficit and Debt The government borrows to finance its deficit. And **government debt** is the total amount of government borrowing. It is the sum of past deficits minus the sum of past surpluses.

When the government budget is in deficit, government debt increases, and when the government budget is in surplus, government debt decreases.

A persistent budget deficit emerged during the mid-1970s, and in such a situation, the deficit begins to feed on itself. A budget deficit increases borrowing; increased borrowing leads to larger debt; a larger debt leads to larger interest payments; and larger interest payments led to a larger deficit and yet larger debt. That is the story of the increasing budget deficit and rising debt of the 1980s.

Similarly, a persistent budget surplus creates a virtuous cycle of falling interest payments, larger surpluses, and falling debt.

Figure 29.4 shows the history of the government of Canada debt since 1940, at the start of World War II. Debt (as a percentage of GDP) was at an all-time high of 113 percent at the end of the war in 1945. Huge wartime deficits had increased Canada's debt to the point that it exceeded GDP. Post-war budget

FIGURE 29.4   The Federal Government Debt

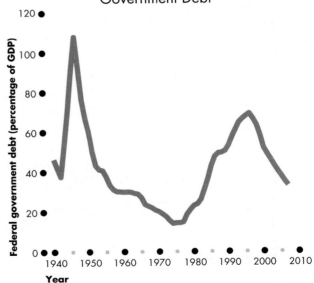

Federal government debt as a percentage of GDP increased during World War II, decreased from 1946 through 1974, increased through 1997, and then began to decrease again.

Source of data: Statistics Canada, CANSIM Tables 380-0002 and 380-0010.

myeconlab animation

Provincial and Local Governments

Bigger than Federal Government

The *total government* sector of Canada includes provincial and local governments as well as the federal government. In 2007, when federal government outlays were $230 billion, provincial and local government outlays were $390 billion and total government outlays were $620 billion.

Most provincial and local government outlays are on public hospitals and public schools, colleges, and universities.

Scale of Different Levels of Government

Figure 1 shows the revenues, outlays, and deficits of the federal government and of total government from 1961 to 2007.

You can see that federal government outlays and revenues and total government outlays and revenues fluctuate in similar ways, but the total government is much larger than the federal government. In other words, the provincial and local governments are a large component of total government. You can also see that total government outlays fluctuate more than federal government outlays.

Both the federal and total government budgets moved into and out of deficit at similar times and both have been in surplus since the late 1990s.

Variation Across Provinces

Provincial government outlays and revenue sources vary a great deal across the provinces. Figure 2 shows the range of variation.

Part (a) shows outlays as a percentage of provincial GDP. You can see that outlays as a percentage of provincial product are the greatest in the northern governments (Nunavut, Yukon, and Northwest Territories). Government outlays of Alberta, Ontario, and British Columbia are the least.

Part (b) shows the sources of provincial revenues as a percentage of total outlays. Again, the northern governments receive the largest transfers from the federal government. Atlantic provinces receive the next largest transfers from the federal government, while Alberta, Ontario, British Columbia, and Saskatchewan receive the least.

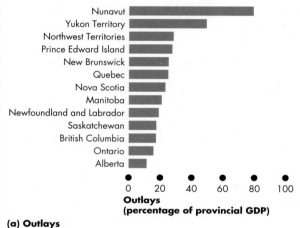

(a) Outlays

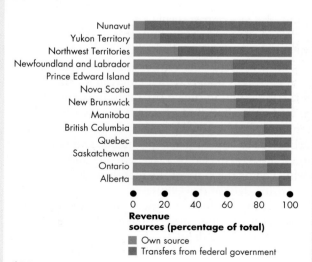

(b) Revenues

Figure 2 Provincial Government Budgets

Source of data: Statistics Canada, CANSIM Tables 384-0002 and 385-0002.

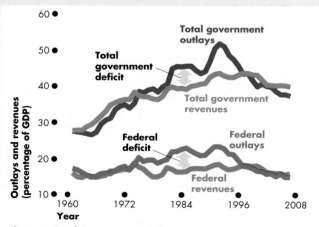

Figure 1 Total Government Budgets

Source of data: Statistics Canada, CANSIM Tables 380-0002 and 380-0007.

Canadian Government Surplus in Global Perspective

Deep Red in the United States and Japan

To compare government budgets across countries, we must take into account the differences in local and regional government arrangements. Some countries, and Canada is one of them, have large state/provincial and local governments. Other countries, and the United Kingdom is one, have larger central government and small local governments. These differences make the international comparison more valid at the level of *total government* rather than at the level of *central* (or *federal*) *government*. The figure shows the budget balances of total government in Canada and nine other countries.

The United States and Japan have the largest budget deficits, as a percentage of GDP. The United Kingdom, France, and Italy come next.

Norway, which has substantial oil wealth, has the largest government budget surplus. Other nations with budget surpluses include Finland, Korea, Sweden, and Australia.

Canada lies in the middle of the countries with budget surpluses and is the only major industrial economy with one.

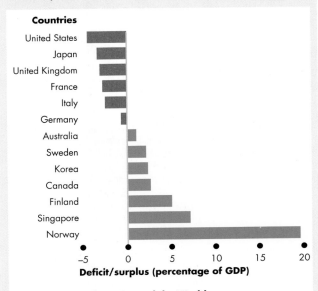

Government Budgets Around the World

Sources of data: International Monetary Fund, *World Economic Outlook*, April 2008, and Statistics Canada, CANSIM Tables 380-0002 and 380-0007.

surpluses lowered the debt-to-GDP ratio through 1974, by which time it stood at 18 percent, its lowest since World War II. Small budget deficits increased the debt-to-GDP ratio slightly through the 1970s, and large budget deficits increased it dramatically between 1981 and 1986. During the late 1980s, the ratio continued to increase but at a more moderate rate. It grew quickly again during the 1990–1991 recession, but its growth rate slowed after 1995 and debt interest as a percentage of GDP decreased.

Debt and Capital When individuals and businesses incur debts, they usually do so to buy capital—assets that yield a return. In fact, the main point of debt is to enable people to buy assets that will earn a return that exceeds the interest paid on the debt. The government is similar to individuals and businesses in this regard. Some government expenditure is investment—the purchase of public capital that yields a return. Highways, major irrigation schemes, public schools and universities, public libraries, and the stock of national defence capital all yield a social rate of return that probably far exceeds the interest rate the government pays on its debt.

But Canadian government debt, which is $500 billion, is much larger than the value of the public capital stock. This fact means that some government debt has been incurred to finance public consumption expenditure.

Review Quiz

1 What are the main items of government revenues and outlays?

2 Under what circumstances does the government have a budget surplus?

3 Explain the connection between a government budget deficit and a government debt.

 Work Study Plan 29.1 and get instant feedback.

Now that you know what the federal budget is and what the main components of revenues and outlays are, it is time to study the *effects* of fiscal policy. We'll begin by learning about the effects of taxes on employment, aggregate supply, and potential GDP. Then we'll look at the demand-side effects of fiscal policy and see how it provides a tool for stabilizing the business cycle.

◆ Supply-Side Effects of Fiscal Policy

Fiscal policy has important effects on employment, potential GDP, and aggregate supply that we'll now examine. These effects are known as **supply-side effects,** and economists who believe these effects to be large ones are generally referred to as *supply-siders.* To study these effects, we'll begin with a refresher on how full employment and potential GDP are determined in the absence of taxes. Then we'll introduce an income tax and see how it changes the economic outcome.

Full Employment and Potential GDP

You learned in Chapter 22 (pp. 521–523) how the full-employment quantity of labour and potential GDP are determined. At full employment, the real wage rate adjusts to make the quantity of labour demanded equal the quantity of labour supplied. Potential GDP is the real GDP that the full-employment quantity of labour produces.

Figure 29.5 illustrates a full-employment situation. In part (a), the demand for labour curve is *LD,* and the supply of labour curve is *LS.* At a real wage rate of $30 an hour and 25 billion hours of labour a year employed, the economy is at full employment.

In Fig. 29.5(b), the production function is *PF.* When 25 billion hours of labour are employed, real GDP (which is also potential GDP) is $1,300 billion.

Let's now see how an income tax changes potential GDP.

The Effects of the Income Tax

The tax on labour income influences potential GDP and aggregate supply by changing the full-employment quantity of labour. The income tax weakens the incentive to work and drives a wedge between the take-home wage of workers and the cost of labour to firms. The result is a smaller quantity of labour and a lower potential GDP.

Figure 29.5 shows this outcome. In the labour market, the income tax has no effect on the demand for labour, which remains at *LD.* The reason is that the quantity of labour that firms plan to hire depends only on how productive labour is and what it costs—its real wage rate.

FIGURE 29.5 The Effects of the Income Tax on Aggregate Supply

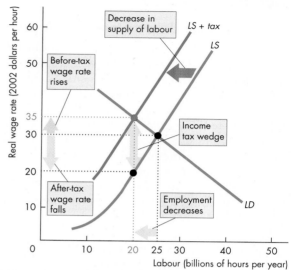

(a) Income tax and the labour market

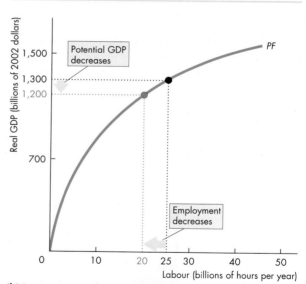

(b) Income tax and potential GDP

In part (a), with no income tax, the real wage rate is $30 an hour and employment is 25 billion hours. In part (b), potential GDP is $1,300 billion. An income tax shifts the supply of labour curve leftward to *LS + tax.* The before-tax wage rate rises to $35 an hour, the after-tax wage rate falls to $20 an hour, and the quantity of labour employed decreases to 20 billion hours. With less labour, potential GDP decreases.

myeconlab animation

But the supply of labour *does* change. With no income tax, the real wage rate is $30 an hour and 25 billion hours of labour a year are employed. An income tax weakens the incentive to work and decreases the supply of labour. The reason is that for each dollar of before-tax earnings, workers must pay the government an amount determined by the income tax code. So workers look at the after-tax wage rate when they decide how much labour to supply. An income tax shifts the supply curve leftward to $LS + tax$. The vertical distance between the LS curve and the $LS + tax$ curve measures the amount of income tax. With the smaller supply of labour, the *before-tax* wage rate rises to $35 an hour but the *after-tax* wage rate falls to $20 an hour. The vertical gap between the before-tax and after-tax wage rates is the **tax wedge**.

The new equilibrium quantity of labour employed is 20 billion hours a year—less than in the no-tax case. Because the full-employment quantity of labour decreases, so does potential GDP. And a decrease in potential GDP decreases aggregate supply.

In this example, the tax rate is high—$15 tax on a $35 wage rate, about 43 percent. A lower tax rate would have a smaller effect on employment and potential GDP.

An increase in the tax rate to above 43 percent would decrease the supply of labour by more than the decrease shown in Fig. 29.5. Equilibrium employment and potential GDP would also decrease still further. A tax cut would increase the supply of labour, increase equilibrium employment, and increase potential GDP.

Taxes on Expenditure and the Tax Wedge

The tax wedge that we've just considered is only a part of the wedge that affects labour-supply decisions. Taxes on consumption expenditure add to the wedge. The reason is that a tax on consumption raises the prices paid for consumption goods and services and is equivalent to a cut in the real wage rate.

The incentive to supply labour depends on the goods and services that an hour of labour can buy. The higher the taxes on goods and services and the lower the after-tax wage rate, the less is the incentive to supply labour. If the income tax rate is 25 percent and the tax rate on consumption expenditure is 10 percent, a dollar earned buys only 65 cents worth of goods and services. The tax wedge is 35 percent.

Some Real-World Tax Wedges

Why Americans Work Longer Hours than Europeans

Edward C. Prescott of Arizona State University, who shared the 2004 Nobel Prize for Economic Science, has estimated the tax wedges for three countries: the United States, the United Kingdom, and France. We have estimated the tax wedge for Canada.

The wedges are a combination of taxes on labour income and taxes on consumption. They include *all* taxes on labour, including social insurance taxes. And the wedges are based on *marginal* tax rates—the tax rates paid on the marginal dollar earned.

The figure shows the tax wedges in these four countries. In the United States, the consumption tax wedge is 13 percent and the income tax wedge is 32 percent. Canada is very similar. In France, the consumption tax wedge is 33 percent and the income tax wedge is 49 percent. The tax wedges in United Kingdom fall between these two.

Does the Tax Wedge Matter?

Differences in potential GDP per person arise partly from productivity differences and partly from choices influenced by the tax wedge. Potential GDP (per person) in France is 14 percent below that of the United States and the entire difference is attributed to the difference in the tax wedge in the two countries. Potential GDP in Canada is 16 percent below that of the United States, but this difference is due to different productivities. Potential GDP in the United Kingdom is 41 percent below that of the United States, and about a third of the difference arises from the different tax wedges and two-thirds from productivity difference.

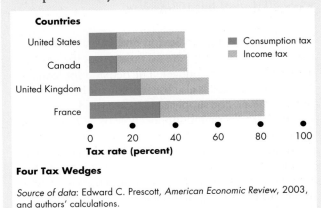

Four Tax Wedges

Source of data: Edward C. Prescott, *American Economic Review*, 2003, and authors' calculations.

Taxes and the Incentive to Save

A tax on interest income weakens the incentive to save and drives a wedge between the after-tax interest rate earned by savers and the interest rate paid by firms. These effects are analogous to those of a tax on labour income. But they are more serious for two reasons.

First, a tax on labour income lowers the quantity of labour employed and lowers potential GDP, while a tax on capital income lowers the quantity of saving and investment and *slows the growth rate of real GDP*.

Second, the true tax rate on interest income is much higher than that on labour income because of the way in which inflation and taxes on interest income interact. Let's examine this interaction.

Effect of Tax Rate on Real Interest Rate

The interest rate that influences investment and saving plans is the *real after-tax interest rate*. The real *after-tax* interest rate subtracts the income tax rate paid on interest income from the real interest rate. But the taxes depend on the nominal interest rate, not the real rate. So the higher the inflation rate, the higher is the true tax rate on interest income. Here is an example. Suppose the real interest rate is 4 percent a year and the tax rate is 40 percent.

If there is no inflation, the nominal interest rate equals the real interest rate. The tax on 4 percent interest is 1.6 percent (40 percent of 4 percent), so the real after-tax interest rate is 4 percent minus 1.6 percent, which equals 2.4 percent.

If the inflation rate is 6 percent a year, the nominal interest rate is 10 percent. The tax on 10 percent interest is 4 percent (40 percent of 10 percent), so the real after-tax interest rate is 4 percent minus 4 percent, which equals zero. The true tax rate in this case is not 40 percent but 100 percent!

Effect of Income Tax on Saving and Investment

In Fig. 29.6, initially there are no taxes. Also, the government has a balanced budget. The demand for loanable funds curve, which is also the investment demand curve, is *DLF*. The supply of loanable funds curve, which is also the saving supply curve, is *SLF*. The equilibrium interest rate is 3 percent a year, and the quantity of funds borrowed and lent is $200 billion a year.

A tax on interest income has no effect on the demand for loanable funds. The quantity of investment and borrowing that firms plan to undertake depends only on how productive capital is and what

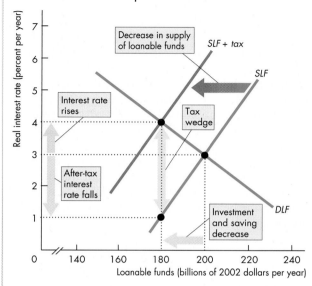

FIGURE 29.6 The Effects of a Tax on Capital Income

The demand for loanable funds and investment demand curve is *DLF*, and the supply of loanable funds and saving supply curve is *SLF*. With no income tax, the real interest rate is 3 percent a year and investment is $200 billion. An income tax shifts the supply curve leftward to *SLF + tax*. The interest rate rises to 4 percent a year, the after-tax interest rate falls to 1 percent a year, and investment decreases to $180 billion. With less investment, the real GDP growth rate decreases.

myeconlab animation

it costs—its real interest rate. But a tax on interest income weakens the incentive to save and lend and decreases the supply of loanable funds. For each dollar of before-tax interest, savers must pay the government an amount determined by the tax code. So savers look at the after-tax real interest rate when they decide how much to save.

When a tax is imposed, saving decreases and the supply of loanable funds curve shifts leftward to *SLF + tax*. The amount of tax payable is measured by the vertical distance between the *SLF* curve and the *SLF + tax* curve. With this smaller supply of loanable funds, the interest rate rises to 4 percent a year but the *after-tax* interest rate falls to 1 percent a year. A tax wedge is driven between the interest rate and the after-tax interest rate, and the equilibrium quantity of loanable funds decreases. Saving and investment also decrease.

Tax Revenues and the Laffer Curve

An interesting consequence of the effect of taxes on employment and saving is that a higher tax *rate* does not always bring greater tax *revenue*. A higher tax rate brings in more revenue per dollar earned. But because a higher tax rate decreases the number of dollars earned, two forces operate in opposite directions on the tax revenue collected.

The relationship between the tax rate and the amount of tax revenue collected is called the **Laffer curve**. The curve is so named because Arthur B. Laffer, a member of Ronald Reagan's Economic Policy Advisory Board, drew such a curve on a table napkin and launched the idea that tax cuts could *increase* tax revenue.

Figure 29.7 shows a Laffer curve. The tax *rate* is on the x-axis, and total tax *revenue* is on the y-axis. For tax rates below T^*, an increase in the tax rate increases tax revenue; at T^*, tax revenue is maximized; and a tax rate increase above T^* decreases tax revenue.

Most people think that Canada is on the upward-sloping part of the Laffer curve. But France might be close to the maximum point or perhaps even beyond it.

The Supply-Side Debate

Before 1980, few economists paid attention to the supply-side effects of taxes on employment and potential GDP. Then, when Ronald Reagan took office as president, a group of supply-siders began to argue the virtues of cutting taxes. Arthur Laffer was one of them. Laffer and his supporters were not held in high esteem among mainstream economists, but they were influential for a period. They correctly argued that tax cuts would increase employment and increase output. But they incorrectly argued that tax cuts would increase tax revenues and decrease the budget deficit. For this prediction to be correct, the United States would have had to be on the "wrong" side of the Laffer curve. Given that U.S. tax rates are among the lowest in the industrial world, it is unlikely that this condition was met. And when the Reagan administration did cut taxes, the budget deficit increased, a fact that reinforces this view.

Supply-side economics became tarnished because of its association with Laffer and came to be called "voodoo economics." But mainstream economists, including Martin Feldstein, a Harvard professor who was Reagan's chief economic advisor, recognized the

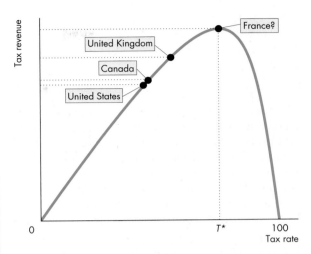

FIGURE 29.7 A Laffer Curve

A Laffer curve shows the relationship between the tax rate and tax revenues. For tax rates below T^*, an increase in the tax rate increases tax revenue. At the tax rate T^*, tax revenue is maximized. For tax rates above T^*, an increase in the tax rate decreases tax revenue.

myeconlab animation

power of tax cuts as incentives but took the standard view that tax cuts without spending cuts would swell the budget deficit and bring serious further problems. This view is now widely accepted by economists of all political persuasions.

Review Quiz

1 How does a tax on labour income influence the equilibrium quantity of employment?
2 How does the tax wedge influence potential GDP?
3 Why are income taxes on capital income more powerful than those on labour income?
4 What is the Laffer curve and why is it unlikely that Canada is on the "wrong" side of it?

myeconlab Work Study Plan 29.2 and get instant feedback.

You now know how taxes influence potential GDP and saving and investment. Next we look at the demand-side effects of fiscal policy and see how it is used as a tool for stabilizing the business cycle.

Stabilizing the Business Cycle

Fiscal policy actions that seek to stabilize the business cycle work by changing aggregate demand and are either

- Discretionary or
- Automatic

A fiscal action initiated by an act of Parliament is called **discretionary fiscal policy**. It requires a change in a spending program or in a tax law. For example, an increase in defence spending or a cut in the income tax rate is a discretionary fiscal policy.

A fiscal action that is triggered by the state of the economy is called **automatic fiscal policy**. For example, an increase in unemployment induces an increase in payments to the unemployed. A fall in incomes induces a decrease in tax revenues.

Changes in government expenditure and changes in taxes have multiplier effects on aggregate demand. Chapter 27 explains the basic idea of the multiplier and the Mathematical Note on pp. 670–673 shows the algebra of the fiscal policy multipliers that we'll now study.

Government Expenditure Multiplier

The **government expenditure multiplier** is the magnification effect of a change in government expenditure on goods and services on aggregate demand. Government expenditure is a component of aggregate expenditure, so when government expenditure changes, aggregate demand changes. Real GDP changes and induces a change in consumption expenditure, which brings a further change in aggregate expenditure. A multiplier process ensues.

A Mackenzie Valley Pipeline Multiplier Canada's Arctic region is rich in natural gas. But to get that gas to market, a $16 billion pipeline must be built. If the project goes ahead (it is controversial because of its impact on the environment), it will have a large multiplier effect in northern Canada. Construction workers will spend much of their income in the Arctic region. Retail stores, schools, health-care centres, hotels and motels, and recreational facilities will open and hire yet more people who will spend yet more income. The initial increase in aggregate expenditure will induce a further increase in aggregate demand.

The Autonomous Tax Multiplier

The **autonomous tax multiplier** is the magnification effect of a change in autonomous taxes on aggregate demand. A *decrease* in taxes *increases* disposable income, which increases consumption expenditure. A decrease in taxes works like an increase in government expenditure. But the magnitude of the autonomous tax multiplier is smaller than the government expenditure multiplier. The reason is that a $1 tax cut generates *less than* $1 of additional expenditure. The marginal propensity to consume determines the increase in consumption expenditure induced by a tax cut. For example, if the marginal propensity to consume is 0.75, then a $1 tax cut increases consumption expenditure by only 75 cents. In this case, the tax multiplier is 0.75 times the magnitude of the government expenditure multiplier.

A GST Cut Multiplier The government has twice cut the GST. These tax cuts had a multiplier effect. With more disposable income, people increased consumption expenditure. This spending increased other people's incomes, which spurred yet more consumption expenditure. These tax cuts and their multiplier effects helped to keep the Canadian economy expanding through 2007 and 2008.

The Balanced Budget Multiplier

The **balanced budget multiplier** is the magnification effect on aggregate demand of a simultaneous change in government expenditure and taxes that leaves the budget balance unchanged. The balanced budget multiplier is positive because a $1 increase in government expenditure increases aggregate demand by more than a $1 increase in taxes decreases aggregate demand. So when both government expenditure and taxes increase by $1, aggregate demand increases.

Discretionary Fiscal Stabilization

If real GDP is below potential GDP, discretionary fiscal policy might be used in an attempt to restore full employment. The government might increase its expenditure on goods and services, cut taxes, or do some of both. These actions would increase aggregate demand. If they were timed correctly and were of the correct magnitude, they could restore full employment. Figure 29.8 shows how. Potential GDP is $1,200 billion, but real GDP is below potential at $1,100 billion and there is a $100 billion *recessionary gap* (see Chapter 26, p. 637). To restore full employment, the government takes a discretionary fiscal policy action. An increase in government expenditure or a tax cut increases aggregate expenditure by ΔE. If this were the only change in spending plans, the AD curve would become $AD_0 + \Delta E$ in Fig. 29.8. But the fiscal policy action sets off a multiplier process, which increases consumption expenditure. As the multiplier process plays out, aggregate demand increases further and the AD curve shifts rightward to AD_1.

With no change in the price level, the economy would move from point A to point B on AD_1. But the increase in aggregate demand combined with the upward-sloping SAS curve brings a rise in the price level. The economy moves to point C, and the economy returns to full employment.

Figure 29.9 illustrates the opposite case in which discretionary fiscal policy is used to eliminate inflationary pressure. The government decreases its expenditure

on goods and services or raises taxes to decrease aggregate demand. In the figure, the fiscal policy action decreases aggregate expenditure by ΔE and the AD curve shifts to $AD_0 - \Delta E$. The initial decrease in aggregate expenditure sets off a multiplier process, which decreases consumption expenditure. The multiplier process decreases aggregate demand further and the AD curve shifts leftward to AD_1.

With no change in the price level, the economy would move from point A to point B on AD_1 in Fig. 29.9. But the decrease in aggregate demand combined with the upward-sloping SAS curve brings a fall in the price level. So the economy moves to point C, where the inflationary gap has been eliminated, inflation has been avoided, and the economy is back at full employment.

Figures 29.8 and 29.9 make fiscal policy look easy: Calculate the recessionary gap or the inflationary gap and the multiplier, change government expenditure or taxes, and eliminate the gap. In reality, things are not that easy.

FIGURE 29.8 Expansionary Fiscal Policy

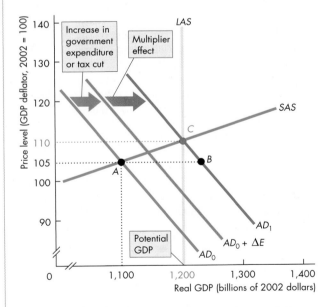

Potential GDP is $1,200 billion, real GDP is $1,100 billion, and there is a $100 billion recessionary gap. An increase in government expenditure or a tax cut increases expenditure by ΔE. A multiplier effect shifts the AD curve rightward to AD_1, the price level rises to 110, real GDP increases to $1,200 billion, and the recessionary gap is eliminated.

myeconlab animation

FIGURE 29.9 Contractionary Fiscal Policy

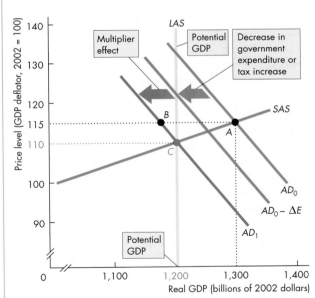

Potential GDP is $1,200 billion, real GDP is $1,300 billion, and there is a $100 billion inflationary gap. A decrease in government expenditure or a rise in taxes decreases expenditure by ΔE. A multiplier effect shifts the AD curve leftward to AD_1, the price level falls to 110, real GDP decreases to $1,200 billion, and the inflationary gap is eliminated.

myeconlab animation

Limitations of Discretionary Fiscal Policy

The use of discretionary fiscal policy is seriously hampered by three time lags:

- Recognition lag
- Law-making lag
- Impact lag

Recognition Lag   The *recognition lag* is the time it takes to figure out that fiscal policy actions are needed. This process has two aspects: assessing the current state of the economy and forecasting its future state.

Law-Making Lag   The *law-making lag* is the time it takes Parliament to pass the laws needed to change taxes or spending. This process takes time because each member of Parliament has a different idea about what is the best tax or spending program to change, so long debates and committee meetings are needed to reconcile conflicting views. The economy might benefit from fiscal stimulation today, but by the time Parliament acts, a different fiscal medicine is needed.

Impact Lag   The *impact lag* is the time it takes from passing a tax or spending change to its effects on real GDP being felt. This lag depends partly on the speed with which government agencies can act and partly on the timing of changes in spending plans by households and businesses.

Economic forecasting has improved in recent years, but it remains inexact and subject to error. So because of these three time lags, discretionary fiscal action might end up moving real GDP away from potential GDP and creating the very problems it seeks to correct.

Let's now look at automatic fiscal policy.

Automatic Stabilizers

Automatic fiscal policy is a consequence of tax revenues and outlays that fluctuate with real GDP. These features of fiscal policy are called **automatic stabilizers** because they work to stabilize real GDP without explicit action by the government. Their name is borrowed from engineering and conjures up images of shock absorbers, thermostats, and sophisticated devices that keep airplanes and ships steady in turbulent air and seas.

The 2008 U.S. Fiscal Stimulus Package
Closing the Output Gap

As recession fears grew in the wake of the U.S. subprime mortgage crisis, U.S. Congress passed the *Economic Stimulus Act of 2008*. This act of *discretionary fiscal policy* was designed to increase aggregate demand and close a recessionary gap.

Tax rebates were the key component of the package and their effect on aggregate demand depends on the extent to which they are spent and saved.

The last time the U.S. federal government boosted aggregate demand with a tax rebate was in 2001 and a statistical investigation of the effects estimated that 70 percent of the rebates were spent within six months of being received.

The rebates in the 2008 fiscal package were targeted predominantly at low-income individuals and families, so the experience of 2001 would be likely to apply: Most of the rebates would be spent.

The cost of the package in 2008 was about $160 billion, so aggregate demand would be expected to increase by close to this amount and then by a multiplier as the initial spending became someone else's income and so boosted their spending.

The figure illustrates the effects of the package. Before the rebates, aggregate demand was AD_0 and real GDP was $11.7 trillion. The rebates increased aggregate demand to $AD_0 + \Delta E$, and a multiplier increased it to AD_1. Real GDP and the price level increased and the recessionary gap narrowed.

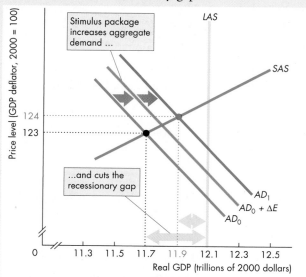

Effects of Fiscal Stimulus Act of 2008

Induced Taxes On the revenues side of the budget, tax laws define tax *rates*, not tax *dollars*. Tax dollars paid depend on tax rates and incomes. But incomes vary with real GDP, so tax revenues depend on real GDP. Taxes that vary with real GDP are called **induced taxes**. When real GDP increases in an expansion, wages and profits rise, so the taxes on these incomes—induced taxes—rise. When real GDP decreases in a recession, wages and profits fall, so the induced taxes on these incomes fall.

Transfer Payments On the outlays side of the budget, the government creates programs that pay benefits to suitably qualified people and businesses. The spending on such programs results in transfer payments that depend on the economic state of individual citizens and businesses. When the economy is in a recession, unemployment is high, the number of people experiencing economic hardship increases, and a larger number of firms and farms experience hard times. Transfer payments increase. When the economy expands, unemployment falls and the number of people, firms, and farms experiencing economic hardship decreases. Transfer payments decrease.

Induced taxes and transfer payments decrease the multiplier effects of changes in autonomous expenditure (such as investment and exports). So they moderate both expansions and recessions and make real GDP more stable. They achieve this outcome by weakening the link between real GDP and disposable income and so reduce the effect of a change in real GDP on consumption expenditure. When real GDP increases, induced taxes increase and transfer payments decrease, so disposable income does not increase by as much as the increase in real GDP. As a result, consumption expenditure does not increase by as much as it otherwise would and the multiplier effect is reduced.

We can see the effects of automatic stabilizers by looking at the way in which the government budget deficit fluctuates over the business cycle.

Budget Deficit Over the Business Cycle Figure 29.10 shows the business cycle in part (a) and fluctuations in the budget balance in part (b) between 1980 and 2008. Both parts highlight recessions by shading those periods. By comparing the two parts of the figure, you can see the relationship between the business cycle and the budget deficit. When the economy is in an expansion, the budget deficit declines. (In the figure, a declining deficit means a deficit that is getting closer to

FIGURE 29.10   The Business Cycle and the Budget Deficit

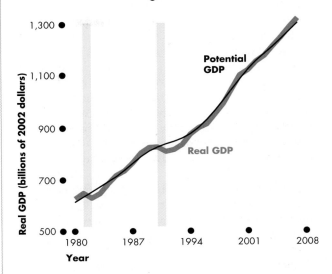

(a) Growth and recessions

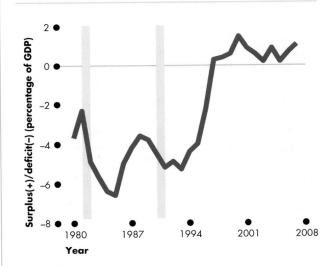

(b) Federal budget balance

As real GDP fluctuates around potential GDP in part (a), the budget deficit fluctuates in part (b). During a recession (shaded years), tax revenues decrease, transfer payments increase, and the budget deficit increases. The deficit also increases *before* a recession as real GDP growth slows and *after* a recession before real GDP growth speeds up.

Sources of data: Statistics Canada, CANSIM Tables 380-0002 and 380-0007, and the Bank of Canada's estimate of the output gap.

myeconlab animation

zero.) As the expansion slows before the recession begins, the budget deficit increases. It continues to increase during the recession and for a period after the recession is over. Then, when the expansion is well under way, the budget deficit declines again.

The budget deficit fluctuates with the business cycle because both revenues and outlays fluctuate with real GDP. As real GDP increases during an expansion, tax revenues increase and transfer payments decrease, so the budget deficit automatically decreases. As real GDP decreases during a recession, tax revenues decrease and transfer payments increase, so the budget deficit automatically increases. Fluctuations in investment and exports have a multiplier effect on real GDP. But fluctuations in the budget deficit decrease the swings in disposable income and make the multiplier effect smaller. They dampen both expansions and recessions.

Cyclical and Structural Balances Because the government budget balance fluctuates with the business cycle, we need a method of measuring the balance that tells us whether it is a temporary cyclical phenomenon or a persistent phenomenon. A government that wants to achieve a balanced budget can ignore a temporary cyclical surplus or deficit because it will vanish when full employment returns. But a surplus or deficit that persists even at full employment cannot be ignored and requires government action to remove it.

To determine whether the budget balance is persistent or temporary and cyclical, economists have developed the concepts of the structural budget balance and the cyclical budget balance. The **structural surplus or deficit** is the budget balance that would occur if the economy were at full employment and real GDP were equal to potential GDP. The **cyclical surplus or deficit** is the actual surplus or deficit minus the structural surplus or deficit. That is, the cyclical surplus or deficit is the part of the budget balance that arises purely because real GDP does not equal potential GDP. For example, suppose that the budget deficit is $100 billion, and that economists have determined that there is a structural deficit of $25 billion. In that case, there is a cyclical deficit of $75 billion.

Figure 29.11 illustrates the concepts of the cyclical surplus or deficit and the structural surplus or deficit. The blue curve shows government outlays. The outlays curve slopes downward because transfer payments, a component of government outlays, decrease

FIGURE 29.11 Cyclical and Structural Surpluses and Deficits

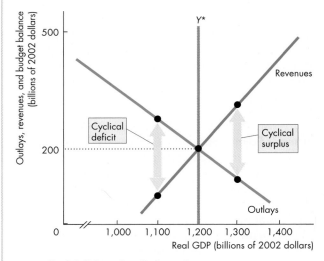

(a) Cyclical deficit and cyclical surplus

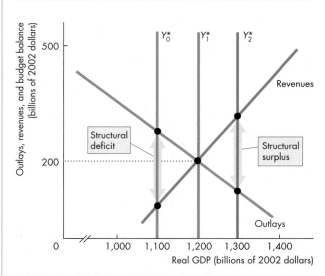

(b) Structural deficit and structural surplus

In part (a), potential GDP is $1,200 billion. When real GDP is less than potential GDP, the budget is in a *cyclical deficit*. When real GDP exceeds potential GDP, the budget is in a *cyclical surplus*. The government has a *balanced budget* when real GDP equals potential GDP. In part (b), if real GDP and potential GDP are $1,100 billion, there is a *structural deficit*. But if real GDP and potential GDP are $1,300 billion, there is a *structural surplus*.

Canada's 2009–10 Budget Deficit

Is It Structural or Cyclical?

Canada's Conservative government, first elected in January 2006 and re-elected in October 2008, has placed a high priority on maintaining a federal budget surplus.

The government wants to maintain a surplus for two reasons. First, it believes that the debt created by the long run of deficits during the 1980s and 1990s remains too large and it wants to see that debt lowered every year. Second, it believes that aiming for a surplus places a discipline on Parliament that can always find reasons to spend ever larger amounts on public projects and social programs.

Given this priority, when Canada began to feel the down draught of the U.S. and global growth slow-down of 2008 and the forecasted recession of 2009, the government faced a dilemma. Should it stick to its surplus priority or join the call for fiscal stimulus to lessen the recession's impact? The government's decision was to permit a cyclical deficit but to maintain a structural balanced budget.

The figure illustrates the situation in Canada in 2009. Potential GDP was (our estimate) $1,370 billion and if actual real GDP remained at that full-

employment level, the budget would be in a small structural surplus.

The forecast for real GDP in 2009 was around $1,330 billion, a recessionary gap of about $40 billion. At that low level of real GDP, the budget moves into a cyclical deficit. A discretionary stimulus would lower the structural surplus and increase the cyclical deficit.

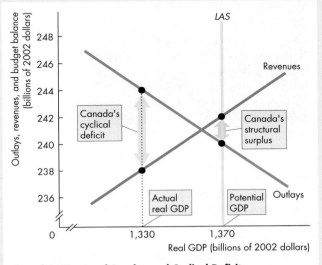

Canada's Structural Surplus and Cyclical Deficit

as real GDP increases. The green curve shows revenues. The revenues curve slopes upward because most components of revenues increase as real GDP increases.

In Fig. 29.11(a), potential GDP is $1,200 billion. If real GDP equals potential GDP, the government has a *balanced budget*. Outlays and revenues each equal $200 billion. If real GDP is less than potential GDP, outlays exceed revenues and there is a *cyclical deficit*. If real GDP is greater than potential GDP, outlays are less than revenues and there is a *cyclical surplus*.

In Fig. 29.11(b), if both real GDP and potential GDP are $1,100 billion ($Y^*_0$), the government has a budget deficit and it is a *structural deficit*. If both real GDP and potential GDP are $1,200 billion ($Y^*_1$), the budget is balanced—a *structural balance* of zero. If both real GDP and potential GDP are $1,300 billion ($Y^*_2$), the government has a budget surplus and it is a *structural surplus*.

Review Quiz

1 How can the federal government use fiscal policy to stabilize the business cycle?

2 Why is the government expenditure multiplier larger than the autonomous tax multiplier?

3 Why does a balanced budget increase in spending and taxes increase aggregate demand?

4 How do induced taxes and transfer payments work as automatic stabilizers to dampen the business cycle?

5 How do we tell whether a budget deficit needs government action to remove it?

myeconlab Work Study Plan 29.3 and get instant feedback.

◆ You've seen how fiscal policy influences potential GDP and real GDP fluctuations. *Reading Between the Lines* on pp. 724–725 applies what you've learned and looks at the attempt by world leaders to coordinate fiscal stimulus and avoid global recession.

Global Coordinated Fiscal Policy

IMF Urges Stimulus as Global Growth Marked Down Sharply

November 6, 2008

IMF forecast cuts world growth by 3/4 percentage points to 2.2 percent for 2009. IMF says policies to stimulate growth can help cushion downturn. ...

The IMF is urging countries to stimulate their economies in the face of a bigger-than-expected slowdown in the global economy triggered by recent financial turmoil. ...

IMF Chief Economist Olivier Blanchard told a news conference: "We think that global fiscal expansion is very much needed at this point. If it comes, then the forecast we have will be on the pessimistic side." ...

Blanchard said the IMF would "advocate at the G-20 a global fiscal expansion as one of the measures that has to be taken fairly soon." Jorg Decressin, of the IMF's Research Department, told the news conference that the United States, Germany, and China were among the countries that have room for additional fiscal stimulus. ...

"There is a clear need for additional macroeconomic policy stimulus relative to what has been announced thus far. ... Room to ease monetary policy should be exploited, especially now that inflation concerns have moderated," [the IMF forecast] stated.

But the forecast said that monetary policy easing may not be enough. "Fiscal stimulus can be effective if it is well targeted, supported by accommodative monetary policy, and implemented in countries that have fiscal space. ...

At a meeting in Toronto on November 6, 2008, Prime Minister Stephen Harper is reported by Bloomberg to have said "governments and central banks face a balancing act deciding how much to stimulate the global economy. There is a very real concern that policy makers may overdo support for the economy, jeopardizing longer-term growth."

Essence of the Story

- The IMF forecasts that all the large industrialized economies will shrink in 2009.

- The IMF Chief Economist is calling for coordinated fiscal stimulus and that it be taken very soon.

- The IMF believes that there is also room to ease monetary policy.

- Prime Minister Stephen Harper said that Canada would take further steps but warned that deciding how much to stimulate the global economy is a balancing act and if policy makers overdo stimulation, longer-term growth might be jeopardized.

Economic Analysis

- The International Monetary Fund (IMF) reported the world real GDP growth rates shown in Fig. 1.

- The average world real GDP growth rate since 2000 is 3.7 percent per year.

- For 2009, the IMF forecasts a growth rate of 2.2 percent, which is similar to that for 2001.

- The outlook for 2009 is unusual in that all the major countries are expected to be in recession with positive world growth coming from the fast-growing developing economies, mainly in Asia.

- To help avoid a deep and long recession, the governments of the G-20 nations (the richest industrial countries and the biggest developing countries) held emergency meetings in Sao Paolo and Washington and discussed the possibility of coordinating fiscal stimulus.

- The United States and China were quick to announce and implement large increases in government expenditure and tax cuts in one of the largest fiscal stimulation measures ever taken.

- Other countries, including Canada, moved more cautiously and Stephen Harper cautioned that stimulus could be overdone.

- Figure 2 shows what Stephen Harper is concerned about.

- World aggregate demand in 2009 is forecasted to be AD_0. The world short-run aggregate supply curve is SAS. Equilibrium real GDP is forecasted to be $44 trillion, which is below potential GDP (here assumed to be $45 trillion).

- A well-judged coordinated fiscal stimulus would shift the AD curve rightward from AD_0 to AD_1. World real GDP would move to potential GDP and the price level would rise (inflation would temporarily rise).

- But the coordinated fiscal stimulus in combination with an expansionary monetary policy (see Chapter 30) might turn out to be more than enough to restore full employment.

- Greater fiscal stimulus (or monetary stimulus) might shift the AD curve further rightward to AD_2. In this case, an inflationary gap will open up and the inflation rate most likely will rise.

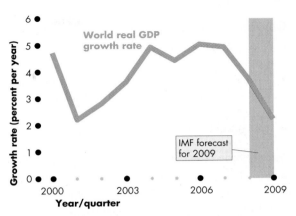

Figure 1 World real GDP growth rate: 2000–2009

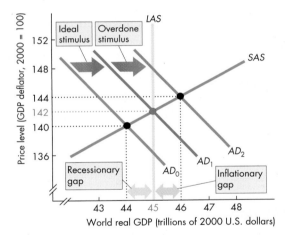

Figure 2 World aggregate supply and aggregate demand

- If the fiscal stimulus turns out to be too large, a further danger is that private investment will get crowded out (see Chapter 23, p. 555–556) and productivity growth will be damaged.

- If crowding out does occur, potential GDP growth will slow and the inflationary gap will become even wider. Rapid and unpredictable inflation will lower investment and slow real GDP growth even further.

- These longer-term consequences of overstimulation are what Stephen Harper is worried about in his remarks reported in the news article.

SUMMARY

Key Points

Government Budgets (pp. 708–713)

- The federal budget is used to achieve macroeconomic objectives.
- Revenues can exceed, equal, or fall short of outlays—the budget can be in surplus, balanced, or in deficit.
- Budget deficits create government debt.

Supply-Side Effects of Fiscal Policy (pp. 714–717)

- Fiscal policy has supply-side effects because taxes weaken the incentive to work and decrease employment and potential GDP.
- The Canadian labour market tax wedge is similar to that in the United States but it is smaller than that in France and the United Kingdom.

- Fiscal policy has supply-side effects because taxes weaken the incentive to save and invest, which lowers the growth rate of real GDP.
- The Laffer curve shows the relationship between the tax rate and the amount of tax revenue collected.

Stabilizing the Business Cycle (pp. 718–723)

- Fiscal stabilization can be discretionary or automatic.
- Discretionary changes in government expenditure or taxes can change aggregate demand but are hampered by law-making lags and the difficulty of correctly diagnosing and forecasting the state of the economy.
- Automatic changes in fiscal policy moderate the business cycle.

Key Figures

Figure 29.5   The Effects of the Income Tax on Aggregate Supply, 714

Figure 29.6   The Effects of a Tax on Capital Income, 716

Figure 29.8   Expansionary Fiscal Policy, 719

Figure 29.9   Contractionary Fiscal Policy, 719

Key Terms

Automatic fiscal policy, 718
Automatic stabilizers, 720
Autonomous tax multiplier, 718
Balanced budget, 709
Balanced budget multiplier, 718
Budget deficit, 709
Budget surplus, 709

Cyclical surplus or deficit, 722
Discretionary fiscal policy, 718
Federal budget, 708
Fiscal policy, 708
Government debt, 711
Government expenditure multiplier, 718

Induced taxes, 721
Laffer curve, 717
Provincial budget, 708
Structural surplus or deficit, 722
Supply-side effects, 714
Tax wedge, 715

PROBLEMS and APPLICATIONS ◆

 Work problems 1–9 in Chapter 29 Study Plan and get instant feedback.
Work problems 10–18 as Homework, a Quiz, or a Test if assigned by your instructor.

1. The government is proposing to raise the tax rate on labour income. Use appropriate diagrams to show the directions of change, not exact magnitudes, of the supply-side effects of such a policy.

   a. What will happen to the supply of labour and the demand for labour and why?
   b. How will the equilibrium quantity of labour employed change and why?
   c. How will the equilibrium before-tax wage rate and after-tax wage rate change and why?
   d. What will happen to potential GDP?
   e. How would your answers to the above questions change if at the same time as raising the tax rate on labour income, the government cut the rate of sales tax to keep the amount of tax collected constant?
   f. What evidence would you present to the government to support the view that a lower tax on labour income will increase employment, potential GDP, and aggregate supply?

2. Suppose that in China, investment is $400 billion, saving is $400 billion, tax revenues are $500 billion, exports are $300 billion, and imports are $200 billion.

   a. Calculate government expenditure.
   b. What is the government budget balance?
   c. Is the government exerting a positive or negative impact on investment?
   d. What fiscal policy action might increase investment and speed economic growth? Explain how the policy action would work.

3. Suppose that instead of taxing nominal capital income, the government changed the tax code so that the inflation rate is subtracted from the interest rate before the taxable income from capital is calculated. Explain and illustrate the effect that this change would have on

   a. The tax rate on capital income.
   b. The supply of loanable funds.
   c. The demand for loanable funds.
   d. Investment and the real interest rate.

4. The economy is in a recession, and the recessionary gap is large.

   a. Describe the discretionary and automatic fiscal policy actions that might occur.
   b. Describe a discretionary fiscal stimulation package that could be used that would not bring a budget deficit.
   c. Explain the risks of discretionary fiscal policy in this situation.

5. The economy is in a recession, the recessionary gap is large, and there is a budget deficit.

   a. Do we know whether the budget deficit is structural or cyclical? Explain your answer.
   b. Do we know whether automatic stabilizers are increasing or decreasing aggregate demand? Explain your answer.
   c. If a discretionary increase in government expenditure occurs, what happens to the structural deficit or surplus? Explain.

6. **Strengthening Canada's Tax Advantage**

   The Government ... announc[ed] $60 billion in tax reductions for individuals, families, and businesses over this and the next five fiscal years. Combined with previous tax relief introduced by the Government, total tax relief over the same period approaches $200 billion. ... The actions in Budget 2008 are affordable, sustainable, and focused on key priorities ... reducing taxes on savings promotes investment, jobs and economic growth. ... The capital cost allowance (CCA) system determines how much of the cost of a capital asset a business may deduct each year for tax purposes. ... [An] accelerated CCA rate ... provides an incentive for ... businesses to accelerate or increase capital investments. ... Canada's scientific research and experimental development tax incentive program provid[ed] over $4 billion in tax assistance in 2007.

   Department of Finance Canada, February 26, 2008

   a. Explain the potential demand-side and supply-side effects of each of the tax policies.
   b. Explain the argument made that the tax cuts are "affordable" and "sustainable."

c. If the government provided $200 billion in tax cuts, does that mean that tax revenues will fall by $200 billion? Explain.

7. Raise Corporate Taxes in Canada, Labour Group Argues

Despite some reductions, corporate tax rates in Canada are still the 11th highest of about 80 developed and developing economies. ... "Canada's corporate income tax rate is on the wrong side of the Laffer curve," a C.D. Howe report said. ... [T]he CLC [Canadian Labour Congress] challenges the argument of business groups that cutting taxes will boost investment. Federal and provincial corporate tax revenues have fallen. ... A $15-billion-a-year loss in corporate tax revenues ... [and] past tax cuts have not been matched by increased business investment, the Canadian Labour Congress argues. ...

CanWest News, September 21, 2007

a. Explain the potential demand-side and supply-side effects of lower corporate tax rates and draw a graph to illustrate these effects.

b. Explain the argument that lower corporate tax rates can increase tax revenue in Canada.

c. Why might Canada's high corporate tax ranking support the C.D. Howe claim about being "on the wrong side of the Laffer curve?" What evidence does the CLC present to refute this claim?

d. If cutting corporate income tax rates resulted in a loss in corporate tax revenues, does that necessarily mean that the lower tax rates did not boost business investment? Explain.

8. Canada May Offer New Economic Stimulus

Finance Minister Jim Flaherty is suggesting the federal government may be willing to provide additional economic stimulus to inject life into Canada's dormant economy—and he's urging the provinces to consider following suit. ... "To the extent that provinces and territories can provide additional stimulus through their policies, that's a benefit to Canadians overall." One area that Canada can move on immediately, Flaherty said, is to speed up infrastructure projects already in the planning stages. ... Flaherty noted that previously introduced federal tax cuts are already adding $1.4 billion in stimulus to the Canadian economy this year and will provide a boost of almost $2 billion in 2009.

CTV News, November 9, 2008

a. Explain Jim Flaherty's statement that "To the extent that provinces and territories can provide additional stimulus through their policies, that's a benefit to Canadians overall."

b. How might Jim Flaherty's plan to "speed up infrastructure projects already in the planning stages" provide stimulus to stabilize the business cycle without imposing deficit pressure on the budget?

c. Explain and use a graph to show how income tax cuts can provide both supply-side and demand-side stimulus.

d. Why might the stimulus provided by the tax cuts be greater in 2009 than in 2008?

e. Explain which would have a larger impact on aggregate demand: a $1.4 billion tax cut or a $1.4 billion increase in government spending.

9. Canada Will Try to Avoid Deficit: Harper

Prime Minister Stephen Harper said ... "The Minister of Finance has been looking at a series of careful measures to try and preserve Canada's balanced budget position. ... But if there's a world-wide agreement we will engage in sufficient stimulus to do our part in carrying global economic demand." He said the government has not yet decided if it would go into deficit spending. ... "We are talking to our American counterparts. On the one hand we can't ignore what the Americans will do[;] on the other hand, we as the government of Canada have to ultimately undertake our own actions... in the best interests of the Canadian economy and the taxpayers. ... The world economy has difficult times ahead," he said. "Canada has so far been sheltered from most of those but will not be sheltered entirely from those problems. ... There is a view that monetary policy alone will not be sufficient to take the global economy through this crisis. ..."

Financial Post, November 15, 2008

a. Explain how Canada could experience a budget deficit even in the absence of discretionary stimulus.

b. Is it possible for Canada to use fiscal stimulus and still avoid a budget deficit? Explain.

c. Explain the potential advantages and disadvantages of coordinating discretionary fiscal policy decisions with other countries.

d. What does Stephen Harper imply about his view of the appropriate roles of monetary policy and fiscal policy?

10. Suppose that in Canada, investment is $160 billion, saving is $140 billion, government expenditure on goods and services is $150 billion, exports are $200 billion, and imports are $250 billion.

   a. What is the amount of tax revenue?
   b. What is the government budget balance?
   c. Is the government exerting a positive or negative impact on investment?
   d. What fiscal policy action might increase investment and speed economic growth? Explain how the policy action would work.

11. Suppose that capital income taxes are based (as they are in Canada and most countries) on nominal interest rates. And suppose that the inflation rate increases by 5 percent. Use appropriate diagrams to explain and illustrate the effect that this change would have on

   a. The tax rate on capital income.
   b. The supply of loanable funds.
   c. The demand for loanable funds.
   d. Equilibrium investment.
   e. The equilibrium real interest rate.

12. The economy is in a boom and the inflationary gap is large.

   a. Describe the discretionary and automatic fiscal policy actions that might occur.
   b. Describe a discretionary fiscal restraint package that could be used that would not produce serious negative supply-side effects.
   c. Explain the risks of discretionary fiscal policy in this situation.

13. The economy is in a boom, the inflationary gap is large, and there is a budget deficit.

   a. Do we know whether the budget deficit is structural or cyclical? Explain your answer.
   b. Do we know whether automatic stabilizers are increasing or decreasing aggregate demand? Explain your answer.
   c. If a discretionary decrease in government expenditure occurs, what happens to the structural balance? Explain your answer.

14. **Clueless Economists Find the Answer**

   "A month ago, when we would normally have released ... an updated Canadian outlook, the economic landscape was in major disarray, and we instead put out a memo titled We Don't Have a Clue and We're Not Going to Pretend That We

Do," economists at the University of Toronto's Institute for Policy Analysis noted. ... "Since that time, the situation has gradually settled down and important new information has been forthcoming such that we now feel that we have enough 'clues' to be able to present forecasts." ... For Canada, they predict the economy contracted at a 0.2-percent annual pace in the summer quarter, will shrink a further 0.2 percent this quarter, and then by a marginal 0.1 percent in the first quarter of 2009, before expanding by 0.4 percent in the spring, and picking up steam in the second half of next year ... an anemic 0.4-percent expansion for all of 2008, down from 2.7 percent in 2007, and then only marginal 0.6-per-cent growth in 2009, after which it projects a strong 3.6-per-cent expansion in 2010.

Ottawa Citizen, November 11, 2008

   a. Explain how economic forecasting can be used to improve discretionary fiscal policy.
   b. How does the uncertainty surrounding economic forecasting limit the effectiveness of discretionary fiscal policy?
   c. Given a forecast of an impending recession, explain how automatic stabilizers may help smooth out the business cycle.
   d. Assuming that automatic stabilizers are not enough to address an impending recession, explain and draw a graph to illustrate how discretionary fiscal policy could be used. What are the potential consequences if these discretionary policies suffer from significant law-making and impact lags?

15. **The Canadian Debt-Strategy Model**

   In its role as fiscal agent to the government, the Bank of Canada provides analysis and advice on decisions about the government's domestic debt portfolio. Debt-management decisions depend on assumptions about future interest rates, macroeconomic outcomes, and fiscal policy, yet when a debt-strategy decision is taken, none of these factors can be known with certainty. ... The debt managers who are responsible for the government's financing strategy have the complex task of choosing a strategy that minimizes the cost of the debt portfolio. ... In any given year, a government must borrow to finance any excess of government expenditures over revenues as well as any maturing debt issued in previous periods.

This borrowing requirement thus depends on past decisions regarding debt issuance and on the government's current surplus or deficit position. The government's position, in turn, depends on the general performance of the macroeconomy and on fiscal policy.

Bank of Canada Review, Summer 2008

a. Explain what is meant by "the cost of the debt portfolio."
b. Explain what factors determine whether or not Canada's government debt is worth the "cost."
c. Explain how annual imbalances impact the government's debt.
d. Explain how a persistent budget deficit can feed itself.
e. Why are managing and forecasting government debt so challenging?

16. **Bracing for Downturn**

Sixteen years of almost uninterrupted job growth has produced an embarrassment of riches in Canada's Employment Insurance account—a surplus, in fact, of $54 billion at current reckoning. But with economic storm clouds gathering south of the border, the Conservative government looks to be preparing for some turbulence ahead. It is creating a special cushion of $2 billion in a side account to help pay for any quick surge in payouts caused by an economic downturn. ...

CBC News, February 26, 2008

a. Explain how Employment Insurance (EI) serves as an automatic stabilizer. How does being prepared for a "quick surge" impact the effectiveness of EI?
b. Explain how EI impacts the budget balance over the business cycle.
c. What is the potential supply-side impact of EI?

17. **Conservative Canada Taking Fiscal Stimulus Slowly**

Canada says it will play its part in a global effort to stimulate the world economy, but Finance Minister Jim Flaherty said on Saturday he still did not foresee running a budget deficit in the current fiscal year. Flaherty said he would include fiscal measures when he presents his fall fiscal and economic update in the last week of November, but it would not likely contain new tax cuts and

it would also try to restrain public sector spending. ... [T]he country might move into a deficit as the result of future, undefined stimulus measures but that would likely only start in the fiscal year that begins April 1. ... Canada is the only one of the Group of Seven big industrial countries still to have a fiscal surplus, and Prime Minister Stephen Harper said this budget position gave it more latitude than many others, especially those with structural deficits. "What we've got to be sure is if we do short-term deficit spending as a deliberate policy—if we do that; we haven't settled on doing that—we will have to be able to demonstrate to Canadians that those deficits will genuinely be short-term and cyclical and we will come out of them quickly," he said.

Reuters, November 15, 2008

a. Explain how fiscal policy may still help stabilize the business cycle even if Canada fails to cut taxes and follows through with plans to "restrain public sector spending."
b. If the government did cut taxes and increase spending, which impact would have a larger multiplier effect? Explain.
c. What major limitation associated with the usage of discretionary fiscal policy is revealed in this article?
d. Explain why Prime Minister Harper believes Canada currently has more "latitude" when designing fiscal policy than other industrial nations.
e. Explain the difference between cyclical and structural deficits.
f. Explain why Prime Minister Harper places so much emphasis on pointing out that any deficit must be "short-term and cyclical."

18. Study *Reading Between the Lines* on pp. 724–725.

a. Describe the fiscal policy proposed by the G-20 finance ministers.
b. Explain the effects of the proposed fiscal policy if it is implemented well.
c. Explain Prime Minister Stephen Harper's concerns about overstimulating the global and Canadian economies.
d. Why are automatic stabilizers not sufficient to boost aggregate demand in the Canadian and global economies in 2009?

30 ◆ Monetary Policy

After studying this chapter, you will be able to

- Describe Canada's monetary policy objective and the framework for setting and achieving it
- Explain how the Bank of Canada makes its interest rate decision and achieves its interest rate target
- Explain the transmission channels through which the Bank of Canada influences the inflation rate
- Explain and compare alternative monetary policy strategies

At eight regularly scheduled meetings a year, the Bank of Canada announces whether the interest rate will rise, fall, or remain constant until the next decision date. And every business day, the Bank operates in financial markets to implement its decision and ensure that its target interest rate is achieved. Financial market traders, economic journalists, and pundits watch the economy for clues about what the Bank will decide at its next meeting.

How does the Bank of Canada make its interest rate decision? What exactly does it do every day to keep the interest rate where it wants it? And how does a change in the Bank's interest rate influence the economy? Can the Bank speed up economic growth and lower unemployment by lowering the interest rate and can the Bank keep inflation in check by raising the interest rate?

The Bank of Canada's monetary policy strategy gradually evolves, and the current strategy isn't the only one that might be used. Is the current monetary policy strategy the best one? What are the benefits and what are the risks associated with the alternative monetary policy strategies?

You learned about the functions of the Bank of Canada and its long-run effects on the price level and the inflation rate in Chapter 24. In this chapter, you will learn about the Bank's monetary policy in both the long run and the short run. You will learn how the Bank influences the interest rate and how a change in the interest rate influences the economy. You will also review the alternative ways in which monetary policy might be conducted. In *Reading Between the Lines* at the end of the chapter, you will see the Bank of Canada in an aggressive move to avoid a deep and prolonged recession in 2008 and 2009.

◆ Monetary Policy Objective and Framework

Canada's monetary policy objective and the framework for setting and achieving that objective stem from the relationship between the Bank of Canada and the government of Canada.

We'll first discuss the objective of monetary policy and then describe the framework and assignment of responsibility for achieving the objective.

Monetary Policy Objective

The objective of monetary policy is ultimately political, and it stems from the mandate of the Bank, which is set out in the Bank of Canada Act.

Bank of Canada Act The objective of monetary policy as set out in the preamble to the Bank of Canada Act of 1935 is to

regulate credit and currency in the best interests of the economic life of the nation ... and to mitigate by its influence fluctuations in the general level of production, trade, prices and employment, so far as may be possible within the scope of monetary action ...

In simple language, these words have come to mean that the Bank's job is to control the quantity of money and interest rates in order to avoid inflation and, when possible, prevent excessive swings in real GDP growth and unemployment.

This emphasis on inflation has been made concrete by an agreement between the Bank and government.

Joint Statement of the Government of Canada and the Bank of Canada

In a joint statement (the most recent of which was made in 2006), the government of Canada and the Bank of Canada have agreed that

- The inflation-control target range will be 1 to 3 percent a year.
- Policy will aim at keeping the trend of inflation at the 2 percent target midpoint.
- The agreement will run for five years and be reviewed before the end of 2011.

A monetary policy strategy in which the central bank commits to an explicit inflation target and to explaining how its actions will achieve that target is called **inflation rate targeting**.

Interpretation of the Agreement The inflation-control target uses the Consumer Price Index (or CPI) as the measure of inflation. So the Bank has agreed to keep trend CPI inflation at a target of 2 percent a year.

But the Bank also pays close attention to *core inflation* (see pp. 502–503), which it calls its *operational guide*. The Bank believes that the core inflation rate provides a better measure of the underlying inflation trend and better predicts future CPI inflation.

Although the Bank watches the core inflation rate closely, it must take into account the possibility that the eight volatile elements that it excludes have a different trend inflation rate from the remaining items. As it turns out, between 1995 and 2000, the core and overall CPI trends were the same. But since 2000, the core rate has run at about 0.5 percent a year below the overall CPI inflation rate.

Actual Inflation The performance of Canada's inflation since the mid-1990s, when the current target was initially set, has been close to target. Figure 30.1 shows just how close.

In part (a), you can see the target range of 1 to 3 percent a year. And you can see that the actual inflation rate has only rarely gone outside the target range. You can also see that the inflation rate has been both above target and below target on occasion, so there is no bias or tendency for inflation to be persistently above or below target.

In part (b), you can see the trend of inflation at the 2 percent target midpoint. The actual path of the CPI was on trend from 1995 through 1998 and again from 2001 through 2007. Between 1999 and 2001, the CPI moved below the 2 percent trend line.

The general message of Fig. 30.1 is that the Bank of Canada has done a remarkable job of holding inflation to its 2 percent target with only small and temporary deviations from that goal.

Rationale for an Inflation-Control Target Two main benefits flow from adopting an inflation-control target. The first benefit is that the purpose of the Bank of Canada's policy actions are more clearly understood

FIGURE 30.1   Inflation-Control Target and Outcome

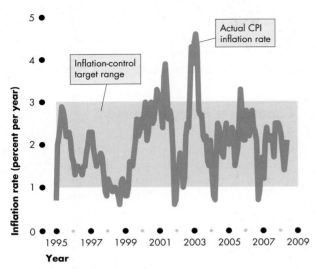

(a) Inflation target and outcome

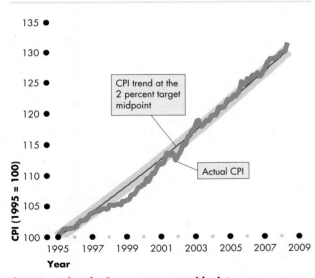

(b) CPI trend at the 2 percent target midpoint

The Bank of Canada and the government of Canada agreed that the inflation-control target range will be 1 percent to 3 percent (part a) and that policy will aim at keeping the trend of inflation at the 2 percent target midpoint (part b).

Sources of data: Statistics Canada, CANSIM Table 326-0022, and Bank of Canada, Joint Statement of the Government of Canada and the Bank of Canada on the Renewal of the Inflation-Control Target, November 23, 2006.

myeconlab animation

by financial market traders. A clearer understanding leads to fewer surprises and mistakes on the part of savers and investors.

The second benefit is that the target provides an anchor for expectations about future inflation. Firmly held expectations of low inflation make the short-run output-inflation (or unemployment-inflation) trade-off as favourable as possible. (see Chapter 28, pp. 686–688). Firmly held (and correct) inflation expectations also help to make better economic decisions, which in turn help to achieve a more efficient allocation of resources and more stable economic growth.

Controversy About the Inflation-Control Target Not everyone agrees that the adoption of an inflation-control target brings benefits. Critics argue that by focusing on inflation, the Bank of Canada sometimes permits the unemployment rate to rise or the real GDP growth rate to suffer.

The fear of these critics is that if the inflation rate begins to edge upward towards and perhaps beyond the upper limit of the target range, the Bank of Canada might reign in aggregate demand and push the economy into recession. Related, the Bank might end up permitting the value of the dollar on the foreign exchange market to rise and making exports suffer.

One response of supporters of inflation targeting is that by keeping inflation low and stable, monetary policy makes its maximum possible contribution towards achieving full employment and sustained economic growth.

Another response is, "Look at the record." The last time the Bank of Canada created a recession was at the beginning of the 1990s when it was faced with the threat of ongoing double-digit inflation. Since that time, monetary policy has been sensitive to the state of employment while maintaining its focus on achieving its inflation target.

Responsibility for Monetary Policy

The government of Canada and the Bank of Canada jointly agree on the monetary policy target, but the Bank of Canada Act places responsibility for the conduct of monetary policy on the Bank's Governing Council.

Governing Council of the Bank of Canada The members of the Bank's Governing Council are the Governor, Senior Deputy Governor, and four Deputy Governors.

All the members of the Governing Council are experts in monetary economics and monetary policymaking and, normally, they are people who have been promoted from within the ranks of economists working in the Bank's research and policy departments.

The current Governor (appointed in 2008) is Mark Carney, an economist who has had wide experience in private sector banking, government departments, and the Bank of Canada.

Bank of Canada Economists   The Bank of Canada employs research economists who write papers on monetary policy and the state of the Canadian and international economies. These economists provide the Governing Council with extensive briefings that guide monetary policy.

Consultations with the Government   The Bank of Canada Act requires regular consultations on monetary policy between the Governor and the Minister of Finance. The Act also lays out what must happen if the Governor and the Minister disagree in a profound way.

In such an event, the Minister would direct the Bank in writing to follow a specified course and the Bank would be obliged to accept the directive. The Governor would most likely resign in such a situation. While in the past there have been disagreements between the government and the Bank, no formal directive has ever been issued.

You now know the objective of monetary policy and can describe the framework and assignment of responsibility for achieving that objective. Your next task is to see how the Bank of Canada conducts its monetary policy.

Review Quiz

1   What is the Bank of Canada's objective of monetary policy?
2   What are the two parts of the inflation-control target?
3   How does the core inflation rate differ from the overall CPI inflation rate?
4   What is the Bank of Canada's record in achieving its inflation-control target?

 Work Study Plan 30.1 and get instant feedback.

◆▶ The Conduct of Monetary Policy

In this section, we describe the way in which the Bank of Canada conducts its monetary policy. We follow this description in the final section with an account of alternative approaches to monetary policy and an evaluation of the Bank's approach.

Choosing a Policy Instrument

As the sole issuer of Canadian money, the Bank of Canada can decide to control the quantity of money (the monetary base), the price of Canadian money on the foreign exchange market (the exchange rate), or the opportunity cost of holding money (the short-term interest rate). If you need a quick refresher, check back to Chapter 24, p. 581 to see how the quantity of money affects the interest rate and to Chapter 25, pp. 611–613 to see how the interest rate or direct intervention in the foreign exchange market affects the exchange rate.

While the Bank of Canada can set any one of these three variables, it cannot set all three. The values of two of them are the consequence of the value at which the third one is set. If the Bank decided to decrease the quantity of money, both the interest rate and the exchange rate would rise. If the Bank decided to raise the interest rate, the quantity of money would decrease and the exchange rate would rise. And if the Bank decided to lower the exchange rate, the quantity of money would increase and the interest rate would fall.

So the Bank must decide which of these three instruments to use. It might decide to select one and stick with it. Or it might switch among them.

The Overnight Rate

The Bank of Canada's choice of policy instrument (which is the same choice as that made by most other major central banks) is a short-term interest rate. Given this choice, the Bank permits the exchange rate and the quantity of money to find their own equilibrium values and has no preset views about what those values should be.

The specific interest rate that the Bank of Canada targets is the **overnight loans rate**, which is the interest rate on overnight loans that members of the Large Value Transfer System or LVTS (the big banks) make to each other (see Chapter 24, p. 575.)

Figure 30.2 shows the overnight loans rate since 1995. You can see that the overnight loans rate was a bit more than 8 percent a year in 1995 and was increased to around 6 percent a year on two occasions. All of these periods with a high overnight rate are ones in which inflation was a concern.

In recent years, the overnight rate has been at historically low levels. The reason is that with inflation well anchored inside its target range, the Bank wanted to lean in the direction of avoiding recession.

Since late 2000, the Bank has established eight fixed dates on which it announces its overnight rate target for the coming period of approximately six weeks. Before 2000, the Bank announced changes in the overnight rate whenever it thought a change was required. And even now, the Bank sometimes acts in an emergency between normal announcement dates.

FIGURE 30.2 The Overnight Loans Rate

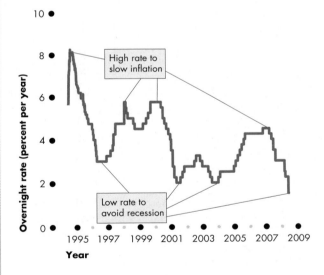

The Bank of Canada sets a target range for the overnight loans rate and then takes actions to keep the rate inside its target range. When the Bank wants to slow inflation, it takes actions that raise the overnight loans rate. When the Bank wants to avoid recession and inflation is low, it takes actions that lower the overnight loans rate.

Source of data: Statistics Canada, CANSIM Table 176-0048.

myeconlab animation

Although the Bank can change the overnight rate by any (reasonable) amount that it chooses, it normally changes the rate by only a quarter of a percentage point.[1]

How does the Bank decide the appropriate level for the overnight rate? And how, having made that decision, does the Bank get the overnight rate to move to the target level? We'll now answer these two questions.

The Bank's Decision-Making Process

Two alternative decision-making processes might be used. They are summarized by the terms:

- Instrument rule
- Targeting rule

Instrument Rule   An **instrument rule** is a decision rule for monetary policy that sets the policy instrument at a level that is based on the current state of the economy. The best known instrument rule is the Taylor rule, which sets the interest rate at a level that depends on the deviation of the inflation rate from target and the size and direction of the output gap. For each percentage point by which inflation is above target, the interest rate is set one percentage point higher. And for each percentage point by which real GDP exceeds potential GDP (the percentage size of the output gap), the interest rate is set another percentage point higher. (We examine the Taylor rule later in this chapter—see p. 747.)

Targeting Rule   A **targeting rule** is a decision rule for monetary policy that sets the policy instrument at a level that makes the forecast of the policy target equal to the target. Where the policy target is the inflation rate and the instrument is the overnight rate, the targeting rule sets the overnight rate at a level that makes the forecast of the inflation rate equal to the target for the inflation rate.

To implement such a targeting rule, a central bank must gather and process a large amount of information about the economy, the way it responds to shocks, and the way it responds to policy. It must then process all this data and come to a judgment about the best level for the policy instrument.

---

[1] A quarter of a percentage point is also called 25 basis points. A basis point is one-hundredth of one percentage point.

The Bank of Canada (along with most other central banks) follows a process that uses a targeting rule.

For the Bank of Canada, the process begins with an exercise that uses a model of the Canadian economy that you can think of as a sophisticated version of the aggregate supply–aggregate demand model (see Chapter 26). The Bank's economists provide the Governor and Governing Council with a baseline forecast that has the overnight loans rate set at a level that hits the inflation target two years in the future.

All the available regional, national, and international data on macroeconomic performance, financial markets, and inflation expectations are reviewed, discussed, and weighed in a careful deliberative process that ends with the Governing Council finding a consensus on the interest rate level to set.

After announcing an interest rate decision, the Bank engages in a public communication to explain the reasons for the Bank's decision.

Hitting the Overnight Rate Target

Once an interest rate decision is made, the Bank of Canada achieves its target by using two tools:

- Operating band
- Open market operations

Operating Band   The **operating band** is the target overnight rate plus or minus 0.25 percentage points. So the operating band is 0.5 percentage points wide. The Bank of Canada creates the operating band by setting two other interest rates: bank rate and the interest rate on reserves.

Bank rate is the interest rate that the Bank of Canada charges big (LVTS-participating) banks on loans. If a bank is short of reserves, it can always obtain reserves from the Bank of Canada but it must pay bank rate on the amount of borrowed reserves.

The Bank of Canada sets bank rate at the target overnight rate plus 0.25 percentage points. So, for example, when the target overnight rate is 4 percent, bank rate is 4.25 percent.

Because the Bank of Canada is willing to lend funds to banks at this interest rate, bank rate acts as a cap on the overnight loans rate. If a bank can borrow from the Bank of Canada at bank rate, it will not borrow from another bank unless the interest rate is lower than or equal to bank rate.

The Bank of Canada pays banks interest on their reserves at the Bank of Canada. The Bank calls these reserves "settlement balances" and the interest rate that they earn is the **settlement balances rate**. The Bank of Canada sets the settlement balances rate at the target overnight rate minus 0.25 percentage points, which also equals the low end of the Bank's target range for the overnight rate. If banks can earn the settlement balances rate from the Bank of Canada, they will not make overnight loans to other banks unless they earn a higher interest rate than what the Bank of Canada is paying.

You can see now that the Bank of Canada can always make the overnight rate remain within 0.25 percentage points of its target. But the Bank wants to do better than that and keep the overnight loans rate at its target, not at one end of the range or the other. The second policy tool is used to move the overnight rate to its target.

Open Market Operations   An **open market operation** is the purchase or sale of government of Canada securities—Treasury bills and government bonds—by the Bank of Canada from or to a chartered bank or the public. When the Bank of Canada buys securities on the open market, it pays for them with newly created reserves that are held by banks. When the Bank of Canada sells securities, the Bank is paid for them with reserves held by banks. So open market operations directly influence the reserves of banks.

During the morning of each business day, banks trade loans with each other. And just before noon, the Bank of Canada conducts open market operations if they are needed.

If the overnight rate is above target, the Bank buys securities to increase reserves, which increases the supply of overnight funds and lowers the overnight rate. If the overnight rate is below target, the Bank sells securities to decrease reserves, which decreases the supply of overnight funds and raises the overnight rate. If the overnight rate is at the target level, the Bank neither buys nor sells.

How an Open Market Operation Works

When the Bank of Canada conducts an open market operation, the reserves of the banking system change. To see why this outcome occurs, we'll trace the effects of an open market operation in which the Bank of Canada buys $100 million of government securities in the open market from CIBC.

After this transaction has been made,

1. CIBC has $100 million less securities, and the Bank of Canada has $100 million more securities.

2. The Bank of Canada pays for the securities by placing $100 million in CIBC's deposit account at the Bank of Canada.

Figure 30.3 shows the effects of these actions on the balance sheets of the Bank of Canada and CIBC. Ownership of the securities passes from CIBC to the Bank of Canada, so CIBC's assets decrease by $100 million and the Bank of Canada's assets increase by $100 million, as shown by the blue arrow running from CIBC to the Bank of Canada.

The Bank of Canada pays for the securities by placing $100 million in CIBC's reserve account at the Bank of Canada, as shown by the green arrow running from the Bank of Canada to CIBC.

The Bank of Canada's assets increase by $100 million, and its liabilities also increase by $100 million. CIBC's total assets are unchanged. It has sold securities in exchange for reserves.

If the Bank of Canada sells $100 million of government securities in the open market, the events that you've just seen occur in reverse.

When the Bank of Canada sells securities,

1. CIBC has $100 million more securities, and the Bank of Canada has $100 million less securities.

2. CIBC pays for the securities by using $100 million of its reserves deposit account at the Bank of Canada.

Figure 30.4 shows the effects of these actions on the balance sheets of the Bank of Canada and CIBC. Ownership of the securities passes from the Bank of Canada to CIBC, so CIBC's assets increase by $100 million and the Bank of Canada's assets decrease by $100 million, as shown by the blue arrow running from the Bank of Canada to CIBC.

CIBC uses $100 million of its reserve account at the Bank of Canada to pay for the securities, as the green arrow running from CIBC to the Bank of Canada shows.

The Bank of Canada's assets decrease by $100 million, and its liabilities also decrease by $100 million. CIBC's total assets are unchanged. It has used reserves to buy securities.

An increase or a decrease in reserves changes the overnight rate by changing the demand for and supply of overnight loans.

FIGURE 30.3 The Bank of Canada Buys Securities

The Bank of Canada

Assets		Liabilities	
Securities	+$100	Reserves of CIBC	+$100

The Bank of Canada buys securities from a bank ... | ... and pays for the securities by increasing the reserves of the bank

CIBC

Assets		Liabilities
Securities	−$100	
Reserves	+$100	

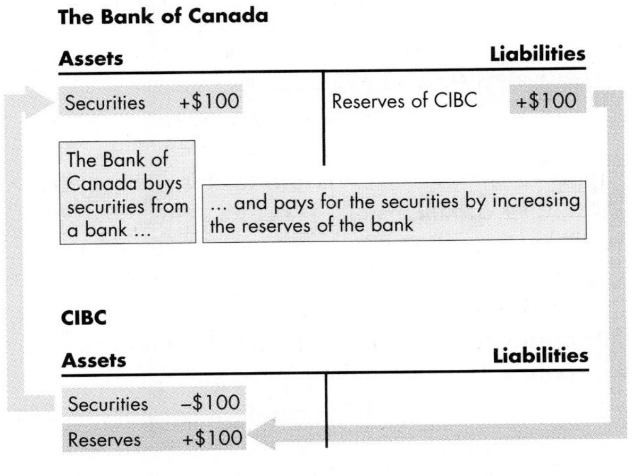

When the Bank of Canada buys securities in the open market, it creates bank reserves. Bank of Canada assets and liabilities increase, and the selling bank exchanges securities for reserves.

myeconlab animation

FIGURE 30.4 The Bank of Canada Sells Securities

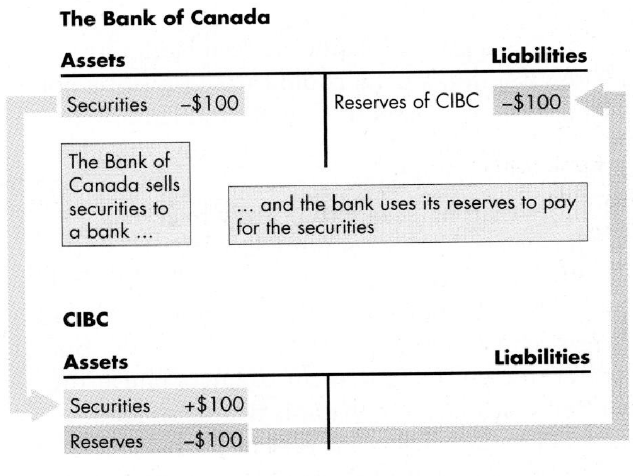

The Bank of Canada

Assets		Liabilities	
Securities	−$100	Reserves of CIBC	−$100

The Bank of Canada sells securities to a bank ... | ... and the bank uses its reserves to pay for the securities

CIBC

Assets		Liabilities
Securities	+$100	
Reserves	−$100	

When the Bank of Canada sells securities in the open market, it reduces bank reserves. Bank of Canada assets and liabilities decrease, and the buying bank exchanges reserves for securities.

myeconlab animation

Equilibrium in the Market for Reserves

To see how an open market operation changes the overnight interest rate, we must see what happens in the market for the reserves of the banks.

Banks hold reserves so they can make payments. The amount that a bank will be called on to pay at any given moment fluctuates and cannot be forecasted accurately. If a bank runs out of reserves and is obliged to make a payment, reserves must be borrowed from the Bank of Canada. So bank rate is the opportunity cost of borrowed reserves.

The more reserves a bank holds, the less likely it is that the bank will need to borrow and pay bank rate. But reserves are costly to hold. The alternative to holding reserves is to lend them. The higher the interest rate at which reserves can be loaned, the higher is the opportunity cost of holding reserves. And the higher the opportunity cost, the greater is the incentive to economize on the quantity of reserves.

So the quantity of reserves demanded by banks depends on the overnight rate. The higher the overnight rate, other things remaining the same, the smaller is the quantity of reserves demanded.

Figure 30.5 shows the demand curve for reserves as the curve labelled *RD*. The *x*-axis measures the quantity of reserves held. If the entire banking system is borrowing from the Bank of Canada, reserves are negative. The *y*-axis measures the overnight rate. You can see that the overnight rate always lies inside the operating band. Why?

The overnight rate cannot exceed bank rate because if it did, a bank could earn a profit by borrowing from the Bank of Canada and lending to another bank. But all banks can borrow from the Bank of Canada at bank rate, so no bank is willing to pay more than bank rate to borrow reserves.

The overnight rate cannot fall below the settlement balances rate because if it did, a bank could earn a profit by borrowing from another bank and increasing its reserves at the Bank of Canada. But all banks can earn the settlement balances rate at the Bank of Canada, so no bank is willing to lend reserves at a rate below the settlement balances rate.

The Bank of Canada's open market operations determine the actual quantity of reserves in the banking system, and equilibrium in the market for reserves determines the actual overnight rate. So by using open market operations, the Bank of Canada can keep the overnight rate on target.

FIGURE 30.5 The Market for Bank Reserves

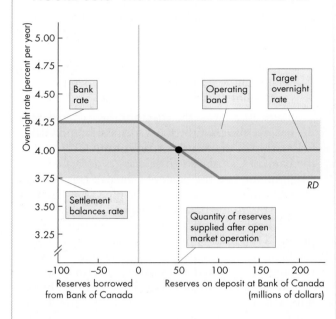

The demand curve for reserves is *RD*. If the overnight rate equals bank rate, banks are indifferent between borrowing reserves and lending reserves. The demand curve is horizontal at bank rate. If the overnight rate equals the settlement balances rate, banks are indifferent between holding reserves and lending reserves. The demand curve is horizontal at the settlement balances rate. Equilibrium, where the quantity of reserves demanded equals the quantity supplied, determines the overnight rate.

 animation

Review Quiz

1   What is the Bank of Canada's monetary policy instrument?
2   Summarize the Bank of Canada's monetary policy decision-making process.
3   What is the operating band? What does it do?
4   What happens when the Bank of Canada buys or sells securities in the open market?
5   How is the overnight rate determined in the market for reserves?

  Work Study Plan 30.2 and get instant feedback.

Monetary Policy Transmission

You've seen that the Bank of Canada's goal is to keep the inflation rate as close as possible to 2 percent a year. And you've seen how the Bank can use its power to set the overnight rate at its desired level. We're now going to trace the events that follow a change in the overnight rate and see how those events lead to the ultimate policy goal. We'll begin with a quick overview of the transmission process and then look at each step a bit more closely.

Quick Overview

When the Bank of Canada lowers the overnight rate, other short-term interest rates and the exchange rate also fall. The quantity of money and the supply of loanable funds increase. The long-term real interest rate falls. The lower real interest rate increases consumption expenditure and investment. And the lower exchange rate makes Canadian exports cheaper and imports more costly, so net exports increase. Easier bank loans reinforce the effect of lower interest rates on aggregate expenditure. Aggregate demand increases, which increases real GDP and the price level relative to what they would have been. Real GDP growth and inflation speed up.

When the Bank raises the overnight rate, as the sequence of events that we've just reviewed plays out, the effects are in the opposite directions.

Figure 30.6 provides a schematic summary of these ripple effects for both a cut and a rise in the overnight rate. These effects stretch out over a period of between one and two years. The interest rate and exchange rate effects are immediate. The effects on money and bank loans follow in a few weeks and run for a few months. Real long-term interest rates change quickly. Spending plans change and real GDP growth slows after about one year. The inflation rate changes between one year and two years after the change in the overnight rate. But these time lags are not entirely predictable and can be longer or shorter.

We're going to look at each stage in the transmission process, starting with the interest rate effects.

Interest Rate Changes

The first effect of a monetary policy decision is a change in the overnight rate. Other interest rates

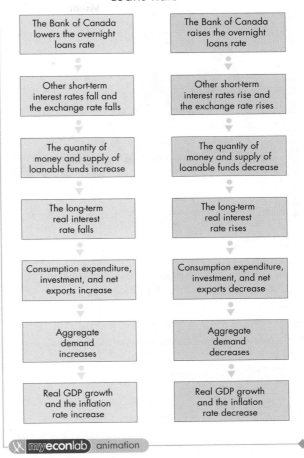

FIGURE 30.6 The Ripple Effects of a Change in the Overnight Loans Rate

myeconlab animation

then change. These interest rate effects occur quickly and relatively predictably.

Figure 30.7 shows the fluctuations in four interest rates:

- The overnight rate
- The short-term bill rate
- The 10-year government bond rate
- The long-term corporate bond rate

Overnight rate As soon as the Bank announces a new setting for the overnight rate, it undertakes the necessary open market operations to hit the target.

Short-Term Bill Rate The short-term bill rate is the interest rate paid by the government of Canada on 3-month Treasury bills. Notice how closely the short-term

FIGURE 30.7   Four Interest Rates

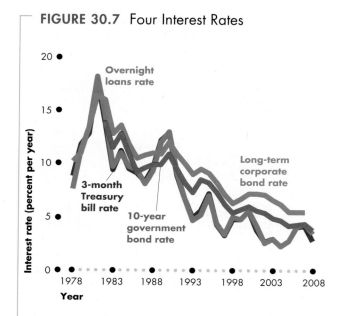

The short-term interest rates—the overnight rate and the short-term bill rate—move closely together. The long-term bond rates are higher than the short-term rates, and they fluctuate less than the short-term rates.

Source of data: Statistics Canada, CANSIM Table 176-0043.

The 10-Year Government Bond Rate   The 10-year government bond rate is the interest rate paid on bonds issued by the government of Canada. The government issues bonds of various maturities to manage its overall borrowing and finance the national debt.

The Long-Term Corporate Bond Rate   The long-term corporate bond rate is the interest rate paid on bonds issued by large corporations. Businesses pay this interest rate on the loans that finance their purchases of new capital, so this interest rate influences investment decisions.

Two features of both of these longer-term bond rates stand out: They are higher than the short-term rates, and they fluctuate less than the short-term rates. The long-term interest rates are higher than the two short-term rates because longer-term loans are riskier than short-term loans. To provide the incentive that brings forth a supply of long-term loans, lenders must be compensated for the additional risk. Without compensation for the additional risk, only short-term loans would be supplied.

Long-term interest rates fluctuate less than short-term rates because expectations about future short-term interest rates as well as current short-term interest rates influence long-term interest rates. The alternative to borrowing or lending long term is to borrow or lend using a sequence of short-term securities. If the long-term interest rate exceeds the expected average of future short-term interest rates, people will lend long term and borrow short term. The long-term interest rate will fall. And if the long-term interest rate is below the expected average of future short-term interest rates, people will borrow long term and lend short term. The long-term interest rate will rise.

These market forces keep the long-term interest rate close to the expected average of future short-term interest rates (plus a premium for the extra risk associated with long-term loans). The expected average future short-term interest rate fluctuates less than the current short-term interest rate.

Exchange Rate Fluctuations

The exchange rate responds to changes in the interest rate in Canada relative to the interest rates in other countries—*the Canadian interest rate differential*. We explain this influence in Chapter 25 (see pp. 601–602).

bill rate follows the overnight rate. The two rates are almost identical. A powerful substitution effect keeps these two interest rates close. Chartered banks have a choice about how to hold their short-term liquid assets, and an overnight loan to another bank is a close substitute for short-term securities such as Treasury bills. If the interest rate on Treasury bills is higher than the overnight rate, the quantity of overnight loans supplied decreases and the demand for Treasury bills increases. The price of Treasury bills rises and the interest rate falls.

Similarly, if the interest rate on Treasury bills is lower than the overnight rate, the quantity of overnight loans supplied increases and the demand for Treasury bills decreases. The price of Treasury bills falls, and the interest rate rises.

When the interest rate on Treasury bills is close to the overnight rate, there is no incentive for a bank to switch between making an overnight loan and buying Treasury bills. Both the Treasury bill market and the overnight loans market are in equilibrium.

When the Bank of Canada raises the overnight rate, the Canadian interest rate differential rises and, other things remaining the same, the Canadian dollar appreciates; when the Bank of Canada lowers the overnight rate, the Canadian interest rate differential falls and, other things remaining the same, the Canadian dollar depreciates.

Many factors other than the Canadian interest rate differential influence the exchange rate, so when the Bank of Canada changes the overnight rate, the exchange rate does not usually change in exactly the way it would with other things remaining the same. So while monetary policy influences the exchange rate, other factors also make the exchange rate change.

Money and Bank Loans

The quantity of money and bank loans change when the Bank of Canada changes the overnight rate target. A rise in the overnight rate decreases the quantity of money and bank loans, and a fall in the overnight rate increases the quantity of money and bank loans. These changes occur for two reasons: The quantity of deposits and loans created by the banking system changes and the quantity of money demanded changes.

You've seen that to change the overnight rate, the Bank of Canada must change the quantity of bank reserves. A change in the quantity of bank reserves changes the monetary base, which in turn changes the quantity of deposits and loans that the banking system can create. A rise in the overnight rate decreases bank reserves and decreases the quantity of deposits and bank loans created; a fall in the overnight rate increases bank reserves and increases the quantity of deposits and bank loans created.

The quantity of money created by the banking system must be held by households and firms. The change in the interest rate changes the quantity of money demanded. A fall in the interest rate increases the quantity of money demanded; a rise in the interest rate decreases the quantity of money demanded.

A change in the quantity of money and the supply of bank loans directly affects consumption and investment plans. With more money and easier access to loans, consumers and firms spend more. With less money and loans harder to get, they spend less.

The Long-Term Real Interest Rate

Demand and supply in the market for loanable funds determine the long-term *real interest rate*, which equals the long-term *nominal* interest rate minus the expected inflation rate. The long-term real interest rate influences expenditure decisions.

In the long run, demand and supply in the loanable funds market depend only on real forces—on saving and investment decisions. But in the short run, when the price level is not fully flexible, the supply of loanable funds is influenced by the supply of bank loans. Changes in the overnight rate change the supply of bank loans, which changes the supply of loanable funds and changes the real interest rate in the loanable funds market.

A fall in the overnight rate that increases the supply of bank loans increases the supply of loanable funds and lowers the equilibrium real interest rate. A rise in the overnight rate that decreases the supply of bank loans decreases the supply of loanable funds and raises the equilibrium real interest rate.

These changes in the real interest rate, along with the other factors we've just described, change expenditure plans.

Expenditure Plans

The ripple effects that follow a change in the overnight rate change three components of aggregate expenditure:

- Consumption expenditure
- Investment
- Net exports

Consumption Expenditure Other things remaining the same, the lower the real interest rate, the greater is the amount of consumption expenditure and the smaller is the amount of saving.

Investment Other things remaining the same, the lower the real interest rate, the greater is the amount of investment.

Net Exports Other things remaining the same, the lower the interest rate, the lower is the exchange rate and the greater are exports and the smaller are imports.

So eventually, a cut in the overnight rate increases aggregate expenditure and a rise in the overnight rate curtails aggregate expenditure. These changes in aggregate expenditure plans change aggregate demand, real GDP, and the price level.

The Change in Aggregate Demand, Real GDP, and the Price Level

The final link in the transmission chain is a change in aggregate demand and a resulting change in real GDP and the price level. By changing real GDP and the price level relative to what they would have been with no change in the overnight rate, the Bank of Canada influences its ultimate goal: the inflation rate. The Bank also influences the output gap.

The Bank of Canada Fights Recession

If inflation is low and real GDP is below potential GDP, the Bank acts to restore full employment and keep inflation steady. Figure 30.8 shows the effects of the Bank's actions, starting in the market for bank reserves and ending in the market for real GDP.

Market for Bank Reserves In Fig. 30.8(a), which shows the market for bank reserves, the Bank lowers the target overnight rate from 5 percent to 4 percent a year. To achieve the new target, the Bank buys

securities and increases the supply of reserves of the banking system from RS_0 to RS_1.

Money Market With increased reserves, the banks create deposits by making loans and the supply of money increases. The short-term interest rate falls and the quantity of money demanded increases. In Fig. 30.8(b), the supply of money increases from MS_0 to MS_1, the interest rate falls from 5 percent to 4 percent a year, and the quantity of money increases from $800 billion to $900 billion. The interest rate in the money market and the overnight rate are kept close to each other by the powerful substitution effect described on p. 740.

Loanable Funds Market Banks create money by making loans. In the long run, an increase in the supply of bank loans is matched by a rise in the price level and the quantity of *real* loans is unchanged. But in the short run, with a sticky price level, an increase in the supply of bank loans increases the supply of (real) loanable funds.

FIGURE 30.8   The Bank of Canada Fights Recession

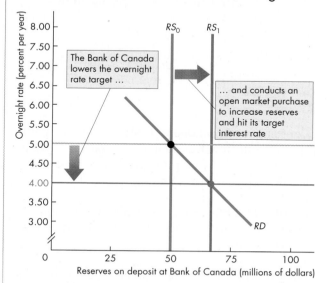

(a) The market for bank reserves

In part (a), the Bank of Canada lowers the overnight rate target from 5 percent to 4 percent a year. The Bank buys securities in an open market operation and increases the supply of reserves from RS_0 to RS_1 to hit the new overnight rate target.

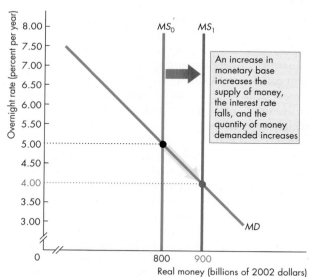

(b) Money market

In part (b), the supply of money increases from MS_0 to MS_1, the short-term interest rate falls, and the quantity of money demanded increases. The short-term interest rate and the overnight rate change by similar amounts.

myeconlab animation

In Fig. 30.8(c), the supply of loanable funds curve shifts rightward from SLF_0 to SLF_1. With the demand for loanable funds at DLF, the real interest rate falls from 6 percent to 5.5 percent a year. (We're assuming a zero inflation rate so that the real interest rate equals the nominal interest rate.) The long-term interest rate changes by a smaller amount than the change in the short-term interest rate for the reason explained on p. 740.

The Market for Real GDP Figure 30.8(d) shows aggregate demand and aggregate supply—the demand for and supply of real GDP. Potential GDP is $1,200 billion, where LAS is located. The short-run aggregate supply curve is SAS, and initially, the aggregate demand curve is AD_0. Real GDP is $1,180 billion, which is less than potential GDP, so there is a recessionary gap.

The increase in the supply of loans and the decrease in the real interest rate increase aggregate planned expenditure. (Not shown in the figure, a fall in the interest rate also lowers the exchange rate,

which increases net exports and aggregate planned expenditure.) The increase in aggregate expenditure, ΔE, increases aggregate demand and shifts the aggregate demand curve rightward to $AD_0 + \Delta E$. A multiplier process begins. The increase in expenditure increases income, which induces an increase in consumption expenditure. Aggregate demand increases further, and the aggregate demand curve eventually shifts rightward to AD_1.

The new equilibrium is at full employment. Real GDP is equal to potential GDP. The price level rises to 115 and then becomes stable at that level. So after a one-time adjustment, there is price stability.

In this example, we have given the Bank of Canada a perfect hit at achieving full employment and keeping the price level stable. It is unlikely that the Bank would be able to achieve the precision of this example. If the Bank stimulated aggregate demand by too little and too late, the economy would experience a recession. And if the Bank hit the gas pedal too hard, it would push the economy from recession to inflation and miss its inflation target.

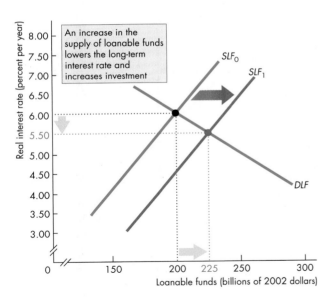

(c) The market for loanable funds

In part (c), an increase in the supply of bank loans increases the supply of loanable funds from SLF_0 to SLF_1 and the real interest rate falls. Investment increases.

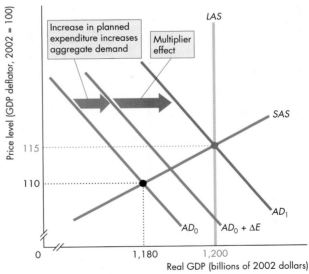

(d) Real GDP and the price level

In part (d), aggregate planned expenditure increases. The aggregate demand curve shifts rightward to $AD_0 + \Delta E$ and eventually to AD_1. Real GDP increases to potential GDP, and the price level rises.

The Bank of Canada Fights High Inflation

If the inflation rate is too high and real GDP is above potential GDP, the Bank takes actions that are designed to lower the inflation rate and restore price stability. Figure 30.9 shows the effects of the Bank's actions, starting in the market for bank reserves and ending in the market for real GDP.

Market for Bank Reserves In Fig. 30.9(a), which shows the market for bank reserves, the Bank raises the target overnight rate from 5 percent to 6 percent a year. To achieve the new target, the Bank sells securities in the open market and decreases the supply of reserves of the banking system from RS_0 to RS_1.

Money Market With decreased reserves, the banks shrink deposits by decreasing loans and the supply of money decreases. The short-term interest rate rises and the quantity of money demanded decreases. In Fig. 30.9(b), the supply of money decreases from MS_0 to MS_1, the interest rate rises from 5 percent to

6 percent a year, and the quantity of money decreases from $800 billion to $700 billion.

Loanable Funds Market With a decrease in reserves, banks must decrease the supply of loans. The supply of (real) loanable funds decreases, and the supply of loanable funds curve shifts leftward in Fig. 30.9(c) from SLF_0 to SLF_1. With the demand for loanable funds at DLF, the real interest rate rises from 6 percent to 6.5 percent a year. (Again, we're assuming a zero inflation rate so that the real interest rate equals the nominal interest rate.)

The Market for Real GDP Figure 30.9(d) shows aggregate demand and aggregate supply in the market for real GDP. Potential GDP is $1,200 billion where LAS is located. The short-run aggregate supply curve is SAS and initially the aggregate demand is AD_0. Real GDP is $1,220 billion, which is greater than potential GDP, so there is an inflationary gap. The Bank is reacting to this inflationary gap.

FIGURE 30.9 The Bank of Canada Fights Inflation

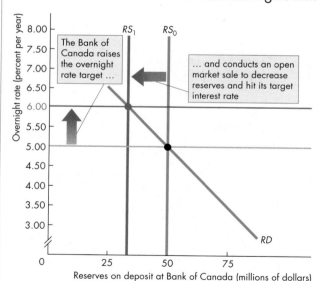

(a) The market for bank reserves

In part (a), the Bank of Canada raises the overnight rate from 5 percent to 6 percent a year. The Bank sells securities in an open market operation to decrease the supply of reserves from RS_0 to RS_1 and hit the new overnight rate target.

 animation

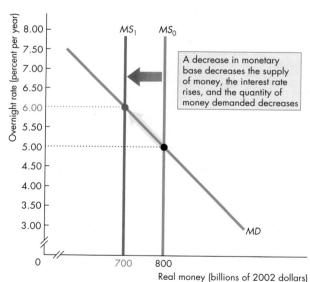

(b) Money market

In part (b), the supply of money decreases from MS_0 to MS_1, the short-term interest rate rises, and the quantity of money demanded decreases. The short-term interest rate and the overnight rate change by similar amounts.

The increase in the short-term interest rate, the decrease in the supply of bank loans, and the increase in the real interest rate decrease aggregate planned expenditure. (A rise in the interest rate also raises the exchange rate, which decreases net exports and aggregate planned expenditure.)

The decrease in aggregate expenditure, ΔE, decreases aggregate demand and shifts the aggregate demand curve to $AD_0 - \Delta E$. A multiplier process begins. The decrease in expenditure decreases income, which induces a decrease in consumption expenditure. Aggregate demand decreases further, and the aggregate demand curve eventually shifts leftward to AD_1.

The economy returns to full employment. Real GDP is equal to potential GDP. The price level falls to 115 and then becomes stable at that level. So after a one-time adjustment, there is price stability.

Again, in this example, we have given the Bank of Canada a perfect hit at achieving full employment and keeping the price level stable. If the Bank decreased aggregate demand by too little and too late,

the economy would have remained with an inflationary gap and the inflation rate would have risen above the rate that is consistent with price stability. And if the Bank hit the brakes too hard, it would push the economy from inflation to recession.

Loose Links and Long and Variable Lags

The ripple effects of monetary policy that we've just analyzed with the precision of an economic model are, in reality, very hard to predict and anticipate.

To achieve price stability and full employment, the Bank needs a combination of good judgment and good luck. Too large a cut in the overnight rate in an underemployed economy can bring inflation, as it did during the 1970s. And too large a rise in the overnight rate in an inflationary economy can create unemployment, as it did in 1981 and 1991. Loose links between the overnight rate and the policy goals make unwanted outcomes inevitable, and long and variable time lags add to the Bank's challenges.

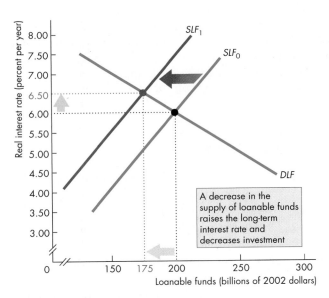

(c) The market for loanable funds

In part (c), a decrease in the supply of bank loans decreases the supply of loanable funds from SLF_0 to SLF_1 and the real interest rate rises. Investment decreases.

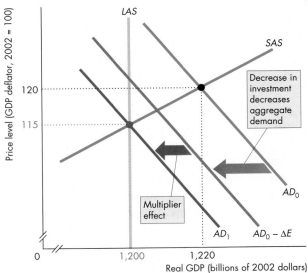

(d) Real GDP and the price level

In part (d), aggregate planned expenditure decreases. Aggregate demand decreases and the AD curve shifts leftward from AD_0 to AD_1. Real GDP decreases to potential GDP, and the price level falls.

A Reality Check

A View of the Long and Variable Lag

You've studied the theory of monetary policy. Does it really work in the way we've described? It does, and the figure provides some evidence to support this claim.

The blue line in the figure is the overnight rate that the Bank of Canada targets *minus* the long-term bond rate. (When the long-term bond rate exceeds the overnight rate, this gap is negative.)

We can view the gap between the overnight rate and the long-term bond rate as a measure of how hard the Bank is trying to steer a change in the economy's course.

When the Bank is more concerned about recession than inflation and is trying to stimulate real GDP growth, it cuts the overnight rate target and the overnight rate minus the long-term bond rate falls.

When the Bank is more concerned about inflation than recession and is trying to restrain real GDP growth, it raises the overnight rate target and the overnight rate minus the long-term bond rate rises.

The red line in the figure is the real GDP growth rate *one year later.* You can see that when the Bank lowers the overnight rate, the real GDP growth rate speeds up one year later, and when the Bank raises the overnight rate, the real GDP growth rate slows one year later.

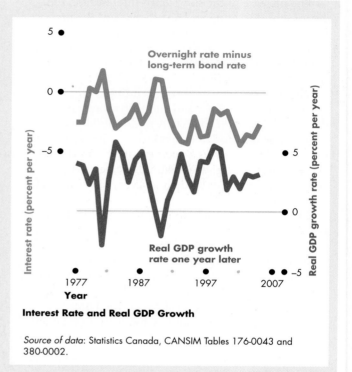

Interest Rate and Real GDP Growth

Source of data: Statistics Canada, CANSIM Tables 176-0043 and 380-0002.

Not shown in the figure are the inflation rate increases and decreases that correspond to the fluctuations in the real GDP growth rate. But the effects on the inflation rate take even longer and are not as strong as the effects on the real GDP growth rate.

Loose Link from Overnight Rate to Spending The real long-term interest rate that influences spending plans is linked only loosely to the overnight rate. Also, the response of the *real* long-term interest rate to a change in the nominal interest rate depends on how inflation expectations change. And the response of expenditure plans to changes in the real interest rate depend on many factors that make the response hard to predict.

Time Lags in the Adjustment Process The Bank of Canada is especially handicapped by the fact that the monetary policy transmission process is long and drawn-out. Also, the economy does not always respond in exactly the same way to a policy change. Further, many factors other than policy are constantly changing and bringing new situations to which policy must respond.

Review Quiz

1 Describe the channels by which monetary policy ripples through the economy and explain why each channel operates.
2 Do interest rates fluctuate in response to the Bank of Canada's actions?
3 How do the Bank's actions change the exchange rate?
4 How do the Bank's actions influence real GDP and how long does it take for real GDP to respond to the Bank's policy changes?
5 How do the Bank's actions influence the inflation rate and how long does it take for inflation to respond to the Bank's policy changes?

 Work Study Plan 30.3 and get instant feedback.

◆ Alternative Monetary Policy Strategies

The Bank of Canada must choose among alternative monetary policy strategies. What are the alternatives, and why has the Bank rejected them in favour of its interest rate strategy?

The Bank might have chosen any of four alternative monetary policy strategies: Two of them are instrument rules, and two are alternative targeting rules. The four alternatives are

- Overnight rate instrument rule
- Monetary base instrument rule
- Exchange rate targeting rule
- Money targeting rule

Overnight Rate Instrument Rule

The idea of setting the overnight rate based on a rule was suggested by Stanford University economist John B. Taylor, and the rule bears his name.

The **Taylor rule** sets the overnight rate in response to only the current inflation rate and the current estimate of the output gap. Calling the overnight rate R, the neutral real overnight rate R^*, the inflation rate π, the target inflation rate π^*, and the output gap (as a percentage of potential GDP) G, the Taylor rule says, set the overnight rate to equal

$$R = R^* + \pi + 0.5(\pi - \pi^*) + 0.5G.$$

Taylor suggests that the neutral real overnight rate is 2 percent a year, so if inflation was on target and the output gap was zero (full employment), with a 2 percent inflation target, the overnight rate would be 4 percent. It would be less than 4 percent if the economy were below full employment and above 4 percent if the economy were above full employment.

If the Bank of Canada had followed the Taylor rule, the overnight rate would have fluctuated by more than it did: On some occasions it would have been higher than the Bank wanted and on other occasions lower. For example, during 2005 when the overnight rate was 2.5 percent, the Taylor rule would have put it at 4.5 percent, and in 2008, when the overnight rate was 1.5 percent, the Taylor rule would have kept it close to 4 percent.

The Bank believes that because it uses much more information than just the current inflation rate and

the output gap, it is able to set the overnight rate more intelligently than Taylor rule would set it.

Monetary Base Instrument Rule

Instead of targeting the overnight rate, the Bank could target the monetary base. The idea of using a rule to set the monetary base was suggested by Carnegie-Mellon University economist Bennet T. McCallum, and a monetary base rule bears his name.

The **McCallum rule** makes the growth rate of the monetary base respond to the long-term average growth rate of real GDP and medium-term changes in the velocity of circulation of the monetary base.

The rule is based on the *quantity theory of money* (see Chapter 24, p 582). McCallum's idea is to make the monetary base grow at a rate equal to the target inflation rate plus the long-term real GDP growth rate minus the medium-term velocity growth rate, so that inflation will be kept close to target.

The Bank of Canada believes that shifts in the demand for money and the demand for monetary base would bring large fluctuations in the interest rate, which in turn would bring large fluctuations in aggregate demand.

Exchange Rate Targeting Rule

The Bank of Canada could intervene in the foreign exchange market to target the exchange rate. A fixed exchange rate is one possible exchange rate target. But with a fixed exchange rate, a country loses control over its inflation rate. The reason is that for internationally traded goods, *purchasing power parity* (see Chapter 25, p. 604) moves domestic prices in line with foreign prices.

The Bank of Canada could avoid a direct inflation link by using a *crawling peg exchange rate* (see Chapter 25, p. 612) as a means of achieving an inflation target. To do so, the Bank would make the exchange rate *change* at a rate equal to the world inflation rate minus the target inflation rate.

Some developing countries that have an inflation problem use this monetary policy strategy to lower the inflation rate.

The Bank of Canada rejects the crawling peg strategy because changes in the *real exchange rate* are unpredictable and even undetectable until after the event and these changes would bring instability to the inflation rate.

Extraordinary Policies for Extraordinary Times

Central Banks Get Creative

The financial crisis that began in the United States in August 2007 quickly spread though the global economy. You are now well equipped to understand the key elements in this crisis. The markets for loanable funds (Chapter 23), money (Chapter 24), and foreign exchange (Chapter 25) interacted in the financial crisis, which quickly became a broader economic crisis through its influence on aggregate demand and aggregate supply (Chapter 26).

The Key Elements of the Crisis

Figure 1 shows the stylized balance sheet of a bank: Deposits plus equity equals reserves plus loans and securities (see p. 572). A bank's equity is the market value of its stock—the value of the bank to its owners.

Three main events can put a bank under stress:

1. Widespread fall in asset prices
2. A significant currency drain
3. A run on the bank

Figure 1 summarizes the problems that each event presents to a bank. A widespread fall in asset prices means that the bank suffers a *capital loss*. It must write down the value of its assets, and the value of the

bank's equity decreases by the same amount as the fall in the value of its securities. If the fall in asset prices is large enough, the bank's equity might fall to zero, in which case the bank is *insolvent*. It fails.

A significant currency drain means that depositors withdraw funds and the bank loses reserves. This event puts the bank in a *liquidity* crisis. It is short of cash reserves, but isn't insolvent.

A run on the bank occurs when depositors lose confidence in the bank and massive withdrawals of deposits occur. The bank loses reserves and must call in loans and sell off securities at unfavourable prices. The banks' equity shrinks.

The red arrows in Fig. 1 summarize the effects of these events and the problems they brought in the 2007–2008 financial crisis.

A widespread fall in asset prices was triggered by the bursting of a house-price bubble that saw house prices in the United States switch from rapidly rising to falling. With falling house prices, sub-prime mortgage defaults occurred and the prices of mortgage-backed securities and derivatives, whose values are based on these securities, began to fall.

People began to withdraw deposits, which created a fear of a massive withdrawal of these funds analogous to a run on a bank. One U.K. bank, Northern Rock, did experience a bank run.

With low reserves and even lower equity, banks turned their attention to securing their balance sheets

Event	Deposits	+ Equity	= Reserves	+ Loans and securities	Problem
Widespread fall in asset prices		▼		▼	Solvency
Currency drain	▼		▼		Liquidity
Run on bank	▼	▼	▼	▼	Liquidity and solvency

Figure 1 The Ingredients of a Financial and Banking Crisis

Money Targeting Rule

As long ago as 1948, Nobel Laureate Milton Friedman proposed a targeting rule for the quantity of money. Friedman's **k-percent rule** makes the quantity of money grow at a rate of k percent a year, where k equals the growth rate of potential GDP.

Friedman's idea remained just that until the 1970s when inflation increased to double-digit rates and the central banks of most major countries—the Bank of Canada among them—adopted the k-percent rule.

The rule worked and inflation rates fell during the early 1980s. But financial innovation brought shifts in the demand for money and central banks began to search for an alternative approach.

Money targeting works when the demand for money is stable and predictable—when the velocity of circulation is stable. In the world of the 1980s, and possibly in the world of today, financial innovation leads to large and unpredictable fluctuations in the demand for money, which make the use of monetary targeting unreliable.

and called in loans. The loanable funds market and the money market dried up.

Because the loanable funds market is global, the same problems quickly spread to other economies, and foreign exchange markets became highly volatile.

Hard-to-get loans, market volatility, and increased uncertainty transmitted the financial and monetary crisis to real expenditure decisions.

The Policy Actions

Five types of policy action dribbled out over a period of more than a year. They were

1. Open market operations
2. Extension of deposit insurance
3. Central bank and government swapping government securities for toxic assets
4. Government buying bank shares
5. Fair value accounting

Figure 2 summarizes these actions, their effects on a bank's balance sheet (red and blue arrows), and the problem that each action sought to address.

An open market operation is the classic policy (described on pp. 736–737) for providing liquidity and enabling a central bank to hit its overnight rate target. With substantial interest rate cuts, heavy open market operations were used to keep the banks well supplied with reserves. This action lowered bank holdings of securities and increased their reserves.

By extending deposit insurance (see p. 695), people with bank deposits had less incentive to withdraw them. Both deposits and bank reserves increased.

Some central banks bought troubled assets that no one could sell (so-called *toxic assets*) and sold good quality government securities in their place. These actions swapped bad loans and securities for good ones and addressed the liquidity problem.

Some governments bought shares in banks. This action boosted bank capital and addressed the insolvency problem.

The final action is not a monetary policy but a change in accounting standards. It relaxed the requirement for institutions to value their assets at current market value—called "mark-to-market"—and permitted them, in rare conditions, to use a model to assess "fair market value."

Taken as a whole, a huge amount of relief was thrown at the financial crisis and events through 2009 will show whether enough was done.

Action	Deposits	+ Equity	= Reserves	+ Loans and securities	Problem addressed
Open market operation			▲	▼	Liquidity
Extension of deposit insurance	▲		▲		Liquidity
Swap government securities for toxic assets			▲	▼	Liquidity
Buy bank shares		▲	▲		Solvency
Fair value accounting		▲		▲	Solvency

Figure 2 Policy Actions in a Financial and Banking Crisis

Why Rules?

You might be wondering why all monetary policy strategies involve rules. Why doesn't the Bank of Canada just do what seems best every day, month, and year, at its *discretion*? The answer is that monetary policy is about managing inflation expectations. In both financial markets and labour markets, people must make long-term commitments and these markets work best when plans are based on correctly anticipated inflation. A well-understood monetary policy rule makes it easier to forecast future inflation.

Review Quiz

1 What are the alternative strategies for conducting monetary policy?
2 Briefly, why does the Bank of Canada reject each of these alternatives?

 Work Study Plan 30.4 and get instant feedback.

◆ You can complete your study of monetary policy in *Reading Between the Lines* on pages 750–751 and see the Bank of Canada's policy challenge in 2008.

Monetary Policy in Action

Bay Street Changes Rules of Rates Game

December 9, 2008

Bay Street's profit margins are starting to come under pressure as official interest rates creep closer to zero, prompting retail banks to change the rules of the game so customers pay more.

While the Bank of Canada on Tuesday cut interest rates to the lowest level since the 1950s, the country's five big banks indicated they would no longer march in lock step with the central bank. Instead, Bay Street is keeping the cost of borrowing for consumers more elevated in a bid to protect corporate earnings, passing on only part of the rate cut to customers.

While the decision of Bay Street to pocket part of the Bank of Canada rate cut is seen as good for shareholders and bad for customers, there is less certainty about how it will impact wider demand, partly because there are few historical precedents. ...

Nancy Hughes-Anthony, head of the Canadian Bankers Association ... said: "The banks are still borrowing in a very volatile marketplace. The Bank of Canada rate is only one component of their cost of funding, and while the cost of borrowing in international markets has come down a bit, it is still higher than before the crisis." ...

This willingness to pass on rate cuts is critical to determining the ability of the Bank of Canada to stimulate the economy in the midst of a downturn.

The central bank's own research shows "it is the real rate of interest that is most relevant" to the purchasing decisions of households, and that it can "influence demand only to the extent that adjustments to the [official] interest rate feed through to the real interest rate. ...

Material reprinted with the express permission of "The National Post Company", a Canwest Partnership.

Essence of the Story

- The Bank of Canada cut the overnight rate target to its lowest level since the 1950s.

- The interest rates on loans from Canada's five big banks did not fall by as much as the Bank of Canada's rate cut.

- The banks borrow in volatile international markets where interest rates have not fallen much.

- The Bank of Canada's research shows that it is the real interest rate that influences the spending decisions of households.

- Changing the overnight rate influences aggregate demand only if it changes the real interest rate faced by borrowers.

Economic Analysis

- In December 2008, the Bank of Canada cut its overnight rate target to 1.5 percent a year, but other interest rates didn't fall by as much as the Bank's rate cut.

- By providing enough reserves to the banks (and by changing the other two interest rates that define the *operating band* (see p. 736), the Bank of Canada was able to achieve it target.

- Figure 1 shows how the Bank achieved the lower overnight rate in the market for reserves. With demand curve RD, the supply of reserves increased from RS_0 to RS_1 and the overnight rate fell to its 1.5 percent target.

- When the Bank of Canada cuts the overnight rate, the supply of loanable funds increases and the economy average real interest rate falls. But the fall in the real interest rate is much smaller than the cut in the overnight rate. Figure 2 shows why.

- Initially, the real interest rate is 3 percent at the intersection of the supply of loanable funds curve SLF_0 and the demand for loanable funds curve DLF. When the Bank lowers the overnight rate, the supply of loanable funds increases and the supply curve shifts rightward to SLF_1. The real interest rate falls, but by much less than the cut in the overnight rate.

- In Fig. 3, real GDP is $1,330 billion and the price level is 118 at the intersection of AD_0 and SAS. Potential GDP is $1,370 billion, so there is a recessionary gap.

- The lower overnight rate and lower real interest rate increase aggregate demand and the AD curve shifts rightward to AD_1. Real GDP increases and the price level rises.

- In 2008, credit markets were not working normally. The perception of risk was unusually high, and institutions normally willing to lend to each other were reluctant to do so.

- In the conditions of 2008, it was possible that a cut in the overnight rate would bring a very small increase in the supply of loanable funds, a small fall in the real interest rate cut, and only a small increase in aggregate demand.

- In this situation, monetary policy is a weak tool for influencing real GDP and the inflation rate.

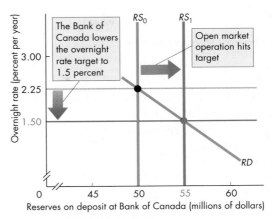

Figure 1 The market for bank reserves

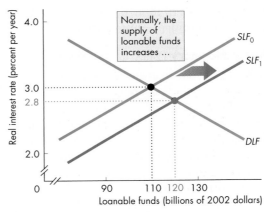

Figure 2 The market for loanable funds

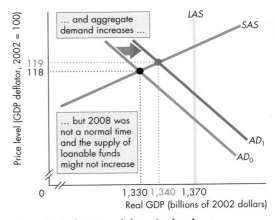

Figure 3 Real GDP and the price level

SUMMARY ◆

Key Points

Monetary Policy Objective and Framework
(pp. 732–734)

- The Bank of Canada Act requires the Bank to use monetary policy to avoid inflation and moderate cycles in real GDP and employment.
- The government of Canada and the Bank of Canada have jointly agreed that the Bank will seek to keep CPI inflation between 1 percent and 3 percent a year and will aim for the 2 percent midpoint.
- The Bank has successfully achieved its inflation-control target.
- The Bank's Governing Council has the responsibility for the conduct of monetary policy, but the Bank and the government must consult regularly.

The Conduct of Monetary Policy (pp. 734–738)

- The Bank of Canada's instrument for monetary policy is the overnight loans rate.
- The Bank of Canada sets the overnight rate target and announces changes on eight dates each year.
- An *instrument rule* for monetary policy makes the instrument respond predictably to the state of the economy. The Bank of Canada does *not* use a mechanical instrument rule.

- A *targeting rule* for monetary policy sets the instrument to make the forecast of the inflation rate equal to the target inflation rate. The Bank of Canada *does* use such a rule.
- The Bank hits its overnight rate target by setting an operating band and using open market operations.
- By buying or selling government securities in the open market, the Bank of Canada is able to change bank reserves and change the overnight rate.

Monetary Policy Transmission (pp. 739–746)

- A change in the overnight rate changes other interest rates, the exchange rate, the quantity of money and loans, aggregate demand, and eventually real GDP and the price level.
- A change in the overnight rate changes real GDP about one year later and changes the inflation rate with an even longer time lag.

Alternative Monetary Policy Strategies (pp. 747–749)

- The main alternatives are the rule for setting the overnight rate, a monetary base rule, exchange rate targeting, or money targeting.
- Rules dominate discretion in monetary policy because they better enable the central bank to manage inflation expectations.

Key Figures

Key Terms

PROBLEMS and APPLICATIONS

1. Suppose that the Bank of Canada is required to keep the inflation rate between 1 percent and 2 percent a year but with no requirement to keep trend inflation at the midpoint of this range. The Bank of Canada achieves its target.
   a. If initially the price level is 100,
      i. Calculate the highest price level that might occur after 10 years.
      ii. Calculate the lowest price level that might occur after 10 years.
      iii. What is the range of uncertainty about the price level after 10 years?
   b. Would this type of inflation goal serve the financial markets well and provide an anchor for inflation expectations?

2. Suppose that the Bank of England decides to follow the Taylor rule. In 2005, the United Kingdom has an inflation rate of 2.1 percent a year and its output gap is –0.3 percent. At what level does the Bank of England set the repo rate (the U.K. equivalent of the overnight rate)?

3. Suppose that the Bank of Canada is following the McCallum rule. The Bank of Canada has an inflation target range of between 1 percent a year and 3 percent a year. The long-term real GDP growth rate in Canada is 2.4 percent a year. If the velocity of circulation of the monetary base is 2, what is the

   a. Highest growth rate of monetary base that will occur?
   b. Lowest growth rate of monetary base that will occur?

4. In Freezone, shown in the figure, the aggregate demand curve is AD, potential GDP is $300 billion, and the short-run aggregate supply curve is SAS_B.

   a. What are the price level and real GDP?
   b. Does Freezone have an unemployment problem or an inflation problem? Why?
   c. What will happen in Freezone if the central bank takes no monetary policy actions?
   d. What monetary policy action would you advise the central bank to take and what do you predict will be the effect of that action?

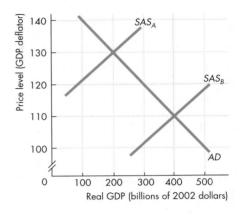

5. Suppose that in Freezone, shown in problem 4, the short-run aggregate supply curve is SAS_A and a drought decreases potential GDP to $250 billion.

   a. What happens in Freezone if the central bank lowers the overnight rate and buys securities on the open market?
   b. What happens in Freezone if the central bank raises the overnight rate and sells securities on the open market?
   c. Do you recommend that the central bank lower or raise the overnight rate? Why?

6. **Bank of Canada Lowers Overnight Rate Target**
   The Bank of Canada today announced that it is lowering its target for the overnight rate by one-quarter of a percentage point to 2 1/4 percent. The operating band for the overnight rate is correspondingly lowered. ... The outlook for growth and inflation in Canada is now more uncertain than usual. ... The weaker outlook for global demand will increase the drag on the Canadian economy coming from exports. ... The marked tightening in Canadian credit conditions in recent weeks will restrain business and housing investment. ... Core inflation is now projected to remain below 2 percent until the end of 2010. Total CPI inflation should peak during the third quarter of 2008, fall below 1 percent in the middle of 2009, and then return to the 2 percent target by the end of 2010. In the face of diminished inflationary pressures, the Bank of Canada lowered its policy interest rate by 50 basis points

on 8 October. ... This extraordinary move, combined with today's announcement, brings the cumulative reduction in our target for the overnight rate to 75 basis points. ...

Bank of Canada, October 31, 2008

a. What is the operating band? Explain how the operating band changed when the target for the overnight rate was lowered by one-quarter of a percentage point to 2.25 percent.
b. Explain the intended effect of the Bank of Canada's cumulative 0.75 percent rate cuts and illustrate your explanation with an appropriate graphical analysis.
c. What is core inflation and why might it be a useful measure of inflation?

7. **Global Bazookas, But No Silver Bullet**

Central bankers unleashed a broadside at the financial markets Wednesday. ... The [U.S.] Federal Reserve and five other central banks cut their interest rates, saying the crisis that has hammered stocks and locked up credit markets has also raised the risk of a serious recession. The Fed said the move ... is the latest in a series of "unprecedented joint actions" taken along with bankers in Canada, Europe, and the United Kingdom in a bid to restore confidence. ... "It is too late to avoid a slowdown, but strong and coordinated policies can avoid even worse scenarios," the IMF said in releasing its annual World Economic Outlook report. ... But no matter how good those plans are, making them work will take time—which is something policymakers seem to sense they don't have much of right now.

Fortune, October 8, 2008

a. How would the exchange rate respond if only the Bank of Canada cut the interest rate?
b. How would the exchange rate respond if the Bank of Canada cut the interest rate in a coordinated monetary policy action with other major central banks?
c. Evaluate the claim that "it is too late to avoid a slowdown." How does this fact complicate decisions on coordinated rate cuts?
d. How might these "unprecedented joint actions" that are meant to "restore confidence" actually end up diminishing confidence?

8. **Canada Moves to Restrict Bank Share Buybacks**

Canada has barred its domestic banks and insurers from buying back their own shares at a time when their priority is to strengthen their balance sheets. ... Governments worldwide have committed more than $1,000bn of state funds to support the financial system over the past month. But they have few tools available to ensure the funds are used to extend cheaper lending to other banks, businesses and individuals, as policymakers want ... local banks were criticized earlier this month for not immediately lowering their prime lending rates after the Bank of Canada reduced its key interest rate by 50 basis points. Finance minister Jim Flaherty said after the interest rate cut: "This isn't just about financial institutions; this is about making sure that credit is available for car loans, for mortgages, for businesses to finance their inventories."

Financial Times, October 28, 2008

a. Explain the intended effect of the Bank of Canada cutting the overnight lending rate by 50 basis points and illustrate your explanation with an appropriate graphical analysis.
b. Explain the factors that are limiting the effectiveness of this monetary stimulus.
c. In light of the limitations associated with both fiscal and monetary policy, explain and evaluate the rationale for using monetary policy as a first line of defence and reserving fiscal policy for deeper downturns when monetary policy has already been exhausted.

9 Suppose the Bank of Canada is required to keep the inflation rate between 0 and 3 percent a year and is also required to keep trend inflation at the midpoint of the range. The Bank of Canada achieves its target.

a. If initially the price level is 100, what is the likely price level after 10 years?
b. Compare this economy with the economy in problem 1. Which economy has the greater certainty about inflation over the longer term? Which has the greater short-term certainty?

10. Suppose that the Reserve Bank of New Zealand is following the Taylor rule. In 2009, it sets the official cash rate (the N.Z. equivalent of the overnight rate) at 4 percent a year. If the inflation rate in New Zealand is 2.0 percent a year, what is its output gap?

11. The figure shows the economy of Freezone. The aggregate demand curve is *AD* and the short-run aggregate supply curve is *SAS*ₐ. Potential GDP is $300 billion.

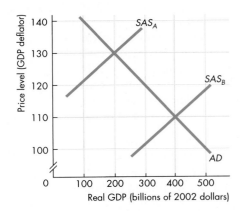

a. What are the price level and real GDP?
b. Does Freezone have an unemployment problem or an inflation problem? Why?
c. What do you predict will happen in Freezone if the central bank takes no monetary policy actions?
d. What monetary policy action would you advise the central bank to take and what do you predict will be the effect of that action?

12. Suppose that in Freezone, shown in problem 11, the short-run aggregate supply curve is *SAS*_B and potential GDP increases to $350 billion.

a. What happens if the central bank lowers the overnight rate and buys securities on the open market?
b. What happens if the central bank raises the overnight rate and sells securities on the open market?
c. Do you recommend that the central bank lower or raise the overnight rate? Why?

13. **Policy and Infrastructure Developments**

Recent disruptions in financial markets have led central banks around the world to re-examine their roles in providing "liquidity" to the financial system. ... Central banks should provide liquidity to financial markets in extraordinary circumstances because markets require liquidity for efficient pricing, illiquidity can contribute to financial system instability with real economic consequences, and a central bank's unique characteristics make it well suited to be the ultimate provider of liquidity to the financial system. A central bank should intervene to address financial market turbulence only when there is a significant market failure and significant financial instability with macroeconomic consequences could be avoided or mitigated. A central bank should price the provision of liquidity to financial markets competitively through auctions. A central bank should have a range of facilities with which to provide liquidity to the financial system, to better focus the provision of liquidity as needed.

Bank of Canada, June 2008

a. What are the primary functions of the Bank of Canada?
b. What does it mean for a central bank to provide "liquidity" to the financial system? How does this compare to the typical monetary policy tools used by the Bank of Canada?
c. Evaluate the claim that "Central banks should provide liquidity to financial markets in extraordinary circumstances."

14. **Canada Inflation Slows, Central Bank Expected to Cut Rates Again**

Inflation slowed dramatically. ... Canada's Consumer Price Index (CPI) increased by 1.8% in the 12-month period from February 2007 to February 2008, the slowest rate of growth in six months ... It's also a dramatic turn from the 12-month increase of 2.2% reported in January. ... Inflation is below the Bank of Canada's 2% target, meaning the Bank of Canada has room to lower interest rates at its next meeting. ... Canada's economy is facing a potential slowdown in the face of a possible U.S. recession. Already this month, the bank lowered its benchmark rate 50 points to 3.5%. "Inflation is under control and that's good news," Stefane Marion, an economist with National Bank Financial in Montreal, told Bloomberg. "Inflation is not an impediment to rate cuts in Canada, contrary to other countries where central bankers might be more hesitant." Unlike most rate cut scenarios, Canada's economy is operating above its production capacity and both core and total consumer price index (CPI) inflation are lower than projected. ... In this case, the rate cut was primarily a precautionary move—putting up its economic dukes to fend off threats of [and reactions to] a possible U.S. recession. ... Domestic demand remains strong because of rising incomes and commodity prices, the bank said. But effects of a weaker U.S. economy will stunt Canada's exports, and the bank projects that growth in 2008 will be weaker than it projected. ...

Money Morning, March 19, 2008

a. Explain the intended effect of the Bank of Canada's rate cuts and illustrate your explanation with an appropriate graphical analysis.
b. Why does the lower rate of inflation provide "room to lower interest rates?" Why are central bankers in other countries "more hesitant" to cut rates?
c. Evaluate the advantages and disadvantages of making "precautionary" monetary policy decisions.

15. **Carney: Bank of Canada's Focus on Inflation Key Amid Commodities Boom**

Keeping inflation in check is vital. ... Bank of Canada governor Mark Carney said Thursday, as he sought to explain the rationale behind last week's controversial decision to keep interest rates steady ... at three percent—a move that surprised many economists who were expecting a cut of a quarter of a percentage point. ... "This is not a question of what people think we say we're going to do. But it's a question of what we ought to do to fulfill our mandate. And that is proper transparency and communication." He said a 10 percent increase in commodity prices since April was enough of a reason for the Bank to change its view. "As a result the bank now judges that the current accommodative stance of monetary policy is appropriate to bring aggregate demand and supply into balance and to achieve the two percent inflation target," Carney said. "Going forward there remain important downside and upside risks to inflation, but these risks are now judged to be evenly balanced." Statistics Canada said Thursday Canada's inflation shot past the two percent level for the first time in four months in May. ... "The demand and supply fundamentals ... give reasons to expect firm commodity prices, but not necessarily persistent—let alone accelerating—commodity price increases," Carney said. The key is to avoid the pitfalls of monetary authorities in the 1970s—the last time commodities rose to such a degree. Interest rates were slashed while it was assumed our growth would continue indefinitely. Carney said that mentality, in large part, led to the 1981 to 1982 recession. "The damage to inflation expectations meant that inflation would remain a real and present danger for years," Carney said.

CNEWS, June 20, 2008

a. Explain the potential consequences of the Bank of Canada cutting rates too much in the face of a potential slowdown.
b. Does Carney predict an inflation spiral?
c. Explain why the Bank of Canada places so much emphasis on managing inflation expectations.
d. Why are public statements by the Bank of Canada actually an important component of successful monetary policy?
e. Evaluate the following statement made by Carney: "This is not a question of what people think we say we're going to do. But it's a question of what we ought to do to fulfill our mandate. And that is proper transparency and communication."

16. Study *Reading Between the Lines* on pp. 750–751 and then answer the following questions.

a. Given the policy action taken by the Bank of Canada, how do you think the Bank's expectation about future real GDP growth and future inflation differ from the most recent actual real GDP growth rate and inflation rate?
b. What would be the normal response to a large cut in the overnight rate in the market for loanable funds and to aggregate demand?
c. What made 2008 unusual and how would you analyze the special features of 2008 in the market for loanable funds?
d. If the Bank of Canada had not cut the overnight rate, what might the consequences have been?

31  International Trade Policy

After studying this chapter, you will be able to

- Explain how markets work with international trade and identify its winners and losers
- Explain the effects of international trade barriers
- Explain and evaluate arguments used to justify restricting international trade

iPods, Wii games, and Roots sweaters are just three of the items you might buy that are not produced in Canada. In fact, most of the goods that you buy are produced abroad, often in Asia, and transported here in container ships or cargo jets. And it's not only goods produced abroad that you buy—it is services too. When you make a technical support call, most likely you'll be talking with someone in India, or to a voice recognition system that was programmed in India. Satellites or fibre cables will carry your conversation along with huge amounts of other voice messages, video images, and data.

All these activities are part of the globalization process that is having a profound effect on our lives. Globalization is controversial and generates heated debate. Many Canadians want to know how we can compete with people whose wages are a fraction of our own.

Why do we go to such lengths to trade and communicate with others in faraway places? You will find some answers in this chapter. And in *Reading Between the Lines* at the end of the chapter, you can apply what you've learned and examine the effects of the softwood lumber deal between Canada and the United States.

How Global Markets Work

Because we trade with people in other countries, the goods and services that we can buy and consume are not limited by what we can produce. The goods and services we buy from other countries are our **imports**; and the goods and services we sell to people in other countries are our **exports**.

International Trade Today

Global trade today is enormous. In 2008, global exports and imports were $35 trillion, which is more than half the value of global production. The United States is the world's largest international trader and accounts for 10 percent of world exports and 15 percent of world imports. Germany and China, which rank second and third behind the United States, lag by a large margin.

In 2008, total Canadian exports were $535 billion, which is about 34 percent of the value of Canadian production. Total Canadian imports were $503 billion, which is about 32 percent of the value of total expenditure in Canada.

Canada trades both goods and services. In 2008, exports of services were about 13 percent of total exports, and imports of services were about 18 percent of total imports.

What Drives International Trade?

Comparative advantage is the fundamental force that drives international trade. Comparative advantage (see Chapter 2, p. 40) is a situation in which a person can perform an activity or produce a good or service at a lower opportunity cost than anyone else. This same idea applies to nations. We can define *national comparative advantage* as a situation in which a nation can perform an activity or produce a good or service at a lower opportunity cost than any other nation.

The opportunity cost of producing a T-shirt is lower in China than in Canada, so China has a comparative advantage in producing T-shirts. The opportunity cost of producing a regional jet is lower in Canada than in China, so Canada has a comparative advantage in producing regional jets.

You saw in Chapter 2 how Liz and Joe reap gains from trade by specializing in the production of the good at which they have a comparative advantage and trading. Both are better off.

Canada's Most Traded Items

Trading Energy for Automobiles

The figure shows Canada's four largest exports and imports by value. Motor vehicles and parts and crude petroleum are large exports *and* imports. But Canada is a *net importer* of motor vehicles and parts and a *net exporter* of crude oil. Natural gas is another big export. So Canadians trade energy products in exchange for motor vehicles and parts.

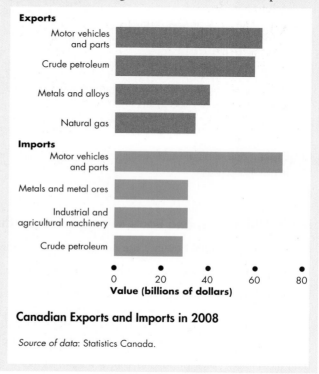

Canadian Exports and Imports in 2008

Source of data: Statistics Canada.

This same principle applies to trade among nations. Because China has a comparative advantage at producing T-shirts and Canada has a comparative advantage at producing regional jets, the people of both countries can gain from specialization and trade. China can buy regional jets from Canada at a lower opportunity cost than that at which Chinese firms can produce them. And Canadians can buy T-shirts from China for a lower opportunity cost than that at which firms in Canada can produce them. Also, through international trade, Chinese producers can get higher prices for their T-shirts and Bombardier can sell regional jets for a higher price. Both countries gain from international trade.

Let's now illustrate the gains from trade that we've just described by studying demand and supply in the global markets for T-shirts and regional jets.

Why Canada Imports T-Shirts

Canada imports T-shirts because the rest of the world has a comparative advantage in producing T-shirts. Figure 31.1 illustrates how this comparative advantage generates international trade and how trade affects the price of a T-shirt and the quantities produced and bought.

The demand curve D_{Can} and the supply curve S_{Can} show the demand and supply in Canada's domestic market only. The demand curve tells us the quantity of T-shirts that Canadians are willing to buy at various prices. The supply curve tells us the quantity of T-shirts that Canadian garment makers are willing to sell at various prices—that is, the quantity supplied at

each price when all T-shirts sold in Canada are produced in Canada.

Figure 31.1(a) shows what the Canadian T-shirt market would be like with no international trade. The price of a shirt would be $8 and 4 million shirts a year would be produced by Canadian garment makers and bought by Canadian consumers.

Figure 31.1(b) shows the market for T-shirts with international trade. Now the price of a T-shirt is determined in the world market, not Canada's domestic market. The world price is less than $8 a T-shirt, which means that the rest of the world has a comparative advantage in producing T-shirts. The world price line shows the world price at $5 a shirt.

The Canadian demand curve D_{Can} tells us that at $5 a shirt, Canadians buy 6 million shirts a year. The Canadian supply curve S_{Can} tells us that at $5 a shirt, Canadian garment makers produce 2 million T-shirts a year. To buy 6 million T-shirts when only 2 million

FIGURE 31.1   A Market with Imports

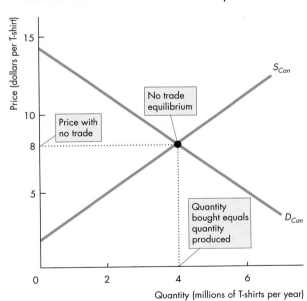

(a) Equilibrium with no international trade

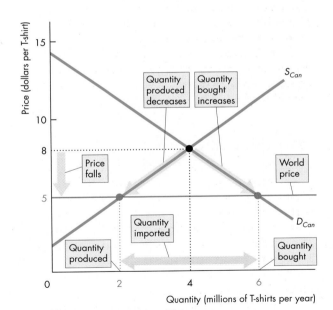

(b) Equilibrium in a market with imports

Part (a) shows the Canadian market for T-shirts with no international trade. The domestic demand curve D_{Can} and domestic supply curve S_{Can} determine the price of a T-shirt at $8 and the quantity produced and bought in Canada at 4 million T-shirts a year.

Part (b) shows the Canadian market for T-shirts with

international trade. World demand and world supply determine the world price of a T-shirt, which is $5. The price in the Canadian market falls to $5 a shirt. Canadian purchases of T-shirts increases to 6 million a year, and Canadian production of T-shirts decreases to 2 million a year. Canada imports 4 million T-shirts a year.

are produced in Canada, we must import T-shirts from the rest of the world. The quantity of T-shirts imported is 4 million a year.

Why Canada Exports Regional Jets

Canada exports regional jets because it has a comparative advantage in producing them. Figure 31.2 illustrates how this comparative advantage generates international trade in airplanes and how this trade affects the price of an airplane and the quantities produced and bought.

The demand curve D_{Can} and the supply curve S_{Can} show the demand and supply in Canada's domestic market only. The demand curve tells us the quantity of regional jet that airlines in Canada are willing to buy at various prices. The supply curve tells us the quantity of regional jets that Bombardier is willing to sell at various prices.

Figure 31.2(a) shows what the Canadian market for regional jets would be like with no international trade. The price of a regional jet would be $100 million and 40 regional jets a year would be produced by Bombardier and bought by Canadian airlines.

Figure 31.2(b) shows the Canadian market for regional jets with international trade. Now the price of a regional jet is determined in the world market and the world price is higher than $100 million, which means that Canada has a comparative advantage in producing regional jets. The world price line shows the world price at $150 million.

The Canadian demand curve D_{Can} tells us that at a price of $150 million, Canadian airlines buy 20 regional jets a year. The Canadian supply curve S_{Can} tells us that at a price of $150 million, Bombardier produces 70 regional jets a year. The quantity produced in Canada (70 a year) minus the quantity purchased by Canadian airlines (20 a year) is the quantity exported, which is 50 regional jets a year.

FIGURE 31.2   A Market with Exports

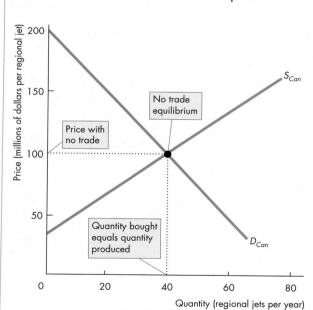

(a) Equilibrium without international trade

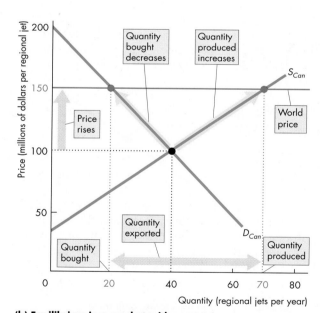

(b) Equilibrium in a market with exports

In part (a), the Canadian market with no international trade, the domestic demand curve D_{Can} and the domestic supply curve S_{Can} determine the price of a regional jet at $100 million and 40 jets are produced and bought each year.

In part (b), the Canadian market with international

trade, world demand and world supply determine the world price of a regional jet at $150 million. The price in Canada rises. Bombardier increases production to 70 a year, and Canadian airlines decrease their purchases to 20 a year. Canada exports 50 regional jets a year.

myeconlab   animation

Winners and Losers from International Trade

International trade has winners but it also has losers. That's why you often hear people complaining about international competition. We're now going to see who wins and who loses from international trade. You will then be able to understand who complains about international competition and why. You will learn why we hear producers complaining about cheap foreign imports. You will also see why we never hear consumers of imported goods and services complaining and why we never hear exporters complaining except when they want greater access to foreign markets.

Gains and Losses from Imports We measure the gains and losses from imports by examining their effect on the price paid and the quantity bought by domestic consumers and the effect on the price received and the quantity sold by domestic producers.

Consumers' Gain from Imports When a country freely imports something from the rest of the world, it is because the rest of the world has a comparative advantage at producing that item. Compared to a situation with no international trade, the price paid by the consumer falls and the quantity consumed increases. It is clear that the consumer gains. The greater the fall in price and increase in quantity consumed, the greater is the gain to the consumer.

Domestic Producers Lose from Imports Compared to a situation with no international trade, the price received by a domestic producer of an item that is imported falls. Also the quantity sold by the domestic producer of an item that is imported decreases. Because the domestic producer of an item that is imported sells a smaller quantity and for a lower price, this producer loses from international trade. Import-competing industries shrink in the face of competition from cheaper foreign-produced imports.

The profits of firms in import-competing industries fall, so these firms cut their workforce. In these industries, unemployment increases and wage rates fall. When these industries have a geographical concentration, such as steel production in Sydney, Nova Scotia, an entire region can suffer economic decline.

Gains and Losses from Exports Just as we did for imports, we can measure the gains and losses from exports by looking their effect on the price paid and quantity bought by domestic consumers and the effect on the price received and quantity sold by domestic producers.

Domestic Consumers Lose from Exports When a country exports something to the rest of the world, it is because the country has a comparative advantage at producing that item. Compared to a situation with no international trade, the price paid by the consumer rises and the quantity consumed in the domestic economy decreases. The domestic consumer loses. The greater the rise in the price and decrease in the quantity bought, the greater is the consumers' loss.

Domestic Producers Gain from Exports Compared to a situation with no international trade, the price received by a domestic producer of an item that is imported rises. Also, the quantity sold by the domestic producer of a good or service that is also exported increases. Because the domestic producer of an item that is exported sells a larger quantity and for a higher price, this producer gains from international trade. Export industries expand in the face of global demand for their product.

The profits of firms that produce exports rise, so these firms expand their workforce. Unemployment in these industries decreases and wage rates rise. When these industries have a geographical concentration, such as oil production in Alberta, an entire region can boom.

Net Gain Producers of exported goods and consumers of imported goods gain. Consumers of exported goods and domestic producers of imported goods lose. But the gains are greater than the losses. In the case of imports, the consumer gains what the producer loses and then gains even more on the cheaper imports. In the case of exports, the producer gains what the consumer loses and then gains even more on the items it exported. So international trade provides a net gain for a country.

Review Quiz

1 Explain the effects of imports and price, quantity, and the gains and losses of consumers and producers.
2 Explain the effects of exports and price, quantity, and the gains and losses of consumers and producers.

 Work Study Plan 31.1 and get instant feedback.

◆ International Trade Restrictions

Governments use four sets of tools to influence international trade and protect domestic industries from foreign competition. They are

- Tariffs
- Import quotas
- Other import barriers
- Export subsidies

Tariffs

A **tariff** is a tax on a good that is imposed by the importing country when an imported good crosses its international boundary. For example, the government of India imposes a 100 percent tariff on wine imported from Ontario. So when an Indian company imports a $10 bottle of Ontario wine, it pays the Indian government a $10 import duty.

The temptation for governments to impose tariffs is a strong one. First, they provide revenue to the government. Second, they enable the government to satisfy the self-interest of the people who earn their incomes in the import-competing industries. But as you will see, tariffs and other restrictions on free international trade decrease the gains from trade and are not in the social interest. Let's see why.

The Effects of a Tariff   To see the effects of a tariff, let's return to the example in which Canada imports T-shirts. With free trade, the T-shirts are imported and sold at the world price. Then, under pressure from Canadian garment makers, the government of Canada imposes a tariff on imported T-shirts. Buyers of T-shirts must now pay the world price plus the tariff. Several consequences follow, as Fig. 31.3 illustrates.

Figure 31.3(a) shows the situation with free international trade. Canada produces 2 million T-shirts a year and imports 4 million a year at the world price

FIGURE 31.3   The Effects of a Tariff

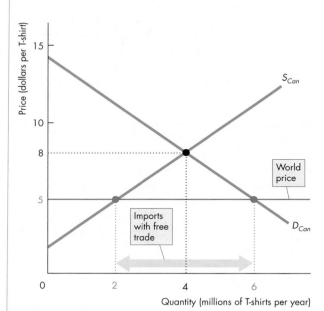

(a) Free trade

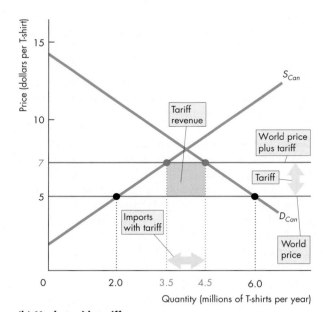

(b) Market with tariff

The world price of a T-shirt is $5. With free trade in part (a), Canadians buy 6 million T-shirts a year. Canadian garment makers produce 2 million T-shirts a year and Canada imports 4 million a year.

With a tariff of $2 per T-shirt in part (b), the price in

Canada rises to $7 a T-shirt. Canadian production increases, Canadian purchases decrease, and the quantity imported decreases. The government collects a tariff revenue of $2 on each T-shirt imported, which is shown by the purple rectangle.

 myeconlab animation

of $5 a shirt. Figure 31.3(b) shows what happens with a tariff set at $2 per T-shirt. The following changes occur in the market for T-shirts:

- The price of a T-shirt in Canada rises by $2.
- The quantity of T-shirts bought in Canada decreases.
- The quantity of T-shirts produced in Canada increases.
- The quantity of T-shirts imported into Canada decreases.
- The Canadian government collects a tariff revenue.

Rise in Price of a T-Shirt To buy a T-shirt, Canadians must pay the world price plus the tariff, so the price of a T-shirt rises by $2 to $7. Figure 31.3(b) shows the new domestic price line, which lies $2 above the world price line.

Decrease in Purchases The higher price of a T-shirt brings a decrease in the quantity demanded along the demand curve. Figure 31.3(b) shows the decrease from 6 million T-shirts a year at $5 a shirt to 4.5 million a year at $7 a shirt.

Increase in Domestic Production The higher price of a T-shirt stimulates domestic production, and Canadian

garment makers increase the quantity supplied along the supply curve. Figure 31.3(b) shows the increase from 2 million T-shirts a year at $5 a shirt to 3.5 million a year at $7 a shirt.

Decrease in Imports T-shirt imports decrease by 3 million, from 4 million to 1 million a year. Both the decrease in purchases and the increase in domestic production contribute to this decrease in imports.

Tariff Revenue The government's tariff revenue is $2 million—$2 per shirt on 1 million imported shirts—shown by the purple rectangle.

Winners, Losers, and the Social Loss from a Tariff A tariff on an imported good creates winners and losers and a social loss. When the government of Canada imposes a tariff on an imported good,

- Canadian consumers of the good lose.
- Canadian producers of the good gain.
- Canadian consumers lose more than Canadian producers gain: Society loses.

Canadian Consumers of the Good Lose Because the price of a T-shirt in Canada rises, the quantity of T-shirts

Canadian Tariffs

Almost Gone

Canadian tariffs were in place before Confederation. They increased sharply in the 1870s and remained high until the 1930s. Since the establishment of the **General Agreement on Tariffs and Trade (GATT)**, in 1947, tariffs have steadily declined in a series of negotiating rounds, the most significant of which are identified in the figure. Tariffs have almost gone, but other trade barriers persist.

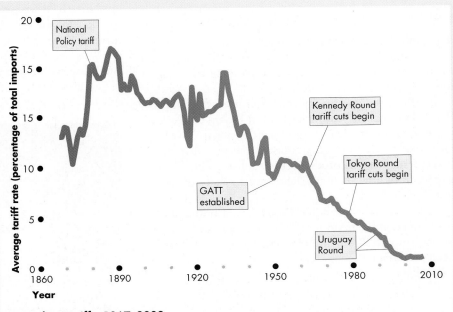

Canadian Tariffs: 1867–2008

Sources of data: Adapted from the Statistics Canada publication "Historical Statistics of Canada." Catalogue 11-516. Released July 29, 1999, and from the Statistics Canada CANSIM database Tables 380-0002 and 380-0034.

demanded decreases. The combination of a higher price and smaller quantity bought makes consumers worse off when a tariff is imposed.

Canadian Producers of the Good Gain   Because the price of an imported T-shirt rises by the amount of the tariff, Canadian T-shirt producers are now able to sell their T-shirts for the world price plus the tariff. At the higher price, the quantity of T-shirts supplied by Canadian producers increases. The combination of a higher price and larger quantity produced increases producers' profits. So Canadian producers gain from the tariff.

Canadian Consumers Lose More Than Canadian Producers Gain: Society Loses   Consumers lose from a tariff for three reasons:

1.   They pay a higher price to domestic producers.
2.   They consume a smaller quantity of the good.
3.   They pay tariff revenue to the government.

The tariff revenue is a loss to consumers but is not a social loss. The government can use the tax revenue to buy public services that consumers value. But the other two sources of consumer loss include some social losses.

There is a social loss because part of the higher price paid to domestic producers pays the higher cost of domestic production. The increased domestic production could have been obtained at lower cost as an import. There is also a social loss from the decreased quantity of the good consumed at the higher price.

Import Quotas

We now look at the second tool for restricting trade: import quotas. An **import quota** is a restriction that limits the maximum quantity of a good that may be imported in a given period. Most countries impose import quotas on a wide range of items. Canada imposes them on food products such as meat, eggs and dairy, and manufactured goods such as textiles and steel.

Import quotas enable the government to satisfy the self-interest of the people who earn their incomes in import-competing industries. But you will discover that like a tariff, an import quota decreases the gains from trade and is not in the social interest.

Failure in Doha
Self-Interest Beats the Social Interest

The **World Trade Organization (WTO)** is an international body established by the world's major trading nations for the purpose of supervising international trade and lowering the barriers to trade.

In 2001, at a meeting of trade ministers from all the WTO member-countries held in Doha, Qatar, an agreement was made to begin negotiations to lower tariff barriers and import quotas that restrict international trade in farm products and services. These negotiations are called the **Doha Development Agenda** or the **Doha Round**.

In the period since 2001, thousands of hours of conferences in Cancún in 2003, Geneva in 2004, and Hong Kong in 2005, and ongoing meetings at WTO headquarters in Geneva, costing millions of taxpayers' dollars, have made disappointing progress.

The rich world, led by the United States, the European Union, and Japan, wants greater access to the markets of developing nations in exchange for allowing those nations greater access to the rich world's markets, especially for farm products.

The developing world, led by Brazil, China, India, and South Africa, wants access to the farm product markets of the rich world, but they also want to protect their infant industries.

With two incompatible positions, these negotiations are stalled and show no signs of a breakthrough. The self-interest of rich and developing nations is preventing the achievement of the social interest.

The Effects of an Import Quota The effects of an import quota are similar to those of a tariff. The price rises, the quantity bought decreases, and the quantity produced in Canada increases. Figure 31.4 illustrates the effects.

Figure 31.4(a) shows the situation with free international trade. Figure 31.4(b) shows what happens with an import quota of 1 million T-shirts a year. The Canadian supply curve of T-shirts becomes the domestic supply curve S_{Can} plus the quantity that the import quota permits. So the supply curve becomes $S_{Can} + quota$. The price of a T-shirt rises to $7, the quantity of T-shirts bought in Canada decreases to 4.5 million a year, the quantity of T-shirts produced in Canada increases to 3.5 million a year, and the quantity of T-shirts imported into Canada decreases to the quota quantity of 1 million a year. All the effects of this quota are identical to the effects of a tariff of $2 per T-shirt, as you can check in Fig. 31.3(b).

Winners, Losers, and the Social Loss from an Import Quota An import quota creates winners and losers that are similar to those of a tariff but with an interesting difference.

When the government imposes an import quota,

- Canadian consumers of the good lose.
- Canadian producers of the good gain.
- Importers of the good gain.
- Society loses.

Canadian Consumers of the Good Lose Because the price of a T-shirt in Canada rises, the quantity of T-shirts demanded decreases. The combination of a higher price and smaller quantity bought makes the consumer worse off. So Canadian consumers lose when an import quota is imposed.

Canadian Producers of the Good Gain Because the price of a T-shirt rises, Canadian T-shirt producers increase

FIGURE 31.4 The Effects of an Import Quota

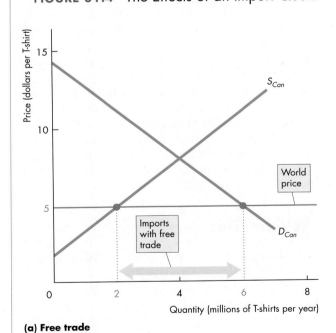

(a) Free trade

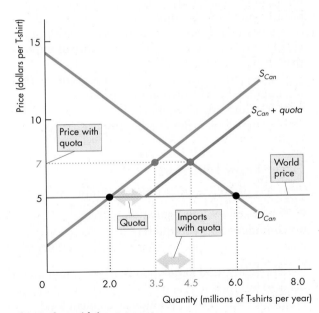

(b) Market with import quota

With free international trade, in part (a), Canadians buy 6 million T-shirts at the world price. Canada produces 2 million T-shirts and imports 4 million a year. With an import quota of 1 million T-shirts a year, in part (b), the supply of

T-shirts in Canada is shown by the curve $S_{Can} + quota$. The price in Canada rises to $7 a T-shirt. Canadian production increases, Canadian purchases decrease, and the quantity of T-shirts imported decreases.

production. The combination of a higher price and a larger quantity produced increases producers' profits. So the Canadian producers gain from the tariff.

Importers of the Good Gain The importer is able to buy the good on the world market at the world market price, and sell the good in the domestic market at the domestic price. Because the domestic price exceeds the world price, the importer gains.

Society Loses Society loses because the loss to consumers exceeds the gains of domestic producers and importers. Just like the social losses from a tariff, there is a social loss because part of the higher price paid to domestic producers pays the higher cost of domestic production, and there is a social loss from the decreased quantity of the good consumed at the higher price.

Tariff and Import Quota Compared You've looked at the effects of a tariff and an import quota and can now see the essential differences between them. A tariff brings in revenue for the government while a quota brings a profit for the importers. All the other effects of a quota are the same as the effects of a tariff, provided the quota is set at the same quantity of imports that results from the tariff.

Tariffs and quotas are equivalent ways of restricting imports, benefiting domestic producers, and harming domestic consumers.

Let's now look at some other import barriers.

Other Import Barriers

Two sets of policies that influence imports are

- Health, safety, and regulation barriers
- Voluntary export restraints

Health, Safety, and Regulation Barriers Thousands of detailed health, safety, and other regulations restrict international trade. For example, Canadian food imports are examined by the Canadian Food Inspection Agency, which "is mandated to safeguard Canada's food supply and the plants and animals upon which safe and high-quality food depends." The discovery of BSE (mad cow disease) in just one cow on May 20, 2003, led to an immediate worldwide ban on Canadian beef exports. The European Union bans imports of most genetically modified foods, such as

Canadian canola. Although regulations of this type are not designed to limit international trade, they have that effect.

Voluntary Export Restraints A *voluntary export restraint* is like a quota allocated to a foreign exporter of a good. This type of trade barrier isn't common. It was initially used during the 1980s when Japan voluntarily limited its exports of car parts to North America.

Export Subsidies

A *subsidy* is a payment by the government to a producer. When the government pays a subsidy, the cost of production falls by the amount of the subsidy so supply increases. An **export subsidy** is a payment by the government to the producer of an exported good so it increases the supply of exports. Export subsidies are illegal under a number of international agreements including the North American Free Trade Agreement (NAFTA) and the rules of the World Trade Organization (WTO).

Although export subsidies are illegal, the subsidies that the U.S. and European Union governments pay to farmers end up increasing domestic production, some of which gets exported. These exports of subsidized farm products make it harder for producers in other countries, notably in Africa and Central and South America, to compete in global markets.

Export subsidies bring gains to domestic producers, but they result in inefficient overproduction of some food products in the rich industrial countries, underproduction in the rest of the world, and create a social loss for the world as a whole.

Review Quiz

1 What tools can a country use to restrict international trade?
2 Explain the effects of a tariff on domestic production, the quantity bought, and the price.
3 Explain who gains and who loses from a tariff and why the losses exceed the gains.
4 Explain the effects of an import quota on domestic production, consumption, and price.
5 Explain who gains and who loses from an import quota and why the losses exceed the gains.

 Work Study Plan 31.2 and get instant feedback.

The Case Against Protection

For as long as nations and international trade have existed, people have debated whether a country is better off with free international trade or with protection from foreign competition. The debate continues, but for most economists, a verdict has been delivered and is the one you have just seen. Free trade promotes prosperity for all countries; protection is inefficient. We've studied the most powerful case for free trade—it brings gains for consumers that exceed any losses incurred by producers, so there is a net gain for society.

But there is a broader range of issues in the free trade versus protection debate. Let's review these issues.

Two classical arguments for restricting international trade are

- The infant-industry argument
- The dumping argument

The Infant-Industry Argument

The **infant-industry argument** for protection is that it is necessary to protect a new industry to enable it to grow into a mature industry that can compete in world markets. The argument is based on the idea of *dynamic comparative advantage*, which can arise from *learning-by-doing* (see Chapter 2, p. 43).

Learning-by-doing, a powerful engine of productivity growth, and on-the-job experience can change comparative advantage. But these facts do not justify protection.

First, the infant-industry argument is valid only if the benefits of learning-by-doing *not only* accrue to the owners and workers of the firms in the infant industry but also *spill over* to other industries and parts of the economy. For example, there are huge productivity gains from learning-by-doing in the manufacture of aircraft.

But almost all of these gains benefit the stockholders and workers of Bombardier and other aircraft producers. Because the people making the decisions, bearing the risk, and doing the work are the ones who benefit, they take the dynamic gains into account when they decide on the scale of their activities. In this case, almost no benefits spill over to other parts of the economy, so there is no need for government assistance to achieve an efficient outcome.

Second, even if the case is made for protecting an infant industry, it is more efficient to do so by giving the firms in the industry a subsidy, which is financed out of taxes. Such a subsidy would encourage the industry to mature and to compete with efficient world producers and keep the price faced by consumers at the world price.

The Dumping Argument

Dumping occurs when a foreign firm sells its exports at a lower price than its cost of production. Dumping might be used by a firm that wants to gain a global monopoly. In this case, the foreign firm sells its output at a price below its cost to drive domestic firms out of business. When the domestic firms have gone, the foreign firm takes advantage of its monopoly position and charges a higher price for its product. Dumping is illegal under the rules of the WTO and is usually regarded as a justification for temporary tariffs, which are called *antidumping duties*.

But there are powerful reasons to resist the dumping argument for protection. First, it is virtually impossible to detect dumping because it is hard to determine a firm's costs. As a result, the test for dumping is whether a firm's export price is below its domestic price. But this test is a weak one because it can be rational for a firm to charge a low price in a market in which the quantity demanded is highly sensitive to price and a higher price in a market in which demand is less price-sensitive.

Second, it is hard to think of a good that is produced by a *global* monopoly. So even if all the domestic firms in some industry were driven out of business, it would always be possible to find alternative foreign sources of supply and to buy the good at a price determined in a competitive market.

Third, if a good or service were a truly global monopoly, the best way of dealing with it would be by regulation—just as in the case of domestic monopolies. Such regulation would require international cooperation.

The two arguments for protection that we've just examined have an element of credibility. The counterarguments are in general stronger, however, so these arguments do not make the case for protection. But they are not the only arguments that you might encounter. There are many other new arguments against globalization and for protection. The most common ones are that protection

- Saves jobs
- Allows us to compete with cheap foreign labour
- Penalizes lax environmental standards
- Prevents rich countries from exploiting developing countries

Saves Jobs

First, free trade does cost some jobs, but it also creates other jobs. It brings about a global rationalization of labour and allocates labour resources to their highest-valued activities. International trade in textiles has cost thousands of jobs in Canada as textile mills and other factories have closed. But thousands of jobs have been created in other countries as textile mills have opened. And thousands of Canadian workers got better-paying jobs than as textile workers because Canadian export industries expanded and created new jobs. More jobs have been created than destroyed.

Although protection saves particular jobs, it does so at a high cost. A striking example of the cost of quotas is that of the quotas on the import of textiles. Quotas imposed under the international agreement called the Multifibre Arrangement (which ended in 2005) protected textile jobs, especially in the United States. The U.S. International Trade Commission (ITC) has estimated that because of import quotas, 72,000 jobs existed in the textile industry that would otherwise have disappeared and that the annual clothing expenditure in the United States was $15.9 billion ($160 per family) higher than it would have been with free trade. Equivalently, the ITC estimated that each textile job saved cost $221,000 a year.

Imports don't only destroy jobs. They create jobs for retailers that sell imported goods and for firms that service those goods. Imports also create jobs by creating incomes in the rest of the world, some of which are spent on U.S.-made goods and services.

Allows Us to Compete with Cheap Foreign Labour

With the removal of tariffs on trade between Canada, the United States, and Mexico, people said we would hear a "giant sucking sound" as jobs rushed to Mexico. Let's see what's wrong with this view.

The labour cost of a unit of output equals the wage rate divided by labour productivity. For example, if a

Canadian autoworker earns $30 an hour and produces 15 units of output an hour, the average labour cost of a unit of output is $2. If a Mexican auto assembly worker earns $3 an hour and produces 1 unit of output an hour, the average labour cost of a unit of output is $3. Other things remaining the same, the higher a worker's productivity, the higher is the worker's wage rate. High-wage workers have high productivity; low-wage workers have low productivity.

Although high-wage Canadian workers are more productive, on average, than low-wage Mexican workers, there are differences across industries. Canadian labour is relatively more productive in some activities than in others. For example, the productivity of Canadian workers in producing financial services and telephone systems is relatively higher than their productivity in the production of metals and some standardized machine parts. The activities in which Canadian workers are relatively more productive than their Mexican counterparts are those in which Canada has a *comparative advantage*.

By engaging in free trade, increasing our production and exports of the goods and services in which we have a comparative advantage and decreasing our production and increasing our imports of the goods and services in which our trading partners have a comparative advantage, we can make ourselves and the citizens of other countries better off.

Penalizes Lax Environmental Standards

Another argument for protection is that many poorer countries, such as China and Mexico, do not have the same environmental policies that we have and, because they are willing to pollute and we are not, we cannot compete with them without tariffs. So if poorer countries want free trade with the richer and "greener" countries, they must raise their environmental standards.

This argument for trade restrictions is weak. First, a poor country cannot afford to be as concerned about its environmental standard as a rich country can. Today, some of the worst pollution of air and water is found in China, Mexico, and the former communist countries of Eastern Europe. But only a few decades ago, London and Los Angeles led the pollution league table. The best hope for cleaner air in Beijing and Mexico City is rapid income growth. Free trade contributes to that growth. As incomes in developing countries grow, they will have the *means* to match their desires to improve their environmental standard. Second, a poor country might have a comparative advantage at doing "dirty" work, which helps it to raise its income and at the same time enables the global economy to achieve a higher environmental standard than would otherwise be possible.

Prevents Rich Countries from Exploiting Developing Countries

Another argument for protection is that international trade must be restricted to prevent the people of the rich industrial world from exploiting the poorer people of the developing countries and forcing them to work for slave wages.

Child labour and near-slave labour are serious problems that are rightly condemned. But by trading with poor countries, we increase the demand for the goods that these countries produce and, more significantly, we increase the demand for their labour. When the demand for labour in developing countries increases, the wage rate also increases. So, rather than exploiting people in developing countries, trade can expand their opportunities and increase their incomes.

The arguments for protection that we've reviewed leave free-trade unscathed. But a new phenomenon is at work in our economy: *offshore outsourcing*. Surely we need protection from this new source of foreign competition. Let's investigate.

Offshore Outsourcing

Roots, Canadian Tire, and BlackBerry: What do these Canadian icons have in common? They all send jobs that could be done in Canada to China, India, Thailand, or even the United States—they are offshoring. What exactly is offshoring?

What Is Offshoring? A firm in Canada can obtain the things that it sells in any of four ways:

1. Hire Canadian labour and produce in Canada.
2. Hire foreign labour and produce in other countries.
3. Buy finished goods, components, or services from other firms in Canada.
4. Buy finished goods, components, or services from other firms in other countries.

Activities 3 and 4 are **outsourcing**, and activities 2 and 4 are **offshoring**. Activity 4 is **offshore outsourcing**. Notice that offshoring includes activities that take place inside Canadian firms. If a Canadian firm opens its own facilities in another country, then it is offshoring.

Offshoring has been going on for hundreds of years, but it expanded rapidly and became a source of concern during the 1990s as many Canadian firms moved information technology services and general office services such as finance, accounting, and human resources management overseas.

Why Did Offshoring of Services Boom During the 1990s? The gains from specialization and trade that you saw in the previous section must be large enough to make it worth incurring the costs of communication and transportation. If the cost of producing a T-shirt in China isn't lower than the cost of producing the T-shirt in Canada by more than the cost of transporting the shirt from China to Canada, then it is more efficient to produce T-shirts in Canada and avoid the transport costs.

The same considerations apply to trade in services. If services are to be produced offshore, then the cost of delivering those services must be low enough to leave the buyer with an overall lower cost. Before the 1990s, the cost of communicating across large distances was too high to make the offshoring of business services efficient. But during the 1990s, when satellites, fibre-optic cables, and computers cut the cost of a phone call between Canada and India to less than a dollar an hour, a huge base of offshore resources became competitive with similar resources in Canada.

What Are the Benefits of Offshoring? Offshoring brings gains from trade identical to those of any other type of trade. We could easily change the names of the items traded from T-shirts and regional jets (the examples in the previous sections of this chapter) to banking services and call centre services (or any other pair of services). A Canadian bank might export banking services to Indian firms, and Indians might provide call centre services to Canadian firms. This type of trade would benefit both Canadians and Indians provided that Canada has a comparative advantage in banking services and India has a comparative advantage in call centre services.

Comparative advantages like these emerged during the 1990s. India has the world's largest educated English-speaking population and is located in a time zone half a day ahead of North America's east coast and midway between Asia and Europe, which facilitates 24/7 operations. When the cost of communicating with a worker in India was several dollars a minute, as it was before the 1990s, tapping these vast resources was just too costly. But at today's cost of a long-distance telephone call or Internet connection, resources in India can be used to produce services in Canada at a lower cost than those services can be produced by using resources located in Canada. Some of the goods and services that Indians buy with the incomes they earn from exporting services, are produced in Canada.

Why Is Offshoring a Concern? Despite the gain from specialization and trade that offshoring brings, many people believe that it also brings costs that eat up the gains. Why?

A major reason is that offshoring is taking jobs in services. The loss of manufacturing jobs to other countries has been going on for decades, but the service sector in Canada has always expanded by enough to create new jobs to replace the lost manufacturing jobs. Now that service jobs are also going overseas, the fear is that there will not be enough jobs for Canadians. This fear is misplaced.

Some service jobs are going overseas, while others are expanding at home. Canada imports call centre services, but it exports education, health care, legal, financial, and a host of other types of services. Jobs in these sectors are expanding and will continue to expand.

The exact number of jobs that have moved to lower-cost offshore locations is not known, and estimates vary. But even the highest estimate is a tiny number compared to the normal rate of job creation.

Winners and Losers Gains from trade do not bring gains for every single person. Canadians, on average, gain from offshore outsourcing. But some people lose. The losers are those who have invested in the human capital to do a specific job that has now gone offshore.

Unemployment benefits provide short-term temporary relief for these displaced workers. But the long-term solution requires retraining and the acquisition of new skills.

Beyond providing short-term relief through unemployment benefits, there is a large role for government in the provision of education and training to enable the labour force of the twenty-first century to be capable of ongoing learning and rapid retooling to take on new jobs that today we can't foresee.

Schools, colleges, and universities will expand and get better at doing their jobs of producing a highly educated and flexible labour force.

Avoiding Trade Wars

We have reviewed the arguments commonly heard in favour of protection and the counterarguments against them. There is one counterargument to protection that is general and quite overwhelming: Protection invites retaliation and can trigger a trade war.

The best example of a trade war occurred during the Great Depression of the 1930s, when the United States introduced the Smoot-Hawley tariff. Country after country retaliated with its own tariff, and in a short period, world trade had almost disappeared. The costs to all countries were large and led to a renewed international resolve to avoid such self-defeating moves in the future. The costs also led to the creation of GATT and are the impetus behind current attempts to liberalize trade.

Why Is International Trade Restricted?

Why, despite all the arguments against protection, is trade restricted? There are two key reasons:

- Tariff revenue
- Rent seeking

Tariff Revenue Government revenue is costly to collect. In the developed countries such as Canada, a well-organized tax collection system is in place that can generate billions of dollars of income tax and sales tax revenues. This tax collection system is made possible by the fact that most economic transactions are done by firms that must keep properly audited financial records. Without such records, the revenue collection agencies (such as the Canada Revenue Agency) would be severely hampered in the work. Even with audited financial accounts, some potential tax revenue is lost. Nonetheless, for industrialized countries, income taxes and sales taxes are the major sources of revenue, and tariffs play a very small role.

But governments in developing countries have a difficult time collecting taxes from their citizens. Much economic activity takes place in an informal economy with few financial records, so only a small amount of revenue is collected from income taxes and sales taxes. The one area in which economic transactions are well recorded and audited is international trade. So this activity is an attractive base for tax collection in these countries and is used much more extensively than it is in developed countries.

Rent Seeking Rent seeking is the major reason why international trade is restricted. **Rent seeking** is lobbying for special treatment by the government to create economic profit or to divert the gains from trade away from others. Free trade increases consumption possibilities *on average*, but not everyone shares in the gain and some people even lose. Free trade brings benefits to some and imposes costs on others, with total benefits exceeding total costs. The uneven distribution of costs and benefits is the principal obstacle to achieving more liberal international trade.

Returning to the example of trade in T-shirts and regional jets, the benefits from free trade accrue to all the people involved in the production of regional jets and to those producers of T-shirts that do not bear the costs of adjusting to a smaller garment industry. These costs are transition costs, not permanent costs. The costs of moving to free trade are borne by the garment producers and their employees who must become producers of other goods and services in which Canada has a comparative advantage.

The number of winners from free trade is large. But because the gains are spread thinly over a large number of people, the gain per person is small. The winners could organize and become a political force lobbying for free trade. But political activity is costly. It uses time and other scarce resources and the gains per person are too small to make the cost of political activity worth bearing.

In contrast, the number of losers from free trade is small, but the loss per person is large. Because the loss per person is large, the people who lose *are* willing to incur considerable expense to lobby against free trade.

Both the winners and losers weigh their benefits and costs and pursue their self-interest. Those who gain from free trade weigh the benefits it brings against the cost of achieving it. Those who lose from free trade and gain from protection weigh the benefit of protection against the cost of maintaining it. Because the protectionists have more at stake, they undertake a larger quantity of political lobbying than do the free traders.

Compensating Losers

If, in total, the gains from free international trade exceed the losses, why don't those who gain compensate those who lose so that everyone is in favour of free trade?

The main reason is that there are serious obstacles to providig direct and correctly calculated compensation. First, the cost of identifying all the losers and estimating the value of their losses would be enormous. Also, it would never be clear whether a person who has fallen on hard times is suffering because of free trade or for other reasons that might be largely under her or his control. Third, some people who look like losers at one point in time might, in fact, end up gaining. The young autoworker who loses her job in Winsdor and becomes a worker in Alberta's oil patch resents the loss of work and the need to move. But a year later, looking back on events, she counts herself fortunate. She has made a move that has increased her income and given her greater job security.

Because we do not, in general, compensate the losers from free international trade, protectionism is a popular and permanent feature of our national economic and political life.

Review Quiz

1 What are the infant-industry and dumping arguments for protection? Are they correct?

2 Can protection save jobs and the environment and prevent workers in developing countries from being exploited?

3 What is offshore outsourcing? Who benefits from it and who loses?

4 What are the main reasons for imposing a tariff?

5 Why don't the winners from free trade win the political argument?

 Work Study Plan 31.3 and get instant feedback.

◆ We end this chapter on global markets in action with *Reading Between the Lines* on pp. 772–773. It applies what you've learned by looking at the U.S. countervailing tariffs on Canadian softwood lumber.

The United States Protects Its Lumber Producers

Softwood Lumber Dispute

August 23, 2006

Disputes on softwood lumber have simmered for more than 20 years, but the most recent conflict boiled over in May 2002, when the United States imposed duties of 27 percent on Canadian softwood lumber, arguing that Canada unfairly subsidized producers of spruce, pine, and fir lumber. ...

The dispute centred on stumpage fees—set amounts charged to companies that harvest timber on public land. Many in the United States see Canadian stumpage fees as being too low, making them de facto subsidies. A U.S. coalition of lumber producers wants the provincial governments to follow the American system and auction off timber rights at market prices.

The bickering between Canada and the United States over softwood lumber is like a case of sibling rivalry. It dates back several decades. Even within Canada there were divisions. The B.C. Lumber Trade Council argued a trade war with the Americans ... would be costly and should be avoided by accommodating U.S. demands. The Free Trade Lumber Council, which includes lumber producers in Quebec and Ontario, wanted to fight it out. What most Canadian foresters and governments do agree on is their goal: free trade in softwood lumber.

Then, on April 26, 2006, came word that Canada and the United Sates had reached a framework agreement that could form the basis for an end to the dispute. The framework agreement called for the United States to return about 80 per cent of the $5 billion in duties that U.S. Customs has collected in the previous four years. Canadian-sourced lumber would also be kept to no more than its current 34 per cent share of the U.S. softwood market. ... Canada will also collect an export tax on softwood lumber exported to the United States if the price drops below $355 a thousand board feet.

Essence of the Story

- The dispute over trade in softwood lumber has simmered for more than 20 years. U.S. lumber producers argued that Canada was unfairly subsidizng producers because stumpage fees are not determined by auction.

- In May 2002, the United States imposed a 27 percent tariff and collected $5 billion in tariff revenue.

- The deal returns 80 percent of the U.S. tariff revenue collected to Canada and maintains Canada's share at 34 percent of the U.S. market.

- If the price drops below $355 a thousand board feet an export tax kicks in.

Economic Analysis

- Before the 2006 agreement, U.S. imports of Canadian lumber had a 27 percent tariff. The tariff damaged the social interest in Canada and the United States.

- Figure 1 shows the U.S. market for lumber. The demand curve D shows the U.S. demand for lumber.

- There are two supply curves: the supply curve of the Canadian producers, S_C, and the supply curve of U.S. producers, S_{US}. We're assuming that Canada can supply any quantity at a price of $100 a load.

- With a 27 percent tariff on the imports, Canadian lumber is supplied to the U.S. market at $100 plus the tariff, $27, so the supply curve of Canadian lumber becomes S_C + tariff.

- At $127 a load, the quantity of lumber bought in the United States is QC_1. Of this amount, QP_1 is produced in the United States and $QC_1 - QP_1$ is imported from Canada.

- The 2006 trade deal removed the tariff but imposed a quota on Canada's imports at its 2006 level—34 percent of the U.S. market.

- Figure 2 shows the U.S. market after the deal. The supply of lumber in the U.S. market is now the U.S. supply plus the quota on Canadian lumber. The supply curve becomes S_{US} + quota.

- The U.S. price remains at $127 a load, the quantity of lumber bought in the United States remains QC_1, the quantity produced in the United States remains QP_1, and imports from Canada remain $QC_1 - QP_1$.

- The only difference that the quota makes is that the tariff revenue becomes a gain to the U.S. importer who buys for $100 a load in Canada and sells for $127 a load in the United States.

- The differences between the tariff and the quota become more interesting and important when the U.S. demand for lumber increases.

- With a quota, an increase in U.S. demand raises the U.S. price and increases both U.S. producer surplus and the deadweight loss. Imports remain constant.

- With a tariff, an increase in U.S. demand leaves the U.S. price, U.S. producer surplus, and the deadweight loss unchanged and imports increase.

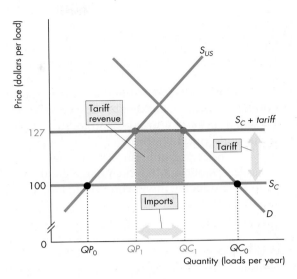

Figure 1 U.S. market with tariff

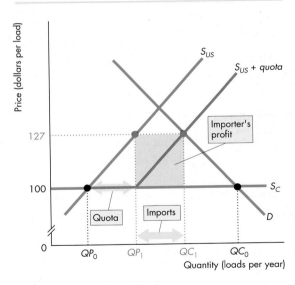

Figure 2 U.S. market with quota

SUMMARY ◆

Key Points

How Global Markets Work (pp. 758–761)

- Comparative advantage drives international trade.
- If the world price of a good is lower than the domestic price, the rest of the world has a comparative advantage in producing that good and the domestic country gains by producing less, consuming more, and importing the good.
- If the world price of a good is higher than the domestic price, the domestic country has a comparative advantage in producing that good and gains by producing more, consuming less, and exporting the good.
- Compared to a no-trade situation, in a market with imports, consumers gain and producers lose, but the gains are greater than the losses.
- Compared to a no-trade situation, in a market with exports, producers gain and consumers lose, but the gains are greater than the losses.

International Trade Restrictions (pp. 762–766)

- Countries restrict international trade by imposing tariffs, import quotas, and other import barriers.

- Trade restrictions raise the domestic price of imported goods, lower the quantity imported, make consumers worse off, make producers better off, and damage the social interest.

The Case Against Protection (pp. 767–771)

- Arguments that protection is necessary for infant industries and to prevent dumping are weak.
- Arguments that protection saves jobs, allows us to compete with cheap foreign labour, is needed to penalize lax environmental standards, and prevents exploitation of developing countries are flawed.
- Offshore outsourcing is just a new way of reaping gains from trade and does not justify protection.
- Trade restrictions are popular because protection brings a small loss per person to a large number of people and a large gain per person to a small number of people. Those who gain have a stronger political voice than those who lose and it is too costly to identify and compensate losers.

Key Figures

Key Terms

PROBLEMS and APPLICATIONS

 Work problems 1–10 in Chapter 31 Study Plan and get instant feedback.
Work problems 11–21 as Homework, a Quiz, or a Test if assigned by your instructor.

1. Canada produces both lumber and wine. Canada exports lumber and imports wine. The rest of the world imports Canadian lumber and exports wine to Canada.

    a. If Canada did not trade with the rest of the world, compare the equilibrium prices of lumber and wine in Canada with the world prices of lumber and wine.
    b. Does Canada or the rest of the world have a comparative advantage in producing lumber? Does Canada or the rest of the world have a comparative advantage in producing wine?
    c. Compare the quantities of wine that Canadian wineries produce and that Canadians buy with and without trade with the rest of the world.
    d. Compare the quantities of lumber that the rest of the world produces and that it buys with and without trade with Canada.
    e. What are the gains from the trade in lumber and wine between Canada and the rest of the world?

2. Wholesalers of roses (the firms that supply local flower shops with roses for Valentine's Day) buy and sell roses in containers that hold 120 stems. The table provides information about the wholesale market for roses. The demand schedule is the wholesalers' demand and the supply schedule is the North American rose growers' supply.

Price (dollars per container)	Quantity demanded	Quantity supplied
	(millions of containers per year)	
100	15	0
125	12	2
150	9	4
175	6	6
200	3	8
225	0	10

North American wholesalers can buy roses at auction in Aalsmeer, Holland, for $125 per container.

    a. Without international trade, what would be the price of a container of roses and how many containers of roses a year would be bought and sold in North America?
    b. At the price in your answer to a, does North America or the rest of the world have a comparative advantage in producing roses?
    c. If North American wholesalers buy roses at the lowest possible price, how many do they buy from local growers and how many do they import?
    d. Draw a graph to illustrate the North American wholesale market for roses. Show the equilibrium in that market with no international trade and the equilibrium with free trade. Mark the quantity of roses produced locally, the quantity imported, and the total quantity bought by North Americans.

3. **Underwater Oil Discovery to Transform Brazil into a Major Exporter**
A huge underwater oil field discovered late last year has the potential to transform South America's largest country into a sizable exporter.
… Just a decade ago the notion that Brazil would become self-sufficient in energy, let alone emerge as an exporter, seemed far-fetched. … Petrobras was formed five decades ago largely as a … company to import oil to support Brazil's growing economy. … Yet two years ago … Brazil reached its long-sought goal of energy self-sufficiency. …
International Herald Tribune, January 11, 2008

    a. Describe Brazil's comparative advantage in producing oil and explain why its comparative advantage has changed.
    b. Draw a graph to illustrate the Brazilian market for oil until a few years ago and explain why it was an importer of oil.
    c. Draw a graph to illustrate the Brazilian market for oil in the near future and explain why Brazil might become an exporter of oil.

4. Use the information on the North American wholesale market for roses in problem 2 to

    a. Explain who gains and who loses from free international trade in roses compared to a situation in which North Americans buy only roses grown locally.
    b. Draw a graph to illustrate the gains and losses from free trade.
    c. Calculate the gain from international trade.

5 **Postcard: Bangalore. Hearts Set on Joining the Global Economy, Indian IT Workers Are Brushing Up on Their Interpersonal Skills**

The huge number of Indian workers staffing the world's tech firms and call centres ... possess cutting-edge technical knowledge, [but] their interpersonal and communication skills lag far behind. ... Enter Bangalore's finishing schools.

Time, May 5, 2008

a. What comparative advantages does this news clip identify?

b. Using the information in this news clip, what services do you predict Bangalore (India) exports and imports?

c. Who will gain and who will lose from the international trade that you described in your answer to b?

6. Use the information on the North American wholesale market for roses in problem 2.

a. If a tariff of $25 per container is imposed on imports of roses, what happens to the North American price of roses, the quantity of roses bought, the quantity produced in North America, and the quantity imported by North American wholesalers?

b. Who gains and who loses from this tariff?

c. Draw a graph to illustrate the gains and losses from the tariff, the tariff revenue, and the deadweight loss created by the tariff.

7. Use the information on the North American wholesale market for roses in problem 2.

a. If an import quota of 5 million containers is imposed on roses, what happens to the North American price of roses, the quantity of roses bought, the quantity produced in North America, and the quantity imported by North American wholesalers?

b. Who gains and who loses from this quota?

c. Draw a graph to illustrate the gains and losses from the import quota, the importers' profit, and the deadweight loss created by the import quota.

8. **Car Sales Go Up as Prices Tumble**

Car affordability [in Australia] is now at its best in 20 years, fueling a surge in sales as prices tumble. ... [In 2000, Australia cut the tariff to 15 percent and] on January 1, 2005, the tariff on imported vehicles fell from 15 to 10 percent.

Courier Mail, February 26, 2005

a. Explain who gains and who loses from the lower tariff on imported cars.

b. Draw a graph to show how the price of a car, the quantity bought, the quantity produced in Australia, and imports of cars changed.

9. **Chinese Tire Maker Rejects U.S. Charge of Defects**

... [R]egulators in the United States ordered the recall of more than 450,000 faulty tires. ... The Chinese company that produced the tires ... disputed the allegations Tuesday and hinted that the recall might be an effort by foreign competitors to hamper the company's exports to the United States. ... Mounting scrutiny of Chinese-made goods has become a source of new trade frictions between the United States and China and fueled worries among regulators, corporations and consumers about the risks associated with many products imported from China. ...

International Herald Tribune, June 26, 2007

a. What does the information in the news clip imply about the comparative advantage of producing tires in the United States and China?

b. Could product quality be a valid argument against free trade?

c. How would the product-quality argument against free trade be open to abuse by domestic producers of the imported good?

10. **Why the World Can't Afford Food**

As [food] stocks dwindled, some countries placed export restrictions on food to protect their own supplies. This in turn drove up prices, punishing countries—especially poor ones—that depend on imports for much of their food.

Time, May 19, 2008

a. What are the benefits to a country from importing food?

b. What costs might arise from relying on imported food?

c. If a country restricts food exports, what effect does this restriction have in that country on the price of food, and the quantities of food produced, consumed, and exported?

d. Draw a graph of the market for food in a country that exports food. Show how the price of food, the quantities of food consumed, produced, and exported change when food exports are restricted.

11. Suppose that the world price of eggs is $1 a dozen, Canada does not trade internationally, and the equilibrium price of eggs in Canada is $3 a dozen. Canada then begins to trade internationally.

    a. How does the price of eggs in Canada change?

    b. Do Canadians buy more or fewer eggs?

    c. Do Canadian egg farmers produce more or fewer eggs?

    d. Does Canada export or import eggs and why?

    e. Would employment in the Canadian egg industry change? If so, how?

12. Suppose that the world price of steel is $100 a tonne, India does not trade internationally, and the equilibrium price of steel in India is $60 a tonne. India then begins to trade internationally.

    a. How does the price of steel in India change?

    b. How does the quantity of steel produced in India change?

    c. How does the quantity of steel bought by India change?

    d. Does India export or import steel and why?

13. A semiconductor is a key component in laptops, cell phones, and iPods. The table provides information about the market for semiconductors in Canada.

Price (dollars per unit)	Quantity demanded	Quantity supplied
	(millions of units per year)	
10	25	0
12	20	20
14	15	40
16	10	60
18	5	80
20	0	100

Producers of semiconductors can get $18 a unit on the world market.

    a. With no international trade, what would be the price of a semiconductor and how many semiconductors a year would be bought and sold in Canada?

    b. At the price in your answer to a, does Canada have a comparative advantage in producing semiconductors?

    c. If Canadian producers of semiconductors sell at the highest possible price, how many do they sell in Canada and how many do they export?

14. **South Korea to Resume U.S. Beef Imports**

South Korea will open its market to most U.S. beef. ... South Korea banned imports of U.S. beef in 2003 amid concerns over a case of mad cow disease in the United States. The ban closed what was then the third-largest market for U.S. beef exporters. ...

CNN, May 29, 2008

    a. Which country, South Korea or the United States, has a comparative advantage in producing beef? What fact in the news clip did you use to answer this question?

    b. Explain how South Korea's import ban on U.S. beef affected beef producers and consumers in South Korea.

    c. Draw a graph of the market for beef in South Korea to illustrate your answer to b. Identify the changes in consumption, production, international trade, and price.

    d. Assuming that South Korea is the only importer of U.S. beef, explain how South Korea's import ban on U.S. beef affected beef producers and consumers in the United States.

    e. Draw a graph of the market for beef in the United States to illustrate your answer to d. Identify the changes in consumption, production, international trade, and price.

15. **Act Now, Eat Later**

... [L]ooming hunger crisis in poor countries ... has its roots in ... misguided policy in the U.S. and Europe of subsidizing the diversion of food crops to produce biofuels like corn-based ethanol ... [That is,] doling out subsidies to put the world's dinner into the gas tank.

Time, May 5, 2008

    a. What is the effect on the world price of corn of the increased use of corn to produce ethanol in the United States and Europe?

    b. How does the change in the world price of corn affect the quantity of corn produced in a poor developing country with a comparative advantage in producing corn, the quantity it consumes, and the quantity that it either exports or imports?

    c. Draw a graph of the market for corn in a poor developing country to illustrate your answer to b. Identify the changes in consumption, production, international trade, and the price that the consumers pay.

16. Before 1995, trade between Canada and Mexico was subject to tariffs. In 1995, Mexico joined NAFTA, and all Canadian and Mexican tariffs are gradually being removed.

    a. Explain how the price that Canadian consumers pay for goods from Mexico and the quantity of Canadian imports from Mexico have changed. Who are the winners from free trade? Who are the losers?
    b. Explain how the quantity of Canadian exports to Mexico and the Canadian government's tariff revenue from trade with Mexico have changed.
    c. Suppose that tomato growers in Ontario lobby the Canadian government to impose an import quota on Mexican tomatoes. Explain who in Canada would gain and who would lose from such a quota.

17. Suppose that in response to huge job losses in the Canadian textile industry, the government of Canada imposes a 100 percent tariff on imports of textiles from China.

    a. Explain how the tariff on textiles will change the price that Canadians pay for textiles, the quantity of textiles imported, and the quantity of textiles produced in Canada.
    b. Explain how the Canadian and Chinese gains from trade will change. Who in Canada will lose and who will gain?

18. With free trade between Australia and Canada, Australia would export beef, but Canada imposes an import quota on Australian beef.

    a. Explain how this quota influences the price that Canadians pay for beef, the quantity of beef produced in Canada, and the Canadian and the Australian gains from trade.
    b. Explain who in Canada gains from the quota on beef imports and who loses.

19. **WTO: Farming Exporters Tell Rich Nations to Open Agriculture Markets**
    Developing countries and food exporters from rich and poor nations on Sunday demanded that the United States and European Union open their farm markets and eliminate trade-distorting subsidies. ... "Those members responsible for the most significant distortions in global agricultural trade—the EU, U.S. and Japan—bear a heavy responsibility," the Cairns Group of agricultural exporters, which includes Canada, New Zealand,

Argentina, South Africa and Thailand, said in a statement. "We can and must now seize this opportunity to secure the main parameters of the Doha round. The costs of failure are too high." ... Zoellick, as former U.S. trade representative, ... said an open and fair trading system would give farmers in developing countries a reason to expand production. Consumers would benefit from lower prices and governments could save on the costs of subsidies and improve their budgets.
    Reuters, July 20, 2008

    a. Explain why farmers in developing countries would expand production if EU, U.S., and Japanese subsidies were eliminated.
    b. Explain why EU, U.S., and Japanese consumers would benefit from lower prices that the removal of subsidies would bring.
    c. What are the costs of failure of the Doha Round? Who loses and who gains?

20. Study *Reading Between the Lines* on pp. 172–173 and answer the following questions.

    a. Why, until 2006, did the United States impose a tariff on softwood lumber imports from Canada?
    b. What were the effects of the U.S. softwood lumber tariff on Canadian and U.S. production and on Canadian exports?
    c. Who were the winners and who were the losers from the U.S. softwood lumber tariff?
    d. When the tariff was replaced by an import quota, how did production and Canadian exports change and who were the winners and losers from the quota?

21. **Vows of New Aid to the Poor Leave the Poor Unimpressed**
    ... [T]he United States, the European Union, and Japan [plan] to eliminate duties and [import] quotas on almost all goods from up to 50 of the world's poor nations. ... The proposal for duty-free, quota-free treatment is so divisive among developing countries that even some negotiators ... are saying that the plan must be broadened.
    New York Times, December 15, 2005

    a. Why do these countries want to eliminate trade barriers for only the poorest countries?
    b. Who will win from the elimination of these trade barriers? Who will lose?
    c. Why is the plan divisive among developing countries?

Tradeoffs and Free Lunches

A policy tradeoff arises if in taking an action to achieve one goal, some other goal must be forgone. The Bank of Canada wants to avoid a rise in the inflation rate and a rise in the unemployment rate. But if the Bank of Canada raises the interest rate to curb inflation, it might lower expenditure and increase unemployment. The Bank of Canada faces a short-run tradeoff between inflation and unemployment.

A policy free lunch arises if in taking actions to pursue one goal, some other (intended or unintended) goal is also achieved. The Bank of Canada wants to keep inflation in check and, at the same time, boost the economic growth rate. If lower inflation brings greater certainty about the future and stimulates saving and investment, the Bank of Canada gets both lower inflation and faster real GDP growth. It enjoys a free lunch.

The first two chapters in this part have described the institutional framework in which fiscal policy (Chapter 29) and monetary policy (Chapter 30) are made, described the instruments of policy, and analyzed the effects of policy. The final chapter (Chapter 31) has explained international trade policy. This exploration of economic policy draws on almost everything you learned in previous chapters.

These policy chapters serve as a capstone on your knowledge of macroeconomics and draw together all the strands in your study of the previous chapters.

Milton Friedman, whom you meet below, has profoundly influenced our understanding of macroeconomic policy, especially monetary policy.

Milton Friedman *was born into a poor immigrant family in New York City in 1912. He was an undergraduate at Rutgers and a graduate student at Columbia University during the Great Depression. From 1977 until his death in 2006, Professor Friedman was a Senior Fellow at the Hoover Institution at Stanford University. But his reputation was built between 1946 and 1983, when he was a leading member of the "Chicago School," an approach to economics developed at the University of Chicago and based on the views that free markets allocate resources efficiently and that stable and low money supply growth delivers macroeconomic stability.*

Friedman has advanced our understanding of the forces that determine macroeconomic performance and clarified the effects of the quantity of money. For this work, he was awarded the 1977 Nobel Prize for Economic Science.

By reasoning from basic economic principles, Friedman (along with Edmund S. Phelps, the 2006 Economics Nobel Laureate) predicted that persistent demand

"Inflation is always and everywhere a monetary phenomenon."

MILTON FRIEDMAN

The Counter-Revolution in Monetary Theory

stimulation would not increase output but would cause inflation.

When output growth slowed and inflation broke out in the 1970s, Friedman seemed like a prophet, and for a time, his policy prescription, known as monetarism, was embraced around the world.

TALKING
WITH

Stephanie Schmitt-Grohé

Stephanie Schmitt-Grohé is Professor of Economics at Columbia University. Born in Germany, she received her first economics degree at Westfälische Wilhelms-Universität Münster in 1987, her M.B.A in Finance at Baruch College, City University of New York in 1989, and her Ph.D. in economics at the University of Chicago in 1994.

Professor Schmitt-Grohé's research covers a wide range of fiscal policy and monetary policy issues that are especially relevant in today's economy as the consequences of the 2007 U.S. mortgage crisis play out.

Working with her husband, Martin Uribe, also a Professor of Economics at Columbia University, she has published papers in leading economics journals on how best to conduct monetary policy and fiscal policy and how to avoid problems that might arise from the inappropriate use of a simple policy rule for setting the overnight rate. She has also contributed to the debate on inflation targeting.

In 2004, Professor Schmitt-Grohé was awarded the Bernácer Prize, awarded annually to a European economist under the age of 40 who has made outstanding contributions in the fields of macroeconomics and finance.

Michael Parkin and Robin Bade talked with Stephanie Schmitt-Grohé about her work and the challenges of conducting stabilization policy.

What attracted you to economics?

When I graduated from high school, I was interested in both chemistry and economics but I wasn't sure which I wanted to study, so I enrolled in both programs. Within the first year of study, I realized that I wanted to pursue a career in economics. I took a class in which we learned how fiat money can have value and how the central bank can control the inflation rate. This seemed very important to me at the time—and still does after so many years.

What led you to focus your research on monetary and fiscal stabilization policy?

I always was very interested in economic policy and both monetary and fiscal stabilization policy have large and clear effects on a society's well-being. The same is certainly true for other areas of economics, but the benefits of macroeconomic stabilization policy are particularly easy to see; and it isn't difficult to find historical examples where bad monetary and fiscal policies unnecessarily lowered the standard of living.

What was your first job as a professional economist? How did you get started?

My first job out of graduate school was at the Board of Governors of the Federal Reserve System in Washington. This was a fabulous experience. Watching the policy-making process, I became motivated to work on having a more consistent and compelling theoretical framework on which to base monetary policy advice, and in particular, learning to develop tools to perform evaluation of alternative monetary policy proposals.

Only a few years out of graduate school, you and your economist husband Martin Uribe accepted a challenge to contribute to an assessment of "dollarization" for Mexico. First, would you explain what dollarization is?

When a country dollarizes, the U.S. dollar becomes legal tender, replacing the domestic currency. Ecuador, for example, is dollarized. In the case of Mexico in 1999, there were proposals, mainly coming from the business community, to replace the peso with the U.S. dollar.

Why might dollarization be a good idea?

Such proposals are typically motivated by the desire to avoid excessive inflation and excessive exchange rate volatility. Dollarization also makes inflationary finance of the Treasury Department impossible.

And what are the costs of dollarization?

One cost is that the country loses the revenues it gains from issuing money. A second cost is that the country loses the ability to conduct monetary stabilization policy. In effect, the domestic central bank can no longer influence the business cycle through interest rate or exchange rate policy. The question that Martin and I wanted to answer was "How costly is it for a country to give up the ability to conduct monetary stabilization policy?" We quickly realized that we didn't have the tools to answer this question in a way that we regarded as satisfying.

Briefly, what did you have to do to enable you to say whether dollarization is a good or bad idea?

We wanted to be able to quantify the loss in economic welfare that comes from not being able to target monetary policy at stabilizing the domestic economy. To do this, we needed to compute two measures of economic welfare, one arising from Mexican monetary policy and another under dollarization. But we wanted our measures to be based on an empirically compelling and sufficiently detailed model of the Mexican business cycle. At that time there were no measurement techniques available that allowed us to perform this task. So over the course of the next five years we developed the tools that we needed. One tool is an algorithm that computes (approximately but with sufficient accuracy) economic welfare under any given monetary policy, including the two of interest to us: Mexican dollarization and actual Mexican monetary policy. A second tool that we developed is another algorithm to compute optimal monetary policy—the best available monetary policy.

Knowing the highest level of economic welfare that can be achieved allows us to judge how close practical policy proposals come to optimal policy.

> Good stabilization policy is not necessarily a policy that smoothes the business cycle ...

And what was your biggest surprise?

I think our biggest surprise in this research program was how small the welfare costs of some very simple policy rules are vis-à-vis the optimal policy. Martin and I have shown in a number of papers that simple interest rate rules are very close to the best that can be achieved.

How would you describe the best stabilization policy for smoothing the business cycle and keeping inflation in check?

Good stabilization policy is not necessarily a policy that smoothes the business cycle, in the sense that it minimizes output fluctuations. On the contrary, it might be that trying to avoid cyclical fluctuations lowers economic welfare. Suppose, for example, that business-cycle fluctuations arise from fluctuations in the growth rate of productivity—as real business cycle theory suggests. Then economic welfare decreases if we limit the cyclical increase in output that comes from the increase in productivity.

The findings of my work with Martin suggest that a simple and highly effective monetary policy is one whereby the central bank raises the short-term interest rate by more than one-for-one when inflation exceeds the targeted level of inflation. Interest rate feedback rules of this type are similar to the Taylor rule, but contrary to Taylor's rule, our results suggest that the central bank should not respond to output variations in setting the short-term nominal interest rate. We find that if the central bank responds to the output gap, economic welfare suffers.

Regarding fiscal policies, the results of several of our papers strongly suggest smoothing out distortionary tax rates and using variations in the level of government debt to address cyclical budget shortfalls.

You've written about avoiding liquidity traps. What is the liquidity trap that we must avoid and how do we do so?

A liquidity trap is a situation in which the nominal interest rate is at zero. At this point, the central bank cannot lower the nominal interest rate any further to stimulate the economy.

In joint work with Jess Benhabib of New York University, Martin and I show that a liquidity trap can be avoided through the coordination of monetary and fiscal policy. In particular, liquidity traps—that is, zero nominal interest rates—can be avoided as equilibrium outcomes if the public becomes convinced that the government follows a fiscal policy that is inconsistent with zero nominal rates.

What is your assessment of the Taylor Rule?

Taylor-type interest rate feedback rules stipulate that the short-term nominal interest rate should be set as an increasing function of deviations of inflation from the target rate and of deviations of output from trend. In particular, the inflation coefficient of such a feedback rule should exceed unity, the so-called Taylor criterion. As mentioned above, in my work with Martin, I have found that simple interest rate rules that respond only to price inflation tend to bring outcomes with welfare levels very close to the optimal policy. In this sense Taylor-type interest rate feedback rules represent good monetary policy. An important caveat relative to Taylor's original specification of interest rate feedback rules is that our research (and that of several others) assigns very little, if any, value to including deviations of output from trend in the interest rate feedback rule. Moreover, such policies of leaning against the wind can under certain circumstances be harmful.

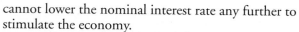

... interest rate rules that respond only to price inflation ... [are] very close to the optimal policy.

... and of inflation targeting?

Different people have different definitions of inflation targeting. This makes answering this question not straightforward. If inflation targeting is interpreted as a monetary policy specification, by which the short-term nominal interest rate responds only (or mainly) to inflation (as opposed to the output gap or other macroeco-

nomic indicators), then the results of our work strongly support an inflation targeting policy.

What are the implications of your work for avoiding and living with the credit market conditions that emerged in August 2007 and dominated the global economy through 2008?

Over the past decade, financial institutions that act like banks have developed. They are not, however, required by law to be under the regulations and supervision of the government in the same way as regular banks are. Going forward, I believe that it is desirable to have an overhaul of the existing regulatory system in order to ensure equal regulation and supervision for all financial institutions.

What advice do you have for a student who is just starting to study economics? Is it a good choice of major? What subjects go well with it?

If you are just starting studying economics, be patient. Economics can be more formal than other social sciences, and because of this, it may take a little while before you can apply what you learn in your economics classes to enhance your understanding of the economy around you. Subjects that are nice complements with economics are statistics and applied math.

Do you have any special advice for young women who might be contemplating a career in economics?

About one-third of newly minted economics Ph.D.s are women, but only about 8 percent of full professors in a Ph.D.-granting economics department are women. Looking at statistics like this can be discouraging. However, from my 15 years of experience of working in this field, I don't see any reason why young women who are about to start a career in economics will not be able to change these statistics.

GLOSSARY

Above full-employment equilibrium A macroeconomic equilibrium in which real GDP exceeds potential GDP. (p. 637)

Absolute advantage A person has an absolute advantage if that person is more productive than another person. (p. 40)

Aggregate demand The relationship between the quantity of real GDP demanded and the price level. (p. 630)

Aggregate planned expenditure The sum of planned consumption expenditure, planned investment, planned government expenditure on goods and services, and planned exports minus planned imports. (p. 650)

Aggregate production function The relationship between real GDP and the quantity of labour when all other influences on production remain the same. (p. 521)

Allocative efficiency A situation in which goods and services are produced at the lowest possible cost and in the quantities that provide the greatest possible benefit. We cannot produce more of any good without giving up some of another good that we *value more highly*. (p. 35)

Automated Clearing Settlement System (ACSS) The system through which all payments not processed by the LVTS are handled. (p. 575)

Automatic fiscal policy A fiscal policy action that is triggered by the state of the economy. (p. 718)

Automatic stabilizers Mechanisms that stabilize real GDP without explicit action by the government. (p. 720)

Autonomous expenditure The sum of those components of aggregate planned expenditure that are not influenced by real GDP. Autonomous expenditure equals the sum of investment, government expenditure, exports, and the autonomous parts of consumption expenditure and imports. (p. 654)

Autonomous tax multiplier The magnification effect of a change in taxes on aggregate demand. (pp. 672, 718)

Balanced budget A government budget in which tax revenues and outlays are equal. (p. 709)

Balanced budget multiplier The magnification effect on aggregate demand of a simultaneous change in government expenditure and taxes that leaves the budget balanced. (pp. 673, 718)

Balance of payments accounts A country's record of international trading, borrowing, and lending. (p. 606)

Bank rate The interest rate that the Bank of Canada charges big (LVTS-participating) banks on loans. (p. 736)

Barter The direct exchange of one good or service for other goods and services. (p. 568)

Below full-employment equilibrium A macroeconomic equilibrium in which potential GDP exceeds real GDP. (p. 636)

Big tradeoff The tradeoff between equality and efficiency. (p. 9)

Bond A promise to make specified payments on specified dates. (p. 545)

Bond market The market in which bonds issued by firms and governments are traded. (p. 545)

Budget deficit A government's budget balance that is negative—outlays exceed tax revenues. (p. 709)

Budget surplus A government's budget balance that is positive—tax revenues exceed outlays. (p. 709)

Business cycle The periodic but irregular up-and-down movement in production. (p. 475)

Canadian-dollar effective exchange rate index (CERI) An average of the exchange rates of the Canadian dollar against the U.S. dollar, the European Union euro, the Japanese yen, the U.K. pound, the Chinese yuan, and the Mexican peso. (p. 596)

Canadian interest rate differential The Canadian interest rate minus the foreign interest rate. (p. 601)

Capital The tools, equipment, buildings, and other constructions that businesses use to produce goods and services. (p. 4)

Capital account A record of foreign investment in Canada minus Canadian investment abroad. (p. 606)

Capital accumulation The growth of capital resources, including human capital. (p. 38)

Central bank A bank's bank and a public authority that regulates the nation's depository institutions and controls the quantity of money. (p. 572)

Ceteris paribus Other things being equal—all other relevant things remaining the same. (p. 24)

Chained-dollar real GDP A measure of real GDP derived by valuing production at the prices of both the current year and the previous year and linking (chaining) those prices back to the prices of the reference base year. (p. 482)

Chained price index for consumption (CPIC) An index of the prices of all the items included in consumption expenditure in GDP; the ratio of nominal consumption expenditure to real consumption expenditure. (p. 502)

Change in demand A change in buyers' plans that occurs when some influence on those plans other than the price of the good changes. It is illustrated by a shift of the demand curve. (p. 60)

Change in supply A change in sellers' plans that occurs when some influence on those plans other than the price of the good changes. It is illustrated by a shift of the supply curve. (p. 65)

Change in the quantity demanded A change in buyers' plans that occurs when the price of a good changes but all other influences on buyers' plans remain unchanged. It is illustrated by a movement along the demand curve. (p. 63)

Change in the quantity supplied A change in sellers' plans that occurs when the price of a good changes but all other influences on sellers' plans remain unchanged. It is illustrated by a movement along the supply curve. (p. 66)

Chartered bank A private firm, chartered under the Bank Act of 1992 to receive deposits and make loans. (p. 571)

Classical A macroeconomist who believes that the economy is self-regulating and that it is always at full employment. (p. 640)

Classical growth theory A theory of economic growth based on the view that the growth of real GDP per person is temporary and that when it rises above subsistence level, a population explosion eventually brings it back to subsistence level. (p. 531)

Comparative advantage A person or country has a comparative advantage in an activity if that person or country can perform the activity at a lower opportunity cost than anyone else or any other country. (p. 40)

Competitive market A market that has many buyers and many sellers, so no single buyer or seller can influence the price. (p. 58)

Complement A good that is used in conjunction with another good (p. 61)

Consumer Price Index (CPI) An index that measures the average of the prices paid by urban consumers for a fixed "basket" of consumer goods and services. (p. 498)

Consumption expenditure The total payment for consumer goods and services. (p. 469)

Consumption function The relationship between consumption expenditure and disposable income, other things remaining the same. (p. 650)

Core inflation rate The inflation rate excluding volatile elements—the underlying inflation trend. (p. 502)

Cost-push inflation An inflation that results from an initial increase in costs. (p. 682)

Crawling peg A policy regime that selects a target path for the exchange rate and uses intervention in the foreign exchange market to achieve that path. (p. 612)

Creditor nation A country that during its entire history has invested more in the rest of the world than other countries have invested in it. (p. 608)

Credit union A cooperative organization that operates under the Co-operative Credit Association Act of 1992 and receives deposits from and makes loans to its members. (p. 571)

Cross-section graph A graph that shows the values of an economic variable for different groups or categories at a point in time. (p. 16)

Crowding-out effect The tendency for a government budget deficit to decrease investment. (p. 556)

Currency The notes and coins held by individuals and businesses. (p. 569)

Currency drain ratio The ratio of currency to deposits. (p. 576)

Current account A record of receipts from exports of goods and services

sold abroad, payments for imports of goods and services from abroad, net interest income paid abroad, and net transfers abroad (such as foreign aid payments). (p. 606)

Cyclical surplus or deficit The actual surplus or deficit minus the structural surplus or deficit. (p. 722)

Cyclical unemployment The higher-than-normal unemployment that arises at a business cycle trough and the unusually low unemployment that exists at a business cycle peak. (p. 496)

Debtor nation A country that during its entire history has borrowed more from the rest of the world than it has lent to other countries. (p. 608)

Demand The entire relationship between the price of a good and the quantity demanded of it when all other influences on buyers' plans remain the same. It is illustrated by a demand curve and described by a demand schedule. (p. 59)

Demand curve A curve that shows the relationship between the quantity demanded of a good and its price when all other influences on consumers' planned purchases remain the same. (p. 60)

Demand for loanable funds The relationship between the quantity of loanable funds demanded and the real interest rate when all other influences on borrowing plans remain the same. (p. 550)

Demand for money The relationship between the quantity of money demanded and the interest rate when all other influences on the amount of money that people wish to hold remain the same. (p. 579)

Demand-pull inflation An inflation that starts because aggregate demand increases. (p. 680)

Depository institution A firm that takes deposits from households and firms and makes loans to other households and firms. (p. 571)

Depreciation The decrease in the value of a firm's capital that results from wear and tear and obsolescence. (p. 470)

Desired reserve ratio The ratio of reserves to deposits that banks want to hold. (p. 576)

Direct relationship A relationship between two variables that move in the same direction. (p. 18)

Discouraged worker A marginally attached worker who has stopped looking for a job because of repeated failure to find one. (p. 494)

Discretionary fiscal policy A fiscal action that is initiated by an act of Parliament. (p. 718)

Disposable income Aggregate income minus taxes plus transfer payments. (pp. 632, 650)

Doha Development Agenda (Doha Round) Negotiations held in Doha, Qatar, to lower tariff barriers and quotas that restrict international trade in farm products and services. (p. 764)

Dumping The sale by a foreign firm of exports at a lower price than the cost of production. (p. 767)

Dynamic comparative advantage A comparative advantage that a person or country possesses as a result of having specialized in a particular activity and then, as a result of learning-by-doing, having become the producer with the lowest opportunity cost. (p. 43)

Economic growth The expansion of production possibilities that results from capital accumulation and technological change. (p. 38)

Economic growth rate The annual percentage change in real GDP. (p. 516)

Economic model A description of some aspect of the economic world that includes only those features of the world that are needed for the purpose at hand. (p. 11)

Economics The social science that studies the *choices* that individuals,

businesses, governments, and entire societies make as they cope with *scarcity* and the *incentives* that influence and reconcile those choices. (p. 2)

Efficiency wage A real wage rate that is set above the equilibrium wage rate. (p. 496)

Employment-to-population ratio The percentage of people of working age who have jobs. (p. 493)

Entrepreneurship The human resource that organizes the other three factors of production: labour, land, and capital. (p. 4)

Equilibrium expenditure The level of aggregate expenditure that occurs when aggregate planned expenditure equals real GDP. (p. 656)

Equilibrium price The price at which the quantity demanded equals the quantity supplied. (p. 68)

Equilibrium quantity The quantity bought and sold at the equilibrium price. (p. 68)

Excess reserves A bank's actual reserves minus its desired reserves. (p. 576)

Exchange rate The price at which one currency exchanges for another in the foreign exchange market. (p. 594)

Expansion A business cycle phase between a trough and a peak—a period in which real GDP increases. (p. 475)

Exports The goods and services that we sell to people in other countries. (pp. 470, 758)

Export subsidy A payment by the government to the producer of an exported good. (p. 766)

Factors of production The productive resources used to produce goods and services. (p. 3)

Federal budget The annual statement of the outlays and tax revenues of the government of Canada, together with the laws and regulations that approve and support those outlays and taxes. (p. 708)

Final good An item that is bought by its final user during a specified time period. (p. 468)

Financial capital The funds that firms use to buy physical capital. (p. 544)

Financial institution A firm that operates on both sides of the market for financial capital. It borrows in one market and lends in another. (p. 546)

Firm An economic unit that hires factors of production and organizes those factors to produce and sell goods and services. (p. 43)

Fiscal policy The government's attempt to achieve macroeconomic objectives such as full employment, sustained long-term economic growth, and price level stability by setting and changing tax rates, making transfer payments, and purchasing goods and services. (pp. 632, 708)

Fixed exchange rate An exchange rate pegged at a value decided by the government or central bank and that blocks the unregulated forces of demand and supply by direct intervention in the foreign exchange market. (p. 611)

Flexible exchange rate An exchange rate that is determined by demand and supply with no direct intervention in the foreign exchange market by the central bank. (p. 611)

Foreign currency The money of other countries, regardless of whether that money is in the form of notes, coins, or bank deposits. (p. 594)

Foreign exchange market The market in which the currency of one country is exchanged for the currency of another. (p. 594)

Frictional unemployment The unemployment that arises from normal labour turnover—from people entering and leaving the labour force and from the ongoing creation and destruction of jobs. (p. 495)

Full employment A situation in which the unemployment rate equals the natural unemployment rate. At full employment, there is no cyclical unemployment—all unemployment is frictional and structural. (p. 496)

Full-employment equilibrium A macroeconomic equilibrium in which real GDP equals potential GDP. (p. 637)

GDP deflator An index of the prices of all the items included in GDP; the ratio of nominal GDP to real GDP. (p. 502)

General Agreement on Tariffs and Trade (GATT) An international agreement signed in 1947 to reduce tariffs on international trade. (p. 763)

Goods and services All the objects that people value and produce to satisfy human wants. (p. 3)

Government debt The total amount that the government has borrowed. It equals the sum of past budget deficits minus the sum of past budget surpluses. (p. 711)

Government expenditure Goods and services bought by government. (p. 470)

Government expenditure multiplier The magnification effect of a change in government expenditure on goods and services on equilibrium expenditure and real GDP. (pp. 672, 718)

Government sector balance An amount equal to net taxes minus government expenditure on goods and services. (p. 609)

Gross domestic product (GDP) The market value of all final goods and services produced within a country during a given time period. (p. 468)

Gross investment The total amount spent on purchases of new capital and on replacing depreciated capital. (pp. 470, 544)

Growth accounting A tool that calculates the contribution to labour productivity growth of each of its sources. (p. 528)

Human capital The knowledge and skill that people obtain from education, on-the-job training, and work experience. (p. 3)

Hyperinflation A rapid inflation that exceeds 50 percent a month. (p. 498)

Import quota A restriction that limits the maximum quantity of a good that may be imported in a given period. (p. 764)

Imports The goods and services that we buy from people in other countries. (pp. 470, 758)

Incentive A reward that encourages an action or a penalty that discourages one. (p. 2)

Induced expenditure The sum of the components of aggregate planned expenditure that vary with real GDP. Induced expenditure equals consumption expenditure minus imports. (p. 654)

Induced taxes Taxes that vary with real GDP. (p. 721)

Infant-industry argument The argument that it is necessary to protect a new industry to enable it to grow into a mature industry that can compete in world markets. (p. 767)

Inferior good A good for which demand decreases as income increases. (p. 62)

Inflationary gap The amount by which real GDP exceeds potential GDP. (p. 637)

Inflation rate The annual percentage change in the price level. (p. 498)

Inflation rate targeting A monetary policy strategy in which the central bank makes a public commitment to achieve an explicit inflation rate and to explain how its policy actions will achieve that target. (p. 732)

Instrument rule A decision rule for monetary policy that sets the policy instrument at a level that is based on the current state of the economy. (p. 735)

Interest The income that capital earns. (p. 4)

Interest rate parity A situation in which the rates of return on assets in different currencies are equal. (p. 604)

Intermediate good An item that is produced by one firm, bought by another firm, and used as a component of a final good or service. (p. 468)

Inverse relationship A relationship between variables that move in opposite directions. (p. 19)

Investment The purchase of new plant, equipment, and buildings, and additions to inventories. (p. 470)

Keynesian A macroeconomist who believes that left alone, the economy would rarely operate at full employment and that to achieve full employment, active help from fiscal policy and monetary policy is required. (p. 640)

Keynesian cycle theory A theory that fluctuations in investment driven by fluctuations in business confidence—summarized in the phrase "animal spirits"—are the main source of fluctuations in aggregate demand. (p. 690)

***k*-percent rule** A rule that makes the quantity of money grow at a rate of k percent a year, where k equals the growth rate of potential GDP. (p. 748)

Labour The work time and work effort that people devote to producing goods and services. (p. 3)

Labour force The sum of the people who are employed and who are unemployed. (p. 491)

Labour force participation rate The percentage of the working-age population who are members of the labour force. (p. 492)

Labour productivity The quantity of real GDP produced by an hour of labour. (p. 525)

Laffer curve The relationship between the tax rate and the amount of tax revenue collected. (p. 717)

Land All the "gifts of nature" that we use to produce goods and services. (p. 3)

Large Value Transfer System (LVTS) An electronic payments system that enables financial institutions and their customers to make large payments instantly and with the sure knowledge that the payment has been made. (p. 575)

Law of demand Other things remaining the same, the higher the price of a good, the smaller is the quantity demanded of it; the lower the price of a good, the larger is the quantity demanded of it. (p. 59)

Law of supply Other things remaining the same, the higher the price of a good, the greater is the quantity supplied of it. (p. 64)

Learning-by-doing People become more productive in an activity (learning) just by repeatedly producing a particular good or service (doing). (p. 43)

Lender of last resort The Bank of Canada is the lender of last resort—depository institutions that are short of reserves can borrow from the Bank of Canada. (p. 573)

Linear relationship A relationship between two variables that is illustrated by a straight line. (p. 18)

Long-run aggregate supply The relationship between the quantity of real GDP supplied and the price level when the money wage rate changes in step with the price level to achieve full employment. (p. 626)

Long-run macroeconomic equilibrium A situation that occurs when real GDP equals potential GDP—the economy is on its long-run aggregate supply curve. (p. 635)

Long-run Phillips curve A curve that shows the relationship between inflation and unemployment when

the actual inflation rate equals the expected inflation rate. (p. 687)

Lucas wedge The dollar value of the accumulated gap between what real GDP per person would have been if the 1960s growth rate had persisted and what real GDP per person turned out to be. (p. 474)

M1 A measure of money that consists of currency and chequable deposits of individuals and businesses. (p. 569)

M2 A measure of money that consists of M1 plus all other deposits. (p. 569)

Macroeconomics The study of the performance of the national economy and the global economy. (p. 2)

Margin When a choice is changed by a small amount or by a little at a time, the choice is made at the margin. (p. 10)

Marginal benefit The benefit that a person receives from consuming one more unit of a good or service. It is measured as the maximum amount that a person is willing to pay for one more unit of the good or service. (pp. 10, 36)

Marginal benefit curve A curve that shows the relationship between the marginal benefit of a good and the quantity of that good consumed. (p. 36)

Marginal cost The opportunity cost of producing one more unit of a good or service. It is the best alternative forgone. It is calculated as the increase in total cost divided by the increase in output. (pp. 10, 35)

Marginally attached worker A person who currently is neither working nor looking for work but has indicated that he or she wants and is available for a job and has looked for work sometime in the recent past. (p. 494)

Marginal propensity to consume The fraction of a change in disposable income that is consumed. It is calculated as the change in consumption

expenditure divided by the change in disposable income. (p. 652)

Marginal propensity to import The fraction of an increase in real GDP that is spent on imports. (p. 653)

Marginal propensity to save The fraction of an increase in disposable income that is saved. It is calculated as the change in saving divided by the change in disposable income. (p. 652)

Market Any arrangement that enables buyers and sellers to get information from and to do business with each other. (p. 44)

Market for loanable funds The aggregate of all the individual markets in which households, firms, governments, banks, and other financial institutions borrow and lend. (p. 548)

McCallum rule A rule that makes the growth rate of the monetary base respond to the long-term average growth rate of real GDP and medium-term changes in the velocity of circulation of the monetary base. (p. 747)

Means of payment A method of settling a debt. (p. 568)

Microeconomics The study of the choices that individuals and businesses make, the way these choices interact in markets, and the influence of governments. (p. 2)

Monetarist A macroeconomist who believes that the economy is self-regulating and that it will normally operate at full employment, provided that monetary policy is not erratic and that the pace of money growth is kept steady. (p. 641)

Monetarist cycle theory A theory that fluctuations in both investment and consumption expenditure, driven by fluctuations in the growth rate of the quantity of money, are the main source of fluctuations in aggregate demand. (p. 690)

Monetary base The sum of Bank of Canada notes, coins, and depository institution deposits at the Bank of Canada. (p. 573)

Monetary policy The Bank of Canada conducts the nation's monetary policy by changing interest rates and adjusting the quantity of money. (p. 632)

Money Any commodity or token that is generally acceptable as a means of payment. (pp. 44, 568)

Money multiplier The ratio of the change in the quantity of money to the change in the monetary base. (p. 577)

Money price The number of dollars that must be given up in exchange for a good or service. (p. 58)

Mortgage A legal contract that gives ownership of a home to the lender in the event that the borrower fails to meet the agreed loan payments (repayments and interest). (p. 545)

Mortgage-backed security A type of bond that entitles its holder to the income from a package of mortgages. (p. 546)

Multiplier The amount by which a change in autonomous expenditure is magnified or multiplied to determine the change in equilibrium expenditure and real GDP. (p. 658)

National saving The sum of private saving (saving by households and businesses) and government saving. (p. 549)

Natural unemployment rate The unemployment rate when the economy is at full employment—natural unemployment as a percentage of the labour force. (p. 496)

Negative relationship A relationship between variables that move in opposite directions. (p. 19)

Neoclassical growth theory A theory of economic growth that proposes that real GDP per person grows because technological change induces

an amount of saving and investment that makes capital per hour of labour grow. (p. 531)

Net borrower A country that is borrowing more from the rest of the world than it is lending to it. (p. 608)

Net exports The value of exports of goods and services minus the value of imports of goods and services. (pp. 470, 609)

Net investment The amount by which the value of capital increases—gross investment minus depreciation. (pp. 470, 544)

Net lender A country that is lending more to the rest of the world than it is borrowing from it. (p. 608)

Net taxes Taxes paid to governments minus cash transfers received from governments. (p. 548)

Net worth The total value of what a financial institution has lent minus the market value of what it has borrowed. (p. 547)

New classical A macroeconomist who holds the view that business cycle fluctuations are the efficient responses of a well-functioning market economy bombarded by shocks that arise from the uneven pace of technological change. (p. 640)

New classical cycle theory A rational expectations theory of the business cycle that regards unexpected fluctuations in aggregate demand as the main source of fluctuations of real GDP around potential GDP. (p. 690)

New growth theory A theory of economic growth based on the idea that real GDP per person grows because of the choices that people make in the pursuit of profit and holds that growth will persist indefinitely. (p. 533)

New Keynesian A macroeconomist who holds the view that not only is the money wage rate sticky but also that the prices of goods and services are sticky. (p. 641)

New Keynesian cycle theory A rational expectations theory of the business cycle that regards unexpected and currently expected fluctuations in aggregate demand as the main source of fluctuations of real GDP around potential GDP. (p. 690)

Nominal exchange rate The value of the Canadian dollar expressed in units of foreign currency per Canadian dollar. (p. 594)

Nominal GDP The value of the final goods and services produced in a given year valued at the prices that prevailed in that same year. It is a more precise name for GDP. (p. 473)

Nominal interest rate The number of dollars that a borrower pays and a lender receives in a year expressed as a percentage of the number of dollars borrowed and lent. (p. 549)

Normal good A good for which demand increases as income increases. (p. 62)

Official reserves The government's holding of foreign currency. (p. 606)

Official settlements account A record of the change in official reserves—the government's holdings of foreign currency. (p. 606)

Offshore outsourcing A Canadian firm buys finished goods, components, or services from other firms in other countries. (p. 769)

Offshoring A Canadian firm hires foreign labour and produces in a foreign country or a Canadian firm buys finished goods, components, or services from firms in other countries. (p. 769)

Open market operation The purchase or sale of government of Canada securities—Treasury bills and bonds—by the Bank of Canada in the open market. (pp. 573, 736)

Operating band The target overnight loans rate plus or minus 0.25 percentage points. (p. 736)

Opportunity cost The highest-valued alternative that we give up to get something. (pp. 9, 33)

Output gap Real GDP minus potential GDP. (pp. 496, 636)

Outsourcing A Canadian firm buys finished goods, components, or services from other firms in Canada or from firms in other countries. (p. 769)

Overnight loans rate The interest rate that banks charge each other on overnight loans of reserves. (p. 734)

Payments system The system through which banks make payments to each other to settle transactions by their customers. (p. 573)

Phillips curve A curve that shows a relationship between inflation and unemployment. (p. 686)

Positive relationship A relationship between two variables that move in the same direction. (p. 18)

Potential GDP The value of production when all the economy's labour, capital, land, and entrepreneurial ability are fully employed; the quantity of real GDP at full employment. (p. 474)

Preferences A description of a person's likes and dislikes. (p. 36)

Price level The average level of prices as measured by a price index. (p. 498)

Private sector balance An amount equal to saving minus investment. (p. 609)

Production efficiency A situation in which goods and services are produced at the lowest possible cost. (p. 33)

Production possibilities frontier The boundary between the combinations of goods and services that can be produced and the combinations that cannot. (p. 32)

Profit The income earned by entrepreneurship. (p. 4)

Property rights Social arrangements that govern the ownership, use, and disposal of anything that people value that are enforceable in the courts. (p. 44)

Provincial budget An annual statement of the revenues and outlays of a provincial government, together with the laws and regulations that approve or support those revenues and outlays. (p. 708)

Purchasing power parity A situation in which the prices in two countries are equal when converted at the exchange rate. (pp. 477, 604)

Quantity demanded The amount of a good or service that consumers plan to buy during a given time period at a particular price. (p. 59)

Quantity supplied The amount of a good or service that producers plan to sell during a given time period at a particular price. (p. 64)

Quantity theory of money The proposition that in the long run, an increase in the quantity of money brings an equal percentage increase in the price level. (p. 582)

Rational expectation The most accurate forecast possible; a forecast that uses all the available information, including knowledge of the relevant economic forces that influence the variable being forecasted. (p. 685)

Real business cycle theory A theory of the business cycle that regards random fluctuations in productivity as the main source of economic fluctuations. (p. 690)

Real exchange rate The relative price of Canadian-produced goods and services to foreign-produced goods and services. (p. 594)

Real GDP The value of final goods and services produced in a given year when valued at the prices of a reference base year. (p. 473)

Real GDP per person Real GDP divided by the population. (pp. 474, 516)

Real interest rate The nominal interest rate adjusted for inflation, which is approximately equal to the nominal interest rate minus the inflation rate. (p. 549)

Real wage rate The money (or nominal) wage rate divided by the price level. The real wage rate is the quantity of goods and services that an hour of labour earns. (p. 522)

Recession A business cycle phase in which real GDP decreases for at least two successive quarters. (p. 475)

Recessionary gap The amount by which potential GDP exceeds real GDP. (p. 636)

Reference base period The period in which the CPI is defined to be 100. (p. 498)

Relative price The ratio of the price of one good or service to the price of another good or service. A relative price is an opportunity cost. (p. 58)

Rent The income that land earns. (p. 4)

Rent seeking The lobbying for special treatment by the government to create economic profit or to divert consumer surplus or producer surplus away from others. The pursuit of wealth by capturing economic rent. (p. 771)

Reserve ratio The fraction of a bank's total deposits that are held in reserves. (p. 576)

Reserves A bank's reserves consist of notes and coins in its vaults plus its deposit at the Bank of Canada. (p. 576)

Rule of 70 A rule that states that the number of years it takes for the level of a variable to double is approximately 70 divided by the annual percentage growth rate of the variable. (p. 516)

Saving The amount of income that households have left after they have paid their taxes and bought their consumption goods and services. (p. 544)

Saving function The relationship between saving and disposable income, other things remaining the same. (p. 650)

Scarcity Our inability to satisfy all our wants. (p. 2)

Scatter diagram A diagram that plots the value of one variable against the value of another. (p. 17)

Self-interest The choices that you think are the best ones available for you are choices made in your self-interest. (p. 5)

Settlement balances rate The interest rate that the Bank of Canada pays on reserves (settlement balances) at the Bank of Canada. (p. 736)

Short-run aggregate supply The relationship between the quantity of real GDP supplied and the price level when the money wage rate, the prices of other resources, and potential GDP remain constant. (p. 627)

Short-run macroeconomic equilibrium A situation that occurs when the quantity of real GDP demanded equals the quantity of real GDP supplied—at the point of intersection of the *AD* curve and the *SAS* curve. (p. 634)

Short-run Phillips curve A curve that shows the tradeoff between inflation and unemployment, when the expected inflation rate and the natural unemployment rate remain the same. (p. 686)

Slope The change in the value of the variable measured on the *y*-axis divided by the change in the value of the variable measured on the *x*-axis. (p. 22)

Social interest Choices that are the best ones for society as a whole. (p. 5)

Speculative bubble A process in which the price is rising because expectations that it will rise bring a rising actual price. (p. 72)

Stagflation The combination of inflation and recession. (pp. 639, 683)

Statistical discrepancy The gap between GDP measured by total expenditure and GDP measured by total income. (p. 472)

Stock A certificate of ownership and claim to the firm's profits. (p. 546)

Stock market A financial market in which shares of stocks of corporations are traded. (p. 546)

Structural surplus or deficit The budget balance that would occur if the economy were at full employment and real GDP were equal to potential GDP. (p. 722)

Structural unemployment The unemployment that arises when changes in technology or international competition change the skills needed to perform jobs or change the locations of jobs. (p. 495)

Subsistence real wage rate The minimum real wage rate needed to maintain life. (p. 531)

Substitute A good that can be used in place of another good. (p. 61)

Supply The entire relationship between the price of a good and the quantity supplied of it when all other influences on producers' planned sales remain the same. It is described by a supply schedule and illustrated by a supply curve. (p. 64)

Supply curve A curve that shows the relationship between the quantity supplied of a good and its price when all other influences on producers' planned sales remain the same. (p. 64)

Supply of loanable funds The relationship between the quantity of loanable funds supplied and the real interest rate when all other influences on lending plans remain the same. (p. 551)

Supply-side effects The effects of fiscal policy on employment, potential GDP, and aggregate supply. (p. 714)

Targeting rule A decision rule for monetary policy that sets the policy instrument at a level that makes the forecast of the ultimate policy target equal to the target. (p. 735)

Tariff A tax that is imposed by the importing country when an imported good crosses its international boundary. (p. 762)

Tax wedge The gap between the before-tax and after-tax wage rates. (p. 715)

Taylor rule A rule that sets the federal funds rate at the equilibrium real interest rate (which Taylor says is 2 percent a year) plus amounts based on the inflation rate and the output gap. (p. 747)

Technological change The development of new goods and of better ways of producing goods and services. (p. 38)

Time-series graph A graph that measures time (for example, months or years) on the *x*-axis and the variable or variables in which we are interested on the *y*-axis. (p. 16)

Tradeoff A constraint that involves giving up one thing to get something else. (p. 8)

Trend The general tendency for a variable to move in one direction. (p. 16)

Trust and mortgage loan company A privately owned depository institution that operates under the Trust and Loan Companies Act of 1992. (p. 571)

Unemployment rate The percentage of the people in the labour force who are unemployed. (p. 492)

Velocity of circulation The average number of times a dollar of money is used annually to buy the goods and services that make up GDP. (p. 582)

Wages The income that labour earns. (p. 4)

Wealth The value of all the things that people own—the market value of their assets—at a point in time. (p. 544)

Working-age population The total number of people age 16 years and over who are not in jail, hospital, or some other form of institutional care. (p. 491)

World Trade Organization (WTO) An international organization that places greater obligations on its member countries to observe the GATT rules. (p. 764)

INDEX

intellectual property, 44
interest, 4
   compound interest, 434, 516–517
   foregone interest, 229
   and income approach, 472
interest rate parity, 604
interest rates
   and asset prices, 548
   bank rate, 736
   Canadian interest rate, 602
   Canadian interest rate differential, 601, 740
   cuts, 632
   cuts in, 750
   foreign interest rates, 601, 602
   long-term corporate bond rate, 740
   long-term real interest rate, 741
   nominal interest rate, 549, 578
   overnight loans rate, 734–735, 735f, 739–740, 739f
   real interest rate, 549–550, 550n, 557, 716, 741
   settlement balances rate, 736
   short-term bill rate, 739–740
   10-year government bond rate, 740
intermediate good, 468
international borrowing and lending, 557
international capital mobility, 557
international substitution, 663
international trade
   balance of payments accounts, 606–608
   borrowers, 608
   comparative advantage, 758
   current account balance, 609
   debtor and creditor nations, 608
   drivers of, 758–759
   encouragement of, 535
   exchange rate. *See* exchange rate
   financing international trade, 606–610
   gains and losses, 761
   lenders, 608
   net exports, 609–610, 609t
   regulatory barriers, 766
   restrictions. *See* international trade restrictions
   statistics, 758
   trade wars, 770
   voluntary export restraint, 766
International Trade Commission (U.S.), 768
international trade restrictions
   case against, 767–771
   cheap foreign labour, competition with, 768
   compensation of losers, 771
   dumping, 767–768
   exploitation, prevention of, 769
   export subsidy, 766
   health and safety barriers, 766
   import quotas, 764–766, 765f
   infant-industry argument, 767
   jobs and, 768
   lax environmental standards, 768–769
   offshore outsourcing, 769–770
   reasons for, 770–771

   rent seeking, 771
   tariff revenue, 770–771
   tariffs, 762–764
   trade wars, avoidance of, 770
intertemporal substitution, 663, 692
inventories
   additions to, as investment, 469–470
   change in, as business investment, 471
   inventory targets, 657
   as physical capital, 544
   and short-run equilibrium, 634
   unplanned inventory changes, 656f
   unwanted inventories, 634, 663
inverse relationship, 19, 20f
investment, 470
   business investment, 471
   and capital, 544, 545f
   funds that finance investment, 548–549
   Great Depression, 662
   gross investment, 470, 544
   income, 708
   miscellaneous investment income, 472
   national saving, 549
   net investment, 470, 544
   real interest rate, 741
   in seven economies, 529t
   taxes, effect of, 716
involuntary part-time rate, 492
involuntary part-time workers, 494

J

Japan, budget deficit in, 713
job leavers, 494
job losers, 494
job losses, 696
JPMorgan Chase, 547

K

k-percent rule, 748
Keynes, John Maynard, 490, 703
Keynesian cycle theory, 690
Keynesian model
   algebra of, 670–673
   described, 640–641
   fixed prices and expenditure plans, 650–653
   multiplier, 658–662
   multiplier and the price level, 663–667
   new Keynesian view, 641
   real GDP with fixed price level, 654–657
Kiva.org, 529
knowledge, and diminishing returns, 533
Korea, economic growth in, 520

L

labour, 3
   demand for labour, 521–522
   full-employment quantity of labour, 628
   quality of labour, 3

   underutilized labour, 494
labour force, 491
   entrants, 494–495
   graph, 491f
   reentrants, 494–495
   status, 446
labour force participation rate, 492–493, 493f
Labour Force Survey, 491
labour market
   aggregate labour market, 521–522
   equilibrium, 522–523, 522f
   indicators, 491–493
   and potential GDP, 523, 523f
   real business cycle theory, 692f
labour productivity, 525
   Asia, faster growth in, 529
   in Canada, 530
   growth accounting, 528–529
   growth of, 525–526, 525f, 528f
   human capital growth, 527
   increase, 525–526, 525f
   physical capital growth, 526
   and potential GDP, 525–526, 525f
   preconditions for growth, 526
   productivity growth slowdown, 474–475
   reasons for growth, 526–530
   slowdown and speedup, 528
   technological advances, 527, 533
labour supply
   aggregate labour market, 522
   and potential GDP, 523–524
Laffer, Arthur B., 717
Laffer curve, 717, 717f
land, 3
Large Value Transfer System (LVTS), 575
law-making lag, 720
law of demand, 59, 597–598
law of diminishing returns, 522
law of supply, 64, 599
learning-by-doing, 43
Lehman Brothers, 547
leisure time, 478
lender of last resort, 573, 695
lenders, 608
Levitt, Steven, 11
life expectancy, 478
line. *See* straight line
linear equation, 26
linear relationship, 18–19, 26, 26f
liquid assets, 571
liquidity, 547, 570, 572
loan markets, 545
loanable funds, 692f
   see also market for loanable funds
loans, 571–572, 575–576, 577f, 741
long and variable lags, 745–746
long run
   aggregate demand, increase in, 666–667

PHOTO CREDITS

READING BETWEEN THE LINES